MEASURING ECONOMIC GROWTH
AND PRODUCTIVITY

MEASURING ECONOMIC GROWTH AND PRODUCTIVITY

FOUNDATIONS, KLEMS PRODUCTION MODELS, AND EXTENSIONS

Edited by

BARBARA M. FRAUMENI

Central University of Finance and Economics, Beijing, China

ACADEMIC PRESS
An imprint of Elsevier

ELSEVIER

Academic Press is an imprint of Elsevier
125 London Wall, London EC2Y 5AS, United Kingdom
525 B Street, Suite 1650, San Diego, CA 92101, United States
50 Hampshire Street, 5th Floor, Cambridge, MA 02139, United States
The Boulevard, Langford Lane, Kidlington, Oxford OX5 1GB, United Kingdom

Notices

Knowledge and best practice in this field are constantly changing. As new research and experience broaden our understanding, changes in research methods, professional practices, or medical treatment may become necessary.

Practitioners and researchers must always rely on their own experience and knowledge in evaluating and using any information, methods, compounds, or experiments described herein. In using such information or methods they should be mindful of their own safety and the safety of others, including parties for whom they have a professional responsibility.

To the fullest extent of the law, neither the Publisher nor the authors, contributors, or editors, assume any liability for any injury and/or damage to persons or property as a matter of products liability, negligence or otherwise, or from any use or operation of any methods, products, instructions, or ideas contained in the material herein.

Library of Congress Cataloging-in-Publication Data
A catalog record for this book is available from the Library of Congress

British Library Cataloguing-in-Publication Data
A catalogue record for this book is available from the British Library

ISBN: 978-0-12-817596-5

For information on all Academic Press publications visit our website at
https://www.elsevier.com/books-and-journals

Publisher: Brian Romer
Acquisition Editor: Brian Romer
Editorial Project Manager: Ruby Smith
Production Project Manager: Bharatwaj Varatharajan
Cover Designer: Matthew Limbert

Typeset by TNQ Technologies

To Dale W. Jorgenson, who taught many of us and inspired all of us in our research

Contents

6. Manufacturing productivity in India: the role of foreign sourcing of inputs and domestic capacity building

K.L. KRISHNA, BISHWANATH GOLDAR, DEB KUSUM DAS,
SURESH CHAND AGGARWAL, ABDUL A. ERUMBAN,
AND PILU CHANDRA DAS

7. An international comparison on TFP changes in ICT industry among Japan, Korea, Taiwan, China, and the United States

CHI-YUAN LIANG AND RUEI-HE JHENG

8. Losing Steam?—An industry origin analysis of China's productivity slowdown

HARRY X. WU

9. Growth origins and patterns in the market economy of mainland Norway, 1997—2014

GANG LIU

10. Progress on Australia and Russia KLEMS

ILYA VOSKOBOYNIKOV, DEREK BURNELL, AND THAI NGUYEN

11. Toward a BEA-BLS integrated industry-level production account for 1947—2016

LUCY P. ELDRIDGE, CORBY GARNER, THOMAS F. HOWELLS,
BRIAN C. MOYER, MATTHEW RUSSELL, JON D. SAMUELS,
ERICH H. STRASSNER, AND DAVID B. WASSHAUSEN

19. Emissions accounting and carbon tax incidence in CGE models: bottom-up versus top-down

RICHARD J. GOETTLE, MUN S. HO, AND PETER J. WILCOXEN

20. Analyzing carbon price policies using a general equilibrium model with household energy demand functions

JING CAO, MUN S. HO, AND WENHAO HU

21. GDP and social welfare: an assessment using regional data

DANIEL T. SLESNICK

22. Accumulation of human and market capital in the United States, 1975—2012: an analysis by gender

BARBARA M. FRAUMENI AND MICHAEL S. CHRISTIAN

Associate Editors

Contributors

Ana Aizcorbe Bureau of Economic Analysis, Washington, DC, United States

Eva Benages Ivie and University of Valencia, Valencia, Spain

Derek Burnell Macroeconomic Statistics Division, The Australian Bureau of Statistics, Belconnen, ACT, Australia

David M. Byrne Federal Reserve Board, Washington, DC, United States

Jing Cao School of Economics and Management, Tsinghua University, Beijing, China

Suresh Chand Aggarwal Department of Business Economics, University of Delhi South Campus, Delhi, India

Pilu Chandra Das Kidderpore College, University of Calcutta, Kolkata, West Bengal, India

Michael S. Christian Education Analytics, Madison, WI, United States

Carol Corrado The Conference Board, New York, United States; Center for Business and Public Policy, McDonough School of Business, Georgetown University, Washington, DC, United States

Deb Kusum Das Department of Economics, Ramjas College, University of Delhi, Delhi, India

Lucy P. Eldridge Office of Productivity and Technology at the United States Bureau of Labor Statistics, Washington, DC, United States

Abdul A. Erumban The Conference Board, Brussels, Belgium; University of Groningen, Groningen, The Netherlands

Barbara M. Fraumeni Central University of Finance and Economics, Haidian, Beijing, China; Hunan University, Changsha, Hunan, China; National Bureau of Economic Research, Cambridge, MA, United States; IZA Institute of Labor Economics, Bonn, Germany

Kyoji Fukao Institute of Economic Research, Hitotsubashi University, Tokyo, Japan

Corby Garner Office of Productivity and Technology at the United States Bureau of Labor Statistics, Washington, DC, United States

Richard J. Goettle Northeastern University, Boston, MA, United States

Bishwanath Goldar Institute of Economic Growth, Delhi, India

Jonathan Haskel Imperial College Business School, London, United Kingdom

Mun S. Ho Harvard-China Project on Energy, Economy, Environment, SEAS, Harvard University, Cambridge, MA, United States

André Hofman University of Santiago de Chile, Santiago, Chile

Thomas F. Howells National Economic, Accounts, United States Bureau of Economic Analysis, Suitland, MD, United States

Wenhao Hu School of Economics, Tianjin University, Tianjin, China

Edward A. Hudson Wellington, New Zealand

Robert Inklaar Faculty of Economics and Business, University of Groningen, Groningen, The Netherlands

Massimiliano Iommi Italian Statistical Institute, Rome, Italy

Kirsten Jäger The Vienna Institute for International Economic Studies, Vienna, Austria

Ruei-He Jheng The Third Research Division, Chung-Hua Institution for Economic Research, Taipei, Taiwan (R.O.C.)

Cecilia Jona-Lasinio LUISS University and Econometric Studies and Economic Forecasting Division, Italian Statistical Institute, Rome, Italy

K.L. Krishna Centre for Delhi School of Economics, Delhi School of Economics, and Madras Institute of Development Studies, Chennai, India

J. Steven Landefeld Consultant and Senior Adviser to the Bureau of Economic Analysis, Huntingtown, MD, United States

Chi-Yuan Liang Research Center for Taiwan Economic Development, National Central University, Taoyuan County, Taiwan (R.O.C.)

Gang Liu Statistics Norway, Oslo, Norway

Matilde Mas University of Valencia and Ivie, Valencia, Spain

Kozo Miyagawa Faculty of Economics, Rissho University, Tokyo, Japan

Tsutomu Miyagawa Faculty of Economics, Gakushuin University, Tokyo, Japan

Brian C. Moyer Office of the Director, United States Bureau of Economic Analysis, Suitland, MD, United States

Thai Nguyen Macroeconomic Statistics Division, The Australian Bureau of Statistics, Sydney, NSW, Australia

Koji Nomura Keio Economic Observatory (KEO), Keio University, Tokyo, Japan; Research Institute of Economy, Trade and Industry (RIETI), Tokyo, Japan

Mary O'Mahony King's Business School, King's College London, London, United Kingdom

Hak Kil Pyo Faculty of Economics, Seoul National University, Seoul, Korea

Marshall Reinsdorf International Monetary Fund, Washington, DC, United States

Keunhee Rhee Korea Productivity Center, Seoul, Korea

Matthew Russell Office of Productivity and Technology at the United States Bureau of Labor Statistics, Washington, DC, United States

Jon D. Samuels National Economic, Accounts, United States Bureau of Economic Analysis, Suitland, MD, United States; Institute of Quantitative Social Science, Harvard University, Cambridge, MA, United States

Paul Schreyer OECD, Paris, France

Daniel E. Sichel Wellesley College and NBER, Wellesley, MA, United States

Daniel T. Slesnick Department of Economics, University of Texas at Austin, Austin, TX, United States

Erich H. Strassner National Economic, Accounts, United States Bureau of Economic Analysis, Suitland, MD, United States

Miho Takizawa Faculty of Economics, Gakushuin University, Tokyo, Japan

Marcel P. Timmer Faculty of Economics and Business, University of Groningen, Groningen, The Netherlands

Bart van Ark The Conference Board, New York, NY, United States; Faculty of Economics and Business, University of Groningen, Groningen, The Netherlands

Ilya Voskoboynikov Laboratory for Research in Inflation and Growth, National Research University Higher School of Economics, Moscow, Russia

Khuong M. Vu National University of Singapore, Singapore

David B. Wasshausen National Economic, Accounts, United States Bureau of Economic Analysis, Suitland, MD, United States

Peter J. Wilcoxen Maxwell School of Citizenship and Public Affairs, Syracuse University, Syracuse, NY, United States

Harry X. Wu National School of Development, Peking University, Beijing, China; Institute of Economic Research, Hitotsubashi University, Kunitachi, Japan

Xianjia Ye Utrecht School of Economics, Utrecht University, Utrecht, The Netherlands

Kun-Young Yun Department of Economics, Yonsei University, Seoul, Korea

Introduction

World and country economic growth is a continuing and major interest to many economists, politicians, policy-makers, media participants, and individuals, as it can impact on the well-being of countries and individuals. However, measuring economic growth is a continuing challenge, particularly with difficult-to-measure factors, such as intangibles, digital and information technology product advances, and productivity, which can impact on growth. In addition, emerging countries such as China and India are taking a greater role in the world economy.

This book serves as a foundational resource for graduate students and researchers worldwide working on growth and productivity and related applications. In addition, policy-makers can use it as a basis to understand how empirical results are produced and to familiarize themselves with empirical analysis and results of experts in this important field.

The chapters in this book demonstrate the significant influence of Dale W. Jorgenson on the research of many economists. Accordingly, this book is dedicated to him with thanks and apitrciation for his direct and indirect (through others) contribution to economic research.

The book starts with foundations, three chapters including a discussion of how economic growth is achieved, the evolution of and the future agenda for national accounts, and the efficiency costs and welfare gains from potential tax reform.

All but one of the next 11 chapters use KLEMS (capital, labor, energy, materials, and services) data, frequently with a KLEMS production model in the analysis.[1] Within these chapters, depending upon the available data and the nature of the analysis, some of the EMS inputs may not be included and others may be added. Chapters cover all Group of 7 (G7) countries (Canada, France, Germany, Italy, Japan, the United Kingdom, and the United States), all Emerging 7 (E7) countries (Brazil, China, India, Indonesia, Mexico, Russia, and Turkey), all EU-12 countries (Austria, Belgium, Czech Republic, Denmark, Finland, France, Germany, Italy, the Netherlands, Spain, Sweden, and the United Kingdom) plus Australia, Chile, Columbia, Norway, South Korea, and Taiwan, for a total of 28 countries. In 2017, these countries account for three-quarters of gross domestic product (GDP) in the world.[2] The leading chapter in the KLEMS section of this book is a comparison of G7 and E7 countries' economic growth and productivity, where the E7 have been projected to account for a greater share of GDP than G7 countries in the near future. Chapter 5 looks at the possible reasons for the

---

[1] KLEMS-type production models were popularized by Dale W. Jorgenson. Professor Jorgenson has organized five biennial World KLEMS conferences that have encouraged the construction of and research using KLEMS databases.
[2] As measured in constant 2011 international dollars, purchasing power parity.

slowdown in economic growth in the EU-12 countries compared to the United States. India may soon be the largest country in the world as measured by population. Chapter 6 describes how reforms initiated since the 1990s, aided by increasing participation in global value chains (GVCs), have strengthened the Indian manufacturing sector. Chapter 7 concludes by suggesting that the governments of China, Japan, South Korea, Taiwan, and the United States should encourage investment in R&D in ICT (information and communications technology). Chapter 8 takes an industry perspective to explain China's productivity slowdown. Chapter 9 uses average labor productivity and multifactor productivity over the subperiods 1997 to 2006 and 2006 to 2014 to look at the differences in growth patterns in mainland Norway. In Chapter 10 the progress toward and the nature of KLEMS database construction for Australia and Russia, both resource-rich countries, is described and contrasted. Chapter 11 describes a joint U.S. Bureau of Economic Analysis/U.S. Bureau of Labor Statistics project to create an internally consistent KLEMS prototype data set from 1947 to 2016 using disparate data sources. The prototype estimates reveal that relatively slow input growth in capital and labor services has curtailed US economic growth for the past decade and a half. Chapter 12 provides benchmark estimates of industry-level price differentials between Japan and the United States based on a bilateral price accounting model anchored to the Japan-US input-output tables. Chapter 13 provides empirical evidence on the impact of the skill-biased technical change associated with the introduction of ICT investment on labor demand in Japan and Korea. Chapter 14 measures the knowledge intensity of industries in six American countries and five European countries, concluding that growth in labor and capital knowledge intensity assets is important in industries that are not knowledge intensive. Altogether, these 11

chapters provide an extensive examination of many factors related to economic growth and productivity.

The last set of chapters in the book extend analysis beyond the core economic and growth considerations, from prices and inflation, GVCs, carbon taxes and policy, welfare, to human capital. Looking at Organisation for Economic Co-operation and Development (OECD) countries, Chapter 15 concludes that mismeasurement of digital product prices entering into a consumption deflator results in an overestimate of growth rates of impacted products. Chapter 16 investigates the direct and indirect impact of knowledge capital and innovation on economic growth and productivity in 10 European countries and the United States. For the United States, Chapter 17 outlines the of construction quality-adjusted price indexes for a digital product: smartphones. The interconnected world, specifically through GVCs, is recognized in Chapter 18. It uses a growth accounting framework to analyze sources of growth and productivity in vertically integrated production that crosses borders. The next two chapters both use a multisector general equilibrium model to examine carbon taxes or carbon price policies, but for different countries. Chapter 19 focuses on the United States; Chapter 20 focuses on China. In Chapter 19 it is demonstrated how different accounting methods: top-down versus bottom-up, can have a large effect on the simulated impact of carbon prices. In Chapter 20, a two-stage translog utility function that explicitly accounts for detailed energy expenditures allows for a simulation to determine if a carbon tax can achieve a country's Paris Climate Change targets. GDP is often thought to be a measure of economic welfare. For several US regions, in Chapter 21, the appropriateness of GDP as a proxy for economic welfare is examined. In the concluding chapter of the book, human capital by gender from 1975 to 2012 is examined in an expanded accounting system, which includes both market and human capital, to look at the trends affecting economic growth and productivity in the United States.

As the managing editor of this book, I was assisted by four associate editors: Carol A. Corrado, Mun S. Ho, Hak K. Pyo, and Bart van Ark. The five editors reviewed the introduction and all but three chapters of the book. These three chapters were reviewed by Charles Yuji Horioka, Cecilia Jona-Lasinio, or Nicholas Oulton. I thank all of the above and the many authors for their efforts to produce this book, which is dedicated to Dale W. Jorgenson.

Barbara M. Fraumeni

Economic growth: a different view

Edward A. Hudson

Wellington, New Zealand

1.1 The emergence of growth

1.1.1 The emergence of growth

Economic growth is the continuing increase in constant dollar GDP per capita. This growth started in England in the 18th century. New production techniques created a series of cheaper and new products, creating a succession of mass markets, starting with cotton goods and progressing through products made using steam power, iron, and steel. The United States took over economic leadership around the turn of the 20th century (see Maddison, 2006) and it too has seen a succession of new products and new industries, resulting in continuing growth.

US real GDP has increased at an average of 3.3% a year since 1890, while GDP per capita has increased at a 2.0% rate. Growth rates have varied considerably—there has not been steady growth. Table 1.1 shows the trends.

1.2 Our approach

1.2.1 Our approach

We first investigated the growth process in Hudson (2015). This chapter extends this earlier investigation, focusing on the United States.

We work at the industry level; this allows us to identify the mechanisms of growth, how the economy has changed, and what has driven these changes. Our industry analysis uses data from the National Economic Accounts, U.S. Bureau of Economic Analysis (BEA). These industry data start in 1947. For much of our analysis we compare growth before and after 1973. 1973 was a transition year as the first oil price shock hastened the end of the rapid growth of the metals and machinery industries, and an acceleration of the shift to electronics and services.

1.3 Industry growth

1.3.1 Changing structure

Different industries have performed in different ways. Table 1.2 shows the growth rates since 1947 for the BEA broad industry categories.

The economy grew at an average of 3.2% a year, but there was a wide range of growth rates for different industries, ranging from 0.8 to 4.7%. These differing growth rates lead to large changes in the sizes of the various industries. Mining in 2016 was less than twice its size in 1947, while Information was 23 times its 1947 size. The changes in detailed industries, not

1

TABLE 1.1   US Economic growth.

	Average annual growth rates					
	1890 to 1913	**1913 to 1929**	**1929 to 1947**	**1947 to 1973**	**1973 to 2016**	**1890 to 2016**
Real GDP	3.9%	3.1%	3.4%	4.0%	2.7%	3.3%
Real GDP per capita	2.0%	1.7%	2.5%	2.5%	1.7%	2.0%

Source: Data from Maddison (2006) and U.S. Bureau of Economic Analysis.

TABLE 1.2   Industry growth relative to GDP.

Relative growth rates of value-added quantity indexes		
	Growth rate relative to real GDP	**Share of current dollar GDP**
	1947–2016	**1973**
Agriculture, forestry, fishing, and hunting	0.9	4%
Mining	0.3	1%
Utilities	0.7	2%
Construction	0.6	5%
Durable goods	1.1	14%
Nondurable goods	0.8	8%
Wholesale trade	1.5	6%
Retail trade	1.0	8%
Transportation and warehousing	0.7	4%
Information	1.5	4%
Finance and insurance	1.3	4%
Real estate and rental and leasing	1.1	10%
Professional and business services	1.4	5%
Educational services	1.1	1%
Health care and social assistance	1.1	3%
Arts, entertainment, and recreation	1.0	1%
Accommodation and food services	0.7	2%
Government	0.6	16%
Other services	0.6	2%
Sum		100%

Source: Based on data from U.S. Bureau of Economic Analysis.

shown here, were even greater—the growth factor for Primary metals was just 1.1, while for Computers and electronic products it was 1076.

There have been large differences in industry performances—economic growth involves continuing change in the structure of spending and production.

1.3.2 Growth before 1947

Kendrick (1961, 1973) tracked growth by industry for the period 1899–1966. GDP increased at an average of 3.4% a year (see Maddison, 2006), but several industries grew at around double this rate. These were Electric machinery, Rubber products, Communications and public utilities, Chemical products, Transportation equipment, and Petroleum and coal products. These were the growth industries of the industrialization of the United States over the first half of the 20th century.

1.3.3 Leading industries 1947–1973

Table 1.3 shows the development of industries leading the economy in the years 1947–1973.

Rapid growth in this period was concentrated in just five industries, accounting for less than 10% of total value added (GDP). These industries continued their rapid growth from earlier in the century. However, four of these five industries slowed after 1973, falling below the GDP growth rate. The one remaining rapid growth industry, Petroleum and coal products, accounted for less than 1% of GDP. With the old growth drivers slowing after 1973, new leading industries were required if GDP growth was to continue.

1.3.4 Growth industries after 1973

Table 1.4 shows the development of industries which led the economy after 1973.

Only one of these seven later growth industries had been a leader in the earlier period. This was joined by six new leaders. Computer and electronic products, some of Information, some of Finance, Air transportation, and some of Professional and business services were relatively new products, now beginning to grow rapidly. Wholesale trade also grew rapidly (reflecting new ways of organizing business rather than being a new product).

Not all industries within Information, Finance and insurance, and Professional and business services were fast-growing, but, due to several data series not starting until after 1973, we could not identify these more detailed industries for Table 1.4. Our estimate is that these fast-

TABLE 1.3 Rapid growth industries 1947–1973.

	Growth rate relative to real GDP		Share of current dollar GDP
	1947–1973	1973–2016	1973
Chemical products	2.0	0.5	1.9%
Machinery	1.6	−0.1	2.2%
Plastics and rubber products	1.5	0.6	0.8%
Petroleum and coal products	1.5	2.7	0.4%
Other transportation equipment	1.4	0.1	1.1%

Note: These are industries with growth exceeding 1.4 times real GDP growth, 1947–73.
Source: Based on data from U.S. Bureau of Economic Analysis.

TABLE 1.4   Industries leading growth after 1973.

	Growth rate relative to real GDP		Share of current dollar GDP
	1947–1973	1973–2016	1973
Computer and electronic products	1.2	5.4	1.5%
Petroleum and coal products	1.5	2.7	0.4%
Information	1.1	1.8	3.8%
Finance and insurance	1.0	1.7	4.0%
Wholesale trade	1.3	1.6	6.4%
Air transportation	na	1.5	0.4%
Professional and business services	1.4	1.4	5.0%

Note: These are industries with growth exceeding 1.4 times real GDP growth, 1973–2016.
Source: Based on data from U.S. Bureau of Economic Analysis.

growing new products represented less than 10% of GDP; this is similar to the share of leading industries in the 1947–1973 period.

1.3.5 Industry changes

Economic growth depends on a few industries growing rapidly; these growth leaders have accounted for only a small part, around 10%, of GDP. Most industries grow at close to the overall rate of GDP growth. A growth leader will ultimately saturate its market and slow. New leading industries have then emerged. The emergence of new growth leaders is critical to overall growth continuing.

History since 1947 shows these mechanisms in action. A new set of growth industries emerged in the 1970s. These electronics and service industries superseded the mechanical and materials industries of the earlier period.

1.4 Growth of demand

1.4.1 Keynes and FDR

Keynes (1936) saw that economies produce in response to spending. Keynes rejected the classical mantra, often expressed as Say's law, that all markets would equilibrate so that the economy would always operate at full capacity. This classical view was that production capacity would create equal demand. Keynes demonstrated the opposite chain of causation—demand ruled, demand would drive production. Actual production would be whichever was less—demand or full capacity.

The Great Depression of the 1930s demonstrated that Keynes was right. Keynes provided the theoretical answer to recovery, but Franklin Delano Roosevelt (FDR) had already demonstrated in practice the primacy of spending. FDR's answer was simply to increase spending, whether by government spending directly or government income support to boost private spending. (In fact, it was not until World War II that defense spending drove GDP to full capacity.)

Keynes' policy recommendation for economic recovery was half right, but only half. Keynes focused on investment and argued for more private and government investment. However, Keynes' own logic implies that any boost to spending would have helped recovery. This could be personal consumption, private investment, government purchases, or exports. (These are all part of the equilibrium condition of Keynesian theory: $Y = C + I + G + X - M$.)

Keynes' insights and FDR's policies demonstrated at the macroeconomic level that demand (spending) leads and supply (production) follows; they apply equally at the industry level at which we are working.

1.4.2 Final demand

Final demand is the sum of personal consumption expenditures, private investment, government purchases, and net exports. Total expenditure is much larger than final demand, as primary and intermediate goods and services are needed in the production of finished goods and services.

Personal consumption is the largest category of final demand, typically accounting for around 65% of GDP. Private investment accounts generally for around 15% with government purchases typically adding a further 20%. Net exports of goods and services have generally been small

although exports and imports each have averaged around 10% of GDP.

1.4.3 Growth in final demand

Most categories of final demand have grown roughly in line with GDP. However, a few types of final demand purchases have grown more rapidly. These rapid growth categories are shown in Table 1.5.

From 1947 to 1973 consumption spending on Motor vehicles, Recreational goods and vehicles, and Health care grew rapidly. This changed after 1973 when Durable equipment, Recreational goods and vehicles, Other durable goods, and Recreation services became leaders.

Private investment grew more rapidly than GDP. The two rapid growth types of investment, both before and after 1973, were Information

TABLE 1.5 Rapid growth types of final demand.

	Growth rate relative to real GDP		Share of current dollar GDP
	1947–1973	1973–2016	1973
Rapid growth within personal consumption			
Motor vehicles and parts	1.6	1.0	3.8%
Furnishings and durable household equipment	1.0	1.5	2.7%
Recreational goods and vehicles	2.0	3.5	1.8%
Other durable goods	1.2	1.7	0.9%
Health care	1.5	1.1	4.7%
Recreation services	0.8	1.6	1.3%
Rapid growth within gross private domestic investment			
Information processing equipment	2.5	4.3	1.4%
Intellectual property products	1.8	2.4	1.6%
Rapid growth in international trade			
Exports	1.0	2.0	6.7%
Imports	1.7	2.0	6.4%

Note: Spending with growth exceeding 1.4 times the real GDP growth rate in either time period.
Source: Based on data from U.S. Bureau of Economic Analysis.

processing equipment and Intellectual property products. Exports grew rapidly but detailed data are not available for the two time periods here. In recent years, exports of financial and information services have grown rapidly.

Rapid growth in final demand has been concentrated in a relatively small number of spending categories, some in personal consumption and some in private investment (and, recently, some in services exports). Some types of final demand grew rapidly both before and after 1973, while some early leaders slowed but were replaced by new types of spending.

1.4.4 Interindustry demand

Final demand drives demand for all the different industries through an input–output process of the type first described by Leontief (1941). Industries supplying rapidly growing producers of finished goods and services will themselves grow relatively rapidly; conversely, industries supplying producers of slowing categories of final demand will tend to have slow growth.

1.5 Development of consumer demand

1.5.1 Importance of consumers

Economic growth, on the expenditure side, is growth in final demand. Personal consumption expenditure accounts for most of GDP while much investment spending is directed to creating capacity for the production of consumer goods and services. In short, consumers are the key to understanding economic growth.

1.5.2 Product innovation

Innovation is central to the growth of consumer spending. New or vastly improved consumer products come from innovation. This could be process innovation which reduces costs,

permitting such a large reduction in prices that a mass market is created; or, it could be product innovation which greatly improves an existing popular product; or, it could be product innovation which creates an entirely new product for which a mass market develops.

Some examples illustrate different ways in which product innovation has occurred. The automobile created a mass market by reducing the time cost of personal travel. Distributed electricity was an entirely new product, allowing the adoption of all sorts of useful electrical machines. Household electrical appliances created huge markets as they drastically reduced the time required for housework. Another set of products, radio and television, provided new types of entertainment services, creating huge new markets. The telegraph created the initial market for rapid personal communication, but subsequent developments such as the telephone and cellular mobile telephones vastly improved and cheapened the service such that the market kept expanding for more than a century.

1.5.3 Creating a mass market

The growth of a popular new product follows a logistic path. This is an S-shaped path of slow growth on introduction, accelerating growth as adoption spreads by a contagion-like process, and then slow growth as the market becomes saturated. Logistic growth is a demand-led process.

The critical outcome, from the point of view of economic growth, is the creation of a mass market. There are several key features in the creation of mass markets.

The emergence of the "consumer society" (the term given by Lebow (1955) although the concept originated as far back as Veblen (1899)) allowed consumer demand to keep increasing even when people's basic needs had already been met. In the consumer society, people seek status or recognition from their peers, or even just self-esteem, from being seen to have the latest products.

Marketing is central in maintaining the consumer society. Marketing informs customers of the product and its benefits, helps persuade potential customers that they need the product, and makes it accessible and easy to purchase. The development of product design, of more effective and diverse advertising on new mass media, and of multiple retail channels have worked together to reinforce the consumer society.

Then, potential customers must have or be able to get the money to buy new products. Consumer spending cannot grow if people simply spend out of their current incomes. Spending growth requires that some customers spend more than their current income. Consumer credit permits this. The development of multiple forms of consumer or household credit has enabled the continuing growth in consumer spending.

1.6 Development of investment demand

1.6.1 Expand capacity

GDP growth typically is led by consumer demand for new and popular goods and services. Capacity to produce these popular new goods and services requires rapid expansion of the capital stock in the growth industries. Demand for these investment goods, whether structures or equipment or intellectual capital products, increases accordingly.

1.6.2 Adoption of new processes

Productive new technologies often are embodied in physical or intellectual capital. As industries throughout the economy strive to adopt these new technologies, the demand for these capital goods can expand rapidly. This leads to increasing demand for these investment goods.

1.6.3 Investment in mainstream industries

The established or mainstream industries, which make up the great bulk of the economy, grow in line with GDP. Even this moderate growth requires continuing expansion of the capital stock.

1.7 Different growth paths

1.7.1 Different behaviors

Some final demand industries grow particularly rapidly. These industries also generate increasing demand for industries supplying them with intermediate goods and services. We look in the following sections at some specific examples of rapidly growing industries—Motor vehicles, Steel, Computers and electronic components, and Computer systems design. Most industries grow roughly in line with GDP, so we look at the features of a typical mainstream industry, Arts, entertainment, and recreation. Finally, a few industries are in relative or absolute decline. These might be former leading industries which have saturated their markets or industries which have been left behind by changing tastes or industries which have been overtaken by foreign competition. We look at an example of a declining industry, Steel.

The industries considered earlier were taken from the National Economic Accounts and are relatively broad. Some of these broad industries show the introduction and adoption of new products but to see the life cycles of important metals and mechanical industries, early growth leaders, we use more detailed data from the U.S. Census Bureau and other sources.

1.7.2 Leading industries

A good example of a growth industry is Motor vehicles. Fig. 1.1 shows Motor vehicles per household along with a logistic curve fit to these

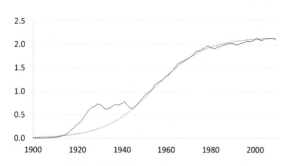

Note: Motor vehicles includes all automobiles, vans, trucks and busses.

FIGURE 1.1 Motor vehicles per household. *Source: Data from U.S. Census Bureau.*

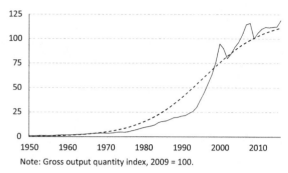

Note: Gross output quantity index, 2009 = 100.

FIGURE 1.3 Computers and electronic components. *Source: Data from U.S. Bureau of Economic Analysis.*

data. (These include all motor vehicles, not just those owned by households.)

The motor vehicle industries took about 100 years to complete their growth cycle. Sales began to accelerate with the introduction of the Ford Model T in 1908, grew rapidly until the 1970s, and then slowed as markets for vehicles became saturated.

This growth of a leading industry pulls its supplying industries along similar growth paths. Steel is a major input to motor vehicles. The growth curve for steel, shown in Fig. 1.2, peaks at the same time as motor vehicles. (In addition, several other steel-using industries, such as appliances, approached market saturation at around this same time.)

A more recent growth industry is Computers and electronic components; Fig. 1.3 shows its growth cycle. Computers experienced rapid growth beginning in the 1970s and are still growing but now at slower rates as their market matures (approaches saturation).

In turn, new growth industries are emerging. A particularly important one is Computer systems design and related services. Its growth curve is given in Fig. 1.4. This industry is still on the rapid growth part of the logistic curve. There is no telling when its rapid growth will stop or what will be the ceiling level of output. Ceilings of anything from 300 to 900 (relative to 2009 = 100) are consistent with the logistic curve to date.

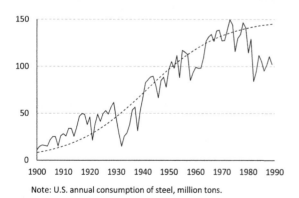

Note: U.S. annual consumption of steel, million tons.

FIGURE 1.2 Consumption of steel. *Source: Data from U.S. Census Bureau and World Steel Association.*

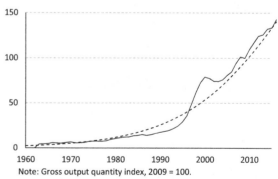

Note: Gross output quantity index, 2009 = 100.

FIGURE 1.4 Computer systems design and related services. *Source: Data from U.S. Bureau of Economic Analysis.*

1.7.3 Length of the growth cycle

The logistic process means that a leading industry will grow rapidly until its market becomes saturated. From that point, demand for the product will grow only with average incomes (or even less rapidly). The previously leading industry will become a mainstream or even declining industry.

The examples above indicate that a long time is required for a major new product to work through its full adoption process. Motor vehicles reached 90% of full market penetration in the 1970s, around 75 years into their life cycle. The logistic curve for Computers and electronic components suggests that penetration reached 93% in 2016, 70 years into its life cycle.

Bowden and Offer (1994) report on the market penetration of many appliances. They distinguish between "time-saving" and "time-using" appliances. (Time-using appliances are those used for entertainment or leisure.) Adoption periods for time-saving appliances are long; for example, the refrigerator took 43 years to reach 75% penetration, the washing machine took 60 years and the vacuum cleaner 76 years. These features are consistent with our analysis of Motor vehicles and Computers. Adoption of time-using appliances typically is much more rapid; for example, black and white television took 14 years to reach 75% adoption, radio took 16 years, and color television took 22 years.

1.7.4 The growth path of mainstream industries

Mainstream industries make up the bulk of the economy. These cater to established markets and, as such, grow with incomes and/or population. Reflecting their demand drivers, their growth is exponential, not logistic. Fig. 1.5 shows the growth of the Arts, entertainment, and recreation industry, together with its exponential trend.

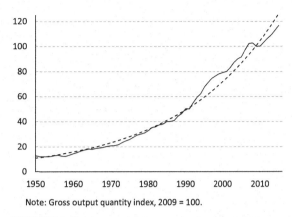

Note: Gross output quantity index, 2009 = 100.

FIGURE 1.5 Arts, entertainment, and recreation. *Source: Data from U.S. Bureau of Economic Analysis.*

1.7.5 The path of declining industries

A few industries are in decline. These typically were once growth or mainstream industries whose products are no longer in demand. A prime example is steel. This industry grew rapidly for decades but many of the markets for the products in which steel is used (products such as motor vehicles, machinery, and appliances) became saturated in the 1970s. Steel consumption then leveled off. Fig. 1.6 shows the trends. Production followed the same trends as consumption, but employment in steel-making has fallen steadily, due to efficiency improvements within the industry.

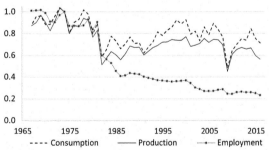

Note: Consumption and production in tons, all series are scaled to 1974 = 1.

FIGURE 1.6 Steel use, production, and employment. *Source: Data from U.S. Census Bureau, U.S. Bureau of Labor Statistics and World Steel Association.*

1.8 Sustaining economic growth

1.8.1 Maintaining demand growth

Growth can be disrupted if spending increases at either an inadequate or an excessive rate relative to productive capacity. Restrictive financial and credit conditions and/or restrictive government spending can lead to falling demand and so to recessions. Conversely, too rapid growth in spending, reflecting overly permissive credit conditions and/or excessive government spending, can lead to accelerating inflation. High or rising inflation leads to inefficient spending and investment decisions and finally to economic disruptions resulting from corrective government policies.

Suitable government policy can keep aggregate demand growing in line with productive capacity. The principal tools open to governments to stabilize growth are fiscal policy (changing government revenues and spending) and monetary policy (changing credit conditions). Fiscal policy led the way out of the Great Depression. Monetary policy was used to bring under control the high inflation of the 1970s. Both policies work by influencing demand—consumer, investment and/or government spending.

1.8.2 Supply growth in leading industries

Leading industries must expand production rapidly to meet the growing demand. This is illustrated by motor vehicles. Kendrick's (1961, 1973) growth accounting of the Transportation equipment industry covers the years of its most rapid growth, 1899–1966. Output increased at an average of 6.4% a year. Factor inputs accounted for around half the increase in output, total factor productivity (TFP) the remainder. Although productivity gains were vital, massive growth in labor and, in particular, capital inputs also was needed.

1.8.3 Growth of production in general

Economic growth requires overall production to keep increasing to sustain the continuing growth in demand. Labor, capital, and productivity have all been essential contributors to this production growth although factor inputs, rather than productivity, have been dominant. Jorgenson (2005) has analyzed the sources of growth for 1948 to 2002 finding that labor quantity accounted for 20% of GDP growth, labor quality 10%, capital quantity and quality 50% with TFP providing the remaining 19%.

1.9 Innovation and growth

1.9.1 The roles of innovation

Innovation is vital to economic growth. Product innovation (innovation on the demand side) leads economic growth while process innovation (innovation on the supply side) helps production increase to meet the growing demand.

1.9.2 The nature of product innovation

Product innovation seeks to design and market new products, or to greatly improve existing products, for which there are large potential markets. This innovation might be directed to creating entirely new products, or to improving the appeal of existing products, or to reducing the price of existing products to such an extent that new mass markets are created.

It typically is individuals or small companies who lead the search for radical new products. These people have little existing business to lose and every incentive to throw the dice for a big win. In contrast, existing businesses tend to focus on incremental improvements or extensions to existing products. (Reluctance to undermine existing success is characterized by Christensen (1997) as "the innovator's dilemma.")

1.9.3 Innovation in production

Jorgenson (2005) calculates that gains in capital quality contributed 10% of GDP growth from 1948 to 2002. These gains presumably were incorporated into new capital and so were introduced through new investment, principally in the mainstream industries. These productivity gains tend to be spread over time as the new technology is gradually adopted and as existing capital is replaced.

In addition, some improvements come from incremental improvements in operating efficiency. Most businesses try to increase margins by reducing unit costs. Reductions in costs are akin to the dual of productivity gains. These improvements typically come from managers and engineers working steadily to reduce costs/improve efficiency.

1.9.4 Research and development

Discussions of economic growth often associate productivity improvement with research and development (R&D) carried out by established businesses or institutions. What matters for economic growth is either highly attractive new or improved consumer products, or production advances which clearly reduce operating costs; these changes may or may not follow from R&D activity. Many product advances come from new or small businesses, many cost reductions come from operating personnel rather than R&D, and many reductions in unit costs come simply from economies of scale. R&D undoubtedly is important, but it is only one among several features underlying growth in production and productivity.

1.10 The outcome

1.10.1 Increasing incomes

Economic growth has generated huge increases in average income. Real GDP per capita increased at an average of 2.0% a year from 1890 to 2016; this corresponds to average real incomes increasing by a factor of 12. These gains in material standards of living have been accompanied by huge gains in health, life expectancy, education, leisure time, and leisure opportunities.

1.10.2 Who gains?

Income never is equally distributed; in fact, market income generally is distributed in a log normal fashion. In the short run, economic growth moves most people to higher incomes. However, some incomes will fall such as a result of people losing jobs or people entering retirement. Low income earners get some protection by the safety net provided by modern-day tax and transfer programs. In the long run, though, the entire distribution moves to the right so that virtually everybody gains from higher incomes as well as from improved health, education, and consumption choices.

1.10.3 Constant change

Labor and capital in growth industries have experienced rapidly rising incomes. However, as leading industries mature this income growth slows. New leading industries emerge, but these new industries typically involve different skills, different capital, and different locations.

Recent experience highlights these processes. Motor vehicles and steel, growth industries until the 1970s, are now static or even in decline. This decline has been concentrated in the Midwestern industrial states. Not only has demand leveled off but some production has moved to lower cost locations. Parallel to this, growth industries in entertainment, finance, electronics, and software have emerged, leading to boom times in different locations.

As mainstream industries make up the bulk of the economy, workers and capital in these industries generally enjoy incomes rising along a moderate trend. Even here, though, there is change as capital substitutes for labor and as productivity advance releases inputs.

Change is continual. Workers and capital in declining industries or workers whose jobs are replaced by capital have either to change occupation and/or industry and/or location or put up with lower incomes. While virtually everyone gains in the long run, the continuing changes in spending and production patterns generate a complex pattern of changes in income and income distribution.

1.11 Our view of economic growth

1.11.1 Our view

Our view of economic growth operates at the industry level. We introduce a demand side, based on people's spending behavior. Growth is driven by demand for innovative products, whether consumer products or investment products, and the industries which cater to these demands. In addition, these growth industries create growing demand for their supplying industries through the input—output mechanism. However, the rapid growth industries account for only around 10% of the economy. The bulk of the economy, the established industries, grows at a moderate rate; demand for their products is driven by population and average incomes. In time, the growth industries will saturate their markets and their growth will slow. Continuing economic growth then depends on the emergence of new mass market products which create new growth industries.

Production capacity increases by using more and better labor, more and better capital, and by improvements in TFP. Production in each industry is the lesser of demand and capacity. In this way, production responds to growing demand; economic growth is demand-driven and supply-enabled.

Innovation is vital for economic growth. We separate innovation into two types—product innovation and process innovation. Product innovation underlies the creation of new products which lead to the new mass markets which are the drivers of growth. Process innovation operates on the supply side by increasing productivity; process innovation contributes to the expansion of supply to accommodate increasing demand.

1.11.2 Hudson—Jorgenson

Our approach could be expressed formally in a model of the type pioneered by Hudson and Jorgenson (1974). The Hudson—Jorgenson framework had multiple industries, a Leontief type of input—output structure but with endogenous price formation and endogenous input—output coefficients including for factor inputs, and an endogenous consumption component of final demand. The characteristics of consumption expenditure and capital formation developed above could be incorporated into this earlier framework.

1.11.3 Schumpeter

Schumpeter (1942) described a long economic growth cycle. Innovation by entrepreneurs, in the pursuit of profit, leads to the introduction of new products. Some of these will be commercially successful. Their markets will grow rapidly until finally they fade and disappear. This final stage is Schumpeter's "creative destruction." New products then appear and go through their own boom and bust cycle. In this way, with a succession of new product cycles, the economy moves forward.

Our concept of leading or growth industries is similar to Schumpeter's. However, we do not view growth as moving in cycles; instead we have identified growth industries at only around 10% of the economy with most of the economy growing at modest rates, in line with GDP. Nor do we stress creative destruction. Our view is that when the markets of growth industries become saturated, their growth simply slows. But, like Schumpeter we view economic growth as depending on a succession of innovative products creating new mass markets.

1.12 Relationship to existing theory

1.12.1 Existing growth theory

The central result of growth theory in the Solow (1956) tradition is that GDP growth converges to a steady rate; in the simple models this rate is $g + n$, the rate of growth of labor effectiveness plus the population growth rate. This theory is mathematically elegant and has some intriguing implications, such as Samuelson's (1965) catenary turnpike establishing that there is a unique optimal growth path and that balanced growth converges to this path. However, this theory does not explain growth—both the growth coefficients are given from outside of the model. More recent developments have tried to ease some of the limitations of the Solow framework. These developments include AK models and endogenous growth theory (see, for example, Romer (1986, 1990) and Lucas (1988)). Capital has been extended to include human capital and no longer exhibits diminishing returns. And, productivity advance, the driver of growth, has been endogenized by appealing to R&D, knowledge, and learning by doing.

1.12.2 Growth accounting

Growth accounting, in particular the KLEMS approach led by Dale Jorgenson, provides a different perspective. Growth accounting separates growth, either of GDP or at the industry level, into contributions by factor quantities and qualities, and TFP. Growth accounting is not a theory of growth; rather, its objective is to better understand the process of growth on the production side.

1.12.3 Scientific theory

Theory in some sciences, such as physics, seeks to predict accurately the outcome of a process. An example is Newton's law of gravity: $F = G \times M1 \times M2 / D^2$ where the gravitation force, F, between two bodies depends on their masses and their distance apart. G is a constant, originally inferred from observations. This model is universally applicable. This theory does not get involved with how gravity works but simply predicts its outcome with universal accuracy (short of radiation moving at light speed).

Conventional growth theory is similar in seeking a standard, universally applicable, mathematical, predictive model. However, conventional growth theory does not generate universally accurate predictions. Economic growth is about people, and people are not universally regular and consistent. Events such as wars, the Great Depression, the Global Financial Crisis, and bad government seem to recur. The United States has survived these events and GDP growth has continued, although at varying rates. It is possible to put a trend through actual growth, but this does not represent accurate prediction. Gordon (2016) makes a similar point with his observation that US growth has decelerated since 1973. As this slowdown began a full 45 years ago, it is hardly a transitory blip.

Neither our approach nor growth accounting aspires to be a universally applicable, predictive theory.

Theory in many natural sciences, such as biology, is different—it seeks to explain a process so we can understand its operation and outcome. An example is Darwin's theory of evolution. This is that species evolve as genetic changes which enhance survival and reproductive success become more common in successive generations of a population. There is no mathematics involved and there are no predictions. However, Darwin's theory provides an explanation of evolution which allows us to understand what is going on.

Endogenous growth theory attributes growth to increased capital, including human capital, and to reported R&D. Although both are important, they are not the whole story. The human sources of growth, such as new product creation, marketing, consumer behavior, and improvements in operating efficiencies, also are important. Conventional theory does not explain economic growth.

Our approach is a theory in the sense of the natural sciences—it clarifies the processes involved with economic growth and allows us to better understand growth. Similarly, growth accounting is concerned with measuring what has happened, not with predicting what will happen. Our approach is complementary to growth accounting—we aim to advance understanding on the demand side, the driver of growth, while growth accounting advances understanding on the production side, the sustainer of growth.

1.12.4 Understanding

The two fundamental questions involved in understanding economic growth are: how does growth happen and why does it happen?

Our analysis shows how economic growth operates. Growth is driven by a succession of new and popular products which lead to a succession of rapid growth industries; these, in addition to the continuing moderate growth of established industries, keep increasing demand. At the same time, production capacity increases, through investment, productivity improvement, and more employment, to meet this rising demand. Growth is demand-led and supply-enabled.

Our approach also shows why growth happened—because of consumer behavior. Consumers always want new and popular products or just cheaper products. Adoption of these new products leads spending growth until their markets become saturated at which time consumers'

imaginations are caught by new products which lead to new rounds of spending growth.

1.13 Other countries

1.13.1 Other countries

We have described the growth of the United States. This growth has been led by rapid growth in spending on a succession of new consumer and investment products. Many, although certainly not all, other countries have also achieved continuing GDP growth. All have used the same processes although the demand drivers and leading industries have differed.

The western European countries have followed the US model of consumption- and investment-led growth; some countries have followed a commodity-led path, exporting essential materials and foodstuffs to industrialized countries; and some countries have followed a low-cost path, exporting low-priced goods to higher income countries.

The US model will continue to be effective as long as consumers rush into new products. The commodity export strategy faces more risks as commodity use in high-income countries slows with the shift from goods to services. The low-priced export strategy also has risks as rising incomes, and so costs, diminish the export price advantage.

1.14 Conclusion

1.14.1 Conclusion

We have set out a different approach to viewing economic growth. We seek to clarify and understand how economic growth works. Unlike conventional growth theory, we do not seek to develop a universally valid predictive model. We are not seeking to replace conventional theory but rather to complement it with a framework which allows better understanding.

The essence of our methodology is to introduce a demand side and to look at growth at the industry level. With this innovation:

- economic growth becomes less of a black box; the processes are revealed;
- demand (or spending) leads the economy; economic growth depends on a succession of innovative products for which mass markets emerge; production responds to demand;
- the nature and role of innovation are clarified; innovation is essential both on the product side (for demand) and the process side (for supply);
- the vital roles of credit and of government stabilization policy become clear;
- it becomes apparent that there is nothing automatic or necessarily steady about economic growth;
- we can better understand the industrial, occupational, income distribution, and geographic changes which are inevitable features of economic growth.

References

Bowden S, Offer A: Household appliances and the use of time: the United States and Britain since the 1920s, *The Economic History Review* 47(4):725–748, 1994.

Christensen CM: *The innovator's dilemma*, Boston, 1997, Harvard Business School Press.

Gordon RJ: *The rise and fall of american growth: the U.S. standard of living since the civil war*, Princeton, 2016, Princeton University Press.

Hudson EA: *Economic growth, how it works and how it transformed the world*, Wilmington DE, 2015, Vernon Press.

Hudson EA, Jorgenson DW: U.S. energy policy and economic growth, 1975-2000, *Bell Journal of Economics, The RAND Corporation* 5(2):461–514, 1974. Autumn 1974.

Jorgenson DW: Accounting for growth in the information Age. In , Amsterdam, 2005, Elsevier, pp 743–815.

Aghion P, Durlauf SN, editors: *Handbook of growth economics*, vol. 1. Part A. Amsterdam, 2005, Elsevier, pp 743–815.

Kendrick JW: *Productivity trends in the United States*, Princeton, 1961, Princeton University Press for the National Bureau of Economic Research.

Kendrick JW: *Postwar productivity trends in the United States, 1948 – 1969*, New York, 1973, Columbia University Press for the National Bureau of Economic Research.

Keynes JM: *The general theory of employment, interest and money*, London, 1936, Macmillan.

Lebow V: Price competition in 1955, *Journal of Retailing* 31(1):5–10, 1955.

Leontief WW: *The structure of American economy, 1919–1929*, Cambridge MA, 1941, Harvard University Press.

Lucas Jr RE: On the mechanics of economic development, *Journal of Monetary Economics* 22(1):3–42, 1988.

Maddison A: *The world economy, vol. 2, Historical statistics*, Paris, 2006, OECD.

Romer PM: Increasing returns and long-run growth, *Journal of Political Economy* 94(5):1002–1037, 1986.

Romer PM: Endogenous technical change, *Journal of Political Economy* 98(5):S71–S102, 1990.

Samuelson PA: A catenary turnpike theorem involving consumption and the golden rule, *The American Economic Review* 55(4):864–866, 1965.

Schumpeter JA: *Capitalism, socialism and democracy*, New York, 1942, Harper & Brothers.

Solow RM: A contribution to the theory of economic growth, *Quarterly Journal of Economics* 70(1):65–94, 1956.

U.S. Bureau of Economic Analysis, National economic accounts, Washington DC, U.S. Department of Commerce.

U.S. Bureau of Labor Statistics: Current employment statistics, Washington DC, U.S. Department of Labor.

U.S. Census Bureau: *Historical statistics of the United States: colonial times to 1970*, Washington DC, 1976, U.S. Department of Commerce.

U.S. Census Bureau: Statistical abstract of the United States, Washington DC: U.S. Department of Commerce.

U.S. Federal Reserve: Industrial production and capacity utilization, Washington DC.

Veblen T: *The theory of the leisure class: an economic study in the evolution of institutions*, New York, 1899, Macmillan.

World Steel Association (formerly International Iron and Steel Institute): Steel statistical yearbook, Brussels.

Expanding the conceptual foundation, scope, and relevance of the US national accounts: the intersection of theory, research, and measurement

J. Steven Landefeld

Consultant and Senior Adviser to the Bureau of Economic Analysis, Huntingtown, MD, United States

2.1 Introduction

This chapter describes the evolution of the US National Accounts with a focus on the intersection of measurement, theory, and economic research. The evolution and durability of National Accounts as the mainstay of macroeconomic analysis and policy stems from the measurement of the US economy across factors of production, industries, products, and geography within a theoretically consistent, comprehensive, unduplicated, double-entry system of economic accounts. Over time, as the economy and economic policy needs have changed, economic theory, measurement, and the national accounts have been continuously updated to track these changes. Much of this success, relative to leading, coincident, and other sets of business cycle indicators, which have been described as "measurement without theory," is attributable to the fact that the National Accounts evolution

has been based on the continuous interaction of theory and measurement.

The organization of this chapter is as follows: First, the importance of basing economic measures on economic theory so that they can be successfully used for hypothesis testing, projections, and economic policy is explained. Second, an overview of the integration of theory and measurement from the perspective of today's National Accounts is presented. Third, the history of the interaction between research, theory, and measurement in the evolution of the US National Accounts is described. Finally, an agenda of next steps for improving the accuracy, timeliness, and relevance of the National Accounts is presented.

2.2 Measurement without theory

Koopmans (1947), in his famous article, "Measurement Without Theory," provided a critical review of Burns and Mitchell's NBER volume *Measuring Business Cycles*. His criticism was that the indicators approach used by the authors was purely empirical. As Koopmans described it, their work was empirical in the sense that: "The various choices as to what to 'look for,' what economic phenomena to observe, and what measures to define and track are made with a minimum of assistance from theoretical conceptions or hypotheses regarding the nature of the economic processes by which the variables studied are generated."

The problems with such indicators are well known to the users and producers of such indicators and to econometricians. Leading and coincident indicators selected for their relationship to aggregate economic activity in the past often are less than helpful as the structure of the economy and the causes of business cycles vary over time. As a result, leading and coincident indicators have to be regularly updated through the addition, deletion, and reweighting of the system indicators. Unfortunately, while the revised US index of leading indicators provide a better ex-ante fit, and better reflect history and the most recent cycle(s), they have been of limited value in correctly predicting downturns in advance.[1]

One of the foundations of econometrics courses is the importance of theory and the problems of measurement and research without theory. Instructors underline the need for classic hypothesis testing and theoretically based modeling. They warn that correlation does not prove causation, and that omitted variables, proxy variables, and changes in underlying relationships can undermine the best-looking results. (A more recent version of this discussion arises in the use of big data for economic projections).

In contrast, the National Accounts—which were being extended and further developed in the 1940s at the time Koopmans wrote this article—were a well-specified set of double-entry economic accounts that provided a comprehensive, unduplicated estimate of overall production, income, and expenditure using consistent principles of economic valuation, aggregation, timing, geography, and transfer of ownership. The components could be aggregated to total production, expenditures, and income.

The circular flow, and double-entry systems, of the national accounts has their foundations in economic theory dating back to Cantillon (1755) and Quesnay's (1766) Tableau Economique. These and later circular flow accounts included the double-entry production and sales of goods and services for households, prices, and the income paid by producers to the factors of production (households). The categories in the accounts arose from a long economic literature on production, consumer spending, capital accumulation, and international trade. The components were also well suited for accurately measuring the overall state of the economy, the impact of changes in the components on the National Income and GDP, and the testing of hypotheses about the determinants of such changes. Prominent examples of theories that could be tested at that time and used in policy included Keynes' marginal propensity to consume, his multiplier, and the effects of war mobilization and demobilization on private consumption, investment, productivity, and inflation.

2.3 Today's national accounts and economic theory

Perhaps the easiest way to describe the integration of theory in today's national accounts is from the perspective of today's national accounts as described in virtually any intermediate

---

[1] See, for example, Diebold and Rudebusch (1991) Filardo (1999).

macroeconomic textbook. Most textbooks start by describing the economy through a circular flow diagram of the accounts, then extending the accounts from simple closed and open economy models to the IS-LM model and the Solow growth model. Mankiw (2016) is particularly good in presenting the underlying theory and model and then presenting empirical evidence regarding key hypotheses. These basic models are normally presented within the National Accounts System and the identities and components in the accounts are used to explain:

- Equilibrium in production and distribution in the short and long run. The equilibrium is shown to be based on firm and household micro-theory and macro-theory and implemented using the National Income and Product Accounts structure and data
- The role of interest rates, prices, and exchange rates in equilibrating markets
- The trade-off between inflation and unemployment
- The accounting identity in an open economy that shows that the difference between aggregate demand and aggregate supply (and saving and investment) is equal to the trade deficit (e.g., the "twin deficits")
- Net National Product (GDP less depreciation, or the capital used up in production which must be replaced) as a measure of sustainable output for the nation.
- The impacts of fiscal and monetary policy including the Keynesian multiplier
- Understanding individual and aggregate consumer behavior
- The determinants of investment by type of investments (equipment, structures, inventories, and intangible assets)

- Changes over time and across business cycles in the distribution across the components of production, income, and expenditures
- The impact of government deficits in the short and long run
- Growth accounting and the determinants of growth over time and across countries
- Inflation and output and the importance of index number theory in aggregation

2.4 Joint evolution of theory, research, and national accounts

Although today's National Accounts seemed to be well-integrated with theory and well-designed to answer economic policy and other questions, their evolution has been a long process.[2] Political economy and National Accounts have always been concerned with political and economic policy using economic theory and data to understand key issues ranging from the gains from free trade to the sources of economic growth. However, the process has been discontinuous with theory, research, and measurement advancing at different rates, but all interacting to improve both economic theory and the accuracy and relevance of the National Accounts. For example, looking at today's textbook presentation, the accounts look like they were designed based on Keynesian models, but while Keynes played a key role as a "theoretician, compiler, supporter and user" of the evolving accounts, the basic structure of the accounts was established in the early 1900s or earlier, well before Keynes' contributions.[3]

Early 1700s to 1900: Early versions of the National Accounts (also known as Social Accounts)

---

[2] For a history of the evolution of the National Accounts, see Kendrick (1970), Carson (1975), Marcuss and Kane (2007), Landefeld (2000), Landefeld, Daley, Greenspan, Baily and Shapiro (2000).

[3] Tilly (2009).

were theoretical models that described the circular flow of commodities and goods and the distribution of income across classes of the population and geography, Boisguillbert (1707) and Cantillon (1755). Quesnay (1766) presented a more highly developed set of circular-flow "Tableaux Economiques" based on double-entry accounting that included elements of the identity between income, product, expenditure, and distribution of income accounts. They also had elements of today's Industry Input−Output Tables. These "Tableaux" were theoretical descriptions of the functioning of an economy that was used by Quesnay and the Physiocrats for an "investigation of the technical and social conditions which allow the repetition of the circular process of production."[4] Marx (1885) later developed a version of the circular-flow Tableaux to describe his own theory of production and income distribution.

In the United States, a number of individuals and organizations made important contributions to the concepts, theory, architecture, and measurement of national income accounts. These included National Income estimates published by Tucker in 1843 and 1855, by Seaman in 1852, and by Spahr in 1885. Spahr (1896) also developed estimates of the distribution of income across households.[5]

1900−32: The budgetary and economic impact of World War I spurred research and analysis on the impact of the war. During this period, the National Bureau of Economic Research (NBER) and others were also interested in measures that would help in evaluating social and political problems. These efforts in the early 1900s included estimates of National Income published by King of the Federal Reserve Board in 1915; Miller in 1918; Anderson in 1921; the National Income Conference Board in 1927; Mitchell, King, Knauth, and McCauley of NBER in 1921; and Walker of the Federal Trade Commission in 1926.[6] Mitchell et al. (1922) also made estimates of the distribution of wealth across households. All these efforts added to the conceptual, theoretical, and empirical development of the official National Accounts.

1933−50: Attempts to better understand and track the Great Depression and the prolonged subsequent recovery, followed by efforts to better plan for post−World War II mobilization and demobilization, were a major impetus for improvements in theory and the national accounts. The President and the Congress needed a consistent and comprehensive measure that would allow them to track the path of the recession and the impact of policies—in the aggregate and by industry—to lift the economy out of recession. The official set of National Income estimates produced by NBER and the US Department of Commerce, under the direction of Simon Kuznets, filled at least part of that need. At the same time, the US and worldwide Great Depression spurred research and new theories on business cycles, including Keynes, with his General Theory of General of Employment, Interest, and Money (1935).[7]

The Great Depression highlighted the problems with the classical model of the economy, which focused on the long-run equilibrium and assumed that flexible prices (prices for goods and services, wages, interest rates, and exchange

---

[4] For a complete discussion of the circular flow, see Gilibert (1998).

[5] See Carson (1975) for a detailed history of the US National and Product Account concentrating on the period 1932−47 with a brief summary of the early estimates, 1843−932.

[6] See Carson (1975), pp. 153−155.

[7] John Maynard, *The General Theory of Employment, Interest, and Money*, 1935, First Harbinger Version, 1964.

rates) would quickly adjust to restore the full employment of labor and capital.[8] The world-wide breadth, depth, and prolonged recovery from the recession prompted calls for a new theory, new fiscal and monetary strategies, and new measures to monitor the economy. (During the Great Depression in the United States, national output fell by 25% and it took nearly 10 years for it to recover its pre-depression peak.)

The Great Depression also highlighted the gaps in economic data to inform economic policy:

> "One reads with dismay of President Hoover and then Roosevelt designing policies to combat the Great Depression of the 1930s on the basis of such sketchy data as stock price indices, freight car loadings, and incomplete indices of industrial production. The fact was that comprehensive measures of national income and output did not exist at the time. The Depression, and with it the growing role of government in the economy, emphasized the need for such measures and led to the development of a comprehensive set of national income accounts."[9]

The original National Accounts produced by Kuznets (1934) and his team were national income accounts broken down by industry. In the initial report to Congress that presented the estimates, Kuznets laid out the basic concepts guiding the development of the estimates as well as the limitations of these market-based accounts. The principles guiding the accounts were largely built on previous work (described above) including the circular flow of expenditure, production and income, double-entry accounting (although quantitative estimates were only produced for national income), unduplicated measures of production, and consistent use of market values. Kuznets also pointed out the shortcomings of market-based national accounts in that they omitted theoretically important components of economic well-being including the value of non-market work in the household, the services of consumer durables, the depletion of natural resources, and the fact that the market prices/weights used in aggregating national output depended on the existing distribution of income.

Interest in Keynesian policy and other fiscal and monetary policies and the need to address World War II mobilization and demobilization issues provided the impetus for developing expenditure, or product, estimates to aid in more complete analysis of the economy. Advances in national accounts and in research and theory developed in this era interacted, with each affecting the other. Many of the principal researchers, including the Kuznets[10] and Keynes, were also intimately involved in the development of the accounts. And many of those at Commerce charged with developing the expenditure accounts had both participated in wartime planning work and had an interest in Keynesian theory and forecasting.[11]

Keynes, for example, worked on the development of the UK accounts and was the author of the volume introducing the UK accounts. Kuznets, who is often remembered for his role in developing the national accounts, was primarily an applied theoretician who used the national accounts and other data in his extensive research on economic growth and development. As might be expected of one with such a background,

---

[8] As Keynes famously said, "Long-run is a misleading guide to current affairs; in the long run we are all dead."

[9] Richard T. Froyen, *Principle of Macroeconomics* (1988)

[10] See articles by Kuznets (1948) and Gilbert, Jaszi, Dennison et al. (1948).

[11] "Forecasts and Models based on Keynesian theory" used the relationship between disposable income and consumption to estimate marginal propensities to consume and future saving and consumption for wartime planning (inflationary gap, etc.).

many of Kuznets' contributions to the construction of the National Income Accounts were theoretical and conceptual. And after leaving Commerce, he was engaged in a spirited debate with the professional staff at Commerce over theoretical issues regarding the appropriate aggregates and measures of capital formation to be included in the expanded National Income and Product Accounts. Milton Gilbert, who was responsible for developing the expenditure estimates, perceived his task as developing a picture of the economy in "Keynesian terms."[12]

The categories chosen for the expenditure accounts $(Y = C + I + G + (X-M))$ reflected wartime planning needs, Keynesian theory, and interest in forecasting and business cycles, but also reflect the long history of economic theory regarding consumer spending, investment and capital formation, international trade, and government's effects on the economy. Their choice provided categories for which this rich body of research and theory could be tested and used in economic policies and the understanding of business cycles and growth. Unlike economic indicators, the expenditure categories for GNP were chosen based on theory and usefulness in testing economic theory for a better understanding of the economy to direct policy. It was not based on the availability of data or the correlation of the available data with GNP. Indeed, much of the data required new and expanded surveys.

Researchers at the NBER continued a long line of research on the distribution of income. Friedman et al. (1948), who directed a two-volume NBER study on the development of income distribution estimates for the United States, noted that such measures were necessary for the measurement of economic welfare and were also of value in better understanding the impact of changes in the distribution of income

on the size and distribution of aggregate demand.[13]

In 1942, the Commerce Department's Office of Business Economics (OBE), then charged with producing the National Accounts, produced initial GNP estimates. GNP was presented in current and constant prices. In 1944, OBE developed estimates of the distribution of income by households. In 1947, OBE released an integrated set of accounts including aggregates for national income, gross and net national product or expenditure, personal income, and disposable income. The accounts were presented with a system of six double-entry accounts. Sectoral accounts were provided for business, government, persons, and the rest of the world. There was also a gross saving and investment account.

1950s: In the 1950s, a number of researchers including Abramovitz (1956), Fabricant (1954), Kendrick (1956), and Solow (1957) explored the sources of economic growth using extensions of the new national accounts. Solow's oft-cited article laid out what is now described as the Solow growth model, which is based on classical production theory, a production function with constant returns to scale (Cobb–Douglas), and Euler's theorem. In equilibrium, factor prices (wages and the real rental price of capital) equal their marginal products and the factor shares of income in national income can be used to measure the inputs of labor and capital to output (GNP) and output (GNP) growth.

$$\Delta Q / Q = \Delta A / A + (RK/Q)^*(\Delta K/K)$$
$$+ (wL/Q)^*(\Delta L/L)$$

where Q is measured by real GNP; R is the real rental price of capital; w is the real wage rate; A is technical change, which is measured as a residual and described as either multi-factor productivity or total factor productivity; (RK/Q)

---

[12] See Carson (1975) p. 169.

[13] Friedman (1948).

and $+(wL/Q)$ are capital and labor's respective shares of National Income; and K is the nation's stock of productive capital. (Note that all of these aggregates are included in today's National Accounts).

Since Solow was measuring long-run growth over the period 1909—49, he used historical estimates from Goldsmith, Kendrick, Douglas, and assumptions and estimates of his own. However, Solow's growth accounting theory and analysis highlighted the importance of these data for the new National Accounts and indicated directions for their extension.

Solow's results also highlighted the analytical and policy importance of such data. He found that 88% of the near doubling of output per man hour during this period was the result of technical change and only 12% was from increased capital per worker. This finding had significant implications for economic policies relating to investment in physical capital and economic growth, investments in technology, and classical models of growth.

However, as Solow noted, some of his assumptions and data might "really drive a purist mad" but provide "some crude and useful conclusions."[14] Indeed his landmark study, and early work by others, provided an important theoretical foundation for improvements and extensions in the new national income and product accounts.

In 1951, as part of an expansion of the GNP accounts, BEA (the Bureau of Economic Analysis)—the successor to OBE—introduced implicit price deflators and the first annual constant-dollar estimates of GNP. BEA introduced quarterly constant-dollar estimates in 1958. These constant-dollar estimates facilitated "the analysis of economic growth, including productivity, for the economy as a whole."[15]

In addition to these advances in the measurement of production and expenditures, in 1953, OBE began periodically updating the income distribution estimates originally developed in 1944. These estimates of the income distribution across income groups were introduced as a special supplement to BEA's National Income estimates.[16] These estimates were an important step forward in providing an understanding of economic welfare derived from the accounts. They were also of use to those studying market demand. However, the need to update the series to incorporate new source data combined with resource constraints led to the series being discontinued in 1965.[17]

1960s: The work by Solow and others was the impetus for decades of work by Dale Jorgenson and others in extending and improving the theoretical and empirical analysis and the underlying data for studies of the sources of growth. This further research demonstrated that although technical change (or multifactor productivity) was an important factor in growth, it accounted for only about 20% of economic growth since WWII with improved measures of capital and labor services accounting for most of growth.

This theoretical and empirical work on accounting for growth ended up providing a blueprint for the expansion and improvement of the US National Accounts for decades.

---

[14] Solow also noted that "(1) better measurement of human capital investments that captured increased labor quality inputs would lower the residual in growth (A, or technical change, included in the GDP production function shown in the text) attributed to technical change and (2) technical change may also have its costs ...." Also, technical change as identified by the residual is quite crude and can contain any omitted variables.

[15] Carson (1987).

[16] BEA (1953).

[17] A new version of the series was introduced in 1973 BEA but publication was ended in 1981. The Bureau once again cited budget constraints.

Jorgenson and Griliches (1967), building on Jorgenson's earlier theoretical work (1966), extended Solow's theoretical model and empirical estimates by expanding the production function to allow for multiple outputs and inputs using: output decomposed into consumption and investment, theoretically superior aggregation indices, unbiased investment goods prices, separate data on capital and labor utilization, theoretically based measures of capital services by type of capital in place of asset prices, and aggregation of labor by quality.

As a result of these innovations, Jorgenson and Griliches were able to show that for the period 1945–65, technical change or total factor productivity (the residual in economic growth computations) accounted for 13% of productivity growth (and 3% of growth in output/GNP). However, for the period 1953–65, total factor productivity accounted for 20% of economic growth, a significantly larger share than for the entire period, but growth in capital and labor inputs still accounted for most economic growth during this subperiod.

Jorgenson and Griliches' article included a list of improvements to National Accounts suggested by theory and their research. This list included:

1. Use of theoretically superlative quantity indexes. Jorgenson and Griliches suggested Divisia indexes. Although the impact was small in their period of analysis, as BEA discovered in the 1980 and 1990s, during periods with significant changes in prices (e.g., oil, agricultural, and computer prices), the impact of "substitution bias" in fixed indexes or implicit deflators could be large. In the 1990s, BEA switched to Chain-Weighted indexes, which is a form of Fisher superlative that uses current period weights for adjacent periods to reduce substitution bias.

2. Improvement of measures of investment and other prices by replacing input prices used to measure output prices with direct output price indexes and by using quality-adjusted prices for automobiles, computers, and other hard-to-measure goods and services.

3. Incorporation of a fully articulated production account, including symmetrically measured capital services and labor services using rates of return, depreciation, and taxes by type of physical and human capital.[18]

   a. Improved classification and aggregation of labor inputs based on data on wage differentials by education, occupation, and gender.

4. New and separate data on labor and capital utilization to control for business cycle effects by adjusting capital and labor services.

5. Further detail, especially disaggregation of output and inputs by individual industry. (Further detail by legal form of business would also facilitate the analysis of tax and other issues.)

Jorgenson and Griliches were not the only researchers concerned with measurement and Denison (1969). Denison constructed a fully articulated growth accounting framework based on the national income and expenditure accounts in *Why Growth Rates Differ* (1967). His debate with Jorgenson and Griliches (1967) was the backdrop for widening research on the appropriate theoretical and empirical basis for measuring growth. Gordon (1968), for example, pointed to

---

[18] Solow's model implicitly used the marginal product of labor and capital (which are equal to the wage rate and the real rental rate, respectively) by using labor and capital shares of income. Jorgenson and Griliches, based on Jorgenson's earlier work, use a more complete cost of capital model where the cost of capital is: $P_k K_k = q_k (r + \delta_k - (\Delta q_k/q_k))K_k$. In other words, the rental price of a capital asset must at least cover the real return the owner of the asset could have made by investing his funds elsewhere, the depreciation in the value of the asset, plus or minus any capital gain or loss on the asset.

problems in the measurement of private capital stocks (exclusion of government-financed capital used in the private sector), which caused large anomalies in capital output ratios used in growth accounting studies covering the period 1929–48.

Although there are necessarily lags in the extensions and changes to official statistics, in response to the continued interest in accounting for growth, the OBE introduced official estimates of tangible wealth in private nonresidential structures and equipment in 1962. In 1964, OBE released input–output tables for 85 industries for the year 1958 that was statistically and definitionally consistent with the NIPA's. They also developed more accurate implicit price deflators in the 1970s (and 1980s).

Increasing interest in the use of econometric models built on national accounts for understanding fiscal and monetary policy, growth, and business cycles resulted in OBE taking over the quarterly econometric model of the US economy developed by Lawrence Klein. BEA enhanced the linkages to the national accounts and enlarged the size of the model.[19]

BEA made a number of expansions in its regional accounts, including urban area estimates, quarterly state personal income estimates, and the development of the OBERS regional projections program. These advances were built on advances in forecasting and computer processing. The beneficiaries of these consistent data and projections were those involved in the allocation of Federal grants to states, state and local tax and planning officials, business planners, and regional economists working to understand the pattern of geographic growth.

1970s: In the 1970s, researchers continued to work on better measuring growth and productivity. Jorgenson and Griliches (1972) updated some of their estimates in response to Denison's critique. Christensen and Jorgenson (1973) introduced the

cost of capital and capital services based on a tax model developed by Jorgenson and Hall (1967 and 1971). Christensen and Jorgenson (1973) also developed an internally consistent system of income, product, and wealth accounts using a more complete theoretical framework and modifications to BEA's official national income, product, and wealth accounts. One of the objectives of Christensen and Jorgenson's accounting system was to provide data from econometric modeling on the behavior of producers and consumers.

Gordon (1970, 1971, 1973, 1978) published a number of papers that critiqued the official price indexes for failing to adjust for quality change in the price indexes for investment deflators and real investment. The absence of such adjustments biased up price indexes and biased down real investment and capital services in accounting for growth. The evidence Gordon presented provided additional support for Jorgenson and Griliches' call for better investment price indexes.

In the 1970s, BEA responded to these research findings—and to increasing inflation—by developing new methods for measuring price changes in a number of components of GNP. BEA expanded the level of detail for prices and started including quarterly estimates. BEA also introduced fixed-weight price and output indexes, which removed the effect of weight shifts captured by shifts in the implicit price deflators but which introduced substitution bias problems into the accounts.

In all of these changes, BEA was cognizant of its role as an official statistical agency, which was to provide a wide variety of users with data that were objective, accurate, and relevant. The Bureau's role was to provide researchers with a statistical tool kit to use in their research and to answer policy questions, but not to conduct the research. Also, one of the key characteristics of National Accounts is that, for the most part,

---

[19] Lienberg, Hirsch, Popkin (1996); Klein (1963); Klein and Popkin (1961).

they are consistently constructed by all of the developed, and many of the developing, countries of the world. Changes to the International System of National Accounts require consensus, and change tends to come slowly.

Another important set of developments in the 1970s was that, after several decades of strong post—WWII growth, there was increasing criticism of growth for growth's sake and of the use of GNP per capita as a shorthand measure of economic and social welfare. As Nordhaus and Tobin (1973) in their famous study, "Is Growth Obsolete?" pointed out, after several decades of policy interest and theoretical and empirical advances in measuring growth, questions were being raised about the desirability and possibility of future growth. Nordhaus and Tobin examined the impact of growth by constructing an expanded measure of economic welfare that corrected for the bigger discrepancies between economic welfare and GNP, many of them going back to Kuznets' warning that National Income and GNP were a measure of market transactions, not economic welfare.

Nordhaus and Tobin began their computation of economic welfare by using Net National Product (GNP less depreciation), which is often used as a measure of the level of consumption that can be sustained by replacing the capital used up in production in each period. They then added imputed values for the services of government capital and consumer durables, leisure time, and nonmarket work.

Against these imputed additions to NNP, they deducted an estimate of those components of GNP that do not directly contribute to welfare but are analogous to other intermediate inputs that are deducted when computing GNP. These deductions included defense spending, police protection, and public health expenditures.[20]

They also deducted an estimate of what Kuznets called the disamenities of modern life (their estimate was of the disamenities of urbanization), and the depreciation on the stock of government and household capital.

Finally, using a neoclassical growth model, Nordhaus and Tobin pointed out that although NNP is a measure of sustainable GNP in a static economy, in an economy with technical change and population growth, one must deduct the amount needed to keep the capital stock growing at the rate of population growth plus the rate of technical change/total factor productivity.

The resulting estimates of Measure of Economic Welfare (MEW) were significantly larger than GNP but grew at a slower rate. Between 1929 and 1965, MEW grew at a 2.3% annual rate and GNP grew at a 3.1% annual rate. Also, the MEW estimates were far less volatile than GNP, actually growing by 5% between 1929 and 1935 during the Great Depression, while the market economy, as measured by GNP, declined by 17%.

Nordhaus and Tobin then used a neoclassical growth model to look at the impact of population growth on economic welfare and on natural resources. They concluded that, although slower growth in population—through its impact on resource use and consumption per capita—would increase welfare somewhat, there was no reason to restrain growth in population. They also concluded that while MEW was a useful measure that provided a different picture of economic welfare, it did not alter the broad picture of growth presented by GNP.

Although the Nordhaus and Tobin's study is among the most cited works on extending the National Accounts to provide a more comprehensive measure of economic welfare, a number of other economists were working in this area at the same time. An NBER Series in Income and

---

[20] These proposals were, and remain, quite controversial. Such expenditures were also described as defensive expenditures. As George Jaszi (1971), OBE's Director, observed (1971), such distinctions could be quite subjective, and even houses could be regarded as defensive expenditures against the weather.

Wealth volume, *The Measurement of Economic and Social Performance*, edited by Milton Moss (1973), is an example of this work, as is the BEA volume, The Economic Accounts of the United States: Retrospect and Prospect (1971).[21]

Notable examples of the work at this time include the contributions of Christensen and Jorgenson (1973), Eisner (1973 and 1978), Juster et al. (1973) and Ruggles and Ruggles (1973). Christenson and Jorgenson developed a theoretical and empirical framework for a complete system of national accounts by integrating the production approach (outputs and inputs) with the welfare approach (income and expenditure). This system required better estimation and integration of capital stocks. Juster proposed an expanded system that included many of the extensions suggested by Tobin and Nordhaus (services of consumer durables and especially the valuation of nonmarket time). Eisner recommended these and other improvements such as the treatment of R&D and other variables as investment and using measures of economic depreciation rather than tax-based depreciation lives. Ruggles and Ruggles also proposed changes to the conceptual design of the accounts and reiterated their long-standing interest in more detailed data in the national accounts.

The Office of Business Economics responded to these interests in expanding the national accounts to better measure economic welfare and the environment by establishing a new program to produce a series of studies that provided estimates of these extensions based on the theoretical and empirical models suggested by these and other researchers. BEA's studies (1980) addressed measurement of nonmarket economic activity in the areas of household work, valuation of the services of consumer durables and government capital, and nonrenewable resources.

These studies demonstrated the feasibility of producing such estimates but also revealed the sensitivity of the estimates to alternative methods and assumptions, gaps in the data, and their impact on the usefulness and relevance of the core accounts. Although a theoretically correct measure of economic welfare would include nonmarket economic activity in their utility function, the magnitude of the associated imputations in GNP and their behavior over time could moderate or swamp business cycle movements, obscure trends in growth in the market sector, and reduce the usefulness of the national accounts for monetary, fiscal, and growth policies. For example, as noted above, the replacement of Nordhaus and Tobin's MEW for GNP would suggest that economic welfare rose, rather than fell, during the Great Depression. As demonstrated by Landefeld and Hines (1985), the capitalization of the additions to investment and GNP and to National Wealth by the addition to proven US crude oil reserves associated with the discovery of oil reserves on the North Slope of Alaska in 1970 would have offset a significant share of the economic problems of the 1970s (even though most of the monetary returns from this discovery would only show up in income and production well into the future).

The nonmarket economics program was discontinued in 1981 for budgetary reasons and the staff was transferred to work on pressing issues in other areas.

1980s: In the 1980s, research continued on production and welfare accounting. Meanwhile, new topics affecting BEA arose. These included the need for accurate measures to better measure and understand the depreciation, capital stocks, inflation and the underground economy; the need for more data to better understand foreign

---

[21] M. Moss, *The Measurement of Economic and Social Performance*, NBER Series in Income and Wealth (1973); and Office of Business Economics, *The Economic Accounts of the United States: Retrospect and Prospect*, U.S., Anniversary Issue of the *Survey of Current Business*, July 1971.

direct investment and the behavior of multinational companies; and better measures of the economic impact of technology.

Hulten and Wykoff's (1981) landmark study of used asset prices (different vintages of capital) to estimate the rate and form of depreciation consistent with Cobb Douglas or fixed coefficients production functions found that, for most assets, depreciation is geometric. This result had important implications for further work by Jorgenson and others working on the analysis of growth and the productivity slowdown.

The large impact of base-year changes in constant-dollar GDP estimates, continued concerns about upward bias in price indexes (and downward bias in real GDP growth), and concerns about the need for quality adjustments in prices stimulated renewed research on several topics—namely, research on price and output index theory and on the use of hedonic indexes to separate quality change from price change, especially for computers.[22]

In other developments in the area of production and welfare accounting, Jorgenson and Fraumeni (1989) extended Jorgenson's system of accounts to include human capital, which allowed for the symmetric treatment of physical and human capital stocks and capital services and labor services as well as a better basis for tracking and estimating the impact of investments in human capital on economic growth.

As documented by Carson (1984), a number of researchers noted anomalies in the stocks and flows of money, GNP, and income that affected key macroeconomic aggregates used in monetary and other macroeconomic policies. These anomalies seemed to be related, in part, to the underground economy, which resulted in calls for BEA to better measure this sector.

Other researchers, including Lipsey (1973–2010), Caves (1971, 1982), and Kindleberger (1968), renewed long-standing interest in foreign direct investment, including the economic transactions of multinational firms.[23] This interest—as well as public concern—was partly stimulated by concerns over rising foreign investment in the United States but was also motivated by interest in the impact of taxes on foreign direct investment and the associated measurement of US and foreign assets and liabilities, affiliated-party exports, imports, receipts, and expenditures.

In addition to interest in the measurement of foreign direct investment, there was growing interest and research on the role of services and the need for greater accuracy and detail in BEA's estimates of service exports and imports.

The statistical response to these various issues included work by BEA and the Bureau of Labor Statistics. One of the most important statistical innovations in the 1980s was the Bureau of Labor Statistics' introduction in 1983 of their Multifactor Productivity Program, which produced Multifactor Productivity estimates for the private business sector and major sectors of the economy. The program was largely based on the sets of accounts laid out by Dale Jorgenson and his coauthors.

BEA's response to these various strands of research, policy, public interest, and changes in the economy was focused on measurement issues related to its core National, International, and Regional Accounts. These included the introduction of BEA's first surveys of US direct investment abroad and international

---

[22] Many researchers looking at the productivity statistics, including Solow (1987), noted that, "You can see the computer age everywhere but in the productivity statistics."

[23] Robert Lipsey was a prolific researcher in the area of foreign direct investment, working closely with BEA staff and suggesting improvements in the data. His publications span four decades, from Lipsey and Weiss (1973) to Lipsey et al. (2010).

transactions in services and the development and introduction of a quality-adjusted hedonic index for computers in collaboration with IBM.

In the regional area, cumulative advances in regional economic theory and modeling resulted in calls for BEA to expand its regional economic impact model and provide more detailed geography. BEA responded by introducing a revised version of its regional model, with its Regional Input-Output Modelling System II (1981, 1986) and by introducing Gross State Product estimates in 1985.

As a result of new developments in macroeconomic theory, expanding research and interest in econometrics and large-scale econometric models, and advances in computers, BEA (1985) expanded its econometric model of GNP to a quarterly model with about 190 stochastic equations. Earlier versions of the model included only 36 stochastic equations.

1990s: In the 1990s, research on productivity continued, with focus on the role of services in slower productivity growth. In the latter half of the 1990s, research by Jorgenson and Stiroh (2000), Sichel and Oliner (2000), and others focused on the acceleration of productivity growth since 1995. There was also renewed concern about accounting for the impact of the economy on the environment.

The economy seemed to suffer from Baumol's disease, with slow growth in productivity in services pulling down overall growth in productivity. Griliches (1994), in his AEA Presidential address, pointed to these problems in the measurement of services productivity. Corrado and Slifman (1999), prompted by measurement concerns voiced by Fed Chairman Greenspan, explored the understatement of services productivity growth. As part of research conducted at BEA and the Federal Reserve Board and by Brookings—through a program cosponsored by NBER and BEA in the 1990s, Triplett and Bosworth (2004) found that properly measured, services productivity, particularly in IT and

computer-using service industries, was registering strong productivity growth.

Internal research at BEA, Diewert, and others on index numbers highlighted the value of introducing chain-weighted output and price indexes (a form of a superlative Fisher index). The use of current and adjacent period weights in a geometric formula eliminates much of the substitution bias embodied in fixed weights. BEA's use of fixed weights resulted in an overstatement of real GDP growth in periods after the base year and an understatement of growth in periods before the base period. The practice also caused significant revisions in the entire GDP time series when BEA updated its fixed base year for constant dollars.

In other developments, Fraumeni (1997) extended Hulten and Wykoff's work on depreciation and integrated it with her work with Dale Jorgenson on a conceptually consistent set of accounts to develop empirically and theoretically superior measures of depreciation in the NIPAs and in BEA's tangible wealth estimates.

A renewal of concern about the environment in the 1980 and 1990s prompted interest in better accounting for the interaction between the economy and the environment. These concerns led to the development of the United Nation's (1993) System of Integrated Economic Environmental Accounts. The BEA developed its own System of Economic and Environmental Satellite Accounts (Landefeld and Carson, 1994). The main difference between these sets of accounts was that the BEA accounts were based more firmly on economic theory and methods and the economic literature, especially with respect to the symmetric treatment of investment and depletion of natural resources, a point made by Nordhaus and Kokkelenberg (1999) and Nordhaus (2006). Although the National Academy of Sciences Panel Study endorsed BEA's work on environmental accounting, work on the project was suspended by the US Congress.

During the benchmark revisions of 1994–95 and 1999, BEA introduced chain-weighted price and output indexes; improved estimates of depreciation, capital stocks, and investments in software; and recognized government investment along with a partial measure of services from government capital. BEA's estimates of the opportunity cost or services of government capital was set equal to the depreciation of government capital (as it was used up in "production"), but no imputation was made for the opportunity cost or return on government capital).

2000s: Research on improved price measures continued at the Federal Reserve Board, BEA, and BLS and by academic researchers. Research also continued on the resurgence in productivity growth since 1995. Researchers and policymakers in the United States and abroad began to emphasize the importance of integrating and improving the consistency of major macroeconomic data, notably the components of the system of national accounts.

Corrado and her coauthors at the Federal Reserve Board conducted research to develop a number of price indexes for IT equipment and services. Researchers at BEA worked independently and with BLS to develop new IT and services prices.

Growing US and international interest in improving the consistency and integration of macroeconomic data expressed itself in the revision of the International Monetary Fund's (IMF) *Balance of Payments Manual* and the International *System of National Accounts* produced by the United Nations, the European Union, the World Bank, and the Organization for Economic and Community Development. The increasing globalization of the world's economies and the increasing importance of coordinated economic policies resulted in increased demands for data that were consistent over time and within and across countries.

The continued importance of growth accounting in economic policy, especially in explaining the recovery of productivity growth and the Great Recession, was also important factor in

harmonizing the various international macro-accounting rules. Over and over since the 1960s, the highly integrated production and welfare accounts developed by Dale Jorgenson had demonstrated their value and were doing so again. The impact of the housing and financial crisis on spending and production leading to the Great Recession underlined the importance of integrated wealth expenditure and production accounts. The importance of integrated accounts and quality-adjusted IT prices were also illustrated by the work of Jorgenson and Stiroh (1999, 2000) and others in explaining the resurgence in US productivity in the 1990s.

The report by Stiglitz, Sen, and Fitoussi (2009, 2010) on defects in GDP as a measure of welfare, the impact of the Great Recession, and the broad secular increase in inequality documented by Piketty and Saez (2003) launched a decade of renewed discussions and research on the measurement of economic welfare. At the same time, on the production side, there was renewed interest in improving the consistency and better integrating the national accounts produced by BEA, BLS, and the Federal Reserve Board.

The Stiglitz panel report reviewed the familiar inadequacies with GDP as a measure of economic welfare and suggested alternatives ranging from extensions to alternatives to GDP. The extensions were similar to those included in the estimates developed during the post–WWII era by such people as Nordhaus and Tobin, Jorgenson and his coauthors, Eisner, Kendrick, and others (see above). The alternatives to GDP included dashboards of economic and welfare indicators and subjective well-being indexes based on survey data.

BEA responded (Landefeld and Villones, 2010) to the renewed interest in accounting for economic welfare by presenting the outlines of a broad plan, GDP and Beyond, that would include improvements within the scope of GDP and through extensions of the scope of GDP through supplemental or satellite accounts. These would include supplemental accounts on: (1) the distribution of personal income at the national and regional level; (2) measures of sustainability such as net domestic product per capita, net investment per capita, and net worth per capita; and (3) other satellite accounts including those for household production, energy, natural resources, and recreation.

In earlier and more recent work, BEA has produced research studies and satellite account estimates for the national and regional distribution of personal income; household production; water and oceans; health care; human capital; natural resource and environmental accounts; and outdoor recreation. BEA has no plans to develop, either weighted or unweighted dashboards of welfare or survey-based measures of subjective well-being.[24]

In order to build on, prioritize, and integrate these various estimates into a set of regularly published supplements, BEA has initiated work on developing a plan and prototype estimates for extended supplemental accounts that better measure economic welfare.[25] In addition to the issues raised by Stiglitz, Sen, and Fitoussi, there have been calls for national accounts statistics that better capture the effects of globalization. BEA is currently working on these issues and hopes to incorporate supplemental global accounts in this plan for extended accounts.

The slow recovery from the Great Recession renewed interest in the determinants of growth, especially the impact of investments in intangible capital such as research and development. Corrado et al. (2005) constructed a set of direct measures of the impact of R&D within a national accounts framework. BEA responded by developing capitalized measures of real and nominal capital expenditures on R&D and treating them as investment rather than as an intermediate expense in GDP.

The other key set of developments since 2000 has been interest in, and work on, better integrating and extending the US National Accounts currently produced by BEA, BLS, and the Federal Reserve within the decentralized statistical system. This interest was paralleled by international interest which resulted in the United Nations (2013) Guidelines on Integrated Economic Statistics (2013). Also, the 2008 version of the SNA made a step forward in the integration of national accounts into a complete and consistent system of accounts by recommending the development of supplemental estimates of capital services.

Jorgenson, Landefeld, and Nordhaus' *A New Architecture for the National Accounts* (2004) presented a framework and methods for a system of integrated market and nonmarket accounts. Jorgenson and Landefeld presented a blueprint for expanded and integrated US economic accounts (2004). Nordhaus (2006) and Abraham and Mackie (2006) presented principles and a framework for nonmarket accounts. The volume also included a number of papers that presented methods and estimates for extending and integrating the national accounts.

Most of the changes for the national accounts proposed by Jorgenson and Landefeld were a summary of the extensions and suggestions in the integrated frameworks put forth earlier by Jorgenson, Fraumeni, and others.[26] The *New Architecture*, Dale Jorgenson's chairmanship of the BEA Advisory Committee, and his work with BLS and the Federal Reserve helped to foster long-term work that evolved from prototypes

---

[24] For a discussion of some of the problems of subjective measures of well-being, see Landefeld and Villones (2009), and BEA Advisory Committee Meeting, "GDP Beyond: Priorities and Plans," November 9, 2018, https://www.bea.gov/about/bea-advisory-committee.

[25] BEA Advisory Committee Meeting, "GDP Beyond: Priorities and Plans," November 9, 2018, https://www.bea.gov/about/bea-advisory-committee.

[26] See, for example, Fraumeni (1999).

to the regular production by BLS and BEA (Integrated aggregate production MFP accounts (2006–16), Integrated industry-level production MFP accounts (2012–15)) and by FRB and BEA of estimates of integrated financial and production accounts (2007–16).[27]

2.5 Conclusion and next steps

This chapter has attempted to demonstrate the successful interaction between economic theory, research, and the development of the US National Accounts. In contrast to Business Cycle Indicators, which were described by Koopmans as measurement without theory, the National Accounts have been built up over time on a large body of economic theory dating back to the 1700s. From the Great Depression and World War II to the productivity slowdown and the Great Recession, there has been a synergy between the accounts and advances in economic theory and research on production and welfare. As a result, today's national accounts—as outlined in standard textbooks—look as though they are inextricably intertwined with modern macroeconomic theory.

Although there are lags between advances in research and theory and developments in the structure of the economy, the accounts seem to have done well over the last 75 plus years in evolving and keeping up. Their very relevance confirms it. That said, a significant volume of work remains. The key next steps include:

- Completing and fully integrating the three components of the US National Accounts produced by BEA, BLS, and the Federal Reserve Board.
- Making the changes in concepts and measurement outlined in the *New Architecture*.

- Better measuring economic welfare through:
  - The regular publication of supplemental accounts such as those on the distribution of income, natural resources and the environment, and human capital;
  - The preparation of an aggregate social welfare measure, such as those developed by Jorgenson or Jones and Klenow; and
  - The development of a set of sustainability measures to highlight such measures already included in the national accounts such as Net Domestic Product and Net Investment.
- Better measuring the impact of globalization and other sectoral changes on production, expenditures, and income, and their distribution (across industries, regions, and households).
  - Some of these changes will require changes in concepts, measures, and methods within the scope of the existing accounts;
  - Others will require supplemental or satellite accounts estimates.
- Continued vigilance in updating the National Accounts to keep them timely, accurate, and relevant.

References

Abramovitz M: Resources and output trends in the U.S. since 1870, *American Economic Review, Papers and Proceedings*, 1956:5–23, 1956. XLVI.

Abraham KG, Mackie C: A framework for nonmarket accounting. In Jorgenson DW, Landefeld JS, Nordhaus WD, editors: *NBER Stidies in Income and Wealth*, 2006, pp 161–192.

Bureau of Economic Analysis: *Income distribution in the United States by size, 1944-1950*, U.S. Office of Business Economics.

Bureau of Economic Analysis: *Measuring non-market activity*, Survey of Current Business.

Bureau of Economic Analysis: *Measuring nonmarket economic activity*, BEA Working Papers.

Boisguillbert P: *Dissertation de la Nature des Richesses*, 1707.

---

[27] See Harper et al. (2009); Teplin et al. (2006); Fleck et al. (2012).

Cantillon R: *Essai Sur La Nature du Commerce en General*, 1755.

Carson CS: The history of the United States national income and product accounts: the development of an analytical tool, *Review of Income and Wealth* 21:153–181, 1975.

Carson CS: *The underground economy: an introduction*vol. 64. Survey of Current Business, pp 2–37.

Carson CS: *Post-world war II history of BEA, attachment to memorandum to Cooper BJ, Director of commerce public affairs*, 1987.

Caves RE: International corporations: the industrial economics of foreign investment, *Economica*, 1971:1–27, 1971.

Caves RE: *Multinational enterprise and economic analysis*, Cambridge University Press.

Christensen LR, Jorgenson DW: Measuring economic performance in the private sector. In Moss M, editor: *The measurement of economic and social performance*Studies in income and wealth, vol. 37.

Corrado C, Slifman L: Decomposition of productivity and unit costs, *The American Economic Review* 89:328–332, 1999.

Corrado C, Hulten C, Sichel D: Measuring capital and technology. In Corrado C, Haltiwanger J, Sichel D, editors: *Measuring capital in the new economy* NBER studies in income and wealth.

Dennison EF: *Why growth rates differ*, The Brookings Institution.

Denison EF: Some major issues in productivity analysis: an examination of of estimates by Jorgenson and Grilliches, *Survey of Current Business* 5:65–94, 1969.

Diebold FX, Rudebusch GD: Forecasting output with the composite leading index: a real-time analysis, *Journal of the American Statistical Association*, 1991:603–610, 1991.

Eisner R: Total incomes in the United States, 1959 and 1969, *Review of Income and Wealth* 24(no. 1):41–70, 1978.

Fabricant S: *Economic progress and economic change, 34th annual report of the national bureau of economic research*, 1954.

Filardo A: *How reliable are recession prediction models? Economic review*, 2nd quarter, Federal Reserve Bank of Kansas City.

Fleck S, Rosenthal S, Russel M, Strassner E, Usher L: *A prototype BEA/BLS industry-level production account for the United States*, Survey of Current Business.

Fraumeni BF: *The measurement of depreciation in the U.S. national income and product accounts*, Survey of Current Business, pp 7–23.

Fraumeni BF: The Jorgenson system of national accounting. In Lau LJ, editor: *Econometrics and the cost of capital: essays in honor of Dale W. Jorgenson*, 1999, pp 111–142.

Friedman M, Brady D, Warburton C, Harriss CL: *Income size distributions in the United States part I and part II, Studies in Income and Wealth*, NBER, 1943.

Froyen RT: *Principle of macroeconomics*, Macmillan.

Gilibert G: *Circular flow, the new palgrave: a dictionary of economics*, Macmillan, pp 424–426.

Gordon RJ: $45 billion of U.S. private investment has been mislaid, *The American Economic Review* 59:221–238, 1968.

Gordon RJ: Adjusting investment deflators for changes in quality, *Proceedings of the American Statistical Association, Business and Economics Section*, 1970:174–183, 1970.

Gordon RJ: Measurement bias in price indexes for capital goods, *Review of Income and Wealth* 17, 1971.

Gordon RJ: The use of unit values to measure deviations of transaction prices from list prices, *Review of Income and Wealth* 19, 1973.

Gordon RJ: *Price changes in durable goods: can we trust government measurements? Electric 95 Perspectives*, 1978, pp 28–38. no. 5.

Grilliches Z: Productivity, R&D and the data constraint, *The American Economic Review*, 1994:1–23, 1994.

Hall RE, Jorgenson DW: Tax policy and investment behavior, *The American Economic Review* (3):391–414, 1967.

Hall RE, Jorgenson DW: Application of the theory of optimum capital accumulation. In Fromm G, editor: *Tax incentives and capital spending*, 1971, pp 9–60.

Harper M, Moulton BR, Rosenthal S, Wasshausen DB: Integrated GDP-productivity accounts, *The American Economic Review*, 2009:74–79, 2009.

Hulten CR, Wykoff FC: The estimation of economic depreciation using vintage asset prices: an application of the Box-Cox power transformation, *Journal of Econometrics* 15: 367–396, 1981.

Jaszi G: An economic accountant's ledger, in the economic accounts of the United States: retrospect and prospect, *Survey of Current Business, 50th Anniversary Issue* 51(7), 1971.

Jorgenson DW: The embodiment hypothesis, *Journal of Political Economy* 74(1):1–17, 1966.

Jorgenson DW, Grilliches Z: The explanation of productivity change, *The Review of Economic Studies* (99):249–280, 1967.

Jorgenson DW, Grilliches Z: *Issues in growth accounting: a reply to Edward F. Dennison*, Survey of Current Business, pp 65–94. no. 5.

Jorgenson DW, Fraumeni BM: The accumulation of human and nonhuman capital, 1948-1964. In Lipsey RE, Tice HS, editors: *The measurement of saving, investment, and wealth*Studies in income and wealth, 1989, pp 227–282.

Jorgenson DW, Stiroh KJ: Information technology and growth, *The American Economic Review* 89(2):109–115, 1999.

Jorgenson DW, Stiroh KJ: Raising the speed limit: U.S. economic growth in the information age, *Brookings Papers on Economic Activity* (1):125–211, 2000.

Juster FT, Courant PN, Duncan JG, Robinson J, Stafford FP: *Time use in economic and social accounts*, University of Michigan Institute for Social Research, 1978.

Kendrick JW: Productivity trends: capital and labor, *Review of Economics and Statistics* (3):248–257, 1956.

Kendrick JW: The historical development of national income accounts, *History of Political Economy* II:284–315, 1970. Fall.

Kindleberger CP: *American business abroad*, 1968.

King WI, Knauth OW, Macauley FR: *Income distribution in the United States, its amount and distribution*, NBER.

Klein LR, Popkin J: An econometric analysis of the postwar relationship between inventory fluctuations and changes in aggregate economic activity. In *Joint economic committee, inventory fluctuations and economic stabilization, part III, 87th congress, 1st session*, 1961, pp 71–89.

Klein LR: *A postwar quarterly model: description and applications, Models of income determination*, 1963, pp 11–57.

Koopmans TC: Measurement without theory, *The Review of Economics and Statistics* 29(3):161–172, 1947.

Kuznets S: *National income, 1929–32, transmitted to congress in response to senate resolution No. 220*, 1934.

Kuznets S: National income: a new version, pp. 151–179. In Gilbert M, Jaszi G, Dennison EF, Shwartz CF, editors: *Objectives of national income measurement: a reply to professor Kuznets, Review of Economics and Statistics*, 1948, pp 179–195.

Landefeld JS, Hines J: National accounting for non-renewable natural resources in the mining industries, *Review of Income and Wealth*, 1985:1–20, 1985.

Landefeld JS, Carson CS: *Integrated economic and environmental satellite accounts*, Survey of Current Business, pp 34–49.

Landefeld JS: *GDP: one of the great innovations of the 20th century (and remarks by Daley W, Greenspan A, Baily MN, Shapiro RJ)*, Survey of Current Business, pp 6–11.

Landefeld JS, Moutlon BR, PLatt JD, Villones SM: GDP and beyond: measuring economic progress and sustainability, *Survey of Current Business* 25, 2010.

Lienberg M, Hirsch AA, Popkin J: *A quarterly econometric model of the United States: a progress report*, Survey of Current Business.

Lipsey RE, Weiss MY: *Multinational firms and the factor intensity of trade*, NBER.

Lipsey RE, Feenstra RE, Branstatter LG, et al.: *Report on the state of available data for the study of international trade and foreign direct investment*, NBER.

Mankiw NG: *Macroeconomics*, Ninth Edition, New York, 2016, Worth Publishers.

Marcuss RD, Kane RE: *U.S. national income and product statistics: born of the great depression and world war II*, Survey of Current Business, pp 32–46.

Marx K: *Das kapital* vol. II.

Moss M: *The measurement of economic and social performance*, NBER Studies in Income and Wealth.

Nordhaus WD, Tobin J: Is growth obsolete? In Moss M, editor: *The measurement of economic and social performance*, NBER, pp 509–564.

Nordhaus WD, Kokkelenberg EC: *Nature's numbers: Expanding the national economic accounts to include the environment, committee on national statistics panel on integrated environmental and economic accounting*, National Academies.

Nordhaus WD: Principles of national accounting for nonmarket accounts, A New Architecture for the U.S. National Accounts. In Jorgenson DW, Landefeld JS, Nordhaus WD, editors: *NBER Studies in Income and Wealth* vol. 66, pp 143–160.

Office of Business Economics: *The economic accounts of the United States: retrospect and prospect, anniversary issue of the survey of current business*, 1971.

Piketty T, Saez E: Income inequality in the United States, 1913–1998. In *The quarterly journal of economics* vol. CXVIII.

Quesnay F: *Analyse de la Formule arithmetique du Tableau economique*, 1766.

Ruggles R, Ruggles N: A proposal for a system of economic and social accounts. In Moss M, editor: *The measurement of social and economic performance*, 1973, pp 111–146.

Sichel D, Oliner S: The resurgence of growth in the late 1990s: is information technology the story? *The Journal of Economic Perspectives*, Fall 2000:3–22, Fall 2000.

Solow R: Technical change and the aggregate production function, *The Review of Economics and Statistics* (3): 312–320, 1957.

Solow R: *We'd better watch out*, New York Times Book Review, p 36.

Spahr CA: *An essay on the present distribution of wealth in the United Sates*, T. J. T. J. Crowell & Company.

Stiglitz JE, Sen A, Fitoussi JP: *Report by the commission on the measurement of economic performance and social progress*, 2009. and *Mismeasuring Our Lives*, 2010.

Stiglitz JE, Sen A, Fitoussii JP: *Report by the commission on the measurement of economic performance and social progress*, 2009. http://europa.eu/eurostat/documents/118025/ 118123/Fitoussi+Commision+report.

Teplin A, Hume-McIntosh S, Solomon G, Meade CI, Moses K, Mouton B: Integrated macroeconomic accounts for the United States: draft SNA-USA. In Jorgenson DW, Landefeld JS, editors: *A new architecture for the U.S. National accounts* NBER studies in income and wealth vol. 66.

Tilly G: John Maynard Keynes and the development of national accounts in Britain, 1895-1941, *Review of Income and Wealth, Series 55*, 2009:331–335, 2009. Number 2.

Triplett JE, Bosworth BP: *Productivity in the U.S. services sector: new sources of economic growth*, Brookings Institution Press, 2004.

United Nations: *Handbook on environmental economic accounting*, 1993.

United Nations. In Landefeld JS, Villones S, Havinga I, Csizmadia M, Singh G, Walton R, editors: *Guidelines on integrated economic statistics*, United Nations.

Further reading

Dennison EF: *Sources of economic growth in the United States and the alternative before Us*, Committee for Economic Development.

Friedman M, Brady D, Warburton C, Harris CL. Conference on research in income and wealth, National Bureau of Economic Research: *Income size distribution on the United States: part I, studies in income and wealth distribution* vol. 5.

Jorgenson DW: Production and welfare: progress in economic measurement, *Journal of Economic Literature* 56(3): 867—919, 2018.

Jorgenson DW, Landefeld JS, Nordhaus WD: *A new architecture for the U.S. National Accounts*, NBER, 2006.

Jorgenson DW, Landefeld JS, Schreyer P: *Measuring economic sustainability and progress*, 2014.

Kendrick JW: *Productivity trends in the United States*, NBER.

Keynes JM: *The general theory of employment, interest, and money*, First Harbinger Version, 1964.

Landefeld JS, Villones S, Holden A: *GDP and beyond: priorities and plans, BEA advisory committee meeting*. https://www.bea.gov/about/bea-advisory-committee.

Martin F, Landefeld JS, Peskin J: Estimates of the service values and opportunity costs of government capital, 1948-78, *Review of Income and Wealth*, 1984:331—349, 1984.

Organization for Economic and Community Development (OECD): *Measuring trade in value-added*, OCED. http://www.oecd.org/sti/ind/measuring-trade-in-value-added.htm.

Ruggles R, Ruggles N: *Integrated economic accounts for the United States, 1947-1980*, Survey of Current Business, pp 1—52. no. 5.

Timmer MP, Dietzenbacher E, Los B, Stehrer R, de Vries GJ: An illustrated user guide to the world input-output database: the case of global automotive production, *Review of International Economics* 23:575—605, 2015.

World input-output data base, Gronigen, 2018, WIOD. http://www.wiod.org/home.

Tax policy and resource allocation

Kun-Young Yun

Department of Economics, Yonsei University, Seoul, Korea

3.1 Introduction

Since Harberger (1962), measuring efficiency cost of taxation has been an important issue in tax policy analyses. The original Harberger model was a simple two-sector static model with fixed supplies of capital and labor. However, the real world is much more complex and, in response to the rising interest in reliable estimates of the economic effects of tax policy, economic models used for the analysis of tax policy have been extended in a number of important directions.

One of the most important innovations is the introduction of dynamic general equilibrium models in which consumers maximize intertemporal welfare and capital is accumulated through investment. Two types of models emerged along this line of developments. One is the overlapping generations (OLG) models introduced by Summers (1981) and Auerbach and Kotlikoff (1987). The other is the infinite time-horizon models of Chamley (1981, 1986) and Jorgenson and Yun (1986a, 1986b).

Another important development is the extension of models by introducing heterogeneous consumers and/or multiple commodities/industries as in Auerbach and Kotlikoff (1987),

Fullerton and Rogers (1993, 1996), and Jorgenson et al. (1997). These innovations enhanced the realism of the models and improved representation of the economy and the tax system. More importantly, the presence of heterogeneous consumers in the model made it possible to analyze distributional effects of tax policy.

Jorgenson and Yun (1986a, 1986b, 1990, 2001, 2013) developed a dynamic general equilibrium model (DGEM) of the US economy, which has been used to evaluate the welfare effects of various tax policies including major tax reform proposals in the United States. Our DGEM consists of four sectors: household, business, government, and the rest of the world. The household sector is populated by identical consumers with infinite life and perfect foresight. In the business sector, labor and capital services are used to produce consumption and investment goods. The government collects taxes, issues debts, purchases goods and services, and makes transfer payments to households and the rest of the world. The rest of the world trades with the United States in consumption goods, investment goods, and labor services.

In our DGEM, the cost of capital approach pioneered by Jorgenson in his celebrated paper

(Jorgenson, 1963) plays a central role by providing a convenient platform for representing the complex structure of taxation of income from capital in the United States. We employ the cost of capital approach to represent corporate income tax, individual taxes on capital income (interests, dividends, and capital gains), property taxes, economic depreciation, and the private returns to capital. Modeling the income tax on labor and the sales taxes on commodities is straightforward.

Section 3.2 describes the cost of capital for the corporate, noncorporate, and household sectors. The cost of capital is used to estimate the social and private rates of return on capital, tax wedges, and the corresponding effective tax rates. Section 3.3 describes the basic structure of DGEM and its parameterization. Section 3.4 describes the equilibrium and dynamics of the model and explains the solution algorithm. In Section 3.5, we measure the marginal and average efficiency costs of tax revenues from various parts of the US tax system. We also consider alternative tax reform proposals and discuss their welfare effects. Section 3.6 concludes the chapter.

3.2 Cost of capital and effective tax rates

3.2.1 Cost of capital

Capital services are consumed by households and used for production in corporate and noncorporate businesses. Tax treatment of income from capital depends upon the sector in which capital is employed. In order to represent these differences, we distinguish the demands for capital services from household,

noncorporate, and corporate sectors. Tax treatment of income from capital also depends upon the type of assets employed in the corporate and noncorporate sectors. The main differences in the tax treatment of assets in the business sectors are in investment tax credits and depreciation allowances for tax purposes. In addition, consumers and producers may treat capital services from different types of assets as less than perfect substitutes. We thus distinguish two types of assets based on durability, short-lived and long-lived assets, in each of the three sectors.[1]

The cost of capital approach introduced by Jorgenson (1963) provides a convenient and versatile vehicle for representing the complex details of the taxation of income from capital. It can easily handle the various tax reform proposals discussed in the tax policy circles around the world as well. The cost of capital approach starts with the assumption that equity holders maximize their wealth by appropriately choosing inputs and outputs in a given period of time and investment strategies over time. For income from corporate capital, equity holders are taxed on dividends and capital gains. The portfolio equilibrium of equity holders requires:

$$\text{Div}_t - \text{TD}_t + \left(1 - t_q^g\right)(E_t - E_{t-1} - N_t) = \rho_t^e E_{t-1}$$

$$(3.1)$$

where Div_t is dividends in period t, TD_t is individual income tax on dividends, t_q^g is marginal tax rate on accrued capital gains, E_t is the value of equity, N_t is the value of new share issues, and ρ_t^e is the equilibrium nominal rate of return to equity. TD_t is proportional to dividends, i.e., $\text{TD}_t = t_q^e \text{Div}_t$, where t_q^e is marginal tax rate on dividends.

[1] In the household sector, short-lived assets include consumer durables and producer durable equipment, and long-lived assets include residential and nonresidential structures and land. In the corporate and noncorporate sectors, short-lived assets include producer durable equipment and long-lived assets include residential and nonresidential structures, farm and nonfarm inventories, and land.

Under the transversality condition that

$$\prod_{s=1}^{\tau+1}\left(1+\frac{\rho^e_{s+t}}{1-t^g_q}\right)^{-1}E_{t+\tau+1}$$ approaches zero as τ

approaches infinity, Eq. (3.1) can be solved for E_t:

$$E_t = \sum_{\tau=0}^{\infty}\prod_{s=1}^{\tau+1}\left(1+\frac{\rho^e_{s+t}}{1-t^g_q}\right)^{-1}\left[\left(\frac{1-t^e_q}{1-t^g_q}-1\right)\right.$$

$$\left.Div_{t+\tau+1}+(Div_{t+\tau+1}-N_{t++1})\right]$$

(3.2)

We assume that dividends are a constant proportion α of corporate cash flow after property and corporate income taxes:

$$Div_t = \alpha\left[P_tQ_t(K_{t-1},L_t)-w_tL_t-(1-k_q\right.$$

$$-t_qz_q)\delta q_tK_{t-1}-t^p_qq_{t-1}K_{t-1}-\beta_q(1-k_q$$

$$\left.-t_qz_q)(i_t-\pi_t)q_{t-1}K_{t-1}-TC_t\right]$$

(3.3)

where P_t is price of output, $Q_t(.)$ is production function, K_{t-1} and L_t are capital and labor inputs, respectively, and w_t is wage rate. k_q and z_q are the rate of investment tax credit and the present value of depreciation allowances for one dollar's worth of investment, respectively, and t_q is corporate income tax rate. δ is rate of economic depreciation, q_t is price of investment good, t^p_q is property tax rate, β_q is debt/capital ratio, i_t and π_t are nominal interest rate and the rate of inflation, respectively, and TC_t is corporate income tax. The subscript q refers to the corporate sector.

Corporations are taxed on income from capital net of depreciation allowances, interest payments, and property taxes, and the tax liability is reduced by investment tax credits, i.e.:

$$TC_t = t_q\left[P_tQ_t-w_tL_t-(1-k_q\right.$$

$$\left.-t_qz_q)q_{t-1}K_{t-1}\beta_qi_t-t^p_qq_{t-1}K_{t-1}\right]\quad(3.4)$$

The cash flow constraint of the corporation is:

$$Div_t-N_t = P_tQ_t-w_tL_t-(1-k_q-t_qz_q)q_tI_t$$

$$-t^p_qq_{t-1}K_{t-1}-\beta_q(1-k_q-t_qz_q)$$

$$[(i_t-\pi_t)q_{t-1}K_{t-1}-q_t(K_t-K_{t-1})]$$

$$-TC_t$$

(3.5)

where investment in period t is given by:

$$I_t = K_t-(1-\delta_q)K_{t-1}\quad(3.6)$$

We assume that corporations keep dividends payout ratio, α, and debt/capital ratio, β_q, constant. It follows that retaining is independent of investment, and the marginal sources of investment funds are debt and new share issues, with debt accounting for the fraction β_q, and new share issues, $1-\beta_q$. An alternative would be to assume that α is endogenous and new share issues are somehow determined independent of investment. Then retaining becomes the marginal source of equity financing. For example, if we assume that new share issues are zero, retaining depends upon investment, and marginal investment funds are financed with debt and retaining.

By substituting Eqs. (3.3)–(3.6) into Eq. (3.2) and taking the derivative of V_t with respect to K_{t+1}, we obtain the first-order condition for maximization of E_t, which can be rearranged to give the cost of capital:

$$\frac{c_t}{q_{t-1}} = \frac{1-k_q-t_qz_q}{1-t_q}\left[r^q_t-\pi_t+(1+\pi_t)\delta\right]+t^p_q$$

(3.7)

where r^q_t is the weighted average of marginal costs of corporate debt and equity:

$$r^q_t-\pi_t = \beta_q[(1-t_q)i_t-\pi_t]+(1-\beta_q)$$

$$\left[\frac{\rho^e_t-(1-t^g_q)\pi_t}{(1-t^e_q)\alpha+(1-t^g_q)(1-\alpha)}\right]\quad(3.8)$$

The cost of capital in Eq. (3.7) is the price of capital services from one dollar's worth of lagged capital stock, which includes compensation for depreciation adjusted for investment tax credit and depreciation allowances for tax purposes. The real social rate return for corporate capital is defined as:

$$\sigma_t^q - \pi_t = \frac{c_t}{q_{t-1}} - (1+\pi_t)\delta. \qquad (3.9)$$

Similarly, the real private rate return for corporate capital is defined as:

$$\rho_t^q - \pi_t = \beta_q\left[\left(1 - t_q^d\right)i_t - \pi_t\right] + (1 - \beta_q)(\rho_t^e - \pi_t) \qquad (3.10)$$

where t_q^d is the marginal tax rate on individual income from interest payments on corporate debt.

Finally, the after-tax real corporate rate of return is defined as:

$$r_t^c - \pi_t = r_t^q - \pi_t + \beta_t t_q i_t \qquad (3.11)$$

We can proceed in a similar manner to derive the cost of capital and the corresponding social and private rates of return on capital employed in the household and noncorporate sectors. In order to avoid repetition, we simply present the results without fully describing the derivation process.[2] The cost of capital for household assets is:

$$\frac{c_t}{q_{t-1}} = r_t^h - \pi_t + (1+\pi_t)\delta + (1 - t_h^e)t_h^p \qquad (3.12)$$

where

$$r_t^h - \pi_t = \beta_h\left[(1 - t_h^e)i_t - \pi_t\right] + (1 - \beta_h)(\rho_t^e - \pi_t). \qquad (3.13)$$

The real social rate of return on household assets is defined as the cost of capital net of economic depreciation adjusted for inflation as

in Eq. (3.9) and the corresponding real private rate of return is:

$$\rho_t^h - \pi_t = \beta_h\left[\left(1 - t_h^d\right)i_t - \pi_t\right] + (1 - \beta_h)(\rho_t^e - \pi_t). \qquad (3.14)$$

The subscripts and superscripts h refer to the household sector.

For the noncorporate businesses, the cost of capital is:

$$\frac{c_t}{q_{t-1}} = \frac{1 - k_m - t_m^e z_m}{1 - t_m^e}\left[r_t^m - \pi_t + (1+\pi_t)\delta\right] + t_m^p \qquad (3.15)$$

where

$$r_t^m - \pi_t = \beta_m\left[(1 - t_m^e)i_t - \pi_t\right] + (1 - \beta_m)\left[\rho_t^e - (1 - t_m^g)\pi_t\right]. \qquad (3.16)$$

The real social rate of return on noncorporate assets, $\sigma^m - \pi_t$, is defined as in (Eq. 3.9), and the corresponding real private rate of return is:

$$\rho_t^m - \pi_t = \beta_m\left[\left(1 - t_m^d\right)i_t - \pi_t\right] + (1 - \beta_m)(\rho_t^e - \pi_t). \qquad (3.17)$$

In Eqs. (3.15)–(3.17), the subscripts and superscripts m refer to the noncorporate sector.

3.2.2 Tax wedges and effective tax rates

Auerbach and Jorgenson (1980) introduced the concept of marginal effective tax rate, which is defined as the ratio between the tax wedge and the social rate of return. It is natural to define the tax wedge as the difference between social and private rates of return. In the case of corporate assets, the effective tax rate is defined as $\frac{\sigma_t^q - \rho_t^q}{\sigma_t^q - \pi_t}$. Similarly, we can define the effective corporate

---

[2] Interested readers are referred to Chapter 2 of Jorgenson and Yun (2001).

income tax rate as $\frac{\sigma_t^q - r_t^c}{\sigma_t^q - \pi_t}$, and the effective individual income tax rate as $\frac{r_t^c - \rho_t^q}{\sigma_t^q - \pi_t}$. The effective tax rates for assets in the household and noncorporate sectors are defined analogously.

Table 3.1 shows the real social rates of return, tax wedges, and effective tax rates for short-lived and long-lived assets in the corporate, noncorporate, all business, and household sectors in the US Notice that the tax wedges in the corporate and noncorporate businesses are substantial in absolute values as well as relative to the real social rates of return. The effective tax rates are 42.7% and 33.5% in the corporate and

noncorporate sectors, respectively. For the entire business sector, the effective tax rate is 40.0%. The substantial tax wedges and the corresponding effective tax rates suggest that taxation of income from capital in the business sector may present a significant barrier to efficient allocation of resources between present and future.

Panel 1 of Table 3.2 presents the tax wedges between short-lived and long-lived assets in the corporate, noncorporate, and all businesses. The interasset tax wedges are defined as the difference between the social rates of return on short-lived and long-lived assets. Considering that the average social rates of return in the corporate and noncorporate businesses are 10.45% and 9.59%, respectively, the interasset tax wedges of 1.49% in the corporate sector and 1.06% in the noncorporate sector may not appear to be large, but they are still significant.

Panel 2 of Table 3.2 shows the intersector tax wedges between the social rates of return on assets in the corporate and noncorporate sectors, corporate and household sectors, and noncorporate and household sectors, respectively. Among these intersector tax wedges, the wedges between corporate and noncorporate sectors have drawn most attention in textbooks and tax policy

TABLE 3.1 Effective tax rates (2010 tax law).

		SROR	TW	ETR
Corporate	S	0.0940	0.0341	0.3631
	L	0.1088	0.0490	0.4501
	A	0.1045	0.0447	0.4275
Noncorporate	S	0.0863	0.0225	0.2612
	L	0.0969	0.0332	0.3421
	A	0.0959	0.0321	0.3351
All business (corporate + noncorporate)	S	0.0930	0.0319	0.3430
	L	0.1045	0.0434	0.4155
	A	0.1018	0.0408	0.4004
Households	A	0.0700	0.0048	0.0680

Property taxes are included in the calculation and the after-corporate-tax real rate of return, $r^c - \pi i$, real interest rate, and the corporate dividend payout ratio are set at their 1970–2010 averages, 6.628%, 4.658%, and 47.86%, respectively. For asset category A (all assets), social and private rates of return are calculated as the averages of short-lived and long-lived assets, where the values of assets are used as the weights. Similarly for the All business sector.
SROR: real social rate of return
TW: tax wedge.
ETR: effective tax rate.
S, short-lived assets.
L: long-lived assets.
A: all assets (short + long).

TABLE 3.2 Tax Wedges (2010 tax law).

Interasset tax wedges (long-short)	
Corporate	0.0149
Noncorporate	0.0106
All business	0.0115

Intersector tax wedges			
	S	L	A
Corporate−noncorporate	0.0076	0.0119	0.0086
Corporate−households	0.0240	0.0389	0.0345
Noncorporate−households	0.0163	0.0269	0.0259

A: all assets (short + long).
L: long-lived assets.
S: short-lived assets.

analyses. Indeed the famous Harberger triangle originally represented the efficiency loss in capital allocation between corporate and noncorporate sectors caused by the double taxation of corporate income.

It is interesting to note that, while corporate tax integration has been an important tax reform issue in the United States and partial integration of the corporate and individual income taxes has been implemented in many other countries, the average tax wedge (for all assets) between corporate and noncorporate sectors of 0.86% is small compared with the tax wedge between corporate and household sectors of 3.45%, or the wedge between noncorporate and household sectors of 2.59%.

3.3 Dynamic general equilibrium model of the US Economy

Tax wedges and effective tax rates are useful for understanding the barriers to efficient resource allocation. However, a narrative on tax distortion is incomplete without information on the displacements of resource allocation caused by the substitution effects of tax wedges. Under the US tax system, there are numerous tax policy instruments, and practically all of them affect relative prices and hence generate substitution effects. Our dynamic general equilibrium model provides a convenient framework for representing the US tax system and measuring the welfare effects of tax distortion.

3.3.1 Consumer behavior

The consumers in the household sector are identical and endowed with infinite life and perfect foresight. The representative consumer maximizes the intertemporal welfare function:

$$V = \frac{1}{1 - \sigma} \sum_{t=1}^{\infty} \prod_{s=1}^{t} \left(\frac{1 + n_s}{1 + \gamma} \right) U_t^{1-\sigma} \qquad (3.18)$$

where σ is the inverse of the elasticity of intertemporal substitution, n_s is the rate of population growth, γ is the subjective rate of time preference, and U_t is the per capita utility function:

$$U_t = F_t(1 - \alpha_T)^t, (t = 1, 2, \ldots) \qquad (3.19)$$

In Eq. (3.19), F_t is per capita full consumption in period t, where population is measured in efficiency unit, and $-\alpha_T$ is the growth rate of labor productivity.

The representative consumer maximizes the intertemporal welfare function subject to the budget constraint:

$$W = \sum_{t=1}^{\infty} \frac{PF_t F_t (1 - \alpha_T)^t \prod_{s=1}^{t}(1 + n_s)}{\prod_{s=1}^{t}(1 + \rho_s)} \qquad (3.20)$$

where W is lifetime wealth, PF_t is price of full consumption, and ρ is nominal private rate of return. The necessary condition for maximization of intertemporal welfare subject to the budget constraint is given by the Euler equation:

$$\frac{F_t}{F_{t-1}} = \left[\frac{PF_{t-1}}{PF_t} \cdot \frac{1 + \rho_t}{(1 + \gamma)(1 - \alpha_T)^\sigma} \right]^{1/\sigma}, \quad t = 1, 2, \ldots \infty \qquad (3.21)$$

Eq. (3.21) plays a central role in determining the optimal path of the economy over time. Specifically, it determines the optimal growth rate of full consumption per capita in efficiency unit. If the level of full consumption in any one period is known, the entire path of full consumption can be determined. Among the infinite number of paths for full consumption that satisfy the Euler equation, the one that satisfies the intertemporal budget constraint will be chosen by the welfare maximizing consumer.

It is useful to note that Eq. (3.21) implies that, in a steady state with a constant rate of inflation, the real private rate of return is constant. In the steady state, full consumption per capita in efficiency unit is constant, i.e., $F_{t-1} = F_t$, and the constant rate of inflation implies that $\frac{PF_t}{PF_{t-1}} = 1 + \pi_t$ is constant, where π_t is the rate of inflation in period t. It follows that the real private rate of return consistent with the steady state is $(1 + \gamma)(1 - \alpha_T)^\sigma - 1$.

The steady-state real private rate of return depends only upon the parameters of the intertemporal welfare function, γ and σ, and the growth rate of labor productivity, $-\alpha_T$. In particular, it is independent of any government policy to the extent that government policy does not affect γ, σ, and α_T. More generally, Eq. (3.21) implies that the growth rate of full consumption per capita is approximately proportional to the difference between real private rate of return and its steady state value.

Once the path of full consumption is determined, the consumer allocates full consumption among consumption goods, capital services, and leisure in each period. In order to represent the allocation of full consumption, we employ translog form of price function for full consumption and the corresponding value share equations introduced by Christensen, Jorgenson, and Lau (1975). The demand for household capital services are further allocated to short-lived and long-lived assets. In order to represent the allocation of household capital services, we employ translog price function for household capital services and the corresponding value share equations.

In the translog price function of full consumption, the price of full consumption, PF_t, is expressed as a function of the consumer prices of consumption goods, capital services, and leisure. The consumer price of consumption goods includes sales taxes and the price of leisure is the wage rate net of marginal tax on labor income. In the translog price function of household capital services, the price of (aggregate) household capital services is expressed as a function of the prices of capital services from short-lived and long-lived assets.

3.3.2 Producer behavior

In the business sector, there are two types of producers, corporate and noncorporate businesses, and two types of outputs, consumption

and investment goods. However, we do not assign separate production processes for corporate and noncorporate businesses, or for consumption and investment goods. Instead we assume that the entire business sector acts like a single producer and employs labor and capital services from corporate and noncorporate businesses to produce consumption and investment goods.

Specifically, we represent the production technology of the entire business sector with a single translog price function of Christensen, Jorgenson, and Lau (1973), where the price of labor services is expressed as a function of the prices of consumption goods, investment goods, corporate and noncorporate capital services, and time. The value share equations corresponding to the price function determine the values of capital services from corporate and noncorporate sectors and the values of consumption and investment goods relative to the value of labor input. As in the household sector, the allocation of corporate and noncorporate capital services between short-lived and long-lived assets is represented by translog price functions and the corresponding value share equations.

The partial derivative of the translog price function for labor with respect to time represents the rate of productivity growth. We require the model to be consistent with a balanced growth equilibrium in which labor productivity grows at a constant rate and value shares and relative prices of inputs and outputs are constant when labor is measured in efficiency unit. It follows that the value shares and the growth rate of labor productivity are independent of time. These conditions constrain the parameters of the translog price function for labor.

3.3.3 Government

We consolidate the federal and state and local governments into a single government sector. Similarly, we consolidate the federal and state and local government enterprises into a single government enterprise sector. The government collects taxes from the household and business sectors, issues debt to finance deficits, and spends its revenues on consumption goods, investment goods, labor services, interest payments on government debt, and transfer payments to households and the rest of the world. The deficit of the government is added to the government debt. Government enterprises employ labor and produce consumption goods, and turn over any surplus to the general government.

The government collects taxes from a variety of sources. In addition to the taxes on income from capital described in Section 3.2, the government levies income tax on labor, sales taxes on consumption and investment goods, property taxes, and wealth taxes. In representing the US tax system in our model, we distinguish marginal and average tax rates. The distinction is particularly important in the taxation of individual income where graduated tax rates apply.

In general, marginal tax rates affect relative prices and average tax rates are used to generate tax revenues. For example, we calculate the price of leisure as the price of labor services times $\left(1-t_L^m\right)$ where t_L^m is the marginal tax rate on labor income. In calculating tax revenue, however, we use the average tax rate, i.e., $R_L = t_L^a \cdot BL$, where R_L is the tax revenue from labor income, t_L^a is the average tax rate, and BL is total labor compensation. In the case of capital income taxation, the prices relevant for resource allocation are the costs of capital derived in Section 3.2. The tax revenue from individual equity income is given by $R_E = t_E^a \cdot BE - ITCM$, where t_E^a is the average tax rate, BE is the tax base, and ITCM is investment tax credits for noncorporate businesses. Similarly, the tax revenue from interest payments on debt is calculated as $R_D = t_D^a \cdot BD$, where t_D^a is the average tax rate, and BD is the tax base.

Since sales taxes and property taxes are proportional, average and marginal tax rates are the same and the calculation of tax revenues is straightforward. In the case of corporate income

tax, the rate structure is graduated. Nevertheless, since most of corporate income is taxed at the maximum rate, we calculate the tax revenue as $R_q = t_q \cdot BQ - ITCQ$, where t_q is the corporate income tax rate, BQ is the tax base, and ITCQ is tax credit for corporate investment.

We assume that the government allocates its total expenditure, net of interest payments on government debt, in constant proportions among consumption goods, investment goods, labor services, and transfer payments to households and the rest of the world. We represent the allocation of government expenditure, net of interest payments, into these five categories of spending with a Cobb–Douglas price function of the aggregate government spending. This representation is useful in the simulation of alternative tax policies in which the path of real government spending need to be controlled.

3.3.4 Rest of the world

The rest of the world trades with the United States in consumption goods, investment goods, and labor services, pays compensation on US claims on the rest of the world, and receives transfer payments from US government. The current account deficit of the rest of the world is added to the US claims on the rest of the world.

3.3.5 Parameter values

We estimate the parameters of the model using time series data of the United States for 1970–2010. This data set, informally referred to as the US Worksheet among Jorgenson and his associates, incorporates the cost of capital into a complete system of US national accounts in accordance with Christensen and Jorgenson (1973). The parameters of the consumer and producer models are estimated by nonlinear three-stage least square method (NL3SLS) developed by Jorgenson and Laffont (1974) and Amemiya (1977). Most of the other parameters are set at historical values. For example, in the allocation of government expenditure, net of interest payment on government debt, the shares of consumption goods, investment goods, labor services, and transfer payments to households and the rest of the world are set at their sample averages. Similarly, we set the dividend payout ratio, α, and the debt/capital ratios in the household and business sectors, β_j ($j = h, m, q$), and the real interest rate at their sample averages.

In the base case simulation, we set all the tax rates at their 2010 values, similarly for investment tax credits and the present values of capital consumption allowances. In all the simulations, we assume that new tax policies are introduced in 2011 and set the total time endowment and the prices of investment goods and the six categories of assets at their 2011 values. Finally, we set the ratio of government expenditure to GDP (SGOV), the proportion of purchases of consumption goods by the rest of the world to domestic purchases (SCR), and the proportion of purchases of investment goods by the rest of the world to domestic supply (SIR) at appropriate values so that the steady-state values of government debt/GDP and the claims on the rest of the world/GDP ratios are reasonable.

3.4 Equilibrium of the model and solution algorithm

3.4.1 Market equilibrium

In a given period, there are four markets that need to be in equilibrium simultaneously. They are the markets for consumption goods, investment goods, labor services, and capital services. In the consumption goods market, households, government, and the rest of the world purchase goods from private businesses and government enterprises. In the investment goods market, households, government, and the rest of the world purchase goods from businesses. In the labor market, businesses, government,

government enterprises, and the rest of the world purchase labor services from households. Finally, in the capital market, the capital stock owned by households is allocated to meet the demands for capital services from the corporate, noncorporate, and household sectors. Due to Walras' law, one of the four market equilibrium conditions is redundant.

3.4.2 Dynamics of the model

When a new economic policy is introduced, the economy jumps on a new transition path which eventually converges to the steady state. Along the transition path, the economy must be in equilibrium in each period and the entire path must be optimal in the sense that it maximizes intertemporal welfare of the consumer subject to the lifetime budget constraint. The transition of the economy from one period to the next is described by the transition of full consumption and the accumulation of capital stock, government debt, and the claims on the rest of the world.

The transition of full consumption is described by the Euler Eq. (3.21). The accumulation of capital stock is represented by:

$$VK = VKL + PI \cdot ID - Dep + Rev \qquad (3.22)$$

where VK is the value of capital stock at the end of the period, VKL is its lagged value, ID is private domestic investment, PI is the price of investment goods inclusive of sales tax, Dep is economic depreciation, and Rev is revaluation of domestic capital. The accumulation of government debt is described by:

$$VG = DG + VGL \qquad (3.23)$$

where VG and VGL are the current and lagged values of government debt, respectively, and DG is government budget deficit. Finally, the claims on the rest of the world evolve according to:

$$VR = DR + (1 + \pi)VRL \qquad (3.24)$$

where VR and VRL are the current and lagged values of the claims on the rest of the world, respectively, and DR is current account deficit of the rest of the world.

Obviously the economy as a whole cannot run deficit or surplus, and the sum of the deficits of the household, business, government, and the rest of the world sectors must be zero. In other words, private savings net of investment are used to finance the deficits of government and the rest of the world:

$$S = PI \cdot ID + DG + DR \qquad (3.25)$$

where S is private saving.

At the beginning of a period on the transition path, the quantities of capital stock, government debt, and claims on the rest of the world are predetermined. However, full consumption is free to jump in the first period of the transition, although it is constrained by the Euler equation thereafter. If we know the value of $FS_0 = F_0 \cdot PF_0^{\frac{1}{\sigma}}$ in the Euler Eq. (3.21), we can solve for FS_1, and the entire transition path of the economy can be calculated. We thus pretend that new policy is introduced in period 0 and start with a guess of FS_0 and solve the model forward. Finding the correct value of FS_0 is the essence of the solution algorithm.

3.4.3 Solution algorithm

In order to evaluate the economic impacts of a new tax policy, we need to establish a reference with which to compare the performance of the economy under an alternative tax policy. We take the US economy under the tax laws of 2011 as the reference. For the year 2011, the lagged values of capital stock, government debt, and the claims on the rest of the world and the amount of total time endowment are

set at their historical values. Since there is no guarantee that the US economy is in a steady state in 2011, we proceed under the assumption that the economy is on a transition path toward a steady state. We refer to the US economy under the 2011 tax law as the *base case*.

In any period on the transition path, once the lagged values of FS (FSL), capital stock (KL), government debt (GL), and the claims on the rest of the world (RL) are known, the equilibrium of the economy can be solved from the market clearing conditions for consumption goods, investment goods, capital stock, and labor services.[3] Since one of the four market clearing conditions is redundant, we drop the labor market clearing condition.

Since our dynamic general equilibrium model of the US economy converges to the steady state, it is convenient to solve for the steady state first. The transition path can then be found by solving for FS_0, or FSL for period 1, that leads the economy to the steady state. Solving for the steady state is similar to solving for the equilibrium for a period on the transition path. However there are two differences. First, in the steady state of the base case, FSL and the lagged values of the three stock variables (KL, GL, RL) are not known. We need to solve for their steady-state values along with three endogenous variables that clear the four markets. Second, the Euler equation for full consumption implies that the real private rate of return on wealth is constant and known.

In our model, total time endowment, rate of inflation in the price investment good, interest rate on debt, and the relative prices of investment good and the six categories of assets are fixed. In order to solve for the steady state of the base case, we start with seven unknowns (FSL, KL, GL, RL, ρ^e, PC, LD), where PC is the

---

[3] In our model, the relative prices of investment good and the six categories of assets are fixed at their 2011 values and the rate of inflation in the price of investment goods is exogenous. The path of total time endowment is also exogenous.

consumer price of consumption goods and LD is labor demand of the business sector. We make use of the Euler equation for full consumption, three market clearing conditions, and the steady state conditions of the three accumulation Eqs. (3.22)−(3.24), and apply Newton's method to solve for the seven unknowns.[4]

The intertemporal welfare function of the consumer does not reflect the welfare effects of government expenditure, net of interest payments on government debts. We thus control the path of real government expenditure, net of interest payments. Similarly, in order to focus on the differential effects of alternative tax policies, we control the paths of government debt and the claims on the rest of the world. In order to constrain government debt and the claims on the rest of the world on reasonable paths, we set SGOV = 0.20168, SCR = −0.0007, and SIR = −0.0022 so that, in the steady state of the base case, government debt/GDP ratio and the claims on the rest of the world/GDP ratio become 0.40 and 0.05, respectively.

Once the steady state values of government debt and the claims on the rest of the world are determined, we construct complete paths of these two variables by connecting their historical values in 2010 and their steady state values. In our model, the economy comes very close to the steady state in less than thirty years after the introduction of a new tax policy. We thus constrain the government debt and the claims on the rest of the world to reach their steady state values in 40 years after the start of the transition. For all practical purposes, it is sufficient to assume that the economy converges to the steady state in 100 years.

With these preparations, we solve for the transition path of the economy with an initial guess of FS_0. Along the transition path, government debt and the claims on the rest of the world are constrained to the paths described above. To control the path of government debt in the base case, we adjust total government expenditure including interest payments on government debt. To control the path of the claims on the rest of the world, we adjust the absolute value of the net exports of consumption goods, investment goods, and labor services.

In a given period on the transition path, FSL, KL, GL, and RL are predetermined and the equilibrium of the base case economy can be determined by solving for the three unknowns (ρ^e, PC, LD) with the three market clearing conditions. However, to cut through the complex interdependence of F, PF, and ρ^e, we add full consumption (F) to the list of the unknowns and add the Euler equation to the simultaneous equation system. Once the equilibrium of one period is found, we move on to the next.

If we solve the entire path of transition starting with an initial guess of $FSL = FS_0$ for period 1, the process is likely to be explosive. To control the explosiveness and make the iteration process manageable, we use the multiple-shooting technique. For example, we divide the 100-year transition path into ten 10-year intervals and solve for the transition path for each of the intervals. In this process, we need to provide each interval with an initial guess for the pair (FSL, KL), except for the first interval for which KL for the first period is set at the historical value. We use Newton's method to solve for FS_0 and the nine pairs of (FSL, KL) that satisfy the Euler equation for full consumption (3.21) and the capital accumulation Eq. (3.22).

We solve for the equilibrium of the economy under an alternative tax policy in a similar manner. The paths of government debt and the claims on the rest of the world are constrained at their paths in the base case. In the base case, the path of real government spending is

---

[4] Steady state condition of a stock variable requires that its real value per capita in efficiency unit remain constant as the economy proceeds from one period to the next.

determined endogenously so that government budget constraint is satisfied. Under an alternative tax policy, however, real government spending and budget deficits are constrained at their base case values. We thus need to adjust total tax revenue in each period to meet the government budget constraint. We consider the adjustment of lump-sum tax, labor income tax, sales tax, and individual income tax.

3.5 Welfare effects of tax reform

3.5.1 Intertemporal expenditure function

Once a transition path of the economy is found, we can evaluate the corresponding level of the intertemporal welfare. Making use of the Euler equation for full consumption, we can express F_t in terms of F_0 and the real private rates of return from period 1 through t, i.e.:

$$F_t = F_0 \prod_{s=1}^{t} \left[\frac{1 + r_s}{(1+\gamma)(1 - \alpha_T)^\sigma} \right]^{\frac{1}{\sigma}}, \quad (t = 1, 2, \ldots)$$

(3.26)

where $r_s = \frac{PF_{s-1}}{PF_s}(1 + \rho_s) - 1$ is the real private rate of return on wealth. Substituting Eq. (3.26) into Eq. (3.19) and then the result into Eq. (3.18), we obtain

$$V = \frac{F_0^{1-\sigma}}{1 - \sigma} D, \quad (3.27)$$

where $\quad D = \sum_{t=1}^{\infty} \left[\frac{1}{(1+\gamma)^{\frac{1}{\sigma}}} \right]^t \prod_{s=1}^{t} (1 + n_s)(1 + r_s)^{\frac{1-\sigma}{\sigma}}.$

Substituting Eq. (3.26) into the intertemporal budget constraint Eq. (3.20), we can express F_0 in terms of full wealth and the future real private rates of return, i.e., $F_0 = \frac{W}{PF_0} \frac{1}{D}$. Substituting this expression in Eq. (3.27) and solving for W, we obtain the intertemporal expenditure function:

$$W(PF_0, D, V) = PF_0 \left[\frac{(1 - \sigma)V}{D^\sigma} \right]^{\frac{1}{1-\sigma}} \quad (3.28)$$

Eq. (3.28) gives the minimum value of lifetime wealth that is required to achieve the intertemporal welfare level of V, where the effects of future real private rates of return are summarized by D.

With the intertemporal expenditure function in our hand, it is straightforward to calculate the welfare effects of an alternative tax policy. Suppose $D = D_0$, $V = V_0$, and $W = W_0$ in the base case. If the economy attains a welfare level of V_1 under an alternative policy, the equivalent variation measure of the welfare effects of the new policy is:

$$EV = W(PF_0, D_0, V_1) - W(PF_0, D_0, V_0)$$
$$= W(PF_0, D_0, V_1) - W_0$$

(3.29)

3.5.2 Efficiency cost of taxation in the United States

In order to estimate the efficiency cost of taxation, we simulate the economy under the alternative tax policy in which the tax rates in part or all of the tax system are reduced and a hypothetical lump-sum tax is collected to keep government debt and government spending on the same trajectories as in the base case. Let the level of intertemporal welfare attainable under the alternative tax policy be V_1. Then Eq. (3.29) gives the equivalent variation measure of the efficiency cost of the part of the tax system that has been replaced by the lump-sum tax. Jorgenson and Yun (2001) define *the average efficiency cost*, say AEC, as the efficiency cost per dollar of tax revenue:

$$AEC = \frac{EV}{TLUMP} \quad (3.30)$$

where TLUMP is the present value of the tax revenue that has been replaced by the lump-sum tax.

In order to calculate TLUMP, we convert the path of lump-sum tax into the path of full consumption and add it to the time path of the full consumption in the base case. Making use of the intertemporal welfare function, we can evaluate the welfare level that can be attained with this composite path of full consumption in the base case and the lump-sum tax under the alternative policy. We use Eq. (3.29) and calculate the present value of lump-sum tax under the alternative tax policy. In this process, we in effect discount the lump-sum tax with the marginal rates of substitution between full consumptions in different time periods in the base case.

We can also measure the marginal efficiency cost of tax revenue by considering a sequence of small changes in the tax policy. Suppose we reduce the tax rates in part of the tax system by 10% interval. In the first simulation, we cut the tax rates by 10%, and evaluate the efficiency cost and call it EV_1. In the second simulation, cut the tax rates by 20% and let the corresponding efficiency cost be EV_2, and so on. The 10th simulation will be the one that sets all the relevant tax rates at zero and measures the total efficiency cost of the taxes under consideration. The *marginal efficiency cost* of the tax revenue is defined as:

$$MEC = \frac{\Delta EV}{\Delta TLUMP} \qquad (3.31)$$

where ΔEV and $\Delta TLUMP$ are the changes in EV and TLUMP due to the incremental changes in the tax rates.

In order to evaluate the efficiency cost of taxation in the United States, we consider 10 overlapping parts of the US tax system and simulate the economy with the corresponding tax rates reduced by 10% intervals until the tax rates are reduced to zero. However, since the efficiency cost of taxation tends to increase more than proportionally with tax rates, we divide the first interval into two and run an additional simulation with the tax rates reduced by 5%.[5] We select 10

sets of taxes in the US tax system: (1) corporate income tax, (2) individual capital income tax, (3) property tax, (4) capital income tax (1 + 2), (5) labor income tax, (6) capital and labor income tax (1 + 2 + 5 = 4 + 5), (7) individual income tax (2 + 5), (8) sales tax, (9) all taxes except for property tax (1 + 2 + 5 + 8), (10) all taxes (1 + 2 + 3 + 5 + 8).

The results are presented in Table 3.3. Since we start with the base case, when the tax rates are first reduced by 5%, MEC and AEC are the same. As the tax rates are further reduced, MEC declines faster than AEC until the tax rates are eventually reduced to zero. These results are consistent with the economic theory that excess burden increases more than proportionally with the marginal tax rates. Table 3.3 indicates that corporate and individual capital income taxes are most inefficient per dollar of tax revenue. In particular, capital income taxes are substantially more inefficient than labor income taxes. Compared to the taxes on capital and labor income, the revenues from property tax and sales taxes are small and so are the associated tax distortions.

For the entire US tax system of 2010, MEC and AEC are 20 cents and 10 cents per dollar of tax revenue, respectively. As noted above, MECs decline faster than the corresponding AECs. In the cases of "all taxes" and "all taxes except for property tax," MECs converges to zero as the tax rates are reduced to zero. However, in all the other cases, MECs do not appear to approach zero even when the relevant tax rates are reduced to zero. The reason is that, when the scope of the tax reduction is limited, there remain substantial nonzero taxes that interact with the taxes being reduced. Capturing the effects of the interaction between taxes is one advantage of general equilibrium analysis.

---

[5] When the taxes are not proportional, both average and marginal tax rates are reduced by the same proportion. In the case of capital income taxes on businesses, investment tax credits are reduced by the same proportion as the tax rates.

TABLE 3.3 Efficiency cost of taxation in the United States: 2010 tax law.

Taxes		Reduction in tax rates (%)										
		5	10	20	30	40	50	60	70	80	90	100
1. Corporate income tax	MEC	0.311	0.302	0.290	0.275	0.261	0.248	0.236	0.225	0.215	0.206	0.197
	AEC	0.311	0.307	0.299	0.291	0.285	0.278	0.273	0.267	0.262	0.258	0.253
2. Individual capital income tax	MEC	0.331	0.322	0.309	0.293	0.277	0.261	0.247	0.233	0.219	0.206	0.193
	AEC	0.331	0.327	0.318	0.310	0.302	0.294	0.286	0.279	0.272	0.265	0.258
3. Property tax	MEC	0.123	0.122	0.120	0.117	0.115	0.112	0.109	0.106	0.103	0.100	0.097
	AEC	0.123	0.123	0.121	0.120	0.119	0.117	0.116	0.114	0.113	0.111	0.110
4. Capital income tax (1 + 2)	MEC	0.318	0.302	0.280	0.253	0.228	0.204	0.182	0.161	0.141	0.122	0.105
	AEC	0.318	0.310	0.296	0.282	0.269	0.257	0.246	0.235	0.225	0.215	0.206
5. Labor income tax	MEC	0.172	0.165	0.156	0.144	0.134	0.125	0.118	0.112	0.107	0.104	0.102
	AEC	0.172	0.169	0.162	0.156	0.151	0.146	0.142	0.138	0.135	0.132	0.129
6. Capital and labor income tax (1 + 2+5 = 4 + 5)	MEC	0.249	0.235	0.216	0.191	0.167	0.145	0.125	0.106	0.088	0.071	0.056
	AEC	0.249	0.243	0.229	0.217	0.206	0.195	0.184	0.175	0.166	0.157	0.149
7. Individual income tax	MEC	0.229	0.220	0.207	0.190	0.174	0.159	0.144	0.131	0.119	0.107	0.097
	AEC	0.229	0.225	0.216	0.207	0.199	0.192	0.184	0.178	0.171	0.165	0.159
8. Sales tax	MEC	0.115	0.114	0.113	0.111	0.109	0.107	0.105	0.103	0.101	0.100	0.098
	AEC	0.115	0.115	0.114	0.113	0.112	0.111	0.110	0.109	0.108	0.107	0.106
9. All taxes (except for property tax)	MEC	0.214	0.201	0.182	0.158	0.135	0.115	0.095	0.078	0.061	0.047	0.033
	AEC	0.214	0.208	0.195	0.183	0.172	0.161	0.151	0.142	0.133	0.125	0.118
10. All taxes	MEC	0.198	0.185	0.165	0.140	0.116	0.094	0.073	0.053	0.034	0.017	0.001
	AEC	0.198	0.192	0.178	0.166	0.154	0.142	0.131	0.121	0.111	0.101	0.092

3.5.3 Welfare effects of tax reform

Table 3.3 suggests some useful directions for tax reform. First of all, the declining MECs in all of the simulations support the widely accepted notion that efficient taxation requires low marginal tax rates applied to broadly defined bases. This classical wisdom is valid for the entire tax system as well as for parts of it. In the first and second sets of simulations in Table 3.3, we find that the MECs for 5% reduction of the tax rates and AECs for 100% reduction are substantially higher than in other simulations. In particular, in terms of excess burden, taxation of income from capital is much more expensive than taxation of labor income.

It follows that reducing the distortion caused by taxation of income from capital need to be an important objective of tax reform in the United States. We may think of two basic approaches. One is to maintain the general framework of the current tax system and pursue incremental changes in the tax policies. The corporate tax cut of 2018 is a good example.

The other approach is to overhaul the entire tax system as in the case of the consumption tax of Hall and Rabushka (1995).

Jorgenson and Yun (2013) consider various alternative tax reform proposals for the United States and evaluate their performance in terms of the improvement in the welfare of the economy. Table 3.4 reproduces some of the simulation results. In the first set of simulations, interasset and intersector tax wedges are eliminated by setting the social rates of return on short-lived and long-lived assets in the corporate and noncorporate sectors to be equal to their capital-weighted average in the steady state of the base case.

In the second set of simulations, we extend the analysis to the household sector and eliminate all

the tax wedges for capital allocation in the entire private sector. This change in tax policy improves the efficiency of the US economy dramatically and produces huge welfare gains. These results are consistent with Table 3.2 which shows that the major tax distortion in the allocation of capital is between the business and household sectors. Since the elimination of the tax wedges in the first two sets of simulation are roughly revenue neutral, the necessary revenue adjustments are small and the welfare effects are not sensitive to the choice of revenue adjustment.

The third set of simulations is for corporate tax integration. We implement corporate tax integration by setting the steady state social rates of return on short-lived and long-lived assets in the corporate sector to be equal to their values

TABLE 3.4 Welfare effects of tax distortion: 2010 tax law (billions of 2011 US dollars).

Eliminated wedges and method of revenue adjustment	Additive[a]	Proportional[b]	
Interasset and intersector distortion: Corporate and noncorporate sectors, all assets			
Lump-sum tax adjustment	303.9	303.9	
Labor income tax adjustment	253.9	248.1	
Sales tax adjustment	223.0	223.0	
Individual income tax adjustment	227.6	226.9	
Interasset and intersector distortion: All sectors, all assets[c]			
Lump-sum tax adjustment	5567.0	5567.0	(6963.6)
Labor income tax adjustment	5558.1	5619.4	(6961.1)
Sales tax adjustment	5550.3	5550.3	(6988.2)
Individual income tax adjustment	5545.4	5612.6	(6980.7)
Corporate tax integration			
Lump-sum tax adjustment	2320.2	2320.2	
Labor income tax adjustment	1715.4	398.3	
Sales tax adjustment	1237.6	1237.6	
Individual income tax adjustment	1422.4	100.0	

[a] *Under the additive tax adjustment, the average and marginal tax rates of labor income and the average tax rates of individual capital income are adjusted in the same percentage points. The marginal tax rates of individual capital income are adjusted in the same proportion as the marginal tax rate of labor income.*
[b] *Under the proportional tax adjustment, average and marginal tax rates are adjusted in the same proportion.*
[c] *The figures in the parentheses represent the welfare effects under the revenue neutral proportional labor income tax.*

in the noncorporate sector in the steady state of the base case, i.e., $\sigma^q = \sigma^m$. Since corporate tax integration shifts tax burden from corporate capital to elsewhere in the tax system, it is not revenue neutral and the welfare effect is sensitive to the method of tax adjustment. Under the hypothetical lump-sum tax adjustment, the welfare effect is as large as 2320.2 billion US dollars. However, it becomes much smaller when realistic tax adjustments are used to offset the revenue shortfall caused by the reduction of corporate income tax.

It is useful to compare the welfare gain from corporate tax integration with lump-sum tax adjustment, 2320.2 billion dollars, with the corresponding welfare gain from the first set of simulations, 303.9 billion dollars. Under corporate tax integration, although intersector tax wedges are eliminated between corporate and noncorporate sectors, interasset tax wedges still remain in both sectors. In contrast, in the first set of simulations, both interasset and intersectoral tax wedges are eliminated. Nevertheless, the welfare gain from corporate tax integration is much larger. This may appear strange from the viewpoint of static Harberger model. The key lies in the fact that corporate tax integration reduces the tax burden on corporate capital, and intertemporal resource allocation is affected.

We finally consider the welfare cost of progressive labor income taxation in the context of the second set of simulations where capital is efficiently allocated across the private sector. In order to evaluate the welfare cost of the progressivity of labor income tax, we set the marginal tax rate of labor income at its average tax rate. This procedure reduces the marginal tax rate of labor income from 25.1% to 9.5%. The welfare effects are presented in the parentheses of Table 3.4. We find that the additional welfare gains from flattening labor income tax are substantial. Since the tax change is roughly revenue neutral, the results are not sensitive to the method of tax adjustment.

3.6 Concluding remarks

In this chapter, we presented the DGEM that Dale Jorgenson and I developed to evaluate the welfare effects of tax policy and government spending. Important features of the DGEM include the cost of capital, translog price functions, NL3SLS estimation of the consumer and producer models, and two-stage allocation of lifetime wealth. The intertemporal expenditure function based on the DGEM plays a central role in the welfare analysis of alternative tax policies.

The cost of capital approach provides an excellent framework for modeling taxation of income from capital. All of the current instruments of capital income taxation in the United States are represented in the cost of capital formulas. Indeed, the cost of capital can accommodate practically any reasonable proposals for taxation of income from capital. The cost of capital approach allows us to measure tax wedges and effective tax rates of income from capital. Although tax wedges and effective tax rates alone do not determine the efficiency costs of tax distortion, they provide useful information about the major sources of tax distortion in the allocation of capital.

Our analyses of the efficiency costs of tax revenues from various parts of the US tax system allow us to gain a general view of the structure of efficiency cost of taxation. We found that taxation of income from capital is most expensive in terms of the efficiency cost per dollar of tax revenue. It seems reasonable to conclude that the first priority of tax reform in the United States is to reduce the distortions caused by taxation of income from capital. In view of our analysis, the corporate tax cut of 2018 in the United States seems to be a step in the right direction.

To evaluate the welfare effects of tax reform proposals in a more realistic setting, we simulated the economy with four alternative tax adjustments. We obtain the largest welfare gain when all the tax wedges for capital allocation are removed and capital is efficiently allocated across the entire private sector. The welfare gain further increases as labor income tax is flattened. One important message from these simulations is that we do not have to reduce the effective tax rate of capital to zero to attain a high level of welfare.

One may be reasonably confident that we can design a number of tax reform proposals that attain high levels of welfare for the economy. However, efficiency is not the only virtue that makes a good tax policy. Equity, however it is defined, is another important virtue a good tax policy must support. In a democratic society, equitable taxation is not only an important virtue in itself, it is also essential for securing political support for tax policy.

In reality, we need to be prepared to sacrifice some efficiency for the equity of tax burden. Indeed it is possible to evaluate distributional effects of efficiency enhancing tax reform proposals. OLG models with multiple consumers distinguished by age and level of income can be used to analyze distributional effects of tax policy across age cohorts and income groups. Jorgenson et al. (1997) and Jorgenson et al. (2013) provide even more flexible framework in which distributional effects of tax policy can be analyzed with consumers distinguished by wage rate and many other attributes. The critical issue is to put together an efficient and equitable tax reform proposal that is attractive to majority of politicians and voters.

References

Amemiya T: The maximum likelihood and the nonlinear three-stage least squares estimator in the general nonlinear simultaneous model, *Econometrica* 89(3): 548–560, 1977.

Auerbach AJ, Jorgenson DW: Inflation-proof depreciation of assets, *Harvard Business Review* 58(5):113–118, 1980.

Auerbach AJ, Kotlikoff LJ: *Dynamic fiscal policy*, Cambridge, 1987, Cambridge University Press.

Chamley C: The welfare cost of capital income taxation in a growing economy, *Journal of Political Economy* 89(3): 468–496, 1981.

Chamley C: Optimal taxation of capital income in general equilibrium with infinite lives, *Econometrica* 54:607–622, 1986.

Christensen LR, Jorgenson DW: Measuring economic performance in the private sector. In Moss M, editor: *The measurement of economic and social performance*, New York, NY, 1973, Columbia University Press, pp 233–251.

Christensen LR, Jorgenson DW, Lau LJ: Transcendental logarithmic production frontiers, *The Review of Economics and Statistics* 55(1):28–45, 1973.

Christensen LR, Jorgenson DW, Lau LJ: Transcendental logarithmic utility functions, *The American Economic Review* 65(3):367–383, 1975.

Fullerton D, Rogers DL: *Who bears the lifetime tax burden?*, Washington, DC, 1993, Brookings Institution.

Fullerton D, Rogers DL: Lifetime effects of fundamental tax reform. In Aaron H, Gale WB, editors: *Economic effects of fundamental tax reform*, Brookings Institution, pp 321–352.

Hall RE, Rabushka A: *The flat tax*, second ed., Stanford, CA, 1995, Hoover Institution Press.

Harberger AC: The incidence of corporate income tax, *Journal of Political Economy* 70:215–240, 1962.

Jorgenson DW: Capital theory and investment behavior, *The American Economic Review* 53(2):247–259, 1963.

Jorgenson DW, Goettle RJ, Ho MS, Wilcoxen PJ: Energy, the environment and US economic growth. In , Waltham MA, 2013, North-Holland, pp 477–552. Dixon PB, Jorgenson DW, editors: *Handbook of computable general equilibrium modeling*, vol. 1A. Waltham MA, 2013, North-Holland, pp 477–552.

Jorgenson DW, Laffont J-J: Efficient estimation of nonlinear simultaneous equations with additive disturbances, *Annals of Economic and Social Measurement* 3(1):615–640, 1974.

Jorgenson DW, Slesnick DT, Wilcoxen PJ: Carbon taxes and economic welfare. In Jorgenson DW, editor: *Measuring social welfare*, Cambridge, MA, 1997, MIT Press, pp 361–400.

Jorgenson DW, Yun KY: The efficiency of capital allocation, *The Scandinavian Journal of Economics* 88(1):85–107, 1986a.

Jorgenson DW, Yun KY: Tax policy and capital allocation, *The Scandinavian Journal of Economics* 88(2):355–377, 1986b.

Jorgenson DW, Yun KY: Tax reform and U.S. economic growth, *Journal of Political Economy* 98(5):S151–S193, 1990. part 2.

Jorgenson DW, Yun KY: *Lifting the burden: tax reform, the cost of capital, and U.S. economic growth*, Cambridge, MA, 2001, MIT Press.

Jorgenson DW, Yun KY: Taxation, efficiency and economic growth. In Dixon PB, Jorgenson DW, editors: *Handbook of computable general equilibrium modeling* vol. 1A, pp 659–741. Waltham MA, North-Holland.

Summers LH: Capital taxation and accumulation in a life-cycle growth model, *The American Economic Review* 71(4):533–544, 1981.

4

Sources of growth in the world economy: a comparison of G7 and E7 economies

Khuong M. Vu

National University of Singapore, Singapore

4.1 Introduction

The world economy has been undergoing transformational changes in recent decades, and these changes are expected to accelerate and be even more profound in the future. More excitingly, the drivers of change are now not only confined to technological progress and globalization trends but also the increasing influence of emerging economic powerhouses.

For decades since the end of the World War II, the G7 group of the world's seven largest economies—the United States, Japan, Germany, the United Kingdom, France, Italy, and Canada—has commanded its dominant influence on the world economy. The accelerated growth of China and India, since they launched economic reforms a few decades ago, have opened the way for the emergence of the increasing strategic influence of large developing economies on the global economic landscape.

Among the world's largest economies ranked by gross domestic product (GDP) share in 2017, the G7 economies were no longer clustered at the top as in the past. Although the United States, Japan, and Germany remain in the list of the seven largest economies, the United Kingdom, France, Italy, and Canada have slipped to the 9th, 10th, 12th, and 17th places, respectively (Table 4.1). In contrast, appearing on the list of the world's largest economies were China (which occupied the 1st place), India (3rd), Indonesia (7th), Brazil (8th), Mexico (11th), Turkey (13th), and South Korea (14th) (Table 4.1). These seven emerging economies turned out to be the world's seven largest economies if the G7 economies and Russia are excluded. This group of seven emerging economies, which will be referred to as the E7 throughout this chapter, has contributed significantly to world economic growth in the past few decades and is expected to play an even more important role in transforming the global economic landscape in the decade to come.

It is, therefore, important to conduct a rigorous investigation of the economic performance of the E7 economies vis-à-vis their G7 peers in the recent past and project the changing dynamics in the world order in the next decade. In this chapter, we aim to conduct this study.

The remainder of this chapter is structured as follows. Section 4.2 looks at the shares and

TABLE 4.1   World's 20 largest economies by GDP in 2017.

Country	Share in world GDP (%)	Rank
China	18.9	1
United States	15.5	2
India	7.2	3
Japan	4.4	4
Germany	3.3	5
Russia	3.2	6
Indonesia	2.6	7
Brazil	2.6	8
United Kingdom	2.3	9
France	2.3	10
Mexico	1.9	11
Italy	1.8	12
Turkey	1.7	13
South Korea	1.6	14
Spain	1.4	15
Saudi Arabia	1.4	16
Canada	1.4	17
Iran	1.3	18
Egypt	1.1	19
Australia	1.0	20

GDP, gross domestic product.
Note: GDP is measured in purchasing power parity, 2017 price level.
Source: Author's calculation using data from Conference Board Total Economy Dataset.

contributions of the E7 economies in the world economy in comparison with their G7 peers. Section 4.3 examines the sources of growth of the E7 and G7 economies during the period 2000—17 while Section 4.4 analyzes their economic catch-up performance over this period. Section 4.5 projects the productivity and GDP growth for the E7 and G7 economies over the next decade to reveal their ranks in the world

economic order in 2027. Section 4.6 summarizes and concludes.

4.2 E7 and G7 in the world economy

This section highlights the salient features of the E7 economies vis-à-vis their G7 peers and the changing dynamics of their shares and contributions to world economy since 2000. While Table 4.2 provides a snapshot of the E7 and G7 economies in 2017, Table 4.3 reports their economic performance and contributions to the world economy during the 2000—17 period.

As shown in Table 4.2, the E7 as a group is more than four times larger than the G7 in population and has also been larger than the G7 in GDP ($45.8 trillion vs. $38.9 trillion). It is interesting to note that China and the United States—the leading members in the E7 and G7, respectively—play a similar role in their respective group, accounting for the dominant shares in both GDP (51.8% for China in the E7 and 50.2% for the United States in the G7) and population (40.8% for China and 42.6% for the United States) (Table 4.2).

Regarding per-capita income, the E7 as a group remains far below the G7 ($13.5 1000 vs. $50.6 1000). This relative low income level is observed for all E7 economies, with the exception of South Korea, which has recently surpassed Italy. Compared to their group average, both China and the United States have a higher income level (127.2% for China and 117.7% for the United States). China, however, is well below its three E7 peers—Mexico, Turkey, and South Korea, while the United States outperforms all other G7 economies (Table 4.2).

From Table 4.3, three observations stand out regarding the dynamics of economic growth observed for the E7 and G7 economies during 2000—17 and its three subperiods—2000—05, 2005—10, and 2010—17. First, the E7 as a group far outperformed the G7 in economic growth during 2000—17 (6.6% vs. 1.7%) and throughout

TABLE 4.2 Selected socioeconomic indicators on E7 and G7 economies in 2017 (countries in each group are sorted by GDP size in decreasing order).

Country	GDP	GDP per capital	Population	GDP	GDP per capital	Population
	$ million	$ 1000	Million		Group = 100	
E7	*45,799*	*13.5*	*3387*	*100.0*	*100.0*	*100.0*
China	23,726	17.2	1380.20	*51.8*	*127.2*	*40.8*
India	9034	7.0	1283.20	*19.7*	*51.8*	*37.9*
Indonesia	3217	12.5	257.3	*7.0*	*92.4*	*7.6*
Brazil	3214	15.3	209.8	*7.0*	*113.1*	*6.2*
Mexico	2439	20.2	120.5	*5.3*	*149.4*	*3.6*
Turkey	2156	25.6	84.3	*4.7*	*189.3*	*2.5*
South Korea	2013	39.1	51.5	*4.4*	*289.1*	*1.5*
G7	*38,851*	*50.6*	*769*	*100.0*	*100.0*	*100.0*
United States	19,485	59.5	327.3	*50.2*	*117.7*	*42.6*
Japan	5462	43.3	126.1	*14.1*	*85.7*	*16.4*
Germany	4143	49.3	84.1	*10.7*	*97.5*	*10.9*
United Kingdom	2884	43.5	66.3	*7.4*	*86.0*	*8.6*
France	2829	42.1	67.2	*7.3*	*83.3*	*8.7*
Italy	2293	37.8	60.6	*5.9*	*74.8*	*7.9*
Canada	1755	47.6	36.9	*4.5*	*94.2*	*4.8*

GDP, gross domestic product.
Notes: Data is for 2017; GDP is measured in purchasing power parity (PPP) dollars.
Source: Author's calculation using data from Conference Board Total Economy Dataset.

the three subperiods: 6.2% versus 2.2% in 2000%−05%; 7.8% versus 0.9% in 2005−10; and 6.1% versus 1.8% in 2010−17. Consequently, as the influence on the world economy rapidly increased for the E7 during 2000−17, it declined for the G7. In fact, the share in the world GDP of the E7 as a group expanded from 22.3% in 2000% to 36.5% in 2017, while the share of the G7 contracted from 43.8% to 31.0% during this period. It should be noted that while the E7's share was nearly 50% smaller than the G7's in 2000, it had overtaken the G7 by 2017.

Second, the E7 and G7 showed contrasting growth patterns during the three subperiods.

With regards to the E7 group, its average growth rate rose from 6.2% in 2000%−05% to 7.8% in 2005−10 and then slowed to 6.1% in 2010−17. In addition, this pattern was observed for its four largest economies: China (9.7%, 11.3%, 7.7%), India (6.2%, 8.0%, 6.6%), Indonesia (4.6%, 5.9%, 5.3%), and Brazil (2.9%, 4.4%, 0.5%). In contrast, the growth rate of the G7 group dropped sharply from 2.2% in the first subperiod to 0.9% in the second before recovering to 1.8% in the third subperiod. With the exception of Germany, this U-shape pattern was also shared by all G7 economies: the United States (2.9%, 1.2%, 2.3%); Japan (1.9%, 0.6%, 1.4%); the United Kingdom (2.8%,

TABLE 4.3 E7 and G7 in the world economy: share in size and growth, 2000–17 (countries in each group are sorted by 2017 GDP share in decreasing order).

		GDP growth									Share in world GDP	
		2000–05			2005–10			2010–17				
			Contribution to			Contribution to			Contribution to			
Economy/Group	2000–17 (%)	(%)	Group	World	(%)	Group	World	(%)	Group	World	2000	2017
E7	**6.6**	**6.2**	**100.0**	**37.4**	**7.8**	**100.0**	**57.8**	**6.1**	**100.0**	**57.8**	**22.3**	**36.5**
China	9.4	9.7	56.0	21.0	11.3	61.6	35.8	7.7	62.2	36.0	7.3	18.9
India	6.9	6.2	19.1	7.1	8.0	19.4	11.2	6.6	20.9	12.1	4.2	7.2
Indonesia	5.3	4.6	6.4	2.4	5.9	5.9	3.4	5.3	6.3	3.6	2.0	2.6
Brazil	2.3	2.9	6.3	2.3	4.4	6.4	3.6	0.5	0.6	0.4	3.3	2.6
Mexico	2.0	1.4	2.4	0.9	1.5	1.5	0.9	2.8	2.8	1.6	2.6	2.0
Turkey	4.9	4.7	4.6	1.7	3.2	2.1	1.2	6.3	4.9	2.8	1.4	1.7
South Korea	3.8	4.6	5.2	1.9	4.0	3.1	1.8	3.0	2.4	1.4	1.6	1.6
G7	**1.7**	**2.2**	**100.0**	**24.1**	**0.9**	**100.0**	**9.0**	**1.8**	**100.0**	**17.1**	**43.8**	**31.0**
United States	2.1	2.9	61.8	14.9	1.2	62.4	5.6	2.3	61.0	10.4	20.3	15.6
Japan	1.3	1.9	12.3	3.0	0.6	9.8	0.9	1.4	10.6	1.8	6.6	4.4
Germany	1.3	0.6	2.8	0.7	1.2	14.5	1.3	1.8	10.6	1.8	5.0	3.3
United Kingdom	1.7	2.8	9.3	2.2	0.4	3.4	0.3	2.0	7.9	1.4	3.2	2.3
France	1.2	1.7	5.8	1.4	0.8	6.9	0.6	1.2	4.9	0.8	3.4	2.3
Italy	0.1	0.9	3.1	0.8	−0.3	−2.5	−0.2	−0.1	−0.3	−0.1	3.4	1.8
Canada	2.0	2.5	4.9	1.2	1.1	5.5	0.5	2.2	5.4	0.9	1.9	1.4

GDP, gross domestic product.
Note: GDP is measured in purchasing power parity; World includes 121 economies. The shares by economy in World's GDP and growth take World = 100.
Source: Author's calculation using data from Conference Board Total Economy Dataset.

0.4%, 2.0%); France (1.7%, 0.8%, 1.2%); Italy (0.9%, −0.3%, −0.1%); and Canada (2.5%, 1.1%, 2.2%) (Table 4.3). The contrasting growth patterns observed for the E7 and G7 groups show that the 2007-08 global financial crisis caused severe losses for the G7 economies but not for the E7 economies, with the exception of Mexico and Turkey. At the same time, it is interesting to note that Germany's growth consistently accelerated during the three subperiods (0.6%, 1.2%, 1.8%), which suggests the positive effect

of the digital revolution that German has prominently embraced in transforming the economy.

Third, in terms of contribution to world economic growth, the E7 has far surpassed the G7 and become the major driving force. The contribution of the E7 increased from 37.4% in 2000%−05% to 57.8% in both 2005−10 and 2010−17, while that of the G7 fluctuated by approximately 20% over the three subperiods, declining from 24.1% in 2000%−05% to 9.0% in 2005−10 and then bouncing back to 17.1% in 2010–17. At the group level, China and the United States were similar in their dominant shares in contributing to group growth, which were approximately 60% in all three subperiods. Moreover, the increasing influence of India on the E7 and the world economy is noticeable. The contribution to growth of this second largest E7 economy steadily climbed up during the three subperiods within the E7 group (19.1%, 19.4%, 20.9%) as well as at the world level (7.1%, 11.2%, and 12.1%). In addition, it is also important to note that India has surpassed the United States in contribution to world growth in two recent subperiods: 2005–10 (11.2% vs. 5.6%) and 2010–17 (12.1% vs. 10.4%) (Table 4.3).

4.3 Sources of growth during 2000–17: E7 versus G7

Applying the growth accounting method augmented by Jorgenson and his collaborators (see Appendix 4.A for elaboration), the GDP growth of a given economy can be decomposed into three main sources: capital input, which consists of information and communications technology (ICT) capital and traditional (non-ICT) capital; labor input, which is a product of labor hours worked and labor quality; and total factor productivity (TFP). Deriving the growth decomposition results from the Conference Board Total Economy Database, Table 4.4 reports the sources of GDP growth during the period of 2000–17 for the E7 and G7 economies. The paragraphs below highlight the key findings that stand out from Table 4.4.

With regards to GDP growth during 2000–17, the E7 far outperformed the G7 on two counts. First, the E7 as a group recorded an average growth of 6.6%, which was nearly four times higher than the G7's 1.7%. Second, the two E7 laggard players—Brazil and Mexico—were on par with the two G7 leading performers—the US and Canada—for which the GDP growth rate was approximately 2%.

Capital accumulation was an important source of growth for both the E7 and G7 economies during 2000–17, which was 3.49 percentage points per annum (ppa) for the E7 and 1.17 for the G7. Interestingly, while the magnitude of the capital input contribution was notably larger for the E7 than for the G7, the share of this source in overall GDP growth was much larger for the G7 (68.8%) than for the E7 (52.9%). In addition, this share was high not only for the G7 economies but also for four higher-income E7 economies—Turkey (79.5%), South Korea (77.6%), Brazil (63.9%), and Mexico (61.5%). This finding tends to suggest that, even for more advanced countries, focusing on innovation alone is not sufficient to sustain desired growth. That is, improving the business environment to foster capital investment remains a strategic priority to promote economic growth not only for lower- but also higher-income economies. This insight is consistent with the findings from previous studies on the importance of capital accumulation in driving economic growth (for example, Jorgenson (1995); Kumar and Russel (2002); Corrado et al. (2009, 2013), and Vu (2013a, 2013b)).[1]

ICT capital has been found to be an increasingly important source of economic growth and productivity performance.[2] The evidence on the

---

[1] In particular, Corrado et al. (2009) show that capital deepening becomes the unambiguously dominant source of growth in labor productivity when intangibles are counted as capital.

[2] For instance, see Jorgenson (2001, 2003), Oliner and Sichel (2000, 2002); Jorgenson and Stiroh (2000); Stiroh (2002); Jorgenson and Motohashi (2005), Jorgenson et al. (2007), Jorgenson and Vu (2005, 2011, 2013, 2016), Bloom et al. (2012); and van Ark (2014).

TABLE 4.4   Source of GDP growth, 2000–17: E7 versus G7 (countries in each group are sorted by GDP growth rate in decreasing order).

Economy	GDP Growth (%)	Total capital input contribution		Contribution of capital input by type					Labor input contribution (ppa)		TFP growth (ppa)
		(ppa)	Share in GDP growth*	(ppa)		Share in total capital input contribution**			Hours	Quality	
				Non-ICT	ICT	Non-ICT	ICT	Total			
E7	6.6	3.49	52.9	2.96	0.53	84.8	15.2	1.06	0.57	0.49	2.06
China	9.4	4.42	47.0	3.84	0.57	86.9	12.9	0.73	0.4	0.33	4.2
India	6.9	3.84	55.7	3.15	0.69	82.0	18.0	1.4	0.9	0.5	1.63
Indonesia	5.3	3.04	57.4	2.84	0.20	93.4	6.6	1.36	0.72	0.63	0.85
Turkey	4.9	3.8	77.6	3.32	0.47	87.4	12.4	1.43	0.89	0.54	−0.3
South Korea	3.8	3.02	79.5	2.02	1.00	66.9	33.1	0.25	0.11	0.13	0.49
Brazil	2.3	1.47	63.9	1.1	0.38	74.8	25.9	1.95	0.58	1.37	−1.11
Mexico	2.0	1.23	61.5	0.97	0.25	78.9	20.3	1.07	0.89	0.18	−0.3
G7	1.7	1.17	68.8	0.72	0.44	61.5	37.6	0.44	0.19	0.25	0.07
United States	2.1	1.31	62.4	0.77	0.54	58.8	41.2	0.48	0.23	0.24	0.35
Canada	2.0	1.59	79.5	1.13	0.47	71.1	29.6	0.8	0.63	0.16	−0.4
United Kingdom	1.8	1.2	66.7	0.86	0.34	71.7	28.3	0.8	0.47	0.33	−0.24
Germany	1.3	0.89	68.5	0.58	0.31	65.2	34.8	0.29	0.12	0.17	0.1
Japan	1.3	1.04	80.0	0.61	0.43	58.7	41.3	0.18	−0.13	0.3	0.06
France	1.2	1.03	85.8	0.69	0.34	67.0	33.0	0.48	0.21	0.27	−0.28
Italy	0.2	0.73	365.0	0.49	0.24	67.1	32.9	0.23	0.04	0.19	−0.82

GDP, gross domestic product; ICT, information and communications technology; TFP, total factor productivity.
Note: ppa = percentage points per annum.
* GDP growth = 100.
** Total capital input contribution = 100.
Source: Author's calculation using data from Conference Board Total Economy Dataset.

contribution of ICT to growth during 2000–17 is solid for both the E7 and G7 economies, which ranged from 0.20 ppa for Indonesia to 1.0 for South Korea in the E7, and from 0.24 for Italy to 0.54 for the United States in the G7. It is important to note that the share of ICT capital in total capital input contribution was notably larger for the G7 group (37.6%) than for the E7 (15.2%). That is, while the magnitude of ICT contribution to growth was comparable between the E7 and G7 economies, its relative role in driving capital accumulation and GDP growth was notably larger for more advanced economies. It should be noted, however, that some G7 economies were lagging in embracing ICT for growth. For example, Chun et al. (2015) find that Japan was behind South Korea in exploiting the synergy between ICT and intangible investments to foster productivity growth in the 2000s.[3]

Labor input, which is a product of employment (hours worked) and labor quality, is a positive source of growth for all the E7 and G7 economies, with the magnitude being nearly twice larger for the E7 than for the G7. While labor quality is a positive source of growth for all the E7 and G7 economies, hours worked was negative only for Japan. This negative contribution of hours worked to Japan's growth was likely due the country's problem of population aging and contraction.[4]

TFP growth was positive and sizable for four E7 economies—China (4.2 ppa), India (1.63), Indonesia (0.85), and South Korea (0.49) but negative for three other E7 economies—Turkey (−0.3 ppa), Brazil (−1.11), and Mexico (−0.3). At the same time, TFP growth was positive for only three G7 economies—the United States (0.35), Germany (0.1), and Japan (0.06); while negative for the four others—Canada (−0.4), the United Kingdom (−0.24), France (−0.28), and Italy (−0.82). At the group aggregate level, TFP growth was large for the E7 (2.06) but marginal for the G7 (0.07), which means that the E7 has become more important than the G7 not only in driving world economic growth but also in improving its overall efficiency of production. The stronger performance of China, India, Indonesia, and the United States on TFP growth tends to suggest that large economies likely have greater potentials to improve their efficiency. One possible reason is the advantage these

economies have in achieving growth through reforms that foster structural change, which has been evidenced to be an important source of growth (Caselli and Coleman (2001); van Ark and Timmer (2003); Fan et al. (2003); Jorgenson and Timmer (2011); Dietrich (2012); Lin (2012; 2016); Vu (2018)).

4.4 E7 economies in the global dynamics of economic catch-up: performance and drivers

4.4.1 Catch-up performance index

To assess the catch-up performance of country i over T-year period $[0, T]$, we construct a catch-up performance index (CUPI) that is defined as follows:

$$CUPI_{0,T}^i = ln\left[\frac{rel\_y_T^i}{rel\_y_0^i}\right]\bigg/ T \qquad (4.1)$$

where $rel\_y_t^i$ is per-capita income of country i in year t relative to the United States[5]:

$$rel\_y_t^i = \frac{y_t^i}{y_t^{US}} \qquad (4.2)$$

Note that y_t^i and y_t^{US}, which are, respectively, the per-capita income of country i and the United States in year t, are measured in purchasing power parity (PPP) dollars at constant prices.

By definition, $CUPI_{0,T}^i > 0$ if country i is catching up $\left(rel\_y_T^i > rel\_y_0^i\right)$, <0 if it is lagging behind $\left(rel\_y_T^i < rel\_y_0^i\right)$, and $=0$ if it is neither catching up nor lagging behind $\left(rel\_y_T^i = rel\_y_0^i\right)$

[3] Corrado et al. (2013) point out the synergy between intangible (non-ICT capital) and ICT capital deepening in fostering growth.

[4] Japan's population declined from 127 million to 126 million in 2017.

[5] Woo (2011) labels this relative income level the "Catch-up Index" (CUI).

4.4.2 Catch-up performance during 2000—17: E7 versus G7

Computing the CUPI during the period 2000—17 for the 121 economies with data available from the TED dataset, we find that 87 economies (72.5%) were catching up and 23 economies (27.5%) were lagging, using the United States as the benchmark. In this catch-up dynamics, six of seven E7 economies (86%) were catching up, while five of six G7 economies (83%) were lagging (Table 4.5). It is also worth noting that China and India, the two major E7 economies, appeared in the top 10 of global catching-up economies during the 2000—17

period, while Indonesia, Turkey, and South Korea were in the top 50.

4.4.3 Drivers of economic catch-up

As presented in Appendix 4.B, the CUPI value of each country can be decomposed into three components: capital deepening, labor participation, and raw TFP. The raw TFP component combines the contribution of labor quality improvement and TFP growth. This component, which will be denoted as Raw Total Factor Productivity (RTFP), provides a broader measure of efficiency improvement in the use of basic production factors: capital and hours worked.

TABLE 4.5   The catch-up performance of E7 and G7 economies, 2000—17 (countries in each group are sorted by CUPI in decreasing order).

Economy	2000—17 CUPI		GDP per capita (US = 100)		Catching up (yes/no)
	Index value	Global rank	2000	2017	
E7					
China	7.54	1	8.0	28.9	Yes
India	4.17	9	5.8	11.8	Yes
Indonesia	2.83	23	13.0	21.0	Yes
Turkey	2.37	30	28.7	43.0	Yes
South Korea	1.96	41	47.1	65.7	Yes
Brazil	0.02	86	25.7	25.7	Yes
Mexico	−0.47	99	36.8	34.0	No
G7					
Japan	0.04	84	72.2	72.8	Yes
United States	0.00	88	100.0	100.0	—
Germany	−0.13	89	84.6	82.7	No
United Kingdom	−0.20	91	75.5	73.0	No
Canada	−0.34	92	84.7	80.0	No
France	−0.63	105	78.7	70.7	No
Italy	−1.49	113	81.9	63.5	No

CUPI, catch-up performance index; GDP, gross domestic performance.
Source: Author's calculation using data from Conference Board Total Economy Dataset.

For a given economy, the values of the three aforementioned components capture the drivers of its catch-up performance during the period of examination. A positive (negative) value of capital deepening means that the country outperformed (underperformed) the United States on enhancing capital intensity, which means it can be a driver (dragger) of the country's catch-up. Similarly, a positive (negative) value of labor participation shows that the country was stronger (weaker) than the United States in labor participation (employment-to-population rate), which enhances (lessens) the country's catch-up

performance. Finally, the RTFP growth captures the country's performance relative to the United States in improving the use efficiency of basic production factors.

Table 4.6 reports the values of CUPI and its three components for the E7 and G7 economies, which reveal several important findings. First, all Asian E7 economies—China, India, Indonesia, and South Korea recorded robust catch-up performance, for which all three drivers—capital deepening, labor participation, and RTFP growth were positive. The sizable magnitude of capital deepening (exceeding 1.0)

TABLE 4.6 Drivers of economic catch-up performance, 2000−17: E7 versus G7 economies (countries in each group are sorted by CUPI in decreasing order).

Country	CUPI	CUPI component (value)			CUPI component (share), CUPI = 100		
		Capital Deepening	Labor participation	RTFP	Capital Deepening	Labor participation	RTFP
E7							
China	**7.54**	3.18	0.41	3.94	42.2	5.5	52.3
India	**4.17**	2.26	0.38	1.53	54.2	9.0	36.8
Indonesia	**2.83**	1.35	0.58	0.90	47.9	20.4	31.7
Turkey	**2.37**	2.11	0.62	−0.36	89.2	26.2	−15.4
South Korea	**1.96**	1.76	0.16	0.03	89.9	8.4	1.7
Brazil	**0.02**	−0.02	0.37	−0.34	−116	2086	−1870
Mexico	**−0.47**	−0.38	0.63	−0.71	81.9	−134.6	152.7
G7							
Japan	**0.04**	0.06	0.21	−0.23	138.9	477.3	−516.2
United States	**0.00**	0.00	0.00	0.00	—	—	—
Germany	**−0.13**	−0.17	0.36	−0.32	130.1	−280.4	250.3
United Kingdom	**−0.20**	−0.09	0.40	−0.50	46.7	−204.5	257.9
Canada	**−0.34**	0.19	0.30	−0.83	−57.4	−89.9	247.3
France	**−0.63**	−0.21	0.19	−0.61	33.5	−29.3	95.7
Italy	**−1.49**	−0.43	0.16	−1.22	29.0	−10.9	81.9

CUPI, catch-up performance index.
Source: Author's calculation using data from Conference Board Total Economy Dataset.

observed for these four economies implies the crucial role of capital accumulation in Asia's economic success.[6]

Second, three non-Asian E7 economies— Turkey, Brazil, and Mexico demonstrated different patterns of catch-up performance compared to their Asian E7 peers. For all three economies, RTFP was a dragger, which means that they were behind the United States on improving the efficiency of using basic production factors. This dragger should be a cause of concern not only for lagging Mexico but also for Turkey and Brazil, which made progress on catch-up. It is noticeable that Turkey's strong catch-up performance was driven heavily by capital deepening, which contributed 89.2% to the country's CUPI. At the same time, Brazil's slight catch-up performance (CUPI = 0.02) was driven merely by labor participation, while its capital deepening and RTFP were draggers.

Third, the G7 economies shared rather similar patterns in their CUPI components. All six economies outperformed the United States in labor participation but lagged in RTFP. With regard to capital deepening, Japan and Canada were slightly stronger than the United States, while Germany, the United Kingdom, France, and Italy lagged.

4.5 Prospects for the E7 and G7 economies in 2027: a projection exercise

This section projects economic growth for the E7 and G7 economies during the decade 2017—27. The projection exercise, which is based on the predicting model introduced in Jorgenson et al. (2002), projects the average labor productivity (ALP) and GDP growth for the period of 2017—27, making assumptions on the

parameters and variables for three scenarios: pessimistic, base-case (which is the most likely to occur), and optimistic. Details of the forecast framework and key assumptions used for this projection exercise are presented in Appendix 4.C.

4.5.1 Salient insights from projection results

Table 4.7 summarizes the projection results, which reveal several important insights. The findings below are based mainly on the projection results from the base-case scenario.

First, as shown in the base-case, the E7 as a group will fair less impressively over the next decade (2017—17) compared to the recent one (2007—17) in both labor productivity growth (4.43% vs. 5.51%) and GDP growth (5.52% vs. 6.34%). Interestingly, this overall pattern is observed for the four Asian E7 economies— China, India, Indonesia, and South Korea but not for the three other E7 economies—Turkey, Brazil, and Mexico, for which growth will accelerate significantly in the next decade. In addition, it should be noted that in the optimistic scenario, for India and Indonesia their labor productivity and GDP growth will also accelerate substantially.

Second, although India will remain behind China in labor productivity growth, it will become the leading player in GDP growth over the next decade, followed by China and Indonesia. However, South Korea will be a less impressive player in the upcoming decade, becoming the slowest-growing economy in the E7 group, which may give an economic imperative for South Korea to engage North Korea in joint economic development efforts more proactively to boost their economic performance.

---

[6] It should be noted, however, that of these four Asian E7 economies, only South Korea has joined the group of high-income nations. South Korea's remarkable catch-up success was driven not only by capital accumulation but also its special emphasis on technological progress through in-house R&D in private sectors (Lee, 2009).

TABLE 4.7 Projected labor productivity and GDP growth, 2017–27: E7 versus G7 (countries in each group are sorted by base-case projected GDP growth over 2017–27 in decreasing order).

Economy	Average labor productivity (ALP) growth				GDP growth			
		Projections, 2017–27			Actual	Projections, 2017–27		
	Actual 2007–17	Pessimistic	Base-case	Optimistic	2007–17	Pessimistic	Base-case	Optimistic
E7	**5.51**	**2.80**	**4.43**	**5.65**	**6.34**	**3.59**	**5.22**	**6.44**
India	5.49	3.42	5.13	6.84	6.72	4.56	6.55	8.55
China	8.09	3.72	5.58	6.69	8.41	3.80	5.69	6.82
Indonesia	3.91	2.09	3.13	4.18	5.47	3.19	4.51	5.83
Turkey	1.53	1.35	2.03	2.44	4.84	3.55	4.23	4.64
Mexico	−0.07	0.37	0.55	0.73	2.02	1.86	2.42	2.98
Brazil	0.96	0.96	1.51	2.06	1.52	1.55	2.25	2.95
South Korea	1.78	0.95	1.42	1.90	3.04	1.38	1.96	2.54
G7	**0.71**	**0.57**	**0.94**	**1.31**	**1.23**	**0.78**	**1.15**	**1.52**
United Kingdom	0.20	0.64	0.96	1.28	1.07	1.10	1.53	1.96
Canada	0.65	0.56	0.85	1.13	1.65	1.06	1.46	1.86
United States	1.06	0.68	1.01	1.35	1.64	1.00	1.42	1.84
France	0.44	0.58	0.87	1.17	0.77	0.65	0.96	1.27
Germany	0.28	0.53	0.79	1.06	1.21	0.61	0.90	1.19
Japan	0.68	0.56	0.84	1.12	0.83	0.19	0.54	0.88
Italy	−0.49	0.16	0.27	0.37	−0.57	0.07	0.19	0.31

GDP, gross domestic product.
Note: GDP share projections for 2027 are based on base-case results.
Source: Author's calculation using data from Conference Board Total Economy Dataset.

Third, compared to 2007–17, as a group, the G7's labor productivity and GDP growth will exhibit two opposite trends in the next decade. While its labor productivity growth will accelerate from 0.71% in 2007–17 to 0.94% in 2017–27, its GDP growth will slow from 1.23% to 1.15%. This pattern is particularly pronounced for three G7 economies: Canada (ALP: 0.65%–0.85%; GDP: 1.65%–1.46%), Germany (ALP: 0.28%–0.79%; GDP: 1.21%–0.9%), and Japan (ALP: 0.68%–0.84%; GDP: 0.83%–0.54%). This contrasting pattern tends to suggest these G7 economies will make good progress in improving labor productivity while population aging remains a formidable problem in hindering their GDP growth. The four other G7 economies will show patterns somehow different from what will be observed at the group level. The United States, which was the strongest player in both ALP and GDP growth during 2007–17, will experience a growth slowdown for both measures in 2017–27, while the United Kingdom, France, and Italy, which were low performers in the past decade, will perform better in both measures in the next decade.

4.5.2 The share of E7 and G7 economies in the world economy in 2027

Projection results presented in Section 4.5.1 allow us to map out the changing positions of the E7 and G7 groups and their member economies in the global economic landscape in the next decade. As shown in Table 4.8, the G7 as a group will expand its share of world GDP by 6.8% points, from 36.5% in 2017% to 43.3% in 2027. In contrast, the share of the G7 will dwindle by 6.2% points, from 31% to 24.8% over the decade. Furthermore, it should be noted that the share in world GDP will expand for only four E7 economies—China (+4.49% points), India (+2.47% points), Indonesia (+0.27% points), and Turkey (+0.13%); while it will shrink for the three other E7 economies: Brazil (−0.28% points), Mexico (−0.19% points), and South Korea (−0.22%). At the same time, this share will also be shrinking for all G7 economies: the United States (−2.81% points), Japan (−1.09% points), Germany (−0.73% points), the United Kingdom (−0.40% points), France (−0.49% points), Italy (−0.50% points), and Canada (−0.25% points) (Table 4.8).

The changing shares of the E7 and G7 economies of world GDP will also affect their global ranking by this measure over the next decade. While the rankings will remain unchanged for four economies—China (1st), India (3rd), Brazil (8th), and South Korea (14th), it will improve for Indonesia (from 7th to 5th) and Turkey (from 13th to 11th) and decline for Mexico (from 11th to 13th). At the same time, this ranking will remain the same for three G7 economies—the United States (2nd), Japan (4th), and Canada (17th), while declining for four other G7 economies: Germany (from 5th to 6th), the United Kingdom (9th to 10th), France (10th to 12th), and Italy (from 12th to 16th) (Table 4.8).

TABLE 4.8 Global ranks and world shares by GDP in 2017 and 2027: E7 versus G7

Group/ Country	Global rank by GDP 2017	Global rank by GDP 2027	Share in world GDP 2017 (I)	Share in world GDP 2027 (II)	Share in world GDP Change (II−I)
E7			**36.5**	**43.3**	**6.8**
China	1	1	18.9	23.4	*4.49*
India	3	3	7.2	9.7	*2.47*
Indonesia	7	5	2.6	2.8	*0.27*
Brazil	8	8	2.6	2.3	*−0.28*
Turkey	13	11	1.7	1.9	*0.13*
Mexico	11	13	1.9	1.8	*−0.19*
South Korea	14	14	1.6	1.4	*−0.22*
G7			31	24.8	−6.2
United States	2	2	15.5	12.7	*−2.81*
Japan	4	4	4.4	3.3	*−1.09*
Germany	5	6	3.3	2.6	*−0.73*
United Kingdom	9	10	2.3	1.9	*−0.40*
France	10	12	2.3	1.8	*−0.49*
Italy	12	16	1.8	1.3	*−0.50*
Canada	17	17	1.4	1.2	*−0.25*
Addendum: G20 economies other than E7 and G7 in 2027					
Russia	6	7	3.2	2.4	*−0.73*
Saudi Arabia	16	9	1.4	2.0	*0.55*
Iran	18	15	1.3	1.4	*0.08*
Egypt	19	18	1.1	1.1	*0.06*
Spain	15	19	1.4	1.1	*−0.33*
Pakistan	24	20	0.9	1.0	*0.10*

GDP, gross domestic product.
Source: Author's calculation using data from Conference Board Total Economy Dataset.

Note that all E7 and G7 economies will remain in the G20 group of the largest 20 economies in 2027. The group, in addition to the E7 and G7 economies, includes Russia, Saudi Arabia, Iran, Egypt, Spain, and Pakistan. It is interesting to see that among these five economies, Saudi Arabia, Iran, Egypt, and Pakistan will ascend significantly in their rankings, while Russia and Spain will experience a decline (Table 4.8).

Figs. 4.1 and 4.2 below exhibit a clearer picture of dynamic change in the global GDP shares of the E7 and G7 economies during 2017–27. Fig. 4.1, which focuses on the two largest economies of each group—China and India of the E7 and the United States and Japan of the G7, shows that China and India will exhibit a consistent clear upward trend, while the United States and Japan a sharp trend in the opposite direction. These four economies will remain as the four largest economies in the world in the next decade.

For the next five economies in each group, which are described in Fig. 4.2, the dynamics are more interesting. Indonesia, which is on a strong rising trend, will overtake Germany to be the fifth largest economy by 2025. Similarly, on a rising trend, Turkey will surpass Italy by 2019, Mexico by 2025, and France by 2026. At the same time, although South Korea and Mexico will exhibit declining trends, they will overtake some G7 economies that will contract faster. South Korea will surpass Italy by 2025, while Mexico will be comparable to France in 2027 (Fig. 4.2).

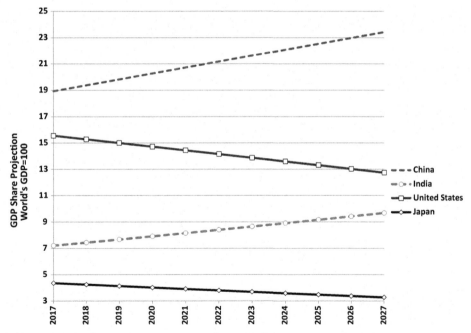

FIGURE 4.1 Trends in the world gross domestic product (GDP) share, 2017–27: E7 versus G7—the top two economies (China and India vs. the United States and Japan).

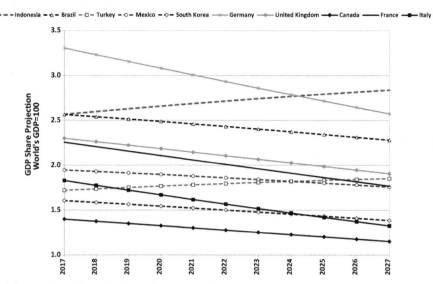

FIGURE 4.2   Trends in the world gross domestic product (GDP) share: E7 versus G7—the next five economies.

4.6 Conclusion

The world economy has experienced profound change in the past few decades and is expected to undergo even more transformational changes in the decades to come. In addition to the rapid technological progress and extensive globalization trends, the increasing influence of the large emerging economies on the global economic landscape has become an important issue that calls for more rigorous research and policy attention. This chapter examines the performance of the seven largest emerging economies—China, India, Indonesia, Brazil, Mexico, Turkey, and South Korea, which together form a group referred to as the E7, comparing them robustly with the G7 group, which include the seven largest industrialized economies—the United States, Japan, Germany, the United Kingdom, France, Italy, and Canada.

To better understand the changing dynamics of the influence of the E7 vis-à-vis G7 economies in the global economic landscape, the study conducts analyses focusing on three important areas of economic performance: sources of growth,

catch-up performance, and future prospects. The investigation reveals a number of valuable insights, including the following.

First, the E7 by far outperformed the G7 in contributing to world growth, with its contribution share reaching approximately 60% during 2005–10 and 2010–17 compared to less than 20% for the G7. Moreover, not only China but also India has well exceeded the United States in contribution to world growth.

Second, capital accumulation exceeded TFP as a source of growth during the 2000–17 period for both the E7 and G7 groups. Interestingly, the contribution of capital accumulation in GDP growth was much larger for the G7 (68.8%) than for the E7 (52.9%). It is important to note that the three largest E7 economies—China, India, and Indonesia, achieved sizable gains in TFP growth, while most G7 economies recorded negative TFP growth. The high TFP growth observed for China, India, and Indonesia tends to suggest that structural change fostered by their reforms has enabled these economies to leverage their advantage of large populations and agricultural sectors.

Third, regarding income level, all E7 economies, with the exception of Mexico, made progress in catching up with the United States during 2000–17 while all G7 economies, except for Japan, lagged. All three potential drivers—capital deepening, labor participation enhancement, and efficiency improvement played a significant role in the catch-up success of the four Asian E7 economies of China, India, Indonesia, and South Korea.

Finally, in projection for 2027, China, the United States, India, and Japan will remain the four largest economies, while Indonesia will overtake Germany to become the fifth largest economy, and Turkey will surpass France and Italy to ascend in rank from 13th to 11th. In addition, it is worth noting that South Korea will perform less impressively in the next decade, while Turkey, Mexico, and Brazil will exhibit improving trends.

It should also be noted that all E7 and G7 economies will remain in the G20 group of the world's 20 largest economies in 2027. In addition to the E7 and G7 economies, the G20 group in 2027 will include three Middle East economies—Saudi Arabia, Iran, and Egypt, one South Asian economy—Pakistan, and one European economy, Spain. It, however, remains to be seen how the on-going developments, which range from the turmoil caused by protectionism and the US–China trade war to the transformational effects of emerging smart technologies such as artificial intelligence and block chain, will affect the performance of the largest economies and the global economic landscape in the decades to come. This issue indeed calls for more in-depth and extensive research.

Appendix 4.A Growth decomposition framework

GDP growth of a given country can be decomposed using an extended production possibility frontier (PPF) model as shown below (see Jorgenson (2001) and Jorgenson et al. (2005) for more details):

$$Y = A.X(K_{nict}, K_{ict}, H, L_Q) \qquad (4.A.1)$$

where gross domestic product Y is produced from an aggregate input function X of capital and labor services. The capital services are rendered by non-ICT capital K_{nict} and ICT capital K_{ict}. The non-ICT capital K_{nict} consists of three non-ICT capital vintages—nonresidential buildings and structures, transport equipment, and machinery and equipment; however, the ICT capital K_{ict} comprises computer hardware, computer software, and telecommunication equipment. The labor services are from labor input L, which is a product of total hours worked H and labor quality index L_Q ($L = H.L_Q$). The TFP A represents a Hicks-neutral augmentation of the aggregate input function.

Under the neoclassical assumptions of competitive markets and constant returns to scale, Eq. (4.A.1) can be transformed into a growth accounting decomposition:

$$\Delta \ln Y = \bar{v}_{K_{ict}}\Delta \ln K_{ict} + \bar{v}_{K_{nict}}\Delta \ln K_{nict} + \bar{v}_L \Delta \ln H$$
$$+ \bar{v}_L \Delta \ln L_Q + \Delta \ln A$$

$$(4.A.2)$$

where $\bar{v}$ is the average share in total factor income of the subscripted input over the period under examination. All variables are expressed in logarithmic first differences ($\Delta \ln$) to represent their growth rates. The assumption of constant returns to scale of the aggregate input function implies that

$$\bar{v}_K = \bar{v}_{K_{ict}} + \bar{v}_{K_{nict}} = 1 - \bar{v}_L.$$

Eq. (4.A.2) implies that GDP output growth can be decomposed into:

- The contribution of capital input $(\bar{v}_{K_{ict}}\Delta \ln K_{ict} + \bar{v}_{K_{nict}}\Delta \ln K_{nict})$, which consists of the contribution of ICT capital services $(\bar{v}_{K_{ict}}\Delta \ln K_{ict})$ and the contribution of non-ICT capital services $(\bar{v}_{K_{nict}}\Delta \ln K_{nict})$;

- The contribution of labor input ($\bar{v}_L \Delta \ln H + \bar{v}_L \Delta \ln L_Q$), which consists of the contribution of total hours worked ($\bar{v}_L \Delta \ln H$) and the contribution of labor quality improvement ($\bar{v}_L \Delta \ln L_Q$); and
- Total factor productivity growth (TFPG) ($\Delta \ln A$).

Appendix 4.B Decomposition of the catch-up performance index

The CUPI, by definition, can be expressed as follows[7]:

$$CUPI^i_{0,T} = \ln\left[\frac{rel_{y^i_T}}{rel_{y^i_0}}\right] / T = \ln\left[\frac{\dfrac{y^i_T}{y^{US}_T}}{\dfrac{y^i_0}{y^{US}_0}}\right] / T$$

$$= \Delta \ln y^i_{0,T} - \Delta \ln y^{US}_{0,T}$$

$$(4.B.1)$$

where $\Delta \ln y^i_{0,T}$ is the average annual growth rate over period $[0, T]$ of country i's per-capita income.

Note that

$$\Delta \ln y^i_{0,T} = \Delta \ln Y^i_{0,T} - \Delta \ln P^i_{0,T} \quad (4.B.2)$$

where $\Delta \ln y^i_{0,T}$, $\Delta \ln Y^i_{0,T}$, and $\Delta \ln P^i_{0,T}$ are the average annual growth rate of country i's GDP per-capita, GDP, and population over the period $[0, T]$, respectively.

As presented in Appendix 4.A, GDP growth for a country can be decomposed into the contribution of capital input, labor hours worked, labor quality, and TFP. To quantify the sources of CUPI, we slightly modify the GDP growth

decomposition framework (4.A.1) in Appendix 4.A into[8]:

$$\Delta \ln Y = \bar{v} \Delta \ln K + (1 - \bar{v}) \Delta \ln H + \Delta \ln B \quad (4.B.3)$$

where

- $\bar{v} \Delta \ln K = \bar{v}_{nict} \Delta \ln K_{nict} + \bar{v}_{ict} \Delta \ln K_{ict}$ is the contribution of total capital input, which consists of ICT and non-ICT capital; $\bar{v}$ is the average income share of capital input over period $[0, T]$.
- $(1 - \bar{v}) \Delta \ln H$ is the contribution of labor hours worked (employment).
- $\Delta \ln B = \Delta \ln L_Q + \Delta \ln A$, which is the combined contribution of labor quality improvement and TFP growth. This combined component captures the contribution of efficiency improvement in the use of basic production factors, which will be referred to as raw TFP and denoted as RTFP in this study.

Combining (4.B.2) and (4.B.3) yields

$$\begin{aligned}
\Delta \ln y &= \Delta \ln Y - \Delta \ln P = [\bar{v} \Delta \ln K \\
&\quad + (1 - \bar{v}) \Delta \ln H + \Delta \ln B] - \Delta \ln P \\
\leftrightarrow \Delta \ln y &= \bar{v}(\Delta \ln K - \Delta \ln P) \\
&\quad + (1 - \bar{v})(\Delta \ln H - \Delta \ln P) + \Delta \ln B \\
\leftrightarrow \Delta \ln y &= \bar{v} . \Delta \ln(K/P) + (1 - \bar{v}) . \Delta \ln(H/P) \\
&\quad + \Delta \ln B
\end{aligned}$$

$$(4.B.4)$$

Eq (4.B.4) means that per-capita income growth rate over a period of a country can be decomposed into three sources:

(i) $\bar{v} . \Delta \ln(K/P)$, the contribution of capital deepening in the population, which will be denoted as *kpopc*;
(ii) $(1 - \bar{v}) \Delta \ln(H/P)$, the contribution of labor force participation expansion, which will be denoted as *lpopc*; and

---

[7] See Vu (2018) for more detailed discussion.

[8] The subscripts of country i over period $[0, T]$ are suppressed for exposition simplicity.

(iii) $\Delta \ln B$, which is the contribution from efficiency improvement in the use of basic production factors, which will be denoted as RTFP.

The CUPI in Eq (4.B.1), therefore, can be expressed as

$$CUPI_{0,T}^{i} = \left(kpopc_{0,T}^{i} - kpopc_{0,T}^{US}\right)$$
$$+ \left(lpopc_{0,T}^{i} - lpopc_{0,T}^{US}\right) \quad (4.B.5)$$
$$+ \left(RTFP_{0,T}^{i} - RTFP_{0,T}^{US}\right)$$

That is, the CUPI for a country can be broken down into three constituent components capturing its performance relative to the United States on the three sources of per-capita growth:

- $\left(kpopc_{0,T}^{i} - kpopc_{0,T}^{US}\right)$, which is the differential in capital deepening rate, which will be referred to in the chapter as "capital deepening";
- $\left(lpopc_{0,T}^{i} - lpopc_{0,T}^{US}\right)$, which is the differential in labor participation rate, which will be referred to in the chapter as "labor participation"; and
- $\left(RTFP_{0,T}^{i} - RTFP_{0,T}^{US}\right)$, which is the differential in RTFP.

Appendix 4.C Growth predicting model and key assumptions

4.C.1 Growth predicting model

The growth predicting model introduced below is based on the projection framework introduced by Jorgenson et al. (2002). GDP growth of a country over a period can be decomposed as

$$\Delta \ln Y = \bar{v} \Delta \ln K - (1 - \bar{v})(\Delta \ln H + \Delta \ln L_Q)$$
$$+ \Delta \ln A$$

$$(4.C.1)$$

where Y, K, H, L_Q, and A are GDP, capital services, hours worked, labor quality, and TFP, respectively, while $\Delta \ln$ in front of a variable

represent its average growth rate over the period of examination; $\bar{v}$ is the average income share of capital input over the period of examination.

From Eq (4.C.1), growth of ALP, which is computed as GDP Y divided by total labor hours worked H, can be decomposed as

$$\Delta \ln ALP = \Delta \ln(Y/H) = \Delta \ln Y - \Delta \ln H$$
$$= \bar{v}(\Delta \ln K - \Delta \ln H)$$
$$+ (1 - \bar{v})\Delta \ln L_Q + \Delta \ln A$$
$$\leftrightarrow \Delta \ln ALP = \bar{v} \Delta \ln k + (1 - \bar{v})\Delta \ln L_Q + \Delta \ln A$$

$$(4.C.2)$$

where $k = K/H$ (ratio of capital services K to labor hours worked H), which is also referred to as capital deepening in a worker.

Three new parameters of the predicting model are defined below.

(i) The capital deepening in the economy is defined the gap between the growth rates of capital stock S and GDP Y:

$$\tau = \Delta \ln S - \Delta \ln Y \quad (4.C.3)$$

In theory, $\tau = 0$ for the economies at the steady state and positive for most developing countries.

(ii) Capital quality K_Q is defined as the ratio of total capital services K to the aggregate capital stock S to capture the value each unit of capital stock can render in generating GDP (Jorgenson and Grilliches, 1967):

$$K_Q = K/S \quad (4.C.4)$$

The shift of capital stock structure from traditional (non-ICT) toward ICT capital in the recent decades has been a major factor driving capital quality K_Q growth, which is computed as

$$\Delta \ln K_Q = \Delta \ln K - \Delta \ln S \quad (4.C.5)$$

Combining (4.C.2) and (4.C.5) yields

$$\Delta \ln K = \Delta \ln K_Q + \tau + \Delta \ln Y \quad (4.C.6)$$

$$\Delta\ln k = \Delta\ln K_Q + \tau + \Delta\ln ALP \qquad (4.C.7)$$

Substituting Eq. (4.C.7) into Eq. (4.C.2), we have

$$\Delta\ln ALP = \bar{v}(\Delta\ln K_Q + \tau + \Delta\ln ALP)$$
$$+ (1 - \bar{v})\Delta\ln L_Q + \Delta\ln A \qquad (4.C.8)$$

$$\leftrightarrow \Delta\ln ALP = \frac{\bar{v}}{1-\bar{v}}\Delta\ln K_Q + \frac{\bar{v}}{1-\bar{v}}\tau + \Delta\ln L_Q$$
$$+ \frac{1}{1-\bar{v}}\Delta\ln A$$

$$(4.C.9)$$

Eq. (4.C.9) provides a model for predicting labor productivity growth of a country during a given future period. GDP growth projected for this period, therefore, will be simply computed as

$$\Delta\ln Y = \Delta\ln ALP + \Delta\ln H \qquad (4.C.10)$$

where $\Delta\ln H$ is the projected growth of labor hours worked during the period.

The growth predicting model in Eq. (4.C.8) offers three advantages. First, the model explicitly indicates the channels for promoting labor productivity growth, which can be done through accelerating growth in capital and labor quality ($\Delta\ln K_Q$ and $\Delta\ln L_Q$), enhancing capital deepening in the economy (τ) and fostering TFP growth ($\Delta\ln A$). Second, the model allows policymakers to examine these sources of growth for the past period to see what changes in policy should be made to accelerate growth and make it more sustainable. Finally, the model makes good use of the information observed for the recent period to set the assumptions on variables and parameters for the predicting model.

4.C.2 Key assumptions

The projections of ALP and GDP growth for the E7 and G7 economies during the next 10-year period, 2017–27, are based on the assumptions on the values that the variables and

parameters in Eqs. (4.C.9) and (4.C.10) will take in this period. The assumptions for the base-case are applied to all the E7 and G7 economies, except for China and Indonesia. The exceptions made for these two countries are based on expectations that China will experience a growth slowdown compared to its extraordinary performance in the recent decades and the looming adverse effect of the US–China trade war and that Indonesia will significantly improve its investment environment in the coming years. The assumptions for the pessimistic and optimistic scenarios are based on some simple adjustments on projected TFP and employment growth.

4.C.2.1 The assumptions for the base-case

(i) The average income share of capital ($\bar{v}$) is equal to the average share observed for the past 7-year period, 2010–17.

(ii) Capital quality growth ($\Delta\ln K_Q$) will be 2/3 of the average rate observed for the past 10-year period, 2007–17, assuming some slowdown in the shift toward ICT assets.

(iii) Capital deepening (τ) will be the same rate observed for the past 10-year period, 2007–17. For China, we reduce this rate by 50% from 1.2% to 0.6%, while for Indonesia, we assume this rate to be 1% instead of −0.016% observed for the past 10-year period.

(iv) Labor quality growth ($\Delta\ln L_Q$) will be the same as the average rate observed for the past 10-year period, 2007–17.

(v) TFP growth ($\Delta\ln A$).

$$\Delta\ln A = (\Delta\ln A20 + \Delta\ln A10 + \Delta\ln A7$$
$$+ \Delta\ln A3)/4$$

$$(4.C.11)$$

where $\Delta\ln A20$, $\Delta\ln A10$, $\Delta\ln A7$, and $\Delta\ln A3$ are, respectively, the average TFP growth rates over the past 20-year (1997–2017), 10-year

(2007−17), 7-year (2010−17), and 3-year (2014−17) periods. The projected TFP growth from Eq. (4.C.11) implies that what observed for TFP growth in recent periods will have a more pronounced effect on TFP growth over the next decade. For China, we assume TFP growth will be only 2/3 of the value estimated from Eq. (4.C.11).

(vi) Employment growth ($\Delta \ln H$).

$$\Delta \ln H = (\Delta \ln H_{2007-17} + \Delta \ln E_{2017-27})/2$$

where $\Delta \ln H_{2007-17}$ is the employment growth rate observed for the country over the past decade, 2007−17, while $\Delta \ln E_{2017-27}$ is the country's projected growth rate of population aged 25−64 extrapolated from the population forecast for 2025 and 2035 provided by United Nations (2017).

4.C.2.2 The assumptions for the pessimistic scenario

The assumptions change from the base-case for TFP growth ($\Delta \ln A$) and employment growth ($\Delta \ln H$), assuming that they will take their min values shown below:

$$\Delta \ln A_{min} = \begin{cases} \left(\dfrac{2}{3}\right)\Delta \ln A \ \text{if} \ \Delta \ln A > 0 \\[2mm] \left(\dfrac{4}{3}\right)\Delta \ln A \ \text{if} \ \Delta \ln A < 0 \end{cases}$$

$$\Delta \ln H_{min} = \begin{cases} \left(\dfrac{2}{3}\right)\Delta \ln H \ \text{if} \ \Delta \ln H > 0 \\[2mm] \left(\dfrac{4}{3}\right)\Delta \ln H \ \text{if} \ \Delta \ln H < 0 \end{cases}$$

4.C.2.3 The assumptions for the optimistic scenario

The assumptions change from the base-case only for TFP growth ($\Delta \ln A$) and employment growth ($\Delta \ln H$), assuming that they will take their maximum values shown below:

$$\Delta \ln A_{max} = \begin{cases} \left(\dfrac{4}{3}\right)\Delta \ln A \ \text{if} \ \Delta \ln A > 0 \\[2mm] \left(\dfrac{2}{3}\right)\Delta \ln A \ \text{if} \Delta \ln A < 0 \end{cases}$$

$$\Delta \ln H_{max} = \begin{cases} \left(\dfrac{4}{3}\right)\Delta \ln H \ \text{if} \ \Delta \ln H > 0 \\[2mm] \left(\dfrac{2}{3}\right)\Delta \ln H \ \text{if} \ \Delta \ln H < 0 \end{cases}$$

References

Bloom N, Sadun R, Reenen JV: Americans Do IT Better: US multinationals and the productivity miracle, *The American Economic Review* 102(1):167−201, 2012.

Caselli F, Coleman WJ: The US structural transformation and regional convergence: a reinterpretation, *Journal of Political Economy* 109:584−616, 2001.

Cardona M, Kretschmer T, Strobel T: ICT and productivity: Conclusions from the empirical literature, *Information Economics and Policy* 25(3):109−125, 2013.

Chun H, Miyagawa T, Pyo HK, Tonogi K: Do intangibles contribute to productivity growth in East Asian countries? Evidence from Japan and Korea. In *RIETI discussion Paper Series, 15-E-055*, 2015.

Colecchia A, Schreyer P: ICT investment and economic growth in the 1990s: is the United States a unique case?: a Comparative Study of Nine OECD Countries, *Review of Economic Dynamics* 5:408−442, 2002.

Corrado C, Hulten C, Sichel D: Intangible capital and U.S. economic growth, *Review of Income and Wealth* 55(3): 658−660, 2009.

Corrado C, Haskel J, Jona-Lasinio C, Iommi M: Innovation and intangible investment in Europe, Japan and the US, *Oxford Review of Economic Policy* 29(2):261−286, 2013.

Daveri F: The new economy in Europe, 1992-2001, *Oxford Review of Economic Policy* 18:345−362, 2002.

Dietrich A: Does growth cause structural change, or is it the other way around? A dynamic panel data analysis for seven OECD countries, *Empirical Economics* 43(3): 915−944, 2012.

Fan S, Zhang X, Robinson S: Structural change and economic growth in China, *Review of Development Economics* 7(3): 360−377, 2003.

Indjikian R, Siegel DS: The Impact of investment in IT on economic performance: implications for developing countries, *World Development* 33(5):681–700, 2005.

Inklaar R, O'Mahony M, Timmer M: ICT and Europe's Productivity Performance: industry-level growth account comparisons with the United States, *Review of Income and Wealth* 51(4):505–536, 2005.

Jorgenson DW, Ho MS, Samuels J, Stiroh KJ: Industry origins of the American productivity resurgence, *Economic Systems Research* 19(3):229–252, 2007.

Jorgenson DW, Ho MS, Stiroh KJ: *Information technology and the American growth resurgence*, Cambridge, MA, 2005, MIT Press.

Jorgenson DW, Ho MS, Stiroh KJ: Projecting productivity growth: lessons from the US growth resurgence, *Federal Reserve Bank of Atlanta Economic Review* 87(3):1–13, 2002.

Jorgenson DW, Motohashi K: Information technology and the Japanese economy, *Journal of the Japanese and International Economies* 194:460–481, 2005.

Jorgenson DW, Stiroh KJ: Raising the speed limit: U.S. economic growth in the information age, *Brookings Papers on Economic Activity* 1:125–211, 2000.

Jorgenson DW, Timmer MP: Structural change in advanced nations: a new set of stylised facts, *Scandinavian Economic Journal* 113(1):1–29, 2011.

Jorgenson DW, Vu KM: Information technology and the world economy, *The Scandinavian Journal of Economics* 107(4):631–650, 2005.

Jorgenson DW, Vu KM: The emergence of the new economic order: growth in the G7 and the G20, *Journal of Policy Modeling* 35(3):389–399, 2013.

Jorgenson DW, Vu KM: The ICT revolution, world economic growth, and policy issues, *Telecommunication Policy* 40: 383–397, 2016.

Jorgenson DW, Vu KM: The rise of developing Asia and the new economic order, *Journal of Policy Modeling* 33(5): 698–716, 2011.

Jorgenson DW: Information technology and the U.S. economy, *The American Economic Review* 91(1):1–32, 2001.

Jorgenson DW: Information technology and the G7 economies, *World Economics* 44:139–170, 2003.

Jorgenson DW: *Productivity: international comparisons of economic growth* (vol. 2). Cambridge, MA, 1995, MIT Press.

Jorgenson DW, Griliches Z: The explanation of productivity change, *The Review of Economic Studies* 34(3):249–283, 1967.

Kumar S, Russell RR: Technological change, technological catch-up, and capital deepening: relative contributions to growth and convergence, *The American Economic Review* 92(3):527–548, 2002.

Lee K: *How Can Korea be a Role Model for Catch-Up Development? A 'Capability-Based View'*, Helsinki, Finland, 2009,

United Nations University — World Institute for Development Economic Research, Research Paper No.2009/34.

Lin JY: *New structural economics: a framework for rethinking development*, Washington, DC, 2012, World Bank.

Lin JY: *The quest for prosperity: how developing economies can take off*, Princeton, 2016, Princeton University Press.

Oliner SD, Sichel DE: Information technology and productivity: where are we now and where are we going? *Federal Reserve Bank of Atlanta Economic Review* 87:15–44, 2002.

Oliner SD, Sichel DE: The resurgence of growth in the late 1990s: is information technology the story? *The Journal of Economic Perspectives* 14(4):3–22, 2000.

O'Mahony M, van Ark B: *EU productivity and competitiveness: an industry perspective*, European Communities.

Schreyer P: *The contribution of information and communication technology to output growth: a study of the G7 countries"*, STI Working Papers 2000/2, Paris, 2000, OECD.

Stiroh KJ: Information technology and the U.S. productivity revival: what do the industry data say? *The American Economic Review* 92(5):1559–1576, 2002.

Timmer MP, van Ark B: Does information and communication technology drive EU-US productivity growth differentials? *Oxford Economic Papers* 57(4):693–716, 2005.

Timmer MP, Ypma G, van Ark B: *IT in the European Union: driving productivity divergence?*, Research Memorandum GD-67, Groningen Growth and Development Centre.

United Nations: *World population prospects 2017*, New York, 2017, United Nations.

van Ark B, Inklaar R, McGuckin RH: ICT and productivity in Europe and the United States: where do the differences come from? *CESifo Economic Studies* 49(3):295, 2003.

van Ark B, Timmer MP: *Asia's productivity performance and potential: the contribution of sectors and structural change*, University of Groningen and the Conference Board.

van Ark B: Productivity and digitalisation in Europe: paving the road to faster growth. In *The conference board and the centre for innovation economics*. http://www.innovation economics.net/index.php/component/attachments/ attachments?id=282&task=view.

Vu KM: Information and communication technology and Singapore's economic growth, *Information Economics and Policy* 25(4):284–300, 2013a.

Vu KM: *The dynamics of economic growth: policy insights from comparative analyses in Asia*, Cheltenham and Northampton, Edward Elgar.

Vu KM: The global dynamics of economic catchup: patterns, drivers, and determinants. In *LKYSPP working papers*, 2018.

Woo WT: Understanding the middle-income trap in economic development: the case of Malaysia, World Economy, *Lecture delivered at the University of Nottingham, Globalization and Economic Policy* 17–34, 2011.

European productivity in the digital age: evidence from EU KLEMS

Robert Inklaar[1], Kirsten Jäger[2], Mary O'Mahony[3], Bart van Ark[4,5]

[1]Faculty of Economics and Business, University of Groningen, Groningen, The Netherlands; [2]The Vienna Institute for International Economic Studies, Vienna, Austria; [3]King's Business School, King's College London, London, United Kingdom; [4]The Conference Board, New York, NY, United States; [5]Faculty of Economics and Business, University of Groningen, Groningen, The Netherlands

5.1 Introduction

Over the past three decades productivity growth in European countries has gradually weakened despite some recovery after recessions and crises. Productivity growth has therefore become a central cause for concern about prospects for future growth in living standards across Europe. Especially when US productivity growth accelerated in the mid-1990s, the lack of a similar development across most of Europe stood out (Timmer et al., 2010). Between 1995 and 2005, GDP per hour worked increased at an average annual rate of 2.5% in the United States compared with 1.4% in the EU-15, the countries that were members of the European Union before 2004.[1]

Since the mid-2000s, US labor productivity growth has been similarly stuck in lower gear. Between 2006 and 2015, US labor productivity grew at an average annual rate of 1.1%, while labor productivity growth in the EU-15 was only 0.7%. The Global Financial Crisis (GFC) depressed productivity growth in part for cyclical reasons. However, as the productivity slowdown started well before the GFC, around 2005, there are good reasons to assume there have been other structural factors at work, including a long-term shortfall of investment (Cette et al., 2016; Fernald et al., 2017) and major business and societal challenges translating digital technology into productivity growth (van Ark and O'Mahony, 2016).

One strand of literature has focused on the declining effectiveness of the overall innovation process, which shows signs of having become both more difficult and more expensive, so that a slowdown in productivity may be unavoidable even in the medium term (Bloom et al., 2018). Others have argued that the productivity effects

---

[1] The Conference Board Total Economy Database, November 2018, https://www.conference-board.org/data/economydatabase/.

of new technology have so far primarily benefited global frontier firms, while other firms have lagged increasingly behind (Andrews et al., 2016; Riley and Bondibene, 2018). However, much of the recent uneven effects of technology on growth may just be temporary as suggested, for example, by Harberger (1998) who distinguishes between a random "mushroom-type" and a broad-based "yeast-like" phase of productivity improvements across industries. Such ideas are not out of line with the more systemic thinking from the evolutionary school of economics about sociotechnological paradigm changes. For example, Perez (2002) distinguishes between the installment and the deployment phases of new technologies with distinctly different growth and productivity effects.

So far, most of the analysis of the recent changes in productivity dynamics has been conducted at the aggregate level. This chapter employs the latest available 2017-version of the EU KLEMS database to examine these trends more closely by focusing on the characteristics of industries and their relative productivity growth performance. A more detailed analysis at industry level can help to detect some of the causes of the slowdown, as well as possible signals of a recovery in specific industries of the economy. We distinguish industries by their intensity of usage of information and communication technology (ICT), intangible capital, degree of offshoring, skill levels, and the average age of their workforces. We consider industry productivity measures until 2015 for an aggregate of 12 European countries, that cover both the largest economies and different regions of Europe, and we provide a more detailed analysis for 9 of these countries. The United States is also included in this analysis as a comparator.

First we include a brief overview of the EU KLEMS database, its history and methodology, and explanations of the sector groupings. This is followed by an overview of output and productivity growth performance at the aggregate economy level, followed by a more detailed analysis of the

performance in the goods versus market services sectors of the economy. We then look at the performance of industries that have been characterized as intensive users on the basis of our taxonomies to detect differences in productivity growth across the European countries and the United States as well as between the first period (1995–2005) and the second period (2006–15) in our analysis. We conclude this chapter with a brief summary of what we know so far, and what next steps the research on the productivity slowdown needs to take, including the issues around improved measurement of productivity in the digital age.

5.2 The EU KLEMS database

5.2.1 A brief history of EU KLEMS

If one was to go back over two decades to the mid-1990s, both the policy concerns regarding economic growth and the evidence base were primarily concerned with unemployment and low labor force participation. The defining feature of the decade starting from 1995—the significant impact of ICT on growth—was only hinted at in a handful of firm-based studies (e.g., Brynjolfsson and Hitt, 1996). The aggregate growth implications of ICT were not understood at the time. Evidence on the key role of high-level skills acquisition was only beginning to emerge in the academic literature and therefore higher education was not high on the policy agenda. Intangible investments were hardly mentioned and were seen as too difficult to measure, while again the focus in the literature was on firm-specific intangibles such as brand development rather than on their macroeconomic importance.

Going forward 5 years to the end of the century, in the context of accelerating productivity growth in the United States, some key papers emerged that argued for a significant impact of ICT on growth (Jorgenson and Stiroh, 2000; Oliner and Sichel, 2000) and that ICT had radically altered the demand for different types of labor in favor of those with university-level education (Autor et al., 1998). Policy makers began to focus much more on productivity and growth in the light of these findings. However, these earlier papers were based on data for the United States and it soon became apparent that the information base required to investigate sources of growth in Europe was not up to the task. There then followed a concerted research effort, mostly financed by the European Commission Framework Programmes, to redress this information deficiency. Using the framework developed by Dale Jorgenson and co-authors, summarized in Jorgenson et al. (1987), EU KLEMS was born.

The EU KLEMS project[2] aimed to produce long time series by sector on outputs, inputs, and productivity for all EU countries using a harmonized methodology, at the (NACE revision 1) industry level. It produced some data series for all EU-25 countries, covering the time period 1970–2007 for up to 70 industries, although the time period, industry detail, and input measures varied by country. It brought together data from national accounts and other official sources such as firm- and individual-level surveys to produce long time series on outputs, inputs, and productivity by country and industry. The database enabled a decomposition of sources of growth into volumes and types of labor (skills), quantities and types of capital (ICT and non-ICT), and total factor productivity (TFP). Details of the methodology and main results were summarized in O'Mahony and Timmer (2009). The database subsequently went through a number of revisions, in particular changing the industrial classification to NACE revision 2, and updates to 2015 for some larger economies.

The economic context in which the database was developed was that, for the macro economy, there was a catching-up process in labor productivity in the EU relative to the United States during the postwar period from the 1950s to the mid-1990s, after which the United States forged ahead. The EU KLEMS database was designed to facilitate research behind these aggregate figures, focusing especially on the industry location of these trends, the sources of differences between the United States and EU (input use or productivity), and cross-country variation. The highlights of the original EU KLEMS work were the findings that the EU productivity gap with the United States was concentrated in market service sectors and that ICT was key to explaining the labor productivity growth gap (see van Ark et al., 2008; Timmer et al., 2010).

Over time national statisticians and academics in other countries expressed interest in developing similar approaches to that in EU KLEMS. This led to the setup of the World KLEMS consortium, which includes all participants in EU KLEMS and partners from China, India, Russia, and countries in Asia, Africa, and Latin America—40 partners in total (Jorgenson et al., 2016).

Since 2008, the EU KLEMS database has been updated a few times. The most comprehensive revision was done in 2016 and 2017, switching to data based on the new European System of National Accounts (ESA10), with data covering the period until 2015. The new data, also available from www.euklems.net, provide a unique opportunity to analyze productivity growth for the total economy and two major sectors in the economy (goods-producing and market services) and cover 12 European economies. Taken together those 12 economies, which include Austria, Belgium, Czech Republic, Denmark, Germany, Finland, France, Italy, the Netherlands, Spain, Sweden, and the United Kingdom and will be named the EU-12, accounted for 90% of the European Union's nominal GDP in 2015.

A preliminary analysis of the data showed that the slow productivity growth, which had been visible in most market services in the decade before, had broadened to the goods-producing

---

[2] www.euklems.net coordinated by the University of Groningen, the Netherlands.

sector for most European economies since the crisis. The manufacturing sector was particularly hard hit by the GFC and had only partially recovered by 2015. The slowing growth trend is driven by a triple combination of modest recovery in employment growth, stagnant growth in capital input, and a further weakening in the TFP growth trend (van Ark and Jäger, 2017). In this chapter we extend the analysis by looking at various industry taxonomies to improve on our preliminary diagnosis of the productivity slowdown, and to use the EU KLEMS data set to pinpoint the main factors accounting for the slowdown.

5.2.2 Growth accounting and methodology

To assess productivity growth at the industry level, we rely on the method of growth accounting. This method has a long history, with a first systematic exposition in Jorgenson et al. (1987) and discussed in more detail in the setting of EU KLEMS in Timmer et al. (2010). Hulten (2010) provides a survey of the growth accounting literature, which includes a discussion of industry growth accounting and a broader discussion on what is and what is not measured in growth accounting.

We proceed here with a brief exposition. We assume an industry in a country at a particular point in time can be characterized by a production function exhibiting constant returns to scale (suppressing country and industry subscripts for brevity):

$$Y_t = A_t F(K_t, L_t, M_t). \quad (5.1)$$

Output Y is produced using (Hicks-neutral) technology A and the inputs are capital K, labor L, and inputs of energy, materials, and services M_t. Assuming Eq. (5.1) takes a translog form and assuming that inputs are paid their marginal products, we can compute productivity growth

as the change in output that is not accounted for by changes in inputs using the following productivity growth index:

$$\Delta \log A_t = \Delta \log Y_t - \overline{w}_t^K \Delta \log K_t - \overline{w}_t^L \Delta \log L_t$$
$$- \overline{w}_t^M \Delta \log M_t. \quad (5.2)$$

Here $\Delta log A_t \equiv log A_t - log A_{t-1}$ is the change operator, $w^X \equiv \frac{p^X X}{p^Y Y}$ is the costs of using input X, $p^X X$, relative to total revenues $p^Y Y$, and the upper bar denotes the two-period average input share, $\overline{w}_t^X = \frac{1}{2}\left(w_t^X + w_{t-1}^X\right)$.

Especially when the aim is to assess the contribution of industries to aggregate growth or, as below, to growth of a group of industries, it is more convenient to work with a value-added measure of productivity growth. We take the value-added volumes V_t from the National Accounts and compute value-added based productivity as:

$$\Delta \log A_t^V = \Delta \log V_t - \overline{s}_t^K \Delta \log K_t - s_t^L \Delta \log L_t. \quad (5.3)$$

The growth of capital input and of labor input is now weighted using the share of input costs in value added, $s_t^X \equiv \frac{p^X X}{p^V V}$. This, in effect, means we move to the value-added production function, rather than the gross output production function from Eq. (5.1), assuming that this production function is separable between intermediate and other inputs.

A key feature of the EU KLEMS database is that inputs of capital and labor are not homogenous, but instead represent a variety of different types of capital and labor, such as buildings and computers for capital and low-skilled and high-skilled workers for labor.[3] To reflect the different types of capital and labor input requires a straightforward extension from Eq. (5.3), where there are $m = 1, ..., M$ types of capital input

---

[3] See Jäger (2018) for more details.

and $n = 1, ..., N$ types of labor input that each earn their marginal products:

$$\Delta \log A_t^V = \Delta \log V_t - \sum_m \bar{s}_{mt}^K \Delta \log K_{mt}$$
$$- \sum_n s_{nt}^L \Delta \log L_{nt}. \quad (5.4)$$

The industry productivity growth rates as computed based on Eq. (5.4) can be aggregated using the share of each industry i in aggregate value added, $v_i = p_i^V V_i / \sum_i p_i^V V_i$:

$$\Delta \log A_t^V = \sum_i \bar{v}_{it} \Delta \log A_{it}^V. \quad (5.5)$$

Note that Eq. (5.5) can be applied for any combination of industries, a key feature in our analysis, below.

While the methodology underlying the EU KLEMS database is, by now, standard, the implementation is far from standardized. National statistical offices in many European countries do not routinely publish productivity accounts. In addition, there are a variety of methods employed to estimate real inputs, especially capital that requires assumptions on the rates and patterns of depreciation. This leads to difficulties in international comparisons of sources of growth. The EU KLEMS project set out to produce productivity accounts using internationally comparable methods and data sources.

In the most recent version of the EU KLEMS database, concepts and methodologies to calculate the various growth and productivity variables were adjusted to the new European System of National Accounts (ESA10) in which the asset boundary was expanded by including research and development as intellectual property assets (Jäger, 2018). Capital stock figures are mostly obtained from Eurostat and are thus consistent with national accounts assumptions on the measurement of capital stock, rather than being fully harmonized. These, plus other adjustments, imply that the latest release is not directly comparable to earlier versions of EU KLEMS. Therefore, in this chapter we only report results from 1995 to 2015.[4]

5.3 Industry taxonomies

Based on our preliminary observations about the possible causes of the productivity slowdown in the past 2 decades, we summarize the industry productivity results using a series of taxonomies, whereby the growth calculations are carried out for groups of industries that share common characteristics. These taxonomies are based largely on the intensity of use of various types of inputs. The taxonomies are as follows.

ICT intensity: In previous studies during the 1990s and early 2000s, the performance of industry productivity has often been compared on the basis of the level of intensity of investment or capital services in information and communication—based hardware and software. This research showed that ICT-intensive industries typically tended to show significantly faster labor productivity growth. However, in contrast to US industries, European industries tended to reveal lower impact from greater ICT intensity on TFP growth (Stiroh, 2002; van Ark et al., 2003). Recently the nature of digital technology has shifted from relying primarily on ICT assets, such as hardware and telecommunication equipment, toward spending on ICT services. The latter refers to data storage and information processing services (including cloud computing), computer systems design, other information

---

[4] For some countries, the start date of the new measures are a few years after 1995—this is indicated in the tables.

services (including Internet publishing), and the usage of data, storage, and communication.[5] The data are obtained from supply—use tables published as part of the World Input-Output Database (www.wiod.org), described in Timmer et al. (2016). Comparing ICT intensity, including those services, to the original ICT assets-only classification reveals a distinctly different taxonomy because ICT hardware has diminished as a share of value added in the past decade while the use of data services has increased, especially in service sectors of the economy (van Ark, 2016).

Intangibles intensity: This industry taxonomy comprises the aggregate of intangibles assets and distinguishes innovative property intensive and economic competency intensive, as explained below. Organizational changes and other forms of intangible investments, such as workforce training and other economic competencies, have long been seen as necessary to benefit from the adoption of new technology (Bresnahan et al., 2002; Bertschek and Kaiser, 2004). The pioneering work of Corrado et al. (2005, 2009) allows the measurement of these assets divided into three categories: computerized information, innovative property, and economic competencies. Computerized information coincides with computer software, which is already included in ICT capital. Innovative property refers to the innovative activity built on a scientific base of knowledge as measured not only by conventional R&D statistics but also by innovation and new products and processes more broadly defined, including new architectural and engineering design, mineral exploration, and new products development costs in the financial industry. Economic competencies include spending on strategic planning, worker training, redesigning or reconfiguring existing products

in existing markets, investment to retain or gain market share, and investment in brand development. The industry divisions are based on the data available from the INTAN Invest platform.[6] Recent work has highlighted the importance of intangible capital in explaining productivity growth in advanced economies (Corrado et al., 2017).

Skill intensity: Industries can also be classified on the basis of the proportion of workers with a university degree. The skill-biased technical change literature shows that the wage of the highly skilled is positively associated with technological changes (Autor et al., 1998). High skills have been widely regarded as complementary to ICT in generating productivity improvements. However, as the technology has become more mature, there is some evidence that high skills are less in demand than previously—firms investing in innovation create opportunities for improving conditions of a wider group of workers. For example, Aghion et al. (2017) argue that low-skilled workers employed in high-tech UK companies enjoy a higher wage premium compared not only to other low-skilled workers but also to the highly skilled.

Age profile of workers: This taxonomy is based on the proportion of workers aged 50 and over. The relationship between age and creative performance has been found to follow a hump-shaped profile in many studies using individual-level data. However, this finding needs to be treated with some caution as this type of analysis may be subject to many endogeneity and selection biases (Frosch, 2011). For example, educational attainment tends to be lower for older workers which may result in a spurious   negative   correlation   between

---

[5] More precisely, computer services refer to the following detailed industries in the North American Industry Classification System (NAICS): data processing, hosting, and related information services (NAICS 51820 and 51913) and computer systems design services and related computer services (NAICS 54152, 54153, and 54159).

[6] See www.intaninvest.net.

innovative performance and age. Also, more mature and less innovative firms tend to attract fewer younger workers. Correcting for these biases using firm-level data tends to shift the age-productivity curve toward older workers (Göbel and Zwick, 2012). Nevertheless, there remains a negative link beyond a certain age (Jones, 2010).

Both the skill taxonomy and the age taxonomy are based on tabulations from the European Labour Force Survey. The skill taxonomy relies on proportions of the workforce who have university degrees or equivalents and the age taxonomy on proportions of the workforce who are aged 50 or over. These data are consistent with the divisions of the workforce by gender, age, and skill that underlie the EU KLEMS labor composition measures.

Offshore intensity: The final classification of industries concentrates on the usage of intermediate inputs and is based on the share of industry intermediate inputs sourced from abroad. Buying inputs from abroad can be an important source of productivity growth, for instance, because they embody new technologies (Keller, 2004) and are thus of higher quality or because new, imported varieties of inputs suit different needs than domestically produced versions. For individual firms, the evidence seems clear that importing more of its inputs improves productivity (e.g., Goldberg et al., 2010; Halpern et al., 2015). The degree of "offshoring intensity" is based on the World Input-Output Database, as described in Timmer et al. (2016). It measures how much an industry relies on foreign intermediate inputs in its production. This can be approached in different ways, since the inputs of industry's suppliers may also be partly sourced abroad. For example, Timmer et al. (2013, 2014) use share of value added created domestically versus abroad. We adopt a simpler

approach, focusing only on the first-stage of the value chain, that is, the degree to which an industry directly sources its inputs from abroad. Choosing this measure over measures that also capture upstream foreign sourcing is unlikely to have a substantial impact on the results: all manufacturing industries score high on our measure, as well as agriculture, mining, transport and storage, and motor vehicle and fuel distribution.

To employ the taxonomies for an analysis of productivity, we need to make a delineation between more and less intensive industries in terms of input usage, offshoring, and other taxonomies. For this purpose, industries were identified as 0 or 1 depending on whether they belonged to the bottom or top half, respectively, of the industries in terms of their intensities. For example, the most intensive ICT-using industries are those with the highest share of value of ICT investment plus purchases of ICT services as a percentage of "synthetic output" (which is value added at industry level plus the intermediate use of those ICT services) in at least four of seven countries for which data were readily available (Finland, France, Germany, Italy, the Netherlands, Sweden, and the United Kingdom). The intangible, skill, age, and offshoring intensities were also based on being above the median of industries for a minimum of four countries out of nine countries (the countries above as well as Austria and Spain).[7]

Table 5.1 summarizes the different taxonomies that we use for the 1-digit market economy industries. The taxonomies on intangibles, skills, and age are not readily available at a greater level of detail than this 1-digit level, while the ICT and offshoring taxonomies are available at the 2-digit level in most cases. For 1-digit industries with more detailed taxonomies, we show the fraction of the 1-digit

[7] In the cases of ICT and offshore intensities, there was more information available for subindustries, so that the average of 0 and 1 for all subindustries was used.

TABLE 5.1 Taxonomies of industries: Market Economy.

	ICT	Intan	InProp	EcComp	Offshore	Skill	Age
Agriculture, forestry, and fishing	0	0	0	0	1	0	1
Mining	0	0	1	0	1	0	1
Manufacturing	0.73	1	1	1	1	0	0
Electricity, gas, and water	1	0	1	0	1	1	1
Construction	0	0	0	0	1	0	0
Wholesale and retail trade	0.67	1	0	1	0.33	0	0
Transportation and storage	0.50	0	0	0	0.50	0	1
Hotels and restaurants	0	0	0	0	0	0	0
Information and communication	1	1	1	1	0	1	0
Finance and insurance	1	1	1	1	0	1	0
Business services	1	1	1	1	0	1	0
Arts, entertainment, and recreation	1	0	0	1	0	1	0
Other services	0	0	0	1	0	0	1
Household services	0	0	0	1	0	0	1

Notes: Industries were identified as 0 or 1 depending on whether they belonged to the bottom or top half, respectively, of the industries in terms of their intensities. In the cases of ICT and offshore intensities, there was more information available for subindustries, so that the average of 0 and 1 for all subindustries was used. The market economy excludes industries mostly in the public sector (education, health, and public administration) and real estate, due to well-known issues in measuring output in these sectors. The table shows whether an industry is classified as intensive according to each criterion. Intan: intangible capital; InProp: innovative properties; EcComp: economic competencies. Fractions indicate that more detailed industries are divided between intensive and nonintensive. Information on intangibles, skill, and age are not available below the level of detail shown in the table.
Sources: see text.

industry that is classified as "intensive" according to this criterion based on the number of underlying 2-digit industries.

The table shows that the intensive industries included in the taxonomies show some overlap, but there are substantial differences too. For example, the ICT taxonomy corresponds closely to the skills and the intangibles taxonomies, though there are notable differences between these. The age taxonomy, which is based on the share of workers aged 50 and over, tends to highlight those industries that are not highlighted in the other taxonomies, such as agriculture and transportation and storage. This is to be expected as age is picking up a factor that is likely to lead to lower performance, whereas the other

taxonomies focus on higher-performing industries. Most taxonomies point at the aggregate manufacturing sector as an intensive sector, except for skill and age. The more detailed ICT intensity classification signals that more than a quarter of manufacturing industries are not ICT-intensive. The information and communication sector, finance and insurance, and business services are intensive on ICT usage, intangibles, and skills but not for offshoring or age. For intangibles, we find that some sectors that did not score on innovation properties did show up for economic competencies: these include wholesale and retail trade, arts/entertainment/creation, and other personal and household services. In contrast, mining and utilities which scored as intensive sectors on the basis of innovative properties dropped out on the basis of economic competencies. The one industry that stands as being not intensive across all taxonomies is hotels and restaurants: it is the only industry that is not ICT-intensive, not intangibles-intensive, not skills-intensive, not prone to offshoring and not employing a relatively old workforce.

In sum, the differences between the taxonomies should provide enough scope for differences in average growth for each classification. Yet the similarities also make clear that any (mono-)causal discussion is not warranted, as there are multiple factors that influence productivity growth and there is no silver bullet that impacts productivity growth beyond all else.

5.4 Aggregate growth accounting

Before turning to the productivity results by industry taxonomy, we consider trends in outputs and inputs for aggregate economic activity. Table 5.2 summarizes value added growth and labor productivity (value added per hour worked) growth for an EU aggregate based on 12 countries,[8] compared to the United States. Between 1998 and 2005, average growth in real value added for both the total economy and the market economy in the United States was about 40% faster than in the EU-12. In the decade since 2005, both regions have witnessed a significant drop in aggregate output growth. The slowdown was partly due to the GFC, but when excluding the most critical years of the crisis (2008—10) and examining the period since 2011, output growth in both the United States

TABLE 5.2 Aggregate growth in real value added and labor productivity, average % per annum.

	Total economy		Market economy	
	1998—2005	2006—15	1998—2005	2006—15
Value Added				
EU-12	2.1	0.9	2.3	0.8
United States	2.9	1.3	3.1	1.2
Labor Productivity (value added per hour)				
EU-12	1.4	0.7	1.7	0.8
United States	2.5	0.8	3.1	1.0

Notes: The 12 EU economies include Austria, Belgium, Czech Republic, Denmark, Germany, Finland, France, Italy, the Netherlands, Spain, Sweden, and the United Kingdom. The EU KLEMS-based growth rates for the total economy results can be slightly different from official estimates as reported in the National Accounts of individual countries or in data sets such as Penn World Tables or the Total Economy Database, as the EU KLEMS growth rates are aggregated up from a sector level, and can therefore be affected by slightly different weighting.
Source: EUKLEMS, 2017, euklems.net.

and EU-12 was about half of that achieved from 1995 to 2005. Similar trends are observable for labor productivity growth. Both regions experienced a large drop in productivity growth during the second period, and the average labor productivity growth for the United States dropped almost to the EU-12 level for both the aggregate and the market economy. Strikingly, the slowdown in productivity for the United States shows no sign of any significant recovery in the most recent years, to 2017.[9]

Fig. 5.1A and B shows contributions from hours worked and labor productivity to output

---

[8] Taken together those 12 economies, which include Austria, Belgium, Czech Republic, Denmark, Germany, Finland, France, Italy, the Netherlands, Spain, Sweden, and the United Kingdom, named EU-12, account for 90% of the European Union's nominal GDP in 2015.

[9] See https://www.conference-board.org/data/economydatabase/.

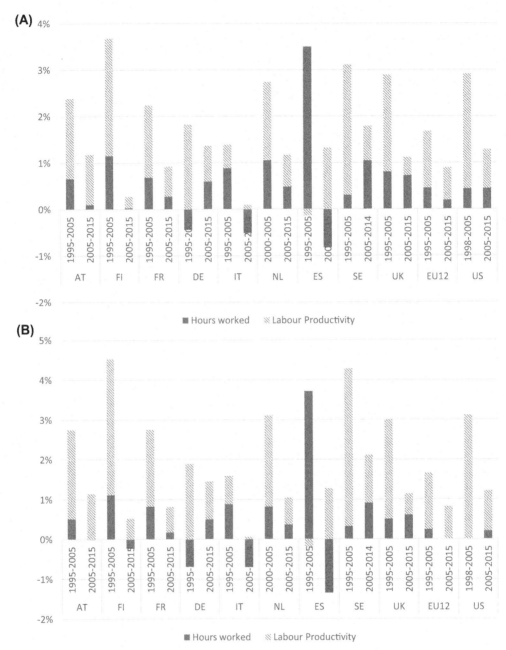

FIGURE 5.1 (A) Hours Worked and Labor Productivity growth rates, Total Economy, % per annum. (B) Hours Worked and Labor Productivity growth rates, Market Economy, % per annum.

growth for the nine largest EU economies separately for the aggregate and market economy, respectively.[10] For the EU-12, hours worked growth rates were slower in the 2006−15 period than during the 1998−2005 period, whereas in the US, hours for the total economy increased at about the same rate during both periods and even slightly improved for the market economy. However, the slump in labor productivity growth, which occurred in both regions, was much more pronounced for the United States than for Europe even though US productivity growth remained marginally higher than in the EU-12 during the 2006−15 period. Similar patterns emerge for most of the individual European countries shown in the diagram with weakening hours and productivity growth rates during the latest period. In Germany and Sweden, the growth in hours worked was higher in the later period and hours worked growth also held up well for the United Kingdom, but for all three economies there was a slowdown in labor productivity growth. The main exception is Spain, where labor productivity growth declined in the earlier period but rose in the later period and vice versa for hours worked which is largely due to the greater exposure of the Spanish economy to boom-and-bust cycles, especially in construction and tourism.

The slowdown in labor productivity growth can partly be explained by reductions in the extent of capital deepening, defined as the growth in capital services per hour worked. Fig. 5.2A and B illustrates the significant slump in this measure, for the EU-12 group, individual EU countries, and the United States. The slowdown in capital deepening was most pronounced in the United Kingdom and the United States which had seen the fastest increases in capital intensity during the earlier

period. Overall the period since the financial crisis is one of widespread reduced investment in capital per worker hour.

Finally, we consider growth rates of TFP. Fig. 5.3A and B shows TFP growth rates for the same time periods and country/region groups as in the previous charts. These figures show a much weaker TFP growth than was evident for labor productivity. In many countries TFP growth was either negative or almost zero in the second period. Countries that experienced the highest growth rates in the earlier period, Finland, the United Kingdom, and the United States, have shown the greatest drop since. Only Germany experienced a slight improvement in TFP growth across the two time periods for both the total and the market economy although at relatively low values. Also Spain, which already had experienced negative TFP growth during the 1996−2005 period, saw that deterioration somewhat lessening during the later period.

In summary the review of the labor productivity, capital deepening, and TFP metrics for the aggregate and market economy highlights that Europe and the United States entered a period of much slower productivity growth from the mid-2000s and that there is little evidence of a recovery after the crisis. Before examining growth according to the industry taxonomies, we first consider TFP growth rates dividing the market economy into goods production and market services. Timmer et al. (2010) highlighted the importance of market services as drivers of growth (in the United States) and slowdown (in most European economies) during the decade from 1995 to 2005, when ICT had its greatest impact on output and labor productivity growth, and arguably also on TFP growth through the use of this technology.

---

[10] For the remainder of the analysis in this chapter, we have excluded separate analysis of three of the smaller European economies (Belgium, Czech Republic, and Denmark) for which up-to-date estimates are available, which are included with the EU-12 aggregate.

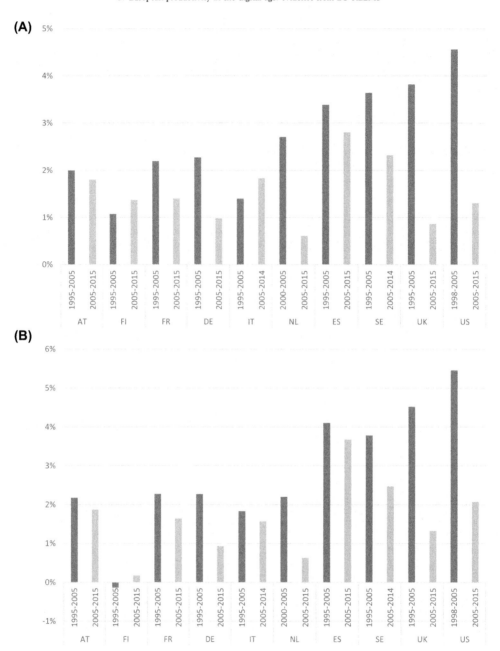

FIGURE 5.2 (A) Growth in Capital per Hour Worked, Total Economy, % per annum. (B) Growth in Capital per Hour Worked, Market Economy, % per annum.

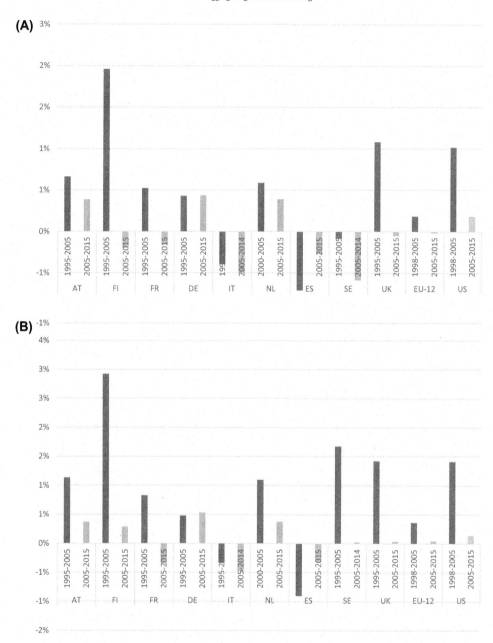

FIGURE 5.3 (A) Growth in Total Factor Productivity, Total Economy, % per annum. (B) Growth in Total Factor Productivity, Market Economy, % per annum.

Table 5.3 shows TFP growth by these major sectors. From 1995 to 2005, TFP growth in the market services sector was much slower than in the goods sector. However, the slowdown during the second period was less dramatic for market services than for manufacturing. In market services, the growth in TFP was moderately positive in the earlier period in most countries, with the exception of Germany, Italy, and Spain. Market services productivity was especially strong in Finland and the United Kingdom. In the later period TFP growth in market services fell to very low numbers or became negative, with the exception of the Netherlands.

TFP growth fell much faster in goods production, but the rates remained largely positive, although in this case the Netherlands and the United Kingdom were showing negative rates. In the United States the TFP decline in the goods sector was also surprisingly strong from 3.5% from 1995 to 2005 to 0.9% from 2006 to 15. However, these observations hide the significant swings in goods-sector productivity over the past decade. For example, van Ark and O'Mahony (2016) showed that manufacturing TFP growth in the EU-12 dropped from 2.4% between 2002 and 2007 to −1% during the most critical recession years from 2008 to 2010 and recovered modestly to 0.9% from 2011 to 2015. In market services, signs of recovery have been limited so far. Therefore the later period cannot be characterized as one in which the market services sector helped to offset the productivity collapse in the goods sector of the economy.

5.5 Growth by sector characteristics

In order to get to a better diagnosis of what have been the key reasons behind the recent productivity dynamics and how to understand

TABLE 5.3 Total factor productivity growth in Market Services and Goods Production, % per annum.

	Market services		Goods	
	1995–2005	2006–15	1995–2005	2006–15
Austria	0.9	0.0	1.9	1.4
Finland	2.1	0.3	4.3	0.3
France	0.2	−0.7	2.4	0.9
Germany	−0.3	0.3	2.1	1.1
Italy*	−0.4	−0.7	0.0	0.1
Netherlands*	1.1	0.7	1.3	−0.5
Spain	−1.9	−0.7	1.3	1.2
Sweden*	1.0	−0.1	3.2	0.4
United Kingdom	1.6	0.2	1.4	−0.2
EU-12*	0.2	−0.1	1.3	0.7
United States*	0.8	0.0	3.5	0.9

*Note: Netherlands 2000–05; EU-12 and United States 1998–2005 instead of 1995–2005; Italy and Sweden 2005–14 instead of 2005–15. *Source: EUKLEMS (2017), euklems.net.*

differences across countries and sectors, we have introduced a range of taxonomies to classify and distinguish industries in EU KLEMS. As a starting point, it is helpful to first analyze the growth experience of the United States between 1998 and 2005 using these taxonomies.[11] As discussed in the previous section, productivity growth in the United States stood out relative to the EU in this first period, as growth was substantially faster than before—or since (Byrne et al., 2016).

Table 5.4 shows the TFP growth rates for the overall market economy and the breakdown in groups of industries according to the different characteristics. Market economy TPF in the United States grew at a rate of 1.4% on average over the 1998–2005 period. Industries producing

---

[11] For most countries, the latest EU KLEMS release provides data since 1995 (or earlier), but for the United States 1998 is the starting year.

TABLE 5.4 Average annual total factor productivity growth in the United States, 1998—2005 (%).

Market economy	1.4
ICT producers	6.0
ICT users	1.6
Total intangibles	2.0
Innovative properties	1.9
Economic competencies	1.8
Offshoring	2.0
Skill	0.9
Age	−0.1

Note: Productivity growth for various taxonomies indicate productivity growth rates of industries that were characterized as above median for all industries for that specific group. *ICT*, Information and communication technology.
Source: EUKLEMS, 2017, euklems.net.

ICT goods and services, which include production of semiconductors, computers, and telecommunication equipment on the goods side and the information and communication industries on the services side, show the fastest TFP growth compared to other groups at 6.0%, substantially higher than the average TFP growth for the market economy as a whole.

ICT-using industries cover the industries that make the most intensive use of ICTs. Unlike earlier ICT classifications, which identified ICT intensity based only on the use of ICT hardware and software capital, the new taxonomy also incorporates information on use of ICT services as intermediate inputs. This aims to capture that firms are increasingly outsourcing ICT activities: rather than maintaining servers and building dedicated software, they purchase access to data centers and cloud-based software services. As Table 5.4 shows, the group of ICT-using

industries contributed positively to high productivity growth in the United States until 2005, slightly above the market sector average.[12]

The three intangible assets taxonomies also show that the most intangible-intensive industries exhibited faster productivity growth than industries that invested less in intangible assets. As shown in Table 5.1, industries scoring high on "intellectual properties" are different from those with high scores on "economic competencies," yet growth of either grouping exceeds market economy growth. This highlights that industries that are in neither grouping—agriculture, construction, transportation and storage, and hotels and restaurants—showed particularly low productivity growth in the United States between 1998 and 2005.

The offshoring taxonomy highlights the productivity performance of industries which have intensively offshored parts of their production process. The relatively high growth in this grouping illustrates that market services were not the only factor in strong US productivity growth during the 1998—2005 period but that globalization played an important role as well.

The two labor-taxonomies highlight that industries that were intensive in usage of high skill levels, and especially of experienced workers over the age of 50 years, were not showing a productivity advantages over industries that did not. One common feature is that these taxonomies both omit manufacturing and wholesale and retail trade. The age-based taxonomy shows a particularly stark result in that TFP growth for industries with relatively many older workers in the United States was below zero.

The discussion so far shows that intensive ICT usages, intangibles. and offshoring were key contributors to the relatively strong TFP growth performance of the market sector in the United States between 1998 and 2005. Yet the more

---

[12] Most industries that are classified as ICT-intensive according to the new "assets + services" framework were also ICT-intensive according to the old asset-based framework.

TABLE 5.5 Average annual total factor productivity growth in Europe and the United States, 1995–2015 (%).

	Market	ICT	Intangibles	InProp	EcComp	Offshore	Skill	Age
Spain	−0.6	−0.2	0.2	0.1	0.2	−0.2	−0.6	−0.6
Italy	−0.4	−0.3	−0.2	−0.4	−0.3	−0.4	−0.7	−0.6
France	0.2	0.1	0.4	0.3	0.4	0.6	−0.3	0.5
Germany	0.5	0.4	0.6	0.4	0.5	1.2	−0.7	0.6
Netherlands	0.6	0.5	1.0	0.4	0.9	0.0	0.6	−0.3
United States	0.7	0.8	1.1	1.1	0.9	0.8	0.6	0.1
United Kingdom	0.7	0.9	1.3	1.1	1.2	0.3	1.3	−0.8
Austria	0.8	0.9	1.0	1.0	0.9	0.6	0.6	0.9
Sweden	0.9	1.2	1.7	1.3	1.5	0.6	0.3	−0.8
Finland	1.6	1.6	2.2	2.0	2.1	1.0	1.3	0.8
Correlation with market economy	1.0	0.96	0.93	0.91	0.93	0.73	0.79	0.44

Notes: The table shows average annual total productivity growth for the group of industries identified in the column heading; see Table 1 for the composition of the industry groups. *Market*, Market economy; *ICT*, Information and communication technology; *InProp*, Innovative properties; *EcComp*, Economic competencies. The period covered is shorter in Italy (1995–2014), the Netherlands (2000–15), Sweden (1995–2014), and the United States (1998–2015).
Source: EUKLEMS, 2017, euklems.net.

pressing questions that motivate this chapter are whether we can use these taxonomies to find a common thread in the productivity performance across European countries and the United States and what factors explain the slowdown after 2005.

Table 5.5 aims to answer the first question, comparing the performance of TFP growth across countries and taxonomies over the full period for the European countries and the United States, sorted by average growth in the market economy (first column) and subsequently for the different taxonomies. Over the full period, most of the countries show average annual TFP growth between 0 and 1%, and with the United States not in an exceptional position relative to the European economies. However, the variation in productivity growth

between European countries is substantial, especially when considering the decline in productivity in Spain and Italy for most groups on the one hand, and the average TFP growth of 1.6% in Finland, as well as strong TFP growth numbers across the groups, on the other hand.[13]

However, there are some common features in terms of the performance of different groups between the countries. In all countries, the industries that are investing more in intangibles, and particularly in intangibles related to economic competencies, show faster productivity growth than the aggregate for the market economy. In most countries, the ICT-intensive industries also show faster productivity growth than the market economy as a whole, whereas the differences are less pronounced for intangible-intensive industries. Conversely, the skill-intensive

[13] Much of the strong productivity growth in Finland during the 1995–2005 period was because of a strong "Nokia effect" in this relatively small economy.

TABLE 5.6 Change in average annual total factor productivity growth: 2005−15 versus 1995−2005.

	Market	ICT	Intangibles	InProp	EcComp	Offshore	Skill	Age
Finland	−2.6	−3.1	−3.2	−3.7	−3.1	−3.1	−2.2	−1.4
Sweden	−1.7	−1.3	−1.3	−1.4	−1.2	−3.0	0.1	−1.9
United Kingdom	−1.4	−1.3	−1.1	−1.8	−1.0	−1.5	−2.2	−3.0
United States	−1.3	−1.4	−1.6	−1.3	−1.4	−2.0	−0.4	0.3
France	−1.2	−1.0	−0.9	−1.2	−1.0	−1.8	−0.8	−1.6
Austria	−0.8	−1.0	−0.5	−0.9	−0.5	−1.2	−1.0	−1.6
Netherlands	−0.7	−0.9	−0.5	−1.3	−0.6	−1.4	−1.0	−2.2
Italy	−0.1	−0.3	0.2	0.0	0.2	−0.7	−0.1	−1.2
Germany	0.1	0.6	0.3	0.6	0.3	−1.0	1.9	−1.5
Spain	0.6	−0.8	0.3	−0.9	0.3	−0.2	−1.3	−0.9
Correlation with market economy	1.00	0.84	0.96	0.84	0.96	0.92	0.47	0.17

Notes: The table shows the change in average annual productivity growth before and after 2005 for the group of industries identified in the column heading; see Table 1 for the composition of the industry groups. *Market*: Market economy; *ICT*, Information and communication technology; *InProp*, Innovative properties; *EcComp*, Economic competencies. The period covered is shorter in Italy (1995−2014), the Netherlands (2000−15), Sweden (1995−2014), and the United States (1998−2015).
Source: EUKLEMS, 2017, euklems.net.

industries and those that employ relatively older workers tend to grow more slowly, or even show declining productivity such as for older-worker−intensive industries in Italy, Spain, the Netherlands, the United Kingdom, and Sweden. Finally, as indicated by the correlations in the bottom row of the table, the cross-country patterns of productivity growth in ICT-intensive and in intangible-intensive industries correspond most closely to the overall growth pattern, suggesting that these industries are most important for characterizing the growth differences across countries.

Table 5.6 addresses the second question, namely the slowdown in productivity growth in most countries after 2005. The first column highlights that TFP growth slowed down between the first and second period in all countries, except Germany and Spain. In most countries the slowdown was in the order of 1 percentage point or more. The degree to which the change in growth for the individual taxonomies

corresponds to the change in aggregate growth is smaller than the correspondence of growth rates in Table 5.5. For example, in approximately half the countries (Sweden, France, the United Kingdom, the United States, and Germany), the slowdown was smaller or the same in ICT-intensive industries compared to the aggregate, while in the other half of countries (Finland, Austria, the Netherlands, Italy, and Spain), the slowdown was larger. The clearest pattern can be seen in industries that invest most intensively in economic competencies and in industries that are offshoring more intensively. The productivity slowdown in industries that invest most intensively in economic competencies is less severe than for the aggregate in nearly all countries, while the slowdown in offshoring-intensive industries is larger than for the aggregate in all countries. The more severe slowdown in offshoring-intensive industries could point to the importance of the broad slowdown in global trade in recent years and the possible impact of a defragmentation of global value chains on productivity growth (Timmer et al., 2016). This would be another sign that firms are exploiting fewer cost reductions from foreign sourcing and specialization.

5.6 Summary and conclusions

Productivity research since the GFC has shown that the productivity slowdown of the past decade or so started well before the crisis—around 2005. However, the recession has exacerbated the productivity crisis which most economies have experienced because of slowing demand, weak investment, and structural rigidities in product, labor, and capital markets (van Ark and Jäger, 2017). In addition, while creating new business models and applications, the complex characteristics of the New Digital Economy, characterized by the combined shifts to mobile technology, cloud computing and storage, and ubiquitous access to broadband, have created important challenges in how to leverage these new technologies to drive productivity growth (van Ark, 2016).

In this chapter we adopted a series of industry taxonomies to detect more precisely the possible causes of differences in productivity growth between European countries and the United States, and the slowdown in productivity growth since 2005. Our findings confirm insights from the literature that the degree of investment in ICT and intangibles assets, and in particularly economic competencies, has accounted for a fair part of the difference between sectors that have shown productivity performance above the average for the market economy vis-à-vis those who performed below that. In contrast, we do not find much evidence that industries which are relatively intensive on the usage of high skills show above average performance and there appears to be signs of a negative impact from the aging workforce.

We also find that the productivity slowdown since 2005 has hit the United States even more than for the average of the European economies together, especially in manufacturing, even though the average US productivity growth rates are still slightly higher than in the EU. Industries that are strong on the intensity of ICT usage and intangibles have generally experienced smaller slowdowns than those that are characterized as less intensive on those characteristics. This implies that the prominent productivity issues in the digital economy have become more visible on a global scale and are less important in distinguishing between US and European productivity performance. While the United States remains a clear technology leader in the digital economy, compared to Europe, the productivity effects from the use of that technology are not superior.

Finally, we find that industries that benefited most from offshoring trends during the period 1995—2005 experienced bigger slowdowns in productivity growth since then. This implies that the slowdown in global trade and possible impact of a defragmentation of global value chains on productivity may have been in play over the past decade.

We emphasize that it is still early days to fully establish the reasons for the productivity slowdown, and that more detailed analysis over time should help to deepen our understanding of the phenomenon. First, we are still in the midst of the transition from the Old Digital Economy (which was characterized by the introduction of the PC in people's lives and business processes, the rise of the Internet, and the beginnings of e-commerce) to the New Digital Economy (which is characterized by the change toward mobile, ubiquitous access to the Internet, the storage and usage of data, and advances in artificial intelligence and robotics). The past decade of slow productivity growth may be characteristic of an adjustment process between two technologies, and a productivity recovery could therefore be around the corner.

Second, even if it is just a matter of time for the effects of the New Digital Economy to show, it is questionable whether the currently agreed measurement framework for productivity will be able to pick up the effects of the New Digital Economy. Most recent studies have argued that increased mismeasurement of output and productivity is unlikely to account for the entire productivity slowdown. However, that does not mean we may not be missing something. Except for well-known measurement issues related to price declines of digital assets and services, which still may account for some underestimation of growth (Byrne et al., 2016), the bigger measurement issues revolve around how to handle the impact of free digital content on the economy. The New Digital Economy may provide benefits that are not being identified in GDP or in the productivity accounts. For example, the user utility of free digital content is not easily captured in a production cost or resources-saving framework, including national and growth accounts. Similarly, output-saving technical change from consumer technologies may change the growth effects from digital technologies (Hulten and Nakamura, 2018). These measurement issues are currently being debated by national accounts statisticians and economists, but their resolution is still some way off.

References

Aghion P, Bergeaud A, Blundell R, Griffith R: *Innovation, firms and wage inequality*, Harvard University.

Andrews D, Criscuolo C, Gal P: *The best versus the rest: the global productivity slowdown, divergence across firms and the role of public policy*, OECD Productivity Working Papers. 5, 2016.

Autor D, Katz LF, Krueger A: Computing inequality: have computers changed the labor market? *Quarterly Journal of Economics* 113(4):1169–1213, 1998.

Bertschek I, Kaiser U: Productivity effects of organizational change: microeconometric evidence, *Management Science* 50(3):394–404, 2004.

Bloom N, Jones CI, Van Reenen J, Webb M: *Are ideas getting harder to find*, March 2018. Version 2.0.

Bresnahan TF, Brynjolfsson E, Hitt LM: Information technology, workplace organization, and the demand for skilled labor: firm-level evidence, *Quarterly Journal of Economics* 117(1):339–376, 2002.

Brynjolfsson E, Hitt LM: Paradox Lost? Firm-level evidence on the returns to information systems, *Management Science* 42(4):541–558, 1996.

Byrne DM, Fernald JG, Reinsdorf MB: Does the United States have a productivity slowdown or a measurement problem? *Brookings Papers on Economic Activity Spring* 109–182, 2016.

Cette G, Fernald J, Mojon B: The pre-great recession slowdown in productivity, *European Economic Review* 88: 3–20, 2016.

Corrado C, Haskel J, Jona-Lasinio C: Knowledge spillovers, ICT and productivity growth, *Oxford Bulletin of Economics & Statistics* 79(4):592–618, 2017.

Corrado C, Hulten C, Sichel DE: Measuring capital and technology: an expanded framework. In Corrado C, Haltiwanger J, Sichel DE, editors: *Measuring capital in the new economy*, University of Chicago Press, pp 11–46.

Corrado C, Hulten C, Sichel DE: Intangible capital and U.S. economic growth, *Review of Income and Wealth* 55: 661–685, 2009.

Fernald JG, Hall RE, Stock JH, Watson MW: The disappointing recovery of output after 2009, *Brookings Papers on Economic Activity* 1–58, 2017.

Frosch KH: Workforce age and innovation: a literature survey, *International Journal of Management Reviews* 13(4): 414–430, 2011.

Göbel C, Zwick T: Age and productivity – sector differences, *De Economist* 160(1):35–57, 2012.

Goldberg PK, Khandelwal AK, Pavcnik N, Topalova P: Imported intermediate inputs and domestic product growth: evidence from India, *Quarterly Journal of Economics* 125(4): 1727–1767, 2010.

Halpern L, Koren M, Szeidl A: Imported inputs and productivity, *The American Economic Review* 105(12): 3660–3703, 2015.

Harberger A: A vision of the growth process, *The American Economic Review* 88(1):1–32, 1998.

Hulten C: Growth accounting. In Hall B, Rosenberg N, editors: *Handbook of the Economics of Innovation*, vol. 2. Elsevier, pp 987–1031.

Hulten C, Nakamura L: *Accounting for growth in the age of the internet: the importance of output-saving technical change*, 2018. NBER Working Paper No. 23315.

Jäger K: *EU KLEMS Growth and productivity accounts, 2017 release, statistical module: description of methodology and country notes*. www.euklems.net.

Jones BF: Age and great inventions, *The Review of Economics and Statistics* 92(1):1–14, 2010.

Jorgenson DW, Fukao K, Timmer MP, editors: *The world economy. growth or stagnation?* Cambridge University Press.

Jorgenson DW, Gollop F, Fraumeni B: *Productivity and U.S. economic growth*, Cambridge and London, 1987, Harvard University Press.

Jorgenson DW, Stiroh K: Raising the speed limit: U.S. economic growth in the information age, *Brookings Papers on Economic Activity* 1:125–211, 2000.

Keller K: International technology diffusion, *Journal of Economic Literature* 42(3):752–782, 2004.

Oliner SD, Sichel DE: The resurgence of growth in the late 1990s: is information technology the story? *The Journal of Economic Perspectives* 14:3–22, 2000.

O'Mahony M, Timmer MP: Output, input and productivity measures at the industry level: the EU KLEMS database, *Economic Journal* 119:F374–F403, 2009.

Perez C: *Technological revolutions and financial capita: the dynamics of bubbles and golden ages*, Edward Elgar.

Riley R, Bondibene CR: *Winners and losers in the knowledge economy: the role of Intangible capital*, NIESR.

Stiroh KJ: Information technology and the US productivity revival: what do the industry data say? *The American Economic Review* 92(5):1559–1576, 2002.

Timmer MP, Inklaar R, O'Mahony M, van Ark B: *Economic growth in Europe*, Cambridge University Press.

Timmer MP, Erumban AA, Los B, Stehrer R, de Vries GJ: Slicing up global value chains, *The Journal of Economic Perspectives* 28:99–118, 2014.

Timmer MP, Los B, Stehrer R, de Vries GJ: An anatomy of the global trade slowdown based on the WIOD 2016 release, *GGDC Research Memorandum* 162, 2016.

Timmer MP, Los B, Stehrer R, de Vries GJ: Fragmentation, incomes and jobs: an analysis of European competitiveness, *Economic Policy* 28:613–661, 2013.

van Ark B: The productivity paradox of the new digital economy, *International Productivity Monitor* 31:1–15, 2016.

van Ark B, Inklaar RC, McGuckin RH: ICT and productivity in Europe and the United States. Where do the differences come from? *CESifo Economic Studies* 49(3):295–318, 2003.

van Ark B, Jäger K: Recent trends in Europe's output and productivity growth performance at the sector level, *International Productivity Monitor* 33:8–23, 2017.

van Ark B, O'Mahony M: Productivity growth in Europe before and since the 2008/2009 economic and financial crisis. In Jorgenson DW, Fukao K, Timmer MP, editors: *The world economy. Growth or stagnation?* Cambridge University Press, pp 111–152.

van Ark B, O'Mahony M, Timmer MP: The productivity gap between Europe and the U.S.: trends and causes, *The Journal of Economic Perspectives* 22(1):25–44, 2008.

Manufacturing productivity in India: the role of foreign sourcing of inputs and domestic capacity building

K.L. Krishna[1], Bishwanath Goldar[2], Deb Kusum Das[3], Suresh Chand Aggarwal[4], Abdul A. Erumban[5,6], Pilu Chandra Das[7]

[1]Centre for Delhi School of Economics, Delhi School of Economics, and Madras Institute of Development Studies, Chennai, India; [2]Institute of Economic Growth, Delhi, India; [3]Department of Economics, Ramjas College, University of Delhi, Delhi, India; [4]Department of Business Economics, University of Delhi South Campus, Delhi, India; [5]The Conference Board, Brussels, Belgium; [6]University of Groningen, Groningen, The Netherlands; [7]Kidderpore College, University of Calcutta, Kolkata, West Bengal, India

6.1 Introduction

Improving manufacturing performance remains a challenge for Indian policymakers. Efforts to increase the sector's dynamism through various policy initiatives such as the "National Manufacturing Policy," the "Make-in-India" program, as well as the "Skill India" program along with several sector-specific initiatives reflect the increased policy focus. The substantial trade policy reforms and industrial deregulations[1] of the early 1990s and subsequent reform measures in the years thereafter have given manufacturing growth a more prominent

---

[1] Following a severe balance of payment crisis, major economic reforms were initiated in India in 1991, which included dismantling of industrial licensing and removal of quantitative restrictions on imports of intermediate and capital goods, etc. The process of economic liberalization continued with the undertaking of several industrial policy reforms in subsequent years along with lowering of trade barriers, aiming to improve productivity and competitiveness of the manufacturing sector. There was substantial liberalization of industrial policy and virtual elimination of protection against imports in the postreform period. The average tariff rate applicable on India's imports on manufactured products was 83% in 1990, which fell to 31.8% in 2001 and further to about 8.6% in 2009 (based on World Bank data on tariff rates). Quantitative restrictions on imports of manufactures were massively reduced in the postreform period. Only about 5% of tariff lines for manufactured products were subject to quantitative restrictions by 2009 (Das, 2016, Table 6.2).

space in policy making. Yet the share of this sector in overall GDP and employment still remains low, leaving it a matter of concern on how it will contribute to India's future growth. While much of India's economic growth has been driven by its services economy, the performance of the manufacturing sector has been modest and still requires better results in terms of output growth, productivity growth, capital intensity, technology absorption, job creation, and export growth.

Two important aspects of India's manufacturing policies are (1) to make the sector internationally competitive, so as to improve the exposure to the international market, and (2) to embrace advanced technology so as to improve productivity and competitiveness of the sector. In this chapter, we make an attempt to understand the determinants of total factor productivity (TFP) performance of the Indian manufacturing sector, with special attention paid to the aforementioned two factors. Specifically, we focus on the sector's integration in the global economy in terms of its participation in the global value chains (GVCs) and its adoption of high-quality capital assets in the production process, in terms of the use of equipment capital. Empirical evidence shows that participation in GVCs has a significant impact on productivity (see, for instance, Constantinescu et al., 2017). The GVCs have figured prominently in the industrialization process in China and several South-east Asian countries. India's export share in world markets (2.1% of global merchandise exports in 2017 according to WTO data) still remains substantially below that of China (16.2%). As far as integration into GVCs is concerned, India remains far behind its peers. It is asserted that poor trade infrastructure remains a barrier to enhancing India's involvement with global supply chains (Tewari et al., 2015).

There is now a vast literature on the role of GVCs especially in the context of international fragmentation of production and industrialization of both developed and the developing world.[2] The onset of cross-country databases such as the World Input-Output Database (WIOD)[3] and the OECD's Trade in Value Added (TiVA)[4] has facilitated extensive scholarly analysis of GVC (Timmer et al., 2015, Timmer et al., 2016, Baldwin and Lopez-Gonzalez, 2015; Constantinescu et al., 2017). Many studies related participation in supply chains to productivity and observed a positive relationship between the two. Baldwin and Yan (2014) found that around 28% of the Canadian manufacturing firms that were exposed to GVCs tended to be more productive and larger in size and paid higher wages. Similarly, Constantinescu et al. (2017) suggest that participation in GVCs is a significant driver of labor productivity. In their study on Central and Eastern European countries (CEECs), Damijan et al. (2013) account for the importance of the 'global supply chains" concept for export restructuring and productivity and observes that FDI has significantly contributed to export restructuring in the CEECs, whereby the effects are shown to be heterogeneous across countries. Formai and

---

[2] See, for instance, Kowalski et al. (2015) which discusses the benefits from GVC participation for developing economies in Asia and Africa/Middle East, and identifies key trade and trade-related policies that would improve a country's ability to integrate into global value chains.

[3] See www.wiod.org.

[4] See http://www.oecd.org/sti/ind/measuring-trade-in-value-added.htm.

Caffarelli (2015) support the widespread perception that importing intermediate goods through GVCs increases productivity in the importing countries. In a study across 20 industries in a panel of 40 countries, Kordalska et al. (2016) observe a positive link between the involvement of sectors in GVCs (measured as a share of foreign value-added in exports) and multifactor productivity growth, mainly in the manufacturing sectors. Kummritz (2016)'s findings also support the former link and show that industry- and country-level value added and labor productivity are systematically higher when participating in GVC.

Raising jobs as well as increasing productivity has also been an important reason for research on GVC participation.[5] OECD (2016) argued that a better understanding of the impact of GVCs on jobs and productivity can be generated by providing new evidence on employment embodied in value-added trade flows. They argue that the impact of GVCs on employment cannot be properly dealt with without taking into account productivity change. The literature, for instance, suggests that productivity gains often offset domestic job losses caused by offshoring. While the short-term impact of productivity growth on job creation can be detrimental, it can lead to creating more and better quality jobs in the long-term.

Several scholars have discussed the role of GVCs in enhancing industrial development in India (Srivastava and Sen, 2015; Athukorala, 2016; Veeramani and Dhir, 2017).[6] The Srivastava-Sen study confirms that at the product level the aircraft parts and automobile parts and components industry became an emerging area of production fragmentation in the trade of manufactured goods in India over the period 1994–2012. Unlike for East Asia, there is no direct empirical evidence to support that FDI has played such a role in such production fragmentation in India. The study also confirms that greater inflexibility in labor laws, better skill development, and the accumulation of human capital in the manufacturing sector need to be addressed. Athukorala (2016) has attributed the weak export growth in India's electronics and electrical goods sector to the country's failure in fitting into global production networks, which have been the prime drivers of export dynamism in China and other successful East Asian countries. Veeramani and Dhir (2017) argue that though India's integration with global production networks has increased over the years, the degree of integration remains significantly below that of other countries. Obviously, all these studies, while acknowledging the importance of participating in GVCs, also recognize India's weak presence in the global manufacturing value chain. Hence it is imperative to understand how the Indian manufacturing sector has benefitted from its limited participation in GVCs so far.

As mentioned earlier, another important channel for improving the productivity performance of the manufacturing sector is the use of high-quality capital assets, or the shift of the

---

[5] Timmer et al. (2016) uses the GVC approach which combines new insights in the international trade literature (trade in tasks) and labor economics to arrive at task approach to employment and earnings. Also refer Grossman and Rossi-Hansberg (2008).

[6] Some other studies that have dealt with the participation of Indian manufacturing industries in GVCs include Tewari et al. (2015), Goldar et al. (2017b), and Goldar et al. (2018).

capital mix to assets of high marginal productivity, such as machinery and equipment. The seminal study by De Long and Summers (1991), for instance, argues that a higher share of equipment in total capital stock has a positive influence on economic growth. More lately, Wilson (2007) and Caselli and Wilson (2004) have also studied the possible linkage between capital composition and productivity. Furthermore, India's industrial deregulations, especially with respect to capacity expansion of existing plants/firms, allow access and freedom to use high-quality capital equipment, including information and communication technology (ICT), in production, which is expected to accelerate productivity growth in India.

This chapter aims to document and explore these channels as determinants of manufacturing productivity performance in India. First, we attempt to examine how manufacturing productivity is impacted by participation in GVCs, measured by foreign value-added share in domestic production. Second, we look at changes in the asset composition of fixed capital stock in Indian manufacturing captured by intertemporal changes in the share of equipment in total fixed capital assets and by the ratio of investment in ICT assets to gross fixed capital formation (GFCF), or ICT intensity. For this research we use a panel data set comprising 13 industries[7] and 22 years beginning in the financial year, 1993/1994.

The determinants of TFP in Indian manufacturing have been analyzed by several authors in the past, and those studies have examined inter alia the roles of trade and industrial policy reforms, infrastructure and investment climate (particularly labor market rigidity), research and development (R&D) and technology purchase, export orientation, and foreign direct investment (see Goldar (2014) for a review of such studies). Our research makes a number of important contributions to existing literature on India's manufacturing productivity, and it deviates from the past studies in three ways. First, by using the India KLEMS data set on manufacturing industries, this study covers both the organized[8] (or formal) and unorganized (or informal) segments of manufacturing, thus complementing previous studies that are largely confined to formal manufacturing using the *Annual Survey of Industries* (ASI) database. Secondly, we use a KLEMS approach to measure gross output—based TFP which is obtained after accounting for contributions not only from factor inputs, labor, and capital but also from intermediate inputs, materials, services, and energy. Thirdly, and more importantly, we consider the role of two variables, which have been hardly considered in the context of India, despite their substantial importance in driving productivity. These are a measure of India's participation in the GVCs—a measure of Indian manufacturing's foreign sourcing of intermediate inputs—and the share of equipment capital in total capital stock—a measure of Indian manufacturing's domestic capacity building.

The rest of the chapter is structured as follows. Section 6.2 documents the trends in TFP growth. In Section 6.3, the determinants of TFP with focus on GVC participation and capital composition are examined. Conclusions are presented in Section 6.4.

---

[7] For actual implementation of the econometric models, data for 12 industries are used, as explained later.

[8] Organized segment of manufacturing covers those industrial units having 10 or more workers with power or 20 or more workers without using power.

6.2 Trends in total factor productivity growth in India

In this section, we document the trends in TFP growth in Indian manufacturing in the postreform period, more specifically from 1993/1994 to 2015/2016.[9] For ease of expression, throughout this chapter, we use the financial year 1993–1994 as 1993 (i.e., 1993/1994–2015/2016 will be expressed as 1993–2015). The 23-year period is divided into two subperiods, 1993–2002, and 2003–15. The year 2003 is taken as a cut-off because there was a substantial step-up in the per capita GDP growth of the Indian economy since 2003.[10] We further divide the post-2002 period into a pre- and a post-2008 period, i.e., 2003–07 and 2008–15. This split is motivated by the emergence of the global financial crisis in 2008.

All data used in this chapter are obtained from India KLEMS database, version 2017 (hereafter referred to as IKD-2017). We made some modifications to the estimates of employment in the post-2011 period, and the price deflators for services input. This data set provides data on gross output, gross value added (GVA), factor inputs—labor, capital, and intermediate inputs—(all at 2011–12 prices), and TFP since 1980, for 27 industries consistent with ISIC revision 3. Of these 27 industries, we focus on the 13 manufacturing industries.

6.2.1 Trends in TFP growth at the industry level

IKD-2017 provides two sets of estimates of TFP—one based on the value-added function and the other on gross output (GO) function. The estimates used here are the ones based on the GO framework where TFP growth is measured as a residual after accounting for the contributions of capital input, labor input, materials inputs, energy input, and services input to gross output growth for each individual industry. That is:

$$\Delta \ln A_{it} = \Delta \ln Y_{it} - \left[\bar{s}_{K,it} \Delta \ln K_{it} + \bar{s}_{L,it} \Delta \ln L_{it} \right.$$
$$\left. + \bar{s}_{E,it} \Delta \ln E_{it} + \bar{s}_{M,it} \Delta \ln M_{it} + \bar{s}_{S,it} \Delta \ln S_{it} \right]$$

$$(6.1)$$

where A is the total factor productivity, Y is the real gross value of output, K capital input (capital services, taking into account capital stock as well as assets composition), L is labor input (taking into account the number of persons employed and educational composition of workers), E is energy input, M is materials input, and S is services input. All variables are taken in natural logs so that the difference between time t and $t-1$ gives us growth rates, Δ is used to represent the change over the previous period. The subscript i is for industry and t is for time (year). The terms $\bar{s}_K, \bar{s}_L, \bar{s}_E, \bar{s}_M$, and $\bar{s}_S$, are, respectively, the income shares of capital, labor, energy, materials, and services inputs in total nominal value of output (the bar over in income shares denotes that average of current year t and previous year $t-1$

---

[9] As mentioned earlier, following a severe balance of payments crisis, major economic reforms were initiated in India in 1991, a year in which the Indian economy faced serious problems (balance of payment crisis; value of imports in US dollars falling by 19% in 1991–92 over previous year). The growth rate in real GDP fell from 5.5% in 1990–91 to only 1.1% in 1991–92. The process of economic liberalization continued with the undertaking of several industrial policy reforms in subsequent years. The period between 1991 and 1993 has been a period of turbulence and transition in the economy, and therefore, while analyzing the postreform performance of the economy, it is ideal to exclude these years. Therefore, throughout this chapter, we consider post-1993 period.

[10] Per capita income growth has accelerated from 4% p.a. during 1993–2002 to 6% p.a. in the post-2003 period.

TABLE 6.1 Growth rates in gross value added and total factor productivity (TFP), by Industry, 1993−2015, and subperiods.

KLEMS industry	Share in nominal manufacturing value added 1993 (%)	Growth rate in single deflated real value added (% p.a.)	TFP growth rate (gross output framework) (% p.a.)				
		1993−2015	1993−2015	1993−2002	2003−15	2003−07	2008−15
Food products, beverages and tobacco products	11.2	6.2	0.5	0.2	0.8	−0.8	1.8
Textiles, textile products, leather and footwear	19.2	6.9	0.8	0.0	1.4	0.5	2.0
Wood and products of wood	4.1	1.6	−2.3	−5.3	0.0	−1.0	0.6
Pulp, paper, paper products, printing and publishing	3.8	5.6	0.8	−0.2	1.5	2.5	0.8
Coke, refined petroleum products and nuclear fuel	4.9	8.5	−0.8	−3.3	1.1	4.5	−1.0
Chemicals and chemical products	10.8	8.2	0.7	−0.2	1.4	1.9	1.1
Rubber and plastic products	3.2	8.8	0.5	0.1	0.8	0.9	0.8
Other nonmetallic mineral products	5.7	7.2	−0.1	−0.3	0.0	−1.2	0.8
Basic metals and fabricated metal products	14.3	5.8	−0.1	1.3	−1.1	−2.5	−0.3
Machinery, nec.	8.2	6.8	0.4	−0.4	1.1	2.7	0.0
Electrical and optical equipment	5.0	8.9	1.2	1.3	1.1	2.2	0.5
Transport equipment	7.1	9.7	0.9	1.0	0.8	1.6	0.3
Manufacturing, nec.; recycling	2.7	8.2	0.6	0.1	1.0	−0.1	1.6
Aggregate manufacturing TFP growth, Domar weighted aggregation			0.6	0.0	1.1	1.5	0.8

Source: Authors' computations based on India KLEMS database, version 2017 (with some modifications to the estimates of employment in the post-2011 period, and the price deflators for services input).

is taken). The detailed methodology of measurement of output, inputs, and factor income shares is explained in India KLEMS data manual available at the website of the Reserve Bank of India (RBI).[11] The average annual growth rates in TFP based on gross output function framework in the 13 manufacturing industries are presented in Table 6.1. The table also provides each

---

[11] The manual for the India KLEMS database for 2017 is available at: https://rbidocs.rbi.org.in/rdocs/PublicationReport/Pdfs/KLEMS27032018E6B6C80028604EBCAFDA3A82ACDE9B10.PDF.

industry's share in nominal GVA in total manufacturing in 1993 and growth rates in single deflated GVA during 1993–2015.

Among the 13 manufacturing industries, the highest growth rate in TFP for the entire period was in the electrical and optical equipment industry which includes electronic items as well as computers, and communication equipment. The rapid changes in technology in ICT and electronic production seem to have helped the sector gain faster productivity growth. Other industries in which the growth rate in TFP has been relatively high include transport equipment; pulp, paper, printing and publishing; textiles, textile products, leather and leather products; and chemicals and chemical products. The impact of high productivity growth in textiles and chemicals on the aggregate manufacturing TFP has been relatively high, as these are large sectors constituting, respectively, 19 and 11% of total manufacturing value added in 1993. The share of electrical and optical equipment was just 5%, and that remained the same in 2015.[12]

Comparing the subperiods, we observe that of the 13 manufacturing industries, 10 had a higher TFP growth during 2003–15 compared to 1993–2002. The acceleration in the growth rate in TFP during this period was relatively strong in coke, refined petroleum products and nuclear fuel; wood and wood products; textiles, textile products, and leather and leather products; paper, paper products and printing and publishing; and manufacturing not elsewhere classified and recycling. Only in the basic metals and metal products and transport equipment sectors the growth rate in TFP came down during 2003–15, and the first even showed a TFP decline during the 2003–15 period.

Comparing the periods 2003–07 and 2008–15, pre- and postcrisis, we find that in some industries (coke, refined petroleum products and nuclear fuel; pulp, paper, paper products, printing and publishing; and machinery not elsewhere classified) there was a substantial decline in TFP growth rate in the latter period. Interestingly, this was countered by a significant hike in the TFP growth rate in some other industries (e.g., food products, beverages and tobacco products; textiles, textile products, leather and footwear; and other nonmetallic mineral products).

Perhaps, the productivity momentum in some industries has been hampered by the global financial crisis, while not all, and some industries may have gained from the stimulus package given by the Indian government in the aftermath of the global financial crisis. Delving into the details of this aspect is beyond the scope of this chapter. However, it is important to note that most industries that had a decline, including chemicals, basic metal and metal products, machinery, electrical and optical equipment, and transport equipment, are relatively more integrated to the GVC, with an above average foreign content in production, compared to other manufacturing sectors.

6.2.2 Trends in TFP growth at the aggregate level, Indian manufacturing

In Fig. 6.1, the trends in TFP growth (along with the 3-year moving average) in the aggregate manufacturing for the period 1993 to 2015 are depicted. These aggregate TFP growth rates have been obtained by using the Domar aggregation of gross output–based industry TFP

---

[12] The share of electrical and optical equipment in aggregate nominal GVA was 5% in 2015, same as in 1993. Share of textiles fell to 13% while the share of chemicals rose to 13% in 2015 from the levels prevailing in 1993.

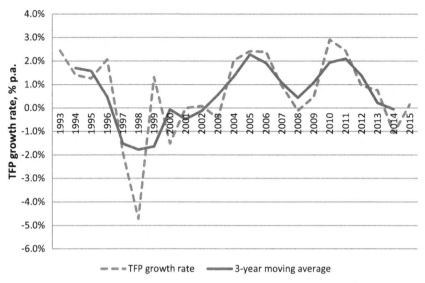

FIGURE 6.1 Total factor productivity (TFP) growth rate and 3-year moving average, Indian manufacturing, Domar aggregation. Note: Industry-level TFP growth rates based on gross output function framework have been aggregated by using Domar weights. *Source: Authors' computations based on India KLEMS database, version 2017 (with modifications as stated below Table 6.1), along with input–output tables and supply–use tables.*

growth measures. The Domar weights for individual industries have been computed with the help of input–output tables and supply–use tables (published by the Central Statistics Office, Government of India).[13] The advantage of using a Domar weighted aggregate of industry TFP is that it accounts for the productivity changes in industries that produce intermediate goods, whose outputs are also inputs for other industries.

The figure shows that there has been a continuously declining trend in TFP growth rate from 1993 until 1999, and it remained negative from 1997 until 2002. Since then TFP growth has been largely positive, barring the last 3 years of our study, when there was very little productivity growth. Productivity growth accelerated since 2003 and the upward trend continued until it dropped in 2007. In the subsequent years which correspond with the global financial crisis, the TFP growth declined, but it started picking up again since 2010. However, there has been a consistent decline in the TFP growth from 2011 until almost the last year in our study period.

In the last row of Table 6.1, we also provide the average TFP growth rates for the aggregate manufacturing for the subperiods combined. The TFP growth was about 0.04% during 1993–2002 which increased to 1.1% during 2003–15. This hike in TFP growth in manufacturing is arguably a lagged impact of

---

[13] For discussion on Domar aggregation, see Domar (1961), Hulten (1978), Gollop (1979), Jorgenson et al. (1987), and Jorgenson et al. (2005), among others. The Domar aggregation procedure has been applied to the Indian economy in Goldar et al. (2017a) and to Indian manufacturing industries in Das and Kalita (2011) and Krishna et al. (2018a). The methodology adopted here follows Krishna et al. (2018a) which contains an explanation of the methodology.

the economic reforms (Hashim et al., 2011). The argument here is that following the massive liberalization reforms in the early 1990s, it is likely that many industries undergo substantial structural change, including intensive creative destruction process coupled with diversion of human resources for learning new technology and markets, which would initially lower the productivity growth, but will see the gains coming in at a later stage. Looking further at the pre- and postglobal financial crisis periods, we see a marked decline of TFP growth rate from 1.5% during 2003−07 to 0.8% during 2008−15. It may be pointed out further that the TFP growth in the last 4 years of the 2008−15 period (i.e., 2012−15) has been rather low at only 0.2% per annum. Thus, the growth rate in TFP at the aggregate level came down in the postcrisis period (but, in some industries, it improved, as noted above), and in the last 4 years of the 2008−15 period under study, that is, 2012−15, the average growth rate in TFP has been as low as 0.2% per annum on average and has dropped back to growth rates about the same as around the turn of the century.

6.3 Determinants of TFP: the role of GVC participation and equipment capital use

To understand how TFP is impacted by India's participation in GVCs and changes in the composition of fixed capital stock, we perform a regression analysis using panel data on manufacturing industries.

Globally, the manufacturing sector has witnessed a substantial production fragmentation since the 2000s, supported by rapid declines in the cost of communication and coordination facilitated by ICT, and the opening up of several emerging markets including India into the global market (Baldwin, 2016). This has increased the use of foreign inputs in domestic production in many developed and developing countries

which is argued to have sorted a productivity-enhancing effect. It is important therefore to undertake an analysis of the effect of GVC participation on TFP in Indian manufacturing.

There are somewhat similar considerations for investigating the role of investment in equipment in raising TFP. A higher share of equipment in total capital stock is argued to be a prominent source of economic growth (De Long and Summers, 1991). Equipment capital, such as machinery and transport equipment, depreciates relatively faster than structures and is characterized by relatively higher levels of marginal productivity. Indeed India's high growth rates in the 1980s and 1990s is argued to be partly due to relatively larger growth-enhancing effect of private equipment investment compared to public equipment investment and nonequipment investment (Sen, 2009). More recently the increased role of ICT equipment has been identified as an especially important driver of productivity growth (see Jorgenson et al., 2005, among others).

Following the extensive liberalization of the Indian economy since the early 1990s, the access of Indian firms to imported high-quality capital equipment, including ICT, has increased. This provides justification for including the share of equipment in capital stock as an explanatory variable in our analysis. In this section, we document the quantitative impacts of foreign input use and equipment investment on TFP in Indian manufacturing, along with some other control variables, identified by the previous literature.

6.3.1 Model specification

The econometric model used for the analysis of determinants of TFP involves regressing a TFP index on a set of explanatory variables that are expected to have an impact on TFP. A particular focus is on the productivity impacts of India's participation in GVCs and changes in the asset composition of fixed capital stock in

Indian manufacturing—intertemporal changes in the share of equipment in total fixed capital assets and in the ratio of investment in ICT assets to GFCF in manufacturing, representing ICT intensity.

In the previous section, we have explained the estimation of annual TFP growth for individual industries using a gross output production function. In our regression specification, we use an index of TFP levels, which are obtained assuming a common TFP level in all industries at 100 in the first year, and then the index for subsequent years are derived as:[14]

$$A_{it} = A_{i,t-1}\exp\left\{\widehat{\Delta \ln A}_{it}\right\} \qquad (6.2)$$

After obtaining the TFP index for each of the manufacturing industries, the following model is specified for estimation from panel data on industries and time, where the dependent variable is the log of TFP index in industry i in year t (lnA_{it}):

$$lnA_{it} = \phi_i + \sum_j \gamma^j X_{it}^j + \xi_{it} \qquad (6.3)$$

In this equation, X is a set of independent variables that are expected to have an influence on TFP, ξ is the random error term and ϕ_i allows

for industry fixed effects.[15] For the actual empirical application, a dynamic version of this model has been estimated by introducing the one-period lagged TFP index as an explanatory variable. Estimation of the model has been done by applying the GMM (generalized method of moments) estimator.

In the econometric model used by Constantinescu et al. (2017) for analyzing the effect of GVCs on productivity using a cross-country panel data set covering 13 sectors in 40 countries over 15 years, the explanatory variables were all trade-related (except fixed effects, country-industry, country-year, and industry-year) and these were taken with 1 year lag. In the analysis presented here also the trade-related explanatory variables have been taken with 1 year lag (to take care of possible endogeneity issues), but for other explanatory variables, the current year values have been used.[16]

6.3.2 Data, variables, and expected relationship with TFP

The econometric model described above has been estimated using panel data on manufacturing industries for the period 1995 to

---

[14] Instead of taking the base year TFP for each industry as 100, one may allow TFP levels to differ across industries based on some measurement of initial relative TFP level and then apply the TFP growth rates to generate a time series. Such an approach is adopted in cross-country assessment of TFP levels in Dabla-Norris et al. (2015), where the initial TFP levels for each industry is taken from Groningen Growth and Development Centre's productivity level database, which provides TFP level for individual industries in each country relative to the United States, in 1997 benchmark PPP. This is not necessary for the analysis presented here because in the econometric model employed (Eq. 6.3), there is a fixed effects term which takes care of the initial period differences in the level of TFP.

[15] Since lnA_{it} in Eq. (6.3) is obtained by assuming the initial TFP level as 100 in each industry and applying the measured TFP growth rates for subsequent years, it does not account for sectoral heterogeneity in productivity levels. Nevertheless, γ^j may rightly be interpreted as the impact of variable X_{it}^j on the level of TFP, and not on the growth rate of TFP. A_{it} for any given year t after the initial year measures the ratio of the level of TFP in industry i in year t to the initial level which is fixed. Therefore, the partial derivative of A_{it} with respect of X_{it}^j shows the impact of the explanatory variable on the current level of TFP.

[16] The issue of endogeneity is probably more serious in the case of trade variables than for other explanatory variables such as ICT intensity. Moreover, since the GMM estimator is used in the present study, it takes care of the issue of endogeneity so that the use of current year values of some of the explanatory variables is not problematic.

2015. In the IKD-2017, data on output, inputs, and TFP are provided for 13 manufacturing industries, of which we use only 12 in our regression analysis. We exclude the coke and petroleum products industry because it has both relatively high imports (crude oil imports) and exports and is in certain ways different in nature than other manufacturing industries. Some studies on India's manufactured exports in the past have also excluded this sector from their analysis (see, e.g., Francis, 2015 and Veeramani et al., 2017).

The key explanatory variables considered in the model are (1) the foreign value-added (FVA) share in domestic production, (2) export intensity, (3) the share of equipment in total fixed capital stock, (4) ICT intensity, and (5) the share of the organized segment of the industry in employment.

The **foreign value-added share** (FVA) serves as an indicator of the extent of participation in GVCs. Access to imported intermediate inputs is argued to have positive effects on output and productivity. This relationship has been established both theoretically and empirically. For instance, the endogenous growth models of Romer (1987, 1990) suggests that the import of new varieties of inputs helps improve productivity and also strengthen the domestic capacity to create a better variety of products. Amiti and Konings (2007), Goldberg et al. (2010), among others, provide empirical support to this argument, respectively, in Indonesia and India. Gopinath and Neiman (2014) emphasize the role of imported inputs in driving fluctuations in aggregate productivity in Argentina. We extend this research by considering the use of foreign-produced value added in the production of domestic manufacturing output. As the participation in GVCs facilitates access to cheaper, wider variety, and high-quality foreign inputs,

it is expected to help improve productivity and reduce costs of production. So, we expect a positive relationship between the FVA variable (hereafter called alternatively as the GVC variable) and TFP.

The FVA has been computed from WIOD (world input—output database) 2016 version, which provides input—output data for 43 countries including India and a rest of the world category, for 56 sectors classified according to the ISIC revision 4, for the period 2000—14. An earlier version of the WIOD provides data for 40 countries and 35 sectors (according to ISIC revision 3) for 1995—2011. There are comparability issues between the two versions, as the 2016 version adheres to SNA-2008 and the old 2012 version is consistent with SNA-1993. However, with our level of aggregation of sectors to India KLEMS sectors, we could avoid several of those inconsistencies of sectoral comparability, yet not the issue of country coverage. In spite of this deficiency, we have extended our measure of FVA to earlier years, so that we have a series running from 1995 until 2014.

To measure the foreign content in domestic production, we apply a decomposition method based on Leontief (1936)'s input—output framework, following Timmer et al. (2014) and Timmer et al. (2015).

$$V = v.(I - B)^{-1}C \qquad (6.4)$$

where V is a vector of value added created in each sector s (s = 1, ..., S) in each country n (n = 1,..., N), involved in the value chain. C is the final output vector, delivered to consumers or investors (i.e., the final demand, absorbed as consumption or investment); v is a diagonal matrix of value added/output ratio and $(I-B)^{-1}$ is the Leontief inverse, with B being the matrix of technology coefficients (the ratio of intermediate input to output, describing how much intermediates are needed to produce a unit of output in a given industry) and I being the identity matrix. The final output vector, C is taken as a diagonal matrix, so that only the consumption of S×N combination of the country-industry is taken on the diagonal. This helps us to decompose the GVC of a final good as a set of all value-adding activities needed in its production. Such a decomposition will provide us the value added from any given country-industry (participating in the value chain), delivered as the final product in the GVC by a given country-industry where the final stage of production took place. The sum across the country-industry (where the products are identified as final product) will be the value added of a given country-industry. Finally, the sum across value added from country-industry participating in the GVC will be the total final output value. This way, we can identify how much of the output in any given industry finalized in a country consists of value added from industries from various countries, including the country where the final output is being produced. Excluding the own country value-added content, we get the foreign content in production. Annexure-I presents period averages of this variable for different industries in India.

In some specifications of the model, the FVA variable has been divided into two parts: FVA content from advanced countries and FVA content from other countries.[17] The productivity-enhancing effect of FVA content from advanced countries is expected to be greater than that from other (relatively less advanced) countries because of the technological advantage the former group of countries enjoys. The imported inputs from technologically advanced economies are expected to be of relatively high quality. The purpose of splitting the GVC variable into two parts in some specifications of the model is to ascertain if this hypothesis is empirically supported by the data on Indian manufacturing.

Export intensity has been widely proved to have a positive relationship on TFP growth through learning by exporting.[18] The variable is computed as total exports (export of intermediate + export of final goods and services) by industries divided by total industry output. The source of data for computation of export intensity is the same as that for GVC participation, i.e., the WIOD database.

The industry-wise time series data on GVC participation and export intensity are obtained for the years 1995–2014. Since these two trade-related variables enter the models with a 1-year lag, the model estimation has been done effectively with data for the period 1995–2015.

The **equipment share in total capital stock** has been computed for each industry using detailed data on asset-wise investment and capital stock. Capital stock for three different asset types—machinery, transport, equipment and construction—are computed using the standard perpetual inventory method, and equipment

---

[17] Advanced economies correspond to the top 10 countries in terms of labor productivity levels and global innovation index scores. These are United States, Switzerland, Sweden, Netherlands, United Kingdom, Germany, Finland, Denmark, France, and Belgium. In order to prepare this list, labor productivity levels are obtained from the Conference Board Total Economy Database (adjusted version), November 2018, and innovation scores are obtained from the Global Innovation Index. In addition to the 10 countries listed above, Japan and Korea have been included. From the total FVA content in domestic production, the FVA content from advanced countries is subtracted to derive the FVA content from other countries.

[18] Econometric evidence in favor of the learning-by-exporting hypothesis in the context of Indian manufacturing has been found by Ranjan and Raychaudhuri (2011). But, several other studies, e.g., Haidar (2012), did not find supportive evidence to this hypothesis. See Goldar et al. (2018), among others, for a review of studies related to this issue.

investment is defined as the sum of the first two.[19]

ICT intensity has been widely researched as a critical variable driving productivity growth. The significant declines in ICT prices over the past decades, owing to the rapid technological change in the ICT producing sector, has helped firms substitute other forms of capital by ICT (see Jorgenson, 2001). The resulting increase in ICT investment helps firms reduce the cost of communication and coordination substantially and to increase their efficiency and productivity by facilitating better organization of production (Erumban and Das, 2016). In addition to better labor productivity growth, emanating from faster ICT capital deepening, the use of ICT generates spillover effect on improving TFP growth. This spillover effect includes network externalities, organizational changes, and lower transaction costs (van Ark et al., 2011). A positive relationship is thus expected between ICT intensity, and TFP. Such a relationship has been found in a number of earlier studies, including studies undertaken for Indian manufacturing (see, for example, Joseph and Abraham, 2007; Kite, 2012, 2013; Sharma and Singh, 2012; and Mitra et al., 2016).

The ICT intensity variable has been computed as the ratio of ICT investment to GFCF (annual ICT investment divided by annual GFCF). This has been computed for each of the 12 manufacturing industries using primarily ASI data (see Krishna et al., 2018b). Industry-wise period averages of ICT intensities are shown in Annexure-I. As this ratio could be computed only for the organized manufacturing sector, this variable should be treated only as a crude measure when applied to the aggregate industry data (organized and unorganized segments combined). Also, estimates are only made for the years 1993–2013, as the required data were not readily available for 2014 and 2015. Hence for these years we assume the intensity levels of 2013. In the literature, ICT investment is mostly considered as the sum of hardware, software, and communication investments. However, the ASI data consist of computing equipment including software only, which means that we may underestimate the ICT intensity in Indian manufacturing. The measure nonetheless is expected to provide us insight on the relative importance of ICT equipment in enhancing productivity across industries and over time.

The formal share in manufacturing, which is measured as the employment share of the organized segment of any given industry in the total employment, has been widely asserted as positively impacting on productivity. The level of TFP in the organized segment of Indian manufacturing is observed to be significantly higher than that in the unorganized segment (see Krishna et al., 2018a), and therefore as the size structure of an industry changes toward the organized segment, the level of TFP should rise. This assertion finds empirical support in a study by Goldar and Kumari (2018) using state-level panel data for 1993–2012. They observe a positive relationship between changes in the value-added share of the organized manufacturing sector and TFP growth. Earlier studies also observe that the presence of the informal sector often pulls down aggregate productivity and growth (Khaturia et al., 2013; De Vries et al., 2012), and that formalization of industries helps them move up in modernity and technology ladders by increased access to capital and technology (Moreno-Monroy et al., 2014) and strengthen productivity performance.

Evidently, a positive relationship is expected between the level of TFP in an industry and the

---

[19] For more details of the method of construction of capital stock for the India KLEMS data series, see the India KLEMS data manual (mentioned earlier in Section 2 of the chapter) available at the RBI website (also see Das et al., 2016). Industry-wise period averages of equipment share in total capital stock are shown in Annexure-I.

TABLE 6.2   Determinants of total factor productivity (TFP), Indian manufacturing, regression results.

Dependent variable: ln(TFP)		Period: 1995–2015		
Explanatory variable	Regression-A1	Regression-A2	Regression-A3	Regression-A4
Lagged ln(TFP)	0.783 (25.58)***	0.783 (24.59)***	0.918 (50.83)***	0.914 (50.34)***
FVA content in production (lagged)	0.075 (1.56)		0.098 (2.02)**	
FVA content from advanced countries (lagged)		0.211 (1.39)		0.293 (2.10)**
FVA content from other countries (lagged)		0.058 (1.12)		0.074 (1.45)
Export intensity (lagged)	−0.038 (−0.87)	−0.044 (−1.00)	−0.0003 (−0.01)	−0.007 (−0.16)
Equipment share in capital stock (in logarithms)	0.039 (1.80)*	0.043 (1.96)*	0.023 (1.70)*	0.020 (1.48)
ICT intensity (in logarithms)	0.005 (0.69)	0.005 (0.69)	0.011 (1.88)*	0.009 (1.46)
Organized sector share in employment	0.075 (1.64)*	0.088 (1.85)*	0.026 (0.78)	0.030 (0.90)
Constant	1.044	1.037	0.426	0.420
Estimation method	Difference GMM	Difference GMM	System GMM	System GMM
Wald Chi-square (Prob.)	802.2 (0.000)	802.8 (0.000)	4781.8 (0.000)	4817.4 (0.000)
No. of observations	228	228	240	240
No. of instruments	229	229	249	249
AR(1)	0.008	0.007	0.009	0.009
AR(2)	0.072	0.061	0.082	0.064
Sargan test, Chi-square (Prob.)	235.0 (0.26)	234.0 (0.26)	253.7 (0.29)	253.3 (0.28)

Note: t-values in parentheses; ***$P < .01$, **$P < .05$, *$P < .1$. *FVA*, Foreign value added; *ICT*, Intensity, Investment in ICT assets divided by gross fixed capital formation. FVA variables and export intensity variable are lagged by 1 year.
Source: Authors' computations.

share of the organized sector employment in the industry. The data on this explanatory variable are obtained from Krishna et al. (2018a) for different years until 2011, and are extended to 2012 to 2015 using a similar methodology.

6.3.3 Regression results

The regression results obtained by estimating a dynamic version of Eq. (6.3) are presented in Table 6.2. Four regression equations have been estimated, two using the difference GMM estimator (Regressions A1 and A2) and another two using the system GMM estimator Regressions A3 and A4). In each pair, the first regression contains the FVA variable without splitting, and the second contains the FVA split into FVA content from advanced countries and that from other countries.

The FVA content (GVC) variable has positive and statistically significant coefficients in models A3 and A4. [20] In A3, where the foreign content in

[20] It is logical to take the alternative hypothesis in the test of statistical significance to be right-sided, and then the coefficient of FVA content in regression A1 and the coefficient of FVA content from advanced countries in regression A2 are statistically significant. The same applies to the coefficients of equipment share in regressions A1 and A2.

production is taken as a single indicator, the GVC participation does make a significant positive effect on TFP. As the foreign content in domestic production goes up for an industry, the TFP levels in the industry increases. The relationship remains positive even when we split the foreign content to advanced and other economies (A4), with a stronger and significant coefficient for advanced economies foreign content, compared to other economies. Our results clearly indicate that the participation in GVCs helps manufacturing industries attain higher productivity levels.[21]

The share of equipment in capital stock has positive coefficients consistently and is statistically significant for all regressions, except in model A4.[22] These results indicate that an increase in the share of equipment in capital stock helps improve TFP, by increasing the quality of capital assets used in production.

The regression results are indicative of a positive effect of organized employment share on TFP, since the coefficient is consistently positive and is statistically significant in two regressions (A3 and A4). It may be inferred that formalization of the manufacturing sector is productivity enhancing. At the same time, it needs to be acknowledged that the results are weak overall.

Of the other explanatory variables, only the lagged TFP is statistically significant, which as expected has a positive sign. ICT intensity has positive coefficient but is not always significant. In model A3, the coefficient for ICT intensity variable is positive and statistically significant at 10% level. This indicates the presence of spillover effects of ICT use on productivity. However, the

relationship is weak. It may be noted that a recent study on ICT and economic growth in India observed the lack of effective use of ICT investment in the manufacturing sector, whereas the ICT contribution to growth in the overall economy is much higher (Erumban and Das, 2016).

The coefficient of export intensity is found to be small and negative, and statistically insignificant in all cases. It seems reasonable to say that the empirical evidence obtained in this study does not point to any strong productivity-enhancing effects of increases in export intensity. This goes against the learning-by-exporting hypothesis. However, since several past studies also did not find empirical support of this hypothesis in Indian manufacturing, the results obtained in this study are not out of sync with the existing literature on productivity—exports nexus.

6.3.4 Robustness checks

To check the robustness of the findings from the regression results reported in Table 6.2, two econometric exercises have been carried out using the dynamic version of the model. In the first exercise, a time trend variable has been introduced in the model, aiming to find out if the regression results change qualitatively when a trend variable is included. Also, both one-period and two-period lagged values of the dependent variable are included in the model as an explanatory variable.

In the second exercise, the estimation is confined only to the organized manufacturing sector, meaning that the model is estimated

---

[21] We also tried the regressions A1 and A2 with current year export intensity. The results are consistent with what is reported in the table and are slightly stronger. The coefficient of the FVA content is found to be statistically significant (even with the two-tailed test), and the same holds true for the coefficient of the FVA content from advanced countries. However, these results are not reported, rather we opt to rely on the lagged results, to evade any potential endogeneity problems.

[22] Taking the alternative hypothesis in the test to be right-sided, the coefficient of equipment share in regression A4 is statistically significant.

TABLE 6.3   Determinants of total factor productivity (TFP), Indian Manufacturing, Additional Regression Results.

Dependent variable: ln(TFP)	Period: 1995–2015 (for organized sector: 1995–2014)			
	Total manufacturing (organized plus unorganized)		Organized manufacturing	
Explanatory variable	Regression-R1	Regression-R2	Regression-R3	Regression-R4
Lagged ln(TFP)	0.977 (20.56)***	0.962 (20.32)***	0.829 (11.53)***	0.821 (11.31)***
2-year lagged ln(TFP)	−0.064 (−1.28)	−0.049 (−0.98)	0.067 (1.01)	0.069 (1.04)
FVA content in production (lagged)	0.063 (0.96)		0.009 (0.13)	
FVA content from advanced countries (lagged)		0.411 (2.73)***		0.230 (1.85)*
FVA content from other countries (lagge		−0.068 (−0.82)		−0.077 (−0.87)
Export intensity (lagged)	−0.009 (−0.19)	−0.020 (−0.44)	0.027 (0.68)	0.021 (0.56)
Equipment share in capital stock (in logarithms)	0.025 (1.74)*	0.020 (1.42)	0.227 (3.63)***	0.219 (4.11)***
ICT intensity (in logarithms)	0.011 (1.85)*	0.009 (1.51)	0.011 (2.31)**	0.010 (2.21)**
Organized sector share in employment	0.017 (0.49)	0.018 (0.52)		
Time trend	0.0006 (0.96)	0.0017 (2.30)**	0.0003 (0.85)	0.0011 (1.51)
Constant	−0.690	−2.963	0.011	−1.459
Estimation method	System GMM	System GMM	System GMM	System GMM
No. of observations:	240	240	228	228
Wald Chi-square (Prob.)	4498.8 (0.000)	4583.9 (0.000)	1531.2 (0.000)	4863.3 (0.000)
No. of instruments	249	249	236	236
AR(1)	0.013	0.012	0.006	0.006
AR(2)	0.106	0.060	0.010	0.079
Sargan test, Chi-square and Prob.	235.4 (0.57)	232.9 (0.60)	245.8 (0.20)	244.6 (0.46)

Note: t-values in parentheses; ***$P < .01$, **$P < .05$, *$P < .1$. Robust standard errors for the estimates for organized manufacturing. *FVA*, Foreign value added; *ICT intensity*, Investment in ICT assets divided by gross fixed capital formation. FVA variables and export intensity variable is lagged by 1 year.
Source: Authors' computations.

with the TFP index for organized manufacturing sector being the dependent variable.[23] As noted earlier, the ICT variable has been constructed for the organized sector manufacturing industries, and therefore, confining the regression only to the organized sector is worth exploring. Moreover, it may be argued that the issue of participation in GVCs and its impact

[23] In this case, the variable on employment share of the organized sector is dropped, as inclusion of this explanatory variable does not seem right.

on productivity is more pertinent for the organized (or formal) sector than for the unorganized or informal sector. This, however, may not necessarily always hold true, as many small- and medium-scale firms also participate in GVC.

The TFP levels in organized manufacturing industries are constructed using Eq. (6.2), with data obtained from Krishna et al. (2018a). Since Krishna et al. (2018a) provide data only until 2011-12, these have been extended using estimates from Goldar (2017) which are for 2-digit industries of National Industrial Classification. It has been necessary for this purpose to map the 2-digit level industries into the KLEMS 13 industry classification and take weighted average of industry-level TFP growth rates where required.

The results of the two exercises described above are reported in Table 6.3. Model estimation has been done by the system GMM estimator. Regressions R1 and R2 are estimates for total manufacturing including a time trend, organized and unorganized segments combined, hence comparable with our original regressions in Table 6.2. The results are found to be mostly similar to those in Table 6.2. The coefficients of ICT intensity and equipment share in capital stock are positive on both regressions and statistically significant in one of them. The coefficient of the FVA content from advanced countries is found to be significant at 1% level, and the magnitude of the coefficient is greater than the coefficient of the FVA content from other countries. By contrast, the coefficient of the FVA content from other countries is negative but statistically insignificant. Thus, the key findings emerging from Table 6.2 remains by and large intact even if a time trend variable is introduced in the equation.

The regression results obtained for organized manufacturing are also by and large supportive of the findings obtained from the regression results presented above (see Models R3 and R4). The coefficient of the FVA content from advanced countries is positive and statistically

significant, and by contrast, the coefficient of the FVA content from other countries is negative and statistically insignificant. The coefficients of equipment share variable and ICT intensity variable are positive and statistically significant.

To summarize, our regression analysis brings out three important insights. The first is that participation in GVCs helps manufacturing industries to improve their productivity performance. Secondly, backward linkages in GVCs with advanced economies have a greater impact on productivity, than with other economies. And thirdly, a shift toward more equipment investment and increases in ICT intensity improve manufacturing productivity.

6.4 Summary and conclusion

The objective of this chapter has been to estimate the impact of India's participation in GVCs, the share of equipment capital in total capital stock, and ICT intensity on TFP in the manufacturing industries in India in the postreform period, 1993–94 (1993) to 2015–16 (2015). The databases used for this purpose are the India KLEMS data set, 2017 version (IKD-2017) with some modifications and World Input-Output Database (WIOD), 2012 and 2016 versions, supplemented by the other relevant data sets. The gross output framework of measuring TFP has been adopted to reveal trends in TFP over the period, 1993–2015 and subperiods.

A panel data model of TFP index as a function of a measure of participation in GVCs, share of equipment in total capital, and ICT intensity as key determinants, together with a few control variables, has been estimated using GMM for 12 manufacturing industries for the years 1993–2015. These 12 manufacturing industries accounted for more than 95% of the total GVA in the manufacturing sector in 1993.

The Domar weighted TFP growth in the manufacturing sector was 0.6% per year, for the entire period, 1993–2015. It was as low as

0.04% per year in 1993–2002, but improved considerably to 1.5% in 2003–07, before decelerating to 0.8% in the postglobal financial crisis period 2008-15.

TFP growth during 1993–2015 at the individual industry level ranged widely between −2.3% in Wood and products of wood and 1.2% in Electrical and optical equipment; the latter industry has a low value added share of only 5%. Several other industries with higher value-added shares achieved TFP growth above the average of 0.6% for the manufacturing sector.

The GMM regression estimates show that the participation in GVCs helped manufacturing industries in India to achieve higher productivity levels. The coefficient of FVA (foreign value added) content in production is significantly positive. When the FVA content is split into value added from advanced countries and value added from other countries in the regression, the former component has a much larger coefficient. The equipment share in capital has a positive and statistically significant coefficient, but the impact of ICT intensity on TFP is rather low and insignificant.

Some robustness checks have confirmed the major findings noted above. Overall, the regression results bring out two important insights. The first is that participation in GVCs helps industries improve their productivity performance. Furthermore, backward linkages in GVCs with advanced economies have a larger impact compared to linkages with other economies. The second insight is that higher equipment shares in total capital stock help in enhancing productivity.

In concluding, there is little doubt that the major economic reforms undertaken in India since 1991 had a positive impact on productivity performance in the manufacturing sector. However, the growth and productivity performance has remained less strong than what was looked-for due to a number of constraints that the sector has faced. These include infrastructural bottlenecks, disadvantages arising from policy constraints and institutional factors such as difficulties in land acquisition, labor market rigidities, high unit labor cost, and lack of competitive advantage compared to the peers such as China. The "Make-in-India" initiative announced in 2014 is intended to boost the manufacturing sector by promoting exports, encouraging FDI, improving productivity, and lowering barriers to doing business. In this context, Veeramani and Dhir (2017) identify two groups of industries that have the potential for export growth and employment generation. The first group consists of traditional unskilled labor-intensive products such as textiles, clothes, footwear, and toys. The second group consists of products where the manufacturing process is internationally fragmented and mainly controlled by multinational enterprises (MNEs) with their global production networks.

Our analysis reveals that the average growth in TFP attained by labor-intensive industries such as food products, beverages and tobacco products, and textiles and leather products over the entire period of analysis has been less impressive than other industries. However, in the more recent period 2008–15, there has been a considerable improvement in TFP in these industries. This may suggest that the traditional labor-intensive industries do hold a good potential in India. Giving a significant push to such industries with the intent of exploring a sizable part of the enhanced production would be advantageous. Regarding the second group of industries, namely the network industries, our findings support the recommendations of Veeramani and Dhir (2017). Rapid development of industries actively participating in GVC is likely to boost manufacturing sector growth and increase India's manufactured exports. In the backdrop of the findings by Veeramani and Dhir (2017) and other similar studies, the results of this chapter have important implications for policies toward the manufacturing sector in India, as more active participation in GVCs by India may have considerable potential for achieving higher growth in employment and productivity.

Abbreviations

ASI Annual Survey of Industries
FDI Foreign direct investment
FVA Foreign value added
GDP Gross domestic product

IKD India KLEMS database
ISIC International Standard Industrial Classification of All Economic Activities
KLEMS Capital-Labor-Energy-Material-Services
MNE Multinational enterprises
OECD Organization for Economic Co-operation and

Industry	FVA content in domestic production (%)			Equipment share in total capital stock (%)			ICT investment divided by gross fixed capital formation (%)		
	1995 −2002	2003 −07	2008 −15	1993 −2002	2003 −07	2008 −15	1993 −2002	2003 −07	2008 −13
Food products, beverages and tobacco products	8.7	9.0	8.9	23.3	23.9	29.6	1.9	1.1	1.0
Textiles, textile products, leather and footwear	10.2	14.5	14.0	43.6	38.7	35.9	2.1	1.2	1.2
Wood and products of wood	8.7	10.1	8.9	14.1	11.8	13.5	3.0	2.1	1.3
Pulp, paper, paper products, printing and publishing	18.0	21.1	21.7	14.7	22.9	30.0	2.9	3.2	1.7
Coke, refined petroleum products and nuclear fuel	35.6	43.4	61.3	81.5	87.5	88.0	0.5	1.1	1.1
Chemicals and chemical products	19.3	25.9	27.3	63.6	61.4	63.6	2.0	2.0	1.5
Rubber and plastic products	17.6	25.4	26.2	49.9	50.1	54.3	2.4	1.3	1.0
Other nonmetallic mineral products	16.2	18.5	24.2	49.7	36.6	46.9	1.0	1.0	0.7
Basic metals and fabricated metal products	19.6	30.8	37.5	61.4	59.7	66.1	1.1	0.9	0.9
Machinery, nec.	21.1	28.4	29.2	42.8	35.1	39.6	5.7	4.8	4.3
Electrical and optical equipment	18.9	31.2	31.2	52.3	48.6	48.6	4.2	4.2	4.5
Transport equipment	19.6	30.3	32.0	62.8	68.2	71.8	2.8	4.4	2.4
Manufacturing, nec; recycling	18.8	26.6	29.3	9.9	11.1	11.5	5.5	4.5	3.9

Source: Authors' computations.

GFCF Gross fixed capital formation
GMM Generalized method of moments
GO Gross output
GVA Gross value added
GVC Global value chain
ICT Information and communication technology

Development
R&D Research and development
RBI Reserve Bank of India
TFP Total factor productivity
WTO World Trade Organization

Annexure-I: summary Statistics for FVA (foreign value-added), equipment share, and ICT (information and communication technology) variables

Acknowledgments

The authors thank Bart van Ark for his comments and suggestions on the previous version of the chapter and Maajid Mehaboob Chakkarathodi and Prachi Madan for able research assistance. The chapter is an outcome of the research project, "Disaggregate Industry-Level Productivity Analysis for India: The KLEMS Approach," being undertaken at the Centre for Development Economics, Delhi School of Economics and supported by the Reserve Bank of India through a financial grant. The authors thank the Ministry of Statistics and Programme Implementation, Government of India, for advice on data issues. The usual disclaimers apply. Corresponding author: Deb Kusum Das, email:dkdas@ramjas.du.ac.in.

References

Amiti M, Konings J: Trade liberalization, intermediate inputs, and productivity: evidence from Indonesia, *The American Economic Review* 97(5):1611–1638, 2007.

Athukorala P-C: Global production sharing and export expansion: emerging opportunities and the Indian experience. In Veeramani C, Nagaraj R, editors: *International trade and industrial development in India: emerging patterns, trends and issues*, Orient Blackswan, 2016, Hyderabad, pp 17–44.

Baldwin R: *The great convergence: information technology and the new globalization*, The Belknap Press of The Harvard University Press.

Baldwin JR, Lopez-Gonzalez J: Supply-chain trade: a portrait of global patterns and several testable hypotheses, *The World Economy* 38(11):1682–1721, 2015.

Baldwin JR, Yan B: *Global value chains and the productivity of Canadian manufacturing firms*, Statistics Canada.

Caselli F, Wilson DJ: Importing technology, *Journal of Monetary Economics* 51(1):1–32, 2004.

Constantinescu C, Mattoo A, Ruta M: *Does vertical specialization increase productivity?*, Policy research working paper, no. 7978, World Bank.

Dabla-Norris ME, Guo MS, Haksar MV, Kim M, Kochhar MK, Wiseman K, Zdzienicka A: *The new normal: a sector-level perspective on productivity trends in advanced economies*, International Monetary Fund.

Damijan JP, Kostevc Č, Rojec M: *Global supply chains at work in central and eastern European countries: impact of FDI on export restructuring and productivity growth*, 2013. VIVES discussion paper, no. 37.

Das DK: *Trade policy and manufacturing performance: exploring the level of trade openness in India's organized manufacturing in the period 1990–2010, study no. 41*, Development Research Group, Department Economic and Policy Research, Reserve Bank of India.

Das DK, Erumban AA, Aggarwal S, Sengupta S: Productivity growth in India under different policy regimes. In Jorgenson D, Timmer MP, Fukao K, editors: *The world economy: growth or stagnation?* Cambridge University Press, pp 234–280.

Das DK, Kalita G: Aggregate productivity growth in Indian manufacturing: an application of Domar aggregation, *Indian Economic Review* 46(2):275–302, 2011.

De Long BJ, Summers L: Equipment investment and economic growth, *Quarterly Journal of Economics* 106(2): 445–502, 1991.

De Vries GJ, Erumban AA, Timmer MP, Voskoboynikov I, Wu HX: Deconstructing the BRICs: structural transformation and aggregate productivity growth, *Journal of Comparative Economics* 40(2):211–227, 2012.

Domar ED: On the measurement of technological change, *Economic Journal* 71, 1961.

Erumban AA, Das DK: Information and communication technology and economic growth in India, *Telecommunications Policy* 40(5):412–431, 2016.

Formai S, Caffarelli FV: *Quantifying the productivity effects of global value chains no. 1564*, Faculty of Economics, University of Cambridge.

Francis S: *India's manufacturing sector export performance during 1999–2013: a focus on missing domestic inter-sectoral linkages*, working paper no. 182, New Delhi, 2015, Institute for Studies in Industrial Development.

Goldar B: Productivity in Indian manufacturing in the post-reform period: a review of studies. In Kathuria V, Raj SN, Sen K, editors: *Productivity in Indian manufacturing: measurement, methods and analysis*, New Delhi, 2014, Routledge, pp 75–105.

Goldar B: Growth, productivity and job creation in Indian manufacturing. In Kapila U, editor: *India's economy: pre-liberalization to GST, essays in honor of Raj Kapila*, New Delhi, 2017, Academic foundation, pp 619–652.

Goldar B, Banga R, Banga K: India's linkages into global value chains: the role of imported services. In Shah S, Bosworth B, Muralidharan K, editors: *India policy forum 2017–18*, New Delhi, 2018, Sage Publications, National Council of Applied Economic Research, pp 107–164.

Goldar B, Kumari A: Growth in output, employment and productivity in the manufacturing sector: a state-wise comparative study of post-liberalization India. In Mitra A, editor:

Economic growth in India and its many dimensions, Orient Blackswan, 2018, Hyderabad, pp 83−116.

Goldar B, Krishna KL, Aggarwal S, Das DK, Erumban AA, Das PC: Productivity growth in India since the 1980s: the KLEMS approach, *Indian Economic Review* 52(1−2): 37−71, 2017a.

Goldar B, Das DK, Sengupta S, Das PC: *Domestic value addition and foreign content: an analysis of India's exports from 1995 to 2011, working paper no. 332*, New Delhi, 2017b, Indian Council for Research on International Economic Relations.

Goldberg KP, Khandelwal AK, Pavcnik N, Topalova P: Imported intermediate inputs and domestic product growth: evidence from India, *Quarterly Journal of Economics* 125(4): 1727−1767, 2010.

Gollop FM: Accounting for intermediate input: the link between sectoral and aggregate measures of productivity growth. In Rees A, Kendrick J, editors: *The measurement and interpretation of productivity*, Washington DC, 1979, National Academy of Sciences.

Gopinath G, Neiman B: Trade adjustment and productivity in large crises, *The American Economic Review* 104(3): 793−831, 2014.

Grossman GM, Rossi-Hansberg E: Trading tasks: a simple theory of offshoring, *The American Economic Review* 98(5):1978−1997, 2008.

Haidar JI: Trade and productivity: self-selection or learning-by-exporting in India, *Economic Modelling* 29(5): 1766−1773, 2012.

Hulten CR: Growth accounting with intermediate inputs, *The Review of Economic Studies* 45:511−518, 1978.

Hashim DA, Kumar A, Virmani A: J-Curve hypothesis of productivity and output growth: a case study of Indian manufacturing in the post reforms period, *Indian Economic Review* 46(1):1−21, 2011.

Jorgenson DW, Gollop FM, Fraumeni BM: *Productivity and US economic growth*, Cambridge, 1987, Harvard University Press.

Jorgenson DW: Information technology and the US economy, *The American Economic Review* 91(1):1−32, 2001.

Jorgenson DW, Ho MS, Stiroh KJ: *Information technology and the American growth resurgence*, Cambridge, 2005, The MIT Press.

Joseph KJ, Abraham V: *Information technology and productivity: evidence from India's manufacturing sector*, Trivandrum, India, 2007, Centre for Development Studies. working paper no. 389.

Khaturia V, Rajesh Raj SN, Sen K: The effects of economic reforms on manufacturing dualism: evidence from India, *Journal of Comparative Economics* 41(4): 1240−1262, 2013.

Kite G: The impact of information technology outsourcing on productivity and output: new evidence from India, *International Conference on Applied Economics*, 2012: 239−248, 2012.

Kite G: The role of information technology outsourcing on output, productivity and technical efficiency: evidence from Indian firms, *Journal of European Economy* 12(3): 260−285, 2013.

Kordalska A, Wolszczak-Derlacz J, Parteka A: Global value chains and productivity gains: a cross-country analysis, *Collegium of Economic Analysis Annals* 41:11−28, 2016.

Kowalski P, Gonzalez JL, Ragoussis A, Ugarte C: *Participation of developing countries in global value chains: Implications for trade and trade-related policies. OECD Trade Policy Papers 179*, Paris, 2015, OECD, https://doi.org/10.1787/5js33lfw0xxn-en.

Krishna KL, Goldar B, Aggarwal S, Das DK, Erumban AA, Das PC: *Productivity growth and levels - a comparison of formal and informal manufacturing in India, working paper no. 291*, Centre for Development Economics, Delhi School of Economics.

Krishna KL, Erumban AA, Goldar B, Das DK, Aggarwal S, Das PC: *ICT investment and economic growth in India: an industry perspective*, Centre for Development Economics, Delhi School of Economics. working paper no. 284.

Kummritz V: *Do global value chains cause industrial development?*, Centre for Trade and Economic Integration. working paper no. 2016-01.

Leontief WW: Quantitative input-output relations in the economic system of the United States, *The Review of Economics and Statistics* 18(3):105−125, 1936.

Mitra A, Sharma C, Véganzonès-Varoudakis M: Infrastructure, ICT and firms' productivity and efficiency: an application to the Indian manufacturing. In Beule FD, Narayanan K, editors: *Globalization in Indian industries: productivity, exports and investment*, Singapore, 2016, Springer, pp 17−42.

Moreno-Monroy AI, Pieters J, Erumban AA: Formal sector subcontracting and informal sector employment in Indian manufacturing, *IZA Journal of Labor & Development* 3(1):22, 2014.

OECD: *Global value chains and trade in value-added: an initial assessment of the impact on jobs and productivity, OECD Trade Policy Papers 190*, OECD Publishing.

Ranjan P, Raychaudhuri J: Self-selection vs. learning: evidence from Indian exporting firms, *Indian Growth and Development Review* 4(1):22−37, 2011.

Romer PM: *Crazy explanations for the productivity slowdown* (vol. 2). National Bureau of Economic Research Macroeconomics Annual, pp 163−202.

Romer PM: Endogenous technological change, *Journal of Political Economy* 98(5.2):S71−S102, 1990.

Sen K: *Trade policy, inequality and performance in Indian manufacturing*, London, 2009, Routledge.

Sharma S, Singh N: *Information technology and productivity in Indian manufacturing*, India Policy Forum, pp 189–238.

Srivastava S, Sen R: Production fragmentation in trade of manufactured goods in India: prospects and challenges, *Asia-Pacific Development Journal* 22(1):33–66, 2015.

Tewari M, Veeramani C, Singh M: *The potential for involving India in regional production networks: analyzing vertically specialized trade patterns between India and ASEAN*, New Delhi, 2015, Indian Council for Research on International Economic Relations. working paper no. 292.

Timmer MP, Erumban AA, Los B, Stehrer R, Vries G: Slicing up global value chains, *The Journal of Economic Perspectives* 28(2):99–118, 2014.

Timmer MP, Erumban AA, Los B, Stehrer R, Vries G: An illustrated user guide to the world input–output database: the case of global automotive production, *Review of International Economics* 23(3):575–605, 2015.

Timmer MP, Los B, Stehrer R, Vries G: An anatomy of the global trade slowdown based on the WIOD 2016, *Release GCDC Research Memorandum* 162, 2016.

Veeramani C, Dhir G: Make what in India? In Dev M, editor: *India development report*, Oxford University Press.

Veeramani C, Lakshmi A, Gupta P: *Intensive and extensive margins of exports: what can India learn from China?*, Mumbai, 2017, Indira Gandhi Institute of Development Research. working paper no. WP-2017-002.

van Ark B, Gupta A, Erumban AA: Measuring the contribution of ICT to economic growth. In van Ark B, editor: *The linked world: how ICT transforming societies, cultures, and economies*, Madrid, 2011, Ariel and Fundación Telefónica.

Wilson DJ: *IT and beyond: the contribution of heterogeneous capital to productivity*, San Francisco, 2007, Federal Reserve Bank of. working paper no. 2004-13.

An international comparison on TFP changes in ICT industry among Japan, Korea, Taiwan, China, and the United States

Chi-Yuan Liang[1], Ruei-He Jheng[2]

[1]Research Center for Taiwan Economic Development, National Central University, Taoyuan County, Taiwan (R.O.C.); [2]The Third Research Division, Chung-Hua Institution for Economic Research, Taipei, Taiwan (R.O.C.)

7.1 Introduction

Information and communications technology (ICT) industries were at the core of transformation of economic systems with a country's rapid growth. The boom of ICT manufacture and the application of ICT products were in highly closed relation with living standard in a country. In addition, the drastic growth in the worldwide ICT market had permitted many countries to attain astounding success by proactive development of their ICT industry. De Prato et al. (2017) analyzed ICT sector within 41 geographical areas and pointed out that the economies percentage shares of ICT sector value added in the United

States, China, Japan, Taiwan, and Korea were 24.7 percent, 23.2 percent, 6.8 percent, 4.6 percent, and 4 percent, respectively. The above five countries were main players of ICT industry in the world. In addition, according to the database of World KLEMS, EU KLEMS, Asia KLEMS, China Industrial Productivity Database 3.0, JIP Database 2015, and DGBAS of Taiwan, the total output value of ICT[1] in China, the United States, Japan, Korea, and Taiwan were 896.7 billion and USD 490.5 billion, 467.5 billion, 321.4 billion, and 240.5 billion, respectively in 2010. China, Korea, and Taiwan registered a remarkable annual growth rate of 24.1 percent, 16.7 percent, and 13.1 percent, respectively, during 1981—2010 in

---

[1] We employ the data of Electrical & optical equipment industries as ICT in this paper.

ICT industry, while that of the United States and Japan were 7.5 percent and 6.1 percent per annum, respectively, in the same period.

China, Korea, and Taiwan seem to be catching up quickly with Japan and the United States in total output value. China even surpassed the United States as number one country in the world in ICT total output value by 2010. It was important to analyze the source of growth in ICT industry among the five countries aforementioned. As Krugman (1994) pointed out that an input-driven growth without total factor productivity (TFP) progress was not sustainable due to law of diminishing return. It is also worthy of studying that whether China, Korea, and Taiwan are catching up Japan and the United States in the TFP level. The current trade war started from March 2018 between the United States and China is not only disputed on commodity but also focused on technology (Liu and Woo, 2018; Lee, 2018). To measure the TFP gap in the ICT industry between China and the United States may shed some light on the technology issue.

The data of total output, inputs, and TFP of ICT industry in the United States, Japan, Korea, and China are available from World KLEMS, EU KLEMS, Asia KLEMS, China Industrial Productivity Database 3.0, and JIP Database 2015. However, the TFP data of Taiwan are unavailable.

And hence, the objective of this paper is: (1) to measure the TFP growth and analyze the sources of ICT growth in Taiwan during 1981—2010, (2) to compare the sources of growth and TFP growth of ICT industry among Japan, Korea, Taiwan, China, and the United States, and (3) to measure the "TFP gap" of ICT industry among the above five countries. The findings might be useful for policy reference and help to clarify the issue of whether the China Manufacturing 2025 posed threat to the United States or not under the trade war.

Following Gollop and Jorgenson (1980) and Jorgenson et al. (1986), the methodology and data compilation employed are basically the same as World KLEMS and Asia KLEMS.

Except introduction, this paper consists of the following sections: (2) Literature Review, (3) Methodology and Data Compilation, (4) Empirical Results, and (5) Conclusion and Suggestion.

7.2 Literature review

When the information age was initiated from the beginning of 1980s, there have been a lot of discussions in literatures on whether the ICT development is being paid off in productivity improvement (Heshmati and Yang, 2006). In addition, the drastic and large size of growth in the worldwide ICT market has permitted many countries to attain astounding success by proactive development of their ICT industry. The "East Asia Miracle" was a sign of success of the respective governments in Singapore, Taiwan, Korea, and Japan in pursuing the ICT-producing sector as a strategic industry while becoming large producers in the worldwide ICT industry (Hanna et al., 1996).

Fukao (2013) employed industry and micro-level data of Japan to examine the reason of Japan's productivity growth has been slow for such a long time and the TFP gap between United States and Japan. The results had showed that the United States experienced an acceleration of TFP growth in ICT-using sectors, but it appears that a similar ICT revolution did not occur in Japan simply because Japan has not accumulated sufficient ICT capital. Henze (2015) analyzed structural change and TFP in Germany's industries. The result shows that the highest TFP growth rates occurred in the electrical and optical equipment industry. The annual growth of TFP of electrical and optical equipment were 2.80 percent, 2.71 percent and 7.72 percent by subperiod 1980—89, 1990—99, and 2000—09, respectively, and the average was 4.3 percent during 1980—2009.

Besides, accumulation of ICT capital and intangible investment in Japan was very slow. Compared with large firms, which enjoyed acceleration in TFP growth, small- and medium-sized enterprises (SMEs) of Japan were left behind in ICT capital and intangible investment, and their productivity growth has been very low. It may imply that the investment and development of ICT would bring about positive effect for TFP growth. Fukao et al. (2011) identify the sources of economic growth based on a KLEMS model for Japan and Korea. They find out that the growth contribution of ICT assets and resource reallocation effects in the two economies. Both Japan and Korea enjoyed high TFP growth in ICT-producing sectors but suffered low TFP growth in ICT-using sectors, and the largest component in ICT investment is computing equipment.

Moreover, there were also a lot of studies for exploring the sources of the US acceleration and good performance of the US economy. Much of this research focuses on the role of ICT. For example, Jorgenson et al. (2006) had pointed out that the overall increase in the US "speed limit" for growth is because of ICT. Bosworth and Triplett (2006) and Corrado et al. (2006) found that non-ICT-producing sectors of the United States saw a sizeable acceleration in TFP within the 2000s, whereas TFP growth slowed in ICT-producing sectors in the 2000s (Acharya, 2016)

Cette et al. (2009) compared TFP in France, Japan, the United Kingdom, and the United States because the four countries have experi-

ICT. The result showed that ICT capital deepening accounts for a large share of the variations in performance. Khalili (2014) analyzed the contribution of ICT to TFP among Asia—Pacific and the European Union (EU) countries. The common point among all of the considered countries is that TFP growth of the countries has been sourced from increasing ICT contribution and the spillover effects of ICT through TFP growth; ICT has significant effects on TFP growth in Sweden, Australia, Denmark, and the EU group of countries.

To sum up, many studies discussed the TPF growth of ICT-using and ICT-producing and the effect of ICT deepening to economy growth for a country but rare to focus on analyzing the TPF change in ICT industry across main countries. In addition, ICT industry was important for Japan, Korea, Taiwan, and China and highly correlated with the United States. We would further discuss the TFP changes of ICT industry among above countries.

7.3 Methodology and data compilation

7.3.1 Methodology

Following the methodology of World KLEMS and Asia KLEMS, we measure sector-level productivity by using the translog production function:

$$
\begin{aligned}
\ln Q = {} & \alpha_0 + \alpha_T T + \alpha_K \ln K + \alpha_L \ln L + \alpha_E \ln E + \alpha_M \ln M \\
& + 1/2\beta_{KK}(\ln K)^2 + \beta_{KL} \ln K \cdot \ln L + \beta_{KE} \ln K \cdot \ln E + \beta_{KM} \ln K \cdot \ln M \\
& + \beta_{KT} \ln KT + 1/2\beta_{LL}(\ln L)^2 + \beta_{LE} \ln L \cdot \ln E + \beta_{KM} \ln K \cdot \ln M + \beta_{LT} \ln LT \qquad (7.1) \\
& + 1/2\beta_{EE}(\ln E)^2 + \beta_{EM} \ln E \cdot \ln M + \beta_{ET} \ln ET \\
& + 1/2\beta_{EE}(\ln M)^2 + \beta_{LT} \ln MT + 1/2\beta_{TT}T^2,
\end{aligned}
$$

enced contrasting advances in productivity, in particular as a result of unequal investment in

which is characterized by constant returns to scale (CRS) if, and only if, the parameters satisfy the condition of coefficient characteristics. In addition, for a well-behaved function, the production should be satisfied by the concavity constraint. That is, the Hessian's matrix is negative semidefinite.[2] Differentiating (Eq. 7.1 with respect to T, the rate of change in TFP can be shown as:

$$R_T = \alpha_T + \beta_{KT} \ln K + \beta_{LT} \ln L + \beta_{ET} \ln E$$
$$+ \beta_{MT} \ln M + \beta_{TT}T \qquad (7.2)$$

For the data at any two discrete points in time, say T and $T - 1$, the average rate of TFP change can be derived from growth accounting, i.e., the difference between successive logarithms of output less a weighted average of the differences between successive logarithms of capital, labor, energy and intermediate inputs with weights given based on average value shares:

assuming specific forms for the functions defining industry aggregate capital (K), labor (L), energy (E), and intermediate input (M). For example, the intermediate input aggregate can be expressed as a translog function of m individual intermediate inputs.

Considering the data at discrete points of time, the difference between successive logarithms of intermediate input is a weighted average of differences between successive logarithms of individual intermediate inputs, and the weights are given by average value shares:

$$\ln M(T) - \ln M(T - 1) = \sum_{i=1}^{m} \overline{S_{M_i}}[\ln M_i(T) - \ln M_i(T - 1)] \qquad (7.6)$$

where

$$\overline{R_T} = \ln Q(T) - \ln Q(T - 1) - \overline{s_K}[\ln K(T) - \ln K(T - 1)] - \overline{s_L}[\ln L(T) - \ln L(T - 1)] \\ - \overline{s_E}[\ln E(T) - \ln E(T - 1)] - \overline{s_M}[\ln M(T) - \ln M(T - 1)] \qquad (7.3)$$

where

$$\overline{s_i} = 1/2[s_i(T) + s_i(T - 1)] \qquad i = K, L, E, M \qquad (7.4)$$

$$\overline{R_T} = 1/2[R_T(T) + R_T(T - 1)] \qquad (7.5)$$

The index of (3) is referred to as the *Tornqvist index of TFP* or the *translog index of TFP*.[3]

The quality changes of inputs caused by input structural changes should be taken into account in calculating the TFP of an industry. We employ Jorgenson and his associates' approach by

$$\overline{S_{M_i}} = \frac{1}{2}[S_{M_i}(T) + S_{M_i}(T - 1)], \quad (i = 1, 2, \cdots, m) \qquad (7.7)$$

Similarly, if aggregate capital, labor, and energy inputs are translog of their components, we can express the difference between successive logarithms in the form

$$\ln K(T) - \ln K(T - 1) = \sum_{i=1}^{k} \overline{S_{K_i}}[\ln K_i(T) - \ln K_i(T - 1)] \qquad (7.8)$$

[2] Please refer to Gollop and Jorgenson (1980), Jorgenson and Liang (1985), Lau (1978), and Liang (1987, 1983) for imposing the "concavity" constraint in translog production (cost) function estimation.

[3] The Tornqvist index, the discrete approximation for the Divisia index, was proven by Diewert (1976) to be exact to the homogeneous translog function and such proof, consequently, provides the translog form a theoretical foundation in productivity analyses.

$$\ln L(T) - \ln L(T-1) = \sum_{i=1}^{l} \overline{S_{L_i}}[\ln L_i(T) - \ln L_i(T-1)] \quad (7.9)$$

$$\ln E(T) - \ln E(T-1) = \sum_{i=1}^{e} \overline{S_{E_i}}[\ln E_i(T) - \ln E_i(T-1)] \quad (7.10)$$

where

$$\overline{S_{K_i}} = \frac{1}{2}[S_{K_i}(T) + S_{K_i}(T-1)], \quad (i = 1, 2, \cdots, k) \quad (7.11)$$

$$\overline{S_{L_i}} = \frac{1}{2}[S_{L_i}(T) + S_{L_i}(T-1)], \quad (i = 1, 2, \cdots, l) \quad (7.12)$$

$$\overline{S_{E_i}} = \frac{1}{2}[S_{E_i}(T) + S_{E_i}(T-1)], \quad (i = 1, 2, \cdots, e) \quad (7.13)$$

7.3.2 Data compilation of Taiwan

The overlap time-series data of total output, inputs, and TFP of ICT industry in the United States, Japan, Korea, and China during 1980–2010 are available from World KLEMS, EU KLEMS, Asia KLEMS, China Industrial Productivity Database 3.0, and JIP Database 2015. However, the TFP data of Taiwan are unavailable. And hence, we employ our own consistent database, starting from 1961 to 2016. But some data of Taiwan such as intelligent investment are not available before 1981. Consequently, the observation period runs from 1981 to 2010 in this paper. For period comparison, we further divide it into four subperiods such as 1981–90,

1990–99, 1999–2007, and 2007–10. The data of factor input and output were compiled as follows:

7.3.2.1 Capital input

Capital input can be decomposed into seven categories: (1) buildings (K_1), (2) other buildings (K_2), (3) transportation equipment (K_3), (4) machineries (K_4), (5) inventory (K_5), (6) land (K_6), and (7) intelligent investment (K_7). Except for land, the time-series capital stock in 1961–2010 is calculated by adding up the net capital formation, which is the difference between the gross capital formation and the depreciation, starting from 1951—the beginning year of the National Income Account in Taiwan. The gross capital formation during 1951–2010 comes from the DGBAS; the types of depreciation are compiled by employing the constant rate depreciation method and the asset lives listed in the *National Wealth Census*.

This method implicitly assumes that no net capital stock existed before 1951. Since the observation period of this paper runs from 1981 to 1990, the above assumption is not so restricted. Because even if net capital stock before 1951 is not zero, it will close to zero by 1981. The time-series land data come from the *Industrial and Commercial Census* in every 5 years by applying interpolation/extrapolation method. We then used the data on various types of capital stock obtained from the *National Wealth Census* in 1988, DGBAS as a reference to adjust the time-series capital stock aforementioned.

The types of capital service price are compiled by using the following equation from Christensen and Jorgenson (1970, 1969):

$$P_{ki} = \frac{1 - \mu(T) \cdot Z_i(T)}{1 - \mu(T)}[P_{Ii}(T-1) \cdot (1 - \mu(T)) \cdot R_r(T) + \delta_i \cdot P_{Ii}(T) - (P_{Ii}(T) - P_{Ii}(T-1))]$$
$$+ P_{Ii}(T) \cdot \tau_i(T), \quad (i = 1, 2, 3, 4,) \quad (7.14)$$

where

μ (T): The effective business income tax rate;
$Z_i(T)$: The present value of depreciation deducted for tax purposes on a dollar's investment in capital i;
$P_{Ii}(T)$: The price index of gross investment in relation to capital i;
δ_i: The depreciation rate in relation to capital i;
$t_i(T)$: The property tax rate for capital i; and
$R_r(T)$: The rate of return for all types of capital.

The effective business income tax rate is the ratio of business income tax divided by the total profit of all sectors. The data on business income tax come from the *Yearbook of the Ministry of Finance*. The total profit (excluding interest and rent) is taken from the *National Income Account*.

By using the constant rate of depreciation method, the present value of deductions in relation to a dollar of investment goods, i, is calculated by means of the following equations:

$$\delta_i + 1 - \left(\frac{s_i}{c_i}\right)^{\frac{1}{N_i}} \quad (given\ s_i = 0.1c_i)$$

$$Z_i(T) = \sum \left[\frac{(1 - \delta_i)^{N_i - 1} \cdot \delta_i}{(1 + r)^{N_i}}\right]$$

(7.15)

where

N: The time span of investment goods i,
δ_i: The constant rate of depreciation of capital i,
r: The 1-year prime rate,
c_i: The cost of investment goods i, and
S_i: The remaining value of investment goods i.

The data on N_i and r come from the *National Wealth Census* (1988) and *Financial Statistics Monthly*, respectively.

The deflator in relation to capital i is the quotient of the gross capital formation at current prices and the gross capital formation at constant 2011 prices. Both of these are provided by the Statistics Bureau of the DGBAS. Based on the corresponding tax code, tax rates for property ($t_i(T)$), buildings (K_1), and other buildings (K_2) are assumed to be 3.0 percent. That for land (K_6) is assumed to be 1.5 percent. No property tax is levied on machineries (K_4), inventory (K_5), and intelligent investment (K_7).

The property tax rate with regard to the transportation equipment (K_3) is calculated as:

$$K_3 = \frac{\text{The license revenue for mobile cars}}{K_3 \text{ at current prices } - \text{ the value of the transportation equipment of all residents}} \quad (7.16)$$

The internal rate of return ($Rr\ (T)$) is calculated by:

$$R_r(T) = \frac{PC - \sum_{i=1}^{6}\left[\frac{1 - \mu(T) \cdot Z_i(T)}{1 - \mu(T)} \cdot (\delta P_{Ii}(T) - P_{Ii}(T))\right] \cdot K_i}{\sum_{i=1}^{6}(1 - \mu(T) \cdot Z_i(T)) \cdot P_{Ii}(T - 1) \cdot K_i(T - 1)} \quad (7.17)$$

Where *PC* denotes the property compensation, which is the sum of rent, interest, and profit depreciation, and is equal to the summation of the products of K_i and P_k:

$$PC = \sum_{i=1}^{4} P_{Ki} \cdot K_i (T - 1) \qquad (7.18)$$

Since the production of unpaid workers tends to be omitted from the survey of National Income and Product Accounts, especially in agriculture or in the quarrying industries and so on, we adjust and calculate this value by using the *Input–Output Table* for various years (i.e., 1976, 1978, 1986, 1991, 1996, 2001, 2006, and 2011).

We interpolate and extrapolate the input–output tables to obtain the time series S_K and S_L for adjusting the S_K and S_L series obtained from the National Income Account. Besides, the data of intelligent investment are also coming from DGBAS. We compile the nominal value and real value of intelligent investment for each industrial sectors and then calculating the deflator of intelligent investment. Furthermore, the beginning year of intelligent investment is 1981 and the depreciation period is 11 years, followed by DGBAS. And hence we also adopt perpetual inventory method and calibrate by using Industry, Commerce, and Service Census in 2011.

7.3.2.2 Labor input

72 categories of labor are classified on the basis of:

a. Sex	(a) Male
	(b) Female
b. Employment status	(a) Employed
	(b) Self-employed and/or unpaid family worker

—cont'd

C. Age	(a) 15–24
	(b) 25–34
	(c) 35–44
	(d) 45–54
	(e) 55–64
	(f) Over 65
D. Education	(a) Junior high school graduate or less
	(b) Senior or vocational high school graduate
	(c) College graduate and above

Wages and labor inputs on the basis of 72 categories during 1981–2010 are compiled from the magnetic tape of the Manpower Survey, DGBAS; total employment is from Manpower Survey, DGBAS, and wage comes from *Labor product and Wage Monthly*, DGBAS. We further incorporate the data of working hour during 1981–2010 into the labor input estimation.

7.3.2.3 Energy input

Energy input consists of coal, oil products, natural gas, and electricity. We calculated the translog index of energy. For this, we needed annual data on quantities and prices of types of energy. Although input–output tables are useful, they are not provided for each year. Moreover, there are no annual data on input–output tables in constant prices. Consequently, we used other data sources instead. The quantities of energy consumed are available in *Energy Balance in Taiwan, ROC*, issued by the Energy Commission, MOEA. Cost shares of types of energy are calculated by using the energy consumption data mentioned above and the data on prices of types of energy. The price of coal products consists of three types of coal and coke and comes from *Commodity Price Monthly* DGBAS, and *Import–Export Trade Monthly*, MOF. The price of coal gas is imputed as 5/9 of the natural gas price. The data on prices of natural gas and oil products are obtained from the *Chinese Petroleum Corporation and Energy Yearbook*, Energy Bureau.

7.3.2.4 Intermediate input

The intermediate inputs are split into five categories: agricultural, industrial, transportation, services, and imports intermediate input. First of all, the value and value share of intermediate input as a whole comes from the *National Income Account*. Since the data on intermediate input in the *National Income Account* include energy input, we subtract the value of energy input from the value of intermediate input. The value of each detailed intermediate input (at current prices) is the product of multiplying value share of each intermediate input $\overline{s_{MI}}$ by the value of total intermediate input M_l. Besides, the value of each intermediate input with constant prices is produced by deflating the value of each intermediate input with a corresponding deflator. Furthermore, the intermediate input deflator of agricultural, industrial, transportation, and services is obtained from DGBAS, and the imports intermediate input deflator comes from Ministry of Finance.

7.3.2.5 Real value added and total output

The time series of total output and value added at nominal prices during 1981−2010 come from the DGBAS. In addition, the real value added of ICT industries are calculated by DGBAS which used the chain-type price index that considered the quality adjustment, i.e., hedonic price. However, DGBAS did not publish the chain-type hedonic price index of total output, and hence we firstly adopted the method of regression to fit the relationship between price index of total output and value added without quality adjustment; then we took chain-type hedonic price index of value added as explain variable to find the chain-type hedonic price index of total output. Real total output and real value added of ICT industries are calculated by nominal total output and nominal value added

deflated with hedonic total output deflator and hedonic value added deflator.

7.3.3 Data compilation of other countries

The data of total output, capital input, labor input, and intermediate input (including energy intermediate input and nonenergy intermediate input) and growth rate of TFP in China, Japan, Korea, and the United States are obtained from World KLEMS Database, Asia KLEMS Database, EU KLEMS Database, China Industrial Productivity Database 3.0, and JIP Database 2015. The relative TFP level of ICT industries adjusted with purchasing power parity in 1995, which are employed to measure the "TFP gap" among five countries during 1995−2010, comes from Motohashi (2007).

7.4 Empirical Results

7.4.1 The growth rate of total output in ICT industries during 1981−2010

According to the database of World KLEMS, Asia KLEMS, and China Industrial Productivity Database, the total output value of ICT industry in the Japan, Korea, Taiwan, China, and United States were 467.5 billion, 321.4 billion, 240.5 billion, 896.7 billion, and USD 490.5 billion, respectively, in 2010.

Table 7.1 presents the international comparison on growth rate of total output (Q), various inputs, and TFP. From row 1, Table 7.1, the following important conclusions emerge:

(1) China had the highest growth rate in total output (Q) during 1981−2010 among five countries (24.1 percent). Korea ranked next (16.7 percent), followed by Taiwan (13.1 percent), the United States (7.5 percent), and Japan (6.1 percent) (see row 1, Table 7.1).

(2) The United States' growth rate of total output had peaked since 1999. It dropped to −0.5

TABLE 7.1 An international comparison on growth rate of total output, capital, labor, intermediate input, and TFP by country, 1981–2010.

	1981–2010					1981–90					1990–99					1999–2007					2007–10				
	Taiwan	Korea	Japan	China	US	Taiwan	Korea	Japan	China	US	Taiwan	Korea	Japan	China	US	Taiwan	Korea	Japan	China	US	Taiwan	Korea	Japan	China	US
Q	13.1	16.7	6.1	24.1	7.5	13.6	20.9	12.9	20.3	7.1	15.0	13.8	4.1	31.9	14.0	12.2	16.5	5.6	24.3	4.0	8.4	13.7	−11.0	13.1	−0.5
K	15.5	13.2	7.4	17.0	4.8	14.8	16.8	14.2	11.8	6.5	20.7	9.5	4.7	17.8	7.6	16.5	15.4	4.7	21.6	1.6	1.0	8.2	0.9	18.8	0.0
L	6.0	3.9	0.6	8.2	−1.2	8.4	11.3	4.8	5.5	0.6	5.2	−1.0	−0.6	7.7	−0.3	5.3	1.2	−0.3	11.8	−3.4	3.3	4.6	−8.4	8.6	−3.5
M	12.3	16.7	3.9	24.9	1.3	14.7	20.5	10.0	21.1	4.0	14.3	13.4	2.8	32.7	9.7	10.0	17.1	2.4	25.3	−4.2	5.2	14.4	−10.7	13.5	−14.8
TFP	1.2	2.0	2.6	2	6.2	−0.2	1.6	2.7	3.8	0.9	3.2	1.3	3.2	6.7	2.7	1.3	3.6	0.7	7.4	2.4	1.1	3.7	−0.2	8.3	

TFP, total factor productivity.
Unit: percent.
Source: Database of World KLEMS and Asia KLEMS, calculated by this paper.

percent per annum during 2007—10 (see row 1, Table 7.1).

(3) Japan's deceleration came even earlier. It started from 1990. It fell to growth rate of 0.5 percent during 2007—10 (see row 1, Table 7.1).

7.4.2 The growth rate of capital (K), labor (L), and intermediate input (M) in ICT industries during 1981—2010

From row 2 to row 4 of Table 7.1, we concluded that:

(1) China had the highest growth rate of capital input (17 percent) during 1981—2010. The followings were Taiwan (15.5 percent), Korea (13.2 percent), Japan (7.4 percent), and the United States (4.8 percent) (see row 2, Table 7.1).

(2) It is worth of noting that the capital input growth rate of the above five countries are fell sharply during 2007—10, owing to Financial Tsunami (see row 2, Table 7.1).

(3) Comparing with the growth rate of capital input, the labor input growth rate in all countries was lower except China. China was the country with the highest annual growth rate of 8.2 percent in labor input during 1981—2010, followed by Taiwan (6.0 percent), Korea (3.9 percent), Japan (0.6 percent), and the United States (−1.2 percent) (see row 3, Table 7.1).

(4) It is noted that the labor input of Japan and the United States registered negative growth since the subperiod of 1990—99. The labor input of ICT decreases to 1.3 percent per annum and 2.2 percent per annum, respectively, in Japan and the United States during 1990—2010 (see row 3, Table 7.1).

(5) Japan and the United States' intermediate input grew with a pace of 3.9 percent per annum and 1.3 percent per annum, respectively, during 1981—2010 (see row 4, Table 7.1).

(6) Compared with Japan and the United States, China, Korea, and Taiwan had much higher growth rate in intermediate input during 1981—2010. China and Korea grew with a pace of 24.9 percent per annum and 16.7 percent per annum, respectively, in intermediate input, while Taiwan increased with a 12.3 percent annually (see row 4, Table 7.1).

Compared with the growth rate of subperiods during 1981—2010, all of the five countries decelerated in intermediate inputs growth. The annual growth rate of intermediate input in Taiwan, Korea, and China decreased from 14.7 percent, 20.5 percent, and 21.1 percent, respectively, during 1981—90 to 5.2 percent, 14.4 percent, and 13.5 percent, respectively, during 2007—10. That of Japan and the United States sharply declined from 10 percent and 4.0 percent during 1981—90 to −10.7 percent and −14.8 percent during 2007—10 (see row 4, Table 7.1).

7.4.3 The growth rate of total factor productivity during 1981—2010

From row 5 of Tables 7.1 and 7.2, the following important conclusions emerge:

(1) For the whole observation period (1981—2010), the United States had the highest TFP growth of 6.2 percent per annum, followed by Japan (2.6 percent), Korea (2.0 percent), China (2.0 percent), and Taiwan (1.2 percent) (see row 5, Table 7.1).

(2) Comparing with the growth rate of subperiods, we found that TFP growth of the United States and Taiwan had accelerated during 1981—2010. The annual TFP growth rate of the United States increased from 3.8 percent during 1981—90 to 8.3 percent during 2007—10, and that of Taiwan and Japan increased from −0.2 percent and 2.7 percent, respectively, during 1981—90 to 2.4 percent and 3.7 percent, respectively, during 2007—10 (see row 5, Table 7.1).

TABLE 7.2 The relative contribution ratio of capital, labor, intermediate input, and TFP to total output growth by country, 1981–2010.

	1981–2010					1981–90					1990–99					1999–2007					2007–10				
	Taiwan	Korea	Japan	China	US	Taiwan	Korea	Japan	China	US	Taiwan	Korea	Japan	China	US	Taiwan	Korea	Japan	China	US	Taiwan	Korea	Japan	China	US
Q	100	100	100	100	100	100	100	100	100	100	100	100	100	100	100	100	100	100	100	100	100	100	100	100	100
K	12.7	10.3	11.3	7.4	8.6	9.4	9.6	5.5	7.7	13.2	17.0	8.7	14.2	8.2	6.1	13.9	11.3	7.9	4.6	2.1	7.7	6.0	7.9	−0.1	2.1
L	6.6	3.0	3.8	4.5	12.4	7.9	10.3	5.4	2.7	4.8	4.7	−1.0	−4.3	2.5	−0.7	0.8	−1.1	4.8	−24.7	3.2	3.4	−115	7.2	215.0	3.2
M	70.1	74.1	41.5	78.7	82.2	72.3	61.8	73.6	33.3	72.0	61.2	71.5	62.1	76.4	42.5	76.5	22.6	84.6	−62.0	42.2	81.4	−986	85.7	1206.7	42.2
TFP	9.3	13.0	43.4	9.4	−4.3	9.1	18.2	15.6	56.1	8.9	15.8	24.0	28.0	12.8	52.0	8.9	69.5	2.8	182.5	48.8	9.1	1195	−0.8	−1326.3	48.8

Unit: percent.

TFP, total factor productivity.

Source: Database of World KLEMS and Asia KLEMS, calculated by this paper.

(3) In contrast, Korea and China had a trend of deceleration in the TFP growth. The annual TFP growth rate of Korea and China declined from 1.6 percent and 2.6 percent, respectively, during 1981–90 to 1.1 percent and −0.2 percent, respectively, during 2007–10 (see row 5, Table 7.1).

7.4.4 The sources of total output growth

Table 7.2 presents the relative contribution ratio of capital input, labor input, and intermediate input to total output growth, respectively, in ICT industries during 1981–2010. Table 7.2 is calibrated from Table 7.1. From Table 7.2, we concluded that:

(1) The relative contribution ratio of capital input to total output growth during 1981–2010, Taiwan ranked the first (13.0 percent), while Japan (11.64 percent) ranked the second. Korea, the United States, and China ranked the third (10.25 percent), the fourth (7.57 percent), and the fifth (7.4 percent), respectively (see row 2, Table 7.2).
(2) The relative contribution ratio of labor input to total output growth, all of the five countries were lower than 7.0 percent during 1981–2010. Taiwan was 6.7 percent, followed by China (4.5 percent), Korea (3.0 percent), Japan (2.5 percent), and the United States (−5.0 percent) (see row 3, Table 7.2).
(3) The relative contribution ratio of intermediate input to total output was very high in China (78.7 percent), Korea (74.06 percent), and Taiwan (72.87 percent) during 1981–2010. Conversely, that of Japan and the United States were 43.43 percent and 9.8 percent, respectively (see row 4, Table 7.2).
(4) During 1981–2010, the relative contribution ratio of TFP to total output growth was the greatest in the United States (87.9 percent); Japan ranked the second (43.4 percent), followed by Korea (13.0 percent), China (9.4 percent), and Taiwan (9.3 percent) (see row 5, Table 7.2). It implies that the growth of

Korea, China, and Taiwan was input driven, while that of the United States and Japan was "TFP driven" during 1981–2010.
(5) However, the relative contribution ratio of TFP to total output increased in Japan, the United States, and Taiwan, while it decreased in China and Korea during 2007–10. For example, the relative contribution ratio of TFP to total output growth in Taiwan increased from −4.3 percent during 1981–90 to 48.8 percent during 2007–10 (see row 5, Table 7.2).

7.4.5 The measurement of relative total factor productivity gap

We refer to Motohashi (2007) and the TFP growth rate in Table 7.1 to measure the relative TFP gap among Japan, Korea, Taiwan, China, and the United States. The findings are as follows.

(1) Due to various TFP growths among countries, the TFP gap in ICT industry between the United States and the rest of four countries got wider during 1995–2010 (see Fig. 7.1).
(2) The relative TFP level of Japan, Korea, Taiwan, China, and the United States were 1, 0.76, 0.79, 0.68, and 0.93, respectively, in 1995. However, due to the different growth rate of TFP among five countries, the relative TFP level of Japan, Korea, Taiwan, China, and the United States were 1.56, 0.99, 1.03, 0.78, and 2.87, respectively in 2010 (see Fig. 7.1).
(3) And the TFP gap in ICT industry between Korea, Taiwan, and Japan got wider during 2003–07 and slightly narrowed during 2008–09 but gradually got wider after 2010 (see Fig. 7.1).
(4) The TFP gap in ICT industry between Korea and Taiwan got wider during 1995–2004 and gradually narrowed after 2005 (see Fig. 7.1).
(5) The TFP gap in ICT industry between China and other four countries got wider after 2005 (see Fig. 7.1).

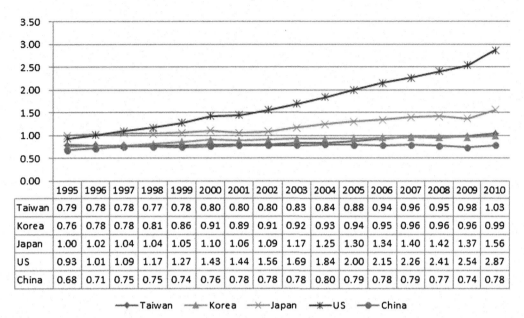

	1995	1996	1997	1998	1999	2000	2001	2002	2003	2004	2005	2006	2007	2008	2009	2010
Taiwan	0.79	0.78	0.78	0.77	0.78	0.80	0.80	0.80	0.83	0.84	0.88	0.94	0.96	0.95	0.98	1.03
Korea	0.76	0.78	0.78	0.81	0.86	0.91	0.89	0.91	0.92	0.93	0.94	0.95	0.96	0.96	0.96	0.99
Japan	1.00	1.02	1.04	1.04	1.05	1.10	1.06	1.09	1.17	1.25	1.30	1.34	1.40	1.42	1.37	1.56
US	0.93	1.01	1.09	1.17	1.27	1.43	1.44	1.56	1.69	1.84	2.00	2.15	2.26	2.41	2.54	2.87
China	0.68	0.71	0.75	0.75	0.74	0.76	0.78	0.78	0.78	0.80	0.79	0.78	0.79	0.77	0.74	0.78

FIGURE 7.1 **Trend of relative total factor productivity (TFP) level by country during 1995–2010.** *Source: Database of World KLEMS and Asia KLEMS, Motohashi (2007), calculated by this paper.*

The above findings imply that China Manufacturing 2025 might not pose threat to the United States under the trade war because of the wider TFP gap between China and the United States.

7.4.6 TFP gap, value-added ratio and R&D expense in total output value

Comparing to the United States and Japan, China, Taiwan, and Korea had lower relative TFP level (see Fig. 7.1). It might lead to lower value-added ratio in China, Taiwan, and Korea, compared to that of the United States and Japan. The value-added ratio of ICT industry in China, Taiwan, and Korea were 16.53 percent, 20.55 percent, and 22.7 percent, respectively, in 2010. In contrast, that of Japan and the United States were 34.53 percent and 62.98 percent, respectively (see Fig. 7.2). Low value-added industry implies low profit, low wage, low competiveness, and low contribution to the economic growth. And vice versa.

Why relative TFP level of ICT industry is different among the United States, Japan, Korea, Taiwan, and China is worthwhile to study further. Stiroh (2002) pointed out that TFP is driven by noninput factors such as technological progress that are not tied to explicit input usage. According to Liang (2009), Taiwan's TFP changes for the whole economy were affected by R&D, and the other factors such as foreign direct investment (FDI), infrastructure, exchange rate, wage rate, industrial policy, and so on. Biber (2017) also pointed out that "R&D investments have an increasing effect on total factor productivity and the increase in the quality of labor capital and ICT capital, which includes technology, is the source of the increase in TFP". Besides, some studies discussed the causality relationship between R&D/patents and TFP/ TFP growth. Rouvinen (2002) constructed a model based on the standard Cobb–Douglas production function and complemented a variable of knowledge stock which is accumulated through current and past R&D investments to

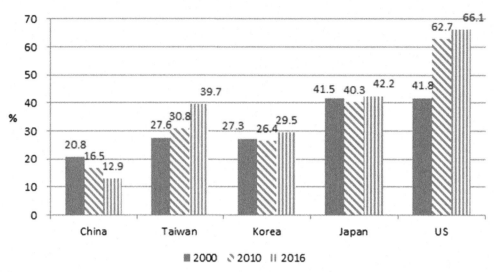

FIGURE 7.2   **Value-added ratio of information and communications technology (ICT) industry.** Note: the value of Japan is 2009, the data of Korea is 2015 and the data of China was estimated by this paper. *Source: OECD.stat and CIP database, calculated by this paper.*

understand the causality relationship between R&D and TFP crossed 12 Organisation for Economic Co-operation and Development (OECD) countries. The results suggested that R&D causes productivity but not vice versa. Westmore (2013) used panel regression techniques to test the relationship between innovation indicators which proxied by R&D expenditure and the number of new patents and multifactor productivity (MFP) growth across 19 OECD countries. The result established an empirical link between R&D/patents between MFP growth. The author also showed that innovation-specific policies such as R&D tax incentives were successful in encouraging the innovative activities associated with higher productivity growth but no evidence of a direct effect of such policies on aggregate productivity growth could be found. Singh and Trieu (1996) used the production function of Cobb—Douglas and to analyze the effects of disaggregated R&D investment expenditures on productivity growth for Japan, Korea, and Taiwan. The result showed that there was evidence that R&D expenditures in Japan, South

Korea, and Taiwan had a positive impact on TFP growth. Lu et al. (2006) adopted panel data of Taiwanese electronics firms to investigate the Granger causality relationship between R&D and productivity growth. They indicated that all variables in the model are stationary and that R&D stock and R&D spatial spillovers Granger cause productivity growth. Cardarelli and Lusinyan (2015) discussed the reason of TFP slowdown in the United States during the mid-2000s. They focused on whether the variation of TFP growth across US states can be associated with cross-state variation in education, R&D and innovation, infrastructure, tax policies, and other institutional and regulatory characteristics. The authors found some support for a positive impact of both business R&D expenditure and government R&D spending to TFP growth which confirmed the most findings that investment in R&D/innovation was an important factor associated with TFP growth. Boeing et al. (2016) analyzed the relationship between R&D/amount of patent applications and TFP in China by firm level with different ownership

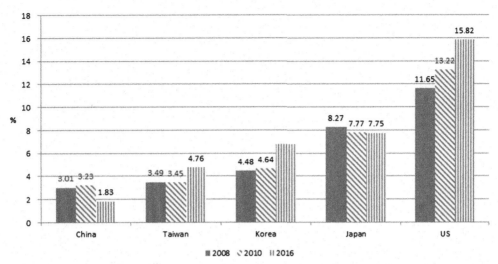

FIGURE 7.3   Average R&D expense in total output value of information and communications technology (ICT) industry by country during 2008, 2010, and 2016. Note: the data of Korea is 2015. *Source: OECD.stat and CIP database, calculated by this paper.*

types. They pointed out that privately owned enterprises generally yield higher benefits from R&D efforts and the strongly increasing amount of patent applications does not directly translate into increasing productivity which may be because economic policy of China puts much more emphasis on quantity instead of quality. Cui and Li (2016) examined the relationship between productivity and innovation by using manufacturers' patent data of the United States. The innovation was proxied by the number of patents. They found TFP was positively correlated with the number of patents granted and the number of citations per granted patent that according with previous studies.

To sum up, most literatures had showed that the R&D has positive relation with TFP and was also a main factor to drive the growth of TFP so it was worthy to understand the R&D expense and number of patents to distinguish the ICT TFP growth among Japan, Korea, Taiwan, China,

and the United States. International comparison on R&D expense of ICT industry in total output is presented in Fig. 7.3. From Fig. 7.3, we found that lower R&D expense might lead to lower TFP in China, Taiwan, and Korea, compared to that of the United States and Japan. The R&D expense in total output of ICT industry in China, Taiwan, and Korea were 3.23 percent, 3.45 percent, and 4.64 percent, respectively in 2010. Conversely, that of the United States and Japan were 13.22 percent and 7.77 percent, respectively.

The number of patents might provide another clue. We compare the number of ICT patents of Computer and Electronic Products[4] and Electrical Equipment, Appliances, and Components[5] granted by US Patent and Trademark Office (USPTO) during 2008–12. The number of patents granted of the United States and Japan were 99,757 and 51,589, respectively, surpassing that of Korea (15,791), Taiwan (15,068), and

[4] NAICS (North American Industry Classification System, NAICS) Classification is 334.

[5] NAICS Classification is 335.

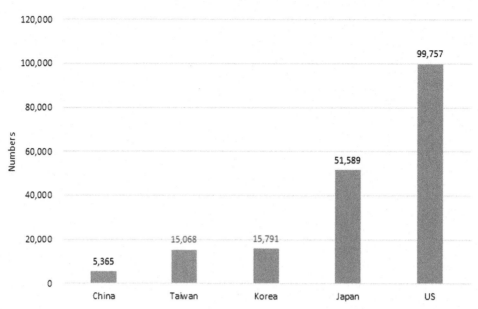

FIGURE 7.4   **Total patents granted during 2008—12 by country.** *Source: U.S. Patent and Trademark Office, calculated by this paper.*

China (5365). In addition, we could also observe the efficiency through an indicator of patents granted divided by total output. The number of patents granted divided by total output of the United States and Japan were 203.9 and 115.6, respectively, surpassing that of Taiwan (64.9), Korea (54.3), and China (7.7) (see Figs. 7.4 and 7.5). It might result in that the difference of competitiveness in ICT industries among five countries.

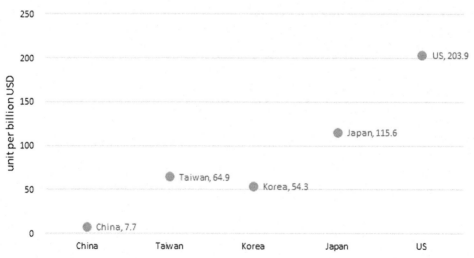

FIGURE 7.5   **Total patents granted divided by total output during 2008—12 by country.** *Source: U.S. Patent and Trademark Office, calculated by this paper.*

Not only the number of patents granted was lower but also the nature or contents of patents within Taiwan, Korea, and China were lower, compared to that of Japan and the United States. For instance, NACS (2014) pointed out that the ICT output of Taiwan was mainly based on original equipment manufacture (OEM), and the patents were mainly concentrated in processing instead of new products so that the impact factor or quality of patent was low.

Some literatures also mentioned other factors that will affect TFP growth. According to Samimi and Arab (2011) and Biber (2017), FDI, trade flows, technology transfer, the degree of protection of intellectual property rights (IPRs), and investment in ICT will also affect TFP growth. In addition, Díaz et al. (2015) maintained that public policies should jointly promote ICT use to improve the TFP of firms. Chou et al. (2014) empirically explore the relationship between IT (information technology) and TFP to show that IT enhances TFP through IT-induced externalities and IT-leveraged innovations. They indicate that TFP can be a competitive advantage that benefits from IT-leveraged innovations.

Furthermore, IPRs were also an vital mechanism to protect and elevate the competitiveness of ICT industries. ICT industries were among the most dynamic and innovative segments of modern economies, and they used IPRs intensively. Advanced ICT firms could learn to use IPR to protect their research investments and defend their competitiveness in global supply chains and maintain industrial status. ICT industry was a key pillar for developing countries such as China, Korea, and Taiwan. The protection of IPR rights should not only be an important part of business strategy but also avoiding trade conflict within countries.

7.4.7 An implication to the US−China trade war

Aforementioned, TFP gap between China and other four countries, especially the United States,

had gotten wider during 1995 to 2010. Although the TFP data of the four countries are not available after 2010, the data of the R&D expense in total output value and value-added ratio might provide clues for the TFP gap among the four countries after 2010.

In general, higher TFP might result from higher R&D expense in total output value. However, we found that China's R&D expense in total output value of the ICT industry was 1.83 percent in 2016. It was much lower than that of the four countries, i.e., Taiwan 4.76 percent, Korea 6.77 percent, Japan 7.75 percent, and the United States 15.82 percent. Furthermore, China's R&D expense in total output value of the ICT industry in 2016, i.e., 1.83 percent, was lower than that of 2010 (3.23 percent) (see Figs 7.3). On the contrary, the R&D expense in total output value of the other three countries in 2016 was higher than that in 2010, with the exception of Japan (also see Figs 7.3).

Moreover, as mentioned before, higher TFP generally will lead to higher value-added ratio. Compared with that in 2010, the value-added ratio of four countries was all higher in 2016 except China (see Figs 7.2).

From the above two clues, we conclude that the TFP gap between China and other three countries was by no means narrowing even after 2010. Therefore, we maintain that the China's TFP in ICT industry is still lagged behind the other three countries, especially the United States, up to recent year. And hence the technology threat of China to the United States which is a hardcore of the US−China trade war might be unfounded.

7.5 Conclusion and suggestion

The objective of this paper is: (1) to measure the TFP growth and analyze the sources of ICT growth in Taiwan during 1981−2010; (2) to compare the sources of growth and TFP growth of ICT industry among Japan, Korea, Taiwan, China, and the United States, and (3) to measure the "TFP gap" of ICT industry among the above five countries. The result also shed some light on the issue of whether the China Manufacturing 2025 posed threat to the United States or not under the trade war between China and the United States.

The major findings and conclusions are:

1) The annual growth rate of ICT total output in China, Korea, and Taiwan were 24.1 percent, 16.7 percent, and 13.1 percent, respectively, during 1981−2010, while that of the United States and Japan were 7.5 percent and 6.1 percent, respectively, in the same period.

2) The TFP growth rate of ICT industry in the United States, Japan, Korea, Taiwan, and China were 6.2 percent, 2.6 percent, 2 percent, 1.2 percent, and 2 percent per year, respectively, during 1981−2010.

3) The relative contribution ratio of TFP of ICT industry in United States, Japan, Korea, China, and Taiwan were 87.9 percent, 43.4 percent, 13.0 percent, 9.4 percent, and 9.3 percent, respectively, during 1981−2010. The growth of the United States and Japan were TFP driven, while that of Korea, China, and Taiwan were input driven in ICT industry during 1981−2010.

4) It is worth noting that contrast with Korea, Taiwan's relative contribution ratio of TFP to total output accelerated during the latest period of 2007−10, becoming the second largest contributor to total output growth.

5) The TFP gap in ICT industry between the United States and the rest of four countries got wider during 1995−2010.

6) Japan's TFP level continued to lead Korea, Taiwan, and China during 1995−2010.

7) The TFP gap in ICT industry between Korea and Taiwan got wider during 1995−2004, while it remarkably narrowed after 2004.

8) China had the lowest TFP level among five countries. The TFP gap in ICT industry between China and other four countries got wider after 2001.

9) From (5), (8) and the clues of comparison on the data of the R&D expense in total output value and value-added ratio among four countries in recent years, the China's TFP in ICT industry is still lagged behind the other three countries especially the United State up to recent year. And hence the technology threat of China to the United States which is a hardcore of US-China trade war might be unfounded.

10) Lower R&D expense and lower number and quality of patents might lead to lower TFP growth in Taiwan, Korea, and China in ICT industry, compared to that of the United States and Japan during 1981−2010.

It is suggested that the governments should encourage R&D in ICT industries and promote ICT application, technology transfer, FDI, and IPR protection in particular for avoiding trade conflict.

References

Acharya RC: ICT use and total factor productivity growth: intangible capital or productive externalities? *Oxford Economic Papers* 68(1):16−39, 2016.

Biber AE: Contribution of total factor productivity in economic growth rate, *Journal of Social Science and Humanities Research* 2(11):68−73, 2017.

Boeing P, Mueller E, Sandner P: China's R&D explosion—analyzing productivity effects across ownership types and over time, *Research Policy* 45(1):159−176, 2016.

Bosworth BP, Triplett JE: *Is the 21st century productivity expansion still in services? And what should be done about it?*, Washington, 2006, Brookings Institution. Manuscript.

Cardarelli R, Lusinyan L: *U.S. total factor productivity slowdown: evidence from the U.S. States*, IMF working paper, international monetary fund, WP/15/116, 2015.

Cette G, Kocoglu Y, Mairesse J: *Productivity growth and levels in France, Japan, the United Kingdom and the United States in the twentieth century*, NBER working paper No. 15577, Cambridge, MA, 2009, National Bureau of Economic Research (NBER).

Chou Y-C, Chuang HC-H, Shao BBM: The impacts of information technology on total factor productivity: a look at externalities and innovations, *International Journal of Production Economics* 158:290–299, 2014.

Christensen LR, Jorgenson DW: The measurement of US real capital input, 1929-1967, *Review of Income and Wealth* 15(4): 293–320, 1969.

Christensen LR, Jorgenson DW: US real product and real factor input, 1929-1967, *Review of Income and Wealth* 16(1): 19–50, 1970.

Comino S, Maria FM, Thumm N: *Intellectual property and innovation in information and communication technology (ICT), No. JRC97541, Joint research centre (Seville site)*, 2015.

Corrado C, Lengermann P, Bartelsman EJ, et al.: Modeling aggregate productivity at a disaggregate level: new results for U.S. sectors and industries. In *Paper presented at 2006 summer institute sponsored by the national Bureau of economic research and the conference on research in income and Wealth, Cambridge, MA*, July 17, 2006. Manuscript.

Cui J, Li X: Innovation and firm productivity: evidence from the US patent data. In *2016 annual meeting, July 31-August 2, 2016, Boston, Massachusetts (No. 235603)*, Agricultural and Applied Economics Association.

De Prato G, López Cobo M, Simon JP: *Dynamics of ICTs: assessing investments in R&D, a global cross-comparison*, 2017.

Díaz-Chao Á, Sainz-González J, Torrent-Sellens J: ICT, innovation, and firm productivity: new evidence from small local firms, *Journal of Business Research* 68(7):1439–1444, 2015.

Diewert WE: Exact and superlative index numbers, *Journal of Econometrics* 4(2):115–145, 1976.

Fukao K, Miyagawa T, Pyo HK, et al.: Estimates of total factor productivity, the contribution of ICT, and resource reallocation Effects in Japan and Korea. In *Global COE hi-stat discussion paper series gd10-177, Tokyo*, Institute of Economic Research, Hitotsubashi University.

Fukao K: Explaining Japan's unproductive two decades, *Asian Economic Policy Review* 8(2):193–213, 2013.

Gollop FM, Jorgenson DW: U.S. productivity growth by industry, 1947-73. In Kendrick KW, Vaccara BN, editors: *New developments in productivity measurement*, Chicago, 1980, University of Chicago press, pp 15–136.

Hanna N, Boyson S, Gunaratne S: *The east asian miracle and information technology: strategic management of technological learning*, World Bank discussion papers 326, 1996.

Henze P: *Structural change and total factor productivity: evidence from Germany*, Economics working paper, No. 2015-03, Kiel, Department of Economics, Kiel University.

Heshmati A, Yang W: *Contribution of ICT to the Chinese economic growth, Ratio Working Papers 91*, 2006.

IDC EMEA: intellectual property rights and competitiveness: challenges for ICT-producing SMEs, Sectoral e-business watch programme, Impact study No. 08/2008, 2008.

Jorgenson DW, Gollop FM, Fraumeni BM: Productivity and sectoral output growth in the United States. In Kendrick JW, editor: *Interindustry differences in productivity growth, Cambridge, MA*, Ballinger.

Jorgenson DW, Ho M, Stiroh K: *The sources of the second surge of U.S. productivity and implications for the future*, New York, 2006, Federal reserve bank of New York manuscript.

Jorgenson DW, Liang C-Y: *On dynamic energy-economic model of Taiwan, R.O.C. project report of energy research and development fund, No. 72Xg313BA, Taipei, Taiwan*, 1985, Energy Committee, Ministry of Economic Affairs.

Khalili F: *The contribution of information communication technology (ICT) to total factor productivity (TFP) and economic growth: evidence from Asia-pacific and EU countries*, Kuala Lumpur, 2014, Degree of doctor of philosophy, Faculty of Economics and Administration, University of Malaya.

Krugman P: *The Myth of Asian's Miracle*, Foreign Affairs, 1994.

Lau LJ: Testing and imposing monotonicity, convexity, and quasi-convexity constraints. In , Amsterdam, 1978, North-Holland, pp 409–453. Fuss M, McFadden DL, editors: *Production economics: A dual approach to theory and applications*, vol. 1. Amsterdam, 1978, North-Holland, pp 409–453.

Liang C-Y: A study on the translog model of aggregate consumer demand for energy in Taiwan, *Academia Economic Papers* 11(2):167–218, 1983.

Liang C-Y: Impacts of alternative electricity development strategies on the economies of NICs: a case study of Taiwan. In *Paper presented at proceedings of the IAEE conference, Alberta,1987; world energy markets: coping with instability, Calgary, Canada*, July 6–8, 1987, pp 217–228.

Liang C-Y: Industrial structure changes and the measurement of total factor productivity growth: the Krugman-Kim-Lau-Young hypothesis revisited, *Academia Economic Papers* 37(3):305–338, 2009.

Liu T, Woo WT: Understanding the U.S.-China trade war, *China Economic Journal* 11(3):319–340, 2018.

Lu W-C, Chen J-R, Wang C-L: Granger causality test on R&D spatial spillovers and productivity growth, *Applied Economics Letters* 13(13):857–861, 2006.

Motohashi K: Assessing Japan's international competitiveness by international productivity level: comparison with China, Korea, Taiwan and the United States. In Jorgenson D, Kuroda M, Motohashi K, editors: *Productivity in Asia: economic growth and competitiveness*, Cheltenham, 2007, Edward Elgar, pp 215–238.

NACS: industrial policy and national competitiveness, National Academy of Civil Service.

Rouvinen P: R&D-productivity dynamics: causality, lags, and 'dry holes', *Journal of Applied Economics* 5(1), 2002.

Samimi AJ, Arab M: Information and communication technology (ICT) & total factor productivity (TFP): evidence from selected countries of the world, *Middle-East Journal of Scientific Research* 10(6):768–776, 2011.

Singh N, Trieu H: *The role of R&D in explaining total factor productivity growth in Japan, South Korea, and Taiwan*, University of California.

Stiroh KJ: Are ICT spillovers driving the new economy? *Review of Income and Wealth* 48(1):33–57, 2002.

Westmore B: *R&D, patenting and growth: the role of public policy economics*, Department working papers No. 1047, ECO/WKP(2013)39, 2013.

Website

Asia KLEMS: DATABASE. http://www.asiaklems.net/data/customize.asp.

Bayntun-Lees A: Industry spotlight: IPR in the ICT industry. Posted on August 10, 2015. http://www.youripinsider.eu/industry-spotlight-ipr-ict-industry/.

Directorate-general of budget, accounting and statistics (DGBAS) of Taiwan: Statistics by categories. https://eng.stat.gov.tw/np.asp?CtNode=1525.

Lee W-C: U.S.-China trade war was turn into technology war, Commercial Times, 2018. https://www.npf.org.tw/1/19891.

OECD.stat: Data by theme. https://stats.oecd.org/.

Research institute of economy, trade and industry (RIETI): CIP database 2015: Introduction to China industrial productivity (CIP) database 3.0. https://www.rieti.go.jp/en/database/CIP2015/index.html.

South-east Asia IPR SME helpdesk: IP considerations for the ICT Industry in Singapore. ASEAN briefing posted on August 10, 2018. https://www.aseanbriefing.com/news/2018/08/10/ip-considerations-ict-industry-singapore.html.

WORLD KLEMS initiative: World KLEMS data. http://www.worldklems.net/data.htm.

8

Losing Steam?—An industry origin analysis of China's productivity slowdown

Harry X. Wu*

National School of Development, Peking University, Beijing, China; Institute of Economic Research, Hitotsubashi University, Kunitachi, Japan

8.1 Introduction

China's persistent slowdown in GDP growth following the global financial crisis (GFC) in 2008 has heated up the long debate about the sustainability of the China model of growth. Despite the government's unprecedented fiscal and monetary stimulus measures, the official statistics, though often critically questioned for exaggerating the real growth performance especially at the time of crisis (Maddison and Wu, 2008; Wu, 2013, 2014a,b), show that China has more than halved its growth pace from an annual average of 13.5% over the period 2005—07, or during its post-WTO (World Trade Organization) heydays, to 6.5% over the period 2015—17 (NBS, 2018). How to properly explain such a decade-long and substantial steam loss

in the engine of the Chinese economy? Is it caused by inactive government (ironically a consequence of the on-going anticorruption campaign), insufficient (imperfect) market, deceleration of potential growth, or some combination of these factors? A productivity analysis is important to understanding the problem in general because these factors should have inevitably affected business performances of enterprises, hence the whole economy.

8.1.1 Why haven't we learned much from the literature?

We have learned little from the vast literature on China's postreform productivity performance using the aggregate production function (APF) growth accounting approach (i.e., taking the

* I thank Barbara Fraumeni as well as participants at the 35th IARIW general conference and seminars at NSD of Peking University and SEM of Tsinghua University for helpful comments and suggestions. What reported in this paper are still interim results of CIP/KLEMS Database Project supported by RIETI's Asian Industrial Productivity Program and IER of Hitotsubashi University. I am very much grateful for excellent research support of Zhan Li, David T. Liang, and George G. Zhang with the revision and update of the CIP 3.0 data (see the data section for details). The usual claims apply.

national GDP growth as the numerator). This is mainly because the available estimates are often distinctly different and even contradictory[1]; therefore without the details of the performance of industries, it is impossible to judge the reliability of the estimates. For example, for the early reform period from the late 1970s to the early 1990s, the available estimates of China's TFP growth rate range from between 1.0 and 1.5% per annum (Woo, 1998; Young, 2003) to around 4% per annum (Borensztein and Ostry, 1996; Bosworth and Collins, 2003; Fan et al., 1999; Hu and Khan, 1997). For the later period prior to GFC, it also remains inconclusive. While Bosworth and Collins (2008) showed that China's TFP growth maintained at 3.9% per annum during 1993—2004, Perkins and Rawski (2008) showed that it declined from 6.7% per annum during 1990—95 to about 3% per annum in 1995—2005. Yet, Brandt and Zhu (2010) suggested an opposite trend from 3.1% per annum in 1988—98 to 4.3% per annum over 1998—2007. On the other hand, empirical studies using parametric approaches are not better alternatives because they could only provide average estimates of the potential productivity growth for certain (long-enough) period, subject to some imposed functional forms.

As commented in Jorgenson et al. (2005), the APF tradition is subject to rather stringent assumptions. It assumes that for all (underlying) industries "value-added functions exist and are identical across industries up to a scalar multiple" and "the aggregation of heterogeneous types of capital and labor must receive the same price in each industry" Obviously, in the case of China, institutional deficiencies and growth-motivated government interventions

have caused severe misallocation of resources (Hsieh and Klenow, 2009). In my 2016 paper, I emphasized that to analyze China's aggregate productivity performance in the light of the role of government, it is essential to have an industry perspective because state interventions are often made through industry-specific policies, and "upstream" industries (those delivering intermediate goods and services such as energy and telecommunications) that are targeted by industrial policies will affect downstream industries through input—output linkages of the economy. I therefore suggested that coherently including industries in a growth accounting framework is the only systematic way to test the hypothesis that government's heavy involvement in resource allocation may solve the growth problem but not the efficiency or productivity problem (Wu, 2016).

8.1.2 Toward a theoretically sound inquiry of China's productivity performance

To this end, not only do we need an appropriate methodological framework that is able to systematically account for the contribution of individual industries to the aggregate productivity performance, but we also need industry productivity accounts that are integrated with the national input and output accounts as well as capital and labor accounts of the economy. This is basically the KLEMS approach[2] that follows in principle the seminal work by Jorgenson and Griliches in 1967 aiming to integrate the neoclassical production theory (Jorgenson, 1963), the growth accounting methodology, and data development

---

[1] See Y. Wu (2011) for a substantive review and a statistical assessment of existing studies and their findings.

[2] KLEMS is used as an acronym for K(C)apital, Labor, Energy, Materials, and Services that are used to produce any product. By the same token, the gross output of an industry equals its costs of "KLEMS" and the gross output of an economy equals the sum of the costs of "KLEMS" of all industries. See O'Mahony and Timmer (2009) for an introduction of the EU-KLEMS database. The on-going CIP Database Project is part of the World KLEMS initiative based in the Harvard University.

and measurement in a holistic and coherent system. The data and measurement work is hence very challenging and it cannot be meaningfully done without the guidance of the theory.

Measurement-wise, this requires a constant quality indexing of all types of the primary inputs (capital and labor) so that the quality change of such inputs cannot be mistakenly counted as TFP growth. One of the most important consequences of such data and measurement advancement is that the so-estimated TFP change is much smaller than otherwise if the heterogeneity of primary inputs is ignored, and hence it is closer to what the theory implied costless source of growth (Hulten, 2001). This idea has been consolidated by empirical studies by Jorgenson and his associates on the postwar US economy (e.g., Jorgenson et al., 1987), among others. The Jorgenson–Griliches approach also means that the estimates by the alternative APF approach cannot be true except if the quality of inputs is the same across industries.

Cao et al. (2009) made an earlier attempt to apply this Jorgenson–Griliches approach to the Chinese economy but suffered from some major data deficiencies. Their estimated annual TFP growth rate is 2.5% for the period 1982–2000, which is somewhat the average of the estimates obtained by the aforementioned studies using the APF framework. However, their estimates for subperiods are hardly acceptable. They suggest an astonishing TFP deceleration from a height of 9.1% per annum in 1982–84 to an absolute drop of 0.3% per annum in 1994–2000. It is difficult to accept that in terms of productivity improvement, despite an unparalleled economy-wide reform propelled by Deng's call

for "bolder reforms" in his southern China trip in 1992, the reform had already lost its momentum in productivity.

The other attempt to analyze China's sources of growth with the Jorgenson–Griliches approach has been made under my leadership. After years of painstaking endeavors to fix data problems, we have constructed the first KLEMS-type database for the Chinese economy, that is, CIP 3.0 (China Industrial Productivity Database 3.0) (CIP, 2015).[3] This China KLEMS data set has a full coverage of the economy with 37 sectors for the period 1980–2010, hence for the first time making it possible to examine China's TFP performance following the economic reform, covering the period both before and after China's WTO participation. In my 2016 paper (Wu, 2016), using CIP 3.0 data I applied the Jorgensonian aggregate production possibility frontier (APPF) growth accounting framework (Jorgenson, 1966) and incorporated it with the Domar aggregation scheme (Domar, 1961) to account for cost heterogeneity of inputs across industries. I obtained preliminary estimates of sources of China's growth including a decomposition of China's TFP growth into industry-origin effect and factor reallocation effect. I showed that China achieved an average TFP growth of 1.24% per annum for the period 1980–2010 as a whole, which is much slower than the existing estimates in the literature and only about half of the estimate by Cao et al. (2009).

8.1.3 Has China's productivity really slowed down?

My results did not support the TFP deceleration in the 1990s as found in Cao et al. (2009).

---

[3] The CIP Project began in 2010, jointly sponsored by the Research Institute of Economy, Trade and Industry (RIETI) of Japan and the Institute of Economic Research (IER) at Hitotsubashi University. It aims to extend my China Growth and Productivity Database Project, initiated in 1995 and heavily involved in Angus Maddison's work on China's post-1949 output and productivity performance in his international comparison of output and productivity project (ICOP) at GGDC, University of Groningen, focusing on the growth of Chinese manufacturing, mining, and utility industries (Maddison, 1998, 2007; Maddison and Wu, 2008), to nonindustrial sectors in a KLEMS compatible framework.

In contrast, I showed that China's TFP growth during the 1990s was most rapid at 1.79% per annum compared to 1.39% in the 1980s. China's post-WTO period (defined as from 2001 to 2007) appeared to have maintained a strong TFP growth at 1.57% per annum, only a slightly slower than that in the 1990s. Nevertheless, I found that China's post-WTO period was the first time for the economy since the reform to have recorded an enormous productivity loss attributed to a considerable negative reallocation effect of capital at -1.15% per annum. Such a misallocation of capital could have wiped out all genuine productivity gains from industries at 0.98% per annum, if there were not a very strong gain from labor reallocation at 1.73% per annum (Wu, 2016: 220).

Although my results showed that China's TFP growth turned significantly negative in the wake of the GFC (-1.80% per annum), the post-GFC period 2008—10 that I covered then was too short to substantiate such any conclusion. However, it is this observation together with the severe misallocation of capital long before the GFC shock that has motivated the present study. Considering the imperative role of Chinese manufacturing in making China the world largest manufacturing factory at a superfast pace, in this study I will focus on the period since the 1990s when significant urban and industrial reforms took place following the Communist Party's decision to adopt a "socialist market economy" model to carry on the reform (CCCPC, 2013), encouraged by Deng's push for "bolder reforms." Thus, 1991 is set up as the beginning of my investigation, just 1 year before Deng's southern China trip (to avoid setting up a time with a major event as the base year). Skipping the heydays of the agricultural reform in the 1980s may help better identify the path of China's industrial reform in terms of its productivity

performance with more reliable data available from the 1990s.

The rest of the paper is organized as follows. Section 8.2 introduces the Jorgensonian APPF-Domar approach to account for the industry-origin and resource reallocation effects on the aggregate growth and productivity performance. Section 8.3 introduces the CIP/China KLEMS database with key steps in the data construction. Section 8.4 introduces industry grouping to distinguish activities of industries by their "distance" from the market or the government and proposes a periodization to help conjectures about the productivity effect of major policy regime shifts. Section 8.5 presents and discusses the empirical results. Finally, Section 8.6 briefly concludes this study.

8.2 The APPF-Domar framework of growth accounting[4]

The long and widely used APF approach, as criticized in Jorgenson, Ho and Stiroh (2005: 362), implicitly assumes that for all (underlying) industries "value-added functions exist and are identical across industries up to a scalar multiple" and that "the aggregation of heterogeneous types of capital and labor must receive the same price in each industry." This is inappropriate to address the productivity problem of the Chinese economy where heavy government interventions and institutional deficiencies have caused severe market distortions. To better deal with China's productivity problem, this study adopts Jorgenson's APPF framework (Jorgenson, 1966) and, following Jorgenson et al. (2005), also incorporates it with Domar's aggregation scheme (Domar, 1961). This approach not only relaxes the stringent assumption that all industries have the same value-added function but also

---

[4] This section is largely based on Wu (2016).

takes into account that industries may pay different prices for the same factor.

This Domar aggregation scheme was introduced into the APPF framework in Jorgenson et al. (1987) to exercise direct aggregation across industries to account for the role of American industries in changes of aggregate inputs. It was later used in Jorgenson and Stiroh (2000), Jorgenson (2001), and Jorgenson et al. (2005) to quantify the role of information technology (IT)-producing and IT-using industries in the US economy.

To simply illustrate this methodology, we can begin with a production function where the gross output of an industry is a function of capital, labor, intermediate inputs, and the shift of the production function indexed by time. We use individual industries as building blocks which allow us to explicitly trace the sources of the aggregate productivity growth and input accumulation to the underlying industries. Focusing on an industry-level production function given by Eq. (8.1), each industry, denoted by j, purchases distinct intermediate inputs, capital, and labor services to produce a set of products:

$$Y_j = f_j(K_j, L_j, X_j, T) \qquad (8.1)$$

where Y is output, K is an index of capital service flows, L is an index of labor service flows, X is an index of intermediate inputs (energy, materials, and services), domestically produced and/or imported, and T is (neutral) technological change that is not embodied in any primary input, that is, the change of total factor productivity (TFP). Note that all input variables are time variant, but this is suppressed for notational convenience.

Under the assumptions of competitive factor markets, full input utilization, and constant returns to scale, the growth of output can be expressed as the cost-weighted growth of inputs and TFP change:

$$\Delta \ln Y_j = \overline{v}_j^K \Delta \ln K_j + \overline{v}_j^L \Delta \ln L_j + \overline{v}_j^X \Delta \ln X_j + v_j^T$$

$$(8.2)$$

where $\overline{v}_j^K$, $\overline{v}_j^L$, and $\overline{v}_j^X$ are two-period averages of the nominal cost weights of capital input, labor input, and input of intermediate materials, respectively, with $v_j^K = \left(P_j^K K_j\right)\big/\left(P_j^Y Y_j\right)$, $v_j^L = \left(P_j^L K_j\right)\big/\left(P_j^Y Y_j\right)$, and $v_j^X = \left(P_j^X K_j\right)\big/\left(P_j^Y Y_j\right)$. Note that under constant returns to scale $v_j^K + v_j^L + v_j^X = 1$, which is controlled by nominal gross output at industry level. Each element in the right-hand side of Eq. (8.2) indicates the proportion of output growth accounted for, respectively, by the growth of capital services $(\overline{v}_j^K \Delta \ln K_j)$, labor services $(\overline{v}_j^L \Delta \ln L_j)$, intermediate materials $(\overline{v}_j^X \Delta \ln X_j)$, and TFP (v_j^T).

One of the advantages of Eq. (8.2) is that it can better account for each input services by different types. For example, it can account for labor services provided by different types of labor with specific demographic, educational, and industrial attributes, attempted in pioneering studies by Griliches (1960), Denison (1962), and Jorgenson and Griliches (1967). It relaxes the usual strong assumption that treats numbers employed or hours worked as a homogenous measure of labor input. The growth of total labor input is thus defined as a Törnqvist quantity index of individual labor types as follows:

$$\Delta \ln L_j = \sum_h \overline{v}_{h,j} \Delta \ln H_{h,j} \qquad (8.3a)$$

where $\Delta \ln H_{h,j}$ indicates the growth of hours worked by each labor type h (with specific gender, age, and educational attainment) and its cost weights $\overline{v}_{h,j}$ given by two-period average shares of each type in the nominal value of labor compensation controlled by the labor income of industry production accounts.

The same user-cost approach is also applied to K and X to account for the contribution of different types of capital asset (Z_z) and intermediate input (X_x) in production with type-specific, two-period average cost weight defined as $\overline{v}_{k,j}$ and $\overline{v}_{x,j}$, respectively:

$$\Delta \ln K_j = \sum_k \overline{v}_{k,j} \Delta \ln Z_{z,j}, \quad \text{and} \quad (8.3b)$$

$$\Delta \ln X_j = \sum_x \overline{v}_{x,j} \Delta \ln X_{x,j} \quad (8.3c)$$

It should be noted that Eq. (8.2) through the whole set of Eq. (8.3) also explicitly express the methodological framework for the CIP industry-level data construction that is linked to and controlled by the national production and income accounts. This point will be discussed again when we discuss the data issues in the following section.

Using the value-added concept, Eq. (8.2) can be rewritten as:

$$\Delta \ln Y_j = \overline{v}_j^V \Delta \ln V_j + \overline{v}_j^X \Delta \ln X_j \quad (8.4)$$

where V_j is the real value-added in j and v_j^V is the nominal share of value-added in industry gross output.

Rearranging Eqs. (8.2) and (8.4), we can derive an expression for the sources of industry value-added growth (i.e., measured in terms of input contributions):

$$\Delta \ln V_j = \frac{\overline{v}_j^K}{\overline{v}_j^V} \Delta \ln K_j + \frac{\overline{v}_j^L}{\overline{v}_j^V} \Delta \ln L_j + \frac{1}{\overline{v}_j^V} v_j^T \quad (8.5)$$

Growth of aggregate value-added by the APPF approach is expressed as weighted industry value-added in a Törnqvist index:

$$\Delta \ln V = \sum_j \overline{w}_j \Delta \ln V_j \quad (8.6)$$

where w_j is the share of industry value-added in aggregate value-added. By combining Eqs. (8.5) and (8.6), we can have a new expression of aggregate value-added growth by weighted

contribution of industry capital growth, industry labor growth, and TFP growth:

$$\Delta \ln V \equiv \sum_j \overline{w}_j \Delta \ln V_j$$

$$= \sum_j \left(\overline{w}_j \frac{\overline{v}_j^K}{\overline{v}_j^V} \Delta \ln K_j + \overline{w}_j \frac{\overline{v}_j^L}{\overline{v}_j^V} \Delta \ln L_j + \overline{w}_j \frac{1}{\overline{v}_j^V} v_j^T \right)$$
$$(8.7)$$

Through this new expression, we have introduced the well-known Domar weights in aggregation (Domar 1961), i.e., a ratio of each industry's share in total value-added (w_j) to the proportion of the industry's value-added in its gross output (v_j^V).

If we maintain the assumption that capital and labor inputs have the same marginal productivity in all industries, we can define aggregate TFP growth as:

$$v^T \equiv \sum_j \overline{w}_j \Delta \ln V_j - \overline{v}^K \Delta \ln K - \overline{v}^L \Delta \ln L \quad (8.8)$$

However, this assumption is not likely to hold in particular in the case of China as argued above. It is therefore interesting to examine the difference between the two measurement approaches. By subtracting Eq. (8.7) from Eq. (8.8) and rearranging the so-derived equation, we can actually show how the aggregate TFP growth is attributable to the productivity performance of individual industries and the effect of capital and labor mobility across industries:

$$v^T = \left(\sum_j \frac{\overline{w}_j}{\overline{v}_j^V} v_j^T \right)$$

$$+ \left(\sum_j \overline{w}_j \frac{\overline{v}_j^K}{\overline{v}_j^V} \Delta \ln K_j - \overline{v}_K \Delta \ln K \right) \quad (8.9)$$

$$+ \left(\sum_j \overline{w}_j \frac{\overline{v}_j^L}{\overline{v}_j^V} \Delta \ln L_j - \overline{v}_L \Delta \ln L \right)$$

Eq. (8.9) expresses the aggregate TFP growth, v^T, in terms of three sources: Domar-weighted industry TFP growth, the reallocation effect of capital across industries, and the reallocation effect of labor across industries. This Domar weighting scheme $(\overline{w}_j \big/ \overline{v}_j^V)$, originated by Domar (1961), plays a key role in the direct aggregation across industries in the Jorgensonian growth accounting framework.

A direct consequence of the Domar aggregation is that the weights do not sum to unity, implying that aggregate productivity growth can be different from the weighted average of industry-level productivity growth. This reflects the fact that productivity change in the production of intermediate inputs does not only have an *own* effect but in addition it leads to reduced or increased prices in downstream industries, and that effect *accumulates* through vertical links. As elaborated by Hulten (1978), the Domar aggregation establishes a consistent link between the industry-level productivity growth and the aggregate productivity growth. Productivity gains of the aggregate economy may exceed the average productivity gains across industries because flows of intermediate inputs between industries contribute to aggregate productivity by allowing productivity gains in successive industries to augment one another. However, the same logic can explain productivity losses.

The next two terms of Eq. (8.9) capture the reallocation effects of capital and labor across industries on the aggregate TFP growth, respectively. The reallocation term is obtained by subtracting cost-weighted aggregate factor input growth from the Domar-weighted input growth across industries. It should be noted that when these terms are not negligible, it indicates that industries do not face the same factor costs, hence suggesting a violation of the stringent assumption of the widely used APF approach. However, one should not expect a significant reallocation effect in an economy where there is a well-developed or fully competitive market system. This is a very useful analytical tool for the Chinese case where government interventions in resource allocation may have caused severe market distortions and thus reduced productivity.

8.3 Major data and measurement issues

This APPF-Domar growth accounting framework requires economy-wide industry-level productivity accounts that are coherently integrated with the national accounts of outputs and inputs. The CIP Database 3.0 is the first of its kind that offers such systematic productivity accounts for the Chinese economy (CIP, 2015).[5] It has a full coverage of the economy with 37 industries for the period 1980–2010. This CIP database is further revised and updated to 2016 for the present study in order to more sufficiently compare China's post-GFC growth and productivity performance with that of the pre-GFC period. It should be, however, noted that my revision and updating for this study are still preliminary and subject to further changes when new input–output accounts are available. In what follows, I shall briefly introduce the key procedures in the construction of CIP 3.0 database while summarizing the recent revision and extension of the data.

8.3.1 How is the CIP database related to official statistics?

Before we proceed further it is necessary to emphasize the basic source-data rule that

---

[5] See Wu and Ito (2015), Wu, Yue and Zhang (2015) (also Wu and Yue, 2012), and Wu (2015) for the construction of output and prices, labor quantitative and compensation matrices, and capital stock and services, respectively.

governs the construction of the CIP database. That is, the CIP Project in principle does not challenge the national aggregates of major input or output variables reported in official statistics. After necessary adjustments for inconsistencies in concept, coverage, and classification in line with the KLEMS principles, such aggregates are used as "control totals" to confine the data construction (filling gaps and repairing broken series etc.) at subnational levels so that the (underlying) coherence between the national aggregates and the values of subnational levels is maintained. In this sense, the industry productivity accounts provided by the CIP database are essentially *reconstructed* official accounts rather than alternative accounts that are independent of the official accounts.

This point is particularly important when considering that Chinese official data may contain severe flaws caused by methodological deficiencies and political incentives as found and discussed in the literature such as by Maddison and Wu (2008) and Wu (2013, 2014a,b), among others. Nevertheless, due to lack of necessary information, it is impossible to tackle such flaws at subnational or industry level of details with alternative estimates. Therefore, CIP data users should always bear in mind that there could be potential biases in their results. For example, if official growth estimates were indeed exaggerated, any CIP data-based TFP estimates are inevitably upward biased.

8.3.2 Gross output, intermediate inputs, and value added

In theory, gross output flows are total (nominal) costs that the economy paid for all services provided by the primary factors (stocks of capital and labor) and intermediate materials in the current period. That is, the value of gross output consists of two components: newly added value that is equal to the compensation for the primary factors, and the cost of intermediate inputs. As elaborated in the methodology section, the two components are indivisible in the production theory. It is the intermediate inputs that not only link and integrate individual industries to produce the final output (value added) as expressed by Eq. (8.7), but also translate productivity changes of individual industries accumulatively into the economy's aggregate productivity performance as expressed by Eq. (8.9). Therefore, a theoretically sound data work to construct output accounts for APPF-Domar growth accounting should not exclude intermediate inputs.

There are no standard annual national accounts in Chinese official statistics that include both output and intermediate inputs. Besides, the limited information provided by the Chinese national accounts neither gives industry details of the manufacturing sector nor shows breakdowns of value added into the compensations of labor and capital. The more useful sources of data are Chinese input—output tables (IOTs) that are available at current prices in the form of full accounts every 5 years since 1987 and also in the reduced form between two consecutive full accounts. The Chinese IOTs since 1987, including corresponding supply and use tables (SUTs), have in principle followed the concept of the United Nations System of National Accounts (SNA). In addition, there is also a set of IOTs for 1981 constructed in line with the concept of Material Product System (MPS) (Wu and Ito, 2015).

Our procedures of constructing Chinese national accounts in CIP 3.0 include four major steps as follows. Firstly, the 1981 IOTs were converted from the MPS standard to the SNA standard to ensure that all available IOTs were conceptually consistent. Meanwhile, the similar conversion is applied to the annual national accounts prior to 1992 that were published in line with the MPS principles to ensure that the national accounts are consistent with the IOTs (Wu and Ito, 2015). Secondly, the aggregate value added or GDP at current prices with broad sector breakdowns of the national accounts was defined as the boundary of all economic activities.[6] Thirdly, the 2011 version of the Chinese Standard Industrial Classification (CSIC) was adopted to reclassify both the IOTs in benchmarks and national accounts in time series into the same 37 industries. The 2011 CSIC basically satisfies the prevailing International Standard Industrial Classification (ISIC Rev. 4, United Nations, 2008), taking into account data availability in Chinese statistics (Appendix Table 8.A1). Finally, using a SUT-RAS program,[7] a time series of Chinese IOTs were constructed by adopting the sectoral aggregates of the national accounts as the "control totals" and the IOTs as the "control structures" at benchmarks, as well as the interpolations between the benchmarks (Wu and Ito, 2015).

There were six reconstructed full IOT accounts available in the CIP 3.0 database (1981, 1987, 1992, 1997, 2002, and 2007), plus four reduced IOT accounts (1990, 1995, 2000, and 2005). There are, however, three new IOTs that were released after CIP 3.0, including a full IOT account for 2012 and two reduced IOT accounts for 2010 and 2015. To construct a new data set for the current study focusing on the period from the early 1990s to the present, I first revisit all the benchmark IOTs from 1992 and then, after necessary revisions, integrate these new IOTs and national accounts with the previous accounts to obtain a new IOT series for the period 1991−2016.[8]

8.3.3 Producer prices and the deflation approach

There is no ready-for-use producer price index (PPI) in Chinese statistics that exactly match our 37-industry output accounts. The official industry PPIs are compiled for the industrial sector only. Official price surveys for the industrial sector are conducted among enterprises that are satisfied by the officially defined output (value of annual sales) threshold. When constructing CIP 3.0, I assumed that enterprises below the threshold faced the same prices as those above it, and the changes of the threshold did not affect such an assumption. PPI for agriculture was constructed using production cost−based farm gate prices of major products and PPI for construction was constructed as weighted average of the prices of capital goods for construction and installation and the nominal wage of construction workers. Finally, PPIs for individual services were constructed based on relevant components of consumer price index (CPI) (Wu and Ito, 2015).

In the revision and update of the price data for this study, taking into account that the price increase of the CPI components for nonmarket services (government administration, education, and health care services) has been considerably slower than the increase of nominal wages of these services especially since the 2000s, the previous CPI component-based PPIs are replaced by nominal wage index to better reflect the reality of price changes of these services.

---

[6] The classification of national accounts evolved over time beginning with the broadest trichotomy, i.e., primary, secondary, and tertiary, to five divisions, and now a classification of 19 sectors. See the following discussion of the classification of employment for details, as well as footnotes 7 and 8.

[7] SUT-RAS is a biproportional method specifically designed for joint projection of SUTs that are immediately consistent (Temurshoev and Timmer, 2011). In Wu and Ito (2015), SUT-RAS is used to project a SUT series for China first and based on which reconstruct a series of IOTs.

[8] It should be noted that since Chinese full IOT accounts are more reliable than reduced IOT accounts, my estimates may be revised particularly for the period between 2012 and 2017 when the 2017 full IOT accounts become available, and structure-wise the period can be more properly anchored.

When the CIP 3.0 database was first used in analysis (Wu, 2016), the nonstandard single-deflation approach was adopted in order to compare the widely used APF framework with official aggregate data taken for granted. This means that an industry's input (purchaser) price was (implicitly) assumed the same as its output (producer) price. In the current study, I abandon this single-deflation approach and accept the standard double-deflation approach in order to better account for the changes of prices, hence the changes of the real value added. With the double-deflation approach, an industry's average input price is estimated as a weighted average of the producer prices of all industries that provide this industry with inputs.

8.3.4 Measuring labor input

The core issue in measuring labor input is how to hold the quality of hours worked constant when there are actually changes in the composition of the age, gender, education, occupation, and industry of the workforce. If this is ignored, in the case of an improving labor quality, the growth of labor input will be underestimated and thereby the growth of TFP will be exaggerated. In theory, the correct solution is to convert economy-wide heterogeneous hours worked into homogenous volume of labor input by weighting different types of labor with their marginal products, in which the aggregate labor costs are ultimately controlled by the national income accounts.

The CIP Project faces two major problems in the data work on labor. One is how to construct the aggregate number of employment by type of labor and distribute them into industries with historical consistencies in concept, coverage, and classification. The other is how to compensate for the services of all types of labor given the available national income accounts for labor. We took four steps to solve the problems and hence accomplish China's first-ever labor accounts with labor quantitative and compensation matrices in time series.

In the first step, using all available population census data (usually with a 10-year interval) as well as one-percent population surveys (with a 5-year interval) between the censuses, we began with a scrutiny of the total employment data in official labor statistics, available at different and inconsistent breakdowns of broad sectors at various levels, and then conducted revisions to restore consistency first for the three broad sectors following the trichotomic classification of the official labor statistics, that is, the primary, secondary, and tertiary sectors,[9] and then for five divisions by further splitting the secondary sector into the industrial and construction sectors, and slitting the tertiary sector into two categories, i.e., "material services" and "nonmaterial services," [10] to match the broadest classification of national accounts in which the longest historical data are available (for details see Wu, 2014a,b).

With the numbers employed in the three broad sectors and in the five divisions in parallel as "control totals," the second step is to reconcile the numbers employed of the 37 CIP industries

[9] The primary sector includes broad agricultural activities, i.e., crop farming, animal husbandry, and fishery; the secondary sector includes mining, manufacturing, utilities, and construction; and the tertiary sector covers all services of both market and nonmarket.

[10] The "material" and "nonmaterial" dichotomy of services is to distinguish services with and without direct "physical extension." Commerce (wholesales and retails), transportation, and post and telecommunication are classified as "material services" because they physically extend the production of goods. The rest services are considered "nonmaterial" because they rely more on human embodied professional knowledge or skills to serve either consumers, businesses, or the society.

with these "control totals." The available industry employment statistics is incomplete because it covers only enterprises that meet the official output threshold measured by annual sales. Since small-sized enterprises tend to use more labor-intensive technologies even within the same industry, we cannot simply assume that the distribution of employment below the threshold is the same as that above the threshold. To solve the problem, following Wu and Yue (2012) we first derived the total numbers employed below the threshold for each broad sector or division, and then redistributed it according to the structure of labor-intensive industries available from various surveys on rural enterprises and small enterprises.

The third step is to construct a quantitative matrix that concurrently cross-classifies total numbers employed by gender, age, education, and industry, and then convert it to a parallel but the same matrix in hours worked. Given the availability of Chinese employment and labor compensation data, this could only be attempted for limited benchmarks for which data from population censuses and surveys are available. As explained in Wu et al. (2015), a full-dimension quantitative matrix for one benchmark could be constructed based on marginal or partial matrices from a population census or survey by the iterative proportional filling approach developed in Wu and Yue (2012). In CIP 3.0 we established seven such full-dimension benchmark matrices (i.e., 1982, 1987, 1990, 1995, 2000, 2005, and 2010). Eventually, after performing interpolations between these benchmark matrices, we constructed China's first-ever full labor accounts in time series.[11]

In CIP 3.0, the conversion from numbers employed to hours worked also began with constructing the same benchmarks using various information on hours worked by industry, region (urban vs. rural), and ownership type (useful when processing other labor information by size of enterprises and degree of state controls), sourced from the 2000 and 2010 population censuses, the 1995 and 2005 one-percent population surveys, and surveys of households and workers provided by the 1988 and 1995 CHIP database (China Household Income Project, see Li et al., 2008) and the 2007 and 2009 RUMiC database (Rural-Urban Migration in China, see Akgüc et al., 2013), together with Wu and Yue (2012)'s work on changes in the government's institutional working hours and stylized facts-based assumptions about the extent to which individual industries within the industrial sector might deviate from the institutional baseline. We then constructed the accounts for hours worked in time series with the same interpolation approach as that used in constructing the accounts for numbers employed (Wu et al., 2015).

The last step is to construct a full-dimension labor compensation matrix that exactly matches the quantitative matrix in numbers and in hours, which is a key step to the estimation of homogenous hours. In CIP 3.0 we used the share of labor compensation in value added of the reconstructed benchmark IOTs to derive income structures in time series, and then based on this we estimated the value of labor compensation for each industry to control for the total amount paid for all types of labor of that industry in a given period of time (Wu and Ito, 2015). Our information on the compensation of each labor type specified by gender, age group, and education level is insufficient. We first run the Mincer function regression models to estimate the partial effect of each of the human capital attributes on the average wage by industry to fill the gaps

---

[11] In constructing the time series for labor, extrapolations are also used to accomplish the part of the series beyond the first and/or the last matrix by assuming the same structure of the nearest matrix holds. This is applied to the series of numbers employed, hours worked, and labor compensation in the following discussions.

or missing cells in each of the benchmark matrices, and then applied interpolations to construct China's labor compensation accounts in time series (Wu et al., 2015).

For the present study, after revisiting the work in CIP 3.0 with minor revisions especially from 1991 onward, we add a new 2015 benchmark using the official 2015 one-percent population survey and the 2013 CHIP database to update the quantitative matrix in numbers employed and hours worked and together with a full IOT accounts for 2012 and two reduced IOT accounts for 2010 and 2015 to update the compensation matrix. With new benchmarks established with these new source data, I have constructed a new version of China's labor accounts for the period 1991—2016.

8.3.5 Measuring capital input

CIP's attempt to construct China's net capital stock at industry level has proved the most challenging of all the data tasks in the project. First of all, unlike the output and labor accounts, there is no "control total" whatsoever that can be used as a boundary of China's capital stock at historical costs or economy-wide "original value of fixed assets" or OVFA as termed in official investment statistics. The available industry-level OVFA is only for the industrial sector and covers only enterprises above the output threshold (refer to the previous discussion of output and labor in this regard). Furthermore, official investment statistics provides no connection at all between OVFA and the official flow concept of "total investment in fixed assets" or TIFA. In fact, as shown in Wu (2014a,b, 2015), although TIFA suffers from severe double counting problem, it has somehow remained in official statistics after China adopted SNA in the early 1990s in parallel to the SNA concept of gross fixed capital formation or GFCF.[12] Yet, even the official GFCF could be exaggerated by improperly including *on-going* capital construction as *completed* investment rather than inventories as required by SNA (Xu, 1999: 62—63).[13]

The CIP work on capital started with the industrial sector. To bypass the problem of double counting and likely overreporting in the official investment statistics, I had to use a bottom-up approach to reconstruct the investment flow by industry. The core variable was OVFA in official industrial statistics covering fixed assets already engaged in production.[14] Since OVFA was reported on an annual basis, the data for the variable must be collected at the end of the year. I therefore assumed that it did not include the fixed assets that had retired before the end of the year, and constructed the nominal investment by taking the first difference of the OVFA series at industry level and adjusted it for assets withdrawn from production services by a hypothetical industry-specific asset retirement

---

[12] Wu (2014a,b) shows that TIFA surpassed GFCF in the beginning of the 2000s and became more than 1.5 times GFCF after about a decade later.

[13] The general SNA principle governing the time of recording and valuating GFCF is "when the ownership of the fixed assets is transferred to the institutional unit that intends to use them in production" (CEC et al., 1993: 223).

[14] OVFA is available in four types of assets: "equipment," "structures for production," "structures for housing and auxiliary services" (typical for state enterprises in centrally planned economies), and "others." In CIP 3.0, "structures for housing and auxiliary services" were dropped and "others" were allocated to equipment and productive structures according to the compositions of equipment and structures (Wu, 2014a,b and 2015). To simplify the discussion in this data brief, we discuss the OVFA-based data construction as if there were only one asset type. The same assumption is applied to the later discussion of the nonindustrial sectors based on NIFA.

function (Wu, 2014a,b, 2015). The resulted nominal investment series was then deflated by industry-specific price deflators constructed based on asset price survey data by the Chinese Ministry of Finance (ECNH, 2002; Wu, 2014a,b, 2015 for details).

To obtain the net capital stock for each industry, CIP 3.0 used a framework that followed the perpetual inventory method (PIM) with an assumed geometric depreciation function. The PIM required industry-specific initial net stock was estimated based on China's first asset census in 1951 (SETC, 2000, Vol. 1; see Wu, 2014a,b for details), and depreciation rate was estimated based on industry-specific asset service lives and the declining balance rate adopted in the US national accounts following the approach developed by Hulten and Wykoff (1981). Finally, the capital stock of the enterprises below the official output threshold for each industry was added by hypothetical capital–labor ratio based on financial information on small enterprises from various economic censuses, assuming that such enterprises used more labor-intensive technology compared to those above the threshold (Wu, 2015).

For the nonindustrial sectors, including agriculture, construction to all services, in the absence of OVFA, the CIP Project adopted official statistics on "newly increased fixed assets" or NIFA. By nature, NIFA is a result of investment in previous periods eventually turned into fixed assets in the current production. Thus, it is closer to the first difference of OVFA than to TIFA or GFCF. However, for the industrial sector NIFA is not available at industry level, thus I cannot investigate how close the two indicators are. There is no clear information on the coverage of NIFA. In CIP 3.0, I assumed that NIFA had a full coverage and deflated it by a deflator constructed as a weighted average of the PPIs of producer-goods (equipment and building materials) industries and CPI to capture labor cost in installation. To construct the net capital stock for each industry of the nonindustrial sectors using the PIM model, I estimated the initial capital stock in 1980 following the steady-state growth model approach (Wu, 2015) and adopted the US industry-specific depreciation rates that were used by the Bureau of Economic Analysis (BEA) (Kaze and Herman, 1997: 72-3 following Hulten and Wykoff, 1981).

Finally, the quantity of services provided by the so-constructed net capital stock for the Chinese economy should be priced by the user cost of capital *a la* Jorgenson (1963) that is equal to the present value of the rents generated by the capital stock with an adjustment for the depreciation of capital. In practice, following Jorgenson and Griliches (1967) I imposed constant returns to scale to obtain an implied nominal rate of returns that ensures the accounting identity between the aggregate of value added and the sum of capital and labor compensation to hold.[15] The estimated asset- and industry-specific user costs were used to weight heterogeneous capital services across Chinese industries so that the aggregate capital input in the Chinese economy could be measured in line with the neo-classical production theory (Wu, 2015).

For the present study, like what I have done for the output and labor input data, data for measuring capital input are also revised and updated using recent official statistics on OVFA and NIFA and the capital compensation matrix in my extended IOT accounts for the period 2010–16.

---

[15] In fact, it is only at this point that the assumption of constant returns is absolutely required for the measurement of TFP (for an elaboration also see Hulten, 2001).

8.4 Industry grouping and periodization

8.4.1 Industry grouping

To better investigate the TFP performance of industries, following Wu (2016) I categorize the CIP 37 industries into eight groups guided by their "distances" from the end market (Table 8.A1). I argue that whether or to what extent the government may use administrative interference and what types of subsidization depend on the distance of an industry from the final demand, especially from the international market. Indirect subsidies, largely in the form of "underpaid costs," are mainly used by local governments to promote export-oriented manufacturers that make semifinished and finished goods (Huang and Tao, 2010; Wu, 2016). Most of them are downstream industries and labor-intensive, therefore crucial for China to timely reap its demographic dividend. However, the state tends to directly get involved in upperstream industries such as energy and primary input materials that are deemed strategically important in supporting downstream industries. In this sense the "distance" from the end market mirrors the "distance" from the government or the magnitude of the state intervention.

I first categorize the 24 industries within the industrial sector into three groups, namely "(broad) energy" including coal and gas mining, petroleum and utilities, "commodities and primary input materials (C&P)" such as basic metals, chemicals and building materials, and "semifinished and finished goods (SF&F)" such as wearing apparel, electrical equipment, and machinery. "C&P" and especially "SF&F" have been the key drivers of China growth since the reform. Their "distances" from the final demand also reflect their positions in the production

chain. The "energy" group is located on the very top of the stream, followed by "C&P," and then "SF&F." Note that the finished goods part of "SF&F" manufacturers is the closest to, if not exactly, the final consumer-market producers, but it cannot be separated because of the limitation of the available data.

All the nonindustrial sectors are divided into five groups though their "location" on the production chain cannot be clearly defined. The agricultural sector not only serves the final demand market but also provides intermediate inputs to food processing and manufacturing industries and as such can be an important channel for government policies. Construction industry also delivers both investment and consumer goods. All service industries are categorized into three groups yet no clear-cut between consumer and producer goods markets. Services I consists of state-monopolized services including financial intermediaries, transportation, and telecommunication services. Services II includes the rest of market services, and Services III is composed of all "nonmarket services" including government administration, education, and health care.

8.4.2 Periodization

Considering major policy regime shifts in China following the reform as well as external shocks to the Chinese economy, I divide the entire period under investigation into five subperiods, namely 1991−96, 1997−2001, 2002−07, 2008−11, and 2011−16 with conjectures about the likely impacts of these changes on China's growth and productivity performance in each subperiod.[16] This may better help understand China's reform-induced industrialization course in which China first emerged as the world

---

[16] The estimated growth rate or contribution to growth for each subperiod reported in Tables 8.1, 8.2, and Tables 8.A2.1 and 8.A2.2 is based on the end time point of the previous subperiod.

largest manufacturing powerhouse, and then struggled with severe imbalance problems in the world economy that has been substantially shaped by China's participation.

The period 1991–96 began with Deng's famous reform-promoting southern China trip in 1992. One year after, the Communist Party's Politburo Standing Committee adopted its own version of the "socialist market economy" model. Domestic market liberalization and further opening up to foreign trade and direct investment suddenly boosted up China's unprecedented investment wave. Meanwhile, the reform of state-owned enterprises (SOEs) was deepened in a state campaign of "*zhua da fang* xiao," literally "enhancing the big (enterprises) while liberalizing the small (enterprises)." Nevertheless, newly emerged private firms absorbed a huge number of state employees who lost their jobs in the SOE reforms. We may expect to see a strong growth and a significant productivity grain during this period.

Next, we use the Asian financial crisis in 1997–98 to mark the beginning of the period 1997–2001 that first suffered from the AFC shock and then a long course of deflation due to huge surplus capacity caused by restless and excessive investment in the previous period.[17] However, this could be also the first time at which China was forced to accept a market-driven restructuring when the government was fiscally poor. We may therefore expect to see an improved TFP performance despite a growth slowdown. At the end of 2001, with a favorable resolution China was accepted as a formal member of the WTO, which was indeed timely to help the economy get rid of its lengthy and painful deflation course.

I then define the period 2002–2007 as China's post-WTO. This period could be characterized by two counteracting forces that shaped the economy. On one hand, China's WTO entry induced a wider and deeper opening up of the economy to the international trade and direct investment market, hence directing the economy toward a more market-driven competition. On the other hand, ironically, China's agitatedly embracing the world economy enhanced the role of the government as well. As consolidated and enlarged state corporations resurged in the name of protecting national interests in the time of an accelerating globalization through fierce international competition, growth-motivated local governments were pressured and then impatiently race for more rapid urbanization and heavy industrialization. We may thus conjecture that China's post-WTO period may have to inevitably sacrifice some productivity growth for a faster output growth.

China's post-WTO period was ended by the GFC. I somehow intend to divide the post-GFC period into two subperiods to distinguish the early post-GFC period 2008–11, characterized by the government's unprecedented fiscal stimulus package to moderate the GFC shock, from the late post-GFC period 2012–16 in which the government struggled to solve the problem of severe structural imbalances in surplus capacity, high debt leverage, environment damage, income inequality, corruption, and social injustices that were in essence caused by severe misallocation of resources for the sake of growth. Nevertheless, political barriers, institutional constraints, and vested interest groups have complicated the problem and obstructed the genuine search for a more efficient and apparently market-based solution. We may expect to see an obvious deceleration of output growth albeit it may still be somewhat disguised by official statistics, and perhaps an absolute decline in TFP.

---

[17] China's retail price index (RPI) declined from 380.8 in 1997 (1978 = 100) to 347.0 in 2002 and meanwhile PPI declined from 315.0 to 292.6 (NBS, 2018).

8.5 Discussion of empirical results

8.5.1 China's growth performance estimated in the APPF framework

We are now ready to examine China's aggregate GDP and TFP performance in the APPF framework. The results are summarized in two panels of Table 8.1 with industry and factor contributions to the real output growth, respectively. In the top line of the table, I show that the Chinese economy achieved a real output growth by 8.4% per annum for the entire period from 1991 to 2016. Of the 8.4% annual growth of GDP, "SF&F," "C&P," and Services II (market services) accounted for about 35, 21, and 21%,[18] respectively, suggesting that China obviously experienced a manufacturing-led rapid expansion that was also accompanied by a rapid rise of market-induced services over the whole period in question.

It should be nonetheless pointed out first that despite that I use basically the same official national accounts data I am unable to obtain the officially claimed growth rate of 9.9% per annum for the period 1991–2016 (NBS, 2018). Apparently, my double-deflation procedures have corrected part of the errors in the official growth rate estimation that in my view are caused by improper measure of price changes and (mis) use of the single-deflation approach, regardless deliberate data manipulations for political purposes. I find that including the earlier reform period from 1980 causes little change to my estimate, i.e., slightly to 8.5% per annum for the period 1980–2016. I can thus confidently confirm that the widely perceived China's persistent 10% annual growth performance since the reform is merely a statistical artifact judged by strict national accounting double procedures in the Jorgensonian APPF framework.

8.5.2 Contribution of industries to China's growth

The upper panel of Table 8.1 shows noteworthy changes in the (weighted) contribution to growth by industry groups over different subperiods. Importantly, these changes reflect a significant restructuring of the economy over time. Driven by unprecedented reforms and opening up the economy experienced the most rapid growth in 1991–96 of the entire period, achieving an aggregate GDP growth rate at 10.2% per annum in which manufacturing played a dominant role with 44.4% that was attributable to "SF&F" (4.54 percentage points or ppts) and 20.5% to "C&P" (2.09 ppts).[19] Such a growth spurt also caused construction industry to surge with a contribution over 10.6% (1.08 ppts) to the growth.

Unfortunately, the Asian financial crisis shocked the economy in 1997 and induced a contraction with a significant structural adjustment. Compared to the period 1991–96, the period 1996–2001 observed the growth contribution by "SF&F" retreated considerably to 30.4% (2.33 ppts) and the contribution of construction industry even turned negative to -1.2% (or -0.09 ppts). In the meantime, the contribution of agriculture changed inversely jumping to 21.9% (1.68 ppts) from 9.3% (0.95 ppts) in the previous period, suggesting a huge number of migrant workers left manufacturing and construction and returned to farming. However, this suggests that the government could somehow accept a more market-based restructuring of the economy during the crisis.

---

[18] The growth contributions in percent are calculated based on the estimates in ppts (percentage points) for individual industries in Table 8.1. The same calculations are conducted hereafter.

[19] For industry details within a group, see Tables 8.A2.1 and 8.A2.2 in Appendix that focus on comparisons between the pre-GFC period 1991–2007 and the post-GFC period 2007–16.

TABLE 8.1 Estimated Industry and Factor Contributions to China's Value-Added Growth (Contributions in percentage points or ppts).

	1991–96	1996–2001	2001–07	2007–11	2011–16	1991–2016
Value-added growth (APPF, %)	10.23	7.66	10.06	8.16	5.61	8.42
Industry contribution (ppts)						
Agriculture	0.95	1.68	0.37	0.12	0.26	0.68
Construction	1.08	−0.09	0.56	0.50	0.29	0.47
Energy group	−0.22	0.39	0.52	0.32	0.35	0.28
Commodities and primary materials (C&P)	2.09	1.88	1.58	1.60	1.74	1.78
Semifinished and finished (SF&F)	4.54	2.33	3.66	2.85	1.05	2.92
Services I (state monopolies)	0.61	0.24	1.72	1.56	1.45	1.12
Services II	1.12	1.32	2.62	2.40	1.39	1.78
Services III (nonmarket)	0.05	−0.08	−0.96	−1.18	−0.93	−0.61
Factor contribution (ppts)						
Capital input:	7.98	4.88	8.48	9.33	7.08	7.52
Net stock	*7.94*	*5.18*	*8.54*	*9.32*	*7.09*	*7.58*
Capital composition	*0.04*	*−0.29*	*−0.06*	*0.01*	*−0.01*	*−0.07*
Labor input:	1.48	1.13	0.65	0.64	0.40	0.86
Hours	*0.63*	*0.97*	*0.59*	*−0.64*	*0.03*	*0.36*
Labor composition	*0.86*	*0.16*	*0.06*	*1.28*	*0.37*	*0.50*
Aggregate TFP	0.77	1.64	0.94	−1.81	−1.86	0.05

Note: The figures in the first line are equal to the sum of industry contributions in the first panel and the sum of factor contributions in the second panel, respectively.

APPF, aggregate production possibility frontier; *TFP*, total factor productivity.

Source: *Author's estimates.*

A new wave of structural changes took place following China's post-WTO period 2001–07. Notwithstanding China's wider and deeper opening up to the international trade and investment under WTO, "SF&F" bounced back with 30.4% (or 3.66 ppts) contribution to the aggregate GDP growth, though not able to resume its pre-AFC position. It is not surprising to see that the role of agriculture dropped to a historical low at 3.7% (0.37 ppts), again suggesting that migrant workers quickly rejoined manufacturing and construction. "C&P"

appeared to be still adjusting for overcapacity, but "energy" maintained its contribution (accordingly up from 0.39 to 0.52 ppts with an overall accelerated growth). The most noteworthy is the substantial increase in the role of the state-dominated Services I, including transportation, telecommunication, and financial services, up considerably by at least fivefold from 3.2 to 17.1% of the aggregate growth (from 0.24 to 1.72 ppts). Meanwhile, the contribution by more market-determined Services II also rose from 17.2 to 26.0% (from 1.32 to 2.62 ppts).

The subsequent changes were caused by the GFC. Despite the government's unprecedented stimulus, China's GDP growth slowed down by nearly 2% points to 8.2% per annum in 2007–11. Thanks to the government's endeavor, this early post-GFC period appears to have largely maintained a pattern of growth contribution within the industrial sector that was similar to that of the previous period after China's WTO entry. Some changes are nonetheless worth a good attention. Firstly, the agricultural sector no longer served as a buffer as during the AFC. Despite the GFC shock, agriculture continued declining and lost 60% of its contribution to growth with only 1.4% (0.12 ppts). Secondly, while "SF&F" maintained its position in the growth of 35.0% (2.85 ppts), "C&P" advanced to 19.6% (1.60 ppts). This suggests that the majority of government capital injections went to "C&P" that was subject to more state interventions rather than "SF&F" that was more exposed to the market. Given already severe surplus capacity in Chinese manufacturing, such a change may reflect the move of the economy toward more intermediate materials–using industries such as real estate and infrastructure construction, which further distorted the structure of the economy.

The late post-GFC period 2011–16 saw a puzzling position swap between more government-influenced "C&P" and more market-exposed "SF&F." While the contribution of "SF&F" dropped sharply to 18.8% (1.05 ppts), "C&P" jumped to 29.4% (1.74 ppts). In the meantime, state-monopolized Services I also increased its contribution to the growth to 25.9% (1.45 ppts), but more market-determined Services II lost some strength to 24.8% (1.39 ppts). These observations will be further examined with the industry origin of the TFP performance in Table 8.2.

8.5.3 Contribution of factors to China's growth

My estimates of China's sources of growth are reported in the lower panel of Table 8.1. A quick glance at the average figures of the entire period in question already confirms the physical investment–driven nature of China's postreform economic growth. Of the 8.4% annual output growth rate, the contribution of the growth of capital and labor inputs was 7.52 ppts and 0.86 ppts, respectively, leaving TFP growth with merely 0.05 ppts. This means that 89.2% of China's real value-added growth relied on capital input growth and 10.2% on labor input growth, hence suggesting little that could be explained by the improvement of TFP. This finding will undoubtedly cause controversies. To develop a convincing explanation, it is important to scrutinize the dynamics of China's sources of growth against a background of major policy regime shifts and macroeconomic shocks. In what follows in this subsection, I focus my productivity analysis on changes in factor contributions in the economy at aggregate level, leaving the industry origin analysis to the next subsection.

As shown in Table 8.1, the period 1996–2001 is the only one that underwent a substantial slowdown in the contribution of capital input growth (63.8%, calculated using the reported 4.88 ppts in Table 8.1, the same hereafter) to a level that was below the average of the entire period (89.2% or 7.52 ppts) and that of the previous period (78.0% or 7.98 ppts). This may well indicate a further reduction in state interventions in the allocation of resources. Notably, during this period the economy was forced to adjust for overcapacity in the wake of AFC, as well as to reduce regulations that were not in line with the WTO principles in order to achieve a favorable resolution for China's application for the WTO membership. Therefore, the Chinese economy could have enjoyed a more market-oriented institutional environment. Besides, the highest contribution of labor input (14.8% or 1.13 ppts) observed over the whole time span of my investigation, which could be China's last harvest of its demographic dividend (Cai, 2010), may also support this point of view. These factors may

TABLE 8.2   Domar-weighted total factor productivity (TFP) growth and reallocation effects in the Chinese economy (growth rate in percent per annum and contributions in ppts corresponding to the growth).

	1991–96	1996–2001	2001–07	2007–11	2011–16	1991–2016
Aggregate TFP growth (%)	0.77	1.64	0.94	−1.81	−1.86	0.05
Industry contribution (ppts)						
1. Domar-weighted TFP growth	0.14	2.05	0.90	−2.59	−2.21	−0.20
Agriculture	0.60	1.21	0.33	−0.06	0.03	0.44
Construction	0.44	−0.57	0.20	−0.10	−0.20	−0.03
Energy group	−0.94	−0.05	−0.49	−0.55	0.04	−0.39
Commodities and primary materials	0.58	1.88	0.27	−0.03	1.18	0.79
Semifinished and finished	2.24	1.80	1.41	0.34	−0.07	1.19
Services I (state monopolies)	−0.97	−1.08	0.68	0.48	0.24	−0.12
Services II	−1.22	−0.73	0.28	−0.72	−1.97	−0.83
Services III (nonmarket)	−0.60	−0.42	−1.78	−1.95	−1.47	−1.24
Factor reallocation contribution (ppts)						
2. Reallocation of capital input (K)	0.02	−0.49	−1.07	−0.13	−0.15	−0.40
3. Reallocation of labor input (L)	0.61	0.08	1.11	0.91	0.49	0.65

Note: The figures in the first line equal to the sum of items 1, 2, and 3.
Source: *Author's estimates.*

help explain why this period achieved the strongest TFP growth, contributing 21.5% (or 8.32 ppts) of the average 7.7% GDP growth.

The GDP growth rate of China's post-WTO period jumped to 10.1% per annum. Nevertheless, it was the growth of capital input that drove the engine of such a growth spurt. We can see that the contribution of capital input growth increased considerably from 63.8 to 84.3% (or 4.88–8.48 ppts), while the contribution of labor input growth decreased from 14.8 to 6.4% (or 1.13 to 0.65 ppts), leaving the contribution of TFP growth with only 9.3% (or 0.94 ppts). Apparently, something institutional happened in the economy that could have engineered the growth acceleration without worrying about the diminishing returns to capital. In other words, it appears to be that the powerful state-directed or influenced investment projects

exceeded the market capacity and crowded out more efficient private enterprises, hence turning China's TFP growth negative.

This pattern remained unchanged over the early post-GFC period despite the shock. While the GDP growth slowed down to 8.2% per annum over the period 2007–11, the growth of capital input accelerated further to 9.33 ppts, which was not only faster than the 8.48 ppts of the previous period, but also unreasonably overtook the pace of the output growth, being equivalent to 114.3 percent of the growth. It continued in the late post-GFC period 2011–16 in which while the GDP growth decelerated significantly to 5.6% per annum, the excessively high growth of capital input maintained, thus making a 126.3% contribution to China's GDP growth. This is the time when researchers and China observers at large began to concern about

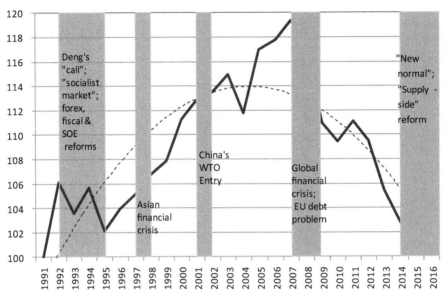

FIGURE 8.1   Losing steam? An index of China's aggregate total factor productivity (1991 = 100). Source: *Constructed based on annual TFP estimates, summarized as averages of subperiods in Table 8.1.*

aggressive advancement of state-owned or connected enterprises at the cost of the private sector (Johansson and Feng, 2016; Du et al., 2014) in the name of adjusting for the "new normal" and implementing "supply-side reforms."[20]

To intuitively trace the path of TFP, I translate annual aggregate TFP growth rates into a level index with the initial point 1991 as the base year as shown in Fig. 8.1. To take into account significant policy regime changes, we mark the initial time point of each regime shift. Note that we do not intend to specify the end point of a policy change, and a "regime period" marked over a span of more than 1 year just indicates that major reforms or policy changes took place consecutively. Fig. 8.1 not only traces China's

actual TFP path alongside marked major policy regime shifts, but more importantly with a provoking underlying (polynomial) trend to highlight China's potential TFP growth path that may help better understand China's TFP performance. It should be born in mind that this trend is estimated given the probable impacts of policies and the prevailing institutional environment.[21]

The rapid TFP spurt in 1992 does not appear to be "normal" because it largely reflects both the "Deng effect" and a recovery from the 1989 Tiananmen shock with a lasting effect over the period 1989—91. This 1992 TFP surge seems to be retarded by two harsh austerity policy attempts in 1993 and 1995 to cool down the

[20] See also the most recent reports in *Economist* on July 20, 2017, and Hong Kong-based *South China Morning Post* on September 21, 2018.

[21] Theoretically, the stage of development can affect the potential TFP growth as well because it determines the room that an economy may gain from imitating existing technologies. However, growth will inevitably slow down at the mature stage when there is little room for imitation and hence income increase will only come from true technological innovations.

overheated economy. The TFP index began to pick up its pace again in 1995 and returned to the underlying trend by the time of China's WTO entry. The estimates of TFP growth in this study have supported our conjecture and rejected the finding by Cao et al. (2009) that there was no TFP growth in the 1990s. I also show that China's post-WTO TFP ride finally peaked in 2007 despite an interruption of another macro-economic policy shock in 2004, but then it shockingly went on along an apparent durable declining path that began with the GFC.

8.5.4 The industry origin of aggregate TFP growth

In order to explicitly account for differences across industries in their impacts on China's aggregate TFP performance, I introduce the Domar weights in the exercise. The TFP growth rates presented in the first line of Table 8.2 are estimated with the stringent assumption that marginal productivities of capital and labor are the same for all industries, which are the same as those presented in the last line of the lower panel of Table 8.1. As expressed in Eq. (8.9), using the Domar weights the estimated aggregate TFP growth rate can be decomposed into three additive components: (1) the change of the Domar-weighted aggregate TFP; (2) the change of capital reallocation effect; and (3) the change of labor reallocation effect. The Domar-weighted TFP growth can be expressed in industry origin and hence help explore the role of individual industries or industry groups in productivity growth. Besides, the two reallocation effects capture the impact of structural changes on productivity growth, which is deemed important in the case of China where strong state interventions cause misallocation of resources.

As Table 8.2 shows, on the average of the entire period 1991–2016, China's TFP growth that could be attributed to industries, as estimated with the Domar weights, is -0.20% per

annum, which means that the pre-GFC positive gains in productivity within industries were completely wiped out by the post-GFC productivity losses. However, the reallocation of labor played a significantly positive role that completely compensated for the TFP loss by the misallocation of capital. In what follows, let us first focus on the roles of industry groups and then return to the factor reallocation effects.

The performances of industry groups are distinctly different, which suggests that treating individual industries homogenous in growth accounting as in the AFP tradition can be rather misleading. On the average of the whole period in question, there are only three groups that played a positive role in productivity growth, i.e., "SF&F" (1.19 ppts), followed by "C&P" (0.79 ppts) and agriculture (0.44 ppts). However, three major loss-making groups, namely Services III (-1.24 ppts), Services II (-0.83 ppts) and "energy" (-0.39 ppts), completely eroded the gains of the positive groups. Such a sharp contrast across industry groups in the Domar-weighted TFP performance can also be observed over different subperiods.

But, before proceeding ahead, we should bear in mind that any change in production cost or market size regardless its cause will change a firm or an industry's productivity performance. In other words, subsidies to reduce the cost of an industry or regulations to protect the market of an industry will raise the industry's productivity, holding all others constant. Nevertheless, how this will be translated into the aggregate TFP is a more complicated issue. In this example, if the crowded out industries are more efficient than those protected, we may expect to see an overall productivity loss.

The agricultural sector was benefited most from the reforms in the 1980s especially from the de facto privatization on farming and deregulations on rural enterprises. In the present study, I show that agriculture contributed significant 0.60 ppts and 1.21 ppts to the Domar-weighted TFP growth at 0.77 and 1.64% per annum in 1991–96 and 1996–2001, respectively. Even in the post-WTO period when the Domar-weighted TFP growth decelerated to 0.94% per annum, agriculture still contributed more than one-third by 0.33 ppts. This means that China was in a process in which the agricultural sector released capital (including land) and labor that had a marginal productivity below the sector's average, hence continuously raising its productivity. But clearly this could not be a source of a long-run growth.

Changes of the roles of the three industrial groups, "SF&F," "C&P," and "energy," in the Domar-weighted TFP growth before and after GFC are worth a careful examination. Before China's WTO entry, Deng's reengineering of the reform drive through the implementation of the "socialist market economy" model seemed to be TFP-promoting. In that course, "SF&F" played the most important role and indeed enjoyed its heydays, contributing 2.24 ppts in 1991–96 and 1.80 ppts in 1996–2001 to the corresponding Domar-weighted TFP growth 0.14 and 2.05% per annum. "C&P" also enjoyed its best TFP performance in the 1990s, contributing 0.58 ppts in 1991–96 and 1.88 ppts in 1996–2001. In a sharp contrast, despite continuous reforms in the 1990s, the "energy" group appeared to be a persistent productivity loser.

The Domar-weighted TFP slowdown following China's WTO participation was almost cross board except for minor improvements in Services I and II and construction. That the total Domar-weighted TFP growth declined from 2.05 ppts in 1996–2001 to 0.90 ppts in 2001–07 looks puzzling because in the meantime GDP accelerated from 7.7% to 10.1% per annum. However, it strongly supports the well-observed increasing government interventions following China's WTO entry, with especially fierce competition between local governments for growth through promoting local urbanization and industrialization (see, for example, Li and Zhou, 2005; Wu, 2008; Xu, 2011). Indeed, while the contribution of "SF&F"

and "C&P" to the TFP growth considerably slowed down, the contribution of construction industry and state-monopolized Services I turned around from -0.57 to 0.20 ppts and from -1.08–0.68 ppts, respectively.

The GFC shock brought about a big change that completely turned this pattern around. In the early post-GFC period 2007–11, the "energy" group remained negative as before, but it surprisingly turned positive in the late post-GFC period 2011–16. Besides, while "C&P" made a huge jump in contribution to the Domar-weighted TFP growth from 0.27 ppts in the post-WTO entry period to 1.18 ppts in the late post-GFC period, "SF&F" first experienced a substantial decline from 1.41 ppts following China's WTO entry to merely 0.34 ppts in the early post-GFC period, and then turned negative at -0.07 ppts in the late post-GFC period.

Given that "energy" and "C&P" are more state dominant (either owned or influenced), my industry-origin findings have to a large extent substantiated the observation of "state advancement, private retreat" (Johansson and Feng, 2016; Du et al., 2014). It appears that private enterprises became the scapegoat in the state campaign to reduce overcapacity. Rising costs forced private firms to withdraw, hence giving more market share to state-owned or government-connected enterprises. Increasing state interventions and the retreat of private firms could be mainly responsible for the loss of productivity in the Chinese economy.

8.5.5 The factor reallocation effect

The distinct differences in TFP performance between industries inevitably induce capital and labor to shift across industries. This is what I find and report in Table 8.2, which may help better understand China's productivity slowdown since the mid-2000s. I show that on the average of the whole period in question, the labor reallocation effect is positive, contributing 0.65 ppts to the aggregate TFP growth, but the capital reallocation effect is negative, contributing -0.40 ppts. In essence, the productivity gain by the reallocation of labor completely compensated for the cost of the misallocation of capital as well as the productivity loss (-0.20 ppts) within industries following Eq. (8.9). To show the dynamic changes in China's TFP, I present the three productivity components in indices in Fig. 8.2.

A quick glance at the indices tells that the reallocation effects of capital and labor moved completely in opposite direction over the entire period in question. The early 1990s was a period in which there was little effect of capital reallocation on productivity despite the reform (0.02 ppts for 1991−96, Table 8.2; the same source hereafter) or the reform-induced changes in investment had not yet really resulted in any noticeable impact on China's productivity growth. The capital reallocation effect turned negative subsequently and substantially in the

late 1990s especially after the AFC shock (-0.49 ppts for 1996−2001) and worsened in the wake of China's WTO entry (-1.07 ppts for 2001-07). As shown in Fig. 8.2, although the magnitude of the capital misallocation reduced after the GFC shock, it had not disappeared by the end of the period. This finding confirms the estimate in my 2016 paper (Wu, 2016) and also that reported in Cao et al. (2009) for the period 1994−2000.

The case of the labor reallocation effect remained generally positive over time. This suggests that on one hand the labor market was much less distorted than the capital market and the economy benefited from increasing labor mobility along with reforms especially the shift from agriculture to industry; on the other hand, since collective bargaining in China was illegal, Chinese labor could be underpaid, hence forced to shift more frequently. Over the post-WTO period 2001−07 the Chinese economy experienced the most significant gain from the

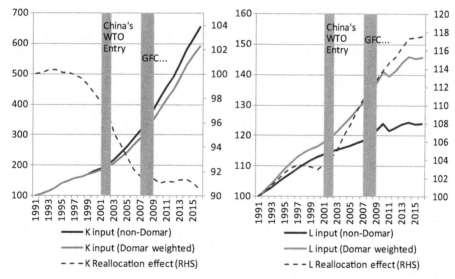

FIGURE 8.2 Domar and non−Domar-weighted factor input and reallocation effects on China's TFP growth (1991 = 100). Source: *Constructed based on annual results that are summarized in Table 8.2.*

reallocation of labor by 1.11 ppts, and this continued with still a strong momentum even in the wake of the GFC, 0.91 ppts for 2007—11 and 0.49 ppts for 2011—16. This finding reflects China's reality and rejects the estimate in Cao et al. (2009) that there was little impact of the reallocation of labor on China's TFP performance throughout the entire period 1980—2000 under their investigation.

Such a magnitude of reallocation effect in the Chinese economy is typically not observed in market economies. For example, based on their empirical work on the US economy in 1977—2000, Jorgenson et al. (2005) showed that firstly, the reallocation effect was generally negligible and secondly, if it was nonnegligible for some subperiods, the capital and labor reallocation effects generally moved in opposite directions. As found in Jorgenson et al. (1987), the reallocation of capital was typically positive and the reallocation of labor was typically negative for the US economy over the period 1948—79. This should be expected because capital grew more rapidly in industries with high capital service prices, hence high returns on capital, whereas labor grew relatively slowly in industries with high marginal compensation. In the case of China, the large magnitude and unexpected sign of capital and labor reallocation effects have important implications. It suggests that Chinese industries indeed face distinctly different factor costs because of too much state interventions and lack of market-based competition that cause serious misallocation of capital in the economy.

8.6 Concluding remarks

In this study I apply the Jorgensonian growth accounting framework, incorporating the Domar aggregation scheme across industries, to a revised and extended CIP database to scrutinize the sources of growth in the Chinese economy following its full-scale industrial reforms that began in the early 1990s. This growth accounting approach provides a highly appropriate analytical tool for investigating the industry origin of the aggregate productivity performance especially its slowdown since the mid-2000s in the Chinese economy.

My findings have confirmed the physical capital investment—driven nature of China's growth during the reform period. I show that of the 8.4% annual GDP growth over the period from 1991 to 2016, the growth of capital input contributed 89.2% and the growth of labor 10.2%, leaving the contribution of TFP growth merely 0.6%. China enjoyed its best TFP performance with an annual growth of 1.64% per annum in the late 1990s when the SOE reforms were deepened, substantial deregulations were carried on to prepare for China's WTO application, and market forces were tolerated in the wake of the Asian financial crisis to adjust for the overcapacity built up in the early 1990s.

However, China's TFP growth began to slowdown following its WTO entry because of increasing state interventions to protect strategic industries and to promote growth. More and more capital resources were directed to state selected industries and crowded out more efficient private enterprises. This made the Chinese economy less capable to adjust for its structural problems in the wake of the GFC. Unlike the substantial productivity improvement when facing the AFC shock, China's productivity growth turned significantly negative following the GFC impact. It is clear that China's TFP decline will not turn positive before the government at all levels is disentangled from the business and the market is allowed to correct for the distorted cost structure of the economy.

8.7 Appendix

TABLE 8.A1 CIP/China KLEMS industrial classification and code.

CIP code	EU-KLEMS code	Grouping	Industry	
1	AtB	Agriculture	Agriculture, forestry, animal husbandry & fishery	AGR
2	10	Energy	Coal mining	CLM
3	11	Energy	Oil & gas excavation	PTM
4	13	C&P	Metal mining	MEM
5	14	C&P	Non-metallic minerals mining	NMM
6	15	Finished	Food and kindred products	F&B
7	16	Finished	Tobacco products	TBC
8	17	C&P	Textile mill products	TEX
9	18	Finished	Apparel and other textile products	WEA
10	19	Finished	Leather and leather products	LEA
11	20	SF&F	Saw mill products, furniture, fixtures	W&F
12	21t22	C&P	Paper products, printing & publishing	P&P
13	23	Energy	Petroleum and coal products	PET
14	24	C&P	Chemicals and allied products	CHE
15	25	SF&F	Rubber and plastics products	R&P
16	26	C&P	Stone, clay, and glass products	BUI
17	27t28	C&P	Primary & fabricated metal industries	MET
18	27t28	SF&F	Metal products (excluding rolling products)	MEP
19	29	Semifinished	Industrial machinery and equipment	MCH
20	31	SF&F	Electric equipment	ELE
21	32	SF&F	Electronic and telecommunication equipment	ICT
22	30t33	SF&F	Instruments and office equipment	INS
23	34t35	Finished	Motor vehicles & other transportation equipment	TRS
24	36t37	Finished	Miscellaneous manufacturing industries	OTH
25	E	Energy	Power, steam, gas and tap water supply	UTL
26	F	Construction	Construction	CON
27	G	Services II	Wholesale and retail trades	SAL
28	H	Services II	Hotels and restaurants	HOT
29	I	Services I	Transport, storage & post services	T&S
30	71t74	Services I	Telecommunication & post	P&T

(Continued)

TABLE 8.A1   CIP/China KLEMS industrial classification and code.—cont'd

CIP code	EU-KLEMS code	Grouping	Industry	
31	J	Services I	Financial intermediations	FIN
32	K	Services II	Real estate services	REA
33	71t74	Services II	Leasing, technical, science & business services	BUS
34	L	Services III	Public administration and defence	ADM
35	M	Services III	Education services	EDU
36	N	Services III	Health and social security services	HEA
37	O&P	Services II	Other services	SER

Note: This is based on Wu's series of works to reclassify official statistics reported under different CSIC systems adopted in CSIC/1972, CSIC/1985, and CSIC/1994 (see Wu and Yue, 2012; Wu and Ito, 2015). The current Chinese classification system CSIC/2011 largely conforms to the 2-digit level industries of the ISIC (Rev. 4) and can be reconciled with the EU-KLEMS system of classification (see Timmer et al., 2007).
Source: *See the text*.

TABLE 8.A2.1   Industry contributions to value-added (VA) and total factor productivity (TFP) growth 1991−2007.

Industry[1]	Value-added			Total factor productivity		
	VA weight	VA growth[2]	Contribution to aggregate VA growth[3]	Domar weight	TFP growth[2]	Contribution to aggregate TFP growth[3,4]
AGR	0.160	5.43	0.96	0.275	2.35	0.69
CLM	0.015	4.38	0.06	0.029	0.35	−0.02
PTM	0.018	−7.25	−0.13	0.027	−12.06	−0.33
MEM	0.005	15.94	0.07	0.013	4.26	0.04
NMM	0.006	12.57	0.08	0.015	3.97	0.06
F&B	0.029	10.78	0.30	0.121	0.59	0.07
TBC	0.010	9.18	0.10	0.016	−0.44	−0.02
TEX	0.024	13.89	0.32	0.104	2.17	0.24
WEA	0.012	13.44	0.14	0.041	0.77	0.03
LEA	0.005	15.52	0.07	0.023	1.22	0.02
W&F	0.007	24.97	0.18	0.028	3.83	0.10
P&P	0.013	14.19	0.18	0.043	1.73	0.07
PET	0.009	7.16	0.04	0.042	−0.55	−0.05
CHE	0.035	17.23	0.61	0.133	2.58	0.34
R&P	0.012	18.29	0.22	0.052	2.13	0.11

TABLE 8.A2.1 Industry contributions to value-added (VA) and total factor productivity (TFP) growth 1991–2007.—cont'd

	Value-added			Total factor productivity		
Industry[1]	VA weight	VA growth[2]	Contribution to aggregate VA growth[3]	Domar weight	TFP growth[2]	Contribution to aggregate TFP growth[3,4]
BUI	0.026	14.49	0.37	0.082	2.62	0.21
MET	0.030	9.74	0.21	0.129	−0.13	−0.09
MEP	0.013	19.78	0.25	0.055	2.66	0.15
MCH	0.032	15.07	0.48	0.113	3.07	0.34
ELE	0.015	19.06	0.28	0.066	2.20	0.12
ICT	0.018	35.39	0.60	0.086	4.71	0.33
INS	0.003	13.61	0.04	0.011	1.31	0.01
TRS	0.019	22.10	0.42	0.077	3.13	0.24
OTH	0.019	23.02	0.44	0.054	4.96	0.30
UTL	0.029	7.02	0.27	0.113	−1.74	−0.10
CON	0.057	9.02	0.52	0.213	0.16	0.03
SAL	0.080	9.52	0.76	0.150	1.28	0.16
HOT	0.021	8.90	0.19	0.054	−1.66	−0.08
T&S	0.056	7.28	0.41	0.109	−2.20	−0.21
P&T	0.016	15.45	0.24	0.028	0.77	0.03
FIN	0.049	5.76	0.26	0.077	−2.06	−0.21
REA	0.042	8.90	0.38	0.055	−9.83	−0.52
BUS	0.022	8.54	0.21	0.048	−1.63	−0.03
ADM	0.034	4.48	0.11	0.069	−2.62	−0.20
EDU	0.027	−10.34	−0.28	0.044	−10.59	−0.47
HEA	0.013	−14.73	−0.20	0.034	−8.86	−0.32
SER	0.021	8.08	0.20	0.046	−1.95	−0.03
Sum	1.000		9.36	2.679		1.02

Notes:

[1] See Table 8.A1 for industry abbreviation.

[2] Value added and TFP growth rates are annualized raw growth rates in percent.

[3] Industry contribution to VA or TFP growth is weighted growth rate in percentage points (ppts).

[4] See Eq. (8.9) for Domar weights.

Source: See Tables 8.1 and 8.2

TABLE 8.A2.2   Industry contributions to value-added and total factor productivity growth 2007—16.

Industry[1]	Value-added			Total factor productivity		
	VA weight	VA growth[2]	Contribution to aggregate VA growth[3]	Domar weight[4]	TFP growth[2]	Contribution to aggregate TFP growth[3,4]
AGR	0.096	2.00	0.20	0.166	−0.08	−0.01
CLM	0.017	7.73	0.12	0.040	0.83	0.01
PTM	0.013	0.56	0.01	0.024	−4.27	−0.11
MEM	0.008	12.53	0.10	0.024	1.37	0.03
NMM	0.005	3.85	0.02	0.014	−0.91	−0.01
F&B	0.029	13.83	0.40	0.155	0.59	0.10
TBC	0.008	9.89	0.08	0.012	0.46	0.01
TEX	0.012	6.54	0.08	0.066	0.81	0.05
WEA	0.008	8.59	0.07	0.036	0.63	0.03
LEA	0.005	8.71	0.04	0.023	0.39	0.01
W&F	0.008	8.03	0.07	0.038	0.05	0.00
P&P	0.009	12.18	0.11	0.038	1.65	0.06
PET	0.012	9.19	0.11	0.065	−0.09	−0.03
CHE	0.032	14.85	0.48	0.167	0.79	0.13
R&P	0.010	11.02	0.11	0.057	1.01	0.06
BUI	0.022	10.79	0.24	0.093	0.56	0.06
MET	0.035	17.67	0.64	0.206	1.57	0.32
MEP	0.012	8.87	0.10	0.060	−0.30	−0.02
MCH	0.030	4.08	0.13	0.138	−0.94	−0.13
ELE	0.017	13.69	0.23	0.099	0.47	0.05
ICT	0.020	14.96	0.31	0.121	1.01	0.13
INS	0.003	5.26	0.02	0.014	−0.02	0.00
TRS	0.024	13.13	0.32	0.121	0.41	0.06
OTH	0.014	−2.28	−0.03	0.043	−4.33	−0.18
UTL	0.024	4.21	0.11	0.123	−0.72	−0.09
CON	0.066	5.76	0.38	0.265	−0.60	−0.15
SAL	0.091	10.19	0.90	0.136	−1.74	−0.25
HOT	0.018	1.41	0.03	0.047	−4.04	−0.19

TABLE 8.A2.2 Industry contributions to value-added and total factor productivity growth 2007—16.—cont'd

	Value-added			Total factor productivity		
Industry[1]	VA weight	VA growth[2]	Contribution to aggregate VA growth[3]	Domar weight[4]	TFP growth[2]	Contribution to aggregate TFP growth[3,4]
T&S	0.044	7.02	0.31	0.114	0.49	0.06
P&T	0.023	13.70	0.31	0.044	3.23	0.14
FIN	0.069	13.29	0.88	0.105	1.67	0.15
REA	0.058	4.47	0.24	0.075	−8.07	−0.62
BUS	0.041	10.85	0.41	0.114	−2.07	−0.27
ADM	0.039	−12.97	−0.50	0.065	−12.90	−0.84
EDU	0.032	−6.76	−0.20	0.044	−8.12	−0.35
HEA	0.018	−21.25	−0.34	0.042	−11.93	−0.49
SER	0.028	9.42	0.26	0.056	−1.65	−0.09
Sum	*1.000*		6.75	3.053		−2.38

Notes:
[1] See Table 8.A1 for industry abbreviation.
[2] Value added and TFP growth rates are annualized raw growth rates in percent.
[3] Industry contribution to VA or TFP growth is weighted growth rate in percentage points (ppts).
[4] See Eq. (8.9) for Domar weights.
Source: See Tables 8.1 and 8.2

References

Akgüc M, Giulietti C, Zimmermann KF: *The RUMIC longitudinal survey: fostering research on labor markets in China*, IZA Discussion Paper (7860). Germany, 2013, Forschungsinstitut zur Zukunft der Arbeit (Institute for the Study of Labor).

Borensztein E, Ostry J: Accounting for China's growth performance, *American Economic Review* (86):224—228, 1996.

Bosworth B, Collins SM: The empirics of growth: an update, *Brookings Papers on Economic Activity* (2):113—179, 2003.

Bosworth B, Collins SM: Accounting for growth: comparing China and India, *Brookings Journal of Economic Perspective* 22(1):45—66, 2008, 2008.

Brandt L, Zhu X: *Accounting for China's Growth*, IZA Discussion Paper (4764). Germany, 2010, Forschungsinstitut zur Zukunft der Arbeit (Institute for the Study of Labor).

Cai F: Demographic transition, demographic dividend, and Lewis turning point in China", *China Economic Journal* 3(2):107—119, 2010.

Cao J, Mun SH, Jorgenson DW, Ren R, Sun L, Yue X: Industrial and aggregate measures of productivity growth in China, 1982—2000, *The Review of Income and Wealth* 55(S1), 2009.

CEC (Commission of the European Communities), IMF, OECD, UN: *World bank: system of national accounts*, 1993, p 223. Brussels/Luxembourg, New York, Paris, Washington, D.C.

CCCPC (The Central Committee of the Communist Party of China): *On the major issues of deepening reforms, adopted by the third plenary session of the eighteenth central committee*, November 12, 2013. Beijing.

CIP (China Industrial Productivity Project): *China industrial productivity database 3.0 (website)*. https://www.rieti.go.jp/en/database/CIP2015/index.html.

Denison EF: *The sources of economic growth in the United States and the alternative before us*, New York, 1962, Committee on Economic Development.

Domar E: On the measurement of technological change", *Economic Journal* 71(284):709—729, 1961.

Du J, Liu X, Ying Z: State advances and private retreats? evidence from the decomposition of the Chinese manufacturing aggregate productivity decomposition in China, *China Economic Review* 31(12):459–474, 2014.

ECNH: Editorial committee of new handbook of regular data and coefficients for assets evaluation. In *New handbook of regular data and coefficients for assets evaluation*, vol. 1. China Statistical Press.

Fan S, Zhang X, Robinson S: *Past and future sources of growth for China*, EPTD Discussion Paper No. 53, Washington, D.C., 1999, International Food Policy Research Institute.

Griliches Z: Measuring inputs in agriculture: a critical survey, *Journal of Farm Economics* 40(5):1398–1427, 1960.

Hsieh C, Klenow PJ: Misallocations and manufacturing TFP in China and India, *Quarterly Journal of Economics* CXXIV(4):1403–1448, 2009.

Hu Z, Khan M: *Why is China growing so fast?*, IMF Staff Papers (44), 1997, pp 103–131.

Huang Y, Tao K: Factor market distortion and the current account surplus in China, *Asian Economic Papers* 9(3):1–36, 2010.

Hulten CR: Growth accounting with intermediate inputs, *Review of Economic Studies* 45(3):511–518, 1978.

Hulten CR: Total factor productivity: a short biography". In Hulten CR, Dean ER, Harper MJ, editors: *New developments in productivity analysis*, Chicago and London, 2001, University of Chicago Press, pp 1–54.

Hulten CR, Wykoff FC: The measurement of economic depreciation". In Hulten CR, editor: *Depreciation, inflation, and the taxation of income from capital*, Washington D.C., 1981, The Urban Institute Press, pp 81–125.

Johansson AC, Feng X: "The state advances, the private sector retreats? Firm effects of China's great stimulus programme,", *Cambridge Journal of Economics* Volume 40(Issue 6):1635–1668, 1 November 2016. https://academic.oup.com/cje/issue/40/6.

Jorgenson DW: Capital theory and investment behavior, *American Economic Review* 53(2):247–259, 1963.

Jorgenson DW: The embodiment hypothesis, *Journal of Political Economy* 74(1):1–17, 1966.

Jorgenson DW: Information technology and the US economy, *American Economic Review* 91(1):1–32, 2001.

Jorgenson DW, Griliches Z: The explanation of productivity change, *Review of Economic Studies* 34(3): 249–283, 1967.

Jorgenson DW, Gollop F, Fraumeni B: *Productivity and U.S. economic growth*, Cambridge, MA, 1987, Harvard University Press.

Jorgenson DW, Ho MS, Stiroh KJ: Information technology and the American growth resurgence, *Productivity* (vol. 3). Cambridge, MA, 2005, MIT Press.

Jorgenson DW, Stiroh KJ: Raising the speed limit: US economic growth in the information age, *Brookings Papers on Economic Activity* (1):125–210, 2000.

Kaze AJ, Herman SW: *Improved estimates of fixed reproducible tangible wealth, 1929–95*, Survey of Current Business, pp 69–92.

Li H, Zhou LA: Political turnover and economic performance: the incentive role of personnel control in China, *Journal of Public Economics* 89(9–10):1743–1762, 2005.

Li S, Luo C, Wei Z, Yue X: Appendix: the 1995 and 2002 household surveys: sampling methods and data description. In Gustafsson B, Li S, Sicular T, editors: *Inequality and public policy in China*, New York, 2008, Cambridge University Press, pp 337–353.

Maddison A: *Chinese economic performance in the long run*, Paris, 1998, OECD Development Centre.

Maddison A: *Chinese economic performance in the long run, 960-2030*, Paris, 2007, OECD Development Centre.

Maddison A, Wu HX: Measuring China's economic performance, *World Economics* 9(2):13–44, 2008.

NBS (National Bureau of Statistics, China): *China statistical yearbook*, Beijing, 2018, State Statistics Press.

O'Mahony M, Timmer MP: Output, input and productivity measures at the industry level: the EU KLEMS database, *The Economic Journal* 119(June):F374–F403, 2009.

Perkins DH, Rawski TG: Forecasting China's economic growth to 2025. In Brandt L, Rawski TG, editors: *China's great economic transformation*, New York, 2008, Cambridge University Press, pp 829–886.

SETC (State Economic and Trade Commission, China): Zhongguo gongye wushi nian (Fifty years of Chinese industry), Beijing, 2000, China Economic Press.

Temurshoev U, Timmer MP: Joint estimation of supply and use tables, *Regional Science* 9(4):863–882, 2011.

Timmer M, Moergastel TV, Stuivenwold E, Ypma G, O'Mahony M, Kangasniemi M: *EU-KLEMS growth and productivity accounts, Version 1.0, PART I: Methodology*, Paris, 2007, OECD.

Woo WT: Chinese economic growth: sources and prospects. In Fouquin M, Lemoine F, editors: *The Chinese economy*, London, 1998, Economica Press.

Wu Y: Total Factor Productivity Growth in China: A Review, *Journal of Chinese Economic and Business Studies* 9(2): 111–126, 2011.

Wu HX: How fast has Chinese industry grown? – the upward bias hypothesis revisited, *China Economic Journal* 6(2–3):80–102, 2013.

Wu HX: China's growth and productivity performance debate revisited – accounting for China's sources of growth in 1949–2012. In *The conference board economics working papers*, EPWP1401, 2014.

Wu HX: The growth of 'non-material services' in China — Maddison's 'zero-labor-productivity-growth' hypothesis revisited, Institute of Economic Research, Hitotsubashi University *The Economic Review* 65(3), 2014b.

Wu HX: *Constructing China's net capital stock and measuring capital service in China*, RIETI Discussion Papers 15-E-006, 2015.

Wu HX: On China's strategic move for the new stage of development — a productivity perspective. In Jorgenson DW, Timmer M, Fulao K, editors: *The world economy: growth or stagnation*, Cambridge, 2016, Cambridge University Press, pp 199−233.

Wu HX, Ito K: *Reconstruction of China's national output and income accounts and supply-use and input-output accounts in time series*, RIETI Discussion Papers 15-E-004, 2015.

Wu HX, Yue X: *Accounting for labor input in Chinese industry, 1949-2009*, RIETI Discussion Papers 12-E-065, 2012.

Wu HX, Yue X, Zhang GG: *Constructing employment and compensation matrices and measuring labor input in China*, RIETI Discussion Papers 15-E-005, 2015.

Wu J: Zhongguo zengzhang moshi jueze (The choice of China's growth model), Shanghai, 2008, Yuandong Book Press.

Xu C: The fundamental institutions of China's reforms and development, *Journal of Economic Literature* 49(4): 1076−1151, 2011.

Xu X: On reform and development of the Chinese system of national economic accounting *(in Chinese)*, Beijing, 1999, Economic Science Press.

Young A: "Gold into Base Metals: Productivity Growth in the People's Republic of China during the Reform Period,", *Journal of Political Economy* 111:1221−1261, 2003.

9

Growth origins and patterns in the market economy of mainland Norway, 1997–2014

Gang Liu[1]

Statistics Norway, Oslo, Norway

9.1 Introduction

From the perspective of a bottom-up approach to exploring economic growth, the aggregate economic growth in a country can be traced back to the sources that are originated at the disaggregated level, such as at the sector or even industry level. This chapter aims to examine in more detail the origins of the (value-added based) aggregate average labor productivity (ALP) growth in the market economy of mainland Norway[2] over the period 1997–2014.

Recent years have witnessed a slowdown of the aggregate ALP growth in the market economy of mainland Norway (see, e.g., Brasch et al., 2015; Liu, 2018a). With the view of identifying possible reasons behind this productivity slowdown, special focus will in this chapter be placed on the changes that had occurred over the two separate subperiods, i.e., 1997–2006 and 2006–14, given that productivity performance in the two subperiods has been found to be quite different (see Liu, 2018a).

It has been demonstrated that the growth patterns of Norwegian structural economic development revealed solely by either total economy in its entirety or conventionally dichotomous goods/services sectors may be misleading, since much of the within-group heterogeneities are not

[1] E-mail address: gang.liu@ssb.no. The author is grateful to Bart van Ark for his insightful and valuable comments and suggestions on an earlier version of this chapter. However, the sole responsibility for any errors or omissions of this chapter lies with the author.

[2] Note that the market economy of mainland Norway does not include offshore oil and gas extraction and maritime sector, as well as nonmarket activities. As a frequently applied concept for the publication of official statistics in Statistics Norway, the definition of the market economy of mainland Norway will be discussed more in detail in Section 9.2.

taken into account (see Liu, 2018a). For instance, important swings of Norwegian oil and gas—related industries cannot be easily caught up simply by aggregate analysis. To make effectively more target-oriented and fine-tuned policy interventions for promoting economic growth, information drawn upon analyses at the disaggregated level are indispensable.

The examination of growth origins in this chapter involves analyzing how the growth of various production inputs and multifactor productivity (MFP) of each sector contributed to the aggregate ALP growth. In addition, those special contributions are highlighted that came from the use of the knowledge-based inputs, such as Information and Communication Technology (ICT) capital, Research and Development (R&D) capital, as well as skilled labor with high education.

Therefore, this chapter not only looks at which sectors contributed most to the aggregate ALP growth and its changes, but also which sectors contributed most to the use of knowledge-based inputs, in recognition that evidences have pointed out that along with recent economic growth, technical change seems to have to a large extent favored the knowledge-based production inputs (e.g., Jorgenson et al., 2005; Timmer et al., 2010; Liu, 2018a).

In this chapter, detailed analyses for the selected six sectors that make up the market economy of mainland Norway are carried out,[3] based on a newly constructed Norwegian KLEMS database (see Liu, 2017). This database compiles detailed and sophisticated output and input statistics at a disaggregated industry level, and thus offers the possibility of yielding much richer information on the sources of economic growth that cannot be acquired only by analysis at aggregate level.

Analyses by means of data at disaggregated level can also facilitate the statistical works in a more general sense, for instance, by directly confronting with each other various detailed statistics at disaggregated level, since measurement errors possibly existing at disaggregated level are sometimes smoothed away at aggregate level. Thus, such analyses have the potential of giving valuable feedback that can be used for enhancing the overall quality of statistical measurement and data compilation.

Just as analyses only at aggregate level may run the risk of losing possibly sizable within-group heterogeneities, analyses merely at disaggregated level may not be capable of giving a succinct interpretation of the overall picture of the growth process. To counterbalance and complement the analyses at the disaggregated level, the Harberger diagram (Harberger, 1998; Timmer et al., 2010) is employed in this chapter as a visualizing method to characterize the overall growth patterns of all industries in the market economy of mainland Norway for the two sub-periods: 1997—2006 and 2006—14.

The rest of the chapter is structured as follows. A brief introduction of the Norwegian KLEMS database, which is the main data source employed for productivity analysis at industry and sector level in this chapter, is given in Section 9.2. Section 9.3 describes the methodology used to determine industries' contributions to the aggregate ALP growth. This is based on the direct aggregation over industries approach that was outlined in Jorgenson et al. (2005).

In Section 9.4 a basic decomposition of the aggregate ALP growth is presented by various sources, such as different capital and labor inputs, and MFP. Section 9.5 then examines the ALP growth trends at the sector level and analyzes the corresponding ALP contribution to

---

[3] The six sectors are ICT production, Manufacturing excluding ICT production, Other goods production (with traditional primary sector included), Distribution services, Finance and business services, and Personal services. The classification and definition of these sectors will be presented in Section 9.2.

the aggregate ALP growth by each sector in the market economy of mainland Norway. As mentioned, a special focus is placed on the changes that had taken place over the two sub-periods (1997–2006 and 2006–14). In the following sections this sector ALP contribution is further investigated.

In Section 9.6, the contribution of input growth in sectors to the aggregate ALP growth is determined for the deepening of Hardware (ITH) capital, Software (ITS) capital, R&D capital, and all Other assets, as well as for the change of labor composition separately. Section 9.7 is devoted to the contributions from sector MFP growth. Section 9.8 investigates by visual diagrams the overall growth patterns of various knowledge-based inputs and the MFP growth across all industries, based on the seminal paper by Harberger (1998). Section 9.9 concludes.

9.2 The Norwegian KLEMS database

The current Norwegian KLEMS database was recently compiled, based in principle on official statistics, such as annual Norwegian national accounts data, including annual supply and use tables. The database provides detailed and sophisticated production input measures including capital (K), labor (L), energy (E), materials (M), and services (S),[4] as well as the output measure, at the disaggregated industry level, for the market economy of mainland Norway over the period 1997–2014 (see Liu, 2017).

For each industry, the labor inputs are further decomposed into hours actually worked and changes of labor composition, and the capital inputs are grouped into Information and Communication Technology (ICT) capital (consisting of Hardware [ITH] and Software [ITS]), Research and Development (R&D) capital, and all other assets (Other), including all assets rather than ICT and R&D capital. These further classifications make it possible for the decomposition of productivity growth into various detailed components.

The variables in the database are organized by means of the modern growth accounting methodology (see Jorgenson and Griliches, 1967; Diewert, 1976; Caves et al., 1982; Jorgenson et al., 1987, 2005). Being well-founded in the neoclassical production theory, the modern growth accounting methodology offers a clear conceptual framework, within which the interactions among different variables in the growth accounts can be analyzed in an internally consistent way. As such, the framework of the modern growth accounting has become an international standard now (see Schreyer, 2001, 2009).

The Norwegian KLEMS database is meant to be used primarily for analyzing productivity trend over time in Norwegian economy, and for productivity comparisons with other countries. Nonetheless, the database can serve for undertaking research in many other areas, such as in skill creation, capital development, technological progress, and R&D activities, as well as in economic growth more generally.

For the purpose of this chapter, by drawing upon the Norwegian KLEMS database, useful statistical indicators will be derived as regards the growth of ALP and MFP, and of various production inputs including the so-called knowledge-based inputs among different industries and sectors that occurred in the market economy of mainland Norway for the period 1997–2014, as well as for the two subperiods: 1997–2006 and 2006–14.

---

[4] The decomposition of intermediate production inputs into energy (E), material (M), and services (S) has not been explicitly employed in the current analysis, given that the focus of this chapter is on value added–based, rather than gross output–based, labor productivity analysis.

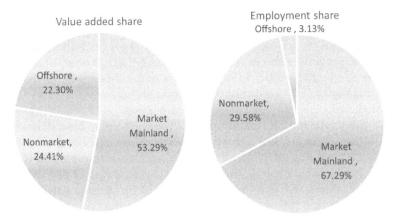

Value added share

Employment share

FIGURE 9.1 Composition of value added and employment in total Norwegian economy, 2014. Note: Nonmarket includes the owner-occupied housing services (KNR2368) and private renting (KNR2369) industries. *Source: Calculations are based on the Norwegian KLEMS database, July 2017.*

The market economy of mainland Norway (Market Mainland) is defined in this chapter by excluding from the total Norwegian economy all nonmarket activities (Nonmarket), the offshore oil and gas extraction and maritime sector (Offshore). The former (i.e., Nonmarket) consists of central and local government activities, such as education, health, defense, and public administration, and activities of the NPISHs. And the latter (i.e., Offshore) comprises the offshore industry extracting oil and gas (KNR2306), the pipeline transport of oil and gas (KNR2348), and the maritime transport (KNR2349). Finally, the industries that provide owner-occupied housing services (KNR2368), as well as private renting (KNR2369), are also excluded.[5]

In Fig. 9.1, the composition of value added and employment in total Norwegian economy in 2014 is displayed. As shown, nonmarket activities (Nonmarket) accounted for quite a large pie, with its value-added share being almost a quarter, and its employment share around 30%, of the total Norwegian economy. Despite a limited share in total employment (3.13%), the

offshore oil and gas extraction and maritime sector (Offshore), however, contributed a significant part of value added (22.30%) in 2014.

The shortage or even absence of market transaction information typically associated with nonmarket activities imposes great challenges for measuring productivity for these activities. Although significant progress has been made in this field, difficulties still remain (see e.g., Atkinson, 2005; Schreyer, 2010). Thus, productivity analysis for nonmarket activities necessitates a different treatment.

On the other hand, exposure to the volatile international oil and gas market frequently gives rise to substantial swings for the Norwegian offshore oil and gas extraction and maritime sector. Owing to its high importance in the Norwegian economy both for now and in the future, productivity analysis for this sector (Offshore) is worthwhile to be treated separately.

Given that the concept of the market economy of mainland Norway has been routinely used in the official statistics and frequently referred to as one of the focal points in public debate in Norwegian society, this chapter will set out the

[5] KNRxxxx are industry codes applied in Statistics Norway, see Table 9.1.

productivity analysis for the market economy of mainland Norway as a first research effort and will leave analyses for nonmarket activities (Nonmarket), as well as the large offshore industries (Offshore) for future research.

Formally, the market economy of mainland Norway comprises in total 57 industries, the names and the corresponding codes of which are listed in Table 9.1.

Traditionally, the main distinction in sectoral studies is made among primary, secondary, and tertiary (services) sectors. However, since the importance of the primary sector has rapidly declined while services sector has become by far the largest sector in Norway, the traditional taxonomy is not sufficient any more for our purpose. Therefore, a more detailed view of the services sector is essential. Moreover, in order to study the development of the ICT-goods–producing sector which has played an important role in recent economic growth, a special focus on this sector is also worthwhile.

With all these considerations being taken, the market economy of mainland Norway in this chapter is thus subdivided exhaustively into the following six mutually exclusive sectors: ICT production (ELECOM); Manufacturing excluding ICT production (MEXELEC); Other goods production (with traditional primary sector included) (OTHERG); Distribution services (DISTR); Finance and business services (FINBU); and Personal services (PERS).

For the purpose of this chapter, we also group the two goods production sectors, i.e., the Manufacturing excluding ICT production and the Other goods production sectors, into a broad (aggregate) *Goods* production sector; and the three services-providing sectors, i.e., the Distribution, the Finance and business services, and the Personal services sectors, into a broad (aggregate) *Services* sector.

In Table 9.1 the detailed description and the corresponding abbreviations of the six sectors are listed. Meanwhile, the precise composition of each sector in terms of the industry codes is also presented. Note that the sector definition/classification applied here is in accordance with that in the EU KLEMS database (see O'Mahony and Timmer, 2009; Timmer et al., 2010), which is of potential use for comparable analysis in the future.

9.3 Methodology: industry contributions to aggregate growth

Normally, general interests from the academia, government, or even the public in a country are frequently shown to be on the performance of aggregate economy and/or sectors which is reflected by a number of headline indicators, among which the most famous may be the GDP and its growth rate.

In the Norwegian KLEMS database, the methodologies are outlined as regards how to measure the performance of individual industries in terms of their outputs, inputs, and productivity growth. Therefore, from a bottom-up perspective to investigating economic growth, linkages between the aggregate indicators and the underlying disaggregate industry measures have to be clarified.

There are several approaches to obtaining measures of aggregate output, inputs, and productivity growth, based on exactly the same underlying detailed industry-level data and the derived industry-specific indicators of performance. These approaches differ in the restrictiveness of their assumptions made and thus give rise to different estimates of the aggregate economic growth and the corresponding conclusions about the sources of economic growth.

The first approach, most restrictive, is an aggregate production function approach; the second, less restrictive, is an aggregate production possibility frontier approach; and the third,

TABLE 9.1   Industries/Sectors in the market economy of mainland Norway.

Industries		Sectors	
Code	Description	Abbreviation	Description
KNR2326	Computer and electronics	ELECOM	ICT production (including electrical machinery manufacturing and post and communication services)
KNR2327	Electrical equipment		
KNR2353	Post and distribution		
KNR2361	Telecommunication		
KNR2362	Information services		
KNR2310	Food products, beverages and tobacco	MEXELEC	Manufacturing (excluding electrical machinery)
KNR2312	Fish farming		
KNR2313	Textiles, wearing apparel, leather		
KNR2315	Manufacture of wood and wood products		
KNR2316	Wood processing		
KNR2317	Graphic production		
KNR2318	Production of coal and refined petroleum		
KNR2319	Chemical raw goods		
KNR2320	Chemical products		
KNR2321	Production of pharmaceutical products		
KNR2322	Rubber and plastic products		
KNR2323	Other chemical and mineral products		
KNR2324	Metal raw goods		
KNR2325	Metal products		
KNR2328	Machinery and equipment		
KNR2329	Production of transport equipment		
KNR2330	Building of ships		
KNR2331	Building of oil platforms and modules		
KNR2332	Other industry production		
KNR2333	Repair/installation of machinery/equipment		
KNR2301	Agriculture, hunting	OTHERG	Other production (including agriculture, mining, utilities and construction)
KNR2302	Forestry		
KNR2303	Fishing		
KNR2304	Aquaculture		

TABLE 9.1 Industries/Sectors in the market economy of mainland Norway.—cont'd

Industries		Sectors	
Code	Description	Abbreviation	Description
KNR2305	Mining and quarrying		
KNR2335	Production of electricity		
KNR2336	Transport and sale of electricity		
KNR2337	Other energy, district heating and gas		
KNR2341	Building development		
KNR2342	Construction		
KNR2344	Wholesale/retail trade, repair of motor vehicles.	DISTR	Distribution (including Trade and transportation)
KNR2346	Passenger transport		
KNR2347	Goods transport		
KNR2350	Domestic maritime transport		
KNR2351	Air transport		
KNR2352	Services connected to transport		
KNR2307	Service activities incidental to oil and gas	FINBU	Finance and business services (excluding housing services)
KNR2358	Publishing business		
KNR2364	Financial services		
KNR2367	Managing real estate		
KNR2370	Architecture/legal/accounting/consulting		
KNR2372	Research and Development		
KNR2373	Marketing/veterinary and other services		
KNR2377	Leasing, travel, other business services		
KNR2338	Water supply, sewerage, waste	PERS	Personal services (including hotels, restaurants and community, social and personal services)
KNR2356	Hotel and restaurant		
KNR2385	Education/training		
KNR2386	Health services		
KNR2387	Social welfare services		
KNR2390	Cultural/sports/leisure activities		
KNR2394	Membership and other private activities		
KNR2397	Paid household works		

Source: Statistics Norway and EU KLEMS database (www.euklems.net).

least restrictive, is a direct aggregation across industries approach.[6]

It is the third approach, i.e., the direct aggregation across industries approach, that was taken in constructing the current Norwegian KLEMS database. Based on this approach, the contribution of each industry to the aggregate growth is given by industry growth multiplied by industry shares of value added.

Suppose the volume of aggregate value added is denoted as GDP, such that the aggregate nominal value of GDP is simply the sum over nominal value added in all industries in a country:

$$P^{GDP} GDP = \sum_j P_j^Z Z_j, \qquad (9.1)$$

where P^{GDP} is the price index of GDP, and P_j^Z is the price index of industry j's value added, the latter being denoted as Z_j.

The volume growth of GDP is then defined as a Törnqvist index, that is, a weighted industry value-added volume growth as the following:

$$\Delta \ln GDP = \sum_j \overline{v}_{Z,j}^{GDP} \Delta \ln Z_j, \qquad (9.2)$$

where $\overline{v}_{Z,j}^{GDP}$ is the period-average share of industry j in nominal value of aggregate value added, and

$$v_{Z,j}^{GDP} = \frac{P_j^Z Z_j}{\sum_j P_j^Z Z_j}. \qquad (9.3)$$

We then define total aggregate hours worked (H) as the sum of industry hours (H_j) worked over all industries, such that $H = \sum_j H_j$.

It follows that the corresponding aggregate ALP can be defined as $\frac{GDP}{H}$.

As shown in Liu (2017), the industry value-added–based ALP is defined as $z_j = \frac{Z_j}{H_j}$, and the corresponding growth decomposition of value-added ALP into its various components as:

$$\Delta \ln z_j = \overline{v}_{ITH,j}^Z \Delta \ln k_j^{ITH} + \overline{v}_{ITS,j}^Z \Delta \ln k_j^{ITS}$$
$$+ \overline{v}_{RD,j}^Z \Delta \ln k_j^{RD} + \overline{v}_{OA,j}^Z \Delta \ln k_j^{OA} \qquad (9.4)$$
$$+ \overline{v}_{L,j}^Z \Delta \ln LC_j + \Delta \ln A_j^Z,$$

where $k_j^{ITH} = \frac{K_j^{ITH}}{H_j}$, $k_j^{ITS} = \frac{K_j^{ITS}}{H_j}$, $k_j^{RD} = \frac{K_j^{RD}}{H_j}$, $k_j^{OA} = \frac{K_j^{OA}}{H_j}$, and $LC_j = \frac{L_j}{H_j}$ are input density (i.e., volume per hour worked) of Hardware (ITH), Software (ITS), R&D (RD), Other assets (OA), and labor services, respectively; $\overline{v}_{ITH,j}^Z$, $\overline{v}_{ITS,j}^Z$, $\overline{v}_{RD,j}^Z$, $\overline{v}_{OA,j}^Z$, and $\overline{v}_{L,j}^Z$ are the corresponding period-average nominal value-added share; A_j^Z is the value-added–based MFP in industry j.

As demonstrated in Stiroh (2002), the aggregate ALP growth can be decomposed into industry contributions as follows:

$$\Delta \ln \frac{GDP}{H} = \sum_j \overline{v}_{Z,j}^{GDP} \Delta \ln z_j$$
$$+ \left(\sum_j \overline{v}_{Z,j}^{GDP} \Delta \ln H_j - \Delta \ln H \right) \qquad (9.5)$$
$$= \sum_j \overline{v}_{Z,j}^{GDP} \Delta \ln z_j + R$$

The term in brackets in Eq. (9.5) is the reallocation of hours (R) and reflects differences in the share of an industry in aggregate value added and its share in aggregate hours worked. This term will be positive when industries with an above-average labor productivity level show positive employment growth or when industries

---

[6] For more comprehensive discussions on the three aggregation approaches, please refer to Jorgenson (1990) and Jorgenson et al. (2005).

with below-average labor productivity have declining employment shares.

Based on Eq. (9.5), we define the contribution of industry j's labor productivity to the overall aggregate ALP growth as:

$$CTLP_{LP,j} = \overline{v}_{Z,j}^{GDP} \Delta \ln z_j \qquad (9.6)$$

By inserting Eq. (9.4) into Eq. (9.5), we have

$$\Delta \ln \frac{GDP}{H} = \sum_j \overline{v}_{Z,j}^{GDP} (\overline{v}_{ITH,j}^{Z} \Delta \ln k_j^{ITH}$$
$$+ \overline{v}_{ITS,j}^{Z} \Delta \ln k_j^{ITS} + \overline{v}_{RD,j}^{Z} \Delta \ln k_j^{RD}$$
$$+ \overline{v}_{OA,j}^{Z} \Delta \ln k_j^{OA} + \overline{v}_{L,j}^{Z} \Delta \ln LC_j$$
$$+ \Delta \ln A_j^{Z}) + R$$
$$(9.7)$$

In this way, the contribution of various inputs and MFP growth from each industry to the aggregate ALP growth can be calculated.

We define the contribution of Hardware (ITH) capital deepening (i.e., volume per hour worked) in industry j to the aggregate ALP growth as:

$$CTLP_{ITH,j} = \overline{v}_{Z,j}^{GDP} * \left(\overline{v}_{ITH,j}^{Z} \Delta \ln k_j^{ITH} \right)$$
$$= \overline{v}_{ITH,j}^{GDP} \Delta \ln k_j^{ITH}, \qquad (9.8)$$

which is the growth of Hardware (ITH) capital per hour worked in industry j weighted by the share of Hardware (ITH) capital compensation in industry j in aggregate nominal value added ($\overline{v}_{ITH,j}^{GDP}$). The weight itself is the product of the share of industry j in aggregate value added ($\overline{v}_{Z,j}^{GDP}$) and the share of Hardware (ITH) capital compensation in industry j's value added ($\overline{v}_{ITH,j}^{Z}$).

Similarly, we define the contribution to the aggregate ALP growth from the deepening of Software (ITS), R&D, and Other assets in industry j, respectively, as:

$$CTLP_{ITS,j} = \overline{v}_{Z,j}^{GDP} * \left(\overline{v}_{ITS,j}^{Z} \Delta \ln k_j^{ITS} \right)$$
$$= \overline{v}_{ITS,j}^{GDP} \Delta \ln k_j^{ITS}, \qquad (9.9)$$

$$CTLP_{RD,j} = \overline{v}_{Z,j}^{GDP} * \left(\overline{v}_{RD,j}^{Z} \Delta \ln k_j^{RD} \right)$$
$$= \overline{v}_{RD,j}^{GDP} \Delta \ln k_j^{RD}, \qquad (9.10)$$

$$CTLP_{OA,j} = \overline{v}_{Z,j}^{GDP} * \left(\overline{v}_{OA,j}^{Z} \Delta \ln k_j^{OA} \right)$$
$$= \overline{v}_{OA,j}^{GDP} \Delta \ln k_j^{OA}, \qquad (9.11)$$

which are the growth of Software (ITS), R&D, and Other assets per hour worked in industry j weighted by the respective share of Software (ITS), R&D, and Other assets compensation in industry j in aggregate nominal value added. The weight applied is the product of the share of industry j in aggregate value added ($\overline{v}_{Z,j}^{GDP}$) and the share of each of the corresponding capital compensation in industry j's value added (i.e., $\overline{v}_{ITS,j}^{Z}$, $\overline{v}_{RD,j}^{Z}$, and $\overline{v}_{OA,j}^{Z}$).

Then, the contribution to the aggregate ALP growth from labor compositional change is defined as:

$$CTLP_{LC,j} = \overline{v}_{Z,j}^{GDP} * \left(\overline{v}_{L,j}^{Z} \Delta \ln LC_j \right)$$
$$= \overline{v}_{L,j}^{GDP} \Delta \ln LC_j, \qquad (9.12)$$

which is the growth of labor services per hour worked in industry j weighted by the share of labor compensation in industry j in aggregate nominal value added ($\overline{v}_{L,j}^{GDP}$). Again, the weight is the product of the share of industry j in aggregate value added ($\overline{v}_{Z,j}^{GDP}$) and the share of labor compensation in industry j's value added ($\overline{v}_{L,j}^{Z}$).

Finally, the contribution to the aggregate ALP growth from industry j's MFP growth is defined as:

$$CTLP_{MFP,j} = \overline{v}_{Z,j}^{GDP} \Delta \ln A_j^{Z}, \qquad (9.13)$$

which is the growth of MFP in industry j weighted by the share of industry j in aggregate value added.

9.4 Aggregate ALP growth decomposed by sources

By following the methodology outlined in Section 9.3, the basic decomposition of the annual aggregate ALP growth in the market economy of mainland Norway is undertaken for different contribution sources. The decomposition results for the entire period (1997—2014), as well as those for the two subperiods (1997—2006 and 2006—14), are presented in Table 9.2.

The first three rows in Table 9.2 indicate the breakdown of the aggregate ALP growth in the market economy of mainland Norway into two general terms, i.e., the weighted growth of industry-level ALP growth and the reallocation term as defined in Eq. (9.5) in Section 9.3. The first row shows that although the aggregate ALP growth in the market economy of mainland Norway was positive over the entire period (2.15% per year on average), it had more than halved from the first subperiod (2.89% per year on average) to the second (1.33% per year on average).

TABLE 9.2   Sources of aggregate ALP (average labor productivity) growth in the market economy of mainland Norway (%).

	1997–2014	1997–2006	2006–14
Aggregate ALP	2.15	2.89	1.33
Reallocation	0.19	0.21	0.18
Industry-weighted ALP	1.96	2.68	1.15
Contribution to industry-weighted ALP			
Labor composition	0.04	0.14	−0.07
Hardware (ITH) capital per hour	0.17	0.39	−0.07
Software (ITS) capital per hour	−0.02	−0.03	0.01
R&D capital per hour	0.03	0.00	0.07
Other assets per hour	0.38	0.64	0.09
Multifactor productivity (MFP)	1.35	1.55	1.13

Notes: The table gives the contributions of industry-level inputs per hour worked and MFP to aggregate ALP growth.
Source: Calculations are based on Norwegian KLEMS database, July 2017.

The second row in Table 9.2 indicates that the reallocation of labor between industries had a positive impact on the aggregate ALP growth as hours worked were reallocated to industries with higher levels of labor productivity. For the entire period, as well as for the two subperiods, this relocation effect remained more or less the same (around 0.2% per year on average). As a result, the industry-weighted ALP growth as given in the third row in Table 9. 2 had also more than halved from the first subperiod (2.68% per year on average) to the second (1.15% per year on average).

In Table 9.2, the industry-weighted ALP growth is further decomposed into the industry-weighted contributions of various factors, such as production inputs (consisting of capital and labor) and the MFP growth, calculated by following Eqs. (9.8)–(9.13), respectively, for each industry. The capital input growth includes the growth of the intensity (i.e., volume per hour) of Hardware (ITH), Software (ITS), R&D capital, and Other assets. The labor input growth is the growth of labor composition change, or in other words, the growth of labor services per hour worked.

As shown, the MFP growth was clearly the dominant one among all factors contributing to the industry-weighted ALP growth for the entire period (1.35% per year on average). It was also the case for the two subperiods as well, although the magnitude of the MFP growth had decreased from the first subperiod (1.55% per year on average) to the second (1.13% per year on average).

Apart from the MFP growth, for the entire period, the largest contribution factor was Other assets deepening (0.38% per year on average), the second largest was Hardware (ITH) capital deepening (0.17% per year on average), the third was the change of labor composition (0.04% per year on average), the fourth was R&D capital deepening (0.03% per year on average), and the fifth, also the smallest one, was Software (ITS) capital deepening, of which the contribution was the only negative one among all factors

(-0.02% per year on average). This ranking order of contribution factors for the entire period also held for the first subperiod.

From the first to the second subperiod, however, the ranking order of contribution factors had dramatically changed. In the second subperiod, apart from the MFP growth, Other assets deepening was still the largest contribution factor, though with a significant contribution reduction in magnitude over the two subperiods (from 0.64% reduced to 0.09% per year on average). On the other hand, R&D and Software (ITS) capital deepening had climbed up to become the second (0.07% per year on average) and the third (0.01% per year on average) largest contribution factors, respectively, in the second subperiod. In particular, the contribution from Software (ITS) capital deepening had, from negative in the first subperiod (-0.03% per year on average), turned out to be positive in the second.

On the contrary, the change of labor composition and Hardware (ITH) capital deepening had dropped substantially to become the fourth (-0.07% per year on average) and the fifth (-0.07% per year on average) largest contribution factors, respectively, in the second subperiod. Even worse, both of their contributions had, from positive in the first subperiod (0.14% and 0.39% per year on average for the change of labor composition and Hardware [ITH] capital deepening, respectively), deteriorated abruptly to become negative in the second subperiod.

In the following sections, the aggregate contributions from various capital and labor inputs and the MFP growth as shown in Table 9.2 will be broken down by the six sectors that make up the total market economy of mainland Norway (see Table 9.1 in Section 9.2). The purpose is to identify the sector growth origins in the market economy of mainland Norway. In addition to the investigation on the entire period, special focus will be put on the changes that had occurred from the first subperiod to the second.

Formally, we first analyze the contributions of sector ALP growth to the aggregate ALP growth

in Section 9.5, and then decompose the industry-weighted contributions further into the origins of various capital and labor inputs by sector in Section 9.6, and into those of the sector MFP growth in Section 9.7.

9.5 Contributions by sector ALP

The estimated ALP growth for the six sectors that make up the total market economy of mainland Norway is reported in the upper panel in Table 9.3, which provides average annual compound growth rates for the entire period (1997−2014), and for the two subperiods (1997−2006 and 2006−14) as well.

Over the entire period, the overall annual ALP growth in (aggregate) *Goods* production sector was higher than that in (aggregate) *Services* sector (2.11% vs. 1.50%). However, the former was lower in the first subperiod (1.86% vs. 2.82%), while much higher in the second subperiod (2.41% vs. 0.09%), than the latter.

Considering the six sectors individually, except for the Manufacturing sector, all other sectors had experienced an ALP growth slowdown over the two subperiods, leading to an overall ALP growth slowdown for the total market economy. Apparently, this ALP growth slowdown was mainly driven by the bad performance of services sector, and especially, by that of the Distribution services sector over the two subperiods.

As shown in Eq. (9.6), the importance of an industry or sector in explaining its contribution to the aggregate ALP growth ($CTLP_{LP,j}$) does depend not only on its productivity growth rate ($\Delta \ln z_j$) but also on its value share in aggregate value added for the total market economy ($\overline{v}_{Z,j}^{GDP}$).

In Table 9.3, the average share in aggregate value added for the six sectors are listed in the middle panel. And the corresponding contribution by each sector to the aggregate ALP growth is calculated by applying Eq. (9.6), and the results are presented in the lower panel in

TABLE 9.3 Contributions by sector ALP (average labor productivity) to aggregate ALP growth (%).

	1997–2014	1997–2006	2006–14
Average annual compound growth in labor productivity			
Total market economy of mainland Norway	2.15	2.89	1.33
ICT production (ELECOM)	*4.90*	*5.21*	*4.51*
Goods	*2.11*	*1.86*	*2.41*
Manufacturing (MEXELEC)	3.28	2.04	5.02
Other goods (OTHERG)	1.02	1.66	0.34
Services	*1.50*	*2.82*	*0.09*
Distribution (DISTR)	2.30	4.35	−0.21
Finance and business (FINBU)	1.60	2.59	0.70
Personal (PERS)	−0.92	−0.52	−1.41
Average share in aggregate value added			
Total market economy of mainland Norway	100	100	100
ICT production (ELECOM)	*7.53*	*8.00*	*7.01*
Goods	*33.34*	*34.37*	*32.20*
Manufacturing (MEXELEC)	16.03	17.66	14.21
Other goods (OTHERG)	17.31	16.71	17.99
Services	*59.11*	*57.64*	*60.79*
Distribution (DISTR)	22.22	23.23	21.09
Finance and business (FINBU)	28.24	25.45	31.39
Personal (PERS)	8.65	8.96	8.31
Contribution to aggregate labor productivity growth			
Total market economy of mainland Norway	2.15	2.89	1.33
ICT production (ELECOM)	*0.37*	*0.42*	*0.32*
Goods	*0.70*	*0.64*	*0.78*
Manufacturing (MEXELEC)	0.53	0.36	0.71
Other goods (OTHERG)	0.18	0.28	0.06
Services	*0.89*	*1.63*	*0.05*
Distribution (DISTR)	0.51	1.01	−0.05
Finance and business (FINBU)	0.45	0.66	0.22
Personal (PERS)	−0.08	−0.05	−0.12
Reallocation effect	0.19	0.21	0.18

Notes: Numbers may not sum exactly due to rounding.
Source: Calculations are based on the Norwegian KLEMS database, July 2017.

Table 9.3, which shows a different picture from the upper panel in the same table.

For instance, over the entire period, the contribution to the aggregate ALP growth by the sector of Finance and Business services was 0.45 percentage points, which is among higher levels if compared to those by other sectors. However, this is not because growth in this sector was particularly high. In fact, the annual ALP growth of this sector was just 1.60%, which was lower than the arithmetic average across all sectors, but due to its large share of value added in the total market economy (28.24%, the largest among all sectors), its contribution was substantially high.

On the other hand, the annual ALP growth in the ICT production sector was much higher (4.90%, the highest among all sectors), but as its share in aggregate value added was only small (7.53%), its contribution to the aggregate ALP growth was only 0.37% over the entire period.

As reflected by the lower panel in Table 9.3, the Distribution and the Finance and business services sectors had experienced the largest contribution decreases over the two subperiods. For example, the contribution from the Distribution services sector had even (from positive, 1.01%) become negative (-0.05%). This is in line with the findings from analyses at detailed industry level. For instance, a half number of industries in the Distribution services sector were among the top 10 industries that had the largest contribution decreases, and two industries in the Finance and business services sector were among the top five industries with largest contribution decreases (see Liu, 2018b).

9.6 Sector contributions by capital and labor inputs

9.6.1 Other assets

Following Eq. (9.11), the contribution to the industry-weighted ALP growth of Other assets

(i.e., all assets other than Hardware [ITH], Software [ITS], and R&D) per hour worked is estimated and then provided in Table 9.4 for the six sectors. The estimates are presented both for the entire period (1997−2014) and for the two subperiods (1997−2006 and 2006−14) as well.

Note that the figures in the first row in Table 9.4 are the same as those in the row with the title of "Other assets per hour" in Table 9.2, which are the contribution to the aggregate ALP growth from Other assets deepening, summed across all industries/sectors in the total market economy of mainland Norway.

As shown in Table 9.4, in terms of Other assets, the largest contribution came from the Finance and business services sector, both for the entire period and for the two subperiods. From the first subperiod to the second, without exception, the contribution of Other assets deepening from all the six sectors had reduced, and that from some had even (from positive) become negative in the second subperiod. Furthermore, the Finance and business services sector had

TABLE 9.4 Contribution of Other assets deepening by sector (%).

	1997−2014	1997−2006	2006−14
Total market economy of mainland Norway	0.38	0.64	0.09
ICT production (ELECOM)	*0.02*	*0.03*	*0.00*
Goods	*0.08*	*0.14*	*0.02*
Manufacturing (MEXELEC)	0.06	0.08	0.04
Other goods (OTHERG)	0.02	0.06	−0.02
Services	*0.28*	*0.46*	*0.07*
Distribution (DISTR)	0.02	0.04	0.00
Finance and business (FINBU)	0.24	0.36	0.10
Personal (PERS)	0.02	0.06	−0.03

Notes: Numbers may not sum exactly due to rounding.
Source: Calculations are based on the Norwegian KLEMS database, July 2017.

the largest contribution decrease among all the six sectors over the two subperiods.

9.6.2 Hardware (ITH)

By means of Eq. (9.8), the contribution by each of the six sectors to the industry-weighted ALP growth of Hardware (ITH) per hour worked is estimated and reported in Table 9.5, both for the entire period (1997–2014), and for the two subperiods (1997–2006 and 2006–14).

As shown in Table 9.5, the contribution from the six sectors were all positive, both for the entire period and for the first subperiod. However, from the first to the second subperiod, the contribution from all the six sectors had reduced to either almost zero for the ICT production and the goods production sectors (i.e., the Manufacturing and the Other goods production sectors), or even negative for all services sectors (i.e., the Distribution, the Finance and business, and the Personal services sectors).

As a result, the summed contribution of the total market economy of mainland Norway had, from positive value in the first subperiod, become negative one in the second (from 0.39% to -0.07%). In addition, the contribution from the ICT production sector had one of the largest decrease, just following those by the Finance and business and the Distribution services sectors over the two subperiods. This could be largely related to the nature of the ongoing technological change in the digital economy, which has shifted from investing in ICT hardware to outsourcing ICT services.

9.6.3 Software (ITS)

The contribution of each of the six sectors to the aggregate ALP growth of Software (ITS) per hour worked is computed by applying Eq. (9.9) in Section 9.3. The estimated results are presented in Table 9.6, both for the entire period (1997–2014) and for the two subperiods (1997–2006 and 2006–14).

Recall that in Table 9.2, "Software (ITS) capital per hour" is the only source that had the

TABLE 9.5 Contribution of Hardware (ITH) deepening by sector (%).

	1997–2014	1997–2006	2006–14
Total market economy of mainland Norway	0.17	0.39	−0.07
ICT production (ELECOM)	*0.04*	*0.07*	*0.00*
Goods	*0.04*	*0.09*	*0.00*
Manufacturing (MEXELEC)	0.03	0.06	0.00
Other goods (OTHERG)	0.01	0.03	0.00
Services	*0.08*	*0.23*	*−0.08*
Distribution (DISTR)	0.04	0.10	−0.02
Finance and business (FINBU)	0.03	0.10	−0.05
Personal (PERS)	0.01	0.03	−0.01

Notes: Numbers may not sum exactly due to rounding.
Source: Calculations are based on the Norwegian KLEMS database, July 2017.

TABLE 9.6 Contribution of Software (ITS) deepening by sector (%).

	1997–2014	1997–2006	2006–14
Total market economy of mainland Norway	−0.02	−0.03	0.01
ICT production (ELECOM)	*−0.01*	*0.01*	*−0.02*
Goods	*0.01*	*0.01*	*0.01*
Manufacturing (MEXELEC)	0.00	0.00	0.00
Other goods (OTHERG)	0.01	0.01	0.01
Services	*−0.01*	*−0.05*	*0.03*
Distribution (DISTR)	−0.01	−0.01	−0.01
Finance and business (FINBU)	0.00	−0.04	0.04
Personal (PERS)	0.00	0.00	0.00

Notes: Numbers may not sum exactly due to rounding.
Source: Calculations are based on the Norwegian KLEMS database, July 2017.

negative contribution to the aggregate ALP growth for the entire period, and for the first subperiod as well. As shown in Table 9.6, this is primarily due to that the contribution from "Software (ITS) capital per hour" was negative for two sectors, i.e., the ICT production and the Distribution services sectors for the entire period, and the Distribution and the Finance and business services sectors for the first subperiod.

Table 9.6 also shows that the contribution from "Software (ITS) capital per hour" of the total market economy of mainland Norway had finally ended up with a positive number in the second subperiod, though small in magnitude, thanks to the substantial increase in the contribution that had been made by the Finance and business services sector over the two subperiods.

In fact, the Finance and business services sector is the only sector of which the contribution had (from negative, -0.04%) become positive (0.04%), while those by the Manufacturing, the Other goods production, the Distribution services, and the Personal services sectors remained more or less the same over the two subperiods. In addition, quite against the whole picture, the contribution by the ICT production sector had, from positive in the first subperiod (0.01%), become negative (-0.02%) over the same two subperiods.

The findings are in line with those from analyses at more detailed industry level (see Liu, 2018b). For instance, four of the top five industries with largest contribution increases were from the Finance and business services sector. On the other hand, three of the five industries with largest contribution decreases were from the ICT production sector, which is also the sector that had the largest contribution decrease over the two subperiods, as shown in Table 9.6.

TABLE 9.7 Contribution of R&D deepening by sector (%).

	1997–2014	1997–2006	2006–14
Total market economy of mainland Norway	0.03	0.00	0.07
ICT production (ELECOM)	*−0.01*	*−0.01*	*0.01*
Goods	*0.01*	*0.00*	*0.02*
Manufacturing (MEXELEC)	0.01	0.00	0.02
Other goods (OTHERG)	0.00	0.00	0.00
Services	*0.02*	*0.00*	*0.04*
Distribution (DISTR)	0.00	0.00	0.00
Finance and business (FINBU)	0.02	0.00	0.04
Personal (PERS)	0.00	0.00	0.00

Notes: Numbers may not sum exactly due to rounding.
Source: Calculations are based on the Norwegian KLEMS database, July 2017.

9.6.4 R&D

Likewise, the contribution of each of the six sectors to the aggregate ALP growth of R&D per hour worked is estimated by using Eq. (9.10) in Section 9.3. The estimated results are provided in Table 9.7, both for the entire period (1997–2014) and for the two subperiods (1997–2006 and 2006–14).

Notice that in Table 9.2, in terms of contribution sources, "R&D capital per hour" is one of the two sources that had improved their contributions to the aggregate ALP growth over the two subperiods.[7] As shown here in Table 9.7, for all the six sectors that make up the total market economy, the contribution of R&D capital deepening had either increased or remained more or less the same over the two subperiods, although all the contributions were relatively small in magnitude.

---

[7] The other source is "Software (ITS) capital per hour" which had even improved its contribution from negative in the first subperiod to become positive in the second (see Table 9. 2).

Compared to other sectors, the Manufacturing, the ICT production, and the Finance and business services sectors had the largest contribution increases over the two subperiods. This is also in line with the findings from analyses at more detailed industry level. For instance, among the top 10 industries with largest contribution increases, 4 were from the Manufacturing sector, 2 from the ICT production sector, and the rest 4from the Finance and business services sector (see Liu, 2018b).

9.6.5 Changes in labor composition

Using Eq. (9.12), the contribution of each of the six sectors to the aggregate ALP growth of labor composition change is estimated and provided in Table 9.8, both for the entire period (1997–2014) and for the two subperiods (1997–2006 and 2006–14).

Similar with most of the other sources as shown in Table 9.2, for the total market economy of mainland Norway, the change of "labor composition" is one source that had positive

TABLE 9.8 Contribution of labor composition change by sector (%).

	1997–2014	1997–2006	2006–14
Total market economy of mainland Norway	0.04	0.14	−0.07
ICT production (ELECOM)	*0.02*	*0.02*	*0.03*
Goods	*−0.06*	*0.02*	*−0.16*
Manufacturing (MEXELEC)	0.01	0.04	−0.03
Other goods (OTHERG)	−0.07	−0.02	−0.13
Services	*0.09*	*0.11*	*0.07*
Distribution (DISTR)	−0.02	0.05	−0.10
Finance and business (FINBU)	0.09	0.04	0.14
Personal (PERS)	0.02	0.02	0.03

Notes: Numbers may not sum exactly due to rounding.
Source: Calculations are based on the Norwegian KLEMS database, July 2017.

contribution to the aggregate ALP growth for the entire period; and had reduced its contribution over the two subperiods. Moreover, its contribution had even from positive in the first subperiod reduced to the negative in the second, which is similar with that by "Hardware (ITH) capital per hour."

However, as for the six sectors considered individually, the contribution of "labor composition change" demonstrated a rather varied picture. As shown in Table 9.8, for the entire period, the contributions were negative only for two sectors (i.e., the Other goods production, and the Distribution services sectors), while positive for the rest four sectors.

Over the two subperiods, although three sectors (i.e., the ICT production, the Finance and business services, and the Personal services sectors) had increased their positive contributions, two sectors (i.e., the Manufacturing and the Distribution services sectors) had reduced their previously positive contributions to become the negative ones, and one sector (i.e., the Other goods production sector)'s contribution had deteriorated in the second subperiod from already a negative one in the first subperiod.

9.7 Contributions by sector MFP

The estimated MFP growth for the six sectors that make up the market economy of mainland Norway is reported in the upper panel in Table 9.9, which provides the estimated average annual compound MFP growth rates for the entire period 1997–2014, as well as for the two subperiods of 1997–2006 and 2006–14.

Similar with ALP growth as shown in Table 9.3, for the total market economy, the MFP growth was positive for the entire period, as well as for the two subperiods, and had decreased from the first to the second subperiod. As shown in Table 9.9, over the entire period, the MFP growth in (aggregate) *Goods* production sector was larger than that in (aggregate) *Services*

TABLE 9.9 Contributions by sector multifactor productivity (%).

	1997—2014	1997—2006	2006—14
Average annual compound growth in multifactor productivity			
Total market economy of mainland Norway	1.35	1.55	1.13
ICT production (ELECOM)	*4.06*	*3.81*	*4.38*
Goods	*1.85*	*1.10*	*2.76*
Manufacturing (MEXELEC)	2.58	1.01	4.78
Other goods (OTHERG)	1.17	1.19	1.16
Services	*0.72*	*1.50*	*−0.12*
Distribution (DISTR)	2.15	3.54	0.44
Finance and business (FINBU)	0.27	0.76	−0.18
Personal (PERS)	−1.53	−1.71	−1.30
Average share in aggregate value added			
Total market economy of mainland Norway	100	100	100
ICT production (ELECOM)	*7.53*	*8.00*	*7.01*
Goods	*33.34*	*34.37*	*32.20*
Manufacturing (MEXELEC)	16.03	17.66	14.21
Other goods (OTHERG)	17.31	16.71	17.99
Services	*59.11*	*57.64*	*60.79*
Distribution (DISTR)	22.22	23.23	21.09
Finance and business (FINBU)	28.24	25.45	31.39
Personal (PERS)	8.65	8.96	8.31
Contribution to industry-weighted multifactor productivity growth			
Total market economy of mainland Norway	1.35	1.55	1.13
ICT production (ELECOM)	*0.31*	*0.30*	*0.31*
Goods	*0.61*	*0.38*	*0.89*
Manufacturing (MEXELEC)	0.41	0.18	0.68
Other goods (OTHERG)	0.20	0.20	0.21
Services	*0.43*	*0.86*	*−0.08*
Distribution (DISTR)	0.48	0.82	0.09
Finance and business (FINBU)	0.08	0.19	−0.06
Personal (PERS)	−0.13	−0.15	−0.11

Notes: Numbers may not sum exactly due to rounding.
Source: Calculations are based on the Norwegian KLEMS database, July 2017.

sector (1.85% *vs.* 0.72%), while during the first subperiod, the former was lower than the latter (1.10% *vs.* 1.50%).

The MFP growth slowdown for the total market economy from the first subperiod to the second was mainly driven by the performance of services sectors, and in particular, by that of the Distribution services sector. The increase of the MFP growth during the second subperiod for the (aggregate) *Goods* production sector came largely from the Manufacturing sector.

Apart from these similarities, there are several dissimilarities between the ALP and MFP growth, especially, when considering the individual performance by the six sectors. While only the Manufacturing sector experienced a growth enhance of ALP over the two subperiods (see Table 9.3), both the Manufacturing and the ICT production sectors, as well as the Personal services sector, had improved their MFP growth, although the MFP growth of the latter was still negative in the second subperiod (see Table 9.9).

As shown in Eq. (9.13), the importance of an industry or sector in explaining the MFP contributions to the aggregate ALP growth ($CTLP_{MFP,j}$) does depend not only on its MFP growth rate ($\Delta \ln A_j^Z$) but also on its value share in aggregate valued added for the total market economy ($\overline{v}_{Z,j}^{GDP}$).

Based on Eq. (9.13), the MFP contributions by the six sectors to the aggregate ALP growth are estimated and presented in the lower panel in Table 9.9, where the use is made of the multiplication of the average share in aggregate value added for each sector (as presented in the middle panel in Table 9.9) with the corresponding sector MFP growth (as shown in the upper panel in Table 9.9).

In terms of the MFP contribution to the aggregate ALP growth, the sector rankings are different from those that are reflected by the

sector MFP growth, since the average sector share of value added has played an important role here. For instance, from the first subperiod to the second, although the MFP growth of the Other goods production sector had decreased (from 1.19% to 1.16%), the estimated MFP contribution by this sector had slightly increased (from 0.20% to 0.21%), simply because this sector is one of the two sectors that had increased its average share in aggregate value added over the two subperiods (from 16.71% to 17.99%) (see Table 9.9).[8]

As shown in Table 9.9, there were four sectors (i.e., the ICT production, the Manufacturing, the Other goods production, and the Personal services sectors) having shown improvements of their MFP contribution over the two subperiods. The MFP contribution for the total market economy of mainland Norway, however, had actually decreased (from 1.55% to 1.13%) over the same two subperiods. The main reason is that the sector contribution from the other services sectors, and especially, that from the Distribution services sector, had revealed a substantial decrease over the two subperiods (from 0.82% to 0.09%), which is in fact the largest contribution decrease, compared to those by all the other sectors over the two subperiods.

On the other hand, the performance of MFP growth in the market economy of mainland Norway was quite exceptional, especially during the second subperiod, if compared with those by other European countries and the USA (see Inklaar et al., 2019). While many other countries suffered heavily from the 2008—09 Global Financial Crisis, the market economy of mainland Norway seemed to have weathered this difficult time relatively well. This might be in part due to the good performance by those industries that are strongly related to the offshore oil and gas extraction and maritime sector.

---

[8] The other sector is the Finance and business services sector, of which the average share in aggregated value added had increased from 25.45% to 31.39% over the two subperiods (see Table 9.9 and Table 9.3).

Indeed, detailed analysis at industry level has shown that from the first to the second subperiod, the top five industries with largest increases in MFP growth are from *Goods* production sector, and in particular, from the Manufacturing sector, such as production of petroleum products, chemical products, and building of ships industries (see Liu, 2018b).

9.8 Growth patterns in diagram

9.8.1 Harberger diagram

In principle, the sector ALP growth can be traced further down to the individual industry origins, which is supposed to offer an increasingly more detailed picture of the sources of economic growth. However, the wealth of industry detail may entail the risk of submerging the broad picture into too much details and thus losing appreciation of the overall pattern of the growth process. To overcome this risk and to complement the analyses as carried out so far, the Harberger diagram will be applied in this chapter as a way to characterize the overall growth pattern of all the 57 industries that make up the market economy of mainland Norway (see Table 9.1).

Harberger diagrams can be used to visualize how widespread various capital deepening, the change of labor composition, and the MFP growth are within an economy, by providing a convenient and succinct graphical summary of the industry pattern of growth (Harberger, 1998). The diagram shows the cumulative contribution of the industries to the aggregate ALP growth on the *y*-axis and the corresponding cumulative share of these industries in aggregate value added on the *x*-axis. The contributions by various sources to the aggregate ALP growth are calculated by following the methodologies as outlined in Section 9.3.

The sources that will be investigated in the following include the knowledge-based inputs that are defined in this chapter, such as Hardware (ITH), Software (ITS), R&D, and the change of labor composition; as well as the MFP growth.

Formally, the industries are first ranked on their contributions by descending order, so that the fastest growing industries are to be found near the origin. The resulting diagrams as revealed can have several different patterns, e.g., showing a more yeast-like or more mushroom-like character, depending on the number of industries contributing positively to the aggregate ALP growth and the distribution of growth rates.

Growth is considered to be yeast-like when it is broad-based and takes place in many industries. Mushroom-like growth indicates a pattern in which only a limited number of industries contribute positively to the aggregate growth. The analogy with yeast and mushrooms comes from the fact that yeast causes bread to expand slowly and evenly, while mushrooms are scattered and pop up almost overnight, in a fashion that it is not easy to predict (Harberger, 1998).

9.8.2 Hardware (ITH)

The Harberger diagram of Hardware (ITH) capital growth for the two subperiods (1997–2006 and 2006–14) is displayed in Fig. 9.2. For the first subperiod, only 4 out of the 57 industries had negative Hardware (ITH) growth, and the total contribution, which was positive, was relatively evenly distributed across the industries. Clearly, the resulting growth pattern can be regarded as being of yeast-like character because Hardware (ITH) investment was widespread across the industries in the market economy of mainland Norway for the first subperiod.

However, a dramatic change had occurred over the two subperiods. In the second subperiod, the growth pattern as shown was starkly different from that for the first subperiod. There were 36 industries having negative growth rates,

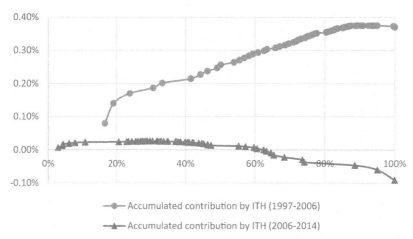

FIGURE 9.2   Harberger diagram of ITH growth in the market economy, 1997—2006 and 2006—14. *Source: Calculations are based on the Norwegian KLEMS database, July 2017.*

indicating that the deceleration of Hardware (ITH) investment was a widespread phenomenon because it took place in most of the total 57 industries, and the deceleration was quite substantial.

As a result, the total contribution of Hardware (ITH) capital deepening ended up with a negative number in the second subperiod, and the revealed pattern is a typical mushroom-like style

because only a limited number of industries contributed positively to the aggregate growth in this subperiod.

9.8.3 Software (ITS)

Fig. 9.3 provides the Harberger diagram of Software (ITS) capital growth for the two subperiods (1997—2006 and 2006—14). As shown, for

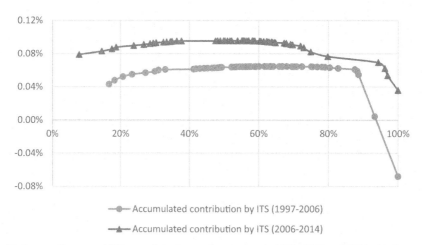

FIGURE 9.3   Harberger diagram of ITS growth in the market economy, 1997—2006 and 2006—14. *Source: Calculations are based on the Norwegian KLEMS database, July 2017.*

the first subperiod, it appears that it is the last added (to the accumulated contribution) industry, i.e., KNR2364 (Financial services), that had dragged down the accumulated total contribution from positive value to the negative one, but the whole pattern is close to a yeast-like one.

During the second subperiod, though less industries had nonnegative growth, compared to the first subperiod, their accumulated contribution, nonetheless, outweighed the accumulated contribution from those industries that had negative growth. The main reason is owing to the outstanding performance by the Finance and business services sector in the second subperiod (also see Table 9.6 and Section 9.6.3), which had the effect of having almost shifted up the whole diagram over the two subperiods. As a result, the total contribution of Software (ITS) capital deepening was therefore a positive number in the second subperiod.

9.8.4 R&D

The Harberger diagram of R&D capital growth for the two subperiods (1997—2006 and 2006—14) is shown in Fig. 9.4. During the first subperiod, there were 20 industries having

negative R&D growth. Despite more industries having nonnegative R&D growth, the contribution from each of these industries was very small in magnitude. Therefore, the total contribution of R&D capital deepening ended up with, though positive, a very small number close to zero.

In the second subperiod, however, there were 41 out of the total 57 industries having nonnegative growth, and the accumulated contribution by those industries with negative growth were very small. The resulting growth pattern for the second subperiod can be regarded as being of more yeast-like character, and the improvement of R&D investment did not concentrate only on a few industries. In fact, it was widespread and took place in the most industries.

9.8.5 Change in labor composition

Fig. 9.5 presents the Harberger diagram of the change of labor composition for the two subperiods (1997—2006 and 2006—14). In the first subperiod, the growth pattern was much closer to a yeast-like one. In fact, only three industries had negative growth, and the total contribution of the change of labor composition became positive.

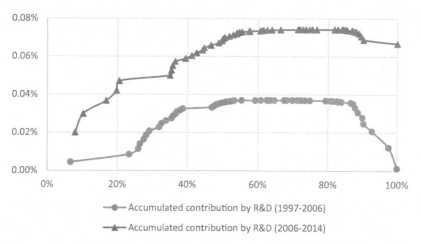

FIGURE 9.4 Harberger diagram of R&D growth in the market economy, 1997—2006 and 2006—14. *Source: Calculations are based on the Norwegian KLEMS database, July 2017.*

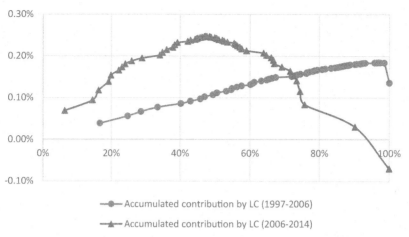

FIGURE 9.5   Harberger diagram of labor composition (LC) change in the market economy, 1997–2006 and 2006–14. *Source: Calculations are based on the Norwegian KLEMS database, July 2017.*

However, in the second subperiod, the growth pattern had a significant change, compared to that in the first subperiod. There were 31 industries having negative growth, and the industries with smallest contribution came either from the Other goods production sector,[9] or from the Distribution services sector[10], which is consistent with the results as discussed in Table 9.8 and Section 9.6.5.

Since the accumulated contribution by industries with negative growth outweighed that by those with positive growth, the total contribution of the change of labor composition in the second subperiod ended up with a negative number. And the resulted growth pattern was closer to a mushroom-like one.

9.8.6 Multifactor productivity

Fig. 9.6 gives the Harberger diagram of industry MFP growth in the market economy of mainland Norway for the two subperiods (1997–2014 and 2006–14).

In the first subperiod, there were 20 industries having negative MFP growth, and the total contribution of MFP growth was positive; while in the second subperiod, there were 19 industries having negative growth, and the total contribution of MFP growth was still positive, although it was lower than that in the first subperiod. The fact that most of industries have positive MFP growth indicates an increasingly more efficient use of both labor and capital in these industries in the market economy of mainland Norway.

From the first to the second subperiod, it seems that the Harberger diagram of MFP growth had just shifted downward, but with little change in terms of the whole pattern. And both diagrams in the two subperiods may suggest that the MFP growth across industries was between a mushroom-like and a yeast-like growth pattern. The reason is that still a limited

[9] Such as KNR2342 (Construction), KNR2301 (Agriculture, Hunting), and KNR2303 (Fishing) (see Liu, 2018b).

[10] Such as KNR2344 (Wholesale/retail trade, repair of motor vehicles), KNR2347 (Goods transport), and KNR2346 (Passenger transport) (see Liu, 2018b).

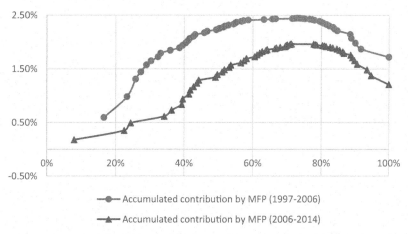

FIGURE 9.6 Harberger diagram of multifactor productivity (MFP) growth in the market economy, 1997–2006 and 2006–14. *Source: Calculations are based on the Norwegian KLEMS database, July 2017.*

number, but already much more than half, of the total 57 industries had contributed positively to the accumulated contribution for both two subperiods.

In spite of this observation, it might well happen that the MFP growth for some industries had (from positive) become negative, while that for some others had just been the opposite from over the two subperiods (also see Section 9.7).

9.9 Concluding remarks

Based on the Norwegian KLEMS database, this chapter investigates the growth origins and visualizes the overall growth patterns in the market economy of mainland Norway for 1997–2014. Over the two subperiods (1997–2006 and 2006–14), the aggregate ALP growth appeared to have more than halved. In fact, among all the six sectors that make up the total market economy of mainland Norway, except for the Manufacturing sector, a decline in ALP growth is found in all the other sectors, among which the Distribution, and the Finance and business services sectors had by far the largest decreases.

When considering the contribution to the aggregate ALP growth from various capital and labor inputs, as well as from the MFP growth, the contribution from the latter was clearly the dominant source, followed by that from Other assets (defined as all assets rather than Hardware, Software and R&D) deepening. Over the two subperiods, however, the contributions from these two sources had declined, with that from Other assets deepening showing the largest decrease among all the sources. On the other hand, the contributions from R&D and Software (ITS) deepening had increased; while those from Hardware (ITH) deepening and labor composition change had decreased substantially, with both from positive numbers becoming negative ones.

The breakdown of the aggregate contributions by the six sectors reveals that the contribution of Hardware (ITH) deepening by all the six sectors had reduced, and those by the Finance and business, and the Distribution services sectors had the largest decreases over the two subperiods. On the contrary, none of the six sectors had experienced a contribution decrease of R&D deepening over the same two subperiods. Except for the ICT production sector, the contribution of Software (ITS) deepening by all the other sectors had experienced a nondecreasing change, and in particular, the contribution by the Finance and business services sector had a substantial increase over the two subperiods.

The breakdown by the six sectors also shows that three sectors (i.e., the ICT production, the Finance and business services, and the Personal services sectors) had increased their positive contributions of labor composition change, while the other three (i.e., the Manufacturing, the Distribution services, and the Other goods production sectors) had reduced their contributions over the two subperiods.

Moreover, there were four sectors having improved their MFP contributions (i.e., the ICT production, the Manufacturing, the Other goods production, and the Personal services sectors), and the other two had only experienced substantial contribution decreases of the MFP growth over the two subperiods (i.e., the Distribution services, and the Finance and business services sectors).

Compared to other European countries and the USA, the performance of MFP growth in the market economy of mainland Norway was exceptionally better, especially during the second subperiod. Although it might be due to the good performance by those Norwegian industries that are strongly related to the large offshore oil and gas extraction and maritime sector, the detailed linkages among them remain to be further explored. Furthermore, the possible correlation between the MFP growth and the knowledge-based inputs (probably by including other knowledge-relevant inputs such as oil and gas exploration and evaluation capital) needs also to be investigated in the future.

By visualizing the overall growth patterns of the knowledge-based inputs and the MFP growth across all industries in the market economy of mainland Norway, the Harberger diagrams demonstrate that over the two subperiods, the growth pattern of Hardware (ITH) had changed from a yeast-like pattern to a mushroom-like one, because growth took place in many industries in the first subperiod, while

only a limited number of industries had positive growth in the second subperiod. In addition, the growth decline was significantly substantial across industries, leading to that the total accumulated contribution had, from positive in the first subperiod, become negative in the second.

Quite different from Hardware (ITH), over the two subperiods, the growth pattern of R&D had become more yeast-like one, and the total accumulated contribution had, from close to zero, become positive. The improvement of R&D investment did not concentrate only on a few industries. In fact, it was broad-based and took place in many industries.

In the first subperiod, the growth pattern of Software (ITS) was close to a yeast-like one. However, the negative growth (but large in absolute value) from just a few industries dragged down the total accumulated contribution to become negative. During the second subperiod, the accumulated contribution from industries with positive growth, nonetheless, outweighed that from those with negative growth.

The growth pattern of labor composition changes was also close to a yeast-like one in the first subperiod, with only a few industries having negative growth, resulting in a positive accumulated contribution. However, it had become close to a mushroom-like pattern in the second subperiod with around half of the total industries having negative growth. Even worse, the accumulated contribution from those with negative growth outweighed that from those with positive ones.

Finally, the Harberger diagrams of the MFP growth demonstrate that from the first subperiod to the second, the diagram seemed to be shifted down without other significant changes, and the total accumulated contribution had, though still positive, declined. Both diagrams in the two subperiods suggest that the MFP growth across industries was between a mushroom-like and a yeast-like growth pattern, simply because still a limited number, but already much more than half, of the total 57 industries had contributed positively to the accumulated contribution for both two subperiods.

The rich and detailed findings from this chapter are of potential use for policy-makings. For instance, the overall growth patterns as displayed by the Harberger diagrams can answer to the question of whether the growth across industries of various knowledge-based inputs and the MFP growth concentrates only in a few industries or otherwise occurs more evenly across the industries. Such information is essential for possible policy intervention and evaluation, for example, when designing R&D promotion policy in the country.

Moreover, the numerous results drawn upon the analyses on the growth origins of the aggregate ALP growth as carried out in this chapter can well be taken to effectively make more target-oriented and fine-tuned policies, with the purpose of promoting the economic growth in the market economy of mainland Norway in the days to come.

Last but not least, recall that the market economy of mainland Norway accounts for only one, though a majority, part of the total Norwegian economy. For a comprehensive understanding of the economic growth in the total Norwegian economy, analyses on nonmarket activities, and the offshore oil and gas extraction and maritime sector, and equally, if not more, important, analyses on the detailed interlinkages among them, are indispensable. All these analyses call for further research in the future.

References

Atkinson T: *Atkinson review: final report — measurement of government output and productivity for the national accounts*, Houndmills, Basingstoke, Hampshire, 2005, Palgrave MacMillan.

Brasch TV, Cappelen Å, Iancu D: *Understanding the productivity slowdown — the importance of entry and exit of workers*, Discussion Papers, No.818, Statistics Norway.

Caves DW, Christensen LR, Diewert WE: The economic theory of index numbers and the measurement of input, output, and productivity, *Econometrica* 50(6):1392–1414, 1982.

Diewert WE: Exact and superlative index numbers, *Journal of Econometrics* 4:114–145, 1976.

Harberger AC: A vision of the growth process, *American Economic Review* 88(1):1–32, 1998.

Inklaar R, Jager K, O'Mahony M, van Ark B: *European productivity in the digital age: evidence from EU KLEMS*, 2019 (Chapter 5).

Jorgenson DW, Griliches Z: The explanation of productivity change, *Review of Economic Studies* 34(3):249–283, 1967.

Jorgenson DW, Gollop FM, Fraumeni BM: *Productivity and U.S. economic growth*, Cambridge, MA, 1987, Harvard Economic Studies.

Jorgenson DW: Productivity and economic growth. In Berndt ER, Triplett JE, editors: *Fifty years of economic measurement, studies in income and wealth*, vol. 54. The University of Chicago Press.

Jorgenson DW, Ho MS, Stiroh KJ: *Information technology and the American growth resurgence*, Cambridge, MA, 2005, MIT Press.

Liu G: *The Norwegian KLEMS growth and productivity a1997–2014*, Documents, 2017/38, Statistics Norway.

Liu G: *Structural development in the market economy of mainland Norway 1997–2014*, Reports, 2018/12, Statistics Norway.

Liu G: *Industry origins of aggregate growth in the market economy of mainland Norway 1997-2014*, Interne dokumenter, 2018/11, Statistics Norway.

O'Mahony M, Timmer MP: Output, input and productivity measures at the industry level: the EU KLEMS database, *Economic Journal* 119(538):F374–F403, 2009.

Schreyer P: *OECD productivity manual: a guide to the measurement of industry-level and aggregate productivity growth*, Paris, 2001, Organization for Economic Co-operation and Development.

Schreyer P: *Measuring capital — OECD manual*, ed 3, Paris, 2009, Organization for Economic Co-operation and Development.

Schreyer P: *Towards measuring the volume output of education and health services: a handbook*, OECD Statistics Working Papers, Paris, 2010, Organization for Economic Co-operation and Development, https://doi.org/10.1787/5kmd34g1zk9x-en.

Stiroh KJ: Information technology and the US productivity revival: what do the industry data say? *American Economic Review* 92(5):1559–1576, 2002.

Timmer MP, Inklaar R, O'Mahony M, van Ark B: *Economic growth in Europe — a comparative industry perspective*, Cambridge University Press.

10

Progress on Australia and Russia KLEMS

Ilya Voskoboynikov[1], Derek Burnell[2], Thai Nguyen[3]

[1]Laboratory for Research in Inflation and Growth, National Research University Higher School of Economics, Moscow, Russia; [2]Macroeconomic Statistics Division, The Australian Bureau of Statistics, Belconnen, ACT, Australia; [3]Macroeconomic Statistics Division, The Australian Bureau of Statistics, Sydney, NSW, Australia

10.1 Introduction

This chapter outlines the progress of KLEMS projects in Australia and Russia and discusses the industry sources of growth of these two economies using the industry growth accounting framework of Jorgenson et al. (1987). For both countries, the extension of growth accounts to the KLEMS framework supports deeper analysis of productivity slowdown conditions since the mid-2000s. For example, Russia KLEMS data help to better understand the economic stagnation in Russia in the last decade not only as the outcome of some domestic challenges but also in the context of global stagnation. Therefore, the development of Russian KLEMS estimates is crucial for the assessment of the economy's dependence of its growth in the export of natural resources. For Australia, KLEMS estimates assist in a better understanding of the impact of structural changes, especially in services industries.

While the development of KLEMS in Australia and Russia is based on the same underlying framework, they differ with respect to data coverage. For example, the Australia KLEMS user cost shares account for taxation, while in Russian KLEMS, the impact of taxes has not been incorporated. Differences can also be found in types of capital covered. In contrast to Australia, Russian KLEMS follows the original EU KLEMS methodology (Timmer et al., 2010), which excludes land, ownership transfer costs, and cultivated biological resources. Russia has aligned the coverage of labor inputs to industry national accounts data. The Russian statistics office (Rosstat) developed employment data, called the Balance of Labor Inputs, which aligns to the National Accounts, using both labor force survey (LFS) and primary reports of firms. For Australia, labor services for productivity estimates are still sourced exclusively from a household-based collection. However, the Australian Bureau of Statistics (ABS) has introduced the experimental Labour Account in 2017 with stronger scope and coverage alignment to the National Accounts.

Measuring Economic Growth and Productivity
https://doi.org/10.1016/B978-0-12-817596-5.00010-X

10.2 Australia KLEMS

10.2.1 Background of KLEMS development in Australia

Since the late 2000s, interest has intensified regarding the sources of economic growth in the Australian economy. This is particularly relevant against the backdrop of declining productivity growth in Australia, particularly over the period 2004—05 to 2011—12. The need for better informed debate has been the case internationally as the productivity slowdown has been widespread. To facilitate this, blueprints for extended economic growth accounting frameworks have become available to meet more detailed and evidence-based economic analysis. KLEMS specifically includes more extensive industry-level growth analysis, including quantifying the contribution to growth of specific asset groupings, such as information technology (IT), as well as labor composition. The additional detail offered by the KLEMS growth accounts has been particularly useful. This is because intermediate inputs, when further split into energy, materials, and services components, inform the within-industry structural changes.

Australian studies have shown that there can be significant heterogeneity in output and productivity growth across industries (ABS, 2018a). Recognizing this, the ABS has extended the growth accounts in the core economic statistical products. Experimental KLEMS estimates for Australian industries were first introduced in 2016, covering KLEMS MFP estimates for 16 industry divisions that comprise the market sector.[1] In current price GVA (gross value added) terms, the 16 industry market sector grouping accounts for around 82% of GVA for all industries in 2017—18. The estimates of KLEMS industry growth accounts are available from 1995—96 to $t-1$, based on the time series of SUTs (supply and use tables) data from 1994—95, where t is the latest full financial year.

Prior to the KLEMS releases, the ABS released annual indexes of labor productivity and multifactor productivity (MFP) for the market sector aggregate since 1999, and for the industry divisions since 2007. Industry MFP statistics are available on both gross value added and gross output (GO) basis.

An important enabler of the KLEMS development is the SUTs.[2] The SUTs provide KLEMS with improved estimates of real output and real intermediate inputs, through double deflation. The SUTs also enable the estimation of volume indices and shares for energy, materials, and services within an integrated growth accounting framework.

There have been two key practical developments that facilitate the KLEMS project. First, recent works (Jorgenson et al., 2005; Timmer et al., 2010) now provide sufficient explicit detail for a coherent structure of the growth accounts. This has allowed the ABS to provide internally coherent systems of both KLEMS and GVA productivity estimates. Second, indices that users once regarded as choices between alternatives are now seen as a different perspective of the same underlying economic story.

10.2.2 KLEMS industry output and inputs

The KLEMS MFP measures are compiled in the standard growth accounting framework, which originates from the neoclassical theory of

---

[1] ABS (2015b). "The market sector covers industries predominantly producing goods and services which are sold at market prices."

[2] The ABS released the first issue of the time series of annual current price SUTs from 1994-95 to 2016-17 in December 2018. See ABS (2018b).

economic growth formulated by Solow (1957). Specifically, industry output is defined as a function of a combination of labor, capital, intermediate inputs, and technology. This was further refined into the modern growth accounting framework by Jorgenson et al. (1987). Following a similar approach, the ABS has developed growth accounts for these variables for the market sector industries. For a given industry, the KLEMS model can be expressed as contribution to output growth components as follows:

$$\Delta \ln GO_t = \tilde{w}_t^K \Delta \ln K_t + \tilde{w}_t^L \Delta \ln L_t + \tilde{w}_t^E \Delta \ln E_t$$
$$+ \tilde{w}_t^M \Delta \ln M_t + \tilde{w}_t^S \Delta \ln S_t + \Delta \ln A_t$$

(10.1)

where $\Delta \ln$ is the growth rate using natural logarithm,

GO_t is real gross output,
K_t is real capital services,
$\tilde{w}_t^K$ is the two period average capital cost share,
L_t is real labor services (hours worked plus labor composition),
$\tilde{w}_t^L$ is the two period average labor cost share,
E_t is real intermediate input: energy,
$\tilde{w}_t^E$ is the two period average energy cost share,
M_t is real intermediate input: materials,
$\tilde{w}_t^M$ is the two period average materials cost share,
S_t is real intermediate input: services,
$\tilde{w}_t^S$ is the two period average services cost share, and
A_t is GO-based MFP.

A brief description of the construction of the variables, some practical challenges, and recent developments are described below.

10.2.2.1 Labor input

The ABS publishes two types of labor input in the Australian KLEMS growth account: hours worked which are sourced from the LFS[3] and labor composition.[4] While the hours worked component implicitly assumes that the workforce is homogenous in terms of its contribution to output, the labor composition component captures changes in the composition of the work force. Such changes are captured through accounting for heterogeneity across different groups of workers by characteristics such as gender, education, and experience.[5] Labor composition data is sourced from the Census of Population and Housing, which is released every 5 years in Australia.

The industry hours worked series is calculated as a simple elemental index based on industry hours worked data. The quality-adjusted labor input (QALI) series is computed as a Törnqvist index based on hours worked weighted by the income share of employed workers in each labor force group. The gap between the QALI and hours worked index represents labor composition.

Labor composition is a key component of labor input growth for Australian market sector, period 1994–95 to 2016–17. Fig. 10.1 shows that the growth in QALI for the period was around 50% higher than the growth in hours worked series. The strength in QALI growth resulted in a 13.3% rise in GVA-based MFP on

---

[3] Industry total hours worked is calculated as total number of employed people multiplied by the average hours worked per worker.

[4] When hours worked and labor composition are combined, they represent quality-adjusted labor input. For details of the conceptual framework for quality-adjusted labor input, see ABS (2005).

[5] Classification of labor force is detailed in ABS (2015a).

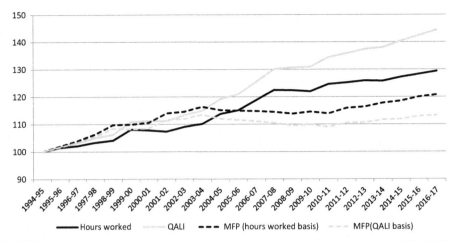

FIGURE 10.1   Labor input and MFP, Market sector—Australia. *Source: ABS (cat. no. 5260.0.55.002).*

a QALI basis, as opposed to 20.8% rise in GVA-based MFP on an hours worked basis for the period. That is, around one-third of the hours worked–based MFP can be attributed to changes in labor composition. GVA-based MFP growth is calculated as the growth of value-added output minus the growth of combined inputs (labor and capital) as follows:

$$\Delta \ln GVA\_MFP_t = \Delta \ln V_t$$
$$- \left(\tilde{z}_t^K \Delta \ln K_t + \tilde{z}_t^L \Delta \ln L_t \right) \qquad (10.2)$$

where GVA_MFP_t is the GVA-based MFP,

V_t is value-added output, and
$\tilde{z}_t^K$ and $\tilde{z}_t^L$ are the respective two period average income shares of capital and labor in total factor income.

One particular challenge facing productivity measurement is related to the alignment of industry output and industry labor input. Comparing employment from household and business surveys reveals significant differences in employed person for a small number of

Australian industries. While much of the variation is due to differences in methodology, scope, coverage, and concept, it may also be attributable to reporting errors. Possible mismatch between industry output and industry employment may be due to survey respondents in LFS reporting the industry based on occupation rather than the industry of employment.

To improve the understanding and account for these differences, the ABS has introduced the experimental Labour Account in 2017. The Labour Account provides a conceptual framework to produce a coherent and consistent set of aggregate labor market statistics. In particular, the Labour Account aligns with the production and residency boundaries of the Australian System of National Accounts (ASNA). The development of the Labour Account provides an important improvement in the alignment between an industry's labor input and output. As a result, the Labour Account estimates of labor input should contribute to improved industry productivity estimates in the future.[6]

---

[6] See, for example, ABS (2018c).

10.2.2.2 Capital input

The ABS distinguishes between many types of assets which include[7]:

- Machinery and equipment (comprising computers, electrical equipment, industrial equipment, other transport equipment, road vehicles, and other plant and equipment),
- Dwellings and nondwelling construction,
- Ownership transfer costs,
- Cultivated biological resources,
- Intellectual property products (comprising artistic originals, computer software, mineral exploration, and research and development [R&D]),
- Inventories, and
- Land.

The industry capital services are calculated as a Törnqvist index of capital services for each asset type. The weights are the shares of each of these assets in total capital income. To estimate the weights, capital income for each asset is calculated as the product of the volume of productive capital stock and the asset's rental price. The capital rental price is derived following the arbitrage equation outlined in Jorgenson et al. (2005).[8] Second, the capital income for each asset is then divided by total capital income, to obtain the weights.[9]

The ABS has made incremental improvements to rental prices since their introduction in 1990. Recognizing heterogeneity in the asset lives and prices, machinery and equipment was decomposed into six types, estimated separately by industry and institutional sector. This step facilitated separate estimation of the rental price for computer equipment. The importance of this improvement cannot be overstated since prices of computers have been declining rapidly, resulting in the large quality improvements of computers correctly attributed to the growth in capital services.

Furthermore, recognizing the distinctly different role of IT capital (computer hardware and software), the ABS implemented the IT/non-IT partition to capital services, as described in Jorgenson et al. (2005) in the productivity growth accounts. This decomposition was first available at industry level with the experimental direct aggregation across industry labor productivity growth accounts from the 2013-14 release of Estimates of Industry Multifactor Productivity[10] and then the experimental KLEMS growth accounts from the first issue in 2014-15.[11] The partition allowed the influence of IT capital to correctly reflect its relatively greater influence in the capital service index (compared to capital stock) supporting deeper analysis of industry's propensity to innovate.[12]

With the breakdown of IT/non-IT capital, hours worked, and labor composition, the KLEMS growth account provides detailed

---

[7] For a complete list of asset types and their details, see Chapter 14 in ABS (2015a).

[8] The arbitrage equation is an expression in which the investor is indifferent between earning a nominal rate of return on an investment or buying a capital asset, renting it out, collecting rent, and selling it. Rental prices can be defined through rearrangement of this expression.

[9] For more detailed discussion of the aggregation, see Chapter 19 in ABS (2015a).

[10] See Table 23 in ABS (2018a).

[11] See ABS (2015b).

[12] This topic was a focus of earlier prominent studies by the Productivity Commission and the Department of Communications Information Technology and the Arts. In particular, supporting a lively debate as to whether the penultimate productivity growth cycle (1993–94 to 1998–99) was due to the ongoing microeconomic reform program or the emerging information technology revolution.

productivity growth accounting decompositions. Finer decompositions are also derivable, since ABS publishes productive capital stock and rental prices by detailed assets.

Although not part of the standard suite of productivity estimates, other asset groupings are also possible. Two useful extensions are to group electrical equipment with IT capital to form the information and communication technology (ICT) capital grouping (since electrical equipment includes significant communications equipment) or to pool intellectual property products (i.e., computer software, mineral exploration, artistic originals, and R&D) and labor composition more broadly as "knowledge capital" similarly to O'Mahony and Timmer (2009), to facilitate globalization analysis.

In the late 1990s, tax parameters were also added to the rental price specification, broadly following Hulten (1990). As one of the policy levers, the Australian tax code can be specific to certain assets types or industries, particularly regarding immediate write-off of capital or the time horizon for various depreciation allowances. Accordingly inclusion of the tax parameters on rental prices can remove certain distortions to the user cost. For example, a policy initiative to stimulate R&D investment via an immediate tax write-off reduced R&D rental prices.

Currently, the ABS rental prices align to international best practice articulated by Jorgenson et al. (2005). That is, by equating gross operating surplus to weighted sum of real productive capital stock, the internal rate of return (IRR) is solved endogenously.

In practice, however, for certain asset classes, especially land (a nondepreciable asset), strong capital gains may offset the IRR resulting in a negative rental price. In such cases, ABS imputes a small positive rental price. The incidence of negative rentals is also reduced by intervention, mainly equating the real IRR to a long-term risk-free borrowing rate of 4%. Due to these interventions, the rental prices are better described as a hybrid between endogenous and exogenous methods.

In view of alternative exogenous IRR approach (see van den Bergen et al., 2007; Baldwin and Gu, 2007), the ABS evaluated the merits of variations to the rental price formula. One issue was whether the increased granularity of productivity statistics warranted a stronger application of the exogenous method of rental price estimation, as per Baldwin and Gu (2007). The ABS also explored whether applying smoothed (expected) capital gains could improve estimation through reduced intervention. This approach needed to be weighed against achieving consistency with other ASNA estimates, such as GFCF implicit price deflators. On balance, the hybrid method strikes a reasonable balance between coherence with the ASNA and various approaches to accommodate the practical requirements of the Törnqvist aggregation method. For example, smoothing capital gains can reduce intervention but at the cost of consistency with capital price deflators used elsewhere in the suite of national accounts.

10.2.2.3 Intermediate inputs

Intermediate inputs play a key role in the production process and are therefore the main component in the GO-based growth account. In 2015−16, intermediate inputs accounted for more than half of the total input cost shares in 12 of the 16 market sector industries. For Manufacturing and Construction, intermediate inputs represent approximately 70% of GO.

The Australian experience with KLEMS is that the role of intermediate inputs in the growth account for many industries has been far from static. An industry's reliance on intermediate inputs may change due to a variety of factors, such as in response to changes in the relative prices of inputs, or to increase flexibility to align the renting or purchase of inputs with production requirements, thus improving utilization rates. For example, a construction company may lease a crane from the rental and hiring industry, which is recorded as a service component in the intermediate inputs of the lessee and as capital services by the lessor in the rental and hiring industry.

The Australian KLEMS separates intermediate inputs into energy, materials, and services, to recognize their distinctively different roles in the production process. In the SUTs, product classes detailed with 5-digit Supply and Use Product Classification (SUPC) are assigned to either energy, materials, or services category based on the primary use of the product within the category. A list of SUPC and assigned categories are detailed in ABS (2015b).

In Australia, the energy component can be useful for monitoring an industry's energy intensity. This variable has benefited from ongoing confrontation with the ABS Energy Accounts within a Supply and Use framework. The reconciliation between ABS Energy Accounts and the SUTs was first achieved on a current prices basis. More recently, the Energy Accounts quantities have been standardized into a single unit (petajoules), assisting the data confrontation exercise. Moreover, ongoing confrontation of petajoules by energy type has strengthened the product to industry alignment.

10.2.2.4 Gross output

GO refers to the value of goods and services produced in the accounting period, including production that remains incomplete at the end of accounting period (ABS, 2015a). GO is sourced from the SUTs for years from 1994-95 onward. The measure of GO requires elaboration for services industries. The GO for transport and storage activity is the recorded transport margin, while the GOs for Wholesale Trade and Retail Trade are the realized trade margins on the goods sold. GO for Finance and Insurance Services is estimated indirectly using financial intermediation services indirectly measured.

10.2.2.5 Index number choice

Index number choice for Australian KLEMS is similar to that of EU KLEMS, outlined in Timmer et al. (2010). The Törnqvist index is the preferred index choice for aggregation, with some exceptions. First, GO indexes are chained Laspeyres index, which are consistent with published aggregate market sector GVA series of the ASNA. Second, the series on intermediate inputs are decomposed into energy, materials, and services. Indexes for each of these intermediate inputs are compiled using a Törnqvist index. However, like GO and GVA, the published intermediate input indices are based on the Laspeyres index formula. To maintain coherence with the National Accounts series on intermediate input, results for energy, materials, and services are scaled using their cost shares to arrive at Laspeyres total intermediate inputs. These adjustments allow additivity in the KLEMS growth accounting framework.

10.2.3 KLEMS results for Australia

10.2.3.1 Input cost shares

Table 10.1 presents the shifts in cost shares of all five factor inputs for market sector industries over the period 1995—96 to 2015—16.

The input cost shares of labor and capital varied considerably across industries. Among the 16 market sector industries, growth in combined cost shares of labor and capital was found in 11 industries, over 1995—96 to 2015—16 period. Particularly, the industries exhibiting rapid growth in primary input cost shares were Administrative and Support Services, Retail Trade, and Professional, Scientific and Technical Services. In these industries, gains in cost shares of the combined labor and capital inputs exceeded 10%. The cost share gains in these industries were predominantly from growth in the labor cost share. These industries had been

TABLE 10.1   KLEMS input cost shares (%), 1995−96 and 2015−16.

	Capital services		Labor services		Energy		Materials		Services	
	1995 −96	2015 −16	1995 −96	2015 −16	1995 −96	2015 −16	1995 −96	2015 −16	1995 −96	2015 −16
Agriculture, Forestry and Fishing	22.7	29.0	14.3	12.6	2.3	4.4	27.1	19.7	33.5	34.2
Mining	39.4	34.7	16.6	15.3	5.4	5.1	9.1	6.7	29.6	38.2
Manufacturing	12.4	9.5	19.3	18.9	5.1	6.7	49.9	44.9	13.3	20.0
Electricity, Gas, Water and Waste Services	31.2	27.3	18.4	13.8	5.2	5.2	6.9	4.0	38.4	49.8
Construction	8.3	9.1	22.5	21.8	2.0	1.2	27.7	21.0	39.6	46.9
Wholesale Trade	19.2	16.4	32.7	33.4	3.0	2.8	7.8	5.7	37.3	41.7
Retail Trade	12.4	15.5	33.6	45.1	1.4	1.8	11.3	6.4	41.3	31.3
Accommodation and Food Services	6.8	10.5	33.7	37.7	2.0	2.5	42.2	26.5	15.3	22.8
Transport, Postal and Warehousing Services	14.8	18.6	26.0	26.7	6.5	8.1	6.1	2.5	46.6	44.1
Information, Media and Telecommunication Services	23.8	25.0	18.3	19.2	1.8	1.8	6.1	4.2	50.1	49.8
Financial and Insurance Services	37.7	42.7	25.2	19.4	0.2	0.5	1.2	0.5	35.7	37.0
Rental, Hiring and Real Estate Services	25.4	29.3	16.1	20.5	1.5	1.8	3.0	0.9	54.0	47.5
Professional, Scientific and Technical Services	2.9	7.1	37.6	44.1	0.7	0.7	4.4	1.1	54.4	47.0
Administrative and Support Services	3.4	2.8	38.5	57.2	0.7	0.3	6.4	1.6	51.0	38.0
Arts and Recreation Services	9.0	13.1	26.3	25.0	0.9	0.7	22.4	17.1	41.5	44.2
Other Services	8.2	6.4	35.8	44.1	0.9	0.6	32.4	23.5	22.8	25.6

Source: ABS (cat. no. 5260.0.55.004).

among the most labor-intensive industries since the start of series in 1995−96.

The cost shares for energy inputs were relatively small across Australian industries. However, a significant increase in energy shares was seen in Agriculture, Forestry and Fishing, as the industry engaged in more capital-intensive farming practices. The cost shares for materials component of intermediate inputs have declined across all industries. While this decline could be due to more efficient materials usage, it is more likely a substitution effect toward services inputs. For example, Manufacturing and Accommodation and Food Services saw an uptake of more digitalized technology requiring the hiring of professional support services.[13]

Services cost shares were large and have been growing for most industry divisions. The increased importance of the services component was due to both within-industry intermediate inputs composition as well as the market sector's

[13] IBIS World reports (unpublished). For a more general discussion on digital uptake, see Australia's Tech Future, Delivering a strong safe and inclusive digital economy (paper 2018/12 at www.industry.gov.au).

increasing orientation toward services industries. Over the last two decades, this trend can also be readily identified in Manufacturing and Construction. More recently, there has been greater interest in the role of outsourcing of labor (such as cleaning and IT consulting services) and capital (such as industrial equipment hire) between industries. Outsourcing reflects arrangements between firms in different industries such as when capital is rented under an operational lease arrangement. This dynamic pattern suggests that productivity analysis, when taking into account the trends in intermediate inputs usage, can explain the divergences between the GVA and GO-based growth accounts.

10.2.3.2 Contributions to output growth

The published KLEMS datacube (ABS cat. no. 5260.0.55.004) provides an opportunity to examine the key drivers of GO for market sector industries. Table 10.2 presents detailed industry growth accounting of GO changes into contributions from growth in labor services, capital services, intermediate inputs, and MFP.

The largest contribution by IT capital was for Financial and Insurance Services; Rental, Hiring and Real Estate Services; and Information, Media and Telecommunication Services. IT capital contribution in Mining has been relatively small compared to contribution from labor driven by a rapid increase in employment during the Australian mining investment boom.

Non-IT capital contributed considerably to GO growth in a number of industries, particularly in Mining. The buildup of non-IT capital was significant during the Mining investment boom with recent years seeing a wind-down of the investment phase as mining firms ramped up their production and increased the utilization rates of newly available infrastructure. During the height of the investment phase, 2005—06 to 2013—14, the contribution from non-IT capital services almost solely explained the growth in GO. Non-IT capital was also significant in Rental, Hiring and Real Estate Services. Firms in this division mainly are engaged in renting and hiring tangible or intellectual propertyassets. For example, they purchase capital and then lease to firms in other industries. Information, Media and Telecommunication Services also recorded strong growth in capital (both IT and non-IT). The fast increase in capital intensity, coupled with a subdued growth in hours worked, resulted in significant capital deepening in this industry.

Hours worked contribution to the output growth showed considerable variation at the industry level. For example, hours worked detracted from GO growth in Agriculture and Wholesale Trade over the period. This reflects the move toward capital-intensive farming practices in Australian agriculture and the increasing popularity of Internet-based wholesaling. In contrast, the contribution of hours worked was strongest in Professional, Scientific and Technical Services, and Administrative and Support Services. The strength in the contribution for these industries was due to the economy's increasing demand for professional services over the past two decades.

Changes in labor composition were notable in Wholesale Trade, and Professional, Scientific and Technical Services, although they were most pronounced in Administrative and Support Services between 2005—06 and 2010—11. This period also saw the reallocation effects of labor to the Mining industry to harness the extraction of minerals that had become economically viable as a result of rising commodity prices. More recently, as commodity prices retreated, offsetting reallocation effects toward the services industries, such as Administrative and Support Services division, were recorded.[14]

---

[14] Experimental estimates of the Stiroh (2002)-based labor reallocation effect are published in Tables 21 and 22 of ABS (2018a).

TABLE 10.2   Annual points contribution to GO growth, 1995—96 to 2015—16.

| Industry | Gross output growth | Contribution from capital services | | Contribution from labor services | | Contribution from intermediate inputs | | | MFP growth[b] |
		IT[a]	Non-IT	Hours worked	Composition	Energy	Materials	Services	
Agriculture, Forestry and Fishing	1.8	0.0	0.1	−0.2	0.0	0.2	0.2	0.3	1.2
Mining	3.4	0.1	3.0	0.5	0.0	0.1	0.1	0.7	−1.0
Manufacturing	0.9	0.1	0.1	−0.2	0.1	0.0	0.4	0.4	0.1
Electricity, Gas, Water and Waste Services	1.3	0.3	0.7	0.3	0.1	0.1	0.1	0.5	−0.7
Construction	4.3	0.1	0.4	0.6	0.0	0.0	1.0	1.9	0.3
Wholesale Trade	3.6	0.2	0.3	−0.3	0.2	0.1	0.2	1.6	1.2
Retail Trade	2.3	0.3	0.5	0.5	0.1	0.0	0.0	0.2	0.7
Accommodation and Food Services	2.7	0.1	0.2	0.4	0.0	0.1	0.4	1.1	0.4
Transport, Postal and Warehousing Services	2.7	0.1	0.5	0.4	0.1	0.2	0.0	1.1	0.3
Information, Media and Telecommunication Services	4.6	0.5	0.8	0.1	0.1	0.1	0.2	2.4	0.4
Financial and Insurance Services	4.6	1.0	0.2	0.3	0.2	0.0	0.0	1.8	1.0
Rental, Hiring and Real Estate Services	3.0	0.6	1.1	0.4	0.1	0.0	0.0	1.5	−0.7
Professional, Scientific and Technical Services	4.5	0.2	0.2	1.4	0.2	0.0	0.0	2.4	0.1
Administrative and Support Services	3.6	0.1	0.1	1.1	0.2	0.0	0.0	1.8	0.2
Arts and Recreation Services	3.2	0.2	0.5	0.8	0.1	0.0	0.3	1.4	−0.2
Other Services	2.0	0.2	0.5	0.3	0.1	0.0	0.3	0.6	0.0

[a] IT capital services refer to computers and software and non-IT capital refers to all other capital services.
[b] Quality-adjusted hours worked basis.
Source: ABS (cat. no. 5260.0.55.004).

The contribution of energy to GO growth was small across most industries. For example, the contribution to output growth was negligible in Manufacturing due to the decline in steel and car manufacturing in Australia. Materials accounted for smaller cost shares over the last two decades (Table 10.1). Despite the declines in cost shares, its contribution to the output growth was still significant in material-intensive industries such as Construction, Manufacturing and Accommodation and Food Services.

Among the intermediate inputs, services component was the key contributor to output growth in many industries. Differences in services contribution appeared to be the major driver of divergences in output growth. Finally, there has been considerable variation in MFP performance across the industries. While noticeable MFP growth was recorded in Agriculture, Forestry and Fishing, and Wholesale Trade, MFP detracted significantly from output growth in Mining, Electricity, Gas, Water and Waste Services, and Rental, Hiring and Real Estate Services.

10.3 Russia KLEMS

10.3.1 Background of Russia KLEMS

The Russia KLEMS initiative was launched in 2007 at National Research University Higher School of Economics (HSE) as a response to concerns on the dependence of growth of the Russian economy on Oil and Gas export revenues. The first release of Russia KLEMS data was published in 2013 as a joint project of HSE and the University of Groningen, and its update and extension, in 2017 (Russia KLEMS, 2017). The published data set covers 34 industries in 1995–2014. With Russia KLEMS Timmer and Voskoboynikov (2014, 2016) showed that Russian growth before the global crisis of 2008 was driven not only by capital input in oil and gas-related industries but also by technology catching up in Manufacturing and market services, especially in Finance. At present Russia KLEMS is the only source of relatively long run series of output, inputs, and productivity in industries in the

international industry classification NACE 1, which describes the Russian economy since 1995. Because of this Russia KLEMS data help to treat economic stagnation in Russia in the last decade not only as the outcome of some domestic challenges but also in the context of global stagnation (Voskoboynikov, 2017). Russia KLEMS data are widely used in the broad set of studies on various aspects of the Russian economy in the comparative perspective.[15]

A big challenge for the Russia KLEMS project is the fact that the Russian statistics office (Rosstat) does not provide backcast estimations of industry-level time series of National Accounts with each major methodology change. Since 1995, there were two such changes. The first one took place in 2003 with the shift of the official statistics to the new industrial classification NACE 1 from the old one, inherited from the pre-SNA period and inconsistent with any international one. The second challenge was the update of national accounts standards in Russia from SNA 93 to SNA 2008. One more is expected with the upcoming transition of the official statistics to NACE 2. The earliest year of the new series in SNA 2008 is 2011 with no officially indicated intention of Rosstat to make backcast estimations. Fig. 10.2 illustrates this point, showing the upward shift in the total GDP trend in 2011 in the official statistics and in Russia KLEMS releases.

Dealing with these and multiple other smaller methodology changes, an independent research center, such as HSE, can be more flexible in data construction, than an official statistics institution. However, a limited access to primary statistics and details of the official statistics methodology makes its maintenance and improvements more complicated.

---

[15] See, among others, Vries et al. (2012); Brock and Ogloblin (2016); Kaitila (2016); Brandt et al. (2017); Zhao and Tang (2018); Okawa and Sanghi (2018); Voskoboynikov (2019). Russia KLEMS data are also in use in the Total Economy Database (https://www.conference-board.org/data/economydatabase/index.cfm?id=27762) and the World Income Output Database (http://www.wiod.org/home).

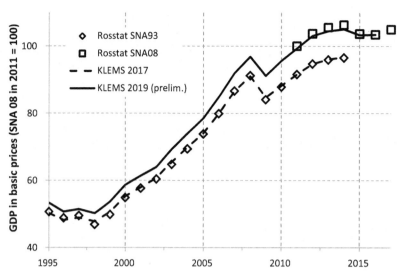

FIGURE 10.2   Real GDP in basic prices. Various releases of the official series and Russia KLEMS. *Sources: ("Russia KLEMS" 2017) (KLEMS-17); own calculations for Russia KELMS 2019 (KLEMS-19, preliminary); Rosstat SNA93 (http://www.gks.ru/free_doc/ new_site/vvp/vvp-god/tab3.xls, last update December 31, 2015; Rosstat (2015; tab. 2.5.1)); Rosstat SNA08 (http://www.gks.ru/free_doc/ new_site/vvp/vvp-god/tab3a.xls, last update April 03, 2018).*

Along with data extensions, three major updates of Russia KLEMS are in progress now. These are the development of labor composition; development of GO-based growth accounts based on the new official SUTs and the adaptation of SNA 2008, including backcast estimations of the Russia KLEMS series.

10.3.2 Russia KLEMS methodology

This subsection reviews shortly major data construction points, thoroughly discussed by Voskoboynikov (2012), and the following updates, such as labor composition and the construction of GO-based growth accounting.

10.3.2.1 *Output*

Output series include GO, intermediate inputs, and value added both in current and comparable prices. Data construction process and sources of Russia KLEMS releases of 2013 and 2017 can be found in Voskoboynikov (2012).

The series are based on the official SNA data with minor adjustments for differences in SNA releases and backcast estimations of industry-level series in 1995—2003 to bridge the old Soviet industrial classification OKONKh and NACE 1. These series correspond to concepts of output in SNA 93, which was adapted in Russia in early 1990s. The industry-level series, based on SNA 93, cover years until 2014 (Rosstat, 2015).

Starting from 2011 Rosstat (2017) publishes the series, which match SNA 2008 standards and correspond to the new series of SUTs. The benchmark SUTs start in 2011 with the following projections. Official SNA 2008 backcast estimations for years before 2011 are not available. The most important issue for output series in this transition from SNA 93 to SNA 2008 is taking into account the own-account production of housing services by owner-occupiers, which fall at real estate activities (industry code 70 in NACE 1). Proper adjustments back to 1995 have been made in the preliminary version of

TABLE 10.3 Sectoral shares of value added and contribution to real growth, 1995–2014 in releases of Russia KLEMS 2017 and 2019.

	Average share of value added (%)		Growth rates (%)		Contributions (p.p.)	
	SNA 93	SNA 08	SNA 93	SNA 08	SNA 93	SNA 08
Total	100.0	100.0	3.47	3.56	3.47	3.56
Market Economy	83.5	78.7	3.60	3.55	3.00	2.79
Agriculture	5.9	5.7	1.39	1.51	0.08	0.09
Extended Oil and Gas sector	22.2	20.2	3.59	3.65	0.80	0.74
Manufacturing	18.7	17.6	2.15	2.06	0.40	0.36
Retail, construction, telecom, hotels and restaurants (RCT)	18.9	18.2	4.07	3.84	0.77	0.70
Finance and business services	8.6	8.3	8.41	8.54	0.72	0.70
Transport	9.3	8.7	2.55	2.33	0.24	0.20
Nonmarket services	16.5	21.3	2.79	3.60	0.46	0.77

Notes: Data of Russia KLEMS 2019 are preliminary. It is based on the last release of Russian National Accounts on the basis of SNA 2008. Growth rates of sectors of KLEMS 2019 release differ from those of KLEMS 2017, because of recent official revisions in Russian national accounts. Extended oil and gas includes mining (code C), fuel (23) and wholesale trade (51); RCT includes construction (F), automotive sales (50), retail (52), hotels (H), post and telecom (64) and social services (O); nonmarket services include real estate activities (70), public administration and defence (L), education (M), and health and social work (N). For the full list of sectors and industries see in Appendix.
Sources: own calculations based on Russia KLEMS: World KLEMS Initiative (website), 2017. http://www.worldklems.net/data/basic/RUS_wk_march_2017.xlsx, and a new release of Russia KLEMS, which is expected in 2019. See main text.

the upcoming release of Russia KLEMS 2019.[16] Table 10.3 and Fig. 10.2 show changes in a real value added in the total economy and its major sectors.

Specifically, Table 10.3 represents average shares of aggregated sectors of the Russian economy in 1995–2014 in the recent and the upcoming releases of Russia KLEMS, which are based on SNA 93 and SNA 2008 correspondingly. Since real estate activities belong to nonmarket economy sector, the extension of this activity led also to the increase of nonmarket services from 16.5% to 21.3%. In turn, this change and the update of sectoral growth rates in line with the recent official release of Russian national accounts leads to slower growth rates in market economy and higher growth in the nonmarket sector and ends up with some upward revision of total growth from 3.47% per year to 3.56.

Starting from 2015 data of the Crimea republic and Sevastopol are included in the SNA series. However, the share of both regions in industry-level series is marginal. That is why no special backward adjustments on this have been made.

10.3.2.2 SUTs: adaptation and backcast estimations

Until recently the lack of official SUTs in NACE 1 was a major obstacle for the

[16] The new release of Russia KLEMS is expected by the end of 2019. Detailed description of this and the following adjustments and sources of the new Russia KLEMS release will be published in a special background paper.

development of GO-based growth accounting for Russia. Fortunately, in March 2017 Rosstat released the first set of benchmark SUTs in NACE 1 for 2011, which covers 178 industries and 248 products.[17] Its projections of SUTs for 2012—15 are less detailed, but enough for the purposes of Russia KLEMS. The next benchmark SUTs for 2016 are expected in 2019.

Taking into account the importance of long run series, we work on the backcast extension of the SUTs series back to 2003, which is the first year after transition of the official statistics to NACE 1. This extension is based on SNA series of GO, intermediate inputs and value added in 2003—10, adjusted for the recent version of SNA, and the RAS projection.[18]

10.3.2.3 Hours worked

Main source of the series of hours worked is the *Balance of Labor Inputs* (BLI), which is harmonized with the Russian National Accounts. It is published from 2005 onward, but only at an aggregate 1-digit industry level. To break it down into finer industry detail and backcast the series back to pre-2005 years, I rely on a combination of data from the *Balance of Labor Force* (BLF) and reports of organizations of *the Full Circle* (FC), which include large, medium, and small firms as well as various public administration organizations. The BLF is the oldest system of labor accounts, existed in the Soviet statistics since early 1920s. It is based on FC with additional estimations for self-employed and workers engaged in commercial

production in husbandries. FC contains more detailed data than the BLF. For 2003 and later, detailed industry shares from BLF, and if necessary from FC, were applied to the aggregate series from the BLI. Before 2003, trends in BLF and FC at the corresponding industries were implemented. BLF and FC give the numbers of employees, and we assume that employee growth proxies for growth in hours. More details can be found in Voskoboynikov (2012).

10.3.2.4 Labor composition

The conventional KLEMS approach (Timmer et al., 2010, tab. 3A.4) assumes the consideration of different labor types. The total amount of hours worked are classified by educational attainment (low-, medium-, and high-skills levels), gender and age (15—29; 30—49; 50 and older), or 18 (= 3 * 2 * 3) labor types in total. Low skills level corresponds to International Standard Classification of Education (ISCED) levels 0—2 and 3C; medium skills, 3 and 4, excluding 3C; and high skills, 5 and 6. In turn, the bridge between ISCED levels and levels of the Russian educational system was suggested by Kapeliushnikov (2008, tab. 1).

Hours worked by individual labor types were obtained by breaking down the total amount of hours worked in an industry with shares of hours worked by a particular labor type. In turn, these shares were based on data of LFS. Next, we used two sources of data on relative wages by type of labor. The first one is the

---

[17] Dale Jorgenson contributed to the restoration of SUTs construction in Russian statistics after a break in 2004—10. In April 1, 2008, he presented the analytical potential of SUTs for the analysis of economic growth and economic policy implications in the Ministry of Economic Development and Trade of the Russian Federation. In 7 years, in April 9, 2015, the head of Rosstat Alexander Surinov acknowledged the role of Professor Jorgenson in the revival of the compilation of SUTs in Russian statistics in his speech in XVI April International Academic Conference at Higher School of Economics in Moscow.

[18] This is the joint effort of Eduard Baranov, Dmitri Piontkovski, and Elena Staritsyna. Detailed description of this methodology of this approach will be published separately a joint paper, which is in progress now.

National Survey of Household Welfare and Participation in Social Programs,[19] conducted by Rosstat in 2003 within the assistance program of the World Bank. The second one is the Survey of Wages by Occupations,[20] provided by Rosstat biannually in 2005–15. Relative wages for years between the surveys and before 2003 were assumed to be equal to ones in the nearest upcoming year, for which data are available.

10.3.2.5 Capital

The series of capital services in Russia KLEMS are constructed on the basis of net stocks of eight types of assets (computing equipment, communication equipment and software, residential structures, nonresidential structures, machinery and equipment, transport, and other assets), standard KLEMS depreciation rates (Timmer et al., 2010, tab. 3.5), and internal rates of return (Voskoboynikov, 2012). The sensitivity analysis of different capital input measures for the Russian economy in terms of GVA-based growth accounting is given by Timmer and Voskoboynikov (2014, 2016, Table 1).

10.3.2.6 Input's shares

The shares of labor and capital in value added are used as weights in the growth accounting and reflect the output elasticity of the inputs. The labor share should reflect the total cost of labor from the perspective of the employer and so include wages but also nonwage employee benefits and an imputed wage for self-employed workers. In Russia, there is a long-standing tradition of nonwage payments. This is well known, and Rosstat provides estimates that are included in the total economy series of the Russian

National Accounts, but not in the industry statistics. That is why industry-level NAS series on labor compensation in industries underestimate labor cost shares. For 2002 and subsequent years, the overall amount of hidden wages at the overall economy level has been allocated among industries in proportion to the industry value added shares of shadow activities according to official imputations.[21] For years before 2002, the hidden wages were allocated in proportion to the industry distribution of shadow value added in 2002. Finally, our estimate of labor income of self-employed is added. For all industries, except Agriculture, I assume that the hourly earnings of self-employed are the same as for employees. For Agriculture, with a high share of low educated workers, I imputed with the total economy average wage for low educated employees based on data from the RLMS survey. Further details can be found in Voskoboynikov (2012).

One of the adjustments in the official statistics with the transition to SNA 2008 is the further elaboration of input shares, taking into account informal activities. Proper backcast adjustments in Russia KLEMS series seem to be substantial and have not been implemented yet.

10.3.3 What we have learned about Russian growth from Russia KLEMS

10.3.3.1 Aggregate view

As shown in Fig. 10.2, Russian economic growth in two recent decades was volatile. The transformational recession with its negative growth rates was followed by outstanding growth. Table 10.4 reports that growth rates

---

[19] In Russian: *Natsional'noe obsledovanie biudzhetov domashnikh biudzhetov domashnikh* (NOBUS).

[20] In Russian: *Obsledovanie zarabotnykh plat po professiiam (OZPP)*.

[21] Rosstat publishes data on adjustments of value added, taking into account informal and shadow economy in industries, starting from 2002 (see, e.g., Rosstat (2010), tab. 2.3.46–2.3.53). According to the methodological note (Rosstat, 2010, section 2.3), official estimations are made on the basis of matching of consumption and income; expert evaluations and indirect imputations.

TABLE 10.4   Growth accounting decomposition of total market economy in 1995–2014 (percentage points).

	1995–2003	2003–07	2007–14	1995–2014
VA growth	3.43	7.14	1.64	3.47
Hours worked	0.07	0.83	−0.12	0.16
Labor product, total	3.36	6.31	1.76	3.30
Labor reallocation	1.19	0.72	0.40	0.72
Intra-industry productivity	2.17	5.59	1.36	2.59
Capital intensity, total	−0.09	2.26	2.40	1.41
ICT	0.16	0.23	0.07	0.10
Machinery and equipment	0.17	1.14	0.81	0.55
Constructions	−0.30	0.46	1.26	0.59
Others	−0.11	0.43	0.27	0.16
Multifactor productivity	2.08	3.26	−1.28	1.00
Labor composition	0.18	0.07	0.24	0.18

Note: data on labor composition differ slightly from results, reported by Timmer and Voskoboynikov (2016, tab. 8.1), because more detailed statistics on hours worked for different categories of workers was used for the present study.
Sources: own calculations, based on Russia KLEMS: World KLEMS Initiative (website), 2017. http://www.worldklems.net/data/basic/RUS_wk_march_2017.xlsx.

were as high as 7.1% per year in 2003–07. Eventually, they ended up with stagnation around 1.6% in 2007–14 and negative growth −0.4% in 2014–17.[22] Most research on growth accounting of the Russian economy has been carried out on the total economy level (e.g., Okawa and Sanghi (2018); see also a recent review in Timmer and Voskoboynikov, 2016). They use different measures of capital input, such as capital stocks and services; take into account capacity utilization (Entov and Lugovoy, 2013) and terms of trade (Kaitila, 2016). This total economy approach, however, is sensitive to strong assumptions of the aggregate production function approach. Specifically, it assumes the same technology in all industries, all types of capital are homogeneous in productivity, so as groups of workers. Finally, the aggregate production function (APF) approach adopts similar prices on inputs and outputs for different industries. Russia KLEMS data set relaxes these assumptions for the Russian economy since 1995 onward in line with the framework of Jorgenson et al. (1987).

In this study I extend results of Voskoboynikov and Timmer and Voskoboynikov (2016) for 2 more years, up to 2014. As can be seen in Fig. 10.2, the period under consideration includes two economic crises, 1998 and 2009, as well as the intercrises period of rapid resurgence. How did the growth structure change? I split the data into three periods, 1995–2003, 2003–07, and 2007–14. In this split I put peaks and troughs of business cycles into the periods to minimize biases, caused by short-term demand effects. Indeed, in case of a sharp output fall, which happened in 1998 and 2009, the reduction of capital utilization might not be fully captured by capital input measures and can be wrongly attributed to the MFP slowdown.

In contrast with the bulk of the growth accounting literature, which stresses the substantial contribution of MFP, our results, shown in Table 10.4, reveal that MFP contributed only 1 percentage point of 3.5% of the yearly average growth of total economy in 1995–2014, or less than one- third. As can be seen from Table 10.4, over time growth becomes more extensive. In 1995–2003 MFP provided 2.1 p.p. of 3.4, or more than 60%, but in the following years MFP contribution declined to about 46%. In the last period, which includes the crisis of 2008, MFP

[22] Growth rates in 2014–17 are retrieved from the website of Rosstat (http://www.gks.ru/free_doc/new_site/vvp/ vvp-god/tab3a.xls, the update of 03.04.2018).

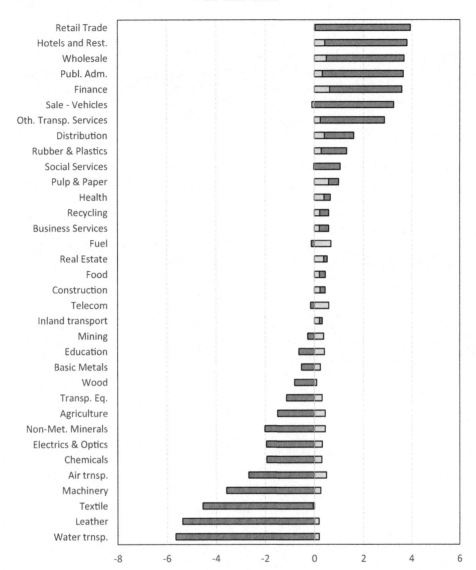

FIGURE 10.3 Growth rates of labor input in 34 industries, 1995–2014. Note: *Dark shaded*, the growth of hours worked; *Light shaded*, the contributions of changes in labor composition. *Source: Calculations on the basis of ("Russia KLEMS" 2017).*

growth turns to be negative. These results suggest that Russia has become ever more dependent on investment to push growth up. While in 1995–2003 the contribution of capital intensity to labor productivity growth was relatively low, in the following years its role increased dramatically. In years of recovery, it accounted for 2.3 p.p., or 36% of labor productivity growth, while in the last global crisis it became the dominant source of growth, growing faster than value added.

Table 10.4 presents the contribution of changes in the labor composition. The main finding here is that in the posttransition Russia, changes in labor composition contribute to labor productivity growth positively. The process of aging leads to the extension of labor shares of experienced and better educated aged workers. At the same time, aged workers with the low level of education and experience retire earlier, giving place to younger generations. This effect can be stronger in high skills—intensive industries and weaker in low skills—intensive ones. Fig. 10.3 shows growth rates of labor services, split into contributions of hours worked and labor composition. If the leading role of such skills-intensive activities as finance, telecom, or air transportation is not surprising, as well as the low position of automotive sales, retail, textile, or wood industries. However, the top positions of fuel or wholesale trade are worth to be commented. The soaring oil prices increased demand on fuel and, as a consequence, the contribution of high qualified workers, especially men aged between 30 and 49. The contribution of this group of workers turns out to be the highest with the largest labor compensation increase and high growth in hours worked, exceeded 5% per year.

The period in question covers years of intensive structural change (Voskoboynikov, 2019). In general, structural change was growth enhancing. Table 10.4 reports that on the average in 1995—2014 labor reallocations contributed to labor productivity growth 0.7 p.p. of total 3%, being reduced in time from 1.2 p.p. in 1995—2003 to 0.4 p.p. in 2007—14. Voskoboynikov (2019) suggested to split formal and informal activities within each industry and calculated the reallocation effects. He found, that expanding informal activities slowdown the value of the reallocation effect. Therefore, the impact of reallocation, which is reported in Table 10.4 with no informal split, seems to be slightly overestimated.

The productivity performance of various sectors has been quite diverse. In Table 10.5 I provide the annual growth rates of labor and capital input and MFP growth of main sectors from 1995 to 2014. This is shown on the left-hand side of the table. The right side of the table reports contributions of each sector to aggregate growth of inputs and MFP. The contributions are calculated as weighted averages of sectoral

TABLE 10.5 Average annual growth rates of inputs and MFP during 1995—2014 in Total Market economy.

	Annual growth rates			Contribution		
	Capital intensity	MFP	Labor composition per hour	Capital intensity	MFP	Labor composition per hour
Total market economy	2.86	1.10	0.32	2.86	1.10	0.32
Agriculture	0.97	2.37	0.43	0.07	0.17	0.03
Extended Oil and Gas sector	2.59	−0.47	0.47	0.69	−0.13	0.12
Manufacturing	2.64	1.34	0.29	0.59	0.30	0.07
Retail, construction, telecom, hotels and restaurants (RCT)	2.98	0.92	0.16	0.67	0.21	0.04
Finance and Business Services	3.05	5.76	0.38	0.32	0.60	0.04
Transport	4.75	−0.31	0.23	0.53	−0.03	0.02

Note: data on labor composition differ slightly from results, reported by Timmer and Voskoboynikov (2016, tab. 8.3), because more detailed statistics on hours worked for different categories of workers was used for the present study.
Sources: Authors' calculations on the basis of Russia KLEMS: World KLEMS Initiative (website), 2017. http://www.worldklems.net/data/basic/RUS_wk_march_2017.xlsx., see main text.

growth rates with corresponding yearly average weights, obtained from Russia KLEMS (2017) and reported in Table 10.3. For example, the contribution of Agriculture to capital intensity growth equals $0.07 = 0.97 \times (5.9/83.5)$.

The fastest MFP growth rates are found in finance and business services. While labor and capital input grew at rates comparable to the market economy as a whole, MFP growth was almost 6% annually, which is more than 4 p.p. higher than the aggregate. This is a remarkable high level of improvements compared to what has been found for advanced countries. MFP growth was also fast for Agriculture, which enjoyed the inflow of modern technology and the outflow of low qualified labor. Another progressive sector is Manufacturing with 1.3% annual growth and this could potentially be a major source of growth for Russia. But it seems that MFP growth was mainly due to a severe contraction and rationalization of the manufacturing sector in the wake of increased competition from advanced nations as Russia gradually opened up to international trade in high-tech in the 1990s.

All sectors, except Agriculture, demonstrate high capital intensity. If in Oil and Gas and Retail this indicates the inflow of investments, in Manufacturing it was accompanied by mass labor outflow (labor outflow in many manufacturing activities can be seen in Fig. 10.3). In turn, the contribution of capital intensity was the highest in Oil and Gas, which is not a surprise, taking into account its high and expanding share in value added and the inflow of rainfall money from Oil and Gas. According to Table 10.5, it is almost one-quarter of market economy. Interestingly, the highest contribution of capital intensity, which falls at Oil and Gas,

corresponds to the lowest contribution of MFP. High rent from soaring oil prices does not create incentives for real costs reduction.

However, such observations remain narrow in focus dealing only with single-deflated real value added decomposition. Because of this the impact of intermediate inputs to Russian growth remains unclear both explicitly (GO-based growth accounting) and implicitly (GVA-based decomposition on the basis of double deflation). In the following subsection, we present some progress in Russia KLEMS in both directions.

10.3.3.2 Recent developments of Russia KLEMS: GO-based growth accounting, labor composition, and double deflation

Until now, Russia KLEMS data set does not provide the full GO-based growth accounting decomposition, because the official statistics stopped developing SUTs in 2003, based on the benchmark SUTs of 1995.[23] The new benchmark tables for 2011 with the following projections to 2012–15 have been published recently. SUTs unveil two opportunities for Russia KLEMS. First, real value added series can be revised, taking into account double deflation. In Russian official statistics, as well as in Russia KLEMS 2017, double deflation has not been adapted. Second, GO-based growth accounting can be implemented. In both cases, the question of interest is to what extent the story of Russian growth, presented above, will survive. In addition, the issue of new data quality is important.

Table 10.6 represents the GVA-based growth accounting decomposition for industry Chemicals and Chemical Products" with both the official and double-deflated real value added. If the volume growth rate of value added is

---

[23] Rosstat published aggregated versions of SUTs at the level of one digit of NACE 1 in 2004–06 with no update of the benchmark tables in NACE 1 (Rosstat, 2007, tab. 4.1, 4.2; 2008, tab. 5.1, 5.2; 2009, tab. 5.1, 5.2) and terminated publications until 2017. These SUTs were not detailed and did not cover the reasonable numbers of years for GO-based decomposition. However, they were used in our projection of the official SUTs back to 2003.

TABLE 10.6 Value added-based growth accounting for Chemicals and chemical products in 2003−14 (p.p.).

	2003 −07	2007 −14	2003 −14
Real value added	3.69	4.03	3.91
Hours worked	−2.82	−2.57	−2.66
Labor productivity	6.52	6.60	6.57
Labor composition	0.13	0.37	0.30
Capital intensity	3.16	3.41	3.04
ICT	0.21	0.12	0.15
Machinery and equipment	2.08	2.19	2.03
Constructions	0.42	0.98	0.65
Other assets	0.45	0.13	0.21
Total factor productivity	3.22	2.82	3.24
Real value added (double deflated)	6.34	−0.39	1.81
Total factor productivity	5.87	−1.60	1.14
Average labor share (%)	59.5	51.6	58.7

Sources: own calculations based on official supply and use tables in 2011−14 (http://www.gks.ru/wps/wcm/connect/rosstat_main/rosstat/ru/statistics/accounts/#; retrieved 20.03.2018) and backcast estimations of SUTs in 2003−10, made by Eduard Baranov, Dmitri Piontkovski and Elena Staritsyna.

calculated with single deflation or derived by the direct observation of volume output series, it will be sensitive to changes in relative prices of GO and intermediate inputs. In case of Russia, the corresponding bias could be substantial. For example, output prices of export-oriented sectors, such as chemicals, are formed mainly on international markets, whereas intermediate input prices (e.g., prices on energy) are formed in the domestic market. These domestic prices might be heavily distorted due to explicit and implicit subsidies. As can be seen from the table, the difference between the single-deflated and the double-deflated real value added growth rates are substantial. In 2003−07 they are almost twice as much as the official ones, while in 2007−14 both have an opposite direction. At

the same time, both the single-deflated and double-deflated versions of growth accounting demonstrate that the contribution of MFP becomes smaller.

Generalization of these observations can be derived from Fig. 10.4, which demonstrates that the discrepancy between the single- and double-deflated real value added growth rates for some industries are substantial, being double-deflated valued in most cases smaller and negative. Although these findings have to be considered as preliminary and only indicative of the potential importance of this issue given that they rely on preliminary backcast projections for the most years of the period and the sensitivity to measurement errors (Hill, 1971), we can assume, that the official/Russia KLEMS 2017 numbers of real value added overestimate economic growth.

Another remarkable feature of decomposition in Table 10.6 is labor composition. Its detailed breaking down is given in Table 10.7 and illustrates a general observation in the previous subsection that the process of labor force aging leads to the positive impact of aged and qualified workers. This can be seen in the form of the positive contribution of aged workers with medium and high education. Because of qualification and experience, they survive in the profession, while the share of low educated workers of the same age disappears. As can be seen, negative growth rates of labor services are slightly attenuated by labor composition. Table 10.7 unveils that this negligible contribution of labor composition masks intensive changes in the structure of hours worked. Indeed, shares of low and medium skills workers of age groups between 15 and 49 decrease. The highest reduction takes place in the share of low skills workers of age 15−29 with negative growth rates 11% per year, while high skills workers contribute positively.

The final step is the GO decomposition, which is given in Table 10.8. It shows that GO growth rates in chemicals in 2003−14 were around 3.5% and relatively stable before and after

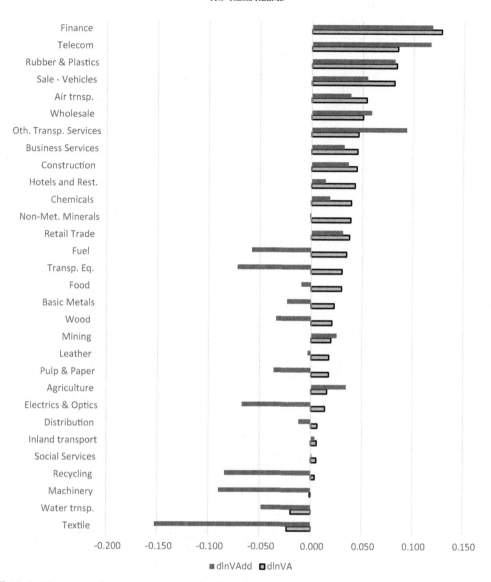

FIGURE 10.4   Yearly growth rates of single- and double-deflated real value added in 30 industries of the market economy, 2003–14. Note: Annual compound growth rates of value added volumes by industry. Single deflation–based volumes (light shaded) and double deflation–based volumes (*dark shaded*). *Source: Author's calculations on the basis of ("Russia KLEMS" 2017) and official Supply and Use tables in 2011–14 (http://www.gks.ru/wps/wcm/connect/rosstat_main/rosstat/ru/statistics/accounts/#; retrieved March 20, 2018) and backcast estimations of SUT's in 2003–2010, made by Eduard Baranov, Dmitri Piontkovski and Elena Staritsyna.*

2007. Intermediate inputs and, specifically, materials contributed the most (1.8 p.p.), which seems reasonable for this industry. The role of machinery and equipment (0.6 p.p.) and services (0.9 p.p.) seems also remarkable. For the period under review, the contribution of MFP is small, but it masks the substantial variation before and after 2007. It was strong (1.6 p.p.) before

TABLE 10.7   Labor composition in chemicals and chemical products, 2003—14.

	2003	2014	Average	Hours worked growth	Contribution	Labor Composition Per hour worked
		Share of value added (%)		Annual growth rates	Percentage points	Percentage points
Total	100.00	100.00	100.00	−2.16	−2.16	0.51
Low skills	3.33	1.39	2.36	−11.10	−0.26	−0.20
Medium skills	66.87	55.34	61.11	−3.41	−2.08	−0.46
High skills	29.80	43.27	36.53	0.52	0.19	1.16
Male	64.13	64.26	64.20	−1.57	−1.01	0.70
Female	35.87	35.74	35.80	−3.21	−1.15	−0.19
Age 15—29	20.18	18.55	19.36	−2.72	−0.53	−0.01
Age 30—49	58.17	52.92	55.55	−3.15	−1.75	−0.27
Age 50+	21.65	28.53	25.09	0.48	0.12	0.79
Low skills, 15—29, male	0.60	0.22	0.41	−13.14	−0.05	−0.04
Medium skills, 15—29, male	10.35	7.91	9.13	−3.68	−0.34	−0.09
High skills, 15—29, male	3.73	4.79	4.26	1.11	0.05	0.16
Low skills, 30—49, male	0.86	0.52	0.69	−7.42	−0.05	−0.03
Medium skills, 30—49, male	24.65	18.86	21.76	−3.81	−0.83	−0.25
High skills, 30—49, male	10.25	14.09	12.17	1.02	0.12	0.45
Low skills, 50+, male	0.80	0.30	0.55	−9.37	−0.05	−0.04
Medium skills, 50+, male	9.12	11.04	10.08	0.57	0.06	0.33
High skills, 50+, male	3.78	6.54	5.16	1.63	0.08	0.22
Low skills, 15—29, female	0.21	0.08	0.14	−13.08	−0.02	−0.02
Medium skills, 15—29, female	2.95	1.95	2.45	−6.63	−0.16	−0.10
High skills, 15—29, female	2.33	3.60	2.97	−0.09	0.00	0.08
Low skills, 30—49, female	0.58	0.14	0.36	−17.58	−0.06	−0.05
Medium skills, 30—49, female	14.76	9.34	12.05	−6.93	−0.84	−0.51
High skills, 30—49, female	7.08	9.97	8.53	−1.12	−0.10	0.13
Low skills, 50+, female	0.29	0.13	0.21	−11.30	−0.02	−0.02
Medium skills, 50+, female	5.04	6.24	5.64	0.35	0.02	0.17
High skills, 50+, female	2.62	4.28	3.45	0.97	0.03	0.13

Source: own calculations based on Labor Force Survey and Wage Survey of Rosstat.

Appendix. List of industries and composition of aggregated sectors

217

TABLE 10.8 GO-based growth accounting for Chemicals and chemical products in 2003–14 (p.p.).

Rowtitle	2003–07	2007–14	2003–14
Gross output	3.58	3.52	3.54
Intermediate inputs	1.80	3.64	3.01
Energy	−0.31	0.71	0.33
Materials	0.87	2.22	1.78
Services	1.24	0.71	0.91
Labor input	−0.43	−0.30	−0.36
Hours worked	−0.47	−0.41	−0.45
Labor composition	0.04	0.11	0.09
Capital input	0.57	0.67	0.57
ICT	0.04	0.02	0.03
Machinery and equipment	0.44	0.52	0.46
Capital intensity, constructions	−0.01	0.11	0.05
Capital intensity, other	0.10	0.02	0.04
MFP (GO-based)	1.64	−0.49	0.32

Source: own calculations based on Russia KLEMS: World KLEMS Initiative (website), 2017. http://www.worldklems.net/data/basic/RUS_wk_march_2017.xlsx, and official Supply and Use tables in 2011–14 (http://www.gks.ru/wps/wcm/connect/rosstat_main/rosstat/ru/statistics/accounts/#; retrieved 20.03.2018) and backcast estimations of SUTs in 2003–10, made by Eduard Baranov, Dmitri Piontkovski, and Elena Staritsyna.

2007 and negative (−0.5) after 2007. This variation is different from the MFP time pattern of single-deflated GVA-based growth accounting. While GVA-based MFP growth variates around 3% both before and after 2007, GO-based MFP growth is positive before 2007 and negative afterward. Negative MFP trend can reflect the lower share of outsourcing in the industry in the years of stagnation. Indeed, while before 2007 the contribution of services dominated and energy dropped, after the crisis the contribution of services became smaller by one-third, while the role of energy and materials grew. All this took place with GO and inputs' growth rates remaining stable. Probably, in years of stagnation many firms, which provided some outsourcing services, withdraw from the market, and producers had to substitute them with own less efficient production.

10.4 Conclusion

The ABS introduced experimental KLEMS MFP estimates in 2016 to support deeper analysis on industry sources of growth and structural changes within industry. The combination of improved data sources and the recent international work articulating the KLEMS framework enabled the release of the Australian estimates. Currently, with the separation of IT/non-IT capital, hours worked/labor composition, and the breakdown of intermediate inputs into energy, materials, and services, the Australian KLEMS framework provides a detailed and informative productivity growth accounting of industry GO growth.

The Russian KLEMS data set was published in 2013 and 2017. It has provided the empirical foundation for the series of studies of sources of economic growth in Russian industries, structural change, and international comparisons. The chapter has reviewed recent developments of the project, which have not been included in the latest release of 2017, such as labor composition and intermediate inputs.

Appendix. List of industries and composition of aggregated sectors

#	Code	Industry	Sector	Aggregated sector
1	AtB	Agriculture, hunting, forestry, and fishing	Agriculture	Market economy
2	23	Coke, refined petroleum products, and nuclear fuel	Extended gas and oil	Market economy

(Continued)

—cont'd

#	Code	Industry	Sector	Aggregated sector
3	C	Mining and quarrying	Extended gas and oil	Market economy
4	51	Wholesale trade and commission trade, except of motor vehicles and motorcycles	Extended gas and oil	Market economy
5	15t16	Food products, beverages, and tobacco	Manufacturing	Market economy
6	17 t18	Textiles, textile products	Manufacturing	Market economy
7	19	Leather and footwear	Manufacturing	Market economy
8	20	Wood and products of wood and cork	Manufacturing	Market economy
9	21t22	Pulp, paper, paper products, printing and publishing	Manufacturing	Market economy
10	24	Chemicals and chemical products	Manufacturing	Market economy
11	25	Rubber and plastics products	Manufacturing	Market economy
12	26	Other nonmetallic mineral products	Manufacturing	Market economy
13	27t28	Basic metals and fabricated metal products	Manufacturing	Market economy
14	29	Machinery, n.e.c.	Manufacturing	Market economy
15	30t33	Electrical and optical equipment	Manufacturing	Market economy
16	34t35	Transport equipment	Manufacturing	Market economy
17	36t37	Manufacturing, n.e.c. and recycling	Manufacturing	Market economy
18	E	Electricity, gas, and water supply	Manufacturing	Market economy
19	F	Construction	Retail, construction, telecom	Market economy
20	50	Sales, maintenance, and repair of motor vehicles and motorcycles; retail sale of fuel	Retail, construction, telecom	Market economy
21	52	Retail trade, except of motor vehicles and motorcycles; repair of household goods	Retail, construction, telecom	Market economy
22	H	Hotels and restaurants	Retail, construction, telecom	Market economy
23	64	Post and telecommunications	Retail, construction, telecom	Market economy
24	O	Other community, social and personal services	Retail, construction, telecom	Market economy
25	J	Financial intermediation	Finance and business services	Market economy
26	71t74	Renting of machinery and equipment and other business activities	Finance and business services	Market economy
27	60	Inland transport	Transport	Market economy

—cont'd

#	Code	Industry	Sector	Aggregated sector
28	61	Water transport	Transport	Market economy
29	62	Air transport	Transport	Market economy
30	63	Supporting and auxiliary transport activities; activities of travel agencies	Transport	Market economy
31	70	Real estate activities	Nonmarket services	Nonmarket economy
32	L	Public administration and defense; compulsory social security	Nonmarket services	Nonmarket economy
33	M	Education	Nonmarket services	Nonmarket economy
34	N	Health and social work	Nonmarket services	Nonmarket economy

n.e.c., not elsewhere classified.

Acknowledgment

The contribution of Ilya Voskoboynikov has been prepared within the framework of the Basic Research Program of National Research University Higher School of Economics.

References

ABS: 1351.0.55.010: *Research paper: quality-adjusted labour inputs* (website), http://www.abs.gov.au/ausstats/abs@.nsf/mf/1351.0.55.010.

ABS: 5216.0: *Australian system of national accounts: concepts, sources and methods* (website), http://www.abs.gov.au/ausstats/abs@.nsf/mf/5216.0.

ABS: 5260.0.55.003: *Information paper: experimental estimates of industry level KLEMS multifactor productivity* (website), http://www.abs.gov.au/ausstats%5Cabs@.nsf/0/249D1E3809315861CA257F09001370F6?Opendocument.

ABS: 5260.0.55.002: *Estimates of industry multifactor productivity, 2016-17* (website), http://www.abs.gov.au/AUSSTATS/abs@.nsf/allprimarymainfeatures/E95A0098761C9EC9CA25807D00172D73?opendocument.

ABS: 5204.0.55.014: *Information paper: Australian national accounts, supply use tables, 2018* (website), http://www.abs.gov.au/ausstats/abs@.nsf/mf/5204.0.55.014.

ABS: 6150.0.55.003: *Labour account Australia, quarterly experimental estimates, September 2017* (website), http://www.abs.gov.au/ausstats/abs@.nsf/Previousproducts/6150.0.55.003Feature%20Article2September%202017?opendo

cument&tabname=Summary&prodno=6150.0.55.003&issue=September%202017&num=&view=.

Baldwin JR, Gu W: Multifactor productivity in Canada: an evaluation of alternative methods of estimating capital services, *The Canadian Productivity Review*, 2007. Available from, https://doi.org/10.2139/ssrn.1507796.

van den Bergen D, van Rooijen-Horsten M, de Haan M, Balk BM: *Productivity measurement at statistics Netherlands*, bpa-no. 2007-19-MNR, Voorburg-Heerlen, 2007, Statistics Netherlands. Available from, https://unstats.un.org/unsd/EconStatKB/KnowledgebaseArticle10109.aspx.

Brandt N, Schreyer P, Zipper V: Productivity measurement with natural capital, *Review of Income and Wealth* 63(S1): S7–S21, 2017. Available from, https://doi.org/10.1111/roiw.12247.

Brock G, Ogloblin C: Russian 1998–2007 TFP decomposed: some inspiration emerging from inherited Soviet legacy, *Economic Change and Restructuring* 52(1):135–151, 2016. Available from, https://doi.org/10.1007/s10644-016-9196-8.

Entov RM, Lugovoy OV: Growth trends in Russia after 1998. In Alexeev M, Weber S, editors: *The oxford handbook of the Russian economy*, Oxford, 2013, Oxford University Press, pp 132–160.

Hill TP: *The measurement of real product: a theoretical and empirical analysis of growth rates, for different industries and countries*, Paris, 1971, OECD.

Hulten CR: The measurement of capital. In Berndt ER, Triplett J, editors: *Fifty years of economic measurement*, Chicago and London, 1990, The University of Chicago Press, pp 119–158.

Jorgenson DW, Gollop FM, Fraumeni BM: *Productivity and U.S. economic growth*, Amsterdam, 1987, North-Holland.

Jorgenson DW, Ho MS, Stiroh KJ: *Information technology and the American growth resurgence*, Cambridge (MA), 2005, MIT Press.

Kaitila V: GDP growth in Russia: different capital stock series and the terms of trade, *Post-communist Economies* 28(2): 129–145, 2016. Available from, https://doi.org/10.1007/s10644-016-9196-8.

Kapeliushnikov: *RI: Zapiska ob otechestvennom chelovecheskom kapitale [Russia's human capital: an assessment]*, Problemy rynka truda [Labor market issues] WP3/2008/01, Moscow, 2008, State University - Higher School of Economics. Available from, https://www.hse.ru/data/2010/05/04/1216406890/WP3_2008_01.pdf.

Okawa Y, Sanghi S: *Potential Growth : outlook and options for the Russian Federation*, Policy Research Working Paper WPS 8663. Washington (D.C.). World Bank Group. Available at, http://documents.worldbank.org/curated/en/437251543855591590/Potential-Growth-Outlook-and-Options-for-the-Russian-Federation.

O'Mahony M, Timmer MP: Output, input and productivity measures at the industry level: the EU KLEMS Database, *Economic Journal* 119(538):F374–F403, 2009.

Rosstat: *Natsional'nye scheta Rossii v 1999-2006 godakh [National accounts of Russia in 1999-2006]*, Moscow, 2007, Federal'naiа sluzhba gosudarstvennoĭ statistiki [Federal State Statistics Service].

Rosstat: *Natsional'nye scheta Rossii v 2000-2007 godakh [National accounts of Russia in 2000-2007]*, Moscow, 2008, Federal'naiа sluzhba gosudarstvennoĭ statistiki [Federal State Statistics Service].

Rosstat: *Natsional'nye scheta Rossii v 2001-2008 godakh [National accounts of Russia in 2001-2008]*, Moscow, 2009, Federal'naiа sluzhba gosudarstvennoĭ statistiki [Federal State Statistics Service].

Rosstat: *Natsional'nye scheta Rossii v 2002-2009 godakh [National accounts of Russia in 2002-2009]*, Moscow, 2010, Federal'naiа sluzhba gosudarstvennoĭ statistiki [Federal State Statistics Service].

Rosstat: *Natsional'nye scheta Rossii v 2007-2014 godakh [National accounts of Russia in 2007-2014], Moscow, 2015* Federal'naiа sluzhba gosudarstvennoĭ statistiki [Federal State Statistics Service].

Rosstat: *Natsional'nye scheta Rossii v 2011-2016 godakh [National accounts of Russia in 2011-2016]*, Moscow, 2017, Federal'naiа sluzhba gosudarstvennoĭ statistiki [Federal State Statistics Service].

Russia KLEMS: *World KLEMS Initiative* (website). http://www.worldklems.net/data/basic/RUS_wk_march_2017.xlsx. Accessed November 2017.

Solow R: Technological change and the aggregate production function, *The Review of Economics and Statistics* 39(3): 312–320, 1957.

Stiroh KJ: Information technology and the US productivity revival: what do the industry data say? *The American Economic Review* 92(5):1559–1576, 2002.

Timmer MP, Inklaar R, O'Mahony M, van Ark B: *Economic growth in Europe*, Cambridge (UK), 2010, Cambridge University Press.

Timmer MP, Voskoboynikov IB: Is mining fuelling long-run growth in Russia? Industry productivity growth trends since 1995, *Review of Income and Wealth* 60(Supplement Issue S2):S398–S422, 2014.

Timmer MP, Voskoboynikov IB: Is mining fuelling long-run growth in Russia? Industry productivity growth trends in 1995-2012. In Jorgenson DW, Fukao K, Timmer MP, editors: *Growth and stagnation in the World economy*, Cambridge (UK), 2016, Cambridge University Press, pp 281–318.

Voskoboynikov IB: New measures of output, labor and capital in industries of the Russian economy, *GGDC Research Memorandum GD-123*, 2012. Available at, http://www.rug.nl/feb/onderzoek/onderzoekscentra/ggdc/index.

Voskoboynikov IB: Sources of Long Run Economic Growth in Russia before and after the Global Financial Crisis, Russian Journal of Economics 3(4):348-365. Available at, https://doi.org/10.1016/j.ruje.2017.12.003.

Voskoboynikov IB: Structural change, expanding informality and labour productivity growth in Russia, *Review of Income and Wealth*, 2019. Forthcoming.

de Vries GJ, Erumban AA, Timmer MP, Voskoboynikov IB, Wu HX: Deconstructing the BRICs: structural transformation and aggregate productivity growth, *Journal of Comparative Economics* 40(2):211–227, 2012. Available from, https://doi.org/10.1016/j.jce.2012.02.004.

Zhao J, Tang J: Industrial structure change and economic growth: a China-Russia comparison, *China Economic Review* 47(February):219–233, 2018. Available at, https://doi.org/10.1016/j.chieco.2017.08.008.

11

Toward a BEA-BLS integrated industry-level production account for 1947–2016

Lucy P. Eldridge[1], Corby Garner[1], Thomas F. Howells[2], Brian C. Moyer[3], Matthew Russell[1], Jon D. Samuels[2,4], Erich H. Strassner[2], David B. Wasshausen[2]

[1]Office of Productivity and Technology at the United States Bureau of Labor Statistics, Washington, DC, United States; [2]National Economic, Accounts, United States Bureau of Economic Analysis, Suitland, MD, United States; [3]Office of the Director, United States Bureau of Economic Analysis, Suitland, MD, United States; [4]Institute of Quantitative Social Science, Harvard University, Cambridge, MA, United States

11.1 Introduction

For students of economic growth, it is important to have complete information on outputs, inputs, and productivity across all sectors of the economy. Since 2012, the Bureau of Economic Analysis (BEA) and the Bureau of Labor Statistics (BLS) have maintained a complete integrated industry-level production account for the United States that combines output and intermediate inputs data from the BEA GDP by Industry accounts with measures of labor and capital inputs from the BLS Productivity Program. Although agencies throughout the decentralized US statistical system have always worked closely together, this was an innovative effort

for BEA and BLS to produce a joint product. The internally consistent production account includes a complete set of prices and quantities of output produced and inputs consumed by US industries, as well as measures of multifactor productivity (MFP), also referred to as total factor productivity. Because GDP and aggregate productivity data begin in 1929 and 1947, respectively, there has been a growing demand to have consistent industry-level data that also span this period. This chapter navigates numerous hurdles to extend the BEA/BLS integrated industry-level production accounts over seven decades, from 1947 to 2016.

Dale W. Jorgenson and J. Steven Landefeld (2006) identified an integration of the nation's national accounts and productivity statistics as a high priority of their "new architecture" for the US national accounts.[1] One of the main applications of integrated GDP and productivity statistics is to provide "growth accounting" that is consistent with official GDP accounts. Growth accounting attributes economic growth to its underlying sources across industries and factors of production, including capital, labor, and MFP. Recently, growth accounting has been applied to identify the role of information technology (as a contributor to aggregate MFP and as a capital input) in economic growth, to measure the role of the upgrading of the labor force on economic growth, to understand the sources of the slow recovery in the United States, and for cross-country comparisons of why economic growth rates differ. Therefore, having integrated and official statistics is of utmost importance.

In response to customer demand, BEA and BLS developed a conceptual framework for creating an integrated production account in 2006.[2] In 2008, BEA and BLS presented a prototype integrated production account for the private nonfarm business sector that included a reconciliation of the BEA and BLS estimates.[3] The initial focus on the private nonfarm sector was an effort to be consistent with the existing

official measures of MFP produced by BLS. The real outputs of government, private households, and nonprofit institutions were removed from the output and input sides of the account because direct measures of output are generally not available for these nonmarket sectors.[4] Including nonmarket sectors tends to dampen estimates of aggregate productivity growth because often productivity growth for these sectors is imposed to be zero by construction. Thus, the official MFP data for the United States focus on the private business sector, which constitutes about 74% of GDP. Although the initial prototype for the BEA/BLS integrated industry-level production account covered the private nonfarm business sector, the ultimate goal was to have a complete accounting of the entire US economy.[5] Therefore, the BEA/BLS integrated industry-level production account that was released in 2012 covered the entire economy and included data for 63 industries.[6] The completeness of this account allows users to identify sources of growth in output, factor inputs, and productivity at the aggregate level; highlight the performance of individual industries; and identify industry contributions to aggregate output and productivity growth. This complete account serves as a valuable

---

[1] This built upon Christensen et al. (1973) research that proposed a set of accounts that incorporate indices of input volume by sector, and Jorgenson et al. (1987) research that extended the accounting system to measures of output by industry.

[2] See Fraumeni et al. (2006) outlined differences in source data and methods that required resolution for a successful account.

[3] See Harper et al. (2008).

[4] Direct measures of output for government enterprises are available; however, subsidies account for a large fraction of government capital income, making estimation of reliable measures of capital for the government sector difficult. Capital measures for nonprofit institutions and government are estimated following methodology outlined in Harper et al. (2008).

[5] This initial prototype also did not include estimates of labor composition at the industry level.

[6] See Fleck et al. (2014).

source of information for assessing the strength of the US economy.[7]

The BEA/BLS integrated industry-level production account originally began with data for 1998 and was based on the North American Industry Classification System (NAICS). The production account includes data for 63 industries that make up the GDP by Industry data from BEA. The NAICS was adopted in 1997 to replace Standard Industrial Classification (SIC) system to harmonize Canada, Mexico, and the US statistical classification systems, as well as account for new and emerging products. To avoid the resource-intensive effort of bridging the SIC/NAICS changes in a consistent manner across all measures of outputs and inputs produced by multiple statistical agencies and to make use of the newly integrated GDP by Industry accounts, the 2012 BEA/BLS integrated production account began with 1998 data. Realizing the value in analyzing past sources of economic growth, BEA and BLS embarked on efforts to extend the dataset back in time. In June 2018, the accounts were extended to include an additional decade of experimental historical data covering 1987–97.[8] However, because GDP and aggregate productivity data begin in 1929 and 1947, respectively, there was significant demand by data users to have consistent industry-level data that also span this period. Yuskavage (2007) described the conversion of the 1947–97 Input-Output Tables from an SIC basis to a NAICS basis. That effort has since been extended and integrated with the expenditure-side GDP data. This time series of make and use tables is an important component of the integrated industry-level production account that we describe in this chapter.

The next section reviews the basic framework for the production account. This is followed by several sections that discuss the construction of the historical data, including necessary estimation assumptions and data limitations. Section 11.3 outlines the measures of GDP by Industry and the annual Make and Use Tables that begin in 1947, as well as measures of intermediate inputs of energy, materials, and purchased services. Section 11.4 explains the work involved to extend industry-level measures of hours worked back to 1947, and the steps involved in capturing changes in labor composition. Section 11.5 presents efforts to create a consistent historical series of capital services at the industry level and explains improvements in the required imputations for capital services in nonmarket industries. Section 11.6 reviews adjustments made to integrate input data with measured output. Sources of growth are presented in Sections 11.7 and 11.8. Section 11.9 concludes and provides next steps for the project.

11.2 Production Account framework

The purpose of the BEA/BLS integrated industry-level production account is to measure the sources of economic growth from the bottom up. Thus, we start with a description of accounting for growth at the industry level. We rely on a long line of literature and begin with the

---

[7] MFP growth rates generated from the BEA/BLS integrated production accounts differ from the productivity data published by BLS because BLS excludes nonmarket sectors and uses a sectoral output concept in the official BLS productivity statistics. Thus, MFP measures from the BEA/BLS integrated accounts presented here will differ from the official MFP measures most noticeably in industries with a high concentration of nonprofit institutions and industries which consume large portions of inputs that are produced within their own industry. Data releases from this BEA/BLS integrated production account typically also include the official productivity data produced by BLS for comparison purposes.

[8] See Garner et al. (2018).

equation that describes the sources of growth of real gross output at the industry level as the weighted sum of the growth in inputs and the growth in MFP. For industry j in a given year:

$$\Delta lnQ_j = w_{K_j}\Delta lnK_j + w_{L_j}\Delta lnL_j + w_{E_j}\Delta lnE_j$$
$$+ w_{M_j}\Delta lnM_j + w_{S_j}\Delta lnS_j + \Delta MFP_j \qquad (11.1)$$

where K, L, E, M, S denote capital, labor, energy, materials, and purchased services, and Δ is the difference between periods t and $t-1$. The growth of KLEMS inputs on the right-hand side and real output on the left-hand side are log growth rates of real constant-quality inputs and output. For each input X, w_x is the associated nominal cost of the input divided by nominal total cost. In discrete time, these cost shares are two-period annual average shares in Eq. (11.1), and in the equations below. We assume that the cost shares sum to one. There is a long literature on this assumption and on the relationship between measured MFP growth using Eq. (11.1) and technological change. This discussion is beyond the scope of this chapter, but many of the issues are summarized in OECD (2001).

In practice, the growth in MFP is unobservable, so it is measured as a residual. MFP growth is the change in output not accounted for by the change in measured inputs. MFP growth is a widely used measure of technological change and innovation and captures quality advances and improvements in the overall production process.

11.3 Output and intermediate inputs including energy, materials, and services

Output and intermediate inputs come directly from the GDP by Industry accounts produced by BEA. BEA's GDP by Industry statistics provides a time series of nominal and real gross output,

intermediate inputs, and value added by industry, prepared based on the 2007 NAICS. These data are fully integrated with expenditure-based GDP estimates from the National Income and Product Accounts (NIPAs). In addition, the data are prepared within a balanced supply–use framework that allows for simultaneous and consistent analysis of industry output, inputs, value added, and final demand. These fully integrated GDP by Industry accounts were first released in January 2014, and covered the period 1997–2012. They have subsequently been updated annually and extended to cover the period 1947–2016.

The estimates of intermediate purchases of energy, materials, and services (EMS) that we employ in this paper are new for the 1947–97 period. That is, while the total intermediate input (price and quantity) by industry are available in the BEA GDP by Industry accounts, information on the price and quantity of energy (E), materials (M), and services (S) for 1947–97 are not.[9] To describe the approach taken to develop historical energy, materials, and services estimates in this chapter, we begin by reviewing the approach taken by Jorgenson et al. (2005). They constructed EMS by assigning a single energy, materials, or services intermediate input category to each individual commodity within their (44 by 44) Use Table. That is, 100% of the Use Table cell gets allocated to E, M, or S. The commodities within the E, M, S categories are aggregated by industry using Tornqvist indexes. This creates a price and quantity of E, M, and S that is consistent with the industry-level intermediate input price and quantity. Because the BEA industry accounts have more detailed underlying information than the published Use Tables, we are able to take advantage of these data to make refined assignments to E, M, or S.

In the account we present here, our E, M, S assignments for the 1947–97 period are related to

---

[9] EMS estimates (price and quantity) are available in the GDP by Industry data for 1997 forward.

the method used for 1997 forward in the official GDP by Industry accounts. In the official accounts for 1997 forward, E, M, S assignments are made using the underlying Use Table at the "working level." The working level of detail for tables beginning in 1997 includes about 5000 goods and services and about 800 industries. At this level of detail, it is possible to directly assign each cell in the use matrix to an E, M, S category (that is, for each detailed commodity and each industry). For 1947–97, "working level" information is not available, and only information at the "summary level" is available. The "summary level" includes a Use Table on the order of about 63 commodities and 63 industries.

The methodology that we use in this paper for 1947–96 allows us to deviate from the assumption that the entire cell of the Use Table published at the summary level gets allocated to a single E, M, or S category. In particular, we assign Use Table cells between 1947 and 1996 using cell-specific E, M, and S ratios at the summary-level (but based on "working level") table in 1997. To be clear, we *are not* using industry-level E, M, S ratios in 1997 and bringing these all the way back in time to 1947. We *are* assuming that within a particular cell of the use table, the same E, M, S ratio holds in 1947 as in 1997. For example, suppose that the working level table in 1997 allows us to estimate that at the summary level 90% of the Oil and gas extraction commodity purchased by the Farm industry was Energy and 10% was Services (like installation services). In our historical data between 1947 and 1997, we assume that this same 90%–10% split applies to purchases of Oil and gas by the Farm industry. We reproduce this methodology for every cell in the Use Table, allowing us to improve on the assumption that 100% of the

Oil and gas by the Farm industry is an Energy purchase, and ensuring consistency with the data from 1997 forward that underlies the official EMS estimates in the GDP by Industry accounts.[10]

An alternative way to gain intuition for our approach is that we basically assign each cell in the 1947–96 Use Table to an E, M, S category, just as in Jorgenson et al. and just as we do at the "working level" in the 1997–2016. But, then we further divide the cells to allow a portion of each cell to be reapportioned as in the 1997 detailed data. While we think that this is an improvement over previous studies that assigned each cell of the use table at the summary level in its entirety to an E, M, S category, we do note that this assumes that *within* each cell of the summary-level use table, there was no structural change across E, M, and S categories between 1947 and 1996. Of course, our method does capture structural change in energy, materials, and services *across* cells in the use table. For example, if the Farm industry has a higher cost share of Oil and gas in 1947 than in 1997, the overall energy share in Farms would be higher in 1947 than in 1997, assuming similar structures for the other intermediate inputs. In summary, this dataset provides the estimates of gross output, and intermediate inputs in current and constant dollars, including energy, materials, and purchased services that we use to implement Eq. (11.1).

We note that the framework described in Eq. (11.1) is based on the concept of industry gross output that underlies BEA's GDP by Industry accounts. The official BLS MFP measures are based on the concept of sectoral output. Sectoral output is equal to gross output less only those intermediate inputs that are produced within that industry or sector; intermediate inputs used in production from outside the industry are not

---

[10] We apply the same price deflator to E, M, and S at the cell level, ensuring that our E, M, and S splits do not impact the GDP by Industry estimates via double deflation.

removed. Thus, sectoral output represents the value of output leaving the sector or industry. For detailed industries, sectoral output is very close to gross output because very few industry outputs are used as intermediate inputs in the same industry.

11.4 Labor input

The measure of labor input that we use accounts for both the change in hours worked by industry and the change in the composition of industry workers. Measuring labor composition is important because an improvement in the composition of the workforce, for example, due to a higher level of educational attainment, represents movement along the production function, not a shift in the production function. If labor composition was not accounted for in the measure of labor input, the contribution of MFP would be confounded with contributions from changes in the characteristics of the workforce. The BLS productivity program regularly publishes measures of hours worked and labor composition for NIPA-level industries from 1987 forward.[11] The next two subsections divide the discussion of labor input into hours worked and labor composition.

11.4.1 Hours worked

Measures of hours worked are developed by the BLS primarily using data on employment and average weekly hours from the BLS Current Employment Statistics (CES) program and

supplemented with data from the Current Populations Survey (CPS) and the National Compensation Survey (NCS).[12] Hours worked for employees are calculated as the product of employment and average weekly hours paid and adjusted to remove paid leave using an adjustment ratio of hours worked to hours paid. We want to capture the total hours actually worked and available for production activities. Hours worked for the self-employed are estimated directly from the CPS. The earliest hours series for subaggregates of the economy published by the BLS begin in 1964 and cover 13 economic sectors.[13] The data become more detailed in 1979 when wholesale trade, retail trade, transportation, and warehousing and utilities are available as individual industry groups. Complete 4-digit NAICS industry coverage begins in 1990. To estimate the historical series of hours worked for employees, components of employment and an adjustment ratio of hours worked to hours paid are created separately.

The CES began collecting data on employment for all workers and hours for production workers in 1947 with the primary interest in understanding the goods-producing economy. Therefore, employment and hours data beginning in 1947 only cover durable and nondurable manufacturing, mining, construction, the aggregate service sector, and a few select industries. Coverage of employment expanded in 1958, and additional hours became available in 1964. CES employment data for most 3-digit SIC subsectors begin in 1972 with continual expansion in service-producing industries through 1990. To fill in the industry gaps in earlier years,

---

[11] https://www.bls.gov/mfp/ Accessed December 1, 2018.

[12] BLS Handbook of Methods: Industry Productivity Measures, https://www.bls.gov/opub/hom/inp/pdf/inp.pdf Accessed December 1, 2018.

[13] Natural resources, construction, durable and nondurable manufacturing, transportation, trade and utilities, information, financial activities, professional business services, education and health, leisure and hospitality, other services, and government. See nonfarm hours in table "U.S. Nonfarm Economy by Sector—employees only" and farm data in "Total U.S. Economy—all workers" at bls.gov/lpc.

data for the first available year that an industry is published are used to determine an industry's size relative to its next larger available parent sector and this share is held constant going back in time.[14] To estimate hours a similar approach is taken, using the available production worker hours and assuming that nonproduction and production workers work similar average weekly hours in a given industry.[15] The historical CES hours-paid data by industry are converted to an hours worked basis using adjustment ratios for 14 major industry groups available from the BLS productivity program beginning with data for 1947.[16]

The CPS are the primary data to estimate hours worked for self-employed workers and are used beginning in 1979.[17] Prior to 1979, data are available for a more aggregate set of 10 SIC sectors back to 1947. To create the more detailed industry data it is assumed that the distribution of self-employed workers within each sector is similar to the all employee distribution of workers. These data are scaled to be consistent with more aggregate measures currently published.

The data on hours for both employees and self-employed are converted from SIC 1987 to NAICS 2002 using SIC to NAICS CES conversion ratios then converted where necessary using CES NAICS 2002 to NAICS 2007 conversion ratios. The BEA National Income and Product Accounts contain NAICS industry employment and hours data for some industries back to 1947, with the level of industry detail improving over time. We convert these data to NAICS 2007, using the CES bridge ratios as well as NAICS 1997 to NAICS 2002 conversion ratios from the Economic Census Core Business Statistics. For consistency with output measures from BEA, the BLS data are scaled to these NIPA measures.

11.4.2 Labor composition

Measures of hours worked treat every hour the same regardless of the worker's experience and education. Labor composition measures account for the effect of shifts in the age, education, and gender composition of the workforce on the efficacy of labor for use in production. Growth in labor input in the production framework can be decomposed into the growth in hours and the growth in labor composition, which accounts for changes in the demographic composition of the labor force.

Eq. (11.2) defines our measure of labor input that accounts for labor composition.

$$\Delta lnL_j = \sum_i \left(s_{i,j}\right) \times \Delta lnHours_{i,j} \qquad (11.2)$$

[14] This is a limiting assumption as industries may not have existed or could be expanding so that their historic importance is overstated. However, this is the only datum available. This is done for total number of employees, production workers, and production worker hours.

[15] Measures of hours for nonproduction workers for 1987 forward use data from the CPS to more accurately capture hours worked. See Eldridge et al. (2004).

[16] Data for 1996 forward use hours worked to hours paid ratios based on the Employment Cost Index (ECI) of the National Compensation Survey. See https://www.bls.gov/lpc/lprhws/lprhwhp.pdf Accessed December 1, 2018. Hours worked to hours paid adjustments use data from the BLS Hours at Work survey for 1982–96 and data on leave practices that were collected from Employer Expenditure surveys. These surveys begin in 1952 and were conducted periodically and only covered major industry groups.

[17] Respondents are assigned to a class of worker based on their primary job from 1979 to 1993; class of worker is collected for primary and secondary jobs beginning in 1994. Data for 1987 are published by industry the BLS productivity program; data from 1979 to 1987 are controlled to published BEA estimates.

where $s_{i,j}$ represents the two-period average share of total compensation earned by worker type i within industry j. It is the i worker types, with specific gender, age, and education groupings, that allow for changes in labor composition to impact the measure of labor input. Intuition for weighting by $s_{i,j}$ can be gained under the assumption that rates of labor compensation correspond to the marginal products of workers. Under this assumption, an hour worked by a (gender, age, education) group of workers is up-weighted if the marginal product of the group is high relative to other groups, and down-weighted if the group has a relatively low marginal product. Thus, a shift to workers of a higher "quality" would manifest as an increase in labor input, even if total hours worked in the economy remained fixed. Alternatively, if all worker types were the same and received the same wage, labor input growth would correspond to the growth rate in hours worked.

For this paper, for the years 1987–2016, workers are disaggregated by sex, eight age groups, six education groups, and employment class (payrolled vs. self-employed) for a total of 192 demographic categories. The estimation process begins by filling out information on employment, hours, and compensation for each demographic category of worker in each of the 63 industries, creating a 12,096 cell matrix for each year. For 1990 and 2000, the matrices are initialized using the US Census (1990) and 2000 1-Percent Public Use Microdata Sample (PUMS) files. Initial estimates are generated for 1991–99 by linear interpolation at the cell level. These initial estimates are iteratively adjusted using the RAS balancing technique to match a series of marginal controls developed from the March supplement to the CPS. For years before 1990 the $t + 1$ balanced matrices are used as the initial cell estimates, and for years after 2000 the $t - 1$ balanced matrices are used. As with the periods 1990–2000, these initial matrices are iteratively adjusted to match controls from the CPS.

After balancing, the matrices are scaled in sequence (1) to employment controls from BEA's National Income and Product Accounts (NIPAs) for 63 industries by employment class, (2) to BLS hours for 63 industries by employment class, (3) to NIPA hours for payrolled workers by 17 aggregate industries, and (4) to NIPA compensation for payrolled workers by 63 industries. In the final step, the hourly compensation of self-employed workers is replaced by the rate for payrolled workers in the same cell. This step is taken because reported compensation of self-employed workers cannot be disentangled from compensation accruing to their capital assets. Additional methodological information is described in Fleck et al. (2014) with updates in Rosenthal et al. (2014).

In preparing the 1987–97 period covered by these accounts, a modified SIC-to-NAICS bridge was constructed to incorporate time-varying weights for manufacturing industries. These dynamic, employment-based weights to go between SIC and NAICS were supplied by the Federal Reserve Board based on research from Bayard and Klimek (2003) which made use of establishment-level microdata from the Census of Manufacturing and the Annual Survey of Manufactures spanning the period from 1963 to 1997. The time-varying weights replaced static weights where available, but were scaled to leave unchanged any weights linking portions of SIC manufacturing industries to NAICS nonmanufacturing industries. For the period between 1997 and 2000, all updated manufacturing weights were interpolated to the static weights from the previous bridge.

The modified SIC-to-NAICS bridge was applied to the US Census (1990) PUMS files to develop the initial 1990 labor composition matrix as well as to the 1987–2002 CPS marginal controls. The bridge was also applied to the SIC-based NIPA employment, hours, and compensation scaling controls for 1987–97; however, these converted results were not used directly. In order to mitigate the possibility of time series breaks, the converted series were used as indicators to backcast a time series beginning with the 1998 levels in the published NAICS-based NIPA tables. Finally, these new NAICS-based employment, hours, and compensation levels were scaled to the SIC-based totals for all industries to ensure that this conversion process left totals unchanged.

In addition to the modified bridge, the 1987–91 March Supplement of the CPS required special handling for the reported level of educational attainment. The current questionnaire allows respondents to select their highest degree attained, which aligns well with the education categories chosen for these accounts. However, prior to 1992, respondents were instead asked for the number of years of schooling, as well as whether the last year of schooling was completed. This inconsistency was addressed by converting the number of years of schooling to an estimated highest degree attained via a frequency matrix described in Jaeger (1997). That work matched CPS respondents who had reported educational attainment under both versions of the questionnaire, and cross tabulated pairs of responses to create conversion weights. With this dataset, we are able to implement Eq. (11.2): $HOURS_{i,j,t}$ is the hours worked by worker type i in industry j and $s_{i,j,t}$ is worker type i's share in total labor compensation in industry j.[18]

The growth rate in labor composition for 1987–2016 is defined as the difference between the growth rate of labor input described above and the growth rate of hours worked (Eq. 11.3):

$$\Delta \ln Labor\ Composition_j \equiv \Delta lnL_j - \Delta lnHours_j$$

$$(11.3)$$

Because this same measure of labor composition is not available for 1947–86, we take the labor composition growth estimates reported in Jorgenson et al. (2018) and add this to the hours

growth estimates based on the hours dataset described above to arrive at labor input measures. The method and data sources used to estimate labor composition in Jorgenson et al. (2018) closely correspond to the methods used in this paper, so that historical data can be easily linked to the 1987–2016 time series. The labor share in gross output is taken from this dataset as well. The BLS has also constructed labor composition measures from 1976 to 2016 using the monthly CPS data and BEA/BLS will work toward incorporating these measures into this integrated account in the future.

11.5 Capital inputs

Capital services data are from the MFP statistics produced by the BLS. The estimate of capital services is produced by first estimating the productive capital stock and then estimating the rental price of capital. The productive capital stock is measured as the sum of past investments net of deterioration and is constructed by BLS as vintage aggregates of real historical investments by US industries using the perpetual inventory method (Fleck et al., 2014). Economic theory dictates aggregating the different capital stocks of assets by using the marginal product of each asset to estimate industry capital input measures. A profit-maximizing firm will accumulate capital up to the point at which its marginal product equals what it would have to pay to obtain the capital service. However, due to firms owning their capital, there is not a clear way to measure these marginal products from observable transactions. Thus, an implicit rental price, or user cost of capital, must be calculated for each asset within an industry. Vintage aggregation provides a mechanism to combine the value of various types and vintages of capital stocks

---

[18] Additional information concerning data sources and methods of measuring labor composition can be found in Zoghi (2010).

over time into a single capital service measure using capital rental prices as weights.

Since some capital assets, such as railroad structures, can last up to 90 years, these vintage aggregations require a sizable amount of investment data over an extended period of time. With the previous release of the BEA/BLS integrated production account, historical vintages of real investment data were created to compute capital service measures by industry. This investment data go back as far as the BEA fixed asset data, 1901, and a measure of productive capital stocks were generated for each of the roughly 100 assets in the capital service measure (Fleck et al., 2014). Because of the need to account for all previous investments, historical stocks covering 1947–2016 for equipment, structures, and intangibles had previously been computed for past releases of the integrated BEA/BLS accounts. However, since inventory and land estimates are nondepreciable, vintage aggregation was not required to estimate those asset pieces. Hence, the historical stocks of inventories and land were not readily available from our previous iterations of the BEA/BLS integrated account. Stocks for these assets for 1947–86 were estimated for the first time for this paper, as are 1947–86 estimates of capital services for federal and state and local governments.

11.5.1 Estimating inventory stocks

Inventories consist of finished goods, work-in-process, and materials and services. They are the stock of goods held in reserve that are intended to be sold (finished goods) or transformed into finished goods (work-in-process or materials and supplies). Stocks of inventories are considered to provide capital services because they represent both an input into the production process and an opportunity cost to the firm. Industry market value of inventories is reported annually in the BEA National Income and Product Accounts. These data are used to

calculate capital stocks directly, because inventories are considered to be nondepreciable assets and thus vintage aggregation is not necessary.

Data on industry investment in inventories are provided quarterly in the BEA National Income and Product Accounts. For all NIPA manufacturing industries, data are available by stage of processing (finished goods, work-in-process, and materials and supplies) starting in 1996. For nonmanufacturing industries, quarterly total inventories are available at the aggregate levels of Farm, Mining-Utilities-Construction, Manufacturing, Wholesale Trade, Retail Trade and All Other sectors. For currently published measures, BLS annualizes the quarterly BEA data, using converted SIC 1987–96 data to create a full 1987–2016 time series. BLS then uses inventory investment data for each industry from the IRS to break out the aggregate nonmanufacturing sectors to the NIPA industry detail.

The differences between the SIC 1972 and 1987 classifications for Farm, Manufacturing, Wholesale Trade, Retail Trade, and "All Other" aggregate sectors are negligible. Therefore, the quarterly inventory series were linked together using the latest definition on a level basis to obtain a series for 1947–86.

A three step process to convert these data to a NAICS 2007 basis was used. Historical SIC data were converted to a NAICS 1997 basis by moving a piece out of manufacturing and into the "Other" sector to better align with the NAICS 1997 treatment of auxiliaries in the NAICS definition. The NAICS 1997-based inventory data for Farm, Mining-Utilities-Construction, Wholesale Trade, Retail Trade, and All Other sectors were linked to the BLS 1987–2016 time series. This rudimentary assumption holds that at the aggregate sector, the differences introduced by the 2002 NAICS were not significantly different from the 1997 NAICS definition at this level of detail. The final step is to break out the aggregate sector data to the NIPA industry detailed level for the nonmanufacturing industries. For the 1947–86 period, BLS used the 1997 ratios of IRS industry inventory investment for each year to distribute the detailed industries from the aggregate.

For industries within the manufacturing sector, we were able to take advantage of historical SIC inventory investment by stage of processing that is available for 1967–86. To complete the time series, manufacturing total inventories for 1947–66 were distributed by using the share of finished goods, work-in-process, and materials and supplies to total manufacturing in 1967. BLS then converted this SIC data to NAICS and linked it to its previous 1987–2016 estimates.

11.5.2 Estimating land stocks

As with inventories, land is not considered to have efficiency decline, and thus vintage aggregation of the land stocks was not necessary for previous versions of the integrated account. For all nonfarm industries, land is estimated by applying a land-structure ratio based on unpublished estimates by the BLS to the value of structures. These ratios are based on data from 2001 for all counties in Ohio. Farm land stock is based on data from the Economic Research Service of the US Department of Agriculture and is available for 1960-forward. For 1947–59, the change in farm land value from 1961 to 60 is applied.

11.5.3 Historical capital rental prices

Capital rental prices equal the price of an asset multiplied by the sum of the rate of depreciation and the appropriate rate of return on the asset,

accounting for both inflation and taxes. Because rental prices are computed separately for each asset category × industry combination, they have significant data requirements. Income components from BEA's GDP-by-Industry data play an integral role in calculating the rental price for each of the 63 industries.

With the release of the historical Input–Output Tables, BEA published a time series of GDP by Industry data for all 63 industries back to 1947 on a NAICS 2007-basis. Additionally, the major components of value added were published beginning in 1987. Some of the underlying estimates of these data are also published on a NAICS-2007 basis starting in 1998.[19]

Of the 18 income pieces needed for the rental price computation, 13 are available in BEA's Historical SIC GDP-by-Industry dataset on a SIC 1972 basis. BLS converted these data to a NAICS 2007-basis to ensure that the data going into the BEA/BLS integrated production account would be consistent. The process for estimating these data is a four-step process similar to that of the earlier work accomplished by the BEA in recoding their SIC National Income and Product Account data back to 1947.[20]

First, each detailed income component from the GDP-by-Industry data was converted to a NAICS 1997-basis by using the variable SIC 1972 to NAICS 1997 bridge previously used by BEA to convert the Input–Output tables to a NAICS 1997 basis. This bridge was first used to publish NAICS-based GDP-by-Industry data that were released in December of 2005, and this bridge serves as the beginning point for the Integrated BEA/BLS production account value added conversion to a NAICS basis.[21] This work provided annual conversion ratios for 1978–86, but due to limited data availability

---

[19] BEA chose not to convert the major components of value-added prior to 1987 due to limited SIC data in the 1947–86 period and data validity concerns. See Yuskavage (2007).

[20] See Garner et al. (2018).

[21] See Yuskavage and Fahim-Nader (2005).

these ratios are held fixed prior to 1978. Future work plans to add more information that better reflects the changing industry dynamics from the 1947–78 period.

Second, the NAICS 1997-based data were then converted to NAICS 2002 using historical data used in previous conversions by the BEA to move estimates to a more current NAICS definition during a comprehensive revision. These bridge ratios were provided to BLS to keep the consistency of the income conversions with the other statistics that BEA had already transitioned. BLS currently uses historical NAICS 2002-based data to create a complete time series of the GDP by Industry income components not published prior to 1998. These NAICS 2002-based data are converted to NAICS 2007 by using conversion ratios based off of the rate of change in the NAICS 2002 to NAICS 2007-based gross operating surplus for each industry for 1987–97. The historical 1947–86 GOS data were linked to the 2002 basis using the overlapping 1987 (NAICS, 1997) and 1987(NAICS, 2002) gross operating surplus data. We linked that series onto the NAICS 2007-based GOS published estimates in 1998.

After initial conversion of the pieces of value added from 1947–86 the fourth and final step of the process was to scale the value-added components, GOS, employee compensation, and taxes on production and imports to ensure consistency with value added so that each subcomponent added up to the aggregate in an integrated and robust way. These adjustment ratios were minor, averaging around 1% across all years and industries.

The last two components needed to compute our rental prices are motor vehicle licenses taxes and property taxes. These data are available at the total economy level and are on a NAICS 2007 basis for the full time series. We used each industry's share of value added to the total economy in 1987 to break out the national tax data to an industry level for 1947–86.

11.5.4 Estimating capital services for government

BLS measures of capital services for government are an aggregation of equipment, structure, and land stock. Capital stocks of equipment and land are derived from BEA government consumption of fixed capital, current-cost net stock, chain-type quantity stock, and current-cost depreciation. All data are available for 1947–2016. Rental prices for each asset category are calculated using the BLS external rate of return for the private nonfarm business sector.

Using the data described above on productive capital stock and rental prices by asset and industry, we construct capital input measures at the industry level by aggregating over assets. This completes our discussion of the estimates of capital input by industry.

11.6 Integration adjustments

Because the data used for this account are produced across statistical agencies and with inconsistent original data sources, a few additional steps were required to produce an account that is integrated with the official GDP by Industry accounts. We describe those details here. The first is that nominal capital services estimates produced by the BLS and the residual capital services estimates based on the GDP by Industry accounts data (calculated as value added less total labor compensation including payments to the self-employed) may be inconsistent because they are produced independently (although with related data). To reconcile these, we keep the nominal value of capital services implicit in the GDP by Industry accounts, and the quantity of capital services estimated by the BLS and make an implicit adjustment to the price of capital services. This yields the capital share and capital input growth rate required to implement Eq. (11.1) in a way that is consistent with the GDP by Industry accounts.

The second issue is that labor compensation is not available in the GDP by Industry accounts before 1987. To derive our measure of labor compensation for 1947–86, we apply the labor share in value added from Jorgenson et al. (2018) to BEA's published industry value added estimates. Capital compensation is calculated as a residual and the implicit prices of labor and capital are adjusted such that the account balances. Future work is under consideration to produce the labor and capital services estimates across agencies so that they hit nominal GDP by Industry as an accounting identity without the need to make integration adjustments.

Our treatment of the government sectors is noteworthy as well. As noted above, BLS's primary focus is on the private business sector. For the purpose of this account an estimate of government land services based on the data sources described in Jorgenson and Landefeld (2006) were used. We then reaggregate total government inputs to create total government inputs in current and constant dollars and this serves as our price and quantity of government output as well. Because we change government output, we adjust real government value added, and thus aggregate value added growth is changed as well. The approach taken to government land is an area for future research.

Our final note here is on the industry level of detail available in this report. From 1963 forward, the official GDP by Industry accounts includes sufficient detail to produce growth accounting estimates for 63 NAICS industries. For 1947–63, less industry detail is available, and we are constrained in this version of the research to present estimates for only 44 industries. Providing additional industry detail for the 1947–63 period is another topic for future research.

11.7 Industry-level sources of growth

Tables 11.1 and 11.2 give the sources of growth at the industry level between 1947 and 2016. Because the output growth numbers have been previously published in the BEA estimates, we focus this write-up on the sources of output growth across industries. The first takeaway is that between 1963 and 2016, the accumulation of inputs (including substitution toward higher quality inputs) accounted for the preponderance of growth for all but 7 of the 63 industries.[22] Specifically, only in the Farms, Primary metals, Textile mills and textile product mills, Apparel and leather and allied products, Computer and electronic products, Petroleum and coal, and Rail transportation industries did growth in MFP account for more than the contribution of input growth. Between 1947 and 1963, six industries had MFP growth that accounted for more than half of output growth: Farms, Support activities for mining, Wood products, Textile mills and textile product mills, Administrative and waste management services, and Arts, entertainment, and recreation.

At the industry level, the accumulation of capital input was most important in the Rental and leasing services and lessors of intangible assets, Data processing, Internet publishing, and other information services, Federal Reserve banks, credit intermediation, and related activities, and Broadcasting and telecommunications industries between 1963 and 2016. Between 1947 and 1963, capital contributed the most to growth in the Rental and leasing services and lessors of intangible assets, Real estate, Information, and Utilities industries. Obviously, information on the sources of growth is useful for classifying intensity of capital used across industries, and this is an important use of this new dataset.

---

[22] This includes industries that had positive MFP growth, but negative output growth, along with industries where MFP growth accounted for more than 50% of output growth.

TABLE 11.1   Sources of industry output growth, 1963–2016.

	Output growth	Capital contribution	Labor contribution	Intermediate contribution	MFP growth
Farms	1.89	0.03	−0.35	0.59	1.61
Forestry, fishing, and related activities	1.11	0.72	0.42	0.13	−0.16
Oil and gas extraction	1.01	0.47	0.16	0.81	−0.44
Mining, except oil and gas	0.90	0.51	−0.15	0.36	0.18
Support activities for mining	1.58	0.23	0.45	0.39	0.51
Utilities	1.09	1.20	0.10	0.30	−0.52
Construction	1.35	0.17	0.66	1.04	−0.52
Wood products	1.48	0.16	−0.02	1.19	0.15
Nonmetallic mineral products	0.88	0.45	−0.04	0.55	−0.07
Primary metals	0.10	0.10	−0.35	0.18	0.18
Fabricated metal products	1.67	0.29	0.13	1.06	0.19
Machinery	2.32	0.70	0.05	1.27	0.30
Computer and electronic products	7.42	0.56	0.14	1.87	4.85
Electrical equipment, appliances, and components	1.22	0.57	−0.21	0.47	0.39
Motor vehicles, bodies and trailers, and parts	2.46	0.36	0.02	1.73	0.34
Other transportation equipment	1.68	0.68	−0.04	1.42	−0.38
Furniture and related products	1.63	0.21	0.09	1.03	0.30
Miscellaneous manufacturing	2.23	0.43	0.26	0.88	0.66
Food and beverage and tobacco products	1.60	0.31	0.04	1.24	0.02
Textile mills and textile product mills	−0.06	0.00	−0.48	−0.38	0.81
Apparel and leather and allied products	−1.22	0.11	−1.05	−0.82	0.54
Paper products	1.14	0.32	−0.08	0.89	0.02
Printing and related support activities	1.43	0.12	0.11	0.78	0.42
Petroleum and coal products	1.33	0.15	−0.05	0.35	0.88
Chemical products	2.41	1.09	0.07	1.44	−0.19
Plastics and rubber products	3.13	0.53	0.41	1.81	0.39
Wholesale trade	4.64	1.51	0.62	1.13	1.37
Retail trade	2.71	0.90	0.63	0.60	0.58
Air transportation	4.07	0.70	0.52	2.02	0.84
Rail transportation	0.10	0.02	−1.39	0.30	1.17

TABLE 11.1 Sources of industry output growth, 1963–2016.—cont'd

	Output growth	Capital contribution	Labor contribution	Intermediate contribution	MFP growth
Water transportation	2.82	0.12	0.13	1.84	0.73
Truck transportation	3.03	0.35	0.82	1.58	0.27
Transit and ground passenger transportation	1.06	0.27	0.67	0.58	−0.45
Pipeline transportation	2.10	0.81	0.04	0.54	0.71
Other transportation and support activities	3.19	0.30	1.17	1.39	0.32
Warehousing and storage	4.95	0.27	1.56	1.26	1.87
Publishing industries, except the Internet (includes software)	3.73	0.92	0.38	1.46	0.97
Motion picture and sound recording industries	3.20	1.27	0.35	0.97	0.61
Broadcasting and telecommunications	5.47	2.21	0.29	2.11	0.86
Data processing, Internet publishing, and other information services	6.65	2.48	1.43	3.30	−0.56
Federal Reserve banks, credit intermediation, and related activities	3.48	2.34	0.69	1.23	−0.78
Securities, commodity contracts, and investments	6.84	0.43	1.82	3.16	1.43
Insurance carriers and related activities	3.60	1.46	0.68	1.54	−0.08
Funds, trusts, and other financial vehicles	4.36	0.32	0.07	3.90	0.05
Real estate	3.38	2.01	0.11	0.98	0.28
Rental and leasing services and lessors of intangible assets	4.67	4.06	0.41	1.17	−0.97
Legal services	1.88	0.77	1.59	0.94	−1.42
Computer systems design and related services	6.57	0.92	4.35	1.80	−0.49
Miscellaneous professional, scientific, and technical services	4.82	1.11	1.44	1.82	0.46
Management of companies and enterprises	3.41	1.05	1.12	1.72	−0.49
Administrative and support services	5.66	0.93	2.30	2.22	0.21
Waste management and remediation services	3.26	0.74	0.80	1.68	0.04
Educational services	3.22	0.25	1.44	1.55	−0.02
Ambulatory health care services	3.77	0.34	2.32	1.45	−0.34
Hospitals and Nursing and residential care	4.15	0.66	1.73	2.54	−0.79
Social assistance	5.69	0.18	2.53	2.53	0.45

(Continued)

TABLE 11.1   Sources of industry output growth, 1963—2016.—cont'd

	Output growth	Capital contribution	Labor contribution	Intermediate contribution	MFP growth
Performing arts, spectator sports, museums, and related activities	3.58	0.10	1.20	1.38	0.89
Amusements, gambling, and recreation industries	3.66	0.87	0.99	1.67	0.12
Accommodation	3.82	0.89	0.48	1.60	0.85
Food services and drinking places	2.67	0.25	0.81	1.66	−0.05
Other services, except government	2.24	0.40	0.15	1.10	0.60
Federal	1.29	0.42	0.24	0.61	0.02
State and local	2.92	0.66	1.23	0.98	0.04

Notes: Average annual percentage growth. A contribution is a share-weighted growth rate.

TABLE 11.2   Sources of industry output growth 1947—63.

	Output growth	Capital contribution	Labor contribution	Intermediate contribution	MFP growth
Farms	2.55	0.16	−1.59	1.39	2.59
Forestry, fishing, and related activities	3.45	1.33	−0.03	2.49	−0.35
Oil and gas extraction	3.35	1.83	0.28	1.09	0.15
Mining, except oil and gas	−0.69	0.26	−1.23	0.29	0.00
Support activities for mining	0.70	0.15	0.16	−0.77	1.15
Utilities	5.39	2.05	0.24	2.00	1.11
Construction	4.95	0.17	0.47	2.77	1.54
Wood products	0.95	0.29	−0.36	0.01	1.01
Nonmetallic mineral products	4.34	0.90	0.33	2.38	0.73
Primary metals	1.60	0.67	0.02	1.41	−0.50
Fabricated metal products	1.81	0.40	0.41	0.70	0.30
Machinery	2.41	1.20	0.34	1.02	−0.15
Computer and electronic products	6.68	0.62	1.56	5.20	−0.70
Electrical equipment, appliances, and components	1.02	1.44	0.53	1.30	−2.23
Motor vehicles, bodies and trailers, and parts	4.31	0.67	0.27	2.57	0.81
Other transportation equipment	6.96	0.83	1.58	2.86	1.70

TABLE 11.2 Sources of industry output growth 1947–63.—cont'd

	Output growth	Capital contribution	Labor contribution	Intermediate contribution	MFP growth
Furniture and related products	3.39	0.14	0.10	1.83	1.32
Miscellaneous manufacturing	2.57	0.27	0.24	0.82	1.25
Food and beverage and tobacco products	2.40	0.19	−0.01	1.53	0.70
Textile mills and textile product mills	2.31	0.06	−0.34	1.32	1.28
Apparel and leather and allied products	2.15	0.19	−0.01	0.96	1.01
Paper products	3.44	0.71	0.47	1.86	0.40
Printing and related support activities	3.43	0.19	0.48	2.70	0.06
Petroleum and coal products	3.26	0.38	0.08	2.56	0.24
Chemical products	6.43	1.17	0.53	2.88	1.85
Plastics and rubber products	5.92	1.21	0.58	3.25	0.87
Wholesale trade	3.70	1.29	0.84	0.35	1.22
Retail trade	3.10	0.58	0.34	1.18	1.00
Transportation and warehousing	1.56	0.61	−0.38	0.56	0.78
Information	3.92	2.05	0.48	1.45	−0.06
Finance and insurance	4.47	1.08	1.29	1.97	0.13
Real estate	4.12	3.49	0.07	0.50	0.06
Rental and leasing services and lessors of intangible assets	5.90	4.02	0.03	1.51	0.35
Professional, scientific, and technical services	6.03	1.57	0.69	2.71	1.05
Management of companies and enterprises	2.59	1.94	0.21	0.79	−0.36
Administrative and waste management services	8.28	1.17	1.15	1.66	4.30
Educational services	5.76	0.67	1.39	3.21	0.49
Health care and social assistance	4.83	1.40	1.81	1.80	−0.18
Arts, entertainment, and recreation	1.07	0.50	0.26	−0.45	0.76
Accommodation	0.78	1.02	0.20	−0.37	−0.07
Food services and drinking places	1.47	0.40	0.42	1.17	−0.51
Other services, except government	3.13	0.38	0.75	1.28	0.73
Federal	2.52	0.16	0.66	1.89	−0.20
State and local	4.63	1.40	2.24	1.10	−0.11

Notes: Average annual percentage growth. A contribution is a share-weighted growth rate.

Not surprisingly, the accumulation of labor input made the largest contributions to growth to industries in the service sector. For example, the industries with the largest labor contributions to growth between 1963 and 2016 were the Computer systems design and related services, Social assistance, Ambulatory health care services, and Administrative and support services. Between 1947 and 1963, State and local government, Health care and social assistance, and Other transportation equipment had the largest labor contributions to industry output growth.

Tables 11.3 and 11.4 present new information on the sources of intermediate input growth across industries. As noted above, this information is new because previously published estimates of intermediate input included the total,

while those used in this account include breakdowns on energy, materials, and services. Between 1963 and 2016, the largest users of energy intermediate (measured as the contribution of energy to gross output growth) were Air transportation, Truck transportation, Water transportation, and Utilities industries. The largest users of materials inputs were the Computers and electronic products industry (likely from constant-quality semiconductor inputs), Motor vehicles, bodies and trailers, and parts, and Other transportation equipment. The Data processing, Internet publishing, and other information services, Securities, commodity contracts, and investments, Funds, trusts, and other financial vehicles, and Administrative and support services industries made extensive use of intermediate inputs of services.

TABLE 11.3   Sources of intermediate input growth 1963–2016.

	Intermediate contribution	Energy intermediate	Materials intermediate	Services intermediate
Farms	0.59	−0.03	0.45	0.17
Forestry, fishing, and related activities	0.13	−0.05	0.03	0.15
Oil and gas extraction	0.81	0.04	0.57	0.19
Mining, except oil and gas	0.36	−0.02	0.20	0.18
Support activities for mining	0.39	0.01	0.02	0.35
Utilities	0.30	0.15	−0.02	0.18
Construction	1.04	0.01	0.77	0.26
Wood products	1.19	0.00	0.90	0.29
Nonmetallic mineral products	0.55	−0.06	0.40	0.21
Primary metals	0.18	−0.10	0.20	0.07
Fabricated metal products	1.06	0.00	0.77	0.29
Machinery	1.27	0.00	1.00	0.27
Computer and electronic products	1.87	0.00	1.61	0.26
Electrical equipment, appliances, and components	0.47	−0.01	0.38	0.11
Motor vehicles, bodies and trailers, and parts	1.73	0.00	1.42	0.31

TABLE 11.3 Sources of intermediate input growth 1963—2016.—cont'd

	Intermediate contribution	Energy intermediate	Materials intermediate	Services intermediate
Other transportation equipment	1.42	0.00	1.13	0.29
Furniture and related products	1.03	0.01	0.75	0.27
Miscellaneous manufacturing	0.88	0.01	0.47	0.41
Food and beverage and tobacco products	1.24	0.01	1.03	0.19
Textile mills and textile product mills	−0.38	−0.06	−0.47	0.14
Apparel and leather and allied products	−0.82	−0.05	−1.09	0.32
Paper products	0.89	0.01	0.66	0.22
Printing and related support activities	0.78	0.00	0.58	0.20
Petroleum and coal products	0.35	−0.02	0.31	0.06
Chemical products	1.44	0.03	0.99	0.43
Plastics and rubber products	1.81	0.04	1.38	0.39
Wholesale trade	1.13	0.01	0.18	0.94
Retail trade	0.60	−0.06	0.04	0.62
Air transportation	2.02	0.54	0.08	1.40
Rail transportation	0.30	0.05	−0.02	0.27
Water transportation	1.84	0.19	0.18	1.48
Truck transportation	1.58	0.34	0.30	0.94
Transit and ground passenger transportation	0.58	0.06	0.04	0.48
Pipeline transportation	0.54	−0.11	0.31	0.34
Other transportation and support activities	1.39	0.08	0.34	0.98
Warehousing and storage	1.26	0.07	0.18	1.01
Publishing industries, except internet (includes software)	1.46	0.01	0.36	1.09
Motion picture and sound recording industries	0.97	0.01	0.08	0.88
Broadcasting and telecommunications	2.11	0.00	0.49	1.63
Data processing, Internet publishing, and other information services	3.30	0.05	0.73	2.53
Federal Reserve banks, credit intermediation, and related activities	1.23	0.00	0.07	1.17
Securities, commodity contracts, and investments	3.16	0.00	0.14	3.03
Insurance carriers and related activities	1.54	−0.02	0.01	1.56

(Continued)

TABLE 11.3   Sources of intermediate input growth 1963–2016.—cont'd

	Intermediate contribution	Energy intermediate	Materials intermediate	Services intermediate
Funds, trusts, and other financial vehicles	3.90	−0.01	0.03	3.88
Real estate	0.98	0.08	0.10	0.80
Rental and leasing services and lessors of intangible assets	1.17	0.03	0.00	1.14
Legal services	0.94	−0.04	0.11	0.87
Computer systems design and related services	1.80	0.03	0.47	1.30
Miscellaneous professional, scientific, and technical services	1.82	0.00	0.36	1.46
Management of companies and enterprises	1.72	0.03	0.18	1.51
Administrative and support services	2.22	0.05	0.44	1.72
Waste management and remediation services	1.68	−0.03	0.59	1.12
Educational services	1.55	0.03	0.35	1.17
Ambulatory health care services	1.45	0.00	0.36	1.10
Hospitals and nursing and residential care	2.54	0.10	0.92	1.52
Social assistance	2.53	0.11	1.00	1.42
Performing arts, spectator sports, museums, and related activities	1.38	−0.02	0.04	1.36
Amusements, gambling, and recreation industries	1.67	0.08	0.39	1.20
Accommodation	1.60	0.07	0.56	0.97
Food services and drinking places	1.66	0.05	0.73	0.88
Other services, except government	1.10	−0.01	0.37	0.73
Federal	0.61	0.02	0.20	0.39
State and local	0.98	0.10	0.26	0.62

Notes: Average annual percentage growth. A contribution is a share-weighted growth rate.

Obviously, these data are extremely useful for analyzing production processes across industries.

Because the tabulations from this account are based on preliminary data, we have chosen to present only the high-level results as a proof of concept. Future data development and research will permit a more fundamental analysis on the sources of growth across industries.

11.8 The sector origins of economic growth

In this section, we describe the sector origins of economic growth using the dataset described above and aggregating over industries. Before moving on to the results, we describe our framework for aggregating across industries. The starting is production possibility frontier model

TABLE 11.4 Sources of intermediate input growth 1947−63.

	Intermediate contribution	Energy intermediate	Materials intermediate	Services intermediate
Farms	1.39	0.10	1.39	−0.11
Forestry, fishing, and related activities	2.49	0.00	2.14	0.36
Oil and gas extraction	1.09	0.00	−0.11	1.21
Mining, except oil and gas	0.29	−0.02	0.25	0.06
Support activities for mining	−0.77	−0.02	−0.48	−0.27
Utilities	2.00	0.95	0.59	0.46
Construction	2.77	0.06	2.36	0.35
Wood products	0.01	−0.01	0.72	−0.70
Nonmetallic mineral products	2.38	0.28	1.87	0.24
Primary metals	1.41	0.13	1.17	0.11
Fabricated metal products	0.70	0.02	0.63	0.05
Machinery	1.02	0.00	0.97	0.04
Computer and electronic products	5.20	0.05	4.26	0.89
Electrical equipment, appliances, and components	1.30	0.02	1.10	0.18
Motor vehicles, bodies and trailers, and parts	2.57	0.01	2.42	0.15
Other transportation equipment	2.86	0.04	2.42	0.40
Furniture and related products	1.83	0.01	1.79	0.03
Miscellaneous manufacturing	0.82	0.01	0.88	−0.07
Food and beverage and tobacco products	1.53	0.00	1.41	0.12
Textile mills and textile product mills	1.32	0.00	1.31	0.01
Apparel and leather and allied products	0.96	−0.01	1.09	−0.12
Paper products	1.86	0.08	1.70	0.07
Printing and related support activities	2.70	0.03	2.20	0.47
Petroleum and coal products	2.56	0.05	2.10	0.41
Chemical products	2.88	0.13	2.24	0.51
Plastics and rubber products	3.25	0.08	2.77	0.39
Wholesale trade	0.35	0.03	0.16	0.17
Retail trade	1.18	0.25	0.46	0.47
Transportation and warehousing	0.56	0.05	−0.06	0.58

(*Continued*)

TABLE 11.4   Sources of intermediate input growth 1947–63.—cont'd

	Intermediate contribution	Energy intermediate	Materials intermediate	Services intermediate
Information	1.45	0.03	0.60	0.81
Finance and insurance	1.97	0.10	0.19	1.68
Real estate	0.50	0.00	0.03	0.47
Rental and leasing services and lessors of intangible assets	1.51	0.02	1.06	0.42
Professional, scientific, and technical services	2.71	0.14	0.51	2.06
Management of companies and enterprises	0.79	0.01	0.10	0.68
Administrative and waste management services	1.66	0.31	0.71	0.64
Educational services	3.21	0.38	0.80	2.03
Health care and social assistance	1.80	0.17	0.97	0.66
Arts, entertainment, and recreation	−0.45	−0.08	0.15	−0.52
Accommodation	−0.37	−0.03	−0.46	0.12
Food services and drinking places	1.17	0.03	1.23	−0.10
Other services, except government	1.28	0.07	0.90	0.30
Federal	1.89	0.09	0.77	1.04
State and local	1.10	0.17	0.33	0.59

Notes: Average annual percentage growth. A contribution is a share-weighted growth rate.

of production described in Jorgenson et al. (2007).

$$\Delta lnV = \sum_{j}\gamma_j\Delta lnV_j \qquad (11.4)$$

Eq. (11.4) says that aggregate value added growth, $\Delta \ln V$, in year t is the share weighted growth in industry-level real value added growth, $\Delta \ln V_j$, where the weights are the average of period t and $t - 1$ shares of each industry's nominal value added in aggregate nominal value added. Because value added growth is not directly measured, we use the growth accounting identity that the growth of gross output (Q_j) equals the weighted growth of intermediate inputs (which itself is an aggregate of the energy, material, and service inputs from industry j, and value added (V_j) to back

out the growth rate of value added. Rearranging Eq. (11.5), which is the growth accounting relationship between gross output, intermediate inputs, and value added, yields Eq. (11.6):

$$\Delta lnQ_j = w_{vj}\Delta lnV_j + w_{Ej}\Delta lnE_j + w_{Mj}\Delta lnM_j + w_{Sj}\Delta lnS_j \qquad (11.5)$$

where the weights are the average of period t and $t - 1$ shares of value added and intermediate input factors in nominal gross output.

$$\Delta lnV_j$$
$$= \frac{\Delta lnQ_j - w_{Ej}\Delta lnE_j - w_{Mj}\Delta lnM_j - w_{Sj}\Delta lnS_j}{w_{vj}} \qquad (11.6)$$

Combining Eqs. (11.1) and (11.6) cancels the intermediate inputs of E, M, S such that

$$\Delta lnV_j = \frac{w_{K_{jt}}\Delta lnK_{jt} + w_{L_{jt}}\Delta lnL_{jt} + \Delta lnMFP_j}{w_{vj}}$$

(11.7)

Combining Eqs. (11.4) and (11.7) yields the bottom-up growth accounting that we use to present results:

$$\Delta lnV = \sum_j \gamma_j \frac{w_{k,j}}{w_{V,j}} \Delta lnK_j + \sum_j \gamma_j \frac{w_{L,j}}{w_{V,j}} \Delta lnL_j$$
$$+ \sum_j \gamma_j \frac{1}{w_{V,j}} \Delta lnMFP_j$$

(11.8)

Equation (Eq. 11.8) is the direct aggregation approach to analyzing the sources of growth. That is, we define $\sum \gamma_j \frac{w_{K,j}}{w_{V,j}} \Delta lnK_j$ as the aggregate contribution of capital to aggregate value added growth. Similarly, $\sum \gamma_j \frac{1}{w_{V,j}} \Delta lnMFP_j$ is the contribution of industry j to aggregate value added growth in addition to also being the industry contribution to aggregate MFP growth, where the weights are typically referred to in the literature as "Domar weights."

Table 11.5 presents the bottom-up sources of US economic growth for the period as a whole and for major subperiods. Between 1947 and 2016, GDP grew by slightly more than 3 percentage points per year based on the integrated account. Of this, capital input accumulation accounted for about half of GDP growth, labor input accounted for a bit more than a quarter, and MFP growth a bit less than a quarter of growth. The data that we have described above allow us to decompose the contributions of capital input by type of capital input, and the contribution of labor input by type of worker. Over the period as a whole, Information technology equipment capital accounted for about 15% of the total capital input contribution, Research and development capital about 10%, and Other capital about 70%.[23]

The fastest growth subperiod that we consider was the decade between 1963 and 1973, but across all subperiods (even the Information technology boom between 1995 and 2000), the contribution of MFP growth never exceeded 35% of GDP growth.

One important use of these data and framework is to put the post-2000 growth period in historical perspective. Our results show that growth during the period that includes the ongoing recovery from the financial crisis and the jobless growth period in the early 2000s was slow even in comparison to the slow growth period between 1973 and 1995 that preceded the IT investment boom. On average MFP during the 2000–16 period was actually higher than MFP growth during the 1973–95 period, putting the current MFP slowdown in historical perspective. Of the approximately 1.10 percentage point difference in GDP growth between the 2000–16 period and the 1973–95 period, capital and labor input both contributed about 0.6 points less during the 2000–16 period than during the 1973–95 period, highlighting the importance of slow input growth over the last 16 years.

Tables 11.6 and 11.7 present information on US economic growth from the bottom-up at the major sector level.[24] Table 11.6 includes information that was previously available from BEA's GDP by Industry accounts, while Table 11.7 includes new information on the sources of growth. Starting with Table 11.6, the Manufacturing sector was the largest contributor to growth over the period as a

---

[23] IT Equipment includes Computers and Communications equipment. Other capital includes structures, land, and other durable equipment.

[24] Sector-level information is created by aggregating contributions described in Eq. (11.6) to the reported sector level.

TABLE 11.5   Growth in aggregate value-added and the sources of growth.

	1947–2016	1947–63	1963–73	1973–95	1995–2000	2000–07	2007–16
Contributions							
Value-added	3.04	3.49	4.42	2.77	4.30	2.37	1.17
Capital input	1.50	1.65	1.97	1.50	1.90	1.34	0.62
IT capital	0.21	0.04	0.07	0.33	0.66	0.27	0.09
R&D capital	0.11	0.13	0.15	0.10	0.09	0.08	0.08
Software capital	0.11	0.00	0.07	0.14	0.25	0.20	0.11
Entertainment originals capital	0.03	0.03	0.02	0.02	0.03	0.03	0.02
Other capital	1.05	1.44	1.66	0.91	0.88	0.76	0.33
Labor input	0.89	0.67	1.14	1.12	1.48	0.46	0.45
College labor	0.58	0.41	0.40	0.74	0.84	0.59	0.56
Noncollege labor	0.31	0.26	0.74	0.38	0.64	−0.13	−0.11
MFP	0.65	1.18	1.31	0.15	0.92	0.57	0.10

Notes: Average annual percentages. Aggregate value added growth is the aggregate of share weighed industry value added growth. The contribution of capital, labor, and TFP is the domar-weighted industry contributions. IT capital is Computer, Communications and other IT capital.

whole; the next largest contributors were the Finance, insurance, real estate, rental and leasing, Other services, and the Trade sectors. It is also instructive to compare the sector sources of the slow growth period after 2000 with the slow growth period between 1973 and 1995. While the slowdown was broad based across sectors, the slowdown in the Manufacturing and Trade sectors accounted from more than half of the slowdown in 2000–16 relative to 1973–95.

The transformation of the economy from Agricultural and Manufacturing toward services is evident in the bottom panel of Table 11.6. In the 1947–63 period, these two sectors accounted about a third of nominal GDP. In the 2007–16 period, these sectors accounted for less than 15% of nominal GDP.

The bottom-up sources of growth are given in Table 11.7. As noted earlier, the accumulation of capital input accounted for the majority of economic growth between 1947 and 2016. The

largest contributor at the sector level was Finance, insurance, real estate, and rental and leasing, which includes owner occupied housing. The Manufacturing sector also made significant capital investments over the period. The key advantage of the sources of growth framework is that it quantifies the impact of these investments on economic growth in a way that is integrated with the national accounts. While the aggregate results presented in Table 11.5 indicate that a major source of the relatively slow growth in 2000–16 was the slowdown in the contribution of capital input, Table 11.7 shows the sector origins of this. Of the approximately 0.60 percentage point slowdown in the contribution of capital input, more than half of this was accounted for by lower capital contributions in the Finance, insurance, real estate, rental and leasing and Manufacturing sectors.

Labor input was the next largest contributor to economic growth over the period as a whole. The aggregate contribution was driven largely

TABLE 11.6 Sector sources of value-added growth.

	1947–2016	1947–63	1963–73	1973–95	1995–2000	2000–07	2007–16
Contributions							
Value-Added	3.04	3.49	4.42	2.77	4.30	2.37	1.17
Agriculture, Forestry, Fishing, Hunting, Mining	0.08	0.15	0.04	0.05	0.05	0.06	0.14
Transportation, Warehousing, Utilities	0.12	0.18	0.23	0.11	0.10	0.02	0.02
Construction	0.08	0.23	0.09	0.03	0.13	−0.04	−0.06
Manufacturing	0.63	0.95	1.27	0.41	0.84	0.32	−0.01
Computer and electronic products	0.18	0.04	0.14	0.24	0.62	0.17	0.07
Trade	0.50	0.52	0.72	0.52	0.90	0.34	0.09
Information	0.18	0.12	0.21	0.19	0.20	0.30	0.14
Finance, Insurance, Real Estate, Rental and Leasing	0.57	0.56	0.68	0.56	0.89	0.57	0.27
Other Services	0.54	0.41	0.61	0.59	0.89	0.49	0.44
Government	0.33	0.36	0.56	0.30	0.28	0.31	0.13
Shares							
Shares in Nominal Value-Added	100.0	100.0	100.0	100.0	100.0	100.0	100.0
Agriculture, Forestry, Fishing, Hunting, Mining	4.3	7.0	4.1	3.8	2.1	2.4	3.3
Transportation, Warehousing, Utilities	5.5	6.7	5.8	5.5	4.8	4.3	4.4
Construction	4.2	4.3	4.5	4.1	4.1	4.6	3.7
Manufacturing	19.3	26.1	23.8	18.4	15.4	12.7	11.6
Computer and electronic products	1.6	1.3	1.6	1.8	2.1	1.6	1.5
Trade	12.9	14.0	13.7	12.9	12.7	11.8	11.2
Information	4.1	3.3	3.7	4.2	4.7	4.7	4.6
Finance, Insurance, Real Estate, Rental and Leasing	15.8	12.4	13.8	16.1	18.5	19.3	19.1
Other Services	17.5	11.6	13.3	17.7	22.6	23.5	24.8
Government	16.5	14.5	17.3	17.4	15.1	16.7	17.4

Notes: Average annual percentages. Aggregate value added growth is the aggregate of share weighed industry value added growth. IT-Producing industries are Computers and electronic products, Data processing, and Computer systems design and related services. IT-using industries are those with an IT intensity share above the median share in 2005. Non-IT are the remaining private sector industries. Government includes government enterprise.

TABLE 11.7   Shares of aggregate value-added growth.

	1947–2016	1947–63	1963–73	1973–95	1995–2000	2000–07	2007–16
Capital input							
Aggregate	1.50	1.65	1.97	1.50	1.90	1.34	0.62
Agriculture, Forestry, Fishing, Hunting, Mining	0.04	0.06	0.04	0.03	0.00	0.00	0.03
Transportation, Warehousing, Utilities	0.07	0.11	0.10	0.06	0.05	0.03	0.04
Construction	0.02	0.02	0.02	0.01	0.05	0.05	−0.01
Manufacturing	0.27	0.39	0.48	0.23	0.26	0.07	0.11
Trade	0.20	0.18	0.27	0.22	0.30	0.22	0.08
Information	0.12	0.10	0.12	0.12	0.22	0.13	0.09
Finance, Insurance, Real Estate, Rental and Leasing	0.47	0.47	0.54	0.50	0.70	0.52	0.12
Other Services	0.18	0.18	0.21	0.19	0.24	0.20	0.08
Government	0.13	0.14	0.18	0.13	0.08	0.13	0.09
Labor input							
Aggregate	0.89	0.67	1.14	1.12	1.48	0.46	0.45
Agriculture, Forestry, Fishing, Hunting, Mining	−0.04	−0.15	−0.06	0.00	0.00	0.01	0.01
Transportation, Warehousing, Utilities	0.02	−0.02	0.03	0.04	0.04	0.00	0.03
Construction	0.06	0.05	0.11	0.06	0.15	0.06	−0.04
Manufacturing	0.06	0.18	0.23	0.01	0.06	−0.21	−0.04
Trade	0.11	0.11	0.20	0.14	0.12	0.04	0.02
Information	0.02	0.02	0.04	0.04	0.11	−0.05	−0.01
Finance, Insurance, Real Estate, Rental and Leasing	0.09	0.08	0.09	0.12	0.16	0.08	0.02
Other Services	0.36	0.14	0.18	0.52	0.63	0.39	0.40
Government	0.20	0.25	0.32	0.20	0.19	0.14	0.06
MFP							
Aggregate	0.65	1.18	1.31	0.15	0.92	0.57	0.10
Agriculture, Forestry, Fishing, Hunting, Mining	0.09	0.23	0.06	0.01	0.06	0.04	0.10
Transportation, Warehousing, Utilities	0.03	0.09	0.10	0.01	0.01	0.00	−0.04
Construction	0.00	0.17	−0.04	−0.03	−0.08	−0.15	−0.01

TABLE 11.7   Shares of aggregate value-added growth.—cont'd

	1947—2016	1947—63	1963—73	1973—95	1995—2000	2000—07	2007—16
Manufacturing	0.30	0.39	0.56	0.17	0.52	0.46	−0.07
Trade	0.18	0.23	0.25	0.16	0.48	0.08	−0.01
Information	0.04	0.00	0.05	0.03	−0.13	0.22	0.06
Finance, Insurance, Real Estate, Rental and Leasing	0.01	0.02	0.05	−0.06	0.03	−0.03	0.13
Other Services	0.00	0.09	0.22	−0.11	0.02	−0.10	−0.05
Government	0.00	−0.03	0.06	−0.03	0.01	0.04	−0.01
Aggregate Value Added Growth	3.04	3.50	4.42	2.77	4.30	2.37	1.17

Notes: Average annual percentages. Aggregate value added growth is the aggregate of share weighed industry value added growth. IT-Producing industries are Computers and electronic products, Data processing, and Computer systems design and related services. IT-using industries are those with an IT intensity share above the median share in 2005. Non-IT are the remaining private sector industries. Government includes government enterprise.

by increases of labor input in the Other services, Government, and Trade sectors. The slowdown in the contribution of labor input in 2000—16 in comparison to 1973—95 was slightly larger than the slowdown in the contribution capital input. Unlike capital input, however, the relatively low contribution of labor input was spread more equally across sectors.

MFP growth between 1947 and 2016 accounted slightly over 20% of aggregate GDP growth. As noted in the data description, the aggregate MFP estimate embeds the underlying assumption for the government sector that output grows at the rate of input.[25] The Agriculture, Manufacturing, and Trade sectors contributed almost all of aggregate MFP growth. Similar to the other sources of growth, we use the long time series to compare MFP growth during the 2000—16 period to 1973—95. Somewhat surprisingly given the recent focus on the productivity slowdown, MFP actually grew faster during 2000—16 than 1973—95. Comparing 2007—16 to 1973—95, MFP grew slowly in both periods, but slightly faster in 1973—95. The Trade sector contributed somewhat less to aggregate MFP growth between 2000 and 2017 than in 1973—95, while the Information and Finance, insurance, real estate, rental and leasing sectors had marginally higher MFP contributions.

11.9 Conclusions and next steps

The purpose of this chapter has been to present research work toward a BEA-BLS Integrated Industry-level Production Account for 1947—16. The methods that we have documented in this chapter link disparate data sources across the BEA and BLS to create an internally consistent KLEMS production account that is also consistent with the official BEA GDP by Industry accounts back to 1947. As presented, there are many assumptions that are necessary to create the historical data, as industry detail is

[25] Technically, only MFP growth for the general government sectors is assumed to be zero. For the government enterprise sectors, we use BEA's published output prices.

limited for many of the data series in the early years. That the results reported in this paper are broadly consistent with Jorgenson et al. (2018), suggests that the approaches taken in this paper are reasonable. It is important to note that the results presented are not yet official data; however, this study provides a proof of concept that an account beginning in 1947 is feasible. These data provide insights on sources of output and productivity growth over a much longer time horizon than was previously available and will be sure to spur important research and further our understanding of the mechanisms underlying economic growth.

To close, a few concrete "next steps" are worth documenting. Firstly, BEA and BLS will continue to analyze industry data for the early years to identify ways to improve the assumptions used to move some of the series back in time. In addition, the labor composition estimates used in this paper are a combination of historical estimates from Jorgenson et al. (2018), and BEA estimates for 1987–16. Yet, BLS produces labor composition estimates that are similar and begin in 1976 using CPS data. Future research is planned to reconcile these estimates and move toward a single labor composition estimate. BEA and BLS will also be completing previous work to release the 1987-forward data as a complete time series. Finally, this paper uses reduced industry detail between 1947 and 1963 due to limited availability of GDP by Industry data from BEA. Future work will investigate the possibility of using the more detailed industry list over the entire time series. Given the work and initial steps presented in this chapter, we are optimistic that these are attainable goals.

Disclaimer

The views expressed in this paper are solely those of the authors, and not necessarily those of the U.S. Bureau of Economic Analysis or the Bureau of Labor Statistics.

Acknowledgments

We have written this paper in honor of Dale Jorgenson, whose seminal work on KLEMS measurement has inspired this paper, and whose research agenda on economic measurement and engagement with the US statistical agencies has been an invaluable resource. We are grateful to Matt Calby, Justin Harper, Eugene Njinkeu, and Ethan Schein of BEA and Kendra Asher, Corey Holman, Mike Jadoo, and Randal Kinoshita of BLS for their work on the estimates presented in this chapter.

References

Bayard K, Klimek S: Creating a historical bridge for manufacturing between the standard industrial classification system and the North American industry classification system. In *The 2003 ASA proceedings: papers presented at the annual meeting of the American Statistical Association: joint statistical meetings, San Francisco*, American Statistical Association.

Christensen LR, Jorgenson DE: Measuring economic performance in the private sector. In Moss M, editor: *The measurement of economic and social performance*, New York, 1973, Columbia University Press, pp 233–351.

Eldridge LP, Manser ME, Otto PF: Alternative measures of supervisory employee hours and productivity growth, *Monthly Labor Review* 127(4):9–28, 2004.

Fleck S, Rosenthal S, Russell M, Strassner EH, Usher L: A prototype BEA/BLS industry-level production account for the United States. In , Chicago, 2014, University of Chicago Press, pp 323–372. Jorgenson DW, Landefeld JS, Schreyer P, editors: *Measuring economic sustainability and progress*, vol. 72. Chicago, 2014, University of Chicago Press, pp 323–372.

Fraumeni BM, Harper MJ, Powers SG, Yuskavage RE: An integrated BEA/BLS production account: a first step and theoretical considerations. In , Chicago and London, 2006, University of Chicago Press, pp 355–435. Jorgenson DW, Landefeld JS, Nordhaus WD, editors: *A new architecture for the U.S. national accounts*, vol. 66. Chicago and London, 2006, University of Chicago Press, pp 355–435.

Garner C, Harper J, Howells III TF, Russell M, Samuels JD: Experimental statistics for 1987–1997, revised statistics for 1998–2015, and initial statistics for 2016, *Survey of Current Business* 98(7):1–17, 2018.

Harper MJ, Moulton BR, Rosenthal S, Wasshausen D: Integrated GDP-productivity accounts. In *The 2009 annual meeting of the American Economic Association*, San Francisco, 2008, American Economic Association.

Jaeger DA: Reconciling the old and new Census Bureau education questions: recommendations for researchers, *Journal of Business & Economic Statistics* 15(1):300–309, 1997.

Jorgenson DW, Gollop F, Fraumeni BM: *Productivity and U.S. economic growth*, Cambridge, 1987, Harvard University Press.

Jorgenson DW, Ho MS, Samuels JD: Educational attainment and the revival of U.S. economic growth. In , Chicago, 2018, University of Chicago Press, pp 23–60. Hulten CR, Ramey VA, editors: *Education, skills, and technical change: Implications for future U.S. GDP growth*, vol. 77. Chicago, 2018, University of Chicago Press, pp 23–60.

Jorgenson DW, Ho MS, Samuels JD, Stiroh KJ: Industry origins of the american productivity resurgence, *Economic Systems Research* 19(3):229–252, 2007.

Jorgenson DW, Landefeld JS: Blueprint for expanded and integrated U.S. accounts: review, assessment, and next steps. In Jorgenson DW, Landefeld JS, Nordhaus WD, editors: *A new architecture for the U.S. national accounts*, Chicago and London, 2006, University of Chicago Press, pp 13–112.

Lyndaker AS, Howells III TF, Strassner EH, Wasshausen DB: Integrated historical input-output and GDP-by-industry accounts, 1947–1996, *Survey of Current Business* 96(2): 1–9, 2016.

OECD: *Measuring productivity*, Paris, 2001, Organization for Economic Cooperation and Development.

Rosenthal S, Russell M, Samuels JD, Strassner EH, Usher L: Integrated industry-level production account for the United States: intellectual property product and the 2007 NAICS. In *The Third world KLEMS conference*, Tokyo, 2014, Research Institute of Economy, Trade and Industry.

Solow RM: Technical change and the aggregate production function, *The Review of Economics and Statistics* 39(3): 312–320, 1957.

Yuskavage RE: Converting historical industry time series data from SIC to NAICS. In *The Federal committee on statistical methodology research conference*, Arlington, 2007, Bureau of Economic Analysis.

Yuskavage RE, Fahim-Nader M: Gross domestic product by industry for 1947-86, *Survey of Current Business* 85(12): 1–15, 2005.

Zoghi C: Measuring labor composition: a comparison of alternate methodologies. In , Chicago, 2010, University of Chicago Press, pp 457–485. Abraham KG, Spletzer JR, Harper MJ, editors: *Labor in the New Economy NBER studies in income and wealth*, vol. 71. Chicago, 2010, University of Chicago Press, pp 457–485.

12

Benchmark 2011 integrated estimates of the Japan–US price-level index for industry outputs

Koji Nomura[1,2,a], Kozo Miyagawa[3,a], Jon D. Samuels[4,5]

[1]Keio Economic Observatory (KEO), Keio University, Tokyo, Japan; [2]Research Institute of Economy, Trade and Industry (RIETI), Tokyo, Japan; [3]Faculty of Economics, Rissho University, Tokyo, Japan; [4]National Economic, Accounts, United States Bureau of Economic Analysis, Suitland, MD, United States; [5]Institute of Quantitative Social Science, Harvard University, Cambridge, MA, United States

12.1 Introduction

Cross-country comparisons of international competitiveness at the industry level are inherently more difficult than aggregate comparisons. The basic issue is that comparing industries is more data demanding than comparing aggregates in general, but this is exacerbated by the fact that price differentials are mainly measured at the level of final expenditures.[1] Price data at the level of final expenditures enable one to compare output across countries at the aggregate level, by estimating the purchasing power parity (PPP) for gross domestic product (GDP) from the expenditure side. One of the main impediments to comparing industries is the lack of adequate data on price differentials of domestic industry outputs and intermediate inputs across countries. This data gap has greatly limited productivity-level comparisons at industry level across countries and in turn, offered little insight into cross-country supply-side efficiency measures and related policy implications (Hamadeh and AbuShanab, 2016; Jorgenson, 2018).

The purpose of this paper is to fill this data gap for the United States and Japan. We employ a bilateral price model to measure 2011 benchmark industry-level price-level indices (PLIs) for outputs. The PLI is defined as the ratio of

---

[a] Nomura and Miyagawa conducted this study as a part of the project on "Productivity Gaps and Industrial Competitiveness" (January 2018–December 2019) at RIETI.

[1] For example, the purchasing power parities (PPPs) compiled within the International Comparisons Program (ICP) in Eurostat-OECD (2012) and World Bank (2014).

the PPP to the market exchange rate. Our starting point is the Isard-type bilateral input–output table (BIOT), that has been developed by the Ministry of Economy, Trade and Industry (METI), government of Japan for the purpose of analyzing the interdependency among Japanese and the US industries since 1985.[2] METI's Japan–US BIOTs are harmonized to a common and detailed classification of industries[3] and provide supplementary tables on international freight and insurance and tariffs by products in both countries. Although the availability of METI's BIOT is a major advantage in forming Japan–US comparisons (that is, data of this nature are not available for most other countries), METI's compilation terminated after the publication of the 2005 BIOT (METI, 2013). In this paper, we estimate the 2011 BIOT by extending the official 2005 BIOT.

Using the 2011 Japan–US BIOT as an anchor, we postulate an accounting model describing the relationships between producer's prices and purchaser's prices for domestically produced and imported products. The model reflects the differences in the trade structure, freight and insurance rates, duty tax rates, wholesale and retail trade margins, and transportation costs in each product.[4] Using demand-side data of purchaser's price differentials for final uses, e.g., the PPP estimates in Eurostat-OECD (2012), and for intermediate uses, e.g., *Survey on Foreign and Domestic Price Differentials for Industrial Goods and Services* in

METI (2012), the producer's price differentials for outputs are estimated based on our Japan–US bilateral price accounting model. That is, the model takes available prices on final demand and intermediate uses and converts these to conceptually appropriate industry output and intermediate input prices that are consistent with the input–output tables (IOTs). The availability of METI's survey on PPPs for intermediate uses is a significant advantage in the Japan–US comparison. This enables us to account for the price differentials for intermediate products like semiconductors, which do not appear in the survey on final demand prices. It is important to note that the PPPs at purchaser's prices are sometimes considerably different for final and intermediate uses even within the same class of product. This could be because the composition and quality of the products may differ between final demand and intermediate input. In our approach, we are able to identify the gap between the two and account for this by constructing the PPPs for industry outputs as a composite of both.

As globalization has deepened since the early 1990s, it has become more important to consider the impact of the differences in the import prices of the traded goods in Japan and the United States. The import prices allow us to parse the price of composite goods into that from domestic supply (which feeds into the industry output price) and that coming from imported goods. Our bilateral price model

[2] The first bilateral table between Japan and the United States for 1970 was developed in Japan at the Institute of Developing Economies (1978) as a joint project with Keio Economic Observatory (KEO), Keio University in 1978. The METI's Japan–US BIOTs were compiled for the benchmark years of Japanese benchmark IOT, i.e., 1985, 1990, 1995, 2000, and 2005.

[3] The 2005 Japan–US IOT in METI (2013) is defined as the symmetric-IOT with common classification of 173 products. This is estimated based on the Japan's 2005 benchmark IOT and the US 2005 Symmetric IOT developed at INFORUM, University of Maryland, which was extended from the 2002 Benchmark SUT by the US Bureau of Economic Analysis (BEA), Department of Commerce.

[4] The original price model approach to determining the product PPPs between Japan and the United States was developed in Jorgenson et al. (1987).

has a submodel to explicitly treat the imports by product from six exogenous economies, i.e., China, Germany, Korea, Malaysia, Taiwan (Republic of China), and Thailand, to Japan and the United States.[5]

Compared to the previous work in Nomura and Miyagawa (1999, 2015), we use more price data than the earlier studies. These additional price data allow us to refine our estimates of the unobserved prices in our price model. The total number of price-differential data we use in this paper is 538 at the elementary level, in which each of the price concepts (i.e., for industry or household use, at producer's or purchaser's prices, and including imports or not) is incorporated into the accounting model to pin down the remainder of the prices for which there are no data. For the case that the appropriate data are not available, or their accuracy cannot be checked, the cost index approach is used. Using the cost index approach, the underlying assumption is that the output price relative corresponds to the input price relative. In measuring costs, we include not only the price differentials of products for intermediate uses (estimated in this paper) but also the prices of labor and capital inputs used in production.[6] By construction, the cost index approach imposes zero total productivity factor (TFP) differential between Japan and the United States.

The accuracy of the estimated PPPs for industry outputs based on the price model approach depends not only on the quality of purchaser-price PPPs of the composite products for different uses but also on measures of the margin rates and other related parameters that are used to translate the available data into conceptually appropriate prices to match the IOT. It should be of note that 2011 as the benchmark year is not necessarily ideal to observe the Japanese economy. The first reason is that the 2011 benchmark estimates in the Japan's system of national accounts (JSNA) depend on the 2011 Economic Census, which was conducted for the first time in the history of Japanese economic statistics. This had the potential to improve the quality of JSNA, but on the other hand, because it was a new Census, the results had the potential to reflect changes in methodologies and approaches to measurement. Another reason is the impact of the East Japan great earthquake disaster on March 11, 2011. The earthquake made it difficult to survey some areas in East Japan and to observe the economy, in general. Although it is hard to evaluate the quality of the 2011 benchmark JSNA at present, there are some indications of measurement error in Japan's benchmark IOT. Nomura and Miyagawa (2018a) pointed out that the wholesale and retail service values in the 2011 benchmark IOT were considerably underestimated. This paper incorporates their alternative estimates of wholesale and retail margins, which are one of the key parameters in the price model. The sensitivity to this revision is discussed in the Appendix.

The remainder of this paper is organized as follows. Section 12.2 presents our representation of the production systems for Japan and the United States that is the basis for our accounting model and an overview of our methodological framework. The detailed equations to describe the bilateral accounting model are provided in the Appendix. In Section 12.3, we describe our data sources for the Japan—US BIOT and for the price differentials that feed into the price accounting model. The results are presented in Section 12.4. Section 12.5 concludes.

---

[5] We are able to include information on these six countries separately from the rest of the world due to data availability.

[6] These are estimated in Jorgenson et al. (2018).

12.2 Framework

We start with a basic description of our framework. Fig. 12.1 provides the Isard-type BIOT. Entries of the table are in nominal values but shown here as price times volume to emphasize how this relates to the price accounting model that we present below. Our BIOT separately identifies the imports from six exogenous economies: China, Germany, Korea, Malaysia, Taiwan, and Thailand, and the rest of the world (ROW). In the Isard-type (noncompetitive import-type IOT) framework (Isard, 1951), all purchases in Japan and the United States from foreign countries are recorded separately from the purchases of domestically produced goods and services. The areas surrounded by dotted squares in Fig. 12.1 represent imports to Japan and the United States. The variables in the BIOT are defined in the Appendix.

The prices of domestically produced products are evaluated at producer's prices (including indirect taxes required for purchasers). The prices of imported products in Japan and the United States, from the United States and Japan, respectively, are evaluated at FOB (free on board) prices (producers' prices plus margin and transportation costs from producers to

Products in	Intermediate uses (N)		Household consumption (H)		Government consumption & Gross capital formation (Z)		Exports to exogenous countries (E)	Gross output (X)
	Japan (J)	the U.S. (U)	Japan (J)	the U.S. (U)	Japan (J)	the U.S. (U)		
Japan (J)	$\frac{p_{J,t}^{d,J}X_{JJ,J}}{e_{J/U}}$	$\frac{p_{JU,t}^{d,J}X_{JU,N}}{e_{J/U}}$	$e_{J/U}p_{J,t}^{d,H}X_{JJ,H}$	$\frac{p_{JU,t}^{d,H}X_{JU,H}}{e_{J/U}}$	$\frac{p_{J,t}^{d,J}X_{JJ,Z}}{e_{J/U}}$	$\frac{p_{JU,t}^{d,J}X_{JU,Z}}{e_{J/U}}$	$p_{JE,t}^{e}X_{JE,tE}$	$\frac{p_{J,t}^{d}X_{J,t}}{e_{J/U}}$
the U.S. (U)	$p_{UJ,t}^{d,J}X_{UJ,N}$	$p_{U,t}^{d,J}X_{UU,N}$	$p_{UJ,t}^{d,H}X_{UJ,H}$	$p_{U,t}^{d,H}X_{UU,H}$	$p_{UJ,t}^{d,J}X_{UJ,Z}$	$p_{U,t}^{d,J}X_{UU,Z}$	$p_{UE,t}^{e}X_{UE,tE}$	$p_{U,t}^{d}X_{U,t}$
Freight and insurance for the Japan-US trade	$\tau_{UJ}^{f}p_{UJ,t}^{fob,J}X_{UJ,N}$	$\frac{\tau_{JU}^{f}p_{JU,t}^{fob,J}X_{JU,N}}{e_{J/U}}$	$\tau_{UJ}^{f}p_{UJ,t}^{fob,J}X_{UJ,H}$	$\frac{\tau_{JU}^{f}p_{JU,t}^{fob,H}X_{JU,H}}{e_{J/U}}$	$\tau_{UJ}^{f}p_{UJ,t}^{fob,J}X_{UJ,G}$	$\frac{\tau_{JU}^{f}p_{JU,t}^{fob,J}X_{JU,Z}}{e_{J/U}}$		
Tariff for the Japan-US trade	$\tau_{UJ}^{r}p_{UJ,t}^{fob,J}X_{UJ,N}$	$\frac{\tau_{JU}^{r}p_{JU,t}^{fob,J}X_{JU,N}}{e_{J/U}}$	$\tau_{UJ}^{r}p_{UJ,t}^{fob,J}X_{UJ,H}$	$\frac{\tau_{JU}^{r}p_{JU,t}^{fob,H}X_{JU,H}}{e_{J/U}}$	$\tau_{UJ}^{r}p_{UJ,t}^{fob,J}X_{UJ,Z}$	$\frac{\tau_{JU}^{r}p_{JU,t}^{fob,J}X_{JU,Z}}{e_{J/U}}$		
Net indirect taxes on imports of the Japan-US trade	$TX_{UJ,J}^{I}$	$TX_{JU,J}^{I}$	$TX_{UJ,tH}^{H}$	$TX_{JU,tH}^{H}$	$TX_{UJ,Z}^{I}$	$TX_{JU,Z}^{I}$		
China (C)	$\frac{p_{CJ,t}^{m,J}X_{CJ,J}}{e_{J/U}}$	$p_{CU,t}^{m,J}X_{CU,N}$	$\frac{p_{CJ,t}^{m,H}X_{CJ,H}}{e_{J/U}}$	$p_{CU,t}^{m,H}X_{CU,H}$	$\frac{p_{CJ,t}^{m,J}X_{CJ,Z}}{e_{J/U}}$	$p_{CU,t}^{m,J}X_{CU,Z}$		
Germany (G)	$\frac{p_{GJ,t}^{m,J}X_{GJ,J}}{e_{J/U}}$	$p_{GU,t}^{m,J}X_{GU,N}$	$\frac{p_{GJ,t}^{m,H}X_{GJ,H}}{e_{J/U}}$	$p_{GU,t}^{m,H}X_{GU,H}$	$\frac{p_{GJ,t}^{m,J}X_{GJ,Z}}{e_{J/U}}$	$p_{GU,t}^{m,J}X_{GU,Z}$		
Korea (K)	$\frac{p_{KJ,t}^{m,J}X_{KJ,J}}{e_{J/U}}$	$p_{KU,t}^{m,J}X_{KU,N}$	$\frac{p_{KJ,t}^{m,H}X_{KJ,H}}{e_{J/U}}$	$p_{KU,t}^{m,H}X_{KU,H}$	$\frac{p_{KJ,t}^{m,J}X_{KJ,Z}}{e_{J/U}}$	$p_{KU,t}^{m,J}X_{KU,Z}$		
Malaysia (M)	$\frac{p_{MJ,t}^{m,J}X_{MJ,J}}{e_{J/U}}$	$p_{MU,t}^{m,J}X_{MU,N}$	$\frac{p_{MJ,t}^{m,H}X_{MJ,H}}{e_{J/U}}$	$p_{MU,t}^{m,H}X_{MU,H}$	$\frac{p_{MJ,t}^{m,J}X_{MJ,Z}}{e_{J/U}}$	$p_{MU,t}^{m,J}X_{MU,Z}$		
Taiwan (W)	$\frac{p_{WJ,t}^{m,J}X_{WJ,J}}{e_{J/U}}$	$p_{WU,t}^{m,J}X_{WU,N}$	$\frac{p_{WJ,t}^{m,H}X_{WJ,H}}{e_{J/U}}$	$p_{WU,t}^{m,H}X_{WU,H}$	$\frac{p_{WJ,t}^{m,J}X_{WJ,Z}}{e_{J/U}}$	$p_{WU,t}^{m,J}X_{WU,Z}$		
Thailand (T)	$\frac{p_{TJ,t}^{m,J}X_{TJ,J}}{e_{J/U}}$	$p_{TU,t}^{m,J}X_{TU,U}$	$\frac{p_{TJ,t}^{m,H}X_{TJ,H}}{e_{J/U}}$	$p_{TU,t}^{m,H}X_{TU,tH}$	$\frac{p_{TJ,t}^{m,J}X_{TJ,Z}}{e_{J/U}}$	$p_{TU,t}^{m,J}X_{TU,tZ}$		
ROW (R)	$\frac{p_{RJ,t}^{m,J}X_{RJ,N}}{e_{J/U}}$	$p_{RU,t}^{m,J}X_{RU,N}$	$\frac{p_{RJ,t}^{m,H}X_{RJ,H}}{e_{J/U}}$	$p_{RU,t}^{m,H}X_{RU,H}$	$\frac{p_{RJ,t}^{m,J}X_{RJ,Z}}{e_{J/U}}$	$p_{RU,t}^{m,J}X_{RU,Z}$		
Value added	$\frac{VA_{J,t}}{e_{J/U}}$	$VA_{U,t}$						
Gross output	$\frac{p_{J,t}^{d}X_{J,t}}{e_{J/U}}$	$p_{U,t}^{d}X_{U,t}$						

(Import from exogenous countries at the price of cif, tariff, and net indirect taxes (E): China, Germany, Korea, Malaysia, Taiwan, Thailand, ROW)

FIGURE 12.1   Japan–US Input–Output Table (the Isard-Type). Note: See Appendix for the definition of the variables.

customs). Thus, the freight and insurance and tariff embedded in imports (in Japan–US trade) and the net indirect taxes required in imported countries (in Japan or the United States) are separately recorded from the FOB-price imports. The imports from exogenous economies are evaluated at the prices including CIF (cost, insurance, and freight), tariff, and the net indirect taxes embedded in imports (in Japan or the United States).

Based on the production system in Fig. 12.1, we specify an accounting model describing producer's prices and purchaser's prices for domestically produced and imported products that take into account the trade structure, freight and insurance rates, duty tax rates, wholesale and retail trade margins, and transportation costs in each product. The details of the equations are provided in the Appendix. Our objects of interest are the following PLIs for each product i, which are defined as price level in Japan relative to the United States, divided by the nominal exchange rate:

$\mathbf{P}_i^d$ PLI for domestic outputs at producer's price,

$\mathbf{P}_i^{d,l}$ PLI for domestic outputs at producer's price (see definition of l below),

$\mathbf{P}_i^{c,l}$ PLI for composite products (domestic products and imports) at producer's price, and

$\mathbf{P}_i^{pc,l}$ PLI for composite products (domestic products and imports) at purchaser's price, where l stands for the demand group.[7] We define six groups of demands, denoting:

N for intermediate uses,

H for household consumption (including consumption by NPISHs),

G for government consumption,

F for investment (gross-fixed capital formation [GFCF] and changes in inventories) by industries and government,

E for exports to exogenous economies, and

M for imports, and the following three broad groups of the demands,

Z for domestic final demand excluding household consumption ($Z = \{G, F\}$),

I for domestic demand by industries and government ($I = \{N, G, F\}$),[8] and

D for domestic demand ($D = \{I, H\} = \{N, H, G, F\}$).

Fig. 12.2 illustrates the relationships among the PLIs and shows four paths used in estimation to go from observed data to the unmeasured the PLIs of interest. The PLI surrounded by each box indicates the observed PLI, and the corresponding directional arrows indicate the estimation used conditional on the observed data.

Path 1 starting with the box on the right shows the case where the producer-price PLI of domestic outputs $\mathbf{P}_i^d$ is available based on surveys. In this case, the difference between $\mathbf{P}_i^{d,l}$ (the arrow to the lower left in Fig. 12.2) and $\mathbf{P}_i^{d,H}$ (the arrow to the upper left) is due to the difference in the treatment of consumption taxes. Next, continuing to move left in the diagram, the producer-price PLI of composite products for intermediate use $\mathbf{P}_i^{c,l}$ and for household use $\mathbf{P}_i^{c,H}$ is derived by taking into account the difference in import prices for Japan and the United

---

[7] To distinguish the price-level index from the prices, we use the bold as $\mathbf{P}_i^d$. These Japan–US PLIs are defined as Japan's price over the United States prices as in Eq. (A12.20). Although they are described as $\mathbf{P}_{J/U,i}^d$ in the Appendix to identify the transactions Japan, the United States, and exogenous economies, the subscript "J/U" is omitted in main text.

[8] Since the government consumption is defined at the actual base, the products for $I = \{N, G, F\}$ mainly refer the products consumed for industries' intermediate uses (N) and investment by industries and government (F). For simplicity, we use I to denote demand for industry uses.

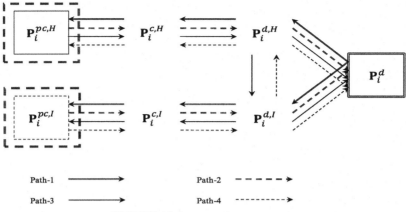

FIGURE 12.2   Price deviation paths.

States (based on Eq. A12.21 in the Appendix). Finally, the purchaser-price PLI of the products for intermediate use $\mathbf{P}_i^{pc,I}$ and for household use $\mathbf{P}_i^{pc,H}$ is estimated by including the difference in the trade margins and the transportation costs by product between Japan and the United States, based on Eq. (A12.30).

Path 2 is the case where data for the purchaser-price PLI of the products for industry use $\mathbf{P}_i^{pc,I}$ and household use $\mathbf{P}_i^{pc,H}$ are available. Based on these data, $\mathbf{P}_i^{c,I}$ and $\mathbf{P}_i^{c,H}$ (the arrow to the right in Fig. 12.2) are calculated based on Eq. (A12.30). And then, $\mathbf{P}_i^{d,I}$ and $\mathbf{P}_i^{d,H}$ are estimated in accordance with Eq. (A12.23), and $\mathbf{P}_i^{d}$ is derived as the aggregate based on Eq. (A12.24).

In Path 3 scenarios, only the purchaser-price PLI of the products for household use $\mathbf{P}_i^{pc,H}$ is available as observations (like the Eurostat-OECD PPPs). By considering the differences in trade margins and the transportation costs, $\mathbf{P}_i^{c,H}$ and $\mathbf{P}_i^{d,H}$ are estimated based on Eqs. (A12.30) and (A12.23), respectively. In this case, $\mathbf{P}_i^{d,I}$ is derived (the arrow pointing down in Fig. 12.2) by considering the difference in consumption taxes and $\mathbf{P}_i^{d}$ is determined using $\mathbf{P}_i^{d,I}$ and $\mathbf{P}_i^{d,H}$ based on Eq. (A12.24). Additionally, $\mathbf{P}_i^{c,I}$ and

$\mathbf{P}_i^{pc,I}$ are estimated by taking into account the difference in import prices, the percentage of imports, the trade margins, and the transportation costs between Japan and the United States. In Path 4 scenarios, $\mathbf{P}_i^{pc,I}$ is observed instead of $\mathbf{P}_i^{pc,H}$ as in the Path 3 scenario, but the process to estimate the other PLIs is similar.

12.3 Data and measurement

12.3.1 2011 Japan–US bilateral input–output table

In measuring the 2005 benchmark PLIs, Nomura and Miyagawa (2015) expanded the 2005 Japan–US BIOT (METI, 2013) to identify the imports from six exogenous economies: China, Germany, Korea, Malaysia, Taiwan (Republic of China), and Thailand and modified the table to account for Japan's consumption tax. Since the introduction of the consumption tax in 1989, in the current JSNA and Japan's benchmark IOT, the values for intermediate uses are recorded as the prices including not only nondeductible consumption taxes but also deductible ones, resulting in an inconsistency between prices recorded in the accounts and the net prices actually paid by purchasers. In addition, consumption taxes (deductible and nondeductible) are not separately estimated from other indirect taxes by industry. Since METI's 2005 Japan—US BIOT follows this price definition used in JSNA, it is difficult to compare Japan's prices with those in the United States. The 2005 BIOT was revised to define output at basic prices in Nomura and Miyagawa (2015), and we follow the same approach.

Using the adjusted 2005 BIOT as the base table, this paper estimates the 2011 BIOT, by considering changes in production and trade from 2005 to 2011. Our adjustments are based on the official national accounts and trade statistics in Japan and the United States. The international trade data of Japan and the United States from the six exogenous countries and the ROW are extended in each product based on the import data by product and by county published in the UN Comtrade Database.

To estimate the model, the trade matrix among Japan and the United States, the six exogenous countries, and the ROW is required as in Eq. (A12.34). In measurement of the PPPs for 2005 in Nomura and Miyagawa (2015), these matrices for industry use and household use were developed based on the 2005 Asian International Input—Output Table published by Institute of Developing Economies (2013), which covers Japan, the United States, China, Korea, Malaysia, Taiwan, and Thailand, and the WIOD (World Input—Output Database) in Timmer et al. (2015), which covers Japan, the United States, China, Germany, Korea, and Taiwan. In this paper, the WIOD is used to update the trade matrices from 2005 to 2011; other trade relationships are assumed to be unchanged due to the lack of the 2011 Asian International IOT.

12.3.2 Elementary-level price-level indices

We use price-differential data obtained from Eurostat-OECD (2012), METI (2012), and many sources published by agencies and ministries of the government of Japan and the private business sector as our starting point.[9] The total number of price data at the elementary level used in this study was 538. Since the number of products in our model based on the 2011 Japan—US BIOT is 174, on average about three price data points are used to estimate the price of one product in our model. In some cases, data with different price concepts at the elementary level are integrated based on our price model, e.g., the PLIs for industry use and household use are integrated as described in Path 2 in Fig. 12.2. Sometimes the price data at the elementary level are highly disaggregated within one of our 174 products of interest. For example in chemical products, the PPPs for highly disaggregated products for intermediate uses are available in METI (2012). In this case, the product-level PLIs are calculated as Törnqvist indices using the elementary-level PLIs. If the weight for the elementary level is unavailable, the product's PLI is calculated as a simple geometric average.

Table 12.1 presents the concepts of the collected data at the elementary level by broad product. Each row corresponds to a sector of Central Product Classification Ver.2. One of the most important data sources is the Eurostat-OECD PPPs. At the most detailed level, the Eurostat-OECD (2011) includes price data for 206 products which are called "basic headings." The survey observes PPPs at purchaser's prices of composite products purchased by households

---

[9] In the context of Japan—US comparisons, a significant advantage is the availability of much richer data on price differentials among major industrialized countries. These have been gathered by the agencies and ministries of the government of Japan since the late 1980s, as a response to an important policy focus on international price differentials after the Plaza Accord of 1985 resulted in the rapid appreciation of the Japanese yen.

TABLE 12.1 Number of data on price differentials at elementary level.

CPC code	Purchaser's price — Intermediate use $P_i^{pc,F}$ — METI PPP survey	Other PPP surveys	Other surveys on unit prices	Total	Household consumption $P_i^{pc,H}$ — Eurostat-OECD PPPs	Other PPP surveys	Other surveys on unit prices	Total	Investment $P_i^{pc,N}$ — Eurostat-OECD PPPs	Producer's price P_i^{pd} — Other surveys on unit prices	Cost index	Reference PPP	Total	Total Total
0 Agriculture, forestry, and fishery					6			6		10		3	13	19
1 Ores and minerals; electricity, gas, and water	10	3		13		1		1		5			5	19
2 Food, beverages and tobacco; textiles, apparel, and leather	1			1	47	5		52				6	6	59
3 Other transportable goods, except metal products, machinery, equipment	76	6	7	89	14	11	1	26	3	3	2		5	123
4 Metal products, machinery, and equipment	121			121	20	6	8	34	18		1		1	174
5 Constructions and construction services									4					4
6 Trade; accommodation, food, and beverage serving; transport	22	5	1	28	9	1	1	11		2			2	41
7 Financial and related services; real estate; rental and leasing services	15			15	5	1	1	7		2	1		3	25
8 Business and production services	19			19	8	5		13	1			5	5	38
9 Community, social, and personal services	8		3	11	20	1		21	1			3	3	36
Total	272	14	11	297	129	31	11	171	27	22	4	17	43	538

Source: Our estimates.

or used as investment. As shown in Table 12.1, 129 price data for households and 27 price data for investment were used to correspond to $\mathbf{P}_i^{pc,H}$ and $\mathbf{P}_i^{pc,F}$, respectively.[10]

For intermediate products, METI's *Survey on Foreign and Domestic Price Differentials for Industrial Goods and Services* is the main data source.[11] This survey has been conducted every year between 1993 and 2012 and every 2 years since 2012. The 2011 survey (METI, 2012), collected price data for 226 goods and 61 services for intermediate uses, and covered six countries namely, Japan, the United States, China, Germany, Korea, and Taiwan. Data in this survey are measured in purchaser's price PPPs. As seen in Table 12.1, 272 data are collected from this survey and used to estimate $\mathbf{P}_i^{pc,N}$, in our framework.

Although these two surveys do not cover all the products, there are rich data on international price differentials based on the surveys implemented by a number of Japanese ministries. We use *Survey of PPPs on Consumer Goods and Services* (METI, 2003), *Survey of PPPs on Drugs and Medical Products* (MHLW, 2003), *Survey of Retail Prices of Food Products in Tokyo and Foreign Major six Cities* (MAFF, 2006), and others.[12] From these surveys, 14 price data for intermediate use and 31 price data for household use are used to estimate $\mathbf{P}_i^{pc,N}$ and $\mathbf{P}_i^{pc,H}$, respectively.[13]

In addition, other surveys on unit prices are used in this study, where appropriate. For example, the output prices of some agricultural products evaluated at producer's price are directly observed from *Table on Value and Quantity* (*Butsuryo Hyo*) which was compiled as a supplementary table of the Japanese 2011 IOT and *Rice Outlook, Oil Crops Outlook*, or *Sugar and Sweeteners Outlook* published by the US Department of Agriculture. The output prices for cattle, poultry, and hog in Japan and the United States are directly obtained from the statistical data on livestock and its products published by the Agriculture and Livestock Industries Corporation, Japan. The output prices of coal, crude oil, and natural gas are obtained from *Trends of the Japanese Mining Industry* published by METI and *Annual Energy Review* published by the US Energy Information Administration. As a result, 22 price data are used to determine $\mathbf{P}_i^d$ directly without having to appeal to the price model. Finally, there are surveys that provide information on unit prices paid by purchasers; these additional surveys provide 11 price data points that are used to measure intermediate and household purchase prices, $\mathbf{P}_i^{pc,N}$ and $\mathbf{P}_i^{pc,H}$, respectively.

In the process to discern the producer's price PLIs for outputs from the purchaser's price PLIs based on the price model, the PLIs of wholesale and retail services have a significant role. Nomura and Miyagawa (2018a) pointed out that the outputs of the wholesale and retail sectors in the 2011 benchmark IOT in Japan appeared to be

---

[10] In Table 12.1, the purchaser's demand price for intermediate uses $\mathbf{P}_i^{pc,N}$ and for investments $\mathbf{P}_i^{pc,F}$ are distinguished. Both of them are treated as $\mathbf{P}_i^{pc,I}$ in the price framework explained in Section 12.2.

[11] The title of METI's survey was revised in 2011 from the previous title: *Survey on Foreign and Domestic Price Differentials for Industrial Intermediate Input*.

[12] In addition, *Survey of PPPs on Transportation and Related Services* (MLIT, 2007), *Survey of PPP on Information Services* (MIAC, 2011), and *Survey of PPPs on Major Consumer Goods and Services* (Cabinet Office, 2001) are used in our study.

[13] These data are estimated for different years and different stages of demand. The differences in timing of the surveys were adjusted using the CPI and PPI in both countries. We have reconciled these data within our price model.

considerably underestimated and provided alternative estimates of wholesale and retail margins based on microdata of Census of Commerce.[14] This paper uses these margin rate and PLI estimates for 2011. These data are counted as two data points in "Other surveys on unit prices" in Table 12.1. A sensitivity analysis to our choice of margins is presented in the Appendix.

The cost approach is also adopted for some products whose prices are difficult to directly observe. In the cost approach, the producer-price PLIs of domestic products are estimated by the PLIs of all intermediate products we estimated in this paper and the estimates of the PLIs for labor and capital inputs estimated in Jorgenson et al. (2018), aggregated using the weights of the cost structures obtained from the 2011 Japan–US BIOT. Fig. 12.3 presents the PPPs for labor and capital inputs at the aggregate level for the period 1990–2015 in Jorgenson et al. (2018). During the recent quarter of century, the PPPs for factor inputs have considerably declined. In particular, the PPP for labor input declined by half.[15] Long-term declines in PPPs for factor inputs translates to declines in PPPs for industry outputs based on the cost approach but obviously only for products that use the cost index approach (21 out of 538 products).

For a small set of products, we apply the reference PPP approach, in which the PPPs of the similar products are applied. In this study, the cost index approach is applied for 21 elementary-level products such as government service, education, and research (that is, we back out the relative output prices by assuming that the gap in total factor productivity between Japan and the United States is zero), and the

reference PPP approach is applied for 17 elementary-level products.

12.3.3 Product-level price-level indices

As shown in Table 12.1, many of the observed price data are based on purchaser's demand prices. Therefore, $\mathbf{P}_i^d$ is estimated in this study by applying our price models to $\mathbf{P}_i^{pc,I}$ and/or $\mathbf{P}_i^{pc,H}$ for a large share of products. Table 12.2 presents the composition of our estimation methods. Each row shows the Central Product Classification Ver.2, and the number in the column corresponds to the number of products classified in each group (the total is the number of all products, 174).

According to Table 12.2, Path 1, which takes $\mathbf{P}_i^d$ as data, was applied to 32 products, which were mainly classified in Agriculture and Mining sector. Since the estimation of $\mathbf{P}_i^d$ is the target of this study, Path 1 based on the directly observed price data is the most preferable approach. The PLIs for 56 products are estimated by Path 2 process, in which $\mathbf{P}_i^{pc,I}$ and $\mathbf{P}_i^{pc,H}$ are observed first, and output prices are estimated via the accounting model. This is the most frequent case among four price deviation paths and can be considered the second best path. Path 3 determines $\mathbf{P}_i^{pc,H}$ first. 38 products, most of which are final consumption goods and services, are estimated by this method. Although Path 4, which takes as data $\mathbf{P}_i^{pc,I}$, is similar to Path 3, this is divided into three subcases depending on the kinds of the observed PLIs. In the first case, written as Path 4.1, the PLI of purchaser's demand price for industries $\mathbf{P}_i^{pc,I}$ is determined using both the PLI of the products

---

[14] In Nomura and Miyagawa (2018b), the output PPP for wholesale service is estimated based on 82 goods for household use and 110 goods for industry use and the output PPP for retail service is estimated based on 87 goods for household use and 19 goods for industry use.

[15] The quality-adjusted price of labor inputs has continued to decline in Japan for 15 years from 1997 to 2012 (Nomura and Shirane, 2014).

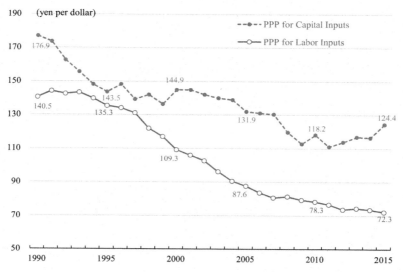

FIGURE 12.3 Purchasing power parities (PPPs) for capital and labor inputs in 1990–2015. *Source: Authors' elaboration of data developed and described in Byrne and Corrado (2017).*

for intermediate use and investment, $\mathbf{P}_i^{pc,N}$ and $\mathbf{P}_i^{pc,F}$, respectively. Path 4.1 is applied only to four products classified in metal products, machinery, and equipment. Path 4.2 uses $\mathbf{P}_i^{pc,N}$ to determine $\mathbf{P}_i^{pc,I}$ and 35 products belong to this case. The PLIs of only nine products are estimated by Path 4.3, which uses only $\mathbf{P}_i^{pc,F}$ to determine $\mathbf{P}_i^{pc,I}$.

12.4 Results

Table 12.3 compares the PPPs for GDP developed in this paper and the Eurostat-OECD PPPs

in 2011. Our estimate of the PPP for GDP, which is derived from aggregating the PPPs for industry-GDP at basic prices, is 109.0 yen per dollar, which closely resembles the Eurostat-OECD PPP (107.5 yen per dollar) in 2011.[16] Compared to the Eurostat-OECD PPP, our expenditure-side estimates are somewhat lower in household consumption and building and construction (B&C) of GFCF (gross-fixed capital formation) and higher in machinery and equipment (M&E) of GFCF.[17]

Fig. 12.4 shows the extrapolated estimates of PPPs for GDP and household consumption from 2011 to 2016, using our benchmark PPP

[16] The close relationship between our estimate of the aggregate PPP for household consumption and the Eurostat-OECD PPP is expected since we used their PPP data for many consumer products at the elementary level. The relationship between our estimate of the PPP for GDP and the Eurostat-OECD measure is slightly more complicated. Conceptually, these measure the same object. But in practice our approach to constructing the PPP for government is based on total quality-adjusted input prices including capital and labor services and intermediate inputs, while the Eurostat-OECD approach is based on reference PPPs applied to the components of gross output. See Box 9.2 in Eurostat-OECD (2012).

[17] In the 2005 PPPs in Nomura and Miyagawa (2015), the gaps in the estimates for M&E of GFCF were much larger as 126.1 yen per dollar of our estimates, compared to 164.0 in the Eurostat-OECD PPP. These gaps are considerably narrowed in the 2011 PPP estimates in Table 12.3.

TABLE 12.2 Number of products by price deviation path.

	Path 1	Path 2	Path 3	Path 4	(Path 4.1)	(Path 4.2)	(Path 4.3)	Total
		Household and industry use $P_i^{pc,H}$ and $P_i^{pc,I}$	Producer's price — Household use $P_i^{pc,H}$	Producer's price — Industry use $P_i^{pc,I}$	Purchaser's price — Intermediate uses and investment $P_i^{pc,N}$ and $P_i^{pc,F}$	Purchaser's price — Intermediate uses $P_i^{pc,N}$	Investment $P_i^{pc,F}$	
	P_i^d							
0 Agriculture, forestry, and fishery	8	2	2					12
1 Ores and minerals; electricity, gas, and water	5	1		3		3		9
2 Food, beverages, and tobacco; textiles, apparel, and leather	2	6	17					25
3 Other transportable goods, except metal products, machinery, equipment	6	11	4	13		13		34
4 Metal products, machinery, and equipment	4	15	5	21	4	12	5	45
5 Constructions and construction services				4			4	4
6 Trade; accommodation, food and beverage serving; transport	2	7	3	2		2		14
7 Financial and related services; real estate; rental and leasing services		4	2	1		1		7
8 Business and production services	3	6	1	1		1		11
9 Community, social, and personal services	2	4	4	3		3		13
Total	32	56	38	48	4	35	9	174

Source: Our estimates. *Note: The number of products (32) in Path 1 includes nine products based on the cost approach and seven products based on the reference PPP approach.*

TABLE 12.3 Aggregated purchasing power parities (PPPs) in 2011.

PPP for	GDP	Household consumption	GFCF	B&C	M&E
Our estimates	109.0	113.4	116.6	113.7	104.0
Eurostat-OECD PPPs	107.5	116.1	110.0	114.0	99.2

2011 exchange rate: 1 US dollar = 79.81 yen

Unit: yen per dollar.

Source: Our estimates. Note: B&C is building and construction and M&E is machinery and equipment.

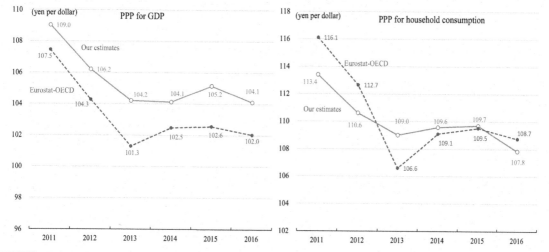

FIGURE 12.4 Extended purchasing power parities (PPPs) for gross domestic product (GDP) and household consumption in 2011–16.

estimates in 2011 and the price indices from the national accounts in Japan (Economic and Social Research Institute [ESRI], Cabinet Office) and the United States (Bureau of Economic Analysis [BEA]) from 2011 to 2016, compared to the Eurostat-OECD estimates. The trends are similar, but our estimate of the PPP for GDP is higher by 2–3 yen per dollar, reflecting the higher benchmark estimates. However, in the PPP estimate for household consumption, our benchmark estimate is slightly lower than the Eurostat-OECD PPP, but they are quite similar in 2014–16. In 2016, our estimates of PPPs for GDP and household consumption are 104.1 and 107.8 yen per dollar, respectively. The current exchange rate of 110.6 yen per dollar as of the beginning of July 2018 is above our aggregate PPP estimate. As a result, both producers and consumers in Japan benefit from price advantages under the current exchange rate. The recent depreciation of the Yen can be tied to the adoption of quantitative easing by the Bank of Japan, followed by the election of Prime Minister Shinzo Abe in December 2012.[18]

Table 12.4 presents the estimated PPP results for 2011 based on the International Standard Industrial Classification (ISIC) classification.[19] The first four columns present the price differentials in domestic outputs (the PPP excluding net indirect taxes, including taxes, for industry use, and for household use), and the next four columns show the PPPs for the composite of domestic and imported products (two PPPs at producer's prices and two at purchaser's prices). And the last two columns indicate the price differentials between Japan and the United States in their imports.[20]

Our estimates show there are large differences among the PPP estimates across concepts, implying that it is important to account for conceptual differences in price measures when making international comparisons. For example, consider Motor vehicles. We use this example to highlight two pertinent issues. The first issue is that observed differences in prices paid by household and industry have important implications for measuring relative prices in domestic product, and the second issue that purchaser's prices embed the margin that must be stripped out in measuring domestic product. This becomes evident in examining the various PPPs for Motor vehicles and trailers. For simplicity, consider as a starting point the observation that the PPP for imports of Motor vehicles and trailers is 79.3 yen per dollar for industry use

and 77.4 yen per dollar for household use. While these are relatively similar, it will become evident that this similarity plays an important role in backing out the PPP for domestic product. The next PPP to consider in this example is the purchase price the purchaser-price PPPs, which cover domestic products and imports. These are 83.9 and 122.8 yen per dollar for industry and household uses, respectively. The model must reconcile these observed prices, that is, the PPP for industry use is slightly above the import PPP, while the PPP for household use is significantly above the PPP. By stripping off the margins paid on sales to households and industry, the model estimates that the internally consistent producer-price PPP of the Motor vehicles and trailers is estimated to be 79.9 and 95.8 yen per dollar for industry and household use, respectively. Finally, as a composite of the products produced for industry and household, the PPP for output is estimated to be 87.9 yen per dollar. At the exchange rate of 79.8 on average in 2011, using the PPP for household purchases of motor vehicles (122.8) yields a considerably different (and conceptually inappropriate) measure of competitiveness compared to the (conceptually appropriate) 87.9 yen per dollar.

In Agriculture, forestry and fishing, the PPP for domestic outputs was 197.7 yen per dollar in 2011, indicating the Japanese producers are considerably inferior in price competitiveness of agricultural products compared to producers in the United States, although some gaps may

---

[18] The historical stories on the price competitiveness and the market exchange rates are provided in Jorgenson et al. (2018).

[19] In some products of 174 products, the unpublished data at the most detailed level (basic headings) of the Eurostat-OECD PPPs are directly used as $\mathbf{P}_i^{pc,H}$. Since they are not in the public domain, we use 42 types of the broad product group for describing the demand-side PLIs. We aggregate to the ISIC classification using Törnqvist aggregation over the 173 industries.

[20] The differences in the quality of products imported by Japan and the United States may be somewhat reflected in the price differentials of imports from exogenous countries, although conceptually this should be counted in the volume differentials.

TABLE 12.4 Purchasing power parities (PPPs) by different price concept in 2011.

	Domestic products				Composite products				Imports	
	PPP_i^{ds}	PPP_i^{d}	PPP_i^{dI}	PPP_i^{dH}	PPP_i^{cI}	PPP_i^{cH}	PPP_i^{pc}	PPP_i^{pcH}	PPP_i^{mI}	PPP_i^{mH}
A—Agriculture, forestry, and fishing	197.7	192.8	237.5	110.1	201.5	104.9	205.4	133.5	97.4	73.9
B—Mining and quarrying	236.1	223.7	214.9	251.6	154.1	–	205.2	–	110.0	–
C—Manufacture	88.6	91.9	92.8	117.4	88.1	103.4	93.0	115.8	79.9	76.8
10—Food products	138.3	142.6	160.4	150.9	134.5	131.4	167.3	168.0	80.7	83.7
11—Beverages	102.1	131.2	138.2	116.9	135.0	115.8	136.5	121.0	108.3	102.7
12—Tobacco products	27.1	69.9	66.7	70.1	–	69.5	–	68.9	–	66.3
13—Textiles	104.6	105.4	107.7	89.7	104.8	–	117.9	–	115.1	68.6
14—Wearing apparel	129.5	134.8	129.5	136.0	–	71.6	–	103.7	61.4	61.5
15—Leather and related products	50.6	52.6	94.9	54.8	–	61.4	–	108.6	62.9	63.5
16—Wood and wood products, except furniture	102.1	102.4	99.1	128.4	92.5	–	98.9	–	76.1	–
17—Paper and paper products	84.2	84.6	85.4	81.0	82.4	–	94.9	–	52.5	45.3
18—Printing and reproduction of recorded media	77.8	78.1	77.0	95.4	77.2	–	80.3	–	–	–
19—Coke and refined petroleum products	103.5	127.8	119.0	151.8	116.2	140.3	117.1	140.8	104.3	96.3
20—Chemicals and chemical products	77.1	77.7	86.8	43.8	81.4	44.8	87.2	82.4	66.9	52.0
21—Pharmaceutical products	74.8	76.1	82.7	65.7	80.6	67.5	75.9	79.7	67.9	67.6
22—Rubber and plastics products	83.1	83.5	79.6	108.2	80.3	–	79.0	–	83.6	98.2
23—Other nonmetallic mineral products	91.1	91.6	94.1	105.9	90.0	–	94.3	–	57.2	64.6
24—Basic metals	77.7	77.7	81.2	69.3	81.9	–	81.7	–	83.9	86.0
25—Fabricated metal products, except M&E	70.2	70.5	72.5	92.5	71.3	–	78.3	–	61.7	–
26—Computer, electronic, and optical products	90.5	91.8	94.0	111.9	88.6	102.6	92.3	91.7	84.9	93.2
27—Electrical equipment	64.4	64.7	61.5	151.7	59.0	–	59.3	–	87.5	86.7
28—Machinery and equipment n.e.c.	119.4	119.6	122.1	129.3	111.7	–	116.2	–	74.8	76.3
29—Motor vehicles and trailers	87.9	88.7	85.9	104.0	79.9	95.8	83.9	122.8	79.3	77.4

Continued

TABLE 12.4 Purchasing power parities (PPPs) by different price concept in 2011.—cont'd

	Domestic products				Composite products				Imports	
	PPP_i^{d*}	PPP_i^{d}	$PPP_i^{d,I}$	$PPP_i^{d,H}$	$PPP_i^{c,I}$	$PPP_i^{c,H}$	$PPP_i^{pc,I}$	$PPP_i^{pc,H}$	$PPP_i^{m,I}$	$PPP_i^{m,H}$
30—Other transport equipment	108.5	108.4	108.4	100.1	—	—	—	—	—	81.6
31—Furniture	117.9	119.1	122.3	108.6	101.6	—	103.6	—	61.4	59.5
32—Other manufacturing	126.1	128.5	103.9	208.9	97.1	127.7	114.9	105.4	83.0	87.9
33—Repair and installation of machinery and equipment	86.6	86.8	82.8	148.6	85.6	—	87.5	—	90.0	—
D—Electricity, gas, steam, and air conditioning supply	208.2	209.6	219.5	204.1	218.7	203.7	218.3	203.7	—	—
E—Water supply	92.4	93.7	92.8	95.9	92.8	95.9	92.9	96.0	—	—
F—Construction	102.2	102.1	105.5	65.3	105.5	65.3	105.5	65.3	—	—
G—Wholesale and retail trade	134.7	138.3	137.8	139.4	133.3	138.4	132.9	138.4	57.9	65.6
H—Transportation and storage	119.4	121.4	106.6	165.6	99.9	153.6	99.7	154.1	70.4	101.1
I—Accommodation and food service activities	103.9	107.5	104.0	109.0	102.6	107.8	102.5	108.0	77.3	78.8
J—Information and communication	119.7	121.6	124.5	104.9	123.1	104.3	124.7	103.7	78.0	74.2
K—Financial and insurance activities	121.6	121.2	118.7	122.1	117.1	120.4	117.4	120.4	81.1	83.9
L—Real estate activities	125.7	127.4	162.1	118.6	162.1	118.6	162.1	118.6	—	—
M—Professional, scientific, and technical activities	99.0	99.2	100.6	113.2	98.7	104.8	98.7	105.4	72.5	74.4
N—Administrative and support service activities	103.8	104.5	101.0	117.4	100.6	116.8	100.6	116.9	—	78.5
O—Public administration and defense	92.4	92.4	92.4	85.9	92.4	85.9	92.4	85.9	—	—
P—Education	117.5	117.5	117.5	117.5	—	117.3	—	117.3	—	—
Q—Human health and social work activities	79.9	79.9	80.6	79.9	80.6	79.9	80.6	79.9	—	—
R—Arts, entertainment, and recreation	103.3	107.0	77.6	120.3	77.5	119.5	77.5	119.6	—	80.7
S—Other service activities	124.1	128.9	106.7	140.6	103.2	138.4	105.7	138.4	86.3	76.6
Total	—	—	108.4	113.2	105.2	110.5	110.0	113.4	86.9	77.6

Unit: Yen per dollar (JPY/USD).
Source: Our estimates. Note: *Industry classification is based on the ISIC Rev.4. The market exchange rate in 2011 is 79.8 yen to the dollar on annual average.*

be explained by unobserved difference in quality.[21] This price gap in output is much larger than the purchaser-price PPP of composite products for household use (133.5 yen per dollar), again emphasizing the importance of accounting for the contribution of imports and margins. In summary, in order to compare price competitiveness by industry, these cases show that it is indispensable to estimate the differentials in output prices, which can differ considerably from the purchaser-price PPPs of composite products that are more readily available in the data. Fig. 12.6 presents the PPPs for industry outputs (excluding the net indirect taxes), PPPjd*, based on 173 industry classification in 2011. There are large differences across ISIC groups in Table 12.4. Most estimates of industry PPPs classified in (A) Agriculture, forestry, and fishery (industries 1–12) are over 150 yen per dollar, with three exceptions of (6) Other nonedible crops (76.1 yen per dollar), (10) Agricultural and forestry services (111.0), and (12) Fishing (71.9).

In manufacturing except foods (industries 33–123), even with the highly appreciated exchange rate (79.8 yen per dollar) in 2011, Japanese industries were still superior in price competitiveness in 25 of 91 industries. The number of industries with superior competitiveness increased to 59 under the current exchange rate (110.6 yen per dollar), indicating the importance of exchange rate movements in determining international competitiveness.[22]

In services (industries 124–173) presented in Fig. 12.6, Japanese industries were inferior in price competitiveness in 44 of 50 industries in 2011, most notably in (129) Gas distribution (the PPP for output is 303.2 yen per dollar), (144) Warehousing and storage (289.1), (128) Electric power generation and distribution (188.9), (136) Real estate (162.1), (170) Barber shops (155.3), and (142) Air transportation (151.0). If these same relative prices held at the current nominal exchange rate (110.6 yen per dollar), 24 of 50 industries would be superior in price competitiveness. In fact, there are some service industries in which Japan already has significant pricing advantages compared to the United States, like (160) Other rental and leasing (the PPP for output is 54.1 yen per dollar), (161) Motor vehicle repair (64.3), and (145) Travel arrangement services (74.9).

The declines in PPP for outputs over time in some service industries are significant. In the PPPs for service outputs in 1990 and 2005 estimated in Nomura and Miyagawa (1999) and (2015), respectively, Japan's price competitiveness was evaluated to be inferior to the United States in 91% (43 of 47 service industries) in 1990 and in 70% (35 of 50) in 2005, using the current exchange rate (110.6 yen per dollar). Our current estimates show that 52% (26 of 50) were inferior in 2011. The PPPs of 74% (37 of 50 service industries) declined from 2005 to 2011.

To try to relate this to industry fundamentals, Fig. 12.5 plots the changes in the PPPs for service outputs between 2005 and 2011 against the two-country average share of compensation of employees (CoE) in gross output for the service

---

[21] Note that the difference in the products observed at our elementary level in Section 12.3.2 is considered. The purchaser's price PPPs for Agriculture, forestry, and fishing are much higher in industry use than that in household use in Table 12.4. This seems contradict that Japan's rice price is much higher than that in the United States. However, this is consistent with that households are defined in Japan's IOT to consume rice not directly from agricultural sector, but from food manufacturing sector as polished rice.

[22] We do not have a full general equilibrium model that determines how prices react to changes in policy that also results in changes to the nominal exchange rate. Therefore, our competitiveness measures reflect the joint determination of the prices and exchange rate, but we are not able to assess how prices would change if the exchange rate changes.

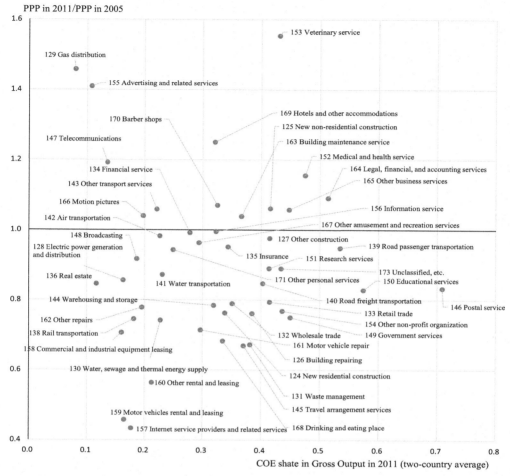

FIGURE 12.5   Changes in purchasing power parities (PPPs) for service outputs from 2005 to 2011.

industries in 2011. One hypothesis is that the fall in labor prices in Japan relative to the United States (Fig. 12.3) enabled relatively labor-intensive service producers in Japan to charge lower prices to purchasers in 2011 than in 2005. This would manifest as a downward sloping line between the change in the PPP level between 2011 and 2005 and the CoE share. Fig. 12.5 shows very limited evidence of this. For example, (159) Motor vehicle rental and leasing and (160) Other rental and leasing in Japan had a low labor share but improved price competitiveness.

Furthermore, a significant share of the PPPs for services increased in 2011 and 2005. Japan's output price in (153) Veterinary service, which has labor cost of over 40% of nominal output increased from 2005 to 2011 relative US production prices. These observations suggest two conclusions: labor costs alone cannot account for the overall decline in the PPPs for services and using the cost approach to measuring PPPs for outputs based on input costs (for example using the labor PPP to estimate the output PPP) likely leads to inappropriate estimates of the output PPPs.

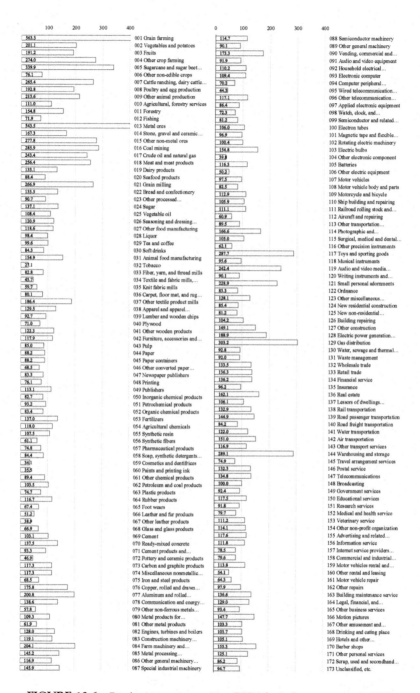

FIGURE 12.6 Purchasing power parities (PPPs) for industry outputs in 2011.

12.5 Conclusion

This paper provides new benchmark estimates of Japan—US industry-level price differentials for 2011, based on a price accounting model that links prices between the United States and Japan and maps available price data to model-consistent industry prices. Price comparisons among countries at the industry level is a challenging task, but constructing measures that are conceptually appropriate are indispensable for evaluating efficiency in production systems and international competitiveness on world markets.

We find that the PPP for GDP, derived from aggregating our estimates of the PPPs for industry-GDP at basic prices, is 109.0 yen per dollar in 2011. In 2011, the Yen appreciated to a historic high of 79.8 yen per dollar. Under the current exchange rate of 110.6 yen per dollar as of the beginning of July 2018, we estimate that Japanese industries are superior in price competitiveness in 59 of 91 industries in the manufacturing sector except foods and in 26 of 50 industries in service sector in comparison to US producers. Some Japanese producers are considerably inferior in price competitiveness in comparison to the United States; in particular, the energy industries providing electricity, gas, and heat and industries producing most agricultural products.

The accuracy of the estimated PPPs for industry outputs depends critically on the quality of the data on margin rates and the other related parameters. In addition, our analysis of the PPPs of service outputs and their relation to labor inputs indicate that the cost approach to measuring PPPs for outputs likely leads to inaccurate estimates. Employing simplifying assumptions on the relationship between prices likely leads to significant biases and incorrect measures of international competitive position. This indicates that improving the measurement of price differentials and the related parameters at the detailed product level is the best path

forward in building conceptually consistent and precise price competitiveness measures across industries and countries.

Appendix: bilateral price model

Producer's prices

To construct the price model describing the production system in Fig. 12.1, we use the following notation for product i:

$p_{k,i}^{d}$ Prices of products produced in country k at producer's prices in currency of country k,

$p_{kE,i}^{d}$ Prices of products produced in country k, purchased by exogenous economies at producer's prices (excluding net indirect taxes on products and consumption tax) in currency of country k,

$p_{k,i}^{d,l}$ Prices of products produced in country k, purchased by industries (I) or household (H) in country k at producers' prices in currency of country k (if $l = I$, the product is purchased by industries for intermediate uses or investment, and the price includes net indirect taxes on products. If $l = H$, the product is purchased by household for final consumption, and the price includes net indirect taxes on products and consumption tax.),

$p_{kk',i}^{d,l}$ Prices of products produced in country k, purchased by industries (I) or household (H) in country k' at producers' prices in currency of country k (if $l = I$, the product is purchased by industries. If $l = H$, the product is purchased by household. The both prices exclude net indirect taxes on products.),

$p_{kk',i}^{m,l}$ Prices of imports from country k, purchased by industries (I) or household (H) in k' country at the CIF prices plus tariff and net indirect taxes on imports in currency of country k' (if $l = I$, the product is purchased by industries and the price excludes consumption tax. If $l = H$, the product is purchased by household and the price includes consumption tax.),

$p_{kk',i}^{fob,l}$ Prices of imports from country k, purchased by industries (I) or household (H) in country k' at the FOB prices in currency of country k (if $l = I$, the product is purchased by industries. If $l = H$, the product is purchased by household.),

$p_{k,i}^{c,l}$ Prices of composite products (domestic products plus imports), purchased by industries (I) or household (H) in country k at producers' prices in currency of country k (if $l = I$, the product is purchased by industries and the price includes net indirect taxes on products. If $l = H$, the product is purchased by household and the price includes net indirect taxes on products and consumption tax.),

$X_{kk',ij}$ Volumes of products produced in country k and purchased by sector j in country k',

$X_{k,i}$ Volumes of products produced in country k,

$\tau_{kk',i}^{f}$ Rates of freight and insurance for imports from country k, purchased in country k',

$\tau_{kk',i}^{r}$ Rates of tariff for imports from country k, purchased in country k',

$\tau_{k,i}^{l}$ Rates of net indirect taxes on products in country k for industries (I) or household (H) (if $l = I$, the rate is for industries and excludes consumption tax.[23] If $l = H$, the rate is for households and includes consumption tax.),

$\tau_{k,i}^{d}$ The effective rates of indirect taxes in country k,

$TX_{k,i}^{d}$ The amount of indirect taxes of domestic products in country k

$e_{k/k'}$ Exchange rate of currency of country k against the currency of country k' (e.g., Japan's exchange rate to the US dollar is $e_{J/U}$),

$T_{k,i}^{e,l}$ Transportation service input for one unit of exports in country k (if $l = I$, the service is input for industries. If $l = H$, the service is input for households.),

$W_{k,i}^{e,l}$ Trade service input for one unit of exports in country k (if $l = I$, the service is input for industries. If $l = H$, the service is input for households.),

$m_{k,i}^{T,e,l}$ Rates of transportation cost (T) of products in country k for exported products (if $l = I$, the rate is for industries. If $l = H$, the rate is for households.),

$m_{k,i}^{W,e,l}$ Rates of trade margin (W) of products in country k for exported products (if $l = I$, the rate is for industries. If $l = H$, the rate is for households.).

We begin with clarifying the treatment of indirect taxes in our model. In Japan's transactions of Fig. 12.1, only households pay the consumption tax. Therefore, we distinguish between the producer's prices of the domestically produced outputs, $p_{J,i}^{d,I}$ (for industry) and $p_{J,i}^{d,H}$ (for household).[24] The rates of net indirect taxes on products for industries and households are also distinguished as $\tau_{J,i}^{I}$ and $\tau_{J,i}^{H}$, respectively. As for the prices of exports, since both the consumption tax and other indirect taxes on products are

[23] The consumption tax on the products purchased by the producers who produce consumption tax exempt products (e.g., medical care) are nondeductible. We describe that the consumption tax is excluded from $\tau_{k,i}^{l}$ in the description of our price model for simplicity, but some nondeductible consumption taxes in domestic final demand excluding household consumption (Z) are considered in our actual estimation.

[24] In addition to the differences in indirect taxes for industry and household uses, our price model permits differences in the basic prices for industry and household uses, reflecting the observed price differentials in different demand types of the product which are classified to the same group. These may indicate that the types or qualities of the same product at the more detail level are different, but we treat them as if they were additive for simplicity of our price model.

deductible, Japan's export prices to the United States ($p_{JU,i}^{d,H}$ and $p_{JU,i}^{d,I}$) are formulated as:

$$p_{JU,i}^{d,l} = p_{J,i}^{d,l} / \left(1 + \tau_{J,i}^l\right) \quad (k = J, U \quad \text{and} \quad l = I, H)$$

$$\text{(A12.1)}$$

On the other hand, the Japanese producer's price $p_{J,i}^d$ is defined as a composite of the producer's prices across all types of demand. The total of the domestic indirect taxes (excluding indirect tax for imported products) of product i is described as:

$$TX_{J,i}^d = \left(\frac{\tau_{J,i}^I}{1 + \tau_{J,i}^I}\right) p_{J,i}^{d,I} \sum_{j \in I} X_{JJ,ij}$$

$$+ \left(\frac{\tau_{J,i}^H}{1 + \tau_{J,i}^H}\right) p_{J,i}^{d,H} X_{JJ,iH} \quad \text{(A12.2)}$$

The first term on the right-hand side represents the amount of other indirect tax paid by industries (I) and the second term is the amount of the consumption tax and other indirect tax paid by households (H). Based on $TX_{J,i}^d$, the effective rate of indirect taxes for domestic product i in Japan is defined as:

$$\tau_{J,i}^d = TX_{J,i}^d / \left(p_{J,i}^d X_{J,i} - TX_{J,i}^d\right), \quad \text{(A12.3)}$$

where $p_{J,i}^d X_{J,i}$ is gross output in Japan. Using $\tau_{J,i}^d$, Japan's export price to the exogenous economies is formulated as:

$$p_{JE,i}^d = p_{J,i}^d / \left(1 + \tau_{J,i}^d\right) \quad \text{(A12.4)}$$

In the case of exports to exogenous economies, that is Eq. (A12.4), we do not distinguish between exports to industry and households due to data constraints, unlike the bilateral trade prices between Japan and the United States which do account for price differences between households and industry. Analogous Eqs. (A12.1)–(A12.4) also hold for the United States.

The IOT in Fig. 12.1 imposes that the value of output is balanced across uses:

$$p_{J,i}^d X_{J,i} = p_{J,i}^{d,I} \sum_{j \in I} X_{JJ,ij} + p_{JU,i}^{d,I} \sum_{j \in I} X_{JU,ij} + p_{J,i}^{d,H} X_{JJ,iH}$$

$$+ p_{JU,i}^{d,H} X_{JU,iH} + p_{JE,i}^d X_{JE,i}$$

$$\text{(A12.5)}$$

The first term on the right-hand side represents industry uses (intermediate uses and investment) in Japan, the second term is the imports by the US industries for the intermediate uses, the third term is the household uses in Japan, the fourth term is the imports by the US households, and the final term accounts for exports to exogenous economies.

Corresponding to the Isard-type BIOT in Fig. 12.1, we define the Chenery–Moses-type IOT (the competitive import-type IOT) for both Japan and the United States. (Chenery, 1953; Moses, 1955). Fig. 12.7 represents this table for Japan (the table for the United States is defined analogously).

Based on the Chenery–Moses-type input–output framework in, the output balance including Japan's uses of imports at current prices is described as:

$$p_{J,i}^d X_{J,i} = \sum_{j \in I} p_{J,i}^{c,I} X_{J,ij} + p_{J,i}^{c,H} X_{J,iH}$$

$$+ \left(\sum_{j \in I} p_{JU,i}^{d,I} X_{JU,ij} + p_{JU,i}^{d,H} X_{JU,iH} + p_{JE,i}^d X_{JE,i}\right)$$

$$- \sum_{k=U,E} \left(\sum_{j \in I} p_{kJ,i}^{m,I} X_{kJ,ij} + p_{kJ,i}^{m,H} X_{kJ,iH}\right),$$

$$\text{(A12.6)}$$

where $X_{J,ij}$ is the domestic demand of product i by sector j in Japan including both domestic products and imports, and $p_{J,i}^{c,I}$ stands for the corresponding prices of the composite products

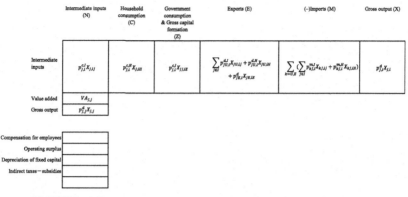

FIGURE 12.7 Japanese input–output table (the Chenery–Moses-type).

(of domestically produced products plus imports). These demand prices are embedded in the accounting identity as:

$$p_{J,i}^{c,l} X_{J,il} = p_{J,i}^{d,l} X_{JJ,il} + p_{UJ,i}^{m,l} X_{UJ,il}$$
$$+ p_{EJ,i}^{m,l} X_{EJ,il} \quad (\, l = I, H) \tag{A12.7}$$

The outputs at constant prices are assumed to be additive among the different demand types;

$$X_{J,i} = \sum_{j \in D} X_{JJ,ij} + \sum_{j \in D} X_{JU,ij} + X_{JE,i}$$
$$= \sum_{j \in D} X_{J,ij} + \sum_{j \in D} X_{JU,ij} + X_{JE,i} \tag{A12.8}$$
$$- \sum_{j \in D} X_{UJ,ij} - \sum_{j \in D} X_{EJ,ij}$$

The former equation corresponds with the nominal balance of Eq. (A12.5) and the latter corresponds to Eq. (A12.6). We also assume additivity among domestic inputs and imports:

$$X_{J,ij} = X_{JJ,ij} + X_{UJ,ij} + X_{EJ,ij} \quad (j \in D). \tag{A12.9}$$

We define the output share at constant prices:

$$w_{Jk,i}^{d,l} = \sum_{j \in I} X_{Jk,ij} / X_{J,i} \ (k = J, U, \ l = I, H) \text{ and } w_{JE,i}^{d}$$
$$= X_{JE,i} / X_{J,i}, \tag{A12.10}$$

where $w_{JJ,i}^{d,I} + w_{JU,i}^{d,I} + w_{JJ,i}^{d,H} + w_{JU,i}^{d,H} + w_{JE,i}^{d} = 1$. Based on Eqs. (A12.5)–(A12.10), Japan's output price of product i is described as:

$$p_{J,i}^{d} = p_{J,i}^{d,I} w_{JJ,i}^{d,I} + p_{JU,i}^{d,I} w_{JU,i}^{d,I} + p_{J,i}^{d,H} w_{JJ,i}^{d,H}$$
$$+ p_{JU,i}^{d,H} w_{JU,i}^{d,H} + p_{JE,i}^{d} w_{JE,i}^{d} \tag{A12.11}$$

By substituting Eqs. (A12.1) and (A12.4) into Eq. (A12.11), we obtain:

$$p_{J,i}^{d} = \left\{ p_{J,i}^{d,I} \left(w_{JJ,i}^{d,I} + \frac{w_{JU,i}^{d,I}}{1 + \tau_{J,i}^{I}} \right) \right.$$
$$\left. + p_{J,i}^{d,H} \left(w_{JJ,i}^{d,H} + \frac{w_{JU,i}^{d,H}}{1 + \tau_{J,i}^{I}} \right) \right\} / \left(1 - \frac{w_{JE,i}^{d}}{1 + \tau_{J,i}^{d}} \right). \tag{A12.12}$$

Thus Japan's output price, $p_{J,i}^{d}$, is measured using $p_{J,i}^{d,I}$ and $p_{J,i}^{d,H}$, the output shares, and the rates of indirect taxes.

On the other hand, in order to clarify the relationship between the US producer's price $p_{UJ,i}^{d,l}$ for sales to Japan and Japan's import prices from the United States, $p_{UJ,i}^{m,l}$, we describe the US FOB price as:

$$p_{UJ,i}^{fob,l} = p_{UJ,i}^{d,l} + p_{UJ,T}^{d,l} T_{U,i}^{e} + p_{UJ,W}^{d,l} W_{U,i}^{e} \ (l = I, H), \tag{A12.13}$$

where $p_{UJ,T}^{d,l}$ and $p_{UJ,W}^{d,l}$ are the prices of US transportation and trade sectors for the exports to Japan, respectively, and $T_{U,i}^{e,l}$ and $W_{U,i}^{e,l}$ are the volumes of transportation and trade services for one unit of exports of product i required in the United States. We define the rate of transportation cost $m_{U,i}^{T,E,l}$ and the rate of trade margin $m_{U,i}^{W,e,l}$ for exported products as,

$$m_{U,i}^{T,e,l} = p_{UJ,T}^{d,l} T_{U,i}^{e} \Big/ p_{UJ,i}^{fob,l} \text{ and } m_{U,i}^{W,e,l}$$
$$= p_{UJ,W}^{d,l} W_{U,i}^{e} \Big/ p_{UJ,i}^{fob,l} \quad (l = I, H),$$

(A12.14)

respectively. From Eqs. (A12.13) and (A12.14), the FOB prices for households and industries are represented as:

$$p_{UJ,i}^{fob,l} = p_{UJ,i}^{d,l} \Big/ \left(1 - m_{U,i}^{T,e,l} - m_{U,i}^{W,e,l}\right) \quad (l = I, H)$$

(A12.15)

The prices of imports for industry and household uses, $p_{UJ,i}^{m,l}$ and $p_{UJ,i}^{m,H}$, are calculated by adding the custom duty and indirect taxes on products to the CIF price as:

$$p_{UJ,i}^{m,l} = e_{J/U}\left(1 + \tau_{J,i}^{l}\right)\left(1 + \tau_{UJ,i}^{r}\right)\left(1 + \tau_{UJ,i}^{f}\right)p_{UJ,i}^{fob,l}$$
$$= e_{J/U}\omega_{UJ,i}^{l} p_{UJ,i}^{d,l} \quad (l = I, H),$$

(A12.16)

where $e_{J/U}$ is the exchange rate of the Japanese yen against the US dollar, $\tau_{UJ,i}^{f}$ and $\tau_{UJ,i}^{r}$ are the rates of the international freight and insurance and the tariff for one unit of product i imported from the United States to Japan, respectively, and $\omega_{kk',i}^{l}$ is defined as insurance and the tariff for one unit of $\left(1 + \tau_{k',i}^{l}\right)\left(1 + \tau_{kk',i}^{r}\right)\left(1 + \tau_{kk',i}^{f}\right)\Big/$ $\left(1 - m_{U,i}^{T,e,l} - m_{U,i}^{W,e,l}\right)$ for l=I,H for notational simplicity.[25]

Meanwhile, the volume share of demand of domestic product and imported product is defined as:

$$w_{kJ,i}^{c,l} = \sum_{j \in l} X_{kJ,ij} \Big/ \sum_{j \in l} X_{J,ij}$$

(A12.17)

$$(k = J, U, E \text{ and } l = I, H),$$

where $w_{JJ,i}^{c,l} + w_{UJ,i}^{c,l} + w_{EJ,i}^{c,l} = 1$ for $l = I, H$. By assigning Eqs. (A12.16) and (A12.17) to Eq. (A12.7), we obtain:

$$p_{J,i}^{c,l} = p_{J,i}^{d,l} w_{JJ,i}^{c,l} + e_{J/U}\omega_{UJ,i}^{l} p_{UJ,i}^{d,l} w_{UJ,i}^{c,l}$$
$$+ p_{EJ,i}^{m,l} w_{EJ,i}^{c,l} \quad (l = I, H)$$

(A12.18)

Similarly, the demand prices in the United States are shown as:

$$p_{U,i}^{c,l} = p_{U,i}^{d,l} w_{UU,i}^{c,l} + \omega_{JU,i}^{l} p_{JU,i}^{d,l} w_{JU,i}^{c,l} \Big/ e_{J/U}$$
$$+ p_{EU,i}^{m,l} w_{EU,i}^{c,l} \quad (l = I, H).$$

(A12.19)

Eqs. (A12.18) and (A12.19) describe the price relationship between the producer's prices of Japan and the United States through bilateral trade.

Based on the definitions of our prices, we define several PLIs between Japan and the United States as,

$$\mathbf{P}_{J/U,i}^{d} = \frac{p_{J,i}^{d}}{e_{J/U}p_{U,i}^{d}}, \quad \mathbf{P}_{J/U,i}^{d,l} = \frac{p_{J,i}^{d,l}}{e_{J/U}p_{U,i}^{d,l}}, \quad \mathbf{P}_{J/U,i}^{c,l}$$
$$= \frac{p_{J,i}^{c,l}}{e_{J/U}p_{U,i}^{c,l}} \quad (l = I, H).$$

(A12.20)

where $\mathbf{P}_{J/U,i}^{d}$ is the PLI of output at producer's price of product i between Japan and the United

[25] The data $\tau_{UJ,i}^{r}$ is based on our extended 2011 Japan–US BIOT and the data $\tau_{UJ,i}^{f}$ is assumed to be identical with the estimates in the 2005 Japan–US BIOT by METI.

States. The second equation describes the definition of the PLIs of output at producer's price for households and for industries, $\mathbf{P}^{d,H}_{J/U,i}$ and $\mathbf{P}^{d,I}_{J/U,i}$, respectively. The third equation describes the PLIs of demand prices at producer's price, $\mathbf{P}^{c,H}_{J/U,i}$ and $\mathbf{P}^{c,I}_{J/U,i}$, respectively. By substituting Eqs. (A12.18) and (A12.19) into (A12.20), the Japan–US PLI of domestic demand prices for households and industries is obtained as follows:

$$\mathbf{P}^{c,l}_{J/U,i} = \frac{\mathbf{P}^{d,l}_{J/U,i}w^{c,l}_{JJ,i} + \omega^{l}_{UJ,i}w^{c,l}_{UJ,i}\big/\left(1+\tau^{l}_{U,i}\right) + \mathbf{P}^{m,l}_{EJ/U,i}w^{c,l}_{EJ,i}}{w^{c,l}_{UU,i} + \mathbf{P}^{d,l}_{J/U,i}\omega^{l}_{JU,i}w^{c,l}_{JU,i}\big/\left(1+\tau^{l}_{J,i}\right) + \mathbf{P}^{m,l}_{EU/U,i}w^{c,l}_{EU,i}} \quad (l=I,H). \quad \text{(A12.21)}$$

$\mathbf{P}^{m,l}_{Ek/U,i}$ is the PLI of the imports from exogenous economies to Japan or the United States, relative to the domestic producer's prices in the United States. These imports PLIs are defined as:

$$\mathbf{P}^{m,l}_{EJ/U,i} = \frac{p^{m,l}_{EJ,i}}{e_{J/U}\, p^{d,l}_{U,i}} \quad \text{and}$$

$$\mathbf{P}^{m,l}_{EU/U,i} = \frac{p^{m,l}_{EU,i}}{p^{d,l}_{U,i}} \quad (l=I,H). \quad \text{(A12.22)}$$

The import price indices for Japan and the United States, $p^{m,l}_{EJ/U,i}$ and $p^{m,l}_{EU/U,i}$, respectively, are endogenous in the model and determined by the submodel, as presented in the subsequent section. From Eq. (A12.21), we obtain:

$$\mathbf{P}^{d,l}_{J/U,i} = \frac{\omega^{l}_{UJ,i}w^{c,l}_{UJ,i}\big/\left(1+\tau^{l}_{U,i}\right) + \mathbf{P}^{m,l}_{EJ/U,i}w^{c,l}_{EJ,i} - \mathbf{P}^{c,l}_{J/U,i}\left(w^{c,l}_{UU,i} + \mathbf{P}^{m,l}_{EU/U,i}w^{c,l}_{EU,i}\right)}{\mathbf{P}^{c,l}_{J/U,i}\omega^{l}_{JU,i}w^{c,l}_{JU,i}\big/\left(1+\tau^{l}_{J,i}\right) - w^{c,l}_{JJ,i}} \quad (l=I,H) \quad \text{(A12.23)}$$

If the PLIs of the demand prices and the imports from exogenous economies are available as data, the PLI of output at producer's price are measured by this equation.

When the PLIs for $\mathbf{P}^{d,I}_{J/U,i}$ and $\mathbf{P}^{d,H}_{J/U,i}$ (PLIs for industry and household) are available in the data, we can measure the PLI of domestic outputs, $\mathbf{P}^{d}_{J/U,i}$, based on Eq. (A12.12) as:

$$P^{d}_{J/U,i} = \left\{ P^{d}_{J/U,i}\left(\frac{P^{d,I}_{U,i}w^{d,I}_{JJ,i}}{P^{d}_{U,i}} + \frac{P^{d,I}_{U,i}w^{d,I}_{JU,i}}{\left(1+\tau^{I}_{J,i}\right)P^{d}_{U,i}}\right) \right.$$
$$\left. + P^{d,H}_{J/U,i}\left(\frac{P^{d,H}_{U,i}w^{d,H}_{JJ,i}}{P^{d}_{U,i}} + \frac{P^{d,H}_{U,i}w^{d,H}_{JU,i}}{\left(1+\tau^{H}_{J,i}\right)P^{d}_{U,i}}\right) \right\}$$
$$\Big/ \left(1 - \frac{w^{d}_{JE,i}}{1+\tau^{d}_{J,i}}\right). \quad \text{(A12.24)}$$

In this equation, $\mathbf{P}^{d}_{J/U,i}$ is defined including the indirect taxes. Since our framework is based on METI's symmetric BIOT, this product-PLI is identical to the industry-PLI ($\mathbf{P}^{d}_{J/U,i} = \mathbf{P}^{d}_{J/U,j}$). To enable us to compare the prices and volumes of outputs, the PLI of j-industry outputs at basic prices $\mathbf{P}^{d*}_{J/U,j}$ as:

$$\mathbf{P}^{d*}_{J/U,i} = \mathbf{P}^{d}_{J/U,i} \frac{1 + \tau^{d}_{U,i}}{1 + \tau^{d}_{J,i}}. \qquad (A12.25)$$

In our study, only the Japan–US differences in the indirect taxes on the consumption of liquor, tobacco, and gasoline are taken into account.

Purchaser's prices

The first section of the Appendix described the price model based on producer's prices. However, the PPP data in the main data sources are measured at purchaser's prices. In this section, we describe the relationship between the producer's prices and purchaser's prices. Some additional notation is required:

$p^{pd,l}_{k,i}$ Prices of products in country k, purchased by industries (I) or household (H) in country k at purchasers' prices in currency of country k (if $l = I$, the product is purchased by industries for intermediate uses or investment. If $l = H$, the product is purchased by household for final consumption.),

$p^{pd,l}_{kk',i}$ Prices of products produced in country k, purchased by industries (I) or household (H) in country k' at purchasers' prices in currency of country k (if $l = I$, the product is purchased by industries. If $l = H$, the product is purchased by household.),

$p^{pm,l}_{kk',i}$ Prices of imports from country k, purchased by industries (I) or household (H) in country k' at purchasers' prices in currency of country k' (if $l = I$, the product is purchased by industries. If $l = H$, the product is purchased by household.),

$T^{l}_{k,i}$ Transportation service input for one unit of imported and domestic products in country k (if $l = I$, the service is input for industries. If $l = H$, the service is input for households.),

$W^{d,l}_{k,i}$ Trade service input for one unit of domestic products in country k (if $l = I$, the

service is input for industries. If $l = H$, the service is input for households.),

$W^{m,l}_{k,i}$ Trade service input for one unit of imports in country k (if $l = I$, the service is input for industries. If $l = H$, the service is input for households.),

$m^{T,l}_{k,i}$ Rates of transportation cost (T) of products in country k for imported and domestic products (if $l = I$, the rate is for industries. If $l = H$, the rate is for households.),

$m^{W,l}_{k,i}$ Rates of trade margin (W) of products in k-country for imported and domestic products (if $l = I$, the rate is for industries. If $l = H$, the rate is for households.),

$m^{W,d,l}_{k,i}$ Rates of trade margin (W) of products in country k for domestic products (if $l = I$, the rate is for industries. If $l = H$, the rate is for households.),

$m^{W,m,l}_{k,i}$ Rates of trade margin (W) of products in country k for imported products (if $l = I$, the rate is for industries. If $l = H$, the rate is for households.)

The purchaser's price paid by industries and households is defined as the sum of the producer-price value, the transportation cost, and the trade margin as:

$$p^{pd,l}_{J,i} = p^{d,l}_{J,i} + p^{d,l}_{J,T}T^{l}_{J,i} + p^{d,l}_{J,W}W^{d,l}_{J,i} \quad (l = I, H),$$
$$(A12.26)$$

where $p^{d,l}_{J,T}$ and $p^{d,l}_{J,W}$ are the output prices of the transportation and trade services in Japan, and $T^{l}_{J,i}$ and $W^{d,l}_{J,i}$ are the transportation and the trade services required for one unit of product i. In our model, since the trade margin rates are distinguished for domestic products and imports, the superscript "d" is added for the trade margin. The rates of transportation cost and trade margin to the purchaser's prices of domestic products are defined as:

$$m^{T,l}_{J,i} = p^{d,l}_{J,T}T^{l}_{J,i} \Big/ p^{pd,l}_{J,i} \quad \text{and} \quad m^{W,d,l}_{J,i}$$
$$= p^{d,l}_{J,W}W^{d,l}_{J,i} \Big/ p^{pd,l}_{J,i} \quad (l = I, H), \qquad (A12.27)$$

respectively, for each of industry or household use. Based on Eqs. (A12.26) and (A12.27), the relationship between producer's prices and purchaser's prices is given by:

$$p_{J,i}^{d,l} = p_{J,i}^{pd,l}\left(1 - m_{J,i}^{T,l} - m_{J,i}^{W,d,l}\right) \quad (l = I, H)$$

(A12.28)

$$m_{k,i}^{W,l} = m_{k,i}^{W,m,l}\sum_{j\in l}\left(p_{k'k,i}^{pm,l}X_{k'k,ij} + p_{Ek,i}^{pm,l}X_{Ek,ij}\right)\Bigg/\sum_{j\in l}p_{k,i}^{pc,l}X_{k,ij}$$

$$+ m_{k,i}^{W,d,l}\cdot\sum_{j\in l}p_{kk,i}^{pd,l}X_{kk,ij}\Bigg/\sum_{j\in l}p_{k,i}^{pc,l}X_{k,ij} \quad (kk' = JU \ or \ UJ \quad and \quad l = I, H).$$

(A12.31)

Analogous equations exist for the United States. The PLI in purchaser's prices for domestic products is described as.

$$\mathbf{P}_{J/U,i}^{pd,l} = \frac{p_{J,i}^{pd,l}}{e_{J/u}\,p_{U,i}^{pd,l}} = \mathbf{P}_{J/U,i}^{d,l}\frac{\left(1 - m_{U,i}^{T,l} - m_{U,i}^{W,d,l}\right)}{\left(1 - m_{J,i}^{T,l} - m_{J,i}^{W,d,l}\right)}$$

$$(l = I, H).$$

(A12.29)

This equation gives the relationship between the producer-price PLI and the purchaser-price PLI of domestic products.

The PLI for composite demand, which reflects the prices of both imports and its domestic counterpart, is represented as:

$$\mathbf{P}_{J/U,i}^{pc,l} = \frac{p_{J,i}^{pc,l}}{e_{J/u}\,p_{U,i}^{pc,l}} = \mathbf{P}_{J/U,i}^{c,l}\frac{\left(1 - m_{U,i}^{T,l} - m_{U,i}^{W,l}\right)}{\left(1 - m_{J,i}^{T,l} - m_{J,i}^{W,l}\right)}$$

$$(l = I, H).$$

(A12.30)

The rate of transportation cost for the component of imports is the same as that for the domestic products. Thus the same rates of $m_{J,i}^{T,l}$ and $m_{U,i}^{T,l}$

are applied in Eqs. (A12.29) and (A12.30). On the other hand, the rate of domestic trade margin for imports $m_{k,i}^{W,m,l}$ is different from that for domestic products $m_{k,i}^{W,d,l}$ in our model. Therefore, Eq. (A12.30) is described using, $m_{J,i}^{W,l}$ and $m_{U,i}^{W,l}$, which are the rates of trade margin for composite products measured as:

Eq. (A12.31) indicates that the rate of trade margin for composite products $m_{k,i}^{W,l}$ is measured as a weighted average of $m_{k,i}^{W,m,l}$ and $m_{k,i}^{W,d,l}$, with weights reflecting the nominal value shares evaluated at the purchaser's prices. This study uses the trade margin rates in Nomura and Miyagawa (2018a).

The PLIs, $\mathbf{P}_{J/U,i}^{pc,l}$ and $\mathbf{P}_{J/U,i}^{pc,H}$ in Eq. (A12.30), reflect the Japan–US relative price differences for demand prices evaluated by purchaser's prices for industry and household uses, respectively. By isolating the PLI of the products for household use, we are able to define the Japan–US PPP for household consumption by product as:

$$\mathbf{PPP}_{J/U,\,i}^{H} = e_{J/u}\mathbf{P}_{J/U,i}^{pc,H}.$$

(A12.32)

If the PPP data, $\mathbf{PPP}_{J/U,i}^{H}$, or the purchaser-price PLI, $\mathbf{P}_{J/U,i}^{pc,H}$, on household consumption between Japan and the United States is available, we can measure the producer-price PLI of demand prices, $\mathbf{P}_{J/U,i}^{c,H}$, from Eq. (A12.30), and then the PLI of domestic products, $\mathbf{P}_{J/U,i}^{d,H}$, can be measured from Eq. (A12.23).

Import prices from exogenous economies

We next describe the role of import prices from exogenous economies (E) to Japan (J) and the United States (U). The estimates of these prices, $p_{EJ,i}^{m,l}$ and $p_{EU,i}^{m,l}$, respectively, are used to infer the producer-price PLI of domestic products $\mathbf{P}_{J/U,i}^{d,l}$ in Eq. (A12.23). Some intuition of this is as follows: suppose we observe the price of paper exported from China into Japan, and we observe the final demand price paid for paper in Japan. In our accounting framework, the gap between the two prices reflects the (unmeasured) production price in Japan (after accounting for trade margins and taxes). We define $p_{EJ,i}^{m,l}$ and $p_{EU,i}^{m,l}$ as the combined import prices from exogenous economies:

$$
\begin{aligned}
p_{Ek',i}^{m,l} &= \sum_k p_{kk',i}^{m,l} v_{kk',i}^{m,l} \\
&= \sum_{k \neq R} e_{k'/k} \omega_{kk',i}^l p_{k,i}^{d,l} v_{kk',i}^{m,l} + p_{Rk',i}^{m,l} v_{Rk',i}^{m,l},
\end{aligned}
$$

$$
(l = I, H, \quad k = C, G, K, M, W, T, R, \text{ and}
$$

$$
k' = J \text{ or } U),
$$

(A12.33)

where the $v_{kk',i}^{m,l}$ stands for the import shares at current prices from country k (the exogenous economies) to country k' (Japan and the United States). The sum of the import shares $\sum_k v_{kk',i}^{m,l}$ is one. $p_{Rk',i}^{m,l}$ is the average price of imported goods from the ROW. $\omega_{kk',i}^l$, which is defined in Eq. (A12.16), is the combined coefficient to transform the output prices in country k to the import prices in country k' from country k. Since it is difficult to obtain the output prices in country k ($p_{k,i}^{d,l}$) directly from statistical data, we construct the following submodel to determine $p_{k,i}^{d,l}$ in six exogenous economies (k) excluding the ROW.[26]

We describe the demand price (of the composite products) in country k as:

$$
\begin{aligned}
p_{k,i}^{c,l} &= p_{k,i}^{d,l} v_{kk,i}^{c,l} + \sum_{k \neq k'} e_{k/k'} \omega_{k'k,i}^l p_{k',i}^{d,l} v_{k'k,i}^{c,l} \\
&\quad + e_{k/J} \omega_{Jk,i}^l p_{J,i}^{d,l} v_{Jk,i}^{c,l} \\
&\quad + e_{k/U} \omega_{Uk,i}^l p_{U,i}^{d,l} v_{Uk,i}^{cl} + p_{Rk,i}^{m,l} v_{Rk',i}^{c,l} \\
&\quad (k = C, G, K, M, W, T, \\
&\quad k' = C, G, K, M, W, T, \text{ and } l = I, H).
\end{aligned}
$$

(A12.34)

where $v_{kk',i}^{c,l}$ is the demand share of the domestic product and the imported product at current prices from country k to country k'. The sum of the demand shares $\sum_k v_{kk',i}^{c,l}$ is one. In this equation, $p_{k,i}^{d,l}$ in the first and second terms of the right hand is the prices to be determined endogenously in the submodel. The third and fourth terms are the import prices from Japan and the United States, respectively, whose output prices, $p_{Jk,i}^{d,l}$ and $p_{Uk,i}^{d,l}$, are predetermined in the main model and are treated as exogenous variables in the submodel. And the final term, $p_{Rk,i}^{m,l}$, is the exogenous prices of imports from the ROW.

In the left-hand side of Eq. (A12.34), the demand-price PPPs in country k, $p_{k,i}^{c,l}$, are observed in Eurostat-OECD (2012), METI (2012), or other PPP surveys. The third and fourth terms of the right-hand side of Eq. (A12.34), i.e., the output prices in Japan and the United States, are predetermined in our main model, as described in Appendices 1 and 2. The fifth term, i.e., the exogenous prices of imports from the ROW, is also usually unobserved. In this paper, the purchaser's price of imports from the ROW in country k is assumed to be identical with the purchaser's price of the composite product of domestic product in country k and imported products from Japan, the United

---

[26] In the submodel, indirect taxes are not considered for simplicity.

States, and other five exogenous countries.[27] For each product i, Eq. (A12.34) is defined for the six countries that we consider. Six endogenous variables of domestic output prices in country k, $p_{k,i}^{d,l}$, are determined simultaneously by solving these six linear equations in each product i.

Some iterations are required between the main model and the submodel. By substituting the output prices ($p_{k,i}^{d,l}$) estimated in the submodel for six countries and the exogenous prices of imports from the ROW ($p_{Rk,i}^{m,l}$) into Eq. (A12.33), the import prices from exogenous economies to Japan and the United States, $p_{EJ,i}^{m,l}$ and $p_{EU,i}^{m,l}$, are affected. These then require the further adjustment in the estimates of $p_{J,i}^{d,l}$ and $p_{U,i}^{d,l}$ in Eq. (A12.23) of the main model, which impacts the third and fourth terms of the right-hand side of Eq. (A12.34) in the submodel. Through a few reiterations between the main model and the submodel, we obtain the final results of all types of PLIs between Japan and the United States.

Sensitivity to margin rates

In this section, we evaluate the sensitivity of the PPPs for industry outputs to our choice of margin rates. Our baseline PPP estimates depend on the margin rates of wholesale and retail services estimated in Nomura and Miyagawa (2018a). They examined the accuracy of the estimates of the trade margin values in the 2011 benchmark IOT in Japan and found the total margin value was underestimated by about 40% due to estimation methods used in the 2011 Economic Census. If lower margin rates are used in the measurement of PPPs via the price model, they induce higher PPPs for industry outputs (Paths 2, 3, and 4 defined in Fig. 12.2). Fig. 12.8 presents the impact on the PPPs for outputs when the margin values were reduced by 40% (on the y-axis) from our baseline estimates (on the x-axis). This low-margin case reduces the price competitiveness measures by more than 50% in 15 industries and by more than 20% in 44 industries.[28] The PPPs based on the (official) low-margin case imply significantly lower productivity levels in Japanese manufacturing than those based on the adjusted margins. These low productivity levels in manufacturing are implausible in comparison to earlier studies of Japan—US productivity gaps.[29]

At the aggregate level, the low-margin case leads to and increase the PPP for GDP to 111.8 yen per dollar, from 109.0 in the baseline scenario, expanding the gap with the expenditure-side PPP for GDP in the Eurostat-OECD (107.5 yen per dollar). However, the impact of the low-margin case at the aggregate level is small compared to the impacts at the industry level presented in Fig. 12.8. This is because higher PPPs for GDP in the manufacturing industries

[27] The estimates of PPP for outputs are sensitive to the assumption on import prices, in the process to parse the observed price of composite goods into that from domestic supply and that coming from imported goods. In measuring PPPs for 1990 in Nomura and Miyagawa (1999), the similar assumption was applied only for the total of six exogenous economies and the ROW. This induced unreasonable estimates in some products. The explicit treatment of six exogenous economies contributes to reduce these events to be happened. However, in some exceptional cases when the estimated results are unreasonable, the import prices from the ROW are adjusted.

[28] For example, the PPP for industry output of (170) Motor vehicles is revised to 120.0 yen per dollar in low-margin case, compared to 97.5 in baseline estimates. The PPP for domestic output estimated in low-margin case seems to be unrealistically high as an evaluation of price competitiveness of the Japanese motor vehicle industry.

[29] Kuroda and Nomura (1999), and Jorgenson and Nomura (2007), as well as Jorgenson et al. (2016).

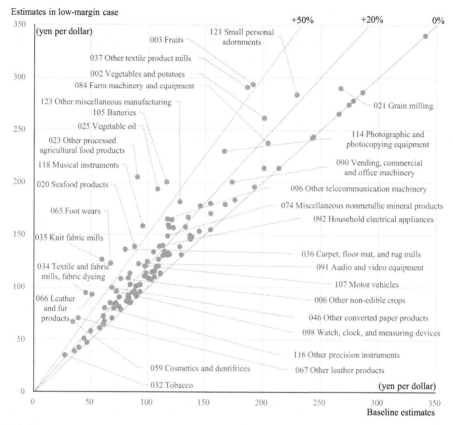

FIGURE 12.8   Purchasing power parities (PPPs) for goods based on the low margin scenario versus the baseline.

are compensated by the revised lower PPPs for GDP of the wholesale and retail industries. The low-margin case has a significant impact on the PPP for wholesale service (95.3 yen per dollar from 133.5 in the baseline estimate) and the PPP for retail service (119.7 from 136.3). These estimates based on the lower margin rates seem to be inconsistent with previous studies, providing additional evidence that those based on the official Japan Census data appear implausible.

Disclaimer

The views expressed in this paper are solely those of the authors and not necessarily that of the RIETI, or the US Bureau of Economic Analysis. The use of the unpublished data collected within the International Comparisons Program is permitted by STD/OECD and Development Economics/The World Bank. The authors are indebted to Hiroshi Shirane (KEO) for his research support.

References

Ark BV, Pilat D: *Productivity levels in Germany, Japan, and the United States: differences and causes, brookings papers on economic activity*, 1993, Microeconomics, pp 1—48.

Cabinet Office: *Survey of PPPs on major consumer goods and services*, 2001, Cabinet Office, Government of Japan.

Chenery HB: In the structure and growth of the Italian economy. In Chenery HB, Clark PG, Cao-Pinna V, editors: *Regional analysis*, 1953, Rome, 1953, U.S. Mutual Security Agency, pp 91—129.

Eurostat-OECD: Eurostat-OECD methodological manual on purchasing power parities. In *Eurostat methodologies and working papers*, 2012, European Union/OECD.

Hamadeh N, AbuShanab H: Uses of purchasing power parities to better inform policy making and poverty measurement. In *IAOS 2016 conference*, 2016, Abu Dhabi, 2016, International Association for Official Statistics.

Institute of Developing Economies: International input-output table Japan-USA 1970. In *IDE statistical data series No.24*, 1978, Institute of Developing Economies.

Institute of Developing Economies: *Asian international input-output table 2005*, 2013, Institute of Developing Economies, Japan External Trade Organization.

Isard W: Interregional and regional input-output analysis: a model of a space economy, *The Review of Economics and Statistics* 33:318–328, 1951.

Jorgenson DW: The world KLEMS initiative: measuring productivity at the industry level. In Grifell-Tatjé E, et al., editors: *The oxford handbook of productivity analysis*, 2018, Oxford, 2018, The Oxford University Press, pp 663–698. Chap. 20.

Jorgenson DW, Kuroda M: Productivity and international competitiveness in Japan and the United States, 1960–1985. In Hulten CR, editor: *Productivity growth in Japan and the United States*, 1990, Chicago, 1990, University of Chicago Press, pp 29–55.

Jorgenson DW, Kuroda M, Nishimizu M: Japan-U.S. Industry-level productivity comparison, 1960–1979, *Journal of the Japanese and International Economies* 1:1–30, 1987.

Jorgenson DW, Nomura K: The industry origins of the Japan-us productivity gap, *Economic System Research* 19(3): 315–341, 2007.

Jorgenson DW, Nomura K, Samuels JD: A half century of trans-Pacific competition: price level indices and productivity gaps for Japanese and U.S. Industries, 1955–2012. In Jorgenson DW, et al., editors: *The world economy — growth or stagnation?*, 2016 Cambridge, 2016, Cambridge University Press, pp 469–507. Chap. 13.

Jorgenson DW, Nomura K, Samuels JD: Progress on measuring the industry origins of the Japan-U.S. Productivity gap. In *Presented in fifth world KLEMS conference at Harvard University*, June 4–5, 2018.

Kuroda M, Nomura K: Productivity comparison and international competitiveness, *Journal of Applied Input-Output Analysis* 5:1–37, 1999.

MAFF: *Survey of retail prices of food products in Tokyo and foreign major six cities*, 2006, Government of Japan, 2006, Ministry of Agriculture, Forestry and Fisheries.

METI: *Survey on foreign and domestic price differentials for industrial goods and services 2011*, 2012, Ministry of Economy, Trade and Industry, Government of Japan.

METI: *2005 Japan-us input-output table*, 2013, Ministry of Economy, Trade and Industry, Government of Japan.

MHLW: *Sourvey of PPPs on drugs and medical products*, 2003, Government of Japan, 2003, Ministry of Health, Labour and Welfare.

MIAC, Survey of PPP on information services: *Ministry of Internal Affairs and Communications*, 2011, Government of Japan.

MLIT: *Survey of PPPs on transportation and related services*, 2007, Government of Japan, 2007, Ministry of Land, Infrastructure and Transportation.

Moses LN: The stability of interregional trading patterns and input-output analysis, *The American Economic Review* 45(5):803–832, 1955.

Nomura K, Miyagawa K: Measurement of US-Japan relative prices of commodities, *Keizai Tokei Kenkyu (Economic Statistics Research)* 27/3:1–38, 1999 (in Japanese).

Nomura K, Miyagawa K: *The Japan-U.S. Price level index for industry outputs*, 2015, pp 1–34. REITI Discussion Paper, 15-E-059.

Nomura K, Miyagawa K: Rebalancing benchmark input-output production system by revision in margin matrix, *Keizai Tokei Kenkyu (Economic Statistics Research)* 46/1: 29–55, 2018a (in Japanese).

Nomura K, Miyagawa K: *Are Japan's prices of distribution services higher than the U.S.?*, 2018, mimeo.

Nomura K, Shirane H: *Measurement of quality-adjusted labor input in Japan, 1955–2012*, KEO Discussion Paper, No.133, 2014, December, 2014, Keio University, pp 1–144 (in Japanese).

Timmer MP, Dietzenbacher E, Los B, et al.: An illustrated user guide to the world input–output database: the case of global automotive production, *Review of International Economics* 23:575–605, 2015.

World Bank: *Purchasing power parities and real expenditures of world economies: summary of results and findings of the 2011 international comparison Program*, 2014, Washington, D.C., 2014, The World Bank.

The impact of information and communications technology investment on employment in Japan and Korea

Kyoji Fukao[1], Tsutomu Miyagawa[2], Hak Kil Pyo[3], Keunhee Rhee[4], Miho Takizawa[2]

[1]Institute of Economic Research, Hitotsubashi University, Tokyo, Japan; [2]Faculty of Economics, Gakushuin University, Tokyo, Japan; [3]Faculty of Economics, Seoul National University, Seoul, Korea; [4]Korea Productivity Center, Seoul, Korea

13.1 Introduction

An interesting development to note is that new growth theory, which highlighted the role of human capital and the convexity of the total capital in growth and development process emerged in the economic literature more or less at the same time as the information and communications technology (ICT) revolution began. ICT capital appears to have played the role of a broad capital encompassing human capital and economies of scale as reviewed in Pyo (2018). Since Solow (1987) highlighted the paradox that "you can see the computer age everywhere but in the productivity statistics," there has been a voluminous debate on how this paradox should be explained. We note in particular two explanations. The first explanation is that the productivity implications of a new technology are only visible with a long lag (Brynjolfsson (1993)).

The second possible explanation is that computers simply are not very productivity-enhancing, since they require time, a scarce complementary human input. In the present chapter, we examine the hypothesis that computers and other ICT technologies have affected human input.

Following the spread of ICT in the 21st century, many studies on inequality between skilled and unskilled labor have focused on the effects of ICT on the wage share of skilled labor. Following Berman et al. (1994), several articles examined skill-biased technological change. Using manufacturing industry data for seven advanced economies, Machin and Van Reenen (1998) show that research and development (R&D) expenditures are associated with an increase in the wage share of nonproduction workers. Chun (2003) examined the effects of ICT adoption and ICT use on the wage share of college graduates. He finds that the firms which adopted and fully implemented new technology can replace high-wage, highly educated workers with lower paid less-educated workers. His empirical results using industry-level data for the United States showed that the introduction of new ICT facilities has increased the wage share of college graduates, which implies that college graduates find it easier to adapt to new technologies. He also showed that in the case of college graduates, ICT is complementary to skills.

O'Mahony et al. (2008) divide studies on ICT and employment into two fields: those on the effects of new technologies such as ICT on labor skills and those on the effects of new technologies on tasks. The first strand of studies starts from Berman et al. (1994), who think that skill-biased technology has increased inequality between skilled and unskilled labor. Using a translog cost function, they estimate an equation where the wage share of nonproduction workers is affected by the relative wage of nonproduction workers and the capital/output ratio. Their estimation results show that the impact of technology on the demand for skilled labor is slowing down, at least in the United States, supporting a transitory interpretation.

O'Mahony et al. (2008) also examined the effects of ICT capital on the wage share of the most educated workers in all countries and found capital-skill complementarity. Focusing on three advanced economies (the United States, the United Kingdom, and France), they divide workers into three groups by educational level. Their estimation results show complementarity between highly educated workers and ICT capital and substitutability between low-skilled workers and ICT capital. They divide high-skilled workers into two groups (ICT occupations and non-ICT occupations) and estimate the wage share equations in each country. Their estimation results show that complementarity effects

between high-skilled labor engaged in ICT occupations and ICT capital are found only in France.

Another study examining the effects of ICT capital on high-skilled labor is that by Michaels et al. (2014). From the EU KLEMS database, they obtain data on the wage and employment of three types of workers (high-education workers, middle-education workers, and low-education workers), value-added, and ICT capital by industry for 11 countries. Like O' Mahony et al. (2008), they find complementarity between high-skilled labor and ICT capital. On the other hand, middle-skilled workers are substitutable for ICT capital.

Spieza et al. (2016) examine the effects of ICT investments on (i) total labor demand, (ii) labor demand by skill level, and (iii) labor demand by industry in selected Organisation for Economic Co-operation and Development (OECD) countries over the period 1990–2012. They report that "ICT investments are estimated to have raised total labor demand in most countries over the period 1990–2007 but to have reduced it after 2007. In the latter period, the decrease in total labor demand has been accompanied by polarization in favor of high and low skills and against medium skills. Yet, the effects on both total labor demand and polarization are estimated to disappear in the long run" (Spieza et al., 2016, p. 4).

The second strand of studies focuses on the effects of new technology on tasks. To examine the effects of computerization on job skill demand, Autor et al. (2003), hereafter Autor, Levy and Murnane (ALM) divided tasks into the following five categories: nonroutine analytical tasks, nonroutine interactive tasks, routine cognitive tasks, routine manual tasks, and nonroutine manual tasks. Their main finding was that "computer technology substitutes for workers in performing routine tasks that can be readily described with programmed rules, while complementing workers in executing non-routine tasks demanding flexibility, creativity, generalized problem-solving capabilities, and complex communications" (Autor et al., 2003, p. 1279). Goos and Manning (2007) and Spitz-Oener (2006) investigated the impact of technology on labor markets in the United Kingdom and West Germany following ALM's approach. They found evidence that job polarization was increasing and that this was related to skill-biased technical change. Ikenaga (2009) and Ikenaga and Kambayashi (2016) analyzed the relationship between changes in task shares and ICT capital. Constructing a dataset with ALM's five task categories by industry using the *Population Census* and the JIP database, the latter find that "although machines seem to have replaced routine cognitive tasks and manual tasks before the introduction of ICT, it appears that ICT reinforces the tendency for routine labor tasks to be replaced by capital. Moreover, ICT induces complementary increases in nonroutine, high-skilled (interactive) tasks" (Ikenaga and Kambayashi, 2016, p. 288).

Following the Global Financial Crisis, economists have been interested not only in inequality between high-skilled and low-skilled labor but also in the decline in the total labor share in advanced countries. Karabarbounis and Neiman (2013) show that the global labor share has declined significantly since the early 1980s in developed countries, highlighting that "larger labor share declines occurred in countries or industries with larger declines in their relative price of investment goods" (Karabarbounis and Neiman, 2013, p. 31). Using KLEMS data, they use the cross-sectional variation in labor shares to estimate the production function for different countries and find that the decline in the relative price of investment explains roughly half of the decline in the global labor share. On the other hand, Elsby et al. (2013) show that "U.S. data provided limited support for neoclassical explanations based on the substitution of capital for (unskilled) labor to exploit technical change embodied in new capital goods" (p. 1).

The central theme of this chapter is the impact of the skill-biased technical change associated with the introduction of ICT investment on labor demand in Japan and Korea. This is a follow-up study to Fukao et al. (2012), which investigated the contribution of ICT investment to total factor productivity in Japan and Korea. The (chapter/study/paper) consists of the specification of the model in Section 13.2, while Section 13.3 presents empirical estimation results using Japanese and Korean. Finally, Section 13.4.

13.2 A model of ICT investment effects on employment

According to O'Mahony et al. (2008), we analyze the impact of ICT on the demand for skills. We consider the following short-run variable cost function in industry i:

$$\mathrm{CV}_i\left(W_i^H, W_i^M, W_i^L, K_i, Y_i, Z_i\right) \qquad (13.1)$$

where $W^H(W^M, W^L)$ is the wage rate of high-skilled (middle-skilled and low-skilled), K is the capital stock, Y is value added, and Z is factors that change the structure of production cost.

Following Berman et al. (1994), we assume a translog cost function with constant returns to scale. Applying Shephard's lemma, we obtain the labor cost share equation for skilled workers. Our empirical specification is based on the following equation:

$$S_i^H = \alpha + \beta \ln\left(\frac{W_i^H}{W_i^L}\right) + \gamma \ln\left(\frac{W_i^M}{W_i^L}\right) + \delta \ln\left(\frac{K_i}{Y_i}\right) + \theta \ln Z_i + \delta_t t,$$

$$(13.2)$$

where S_i^H is the labor cost share of skilled workers. Following O'Mahony et al. (2008), we replace the relative wage term by time dummies (D_t) to deal with the endogeneity issue associated with wages.[1] In addition, we assume that ICT over capital represents Z. Eventually, we can rewrite Eq. (13.2) as follows:

$$S_i^H = \alpha + \delta \ln\left(\frac{K_i}{Y_i}\right) + \theta \ln\left(\frac{ICT_i}{K_i}\right) + \eta_t D_t + \varepsilon_i$$

$$(13.3)$$

where ICT_{it} represents the ICT capital stock and ε_{it} is the error term.

The coefficient on the capital−output ratio (δ) shows the degree of complementarity or substitutability between capital and skills. δ will be positive if capital and skills are complementary. The coefficient of ICT−capital ratio (θ) captures the impact of ICT on the wage structure. If ICT capital increases the demand for skilled workers, θ will be positive in the labor cost share equation for skilled workers.

We use both Japanese and Korean dataset for estimating the labor cost share equation. These datasets comprise annual series from 1979 to 2015. We split the dataset into two subsets. The one is from 1979 to 2000 for comparing with the results of O'Mahony et al. (2008); the other is from 1995 to 2015 for tracing the impact of ICT investments on employment in Korea and Japan after the main ICT investments started from the mid-1990s. The latter period also includes the Asian financial crisis, which was particularly severe in Korea, as well as the Global Financial Crisis of 2007−08. To test the impact of ICT capital by skill category, we estimate Eq. (13.3) using industry-level data for all skill groups. γ and θ are assumed to be identical across industries.

13.3 Empirical results for Japan and Korea

13.3.1 Trends in wage shares and ICT capital intensity

Both Japan and Korea use the same industry classification. We have our own KLEMS databases called Japan Industrial Productivity (JIP) Database and Korea Industrial Productivity (KIP) Database, respectively, and both classifications are summarized into 38 industries to harmonize with the EU KLEMS database.

13.3.1.1 Labor share

For Japan, we obtain employment and wage data by gender (male and female), by age group (5-year brackets from 15 to 64, and over 65), by industry, and by education level (middle-school graduates, high-school graduates, vocational school and junior college graduates, and college graduates) from the *National Population Census* the *Basic Survey on Employment Structure* and the *Basic Survey on Wage Structure*. However, when we estimate (the cost share function/cost share functions), we categorize our data into three education levels (high = college graduates; middle = high-school graduates, and vocational school and junior college graduates; and low - = middle-school graduates).

Table 13.1 shows that the wage share of the high-skilled group has steadily increased in Japan. In fact, this upward trend can be observed even before the start of the IT revolution in the mid-1990s, which is consistent with Sakurai (2001). Moreover, the trend does not appear to have been dramatically affected by the ICT revolution, with the increase in the wage share of

---

[1] In several extant studies (e.g., Chun, 2003; O'Mahony et al., 2008; Michaels et al., 2014), the time-specific effect is employed to account for the level of the relative wage. This empirical strategy is based on a set of assumptions, namely, that (i) labor is mobile across industries, (ii) labor markets are not locally segmented but nationally unified, and (iii) the relative wage is correlated with economic activity.

TABLE 13.1 Wage shares by skill category: Japan.

	1970	1980	1990	2000	2010	2015
All						
High-skilled	13.1%	20.3%	26.9%	31.0%	36.9%	38.6%
Middle-skilled	45.9%	51.5%	56.6%	61.4%	60.0%	59.3%
Low-skilled	41.0%	28.2%	16.5%	7.7%	3.2%	2.1%
Manufacturing						
High-skilled	10.2%	14.7%	19.0%	23.0%	30.0%	31.0%
Middle-skilled	36.1%	43.4%	54.8%	63.6%	64.9%	66.1%
Low-skilled	53.7%	41.9%	26.2%	13.4%	5.1%	2.9%
Nonmanufacturing						
High-skilled	14.2%	22.0%	29.2%	33.2%	38.6%	40.4%
Middle-skilled	49.5%	54.0%	57.2%	60.7%	58.7%	57.7%
Low-skilled	36.3%	23.9%	13.6%	6.1%	2.7%	1.9%

Note: High skilled: college graduates. Middle skilled: high-school graduates, vocational school and junior college graduates. Low skilled: middle-school graduates.

high-skilled continuing at more or less the same pace. The upward trend in the wage share of high-skilled workers throughout the entire period also reflects demographic developments. As Japanese firms tend to pay higher wages to older generations, the increase in the wage share of older workers in the skilled group leads to the increase in the wage share of the skilled group as a whole. The wage shares of the high-skilled group in manufacturing industries are relatively higher than those in nonmanufacturing industries. The table also shows that the wage share of high-skilled group is higher in the manufacturing sector than the nonmanufacturing sector.

In Korea, the employment and wage shares of different groups change over time, and therefore, we have followed the EU KLEMS method of labor decomposition by gender (male and female), by age (below 30 group, 30—49 years old group, and 50 and above group), and by education level (below middle-school graduates, high-school graduates, and college graduates), compiling a total of 18 cohorts' data. At the stage of estimating wage share equations, O'Mahony et al. (2008) use further breakdowns in intermediate skill group into associate, some college and high-school subgroups, but since we do not have subgroup data, we have used age groups (15—29, 30—49, and 50 and over) as subgroups instead of skill subgroups.

Table 13.2 presents the results for Korea for the period 1970—2015. The table shows that the wage share of high-skilled labor has increased substantially from 40.7% in 1970 to 68.7% in 2015 in all industries, from 14.4% to 50.5% in manufacturing, and from 47.4% to 75.5% in nonmanufacturing. By 2015, the share of low-skilled labor had fallen to less than 5%. This might reflect an overestimation bias in estimating skill level by education index only because by and large college education has been vastly expanded in Korea during the period of 1970—2015.

TABLE 13.2 Wage shares by skill category: Korea.

	1970	1980	1990	2000	2010	2015
All						
High-skilled	40.7%	38.0%	41.6%	51.3%	66.8%	68.7%
Middle-skilled	25.4%	34.1%	40.0%	38.1%	29.4%	28.5%
Low-skilled	33.7%	27.7%	18.3%	10.5%	3.8%	2.8%
Manufacturing						
High-skilled	14.4%	18.9%	23.9%	30.7%	46.1%	50.5%
Middle-skilled	27.1%	37.1%	49.0%	52.5%	48.2%	46.0%
Low-skilled	58.4%	43.8%	26.9%	16.8%	5.7%	3.5%
Nonmanufacturing						
High-skilled	47.4%	45.9%	49.1%	58.9%	74.3%	75.5%
Middle-skilled	25.0%	32.8%	36.2%	32.9%	22.7%	22.0%
Low-skilled	27.4%	21.1%	14.6%	8.2%	3.1%	2.5%

Note: High skilled: college graduates. Middle skilled: high-school graduates, vocational school and junior college graduates. Low skilled: middle-school or elementary school graduates.

13.3.1.2 Capital stock

Following O'Mahony et al. (2008), we measure output as real value added and decompose the real capital stock into ICT components (computers, software, and communications) and non-ICT components (structures, non-ICT equipment, and vehicles) in line with the definitions in EU KLEMS (2007). For Japan, we construct the capital stock series from 1995 to 2015 based on the System of National Accounts (SNA), because the Japanese SNA (JSNA) has published ICT capital stock (information and communication equipment and software) since 2016. However, the JSNA consists of 29 industries. Subsequently, we harmonize the JSNA data with our industry classification by using JIP, because the industry classification of the JIP database is more sophisticated.[2] As the JSNA does not provide ICT data before 1994, we use the capital stock data in the EU KLEMS database released in November 2009 to estimate ICT data for the period 1979–2000.

For Korea, we estimate the capital stock of each type of asset based on the modified perpetual inventory method using the estimates by the National Wealth Survey (NWS) for 1968 as the initial value and the three subsequent NWS estimates for 1977, 1987, and 1997 as benchmark estimates. We assume lower geometric depreciation rates than EU KLEMS (2007) following Korea Productivity Center (2017) in order to avoid the underestimation of productive service flows of ICT assets.[3] The adoption of geometric depreciation rates makes age–price profile converge with age–efficiency profile, and therefore, productive stock becomes consistent with net stock as outlined in OECD (2009). Using geometric depreciation rates means that the age–price profile of assets is closer to their age–efficiency profile, so that the productive stock of assets is consistent with the net stock.

Figs. 13.1 and 13.2 show developments in the capital/output ratio and the share of ICT capital stock in the total capital stock in Japan. The

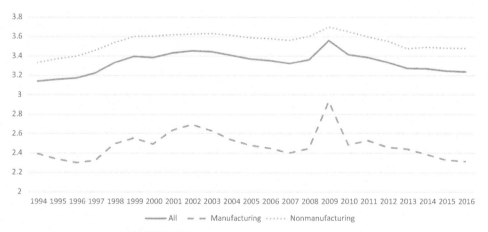

FIGURE 13.1 Capital–output (K/Y) ratio: Japan.

[2] We do not use the JIP data because its database covers the period from 1970 to 2012. When we split an industry in the JSNA into multiple industries from 2013 to 2015 by using the share of capital in the JIP database, we use the average share in the JIP database from 2010 to 2012.

[3] Specifically, we assume a depreciation rate of 9.2% (vis-à-vis the 31.5% assume in EU KLEMS (2007) for computer equipment, 9.2% (vis-à-vis 11.5%) for communication equipment, and 24.7% (vis-à-vis 31.5%) for software.

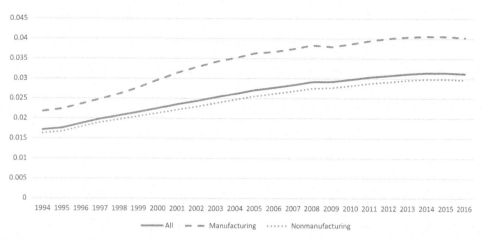

FIGURE 13.2 Intensity of information and communications technology (ICT) components in total capital (ICT/K) ratio: Japan.

capital/output ratio gradually increased in the 1990s before moving sideways in the 2000s. The spike in 2009 was due to the sharp decline in output during the Global Financial Crisis. It then gradually declined in the 2010s as Japanese firms restrained capital investment. Turning to the share of ICT capital in the total capital stock, this has steadily increased throughout the observation period. However, the share remains very low, reflecting the high rate of depreciation of ICT capital compared to other types of capital. Nevertheless, the rising trend implies that

Japanese firms have responded to the IT revolution by increasing their investment in technology.

Figs. 13.3 and 13.4 show developments in the capital/output ratio and the share of ICT capital stock in the total capital stock in Korea. The capital/output ratio increased gradually in the 1990s and continued to rise in the 2000s, which differs from the trend in Japan. The capital/output ratio of the nonmanufacturing sector is higher than that of the manufacturing sector. However, the share of ICT capital in total capital

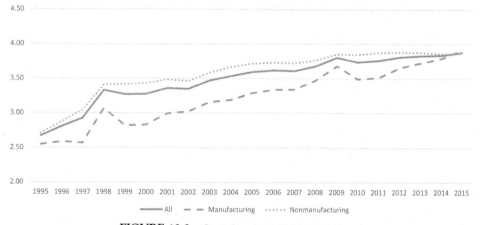

FIGURE 13.3 Capital–output (K/Y) ratio: Korea.

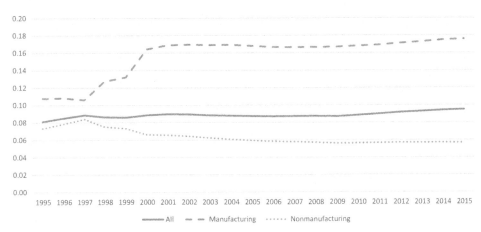

FIGURE 13.4 Intensity of information and communications technology (ICT) components in total capital (ICT/K) ratio: Korea.

is higher in manufacturing than in nonmanufacturing, as observed in the data for Japan. However, the difference between the shares in Korea is much larger than in Japan.

13.3.2 Estimation results of the wage share equations

13.3.2.1 Estimation results for Japan

Table 13.3 shows the estimation results of the wage share equations for Japan for the period 1979–2000. First, we use ordinary least squares (OLS) for the estimation. We also use fixed effects (FE) in order to control heterogeneity among industries.[4] The OLS for all industries show that capital and labor are complementary in the case of middle- and low-skilled workers. On the other hand, in nonmanufacturing industries, capital and labor are substitutes in the case of low-skilled workers. For manufacturing industries, we find that capital and labor are substitutes in the case of high-skilled workers but complements in the case of low-skilled workers. Next, the coefficients on the intensity of ICT components in total capital (ICT/K) ratio for all

industries are positive and significant for middle- and low-skilled workers, which indicates that ICT and middle- and low-skilled labor are complement to each other. This finding is the main difference between our results and O'Mahony et al.'s (2008) as shown in Table 13.7. For nonmanufacturing industries, we find that ICT and high- and low-skilled workers are substitutes. Unfortunately, our estimation results in this period are not consistent with hypothesis induced from the model. We think that the technological progress in this period is different from the current ICT technologies. Koike (1991) pointed out that the advanced technologies are factory or establishment based. Our estimation results show that these technologies are supported by middle-skilled or low-skilled labors in the factories or establishments.

The lower part of Table 13.3 shows the results of the FE estimates. For all industries, we find that capital and high-skilled workers are substitutes, while capital and middle- and low-skilled workers are complements. Next, the results for the ICT/K ratio indicate that this has a positive impact on the wage share of

---

[4] We assume here that technology is exogenous.

TABLE 13.3 Estimation of wage share equations for Japan, 1979–2000.

	All industries				Manufacturing				Nonmanufacturing		
	High	Middle	Low		High	Middle	Low		High	Middle	Low
OLS											
K/Y	0.000	0.009**	0.192***	K/Y	−0.007***	0.001	0.682***	K/Y	−0.007	0.015***	−0.017***
	(0.004)	(0.004)	(0.021)		(0.005)	(0.002)	(0.046)		(0.007)	(0.005)	(0.006)
ICT/K	0.000	0.025***	0.026*	ICT/K	0.030	−0.002	−0.009	ICT/K	−0.010**	0.035***	−0.022***
	(0.003)	(0.003)	(0.015)		(0.004)	(0.002)	(0.036)		(0.005)	(0.004)	(0.004)
Year dummies	Yes	Yes	Yes	Year dummies	Yes	Yes	Yes	Year dummies	Yes	Yes	Yes
R2	0.0873	0.2318	0.1544	R2	0.3285	0.7735	0.4463	R2	0.0741	0.2174	0.2511
Obs.	815	815	815	obs.	397	397	397	obs.	418	418	418
Fixed effect											
K/Y	−0.010***	0.008**	0.784***	K/Y	−0.008***	0.015***	1.039***	K/Y	−0.019***	0.027***	0.065***
	(0.001)	(0.003)	(0.038)		(0.001)	(0.003)	(0.062)		(0.003)	(0.007)	(0.007)
ICT/K	0.006***	−0.006	0.043	ICT/K	−0.012***	0.017***	−0.069	ICT/K	0.013***	−0.020***	0.045***
	(0.002)	(0.005)	(0.056)		(0.002)	(0.006)	(0.136)		(0.003)	(0.006)	(0.006)
Year dummies	Yes	Yes	Yes	Year dummies	Yes	Yes	Yes	Year dummies	Yes	Yes	Yes
Obs.	815	815	815	obs.	397	397	397	obs.	418	418	418

high-skilled workers in all industries and the wage share of high- and low-skilled workers in nonmanufacturing industries. This result is similar to Sakurai (2001). Sakurai (2001) examines the effects of skill-biased technical change on the wage structure using Japanese industry-level data. From cross-sectional regressions of the wage share equation developed by Berman et al. (1994), he shows that computer investment contributed to the increase in the wage share of nonproduction workers in all industries.

Table 13.4 shows the estimation results of the wage share equations for Japan for the period 1995–2015. Although the results are diverse in both OLS and FE estimates, the coefficients on the K/Y ratio of low-skilled workers are negative and significant in all estimates. This may

show that capital and low-skilled labor are substitutes (i.e., low-skilled workers are replaced by automation). Looking at the link between ICT and labor by skill category, we find that the coefficients are negative and significant for middle-skilled workers, and that the coefficient is particularly large in the case of nonmanufacturing industries. This implies that there is a negative correlation between the level of installed ICT capital and the labor cost share of middle-skilled workers. On the other hand, capital and labor are complementary in the case of high-skilled workers. In manufacturing industries, the ICT/K ratio has a negative impact on the wage share of low-skilled workers, which implies low-skilled workers are replaced by ICT investment.

TABLE 13.4 Estimation of wage share equations for Japan, 1995–2015.

	All industries				Manufacturing				Nonmanufacturing		
	High	Middle	Low		High	Middle	Low		High	Middle	Low
OLS											
K/Y	0.044***	−0.035***	−0.009***	K/Y	0.018**	−0.010	−0.009**	K/Y	0.090***	−0.068***	−0.022
	(0.006)	(0.005)	(0.002)		(0.009)	(0.007)	(0.003)		(0.010)	(0.009)	(0.004)
ICT/K	0.071***	−0.047***	−0.024***	ICT/K	0.045***	−0.030***	−0.016***	ICT/K	0.110***	−0.075***	−0.035
	(0.004)	(0.004)	(0.002)		(0.004)	(0.003)	(0.002)		(0.008)	(0.007)	(0.003)
Year dummies	Yes	Yes	Yes	Year dummies	Yes	Yes	Yes	Year dummies	Yes	Yes	Yes
R2	0.2969	0.1731	0.4564	R2	0.3439	0.1815	0.6909	R2	0.3844	0.2514	0.4153
Obs.	798	798	798	obs.	399	399	399	obs.	399	399	399
Fixed effect											
K/Y	−0.036***	0.060***	−0.023***	K/Y	−0.048***	0.062***	−0.014***	K/Y	−0.005	0.059***	−0.054
	(0.005)	(0.006)	(0.004)		(0.007)	(0.008)	(0.004)		(0.007)	(0.012)	(0.007)
ICT/K	0.003	−0.007	0.004	ICT/K	−0.005	0.015	−0.010**	ICT/K	0.012**	−0.032***	0.019
	(0.004)	(0.006)	(0.004)		(0.010)	(0.011)	(0.005)		(0.005)	(0.008)	(0.005)
Year dummies	Yes	Yes	Yes	Year dummies	Yes	Yes	Yes	Year dummies	Yes	Yes	Yes
Obs.	798	798	798	obs.	399	399	399	obs.	399	399	399

Summarizing our results for Japan, we find a polarization in favor of high and low skills and against medium skills in nonmanufacturing industries after 1995. The demand for labor with middle-skills has been decreasing in nonmanufacturing industries. Further, from the results after 1995, we also find a demand shift from unskilled to skilled workers caused by the skill-biased technical change associated with the introduction of ICT capital in manufacturing industries.

13.3.2.2 Estimation results for Korea

The estimation results for Korea are shown in Tables 13.5 and 13.6. Table 13.5 presents the results of estimating wage share equations for the period 1979–2000 in order to allow comparisons

with O'Mahony et al. (2008). First, the effect of higher capital–output ratio (K/Y) shows an insignificant almost zero effect on the wage share of higher skilled labor, implying that there exists neither substitutability nor complementarity effect. However, it shows a statistically significant substitutability effect on the medium-aged subgroup (30–49) of the medium-skilled group, implying that in this subgroup, a higher capital–output ratio has produced a negative effect on their wage share. On the other hand, the higher capital–output ratio has produced a positive substitutability effect on the wage share of unskilled labor, as in the case of the United States and the United Kingdom in O'Mahony et al. (2008) as shown in Table 13.7. The effect of the increase in the ICT/K has produced a significant

TABLE 13.5 Estimation of wage share equations for Korea, 1979–2000.

	High	Mid1 (15–29 years)	Mid2 (30–49 years)	Mid3 (50 years and over)	Low
K/Y	0.000	0.000	−0.004***	0.000	0.003
	(−0.001)	(0.000)	(−0.001)	(0.000)	(−0.001)
ICT/K	0.151***	−0.017	0.015	−0.035***	−0.113
	(−0.054)	(−0.023)	(−0.038)	(−0.009)	(−0.061)
Year dummies	Yes	Yes	Yes	Yes	Yes
R2	0.52	0.59	0.54	0.48	0.65
Obs.	836	836	836	836	836

TABLE 13.6 Estimation of wage share equations for Korea, 1995–2015.

	High	Mid1 (15–29 years)	Mid2 (30–49 years)	Mid3 (50 over)	Low
K/Y	−0.003***	0.002***	0	0	0.001**
	(−0.001)	(0.000)	(0.000)	(0.000)	(0.000)
ICT/K	0.03	−0.061***	0.061***	0.044***	−0.074***
	(−0.023)	(−0.011)	(−0.017)	(−0.012)	(−0.017)
Year dummies	Yes	Yes	Yes	Yes	Yes
R2	0.81	0.85	0.41	0.69	0.75
Obs.	798	798	798	798	798

positive effect on higher skilled wages, implying capital-skill complementarity, as observed in O'Mahony et al. (2008). However, it has produced an insignificant negative effect on lower skilled wages, implying that the higher ICT capital intensity has produced a substitution effect on low-skilled group workers. It is interesting to note that its effect on the medium-skilled group is significantly negative, suggesting that it has produced a substitution effect on medium-skill group 3 (50 and over). O'Mahony et al. (2008) also report mixed effects of ICT capital intensity on the wage shares of the intermediate-skilled groups in the estimates of the United States and France as shown in Table 13.7.

Table 13.6 reports the estimation results of the wage share equations for the period 1995–2015, which includes the period from 1995 to 99, when investment in ICT boomed period, the downturn in ICT investments from 2000 to 03, and the Global Financial Crisis of 2007–08. The effect of higher capital–output ratio (K/Y) has produced a negative dampening effect on the wage share of the high-skilled group, which contradicts the finding of O'Mahony et al. (2008), but a significant positive effect on the wage shares of the low-skilled group, which is

TABLE 13.7 Japan results, Korea results, and O'Mahony et al. (2008) results.

(1)

Japan

	High	Middle	Low
K/Y	-0.010***	0.008**	0.784***
	(0.001)	(0.003)	(0.038)
ICT/K	0.006***	-0.006	0.043
	(0.002)	(0.005)	(0.056)

(2)

Korea

	High	Mid1 (15–29 years)	Mid2 (30–49 years)	Mid3 (50 years and over)	Low
K/Y	0.000	0.000	-0.004***	0.000	0.003
	(-0.001)	(0.000)	(-0.001)	(0.000)	(-0.001)
ICT/K	0.151***	-0.017	0.015	-0.035***	-0.113
	(-0.054)	(-0.023)	(-0.038)	(-0.009)	(-0.061)

(3)

United States (O'Mahony et al., 2008)

	High	Intermediate			Unskilled
		Associate	Some college	High school	
K/Y	0.089*	-0.013*	-0.000	-0.113*	0.037*
	(-0.006)	(-0.001)	(-0.004)	(-0.006)	(-0.003)
ICT/K	0.013*	0.006*	0.008*	-0.004*	-0.023*
	(-0.001)	(0.000)	(-0.001)	(-0.002)	(-0.001)

United Kingdom (O'Mahony et al., 2008)

	High	Intermediate			Unskilled
		NVQ4	NVQ3	NVQ1-2	
K/Y	0.040*	-0.007*	-0.049*	-0.059*	0.076*
	(-0.007)	(-0.003)	(-0.009)	(-0.007)	(-0.011)
ICT/K	0.015*	0.008*	0.021*	0.008*	-0.052*
	(-0.002)	(-0.001)	(-0.003)	(-0.002)	(-0.003)

France (O'Mahony et al., 2008)

	High	Intermediate				Unskilled
		BC2	BC	Vocs	Geds	
K/Y	0.048*	0.052*	-0.023*	-0.051*	-0.013*	-0.012*
	(-0.004)	(-0.004)	(-0.004)	(-0.005)	(-0.003)	(-0.006)
ICT/K	0.002	0.034*	-0.005	0.037*	-0.003	-0.066*
	(-0.004)	(-0.003)	(-0.004)	(-0.004)	(-0.002)	(-0.005)

Note: Column (1) shows the FE results for Japan for the period 1979–2000, shown in Table 13.3. Column (2) shows the OLS results for Korea for period 1979–2000, shown in Table 13.5. Column (3) shows Table 2 in O'Mahony et al. (2008).

consistent with O'Mahony et al. (2008) as shown in Table 13.7. On the other hand, the effect of higher ICT intensity has produced an insignificant positive effect on higher skilled wages, implying a weak technology-skill complementarity, and a significant negative effect on the low-skilled group's wage shares, implying a strong technology-skill substitutability. However, its effect on the intermediate-skilled groups' wage shares are mixed, with a positive effect on medium-skilled group 2 (30−49 years) and group 3 (50 and over) but a negative effect on medium-skilled group 1 (15−29 years). Therefore, our estimates of the effect of the ICT intensity on wage shares are in general consistent with O'Mahony et al. (2008), in the sense that we find both capital-skill complementarity and technology-skill substitutability in lower skilled groups' wage shares in the Korean economy during the later period of 1995−2015.

13.4 Conclusion

In this chapter, we attempted to provide further evidence on the conflicting views on the effect of ICT investment on employment. The empirical results of the fixed effect estimates for Japan indicate that capital and high-skilled workers are substitutes, while capital and middle- and low-skilled workers are complements. The accumulation of capital increased the demand for middle and low-skilled labor in the period 1979−2000 in Japan.

The ICT/K ratio has a positive impact on the wage share of high-skilled workers in all industries and the wage share of high and low-skilled workers in manufacturing industries. The effect of higher capital−output ratio (K/Y) has produced a negative dampening effect on the wage share of the high-skilled group, which contradicts the finding of O'Mahony et al. (2008), but a significant positive effect on the wage shares of the low-skilled group, which is consistent with O'Mahony et al. (2008).

As for the relationship between technology (ICT) and skill in Japan, we find that the coefficients of middle-skilled workers are negative and significant, especially in nonmanufacturing industries in Japan. This implies that there is a negative correlation between the level of installed ICT capital and the labor cost share for middle-skilled workers. Our estimates of the effect of the ICT intensity on wage shares are in general consistent with O'Mahony et al. (2008), in the sense that we find both capital-skill complementarity and technology-skill substitutability in lower skilled groups' wage shares in the Korean economy during the later period of 1995−2015.

The empirical results for Korea show a statistically significant substitutability effect of higher capital−output ratio on the wage share of medium-aged subgroup (30−49) of the medium-skilled group, implying that in this subgroup, a higher capital−output ratio has produced a negative effect on their wage share. On the other hand, the higher capital−output ratio has produced a positive substitutability effect on the wage share of unskilled labor, as in the case of the United States and the United Kingdom in O'Mahony et al. (2008). The effect of the increase in the ICT/K has produced a significant positive effect on higher skilled wages, implying capital-skill complementarity, as observed in O'Mahony et al. (2008). However, it has produced an insignificant negative effect on lower skilled wages, implying that the higher ICT capital intensity has produced a substitutability effect on low-skilled group workers. On the other hand, it is interesting to note that its effect on the medium-skilled group is significantly negative, suggesting that it has produced a substitutability effect on medium-skill group 3 (50 and over). O'Mahony et al. (2008) also report mixed effects in the intermediate-skilled groups in the estimates of the United States and France.

For the period 1995−2015 in Korea, which includes a high ICT boom period (1995−99), a downturn in ICT investments from 2000 to 03, and the Global Financial Crisis of 2007—08, the effect of higher capital—output ratio (K/Y) has produced a negative dampening effect on the wage share of the high-skilled group. It contradicts with the finding of O'Mahony et al. (2008), but a significant positive effect on the wage shares of the low-skilled group, which is consistent with O'Mahony et al. (2008). On the other hand, the effect of higher ICT intensity has produced an insignificant positive effect on higher skilled wages, implying technology-skill complementarity, and a significant negative effect on the low-skilled group's wage shares, implying technology-skill substitutability. However, its effect on the intermediate-skilled groups' wage shares is mixed, with a positive effect on medium-skilled group 2 (30—49 years) and group 3 (50 and over) but a negative effect on medium-skilled group 1 (15—29 years). Therefore, our estimates of the effect of the ICT intensity on wage shares in Korea are in general consistent with O'Mahony et al. (2008), in the sense that we find capital-skill complementarity and technology-skill substitutability in the Korean economy during the later period of 1995—2015.

Appendix: industry classification

Code	Industry
1	Agriculture, forestry, and fishing
2	Mining and quarrying
3	Food, beverages, and tobacco products
4	Textile and leather products
5	Wood and paper products, printing and reproduction of recorded media
6	Petroleum and coal products
7	Chemicals and chemical products
8	Pharmaceutical products
9	Rubber and plastics product
10	Nonmetallic mineral products
11	Basic metal products
12	Fabricated metal products
13	Electronic components
14	Computers and peripheral equipment
15	Communication equipment
16	Precision instruments
17	Electrical equipment
18	Machinery and equipment
19	Motor vehicles, trailers, and semitrailers
20	Other transport equipment
21	Other manufactured products and outsourcing
22	Electricity, gas, and water supply
23	Water supply, waste management, and remediation activities
24	Construction
25	Wholesale and retail trade
26	Transportation and storage
27	Restaurants and hotels
28	Publishing, broadcasting, movies, information services
29	Telecommunication
30	IT and other information services
31	Finance and insurance
32	Real estate and leasing
33	Professional, scientific, and technical services
34	Business support services
35	Public administration and defense
36	Education
37	Health and social work
38	Cultural and other services

References

Antràs P: Is the U.S. aggregate production function Cobb-Douglas? New estimates of the elasticity of substitution, *Contributions to Macroeconomics* 4(1), 2004. https://doi.org/10.2202/1534-6005.1161.

Autor D, Levy F, Murnane RJ: The skill content of recent technological change: an empirical exploration, *Quarterly Journal of Economics* 118(4):1279–1333, 2003.

Berman E, Bound J, Griliches Z: Change in the demand for skilled labor within U.S. manufacturing: evidence from the Annual survey of manufacturers, *Quarterly Journal of Economics* 109(2):367–397, 1994.

Brynjolfsson E: The productivity paradox of information technology, *Communication of the ACM* 36(12):66–77, 1993.

Chun H: Information technology and the demand for educated workers: disentangling the impacts of adoption versus use, *The Review of Economics and Statistics* 85(1):1–8, 2003.

Elsby MWL, Hobijn B, Sahin A: The decline of the U.S. labor share, *Brookings Papers on Economic Activity* 47(2):1–63, 2013.

EU KLEMS: *EU KLEMS growth and productivity accounts, Version 1.0, Part I Methodology*, 2007.

Fukao K, Miyagawa T, Pyo H, Rhee K: Estimates of total factor productivity, the contribution of ICT, and resource allocation effects in Japan and Korea. In Mas M, R Stehrer R, editors: *Industrial productivity in Europe: growth and crisis*, Northampton, MA, 2012, Edward Elgar, pp 264–305.

Goos M, Manning A: Lousy and lovely jobs: the rising polarization of work in Britain, *The Review of Economics and Statistics* 89(1):118–133, 2007.

Ikenaga T: Rodo shijo no nikyokuka: IT no donyu to gyomu naiyo no henka ni tsuite [Polarization of the Japanese labor market: the adoption of IT and changes in task contents], *The Japanese Journal of Labour studies* 584:73–90, 2009.

Ikenaga T, Kambayashi R: Task polarization in the Japanese labor market: evidence of a long-term trend, *Industrial Relations* 55(2):267–293, 2016.

Karabarbounis L, Neiman B: *The global decline of the labor share*, NBER. Working Paper No. 19136.

Koike K: *Shigoto no keizaigaku [Economics of tasks]*, Tokyo, 1991, Toyo Keizai Shinposha (in Japanese.

Korea Productivity Center: *International comparison of total factor productivity*, Seoul, 2017, Korea Productivity Center (in Korean.

Machin S, Van Reenen J: Technology and changes in skill structure: evidence from seven OECD countries, *Quarterly Journal of Economics* 113(4):1215–1244, 1998.

Michaels G, Natraj A, Van Reenen J: Has ICT polarized skill demand? Evidence from eleven countries over 25 years, *The Review of Economics and Statistics* 96(1):60–77, 2014.

OECD: *Measuring capital – OECD manual 2009*, ed 3, Paris, 2009, OECD Publishing.

O'Mahony M, Robinson C, Vecchi M: The impact of ICT on the demand for skilled labour: a cross-country comparison, *Labour Economics* 15:1435–1450, 2008.

Pyo Hak K: Chapter 23 Productivity and economic development. In Tatje E, Lovell K, Sickles R, editors: *Oxford handbook of productivity analysis*, London, 2018, Oxford University Press, Edward Elgar.

Sakurai K: Biased technological change and Japanese manufacturing employment, *Journal of the Japanese and International Economies* 15:298–322, 2001.

Solow R: We'd better watch out. In Cohen SS, Zysman J, editors: *New York Times book review on* The myth of the post-industrial economy, New York, July 12, 1987, Basic Books.

Spieza V, Polder M, Presidente G: *ICTs and jobs: complements or substitutes? The effects of ICT investment on labour demand by skills and by industry in selected OECD countries*, OECD report for the working party on measurement and analysis of the digital economy, 2016.

Spitz-Oener A: Technical change, job tasks, and rising educational demands: looking outside the wage structure, *Journal of Labor Economics* 24(2):235–270, 2006.

Economic valuation of knowledge-based capital: an International comparison

Matilde Mas[1], André Hofman[2], Eva Benages[3]

[1]University of Valencia and Ivie, Valencia, Spain; [2]University of Santiago de Chile, Santiago, Chile; [3]Ivie and University of Valencia, Valencia, Spain

14.1 Introduction

Knowledge economy is the term applied to describe an economy where a considerable share of production is based on accumulated knowledge. Despite this term being frequently used, there is no metric that accurately measures how much economic value stems from knowledge. The most widely used approach classifies productive activities into several categories according to technological intensity, usually on the basis of R&D expenditure or high-skilled labor.[1] Calculations are then made on the percentage that these activities represent in total employment or production.

It is clear that knowledge is generated and disseminated by educated and intelligent individuals. However, it is not only our discoveries of today that matter but the knowledge accumulated by humanity over time. Thus, when measuring the weight of knowledge in the production of goods or services, we should concentrate not only on current discoveries but on all human capital used in the process, both directly and indirectly, i.e., including that which has been incorporated into capital goods and intermediate products.

There are three important limitations regarding conventional measures of knowledge intensity. The first is that it focuses on the current creation of knowledge rather than how the productive system uses it, which is crucial to analyzing certain problems. The second is that it uses classifications of knowledge intensity in activities based on a single factor: R&D expenditure in the case of manufacturing, and human capital with higher education in services industries. Knowledge, however, is incorporated into production through various channels: qualified labor in general, some capital assets, and

---

[1] See, for example, the definition of KIS (Knowledge Intensive Services) and HTech (High Technology Manufacturing) or KIA classification (Knowledge Intensive Activities), which are used by Eurostat (2013). OECD (2015) uses these classifications as well. See also Tradecan (Trade Competitive Analysis of Nations) methodology, which was developed in 1990 by the Economic Commission for Latin America and the Caribbean (ECLAC).

intermediate inputs. The weight that each of these carries in industries is different, and, therefore, classifying activities based on a single criterion could bias the results. The third major limitation is that the incorporation of knowledge varies from one country to another within the same industry. The reality is that knowledge is (more or less) present in all industries and not only in those defined as high or medium technology in the usual classifications, which in turn have different degrees of knowledge intensity by country.

Other studies examine the knowledge economy through a set of indicators which includes several profiles of the presence of knowledge in productive activities. In some cases, synthetic indices of the development of knowledge—both in the economic system and society—are elaborated, including multiple variables which are aggregated according to statistical criteria or ad hoc weights. However, many of these indices are usually partial[2] and have an ambiguous meaning, given that they are not derived from a metric based on clear definitions and evaluation criteria, nor on a precise structure of relationships between variables. In this sense, business accounting and the system of national accounts have advantages for the aggregation, which is based on the relative prices of goods or factors.

This chapter explores whether it is possible to assess the intensity with which knowledge is used—not its generation or creation—within economies by means of a methodology that is integrated into the conceptual schema, measurement criteria, and information systems of national accounts. To answer this question, we can take two different approaches: the development of *knowledge satellite accounts*, and the development of *knowledge accounting*.

Regarding the first option, the complexity and data requirements of satellite accounts are considerable, given that they aspire to build an integrated system that quantifies all dimensions and elements present in the dynamics of a knowledge-based economy. Because of that, although some official statistics institutes have taken preliminary steps in developing such knowledge satellite accounts,[3] they are not available for the majority of countries.

The second alternative takes advantage of the important theoretical and empirical advances achieved in the measurement of physical and human capital.[4] We have chosen to go in this direction, proposing to measure the weight of knowledge in GDP by calculating the market value of a set of knowledge-based inputs which are incorporated in the production processes. The idea is to assess the contribution of these knowledge-based inputs to the GDP generation and obtain a measure of what we have called *knowledge-based GDP*. The cornerstone of this approach is the analytical structure of *growth accounting*, which allows us to differentiate the value of various types of physical and human capital service inputs and their contribution to GDP growth. This methodology was initially proposed by Pérez and Benages (2012) and applied to all the European countries included in the EU KLEMS database. Maudos et al. (2017) updated and expanded this methodology

---

[2] Some examples are the KEI and KAM indicators published by the World Bank (see Chen and Dahlman (2006) and World Bank (2008a, 2008b) for more details) or the Digital Economy and Society Index (DESI) developed by the European Commission (see more details at: https://ec.europa.eu/digital-single-market/en/desi). All of them take into account different economic and social dimensions to measure the development of the knowledge economy, but exclude some important areas, such as physical capital endowments, institutional characteristics of the labor markets, etc., which may be relevant.

[3] See de Haan and van Rooijen-Horsten (2003) and van Rooijen-Horsten et al. (2008).

[4] See Jorgenson et al. (1987).

applying it to the Spanish regions for which KLEMS-type data are available. And Mas et al. (2019) revised and extended it to a set of four Latin-American countries.

The proposed methodology, described in detail in the next section, can be applied today to those economies whose national accounts systems offer industry data on various types of labor and capital services and their corresponding compensation. Databases that allow these estimates to be carried out have been created and harmonized by projects developed within the framework of WORLD KLEMS, devoted to examining productivity and sources of economic growth.[5] In our case, we will make use of two recently released databases. The first is LA KLEMS (http://laklems.net/), containing information for four Latin-American countries: Brazil, Chile, Colombia, and Mexico. From the recently updated version of EU KLEMS (http://euklems.net/) we take the information for the big five EU countries: France, Germany, Italy, Spain, and the United Kingdom. The information for the United States and Canada stems mainly from the USA KLEMS and Canada KLEMS databases (both available at http://www.worldklems.net/data.htm), although information from BLS (Bureau of Labor Statistics), BEA (Bureau of Economic Analysis), and Statistics Canada is also used to update and supplement these two databases, when necessary.

There are many questions we are interested in answering in this study. Is the value added generated by the factors of production incorporating knowledge high enough to speak of *knowledge economies*? What differences can we observe in the weight of knowledge among industries and among countries? What is the time evolution of knowledge intensity by industry and by economy? Do activities and countries converge in knowledge intensity?

To address these issues, the chapter is structured as follows. Section 14.2 explores the methodological approach adopted in the context of related economic literature, while Section 14.3 revises the statistical data, their sources, and coverage. Section 14.4 presents the results at the aggregate level, whereas Section 14.5 presents them for the nine industries for which information is available. Finally, Section 14.6 sets out the main conclusions.

14.2 Calculating knowledge intensity: methodological approach

The most widely used approach for measuring knowledge intensity in economies is based on classifying manufacturing industries according to technology intensity—measured by the weight of R&D expenditure in relation to GDP—and services industries according to the use of human capital—measured by the percentage of staff with higher education.[6] The first one, the weight of R&D, responds better to the objective of analyzing the intensity in which knowledge is created rather than how much knowledge is used. In fact, the classification of manufacturing according to technological intensity was conceived for another purpose: to assess the origin of exogenous technological progress and its role in growth and competitiveness. The focus on R&D activities is justified since technology-intensive companies and industries show a high innovative and commercial dynamism and are especially productive.[7]

It is clear that R&D activities play a key role in generating knowledge. This knowledge is incor-

---

[5] See http://www.worldklems.net/.

[6] See Eurostat (2013) and OECD (2015).

[7] See Hatzichoronoglou (1997)

porated in the capital assets used in the production process. Machinery and other capital goods are the key vehicles for the use of knowledge. These capital goods are previously produced incorporating the knowledge used in their own production process and are almost always intensive in human capital and in the use of other machinery. The same can be said of some intermediate products, although the degree in which they incorporate knowledge varies to a greater extent than in the case of machinery.

Since our objective is to measure the weight of knowledge used in current production, we should not concentrate solely on the discoveries of today but rather on all the knowledge accumulated in capital assets throughout time. It is not a question of *measuring knowledge* but rather which part of the economic value of production remunerates the knowledge accumulated in the used inputs.

The refinement provided by the concept of productive capital offers a greater precision for measuring capital services and allows us to approximate the accounting of knowledge incorporated in the capital stock. Other analytical and statistical improvements in the methodology for measuring assets and their productive services are a consequence of a greater accuracy in aggregation procedures, using Tornqvist indices.[8] On account of these developments, an improved analysis is now available using sources of growth as well as key variables to estimate the value of production of assets incorporating knowledge. Developments currently underway

extend the capital assets to take into account the contribution of intangible assets, many of which are also the result of knowledge accumulated by companies and their organizations.[9] A more accurate measurement of physical and human capital services better assesses the knowledge incorporated in the factors and reduces the weight of the Solow residual.[10] These advances in growth accounting illustrate that, when the contributions of productive factors are measured more precisely, incorporated knowledge is more relevant than total factor productivity when explaining improvements in labor productivity.[11]

The methodological and statistical framework of advanced versions of *growth accounting* offers an appropriate scheme to build an *accounting of the use of knowledge in production*. We can consider that knowledge is incorporated into production through the use of different kinds of labor, capital, and intermediate inputs. However, to simplify the presentation of the methodology, and relate it to subsequent empirical findings, we only show the case in which the measurement of the product is gross domestic product (GDP) or gross value added (GVA), although the approach will be replicable in similar terms to the case of total production. Thus, we do not consider knowledge incorporated into intermediate inputs, but only content in primary inputs, labor, and capital. Taking this into account, to assess the contribution of productive factors based on knowledge, first we have to identify which factors contain knowledge, measure the

---

[8] See Jorgenson et al. (1987) and OECD (2009, 2001).

[9] See Corrado et al. (2017, 2013, 2006), Fukao et al. (2007), Hulten (2008), Marrano and Haskel (2006), Marrano et al. (2007), and Van Ark and Hulten (2007). From our work's perspective, the services of intangible assets increase the value added generated but the income they yield could be allocated to the heart of the organizations, both to the owners of capital and labor. It is because these assets, by their nature, do not have an external market that determines their price. Therefore, their contribution can be considered to be accounted through the remuneration of other factors.

[10] See Solow (1957, 1956).

[11] See Aravena et al. (2018), Coremberg and Pérez (2010), Oulton (2016), and Pérez and Benages (2017) on how a more accurate measurement of productive factors impacts total factor productivity.

amount used in different activities, and value their services with appropriate prices.

From this point of view, knowledge intensity in an industry is defined as the value of the knowledge services used in relation to the value of its production. Thus, it can take any value in the interval [0,1]. Industries are therefore not classified into categories of greater or lesser intensity, avoiding the discontinuity caused by thresholds which arbitrarily separate some groups from others. However, certain arbitrariness is unavoidable when considering which assets include knowledge and which do not.

One possibility is to take a very restrictive approach and include only ICT capital (on the asset side) and only workers with the highest level of tertiary education (on the labor side) as knowledge-contributing factors. This is the approach followed in Mas et al. (2019). Here, however, we will follow Pérez and Benages (2012), taking a broader view in which knowledge-based factors are understood to include not only high-skilled but also medium-skilled workers (higher and upper secondary education), and not only ICT but all types of machinery and equipment. Low-skilled workers and real estate capital are not considered to incorporate significant knowledge and so are excluded.

As already mentioned, the knowledge intensity of an industry can take any value in the interval [0,1]. One of the implications of this is that, unlike the conventional approach, knowledge intensity in an industry is not constant over time or among countries. Another implication is that the knowledge intensity of an economy is obtained from the knowledge intensity in each of its industries, as well as from the weight of value added of each branch of activity in the aggregate GVA.

Assuming that there are m types of labor and n types of capital and some of these provide knowledge services and others do not, let L_{ij} be the amount of labor of type i used in sector j; K_{hj} the amount of capital of type h used in the same sector j; P_{ij}^L is the unitary wage paid for the labor of type i in sector j; and P_{hj}^K is the user cost of type h capital in sector j. Defining the value added in real terms produced by sector j as V_j and being P_j^V its price, the value added of sector j in nominal terms ($V_j P_j^V$, to simplify the notation, Y_j) is distributed between the different inputs included in the production process so that,

$$Y_j = V_j P_j^V = \sum_{i=1}^{m} L_{ij} * P_{ij}^L + \sum_{h=1}^{n} K_{hj} * P_{hj}^K \quad (14.1)$$

Let us assume that the price of the amount used for each type of labor depends on its productivity, and that the basis for differences in productivity is the human capital that each type contains. Under these hypotheses, wages can approximate the economic value of the amount of knowledge per unit of each type of labor. According to this criterion, we can consider that the type of labor that offers a lower wage (for workers with lower education levels) does not incorporate knowledge. While the other types of labor do incorporate knowledge, though at different rates according to the number of years or level of education. If we generalize to allow f type of low-skilled labor, the value of labor is decomposed into two parts, the second of which measures the value of human capital services:

$$\sum_{i=1}^{m} L_{ij} * P_{ij}^L = \sum_{i=1}^{f} L_{ij} * P_{ij}^L + \sum_{i=f+1}^{m} L_{ij} * P_{ij}^L \quad (14.2)$$

Thus, the value of knowledge incorporated through labor (knowledge-intensive labor, KIL) would be given by:

$$KIL_j = \sum_{i=f+1}^{m} L_{ij} * P_{ij}^L \quad (14.3)$$

The unit value of productive services providing different kinds of labor that incorporate knowledge is not the same. For example, the production services of workers with higher education are more intensive in knowledge than in the case of workers with upper secondary education. By multiplying the amount of each type of labor by its wages, knowledge intensity can be accurately calculated when the wages are a reflection of this intensity. This criterion implies that the value of knowledge that qualified workers have does not depend on education per se but rather on their experience and how it is used by the productive system in general, which is reflected in their wages.

In terms of capital, we assume that the productivity of each asset is reflected in its user cost, which is taken into account in the calculation of the productive capital. The differences in the user cost have become more relevant due to the growing importance of ICT investment, which was a key driving force behind the disaggregation of assets and the distinction between net and productive capital.[12]

The capital user cost has three components: the financial opportunity cost or rate of return, the depreciation rate resulting from the service life of the corresponding asset, and earnings or losses of capital arising from variations in its price. In the long-term, i.e., in the absence of price changes associated with the business cycle,[13] the component of the user cost that most differentiates certain assets from others is the depreciation rate, which depends on the average service life of the assets. The service life of machinery is shorter than housing or infrastructure, while that of ICT assets is shorter than the majority of machinery and transport equipment. The materials that make up the assets and, in particular, the complexity and vulnerability to obsolescence (i.e., the technology incorporated) make the economic life shorter (and depreciation faster). Assets that contain more knowledge tend to have a shorter economic life and a more intense depreciation, although there can

be exceptions to this rule. In the language of capital theory, more depreciation means greater user cost that should be offset by a greater flow per unit of time of the asset's productive services, because otherwise the decision to invest in it would not be justified.

We assume that the content of knowledge in assets increases proportionately with its user cost. We use as a starting point the hypothesis that assets with a lower user cost—produced by the construction sector—do not incorporate knowledge in a significant way. On the other hand, we can assume that machinery and equipment do, although with the relative intensity reflected by their user cost (e.g., much higher in ICT assets). As before, a more restrictive view for capital would consider that only ICT and intangible assets incorporate knowledge in the production process.

The value added generated by physical capital is broken down into two broad categories: those that do not incorporate knowledge significantly (g assets) and those that do (n-g assets):

$$\sum_{h=1}^{n} K_{hj} * P_{hj}^{K} = \sum_{h=1}^{g} K_{hj} * P_{hj}^{K} + \sum_{h=g+1}^{n} K_{hj} * P_{hj}^{K}$$

(14.4)

Then, the value of knowledge incorporated through physical assets (knowledge-intensive capital, KIK) would be given by:

$$KIK_j = \sum_{h=g+1}^{n} K_{hj} * P_{hj}^{K}$$
(14.5)

And the value of knowledge-intensive factors or value added based on knowledge (knowledge-intensive value added, Y_j^K) of activity j will therefore be:

$$Y_j^K = KIL_j + KIK_j$$
(14.6)

---

[12] See OECD (2009, 2001).

[13] See Schreyer (2009).

The relative knowledge intensity of activity j is defined as

$$Y_j^K / Y_j = [KIL_j + KIK_j]/V_j P_j^V \qquad (14.7)$$

Given the knowledge content of each industry, the knowledge intensity of an economy depends on the weight of the various branches in the aggregate. If q industries exist, the knowledge intensity of the economy as a whole (Ç) is defined as,

$$Ç = \sum_{j=1}^{q} Y_j^K / Y_j \left[Y_j \Big/ \sum_{j=1}^{q} Y_j \right] \qquad (14.8)$$

The exercises presented in Sections 14.4 and 14.5 adopt the less restrictive approach to measuring the knowledge economy presented in this section. That is, for labor they consider high- and medium-skilled workers (higher and upper secondary education) as knowledge-intensive, and for capital, ICT and machinery and equipment capital, following the spirit of the KLEMS project. It would have been interesting to include other intangible assets, besides software, which are already included in the 2008 System of National Accounts, such as R&D. However, although two LA KLEMS countries (Chile and Mexico) have released the required information, it is not yet included in the LA KLEMS database, as explained in the next section, which describes the data.

14.3 Statistical data: sources and coverage

The estimates of knowledge intensity following the methodology described previously and presented in Sections 14.4 and 14.5 are mainly based on data from KLEMS databases: LA KLEMS for the four Latin-American countries, EU KLEMS for the European countries, and USA KLEMS and Canada KLEMS for the North American countries.[14] These databases contain information by industry on variables related to productivity and economic growth: value added, output, employment and skills, gross capital formation by assets and accumulated capital, capital and labor compensation, etc. At the moment, LA KLEMS data are available for the period 1990–2015, whereas the EU KLEMS database covers the period 1995–2015. Canada and the United States offer similar time coverage for general output magnitudes as well, but the coverage varies depending on the selected variable and its detail. That is why additional sources have been used to supplement the data for these two countries. Taking all this into account, in this chapter we focus on the period 2000–15, for which data are available for most of the countries considered.

Thus, the KLEMS databases offer all the variables needed to apply the methodology outlined in Section 14.2: value added, capital compensation, and labor compensation by educational attainment level. However, there are particular problems concerning each variable that need to be solved before the described methodology can be applied. Regarding capital compensation, although previous releases of EU and USA KLEMS included a disaggregation of capital compensation by asset, recent releases include only total compensation by industry. The same is true of LA KLEMS countries and Canada. We have therefore had to estimate the capital compensation for each asset. This estimation has been made following the KLEMS method (Timmer et al., 2007) and taking as a basis the information on GFCF deflators, capital stock, and depreciation rates included in the KLEMS databases.

---

[14] For the United States and Canada, it was necessary to use additional data sources (BEA, BLS, Statistics Canada, and OECD) in order to update and supplement the KLEMS database.

TABLE 14.1   Capital assets considered for the estimation of knowledge-based GVA.

KLEMS assets
ICT assets
Software
Computing equipment
Communication equipment
Non-ICT assets
Transport equipment
Machinery and equipment (excluding ICT)
Non-residential structures
Residential structures

Source: Own elaboration.

With regard to labor-related variables, in the case of EU KLEMS data, we have had to link up labor input files from different EU KLEMS releases to construct long time series. This has been done by using data from the most recent release and extending the series further back in time using the growth rates from previous releases. Some problems arise, however, as the labor input files with detailed industry data are not fully compatible across EU KLEMS releases. This is particularly true for the United Kingdom, where additional adjustments have been required.

Labor data are classified by educational attainment, distinguishing between three levels: high, medium, and low. For our purposes, we consider that workers with high and medium education levels contribute knowledge to the production process, whereas the rest do not. In the case of physical capital, the LA KLEMS database distinguishes seven capital assets: three ICT assets and four non-ICT assets (see Table 14.1). However, the EU, Canada, and USA KLEMS

databases also include two additional intangible assets (R&D and other intellectual property products) that were included in National Accounts by ESA 2010 but are not yet included in the LA KLEMS database.[15] To make the data comparable, these intangible assets have not been considered when calculating knowledge-based GVA for the EU and North American countries; only the assets shown in Table 14.1 are included in the estimation. As stated before, ICT assets, transport equipment, and other machinery and equipment are classified as knowledge-based capital assets, whereas residential and non-residential structures are considered to have lower knowledge intensity.

Knowledge-based GVA thus includes the remuneration of highly and medium-educated workers, on the one hand, and ICT and machinery and equipment capital on the other.

As explained in Section 14.2, knowledge intensity is measured at the sectoral level. However, the industry classification of the EU and USA KLEMS databases is different from that of the Canada and LA KLEMS data. While the former have been updated according to the most recent industry classifications (ISIC Rev. 4/NACE Rev. 2), the Canada and LA KLEMS databases still follow previous classifications (based on ISIC Rev. 3.1/NACE Rev. 1). For that reason, although greater industry detail is available for some countries, only nine individual industries are considered in this chapter, in order to have a common industry classification for all the countries analyzed. Table 14.2 shows a list of these industries.

Table 14.3 provides an overview of the two sets of variables involved in the methodology presented in Section 14.2: capital and labor inputs classified by capital assets and by types of labor according to the level of educational attainment.

---

[15] Among LA KLEMS countries, only Chile and Mexico have already incorporated R&D and other intellectual property products as gross fixed capital formation (GFCF) in their official National Accounts figures.

TABLE 14.2   Industry classification (available for all countries).

Agriculture, forestry, and fishing

Mining and quarrying

Manufacturing

Electricity, gas, and water supply

Construction

Wholesale and retail trade; accommodation and food service

Transportation and communications

Financial, real state, and business services

Other services

Source: Own elaboration.

Regarding capital input, Table 14.3 shows the composition of gross fixed capital formation (capital flows) in the countries considered. Because of the variability of this variable, the table shows the average structure for the whole period analyzed (2000–15). As expected, the share of ICT investment is lowest in the Latin-American economies, around 6.5% on average. Among the other countries, in most the share is more than twice the Latin-American average. The United States has the highest share of ICT assets (19%), followed by France (16.7%), the United Kingdom (16.7%), and Italy (13.1%).

In all the countries analyzed, residential and non-residential structures are by far the largest category of capital assets, reaching a high share of 72.4% in Colombia, 22 percentage points above the country with the lowest share, the United States (50.3%). In general, except for Canada and Spain, real estate assets are more important in the Latin-American countries, whereas the European countries and the United States show lower shares, about 50%–60% of total investment. Machinery and equipment (including transport equipment) accounts for around 30% of total investment in Brazil, Mexico, Germany, Italy, and the United States, whereas its share is 10 percentage points lower in Colombia, Canada, France,

Spain, and the United Kingdom. The analysis of this structure is important because capital stock stems from the accumulation of GFCF flows. Therefore, the structure of capital stock and capital compensation in each country is determined, at least in part, by GFCF characteristics.

As expected, due to its lower base level, ICT investment has experienced a higher rate of growth than non-ICT assets in all the countries over the period 2000–15. The difference between the two is especially marked in Chile (10.3% ICT vs. 5% non-ICT) and Spain (5.6% vs. −0.8%). It seems that, in general, ICT investment grows at a higher rate in countries that have lower points of departure in terms of accumulated stock, as is the case of the Latin-American countries. The same applies to non-ICT investment. Regarding non-ICT assets, the high growth rate in Colombia (9.7%) is worth noting.

Table 14.3 also shows information about labor (in terms of total hours worked), according to the level of educational attainment (part 2 of the table). Canada and the United States have the lowest share of unskilled labor. In general, the labor structure in these two countries, and also in the EU countries, is based more on educated labor. Among LA KLEMS countries, only Chile shows a similar structure, with higher shares for high-skilled than for low-skilled workers. Nevertheless there are important differences among countries: Italy and Spain stand out for the high shares of less educated labor (33.4% and 35.3%, respectively) when compared to their European neighbors. Germany and Canada have the highest shares of medium-skilled labor (59% and 69.5%, respectively), whereas this category is much smaller in other countries, particularly in Spain (24%). Thus, the structure of labor differs among countries and these differences will play an important role in determining the intensity of the use of knowledge in the economy.

The general pattern since 2000 has been, as expected, a decrease in the share of the lower levels in favor of the other two. However, whereas in

TABLE 14.3 Descriptive Statistics.

(1) Gross fixed capital formation										
(a) GFCF structure by assets, 2000-2015[a] (%)	**USA**	**Canada**	**Brazil**	**Chile**	**Colombia**	**Mexico**	**France**	**Germany**	**Italy**	**Spain**	**UK**
ICT	**19.02**	**12.61**	**6.07**	**8.00**	**7.06**	**4.27**	**14.72**	**9.91**	**13.11**	**11.02**	**14.74**
Software	11.26	5.87	2.47	3.70	0.87	0.16	12.23	4.56	8.84	4.87	11.19
Computing equipment	3.74	3.69	1.13	2.15	1.64	1.72	1.17	3.10	2.08	2.34	2.97
Communication equipment	4.02	3.05	2.47	2.15	4.56	2.39	1.32	2.25	2.20	3.81	0.58
Non-ICT	**80.98**	**87.39**	**93.93**	**92.00**	**92.94**	**95.73**	**85.28**	**90.09**	**86.89**	**88.98**	**85.26**
Transport equipment	7.52	7.06	11.59	–	8.91	8.71	7.55	14.08	4.97	8.74	5.43
Machinery and equipment (exclusively ICT)	23.17	13.11	22.12	25.12	11.59	25.48	16.34	23.17	27.46	14.39	20.28
Nonresidential structures	26.84	36.22	32.29	43.99	46.58	32.01	30.66	22.33	25.14	31.90	36.85
Residential structures	23.45	31.01	27.93	22.90	25.86	29.54	30.73	30.51	29.31	33.95	22.70
Total	**100.00**	**100.00**	**100.00**	**100.00**	**100.00**	**100.00**	**100.00**	**100.00**	**100.00**	**100.00**	**100.00**
(b) GFCF. Average annual growth rates (2000-2015[a])	**USA**	**Canada**	**Brazil**	**Chile**	**Colombia**	**Mexico**	**France**	**Germany**	**Italy**	**Spain**	**UK**
ICT	**3.92**	**3.45**	**6.63**	**10.30**	**10.85**	**4.94**	**3.59**	**3.24**	**0.14**	**5.64**	**4.56**
Software	4.11	3.12	7.76	14.30	13.58	3.99	3.74	3.70	0.05	5.02	4.27
Computing equipment	5.84	7.83	7.63	8.06	14.25	4.10	5.63	8.03	−0.33	6.53	4.99
Communication equipment	2.09	−1.32	4.09	7.78	9.52	5.29	0.39	−0.59	0.94	6.09	7.45
Non-ICT	**0.30**	**3.27**	**4.41**	**4.98**	**9.74**	**2.18**	**0.35**	**0.25**	**−1.93**	**−0.81**	**0.59**
Transport equipment	2.98	0.21	7.91	–	11.98	4.18	0.76	1.34	−5.07	1.42	3.25
Machinery and equipment (exclusively ICT)	1.90	2.21	5.19	7.74	11.27	4.25	−0.08	1.51	−1.06	0.22	−0.57
Nonresidential structures	−0.88	3.75	3.70	5.04	8.39	0.40	0.43	−0.90	−2.86	−0.65	1.11
Residential structures	−0.85	3.81	3.18	1.48	11.35	1.82	0.40	−0.26	−1.10	−2.19	0.17
Total	**0.89**	**3.29**	**4.65**	**5.36**	**9.26**	**2.31**	**0.81**	**0.49**	**−1.68**	**−0.14**	**1.09**
(2) Labor											
(a) Labor share by level of education, 2015 (%)	**USA**	**Canada**	**Brazil**	**Chile**	**Colombia**	**Mexico**	**France**	**Germany**	**Italy**	**Spain**	**UK**
High	37.95	28.46	18.41	35.20	21.73	13.45	38.07	28.20	19.43	40.74	42.41
Medium	54.24	69.51	42.48	45.93	42.34	46.54	45.17	59.05	47.18	24.00	41.02
Low	7.81	2.04	39.12	18.87	35.93	40.01	16.76	12.75	33.40	35.26	16.56
Total	**100.00**	**100.00**	**100.00**	**100.00**	**100.00**	**100.00**	**100.00**	**100.00**	**100.00**	**100.00**	**100.00**

TABLE 14.3 Descriptive statistics.—cont'd

	(2) Labour										
(b) Labor. Average annual growth rates (2000–2015)	**USA**	**Canada**	**Brazil**	**Chile**	**Colombia**	**Mexico**	**France**	**Germany**	**Italy**	**Spain**	**UK**
High	2.11	3.39	6.78	4.25	5.92	1.03	2.84	1.53	3.31	3.32	3.66
Medium	−0.46	0.48	3.13	0.24	3.38	2.54	0.50	−0.08	0.67	1.84	0.11
Low	−1.61	−3.05	−0.74	1.54	1.57	0.20	−3.67	−1.64	−2.21	−2.34	−2.80
Total	**0.30**	**1.08**	**1.75**	**1.64**	**3.10**	**1.31**	**0.28**	**0.11**	**−0.07**	**0.48**	**0.70**

Note: In the case of Chile, transport equipment is included in machinery and equipment (exclusively ICT)
[a] 2013 for Brazil and 2014 for Colombia and Italy.
Source: Bureau of Economic Analysis (BEA): Industry economic accounts, 2018. Available at: https://www.bea.gov/data/economic-accounts/industry. Bureau of Labor Statistics (BLS): Current employment statistics (CES), 2018. Available at: https://www.bls.gov/ces/. EU KLEMS: EU KLEMS growth and productivity accounts, 2018. Available at: http://www.euklems.net/. LA KLEMS: Productividad y crecimiento económico en América Latina, 2018. Available at: https://www.cepal.org/cgi-bin/getprod.asp?xml=/la-klems/noticias/paginas/9/40269/P40269.xml&xsl=/la-klems/tpl/p18f-st.xsl&base=/la-klems/tpl/topbottom.xsl. OECD, Statistics Canada, World KLEMS and own elaboration.

the European and North American countries the proportion of less qualified labor has decreased in terms of hours worked, in Chile, Colombia, and Mexico the hours worked by this group have increased. In the majority of countries, in general, job creation is concentrated among workers with higher educational levels, who, according to the described methodology, are the main contributors to knowledge.

14.4 Knowledge intensity estimates: aggregated results

This section presents the main aggregated results of the exercises proposed in Section 14.2 for measuring the knowledge economy. Fig. 14.1 provides an overview of the knowledge economy's share of total GVA (as given by Eq. 14.8) during the 2000–15 period. Panel A shows the profiles followed by the six American countries and panel B shows the same information for the five European countries. The first conclusion that we can draw from this figure is that the

considered economies are currently extensively based on knowledge, using more than half of GVA[16] to remunerate factors which incorporate knowledge to the production process.

Within the American countries, as expected, the United States and Canada have the highest shares, slightly higher in the United States than in Canada. However, both of them show a declining trend over the period. On average, for the whole period 2000–15, in the North American countries the knowledge economy accounted for around 73% of total GVA. This figure contrasts with the share of the knowledge economy in the four Latin-American countries. Chile has by far the highest share, averaging around 63%, but with a very volatile profile. From the start of the great recession the share of the knowledge economy in Chile increased and by the end of the period was approaching the level of the United States and Canada (if we exclude the slight decline in 2015). Of the other three Latin-American countries, Brazil used to be the one with the highest share, but its position worsened from 2008 onward. Mexico

[16] The only exception is Colombia, but its knowledge-based GVA accounts for 46% of total GVA.

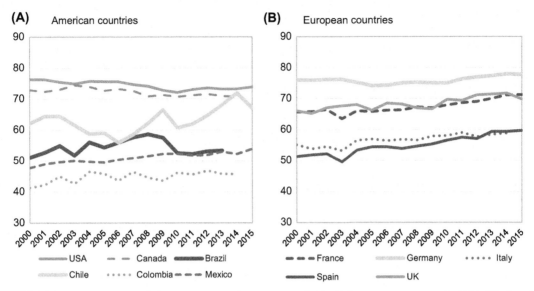

FIGURE 14.1 Knowledge-based GVA. International comparison, 2000–15 (percentage over total GVA). (A) American countries. (B) European countries. *Source: Bureau of Economic Analysis (BEA): Industry economic accounts, 2018. Available at: https://www.bea.gov/data/economic-accounts/industry. Bureau of Labor Statistics (BLS): Current employment statistics (CES), 2018. Available at: https://www.bls.gov/ces/. EU KLEMS: EU KLEMS growth and productivity accounts, 2018. Available at: http://www. euklems.net/. LA KLEMS: Productividad y crecimiento económico en América Latina, 2018. Available at: https://www.cepal.org/cgi-bin/getprod.asp?xml=/la-klems/noticias/paginas/9/40269/P40269.xml&xsl=/la-klems/tpl/p18f-st.xsl&base=/la-klems/tpl/top-bottom.xsl. World KLEMS, Statistics Canada and own elaboration.*

follows, with a share close to 55% and a rising profile, while the knowledge economy's share of total GVA was lowest in Colombia, which also shows only a weak tendency toward improvement.

Of the five European countries (Fig. 14.1, panel B), Germany leads, outperforming even the United States, with a knowledge economy that accounts for close to 80% of total GVA and a stable or even slightly increasing tendency. The other four countries have lower shares than the two North American countries and are clustered in two groups. France and the United Kingdom share a common pattern, showing a positive trend and with shares close to 70% by the end of the period. Italy and Spain form the second cluster, with the knowledge economy

likewise increasing its share of GVA, approaching a lower value of around 60% by the end of the period.

Fig. 14.2 summarizes the position of the 11 countries, at the beginning and at the end of the period, in terms of the knowledge economy's share of total GVA. The following comments are in order. At the beginning of the period the two North American countries and Germany had the highest share, with the United States taking the lead. The United Kingdom and France followed. Already in 2000 Chile held sixth place in the ranking, ahead of Italy and Spain, which ranked last among the five European countries. The last places were taken by Brazil, Mexico, and Colombia. In that year, the distance between the leader, the United States, and the country

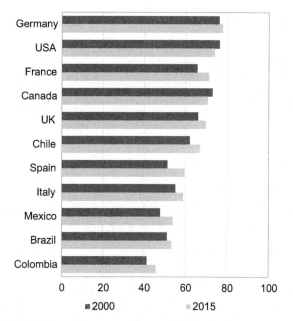

FIGURE 14.2 Knowledge-based GVA. International comparison, 2000 and 2015 (percentage over total GVA). Note: Countries are ranked according to Knowledge-GVA share in 2015. 2013 is the last available year in the case of Brazil and 2014 in the case of Colombia, Canada, and Italy. *Source: BEA, EU KLEMS: EU KLEMS growth and productivity accounts, 2018. Available at: http://www.euklems.net/. LA KLEMS: Productividad y crecimiento económico en América Latina, 2018. Available at: https://www.cepal.org/cgi-bin/getprod. asp?xml=/la-klems/noticias/paginas/9/40269/P40269.xml&xsl=/ la-klems/tpl/p18f-st.xsl&base=/la-klems/tpl/top-bottom.xsl. Statistics Canada, World KLEMS and own elaboration.*

at the bottom of the ranking, Colombia, reached 35 percentage points.

Fifteen years later, in 2015, Germany was the leader, having overtaken the United States, while France had surpassed Canada, which was relegated to fourth position. The United Kingdom had dropped one place, from fourth to fifth, and Chile ranked sixth. Spain and Italy followed, but with Spain overtaking Italy, which slipped into eighth position. Mexico, Brazil, and Colombia still ranked at the bottom, but with Mexico slightly outperforming Brazil. An interesting point is that the two North American countries are the only ones to have seen a decline in the knowledge economy's share of GVA over the period. In 2015 the distance between the leader (Germany) and the country at the bottom (still Colombia) was slightly smaller than in 2000, at 32 percentage points.

Fig. 14.3 shows the dynamics of knowledge-based GVA, measured in real terms, over the 2000–15 period in the 11 countries considered. The four Latin-American countries show the fastest growth, with Colombia and Chile taking the lead, followed by Brazil and Mexico (panel A). Canada and especially the United States followed a slower path than either the four Latin-American countries or Spain, which was the most dynamic of the European countries (panel B). Even the United Kingdom and France had higher rates of growth than the United States over the period. The most sluggish growth rates are those of Germany and especially Italy, which had the slowest growth of all the 11 countries. Overall, Fig. 14.3 confirms that there was some convergence over the period, with the countries ranked lowest in 2000 growing faster than the leaders. Italy is the only exception to this general convergence behavior.

The information provided by Fig. 14.4 qualifies the above conclusions. It shows the dynamics of non-knowledge GVA, also in real terms. The first thing that draws attention when comparing this information with that provided by Fig. 14.3 is the much more dynamic behavior of the American countries (panel A), compared to the European ones (panel B), whose profile is almost flat or, in the case of Italy, even declining. In contrast, panel (A) shows the dynamic behavior of the American countries, with Colombia, Brazil, and Chile in the lead (as with the knowledge economy in Fig. 14.3), although even the United States and Canada show faster growth in the non-knowledge than in the knowledge economy.

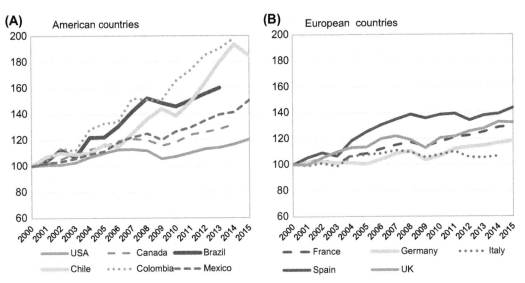

FIGURE 14.3   Real knowledge-based GVA. International comparison, 2000–15 (2000 = 100). (A) American countries. (B) European countries. *Source: Bureau of Economic Analysis (BEA): Industry economic accounts, 2018. Available at: https://www.bea. gov/data/economic-accounts/industry. Bureau of Labor Statistics (BLS): Current employment statistics (CES), 2018. Available at: https://www.bls.gov/ces/. EU KLEMS: EU KLEMS growth and productivity accounts, 2018. Available at: http://www.euklems.net/. LA KLEMS: Productividad y crecimiento económico en América Latina, 2018. Available at: https://www.cepal.org/cgi-bin/getprod.asp? xml=/la-klems/noticias/paginas/9/40269/P40269.xml&xsl=/la-klems/tpl/p18f-st.xsl&base=/la-klems/tpl/top-bottom.xsl, Statistics Canada, World KLEMS and own elaboration.*

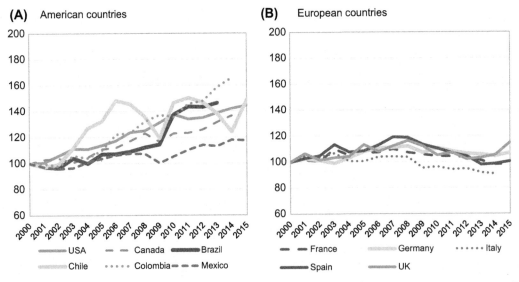

FIGURE 14.4   Real non-knowledge GVA. International comparison, 2000–15 (2000 = 100). (A) American countries. (B) European countries. *Source: Bureau of Economic Analysis (BEA): Industry economic accounts, 2018. Available at: https://www.bea.gov/ data/economic-accounts/industry. Bureau of Labor Statistics (BLS): Current employment statistics (CES), 2018. Available at: https:// www.bls.gov/ces/. EU KLEMS: EU KLEMS growth and productivity accounts, 2018. Available at: http://www.euklems.net/. LA KLEMS: Productividad y crecimiento económico en América Latina, 2018. Available at: https://www.cepal.org/cgi-bin/getprod.asp?xml=/la-klems/ noticias/paginas/9/40269/P40269.xml&xsl=/la-klems/tpl/p18f-st.xsl&base=/la-klems/tpl/top-bottom.xsl.   Statistics   Canada,   World KLEMS and own elaboration.*

Overall, the picture given by the two figures is of less dynamic European countries, especially in non-knowledge-based GVA, in contrast to very dynamic Latin-American countries. The United States and to a lesser extent Canada show a more dynamic behavior than the European countries, especially in the non-knowledge economy.

A complementary way of observing the same phenomenon is provided by Fig. 14.5, which depicts the annual rates of growth of knowledge and non-knowledge GVA over the period 2000–15. The four Latin-American countries take first place in both aggregations, and the rate of growth of the knowledge economy is higher than that of the non-knowledge economy in all cases. Canada and the United States experienced fairly high rates of growth for both components, but higher in the non-knowledge than in the knowledge part of the economy, especially in the case of the United States. The opposite is true of the European countries. Spain, France, and Italy experienced either nil or negative rates of growth of the non-knowledge economy, while the United Kingdom and Germany had positive growth in non-knowledge GVA but still lower than the growth in knowledge-based GVA.

Figs. 14.3–14.5 provide the rates of growth of knowledge and non-knowledge-based GVA considered individually. Fig. 14.6 combines this information with each component's share of total GVA, showing each one's contribution to total GVA growth. This information is provided for the whole period 2000–15 (panel A) and also separately for the prerecession (panel B) and postrecession (panel C) years.

Regardless of the period analyzed, Colombia, Chile, and Brazil have the highest rates of GVA growth and also the highest contribution of the knowledge economy (in percentage points). Mexico shows more modest results, especially when compared with the other three Latin-American countries. The United States and Canada stand in the middle range, both in growth

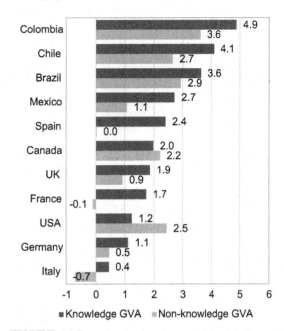

FIGURE 14.5 Average growth rate of knowledge and non-knowledge GVA. International comparison, 2000–15* (percentage). *2000–13 for Brazil, 2000–14 for Canada, Colombia, and Italy. Note: Countries are ranked according to knowledge GVA growth. *Source: Bureau of Economic Analysis (BEA): Industry economic accounts, 2018. Available at: https://www.bea.gov/data/economic-accounts/industry. Bureau of Labor Statistics (BLS): Current employment statistics (CES), 2018. Available at: https://www.bls.gov/ces/. EU KLEMS: EU KLEMS growth and productivity accounts, 2018. Available at: http://www.euklems.net/. LA KLEMS: Productividad y crecimiento económico en América Latina, 2018. Available at: https://www.cepal.org/cgi-bin/getprod.asp?xml=/la-klems/noticias/paginas/9/40269/P40269.xml&xsl=/la-klems/tpl/p18f-st.xsl&base=/la-klems/tpl/top-bottom.xsl. Statistics Canada, World KLEMS and own elaboration.*

rates and in the contribution of the knowledge economy. However, their behavior was more positive in the expansion years (2000–07) than in the years that followed. The five European countries show a more contrasting trajectory. For the whole 2000–15 period, the rate of GVA growth was similar in France, Germany, Spain, and the United Kingdom, and in all cases the (almost) only source of that growth was the knowledge-based economy. Italy is the

FIGURE 14.6 GVA annual growth rate: knowledge and non-knowledge contribution. International comparison, 2000–15* (percentage). (A) 2000–15*. *2000–13 for Brazil, 2000 –14 for Colombia, Canada, and Italy. (B) 2000 –07. (C) 2007–15**. **2007–13 for Brazil, 2007–14 for Colombia, Canada, and Italy. *Source: Bureau of Economic Analysis (BEA): Industry economic accounts, 2018. Available at: https://www.bea.gov/data/economic-accounts/industry. Bureau of Labor Statistics (BLS): Current employment statistics (CES), 2018. Available at: https://www.bls.gov/ces/. EU KLEMS: EU KLEMS growth and productivity accounts, 2018. Available at: http://www.euklems.net/. LA KLEMS: Productividad y crecimiento económico en América Latina, 2018. Available at: https:// www.cepal.org/cgi-bin/getprod.asp?xml=/la-klems/ noticias/paginas/9/40269/P40269.xml&xsl=/la-klems/tpl/p18f-st.xsl&base=/la-klems/tpl/top-bottom.xsl. Statistics Canada, World KLEMS and own elaboration.*

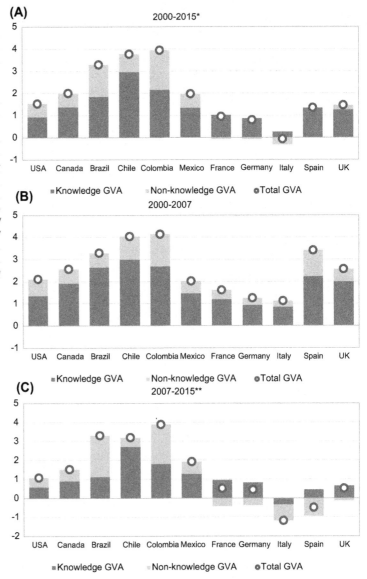

exception, presenting the lowest rate of GVA growth, together with a negative contribution of the non-knowledge economy.

There is a sharp contrast in the behavior of the five European countries between the pre- and postrecession years. During the expansion years (panel B), Spain and the United Kingdom were the fastest-growing countries, almost doubling the rates of growth of the other three, but in all five the knowledge economy made an important contribution to growth. The consequences of the great recession after 2007 (panel C) were dramatic for the European countries, especially for Spain and Italy, which presented a negative average annual rate of growth for the whole 2007–15 period. And all five countries had negative contributions of the non-knowledge economy throughout those years, indicating that the non-knowledge part of the economy is more vulnerable to difficult times than its knowledge counterpart.

To finish the presentation of the aggregated results, Fig. 14.7 shows knowledge-based GVA per capita (expressed in 2010 US dollars PPP per person) at the beginning and end of the period. The two North American countries lead the ranking, with the United States in first place. They are followed by the five European countries in this order: Germany, France, the United Kingdom, Italy, and Spain. The four Latin-American countries present lower values, with Chile ranking highest in this group, followed by Mexico, Brazil, and Colombia. However, it is worth noting that all 11 countries experienced an improvement in this variable between 2000 and 2015.

Despite the positive performance of the knowledge-based economy in all the countries and the strong growth trend shown by the less developed ones (namely, the Latin-American countries), the convergence between them is only moderate, as can be observed in Fig. 14.8, which shows the coefficient of variation for knowledge, non-knowledge, and total GVA per capita, considering all the countries analyzed. There is only a slight convergence in knowledge-based GVA per capita and a somewhat stronger convergence in non-knowledge GVA per capita.

14.4.1 Disaggregation of knowledge-based GVA by source

As already explained in Section 14.2, our approach to the knowledge-based economy assumes that knowledge is embedded in the two factors of production—labor and capital—and

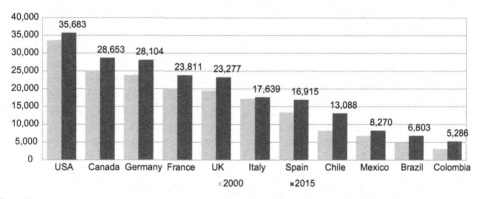

FIGURE 14.7   Knowledge-based GVA per capita, 2000 and 2015* (2010 US Dollars PPP per person). * 2013 for Brazil and 2014 for Colombia, Canada, and Italy. *Source: Bureau of Economic Analysis (BEA): Industry economic accounts, 2018. Available at: https://www.bea.gov/data/economic-accounts/industry. Bureau of Labor Statistics (BLS): Current employment statistics (CES), 2018. Available at: https://www.bls.gov/ces/. EU KLEMS: EU KLEMS growth and productivity accounts, 2018. Available at: http://www. euklems.net/. LA KLEMS: Productividad y crecimiento económico en América Latina, 2018. Available at: https://www.cepal.org/cgi-bin/getprod.asp?xml=/la-klems/noticias/paginas/9/40269/P40269.xml&xsl=/la-klems/tpl/p18f-st.xsl&base=/la-klems/tpl/top-bottom.xsl. OECD, Statistics Canada, United Nations, World KLEMS and own elaboration.*

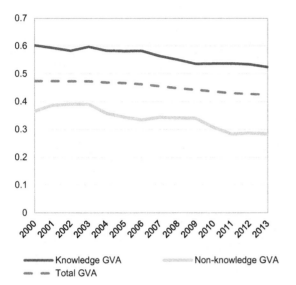

FIGURE 14.8 Convergence in the knowledge and non-knowledge-based GVA per capita among countries. International comparison, 2000–13 (coefficient of variation). *Source: Bureau of Economic Analysis (BEA): Industry economic accounts, 2018. Available at: https://www.bea.gov/data/economic-accounts/industry. Bureau of Labor Statistics (BLS): Current employment statistics (CES), 2018. Available at: https://www.bls.gov/ces/. EU KLEMS: EU KLEMS growth and productivity accounts, 2018. Available at: http://www.euklems.net/. LA KLEMS: Productividad y crecimiento económico en América Latina, 2018. Available at: https://www.cepal.org/cgi-bin/getprod.asp?xml=/la-klems/noticias/paginas/9/40269/P40269.xml&xsl=/la-klems/tpl/p18f-st.xsl&base=/la-klems/tpl/top-bottom.xsl. OECD, Statistics Canada, United Nations, World KLEMS and own elaboration.*

that the contribution of each individual asset is determined by the prices of the services it provides. Fig. 14.9 and Table 14.4 show the knowledge and non-knowledge compensation, as a percentage of GVA, of all the six components considered (in addition to knowledge and non-knowledge capital and labor, the figure also distinguishes between ICT and non-ICT knowledge-based capital and between high- and medium-skilled knowledge-intensive labor), at the start and end of the period (2000 and 2015). ICT-knowledge–intensive capital has the lowest share, below 5% in all countries. The component with the second lowest share is

Non-knowledge-intensive labor, which in 2015 ranges between 15.3% in Italy and 0.8% in Canada. The contributions of the remaining four components of the decomposition vary between countries and years.

Focusing on the last year (2015), the Latin-American countries account for the relatively higher weight of *Non-knowledge-intensive capital* and the relatively lower weight of medium-skilled labor. The share of medium-skilled labor is larger in Germany and also in Canada and Italy, whereas in Spain, France, and the United Kingdom high-skilled workers have a larger share. In the United States, the contribution of ICT capital is the highest of all the countries and that of low-skilled workers, the lowest after Canada. In Canada, the component with the largest contribution is medium-skilled labor, followed by *Non-knowledge-intensive capital*. However, as said before, there are important differences among countries and it is difficult to find common patterns.

Fig. 14.10 shows the annual rates of growth for each of the six components between 2000 and 2015. Panel (A) of this figure provides the information for the components of capital compensation. As can be seen, the Latin-American countries have the highest rates of growth of all three components, except for Brazil, which has the highest negative growth rate in the ICT-knowledge–intensive component. Canada and the United States experienced lower but positive growth rates throughout the period for all three components of capital. The European countries, in contrast, have negative rates in some of them. The United Kingdom, Italy, and France, for example, show negative growth rates in machinery and equipment, while Germany and Italy have negative rates in ICT capital. In the case of Spain, all the components of capital compensation increased, but at a slower rate than in the American countries.

Regarding labor, panel (B) confirms that three of the Latin-American countries once again experienced the highest rates of growth. In the case of

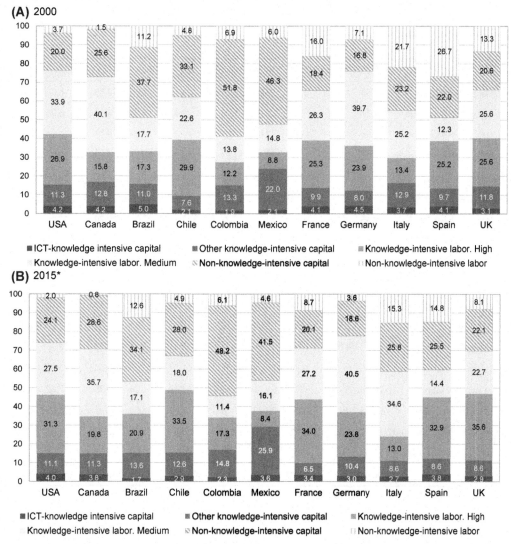

FIGURE 14.9 Knowledge and non-knowledge compensation over GVA. International comparison, 2000 and 2015* (percentage). (A) 2000. (B) 2015*. * 2013 for Brazil and 2014 for Canada, Colombia, and Italy. *Source: Bureau of Economic Analysis (BEA): Industry economic accounts, 2018. Available at: https://www.bea.gov/data/economic-accounts/industry. Bureau of Labor Statistics (BLS): Current employment statistics (CES), 2018. Available at: https://www.bls.gov/ces/. EU KLEMS: EU KLEMS growth and productivity accounts, 2018. Available at: http://www.euklems.net/. LA KLEMS: Productividad y crecimiento económico en América Latina, 2018. Available at: https://www.cepal.org/cgi-bin/getprod.asp?xml=/la-klems/noticias/paginas/9/40269/P40269.xml&xsl=/la-klems/tpl/ p18f-st.xsl&base=/la-klems/tpl/top-bottom.xsl. Statistics Canada, World KLEMS and own elaboration.*

Mexico, labor compensation growth was positive but much lower. For the rest of the countries, the common feature is the fall in *Non-knowledge-intensive labor*, that is, the compensation that

corresponds to workers with the lowest levels of skills.

Taking into account the information provided in this section (Table 14.4 and Figs. 14.9 and

TABLE 14.4   Knowledge and non-knowledge compensation over GVA. International comparison, 2000 and 2015[a] (percentage).

(a) 2000

	USA	Canada	Brazil	Chile	Colombia	Mexico	France	Germany	Italy	Spain	UK
Knowledge-intensive capital	15.55	17.02	16.03	9.67	15.28	24.14	14.00	12.55	16.58	13.77	14.89
ICT-knowledge—intensive capital	*4.21*	*4.21*	*5.03*	*2.07*	*1.93*	*2.12*	*4.08*	*4.50*	*3.71*	*4.10*	*3.11*
Other knowledge—intensive capital	*11.34*	*12.81*	*11.00*	*7.60*	*13.35*	*22.01*	*9.92*	*8.05*	*12.86*	*9.68*	*11.78*
Non-knowledge-intensive capital	19.97	25.62	37.68	33.10	51.81	46.26	18.37	16.80	23.20	21.98	20.58
Knowledge-intensive labor	60.80	55.88	35.05	52.43	26.03	23.60	51.68	63.57	38.56	37.53	51.19
Knowledge-intensive labor. High	*26.95*	*15.81*	*17.32*	*29.88*	*12.25*	*8.75*	*25.33*	*23.87*	*13.36*	*25.25*	*25.63*
Knowledge-intensive labor. Medium	*33.85*	*40.06*	*17.73*	*22.55*	*13.78*	*14.85*	*26.34*	*39.70*	*25.20*	*12.28*	*25.56*
Non-knowledge-intensive labor	3.68	1.49	11.23	4.80	6.88	6.00	15.96	7.08	21.67	26.71	13.34
Total GVA	**100.00**	**100.00**	**100.00**	**100.00**	**100.00**	**100.00**	**100.00**	**100.00**	**100.00**	**100.00**	**100.00**

(b) 2015[a]

	USA	Canada	Brazil	Chile	Colombia	Mexico	France	Germany	Italy	Spain	UK
Knowledge-intensive capital	15.13	15.05	15.30	15.51	17.01	29.44	9.98	13.44	11.23	12.40	11.51
ICT-knowledge—intensive capital	*4.01*	*3.76*	*1.65*	*2.88*	*2.25*	*3.56*	*3.45*	*3.03*	*2.68*	*3.84*	*2.89*
Other knowledge—intensive capital	*11.12*	*11.30*	*13.65*	*12.63*	*14.76*	*25.88*	*6.54*	*10.42*	*8.55*	*8.56*	*8.62*
Non-knowledge-intensive capital	24.06	28.60	34.07	28.05	48.16	41.53	20.08	18.58	25.80	25.49	22.10
Knowledge-intensive labor	58.78	55.58	38.04	51.51	28.69	24.46	61.26	64.35	47.62	47.28	58.32
Knowledge-intensive labor. High	*31.28*	*19.84*	*20.95*	*33.49*	*17.31*	*8.40*	*34.03*	*23.81*	*12.98*	*32.87*	*35.61*
Knowledge-intensive labor. Medium	*27.51*	*35.74*	*17.09*	*18.02*	*11.38*	*16.07*	*27.23*	*40.54*	*34.63*	*14.42*	*22.71*
Non-knowledge-intensive labor	2.03	0.76	12.59	4.93	6.14	4.56	8.68	3.63	15.35	14.83	8.08
Total GVA	**100.00**	**100.00**	**100.00**	**100.00**	**100.00**	**100.00**	**100.00**	**100.00**	**100.00**	**100.00**	**100.00**

[a] *2013 for Brazil and 2014 for Canada, Colombia, and Italy.*
Source: Bureau of Economic Analysis (BEA): Industry economic accounts, 2018. Available at: https://www.bea.gov/data/economic-accounts/industry. Bureau of Labor Statistics (BLS): Current employment statistics (CES), 2018. Available at: https://www.bls.gov/ces/. EU KLEMS: EU KLEMS growth and productivity accounts, 2018. Available at: http://www.euklems.net/. LA KLEMS: Productividad y crecimiento económico en América Latina, 2018. Available at: https://www.cepal.org/cgi-bin/getprod.asp?xml=/la-klems/noticias/paginas/9/40269/P40269.xml&xsl=/la-klems/tpl/p18f-st.xsl&base=/la-klems/tpl/top-bottom.xsl. Statistics Canada, World KLEMS and own elaboration.

14.10), Table 14.5 provides a disaggregation of each of the factors that contribute to GVA growth, distinguishing between capital and labor compensation, and their components. It should be noted that since the information in Table 14.5 is provided at the highest level of disaggregation, the contribution of the knowledge-based and non-knowledge-based

economy can be computed in a very flexible way. In fact, we can easily move from the narrowest to the broadest definition of knowledge-based GVA by either focusing solely on ICT capital and high-skilled labor compensation for the narrow definition, as in Mas et al. (2019), or also including compensation corresponding to machinery and equipment and medium-skilled labor for the

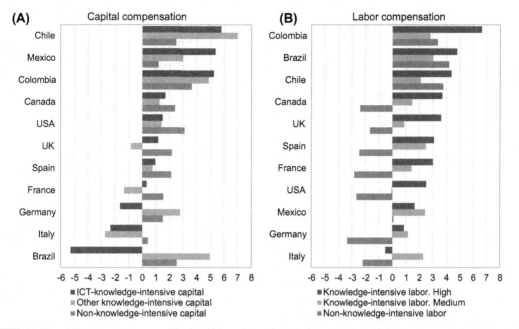

FIGURE 14.10 Average growth rate of knowledge and non-knowledge capital and labor's compensation. International comparison, 2000—15* (percentage). (A) Capital compensation. (B) Labor compensation. * 2000—13 for Brazil, 2000—14 for Canada, Colombia, and Italy. Note: In panel (A) countries are ranked according to ICT-knowledge—intensive capital growth. In panel (B), countries are ranked according to high-skilled labor. *Source: Bureau of Economic Analysis (BEA): Industry economic accounts, 2018. Available at: https://www.bea.gov/data/economic-accounts/industry. Bureau of Labor Statistics (BLS): Current employment statistics (CES), 2018. Available at: https://www.bls.gov/ces/. EU KLEMS: EU KLEMS growth and productivity accounts, 2018. Available at: http://www.euklems.net/. LA KLEMS: Productividad y crecimiento económico en América Latina, 2018. Available at: https://www. cepal.org/cgi-bin/getprod.asp?xml=/la-klems/noticias/paginas/9/40269/P40269.xml&xsl=/la-klems/tpl/p18f-st.xsl&base=/la-klems/tpl/ top-bottom.xsl. Statistics Canada, World KLEMS and own elaboration.*

broader perspective, which is the one proposed here (following Pérez and Benages (2012)).

Panel (A) of Table 14.5 shows the contributions to total GVA growth of each type of capital and labor for the whole period 2000—15. The first conclusion to be highlighted is that in almost all the countries (except Mexico), *Knowledge-intensive labor* made a higher contribution to GVA growth than *Knowledge-intensive capital*. Within *Knowledge-intensive labor*, in most of the countries (the exceptions being Mexico, Germany, and Italy) the contribution from high-skilled workers was larger than that from medium-skilled workers.

Second, the contribution of *Knowledge-intensive capital* has been negative in three of

the European countries, namely, France, the United Kingdom, and Italy. In the case of France and the United Kingdom, this was due to the *Other knowledge—intensive capital* component (machinery and equipment, basically), while in Italy both components of knowledge-intensive capital (machinery and equipment and also ICT capital) had a negative contribution. Germany and Brazil were the other two countries with a negative ICT capital contribution, although offset by the growth of machinery and equipment capital. In the remaining eight countries the ICT capital contribution was positive.

Third, in a set of countries the contribution of *Non-knowledge-intensive capital* was higher than its *Knowledge-intensive* counterpart. This is the

TABLE 14.5 GVA annual growth rate: knowledge and non-knowledge contributions. International comparison, 2000–15[a] (percentage).

	USA	Canada	Brazil	Chile	Colombia	Mexico	France	Germany	Italy	Spain	UK
(a) 2000–15[a]											
Knowledge-intensive capital	0.23	0.20	0.33	0.86	0.79	0.93	−0.27	0.21	−0.37	0.10	−0.06
ICT-knowledge–intensive capital	*0.06*	*0.06*	*−0.20*	*0.15*	*0.12*	*0.20*	*0.01*	*−0.06*	*−0.07*	*0.04*	*0.04*
Other knowledge–intensive capital	*0.17*	*0.13*	*0.52*	*0.71*	*0.68*	*0.73*	*−0.28*	*0.27*	*−0.30*	*0.07*	*−0.10*
Non-knowledge-intensive capital	0.68	0.66	0.99	0.58	1.58	0.65	0.29	0.11	0.09	0.53	0.39
Knowledge-intensive labor	0.70	1.18	1.52	2.11	1.36	0.41	1.28	0.66	0.63	1.23	1.31
Knowledge-intensive labor. High	*0.73*	*0.66*	*1.03*	*1.50*	*1.03*	*0.08*	*0.91*	*0.20*	*−0.06*	*0.90*	*1.11*
Knowledge-intensive labor. Medium	*−0.02*	*0.52*	*0.48*	*0.61*	*0.33*	*0.33*	*0.38*	*0.46*	*0.69*	*0.33*	*0.20*
Non-knowledge-intensive labor	−0.08	−0.03	0.46	0.22	0.21	−0.02	−0.36	−0.18	−0.41	−0.52	−0.18
Total GVA	**1.53**	**2.00**	**3.29**	**3.77**	**3.94**	**1.97**	**0.95**	**0.79**	**−0.06**	**1.34**	**1.46**
(b) 2000–07											
Knowledge-intensive capital	0.36	0.36	0.81	0.85	1.50	1.02	−0.03	0.75	−0.07	0.29	−0.04
ICT-knowledge–intensive capital	*0.11*	*0.16*	*−0.37*	*0.27*	*0.20*	*0.21*	*0.06*	*0.07*	*−0.03*	*0.10*	*0.09*
Other knowledge–intensive capital	*0.25*	*0.21*	*1.18*	*0.58*	*1.29*	*0.81*	*−0.10*	*0.68*	*−0.04*	*0.19*	*−0.14*
Non-knowledge-intensive capital	0.79	0.69	0.75	1.04	1.01	0.65	0.55	0.38	0.29	1.17	0.61
Knowledge-intensive labor	0.99	1.55	1.83	2.15	1.19	0.44	1.22	0.18	0.92	1.94	2.04
Knowledge-intensive labor. High	*0.81*	*0.74*	*1.08*	*1.13*	*0.84*	*−0.01*	*0.68*	*0.46*	*0.08*	*1.25*	*1.21*
Knowledge-intensive labor. Medium	*0.18*	*0.81*	*0.75*	*1.02*	*0.34*	*0.45*	*0.54*	*−0.28*	*0.84*	*0.69*	*0.83*
Non-knowledge-intensive labor	−0.02	−0.04	−0.10	0.00	0.44	−0.08	−0.13	−0.06	−0.02	0.01	−0.05
Total GVA	**2.11**	**2.57**	**3.29**	**4.03**	**4.13**	**2.02**	**1.62**	**1.25**	**1.12**	**3.41**	**2.56**
(c) 2007–15[b]											
Knowledge-intensive capital	0.11	0.05	−0.12	0.87	0.28	0.87	−0.34	−0.23	−0.62	−0.06	−0.04
ICT-knowledge–intensive capital	*0.03*	*−0.02*	*−0.02*	*0.06*	*0.06*	*0.18*	*−0.03*	*−0.16*	*−0.11*	*−0.01*	*−0.01*
Other knowledge–intensive capital	*0.09*	*0.06*	*−0.11*	*0.81*	*0.22*	*0.69*	*−0.31*	*−0.07*	*−0.51*	*−0.04*	*−0.03*
Non-knowledge-intensive capital	0.61	0.64	1.14	0.13	2.06	0.61	0.07	−0.12	−0.09	−0.08	0.12

TABLE 14.5 GVA annual growth rate: knowledge and non-knowledge contributions. International comparison, 2000—15[a] (percentage).—cont'd

	USA	Canada	Brazil	Chile	Colombia	Mexico	France	Germany	Italy	Spain	UK
Knowledge-intensive labor	0.47	0.85	1.25	1.84	1.52	0.40	1.29	1.05	0.28	0.50	0.69
Knowledge-intensive labor. High	*0.65*	*0.56*	*0.98*	*1.57*	*1.20*	*0.17*	*1.06*	*−0.02*	*−0.21*	*0.49*	*0.99*
Knowledge-intensive labor. Medium	*−0.18*	*0.29*	*0.26*	*0.26*	*0.32*	*0.23*	*0.23*	*1.07*	*0.49*	*0.01*	*−0.30*
Non-knowledge-intensive labor	−0.11	−0.01	1.03	0.35	0.03	0.03	−0.51	−0.26	−0.75	−0.88	−0.26
Total GVA	**1.08**	**1.52**	**3.29**	**3.19**	**3.89**	**1.91**	**0.51**	**0.44**	**−1.19**	**−0.50**	**0.51**

[a] *2000—13 for Brazil, 2000—14 for Colombia, Canada, and Italy.*
[b] *2007—13 for Brazil, 2007—14 for Colombia, Canada, and Italy.*
Source: Bureau of Economic Analysis (BEA): Industry economic accounts, 2018. Available at: https://www.bea.gov/data/economic-accounts/industry. Bureau of Labor Statistics (BLS): Current employment statistics (CES), 2018. Available at: https://www.bls.gov/ces/. EU KLEMS: EU KLEMS growth and productivity accounts, 2018. Available at: http://www.euklems.net/. LA KLEMS: Productividad y crecimiento económico en América Latina, 2018. Available at: https://www.cepal.org/cgi-bin/getprod.asp?xml=/la-klems/noticias/paginas/9/40269/P40269.xml&xsl=/la-klems/tpl/p18f-st.xsl&base=/la-klems/tpl/top-bottom.xsl. Statistics Canada, World KLEMS and own elaboration.

case for Brazil, Colombia, the United States, Canada, France, Italy, Spain, and the United Kingdom. However, in none of the countries, without exception, was the contribution of *Non-knowledge-intensive labor* higher than its *Knowledge-intensive* counterpart. In fact, in the majority of countries the contribution of *Non-knowledge-intensive labor* to GVA growth was negative. The exceptions were three Latin-American countries (Brazil, Chile, and Colombia), where it was positive.

Table 14.5 also provides the information disaggregated in two subperiods. The first covers the expansion years 2000—07 (panel B) and the second, the postrecession years 2007—15 (panel C). It is worth noticing the consequences of the economic crisis in the European countries. First, the contribution of *Knowledge-intensive capital* was negative in all five European countries after 2007, while in the non-European countries it was positive (with the sole exception of Brazil). This result is attributable to both the ICT and the machinery and equipment components, which contributed negatively in all five countries.

Second, another common feature was the negative contribution of *Non-knowledge-intensive labor* in the five European countries, and also in the United States and Canada. In all countries, however (with the exception of Italy and Germany, though only marginally in the latter case), the contribution of high-skilled workers was positive, showing that the most highly educated labor makes a positive contribution to growth, even in an economic downturn.

14.5 Knowledge intensity estimates: industry results

A distinctive characteristic of the KLEMS methodology is the emphasis it puts on the importance of industry disaggregation. In fact, the results presented in the previous section come from the aggregation of industry data, as described in Section 14.2 (see Eq. 14.8). However, the available level of industry disaggregation is not homogenous for all countries, as explained in Section 14.3. For comparability purposes, a common classification of nine industries (listed in Table 14.2) has been adopted, as this is the highest level of industry disaggregation that is available for all the countries considered.

Fig. 14.11 shows how the knowledge economy is distributed, in 2000 and 2015, among the nine sectors considered. In all countries, *Other services* (which includes Public Administration, Education, Health, Social services, Arts, entertainment, and recreation, and Other services) is the sector that absorbs the highest share of the knowledge economy, reaching up to 30% in the United States, Canada, Brazil, France, and Spain. The only exception is Mexico, where *Manufacturing* is first and *Other services* second. The second most important sector in most of the countries is *Financial, real estate, and business services*. The exceptions are Brazil and Germany, where the second position is taken by *Manufacturing*; Colombia, where *Wholesale and retail trade, accommodation and food service* is in second place; and Mexico, as already mentioned. Summing up, the four sectors just mentioned are the ones that absorb the highest share of the total knowledge economy, while the other five sectors have a much smaller share, especially *Agriculture* and *Mining and quarrying* in the European countries and the United States and *Electricity, gas, and water supply* in the Latin-American countries and Canada.

It is to be expected that the largest sectors of the economy, such as Other services, should also absorb the largest shares of both the knowledge and the non-knowledge economy. It is interesting, therefore, to consider the complementary view offered by Fig. 14.12, which shows the share of knowledge-based GVA within each industry (that is, assuming that the GVA for each industry takes a value of 100). The first thing to notice is that while for some countries the differences between industries are noteworthy, in others the penetration of knowledge is more homogenous among the nine sectors considered.

Broadly speaking, the more developed a country is, the more evenly spread the knowledge economy is across all the sectors of the economy. France, Germany, the United Kingdom, Canada, and the United States illustrate this assertion.

The second thing to notice is that there are notable differences between countries in the ranking of sectors by knowledge content. Even so, *Mining and quarrying* and *Electricity, gas, and water supply* are the least knowledge-intensive sectors in most (though not all) of the 11 countries. Also worth noting is the low knowledge intensity of one of the sectors that accounts for a large proportion of total knowledge-based GVA (see Fig. 14.11), namely *Financial, real estate, and business services*.

Table 14.6 completes the information from the industry disaggregation perspective, offering for each country and industry the share of GVA of each individual component of the *Knowledge-intensive economy* (capital and labor) for 2015 and confirming the big differences between countries and sectors. At this point it is interesting to check whether these differences have increased or decreased over the period analyzed.

Fig. 14.13 shows the dispersion (measured by the coefficient of variation) of knowledge-based GVA shares within sectors (shown in Fig. 14.12 for 2000 and 2015) in the different countries during the period 2000−15. First, this figure confirms that the more developed economies have a more homogenous penetration of knowledge in the different sectors. Second, it shows no general pattern of convergence toward less dispersion between sectors. Of the more developed countries only Spain shows a definite pattern of convergence over the period, and the United States and the United Kingdom since 2009. Of the four Latin-American countries, only Chile shows a well-defined pattern of reduction of inequalities (despite the reversal of this trend in the last year), while in Mexico the tendency is the opposite from 2009 onward.

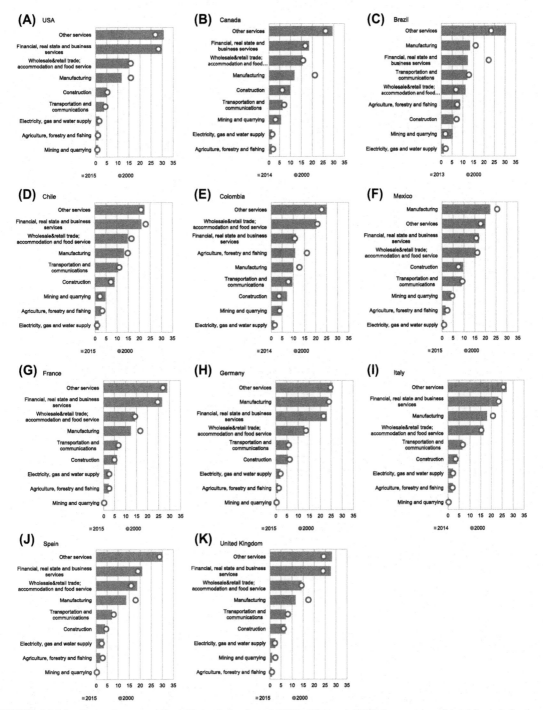

FIGURE 14.11 Sectoral composition of knowledge-based GVA. 2000 and 2015* (percentage of total knowledge-based GVA). Total economy = 100. (A) USA. (B) Canada. (C) Brazil. (D) Chile. (E) Colombia. (F) Mexico. (G) France. (H) Germany. (I) Italy. (J) Spain. (K) United Kingdom. * 2013 for Brazil (2014) for Canada, Colombia, and Italy. *Source: Bureau of Economic Analysis (BEA): Industry economic accounts, 2018. Available at: https://www.bea.gov/data/economic-accounts/industry. Bureau of Labor Statistics (BLS): Current employment statistics (CES), 2018. Available at: https://www.bls.gov/ces/. EU KLEMS: EU KLEMS growth and productivity accounts, 2018. Available at: http://www.euklems.net/. LA KLEMS: Productividad y crecimiento económico en América Latina, 2018. Available at: https://www.cepal.org/cgi-bin/getprod.asp?xml=/la-klems/noticias/paginas/9/40269/P40269.xml&xsl=/la-klems/tpl/p18f-st.xsl&base=/la-klems/tpl/top-bottom.xsl. Statistics Canada, World KLEMS and own elaboration.*

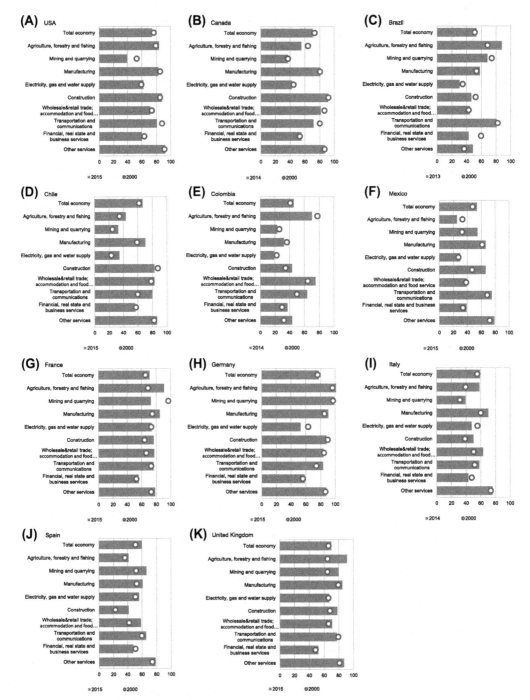

FIGURE 14.12 Knowledge-based GVA by industry. 2000 and 2015* (percentage of each industry's GVA). Total industry = 100. (A) USA. (B) Canada. (C) Brazil. (D) Chile. (E) Colombia. (F) Mexico. (G) France. (H) Germany. (I) Italy. (J) Spain. (K) United Kingdom. * 2013 for Brazil (2014) for Canada, Colombia, and Italy. Note: In Germany knowledge-GVA share in 2015 is above 100% in the case of Agriculture, forestry, and fishing because capital compensation of non-knowledge assets is negative. *Source: Bureau of Economic Analysis (BEA): Industry economic accounts, 2018. Available at: https://www.bea.gov/data/economic-accounts/ industry. Bureau of Labor Statistics (BLS): Current employment statistics (CES), 2018. Available at: https://www.bls.gov/ces/. EU KLEMS: EU KLEMS growth and productivity accounts, 2018. Available at: http://www.euklems.net/. LA KLEMS: Productividad y crecimiento económico en América Latina, 2018. Available at: https://www.cepal.org/cgi-bin/getprod.asp?xml=/la-klems/noticias/paginas/9/40269/ P40269.xml&xsl=/la-klems/tpl/p18f-st.xsl&base=/la-klems/tpl/top-bottom.xsl. Statistics Canada, World KLEMS and own elaboration.*

TABLE 14.6 Knowledge and non-knowledge compensation over GVA by industry. International comparison, 2015[a] (percentage of each industry GVA).

	Knowledge-intensive capital				Knowledge-intensive labor				
	Total	ICT-knowledge−intensive capital	Other knowledge−intensive capital	Non-knowledge-intensive capital	Total	Knowledge-intensive labor. High	Knowledge-intensive labor. Medium	Non-knowledge-intensive labor	Total GVA
United States									
Total economy	15.13	4.01	11.12	24.06	58.78	31.28	27.51	2.03	100.00
Agriculture, forestry, and fishing	38.67	0.27	38.40	10.67	45.03	16.01	29.02	5.62	100.00
Mining and quarrying	12.50	1.21	11.29	58.93	27.04	14.95	12.09	1.53	100.00
Manufacturing	27.93	3.41	24.52	14.51	54.90	24.63	30.26	2.66	100.00
Electricity, gas, and water supply	31.10	1.71	29.39	36.91	31.19	14.55	16.64	0.80	100.00
Construction	16.48	0.83	15.65	5.83	71.22	17.50	53.72	6.48	100.00
Wholesale, retail trade; accommodation and food service	19.45	5.02	14.43	25.09	52.00	16.36	35.64	3.46	100.00
Transportation and communications	17.67	1.98	15.68	15.42	62.97	18.62	44.35	3.95	100.00
Financial, real state, and business services	13.01	6.39	6.62	39.07	47.01	33.82	13.19	0.91	100.00
Other services	7.45	1.47	5.98	6.24	84.86	47.27	37.59	1.45	100.00
Canada									
Total economy	15.05	3.76	11.30	28.60	55.58	19.84	35.74	0.76	100.00
Agriculture, forestry, and fishing	33.01	0.59	32.41	42.70	22.34	2.47	19.87	1.96	100.00
Mining and quarrying	19.96	0.66	19.30	62.37	17.39	4.54	12.85	0.28	100.00
Manufacturing	24.48	3.71	20.77	17.70	56.41	13.98	42.43	1.42	100.00
Electricity, gas, and water supply	16.87	5.40	11.47	57.31	25.79	8.86	16.93	0.03	100.00
Construction	17.07	1.05	16.02	5.84	74.67	8.54	66.13	2.41	100.00

(Continued)

TABLE 14.6   Knowledge and non-knowledge compensation over GVA by industry. International comparison, 2015[a] (percentage of each industry GVA).—cont'd

	Knowledge-intensive capital				Knowledge-intensive labor				
	Total	ICT-knowledge −intensive capital	Other knowledge −intensive capital	Non-knowledge-intensive capital	Total	Knowledge-intensive labor. High	Knowledge-intensive labor. Medium	Non-knowledge-intensive labor	Total GVA
Wholesale, retail trade; accommodation and food service	13.35	4.60	8.75	17.50	68.09	14.43	53.66	1.05	100.00
Transportation and communications	18.01	7.43	10.58	27.43	53.64	11.81	41.83	0.92	100.00
Financial, real state, and business services	14.26	4.63	9.63	44.66	40.94	22.34	18.60	0.14	100.00
Other services	7.64	3.78	3.86	12.16	79.63	37.89	41.74	0.58	100.00
Brazil									
Total economy	15.30	1.65	13.65	34.07	38.04	20.95	17.09	12.59	100.00
Agriculture, forestry, and fishing	81.19	2.03	79.17	0.00	6.73	1.99	4.74	12.08	100.00
Mining and quarrying	55.16	3.18	51.98	28.03	13.29	6.27	7.02	3.52	100.00
Manufacturing	10.26	3.08	7.17	24.28	47.68	18.74	28.94	17.78	100.00
Electricity, gas, and water supply	4.18	1.80	2.38	64.84	26.38	15.45	10.93	4.60	100.00
Construction	25.45	2.09	23.36	30.25	21.14	6.34	14.80	23.16	100.00
Wholesale, retail trade; accommodation and food service	5.30	0.73	4.58	40.30	39.20	12.28	26.92	15.20	100.00
Transportation and communications	48.63	7.34	41.29	2.39	32.26	10.13	22.13	16.72	100.00
Financial, real state and business services	2.71	0.54	2.17	51.37	40.27	30.01	10.26	5.66	100.00
Other services	2.32	0.31	2.01	39.81	46.39	31.69	14.70	11.49	100.00

TABLE 14.6 Knowledge and non-knowledge compensation over GVA by industry. International comparison, 2015[a] (percentage of each industry GVA).—cont'd

| | Knowledge-intensive capital | | | | Knowledge-intensive labor | | | | |
	Total	ICT-knowledge-intensive capital	Other knowledge-intensive capital	Non-knowledge-intensive capital	Total	Knowledge-intensive labor. High	Knowledge-intensive labor. Medium	Non-knowledge-intensive labor	Total GVA
Chile									
Total economy	15.51	2.88	12.63	28.05	51.51	33.49	18.02	4.93	100.00
Agriculture, forestry, and fishing	11.85	1.79	10.06	34.78	31.85	13.86	17.99	21.52	100.00
Mining and quarrying	21.87	2.81	19.06	66.61	10.98	6.48	4.49	0.54	100.00
Manufacturing	38.70	5.53	33.16	26.00	31.82	17.05	14.77	3.49	100.00
Electricity, gas, and water supply	26.70	4.44	22.25	64.96	7.85	5.18	2.67	0.49	100.00
Construction	24.07	1.84	22.22	5.07	58.72	30.17	28.55	12.14	100.00
Wholesale, retail trade; accommodation and food service	7.18	3.29	3.89	8.69	75.63	36.73	38.90	8.50	100.00
Transportation and communications	27.77	3.95	23.82	14.13	51.90	19.03	32.87	6.20	100.00
Financial, real state, and business services	5.68	2.42	3.26	42.54	50.83	42.43	8.40	0.95	100.00
Other services	4.39	1.27	3.12	9.01	81.90	63.76	18.14	4.70	100.00
Colombia									
Total economy	17.01	2.25	14.76	48.16	28.69	17.31	11.38	6.14	100.00
Agriculture, forestry, and fishing	51.01	0.15	50.86	19.32	19.32	10.61	8.71	10.36	100.00
Mining and quarrying	14.28	1.44	12.84	75.03	9.16	4.68	4.47	1.54	100.00
Manufacturing	7.39	0.35	7.05	57.72	25.26	9.48	15.78	9.63	100.00
Electricity, gas, and water supply	5.35	0.23	5.12	74.14	13.81	5.43	8.38	6.70	100.00
Construction	23.84	0.07	23.77	51.83	19.69	9.79	9.90	4.65	100.00

(Continued)

TABLE 14.6   Knowledge and non-knowledge compensation over GVA by industry. International comparison, 2015[a] (percentage of each industry GVA).—cont'd

	Knowledge-intensive capital				Knowledge-intensive labor				
	Total	ICT-knowledge −intensive capital	Other knowledge −intensive capital	Non-knowledge-intensive capital	Total	Knowledge-intensive labor. High	Knowledge-intensive labor. Medium	Non-knowledge-intensive labor	Total GVA
Wholesale, retail trade; accommodation and food service	38.62	2.82	35.79	17.67	36.42	20.83	15.59	7.30	100.00
Transportation and communications	38.86	21.43	17.43	35.08	24.89	21.98	2.91	1.16	100.00
Financial, real state, and business services	2.06	0.98	1.08	62.34	35.26	32.13	3.13	0.34	100.00
Other services	5.32	0.38	4.94	47.55	38.22	20.75	17.48	8.91	100.00
Mexico									
Total economy	29.44	3.56	25.88	41.53	24.46	8.40	16.07	4.56	100.00
Agriculture, forestry, and fishing	18.48	0.43	18.05	64.51	6.58	0.33	6.25	10.43	100.00
Mining and quarrying	47.13	1.37	45.76	43.44	7.57	1.74	5.83	1.86	100.00
Manufacturing	45.33	2.37	42.96	30.14	20.95	4.40	16.54	3.58	100.00
Electricity, gas, and water supply	7.13	0.37	6.77	68.99	22.81	7.88	14.92	1.07	100.00
Construction	46.80	8.82	37.98	22.76	19.37	9.96	9.42	11.06	100.00
Wholesale, retail trade; accommodation and food service	27.08	3.03	24.04	58.17	11.90	2.29	9.62	2.85	100.00
Transportation and communications	50.06	0.87	49.19	19.93	25.07	8.94	16.13	4.94	100.00
Financial, real state, and business services	20.62	6.18	14.44	59.13	18.46	5.91	12.55	1.79	100.00
Other services	7.32	1.60	5.72	12.06	71.45	30.44	41.01	9.17	100.00

TABLE 14.6 Knowledge and non-knowledge compensation over GVA by industry. International comparison, 2015[a] (percentage of each industry GVA).—cont'd

	Knowledge-intensive capital				Knowledge-intensive labor				
	Total	ICT-knowledge−intensive capital	Other knowledge−intensive capital	Non-knowledge-intensive capital	Total	Knowledge-intensive labor. High	Knowledge-intensive labor. Medium	Non-knowledge-intensive labor	Total GVA
France									
Total economy	9.98	3.45	6.54	20.08	61.26	34.03	27.23	8.68	100.00
Agriculture, forestry, and fishing	5.29	0.12	5.17	−10.78	85.71	23.35	62.36	19.79	100.00
Mining and quarrying	30.34	4.35	25.99	16.72	42.60	18.45	24.15	10.34	100.00
Manufacturing	19.45	5.72	13.72	6.26	65.63	34.49	31.14	8.66	100.00
Electricity, gas, and water supply	36.69	2.42	34.28	21.39	36.99	21.17	15.82	4.93	100.00
Construction	6.97	1.26	5.72	6.65	69.85	19.18	50.68	16.52	100.00
Wholesale, retail trade; accommodation and food service	7.41	1.93	5.48	8.52	69.99	29.73	40.25	14.08	100.00
Transportation and communications	24.54	4.37	20.16	10.91	51.92	22.98	28.95	12.62	100.00
Financial, real state, and business services	8.66	5.55	3.11	40.40	47.31	34.30	13.01	3.63	100.00
Other services	4.21	1.18	3.03	12.08	74.22	43.41	30.81	9.49	100.00
Germany									
Total economy	13.44	3.03	10.42	18.58	64.35	23.81	40.54	3.63	100.00
Agriculture, forestry and fishing	26.29	0.75	25.54	−26.41	92.42	36.46	55.95	7.70	100.00
Mining and quarrying	8.94	1.74	7.20	−6.10	89.73	32.70	57.03	7.43	100.00
Manufacturing	19.76	2.36	17.39	4.55	70.91	26.46	44.45	4.79	100.00

(Continued)

TABLE 14.6   Knowledge and non-knowledge compensation over GVA by industry. International comparison, 2015[a] (percentage of each industry GVA).—cont'd

	Knowledge-intensive capital				Knowledge-intensive labor				
	Total	ICT-knowledge −intensive capital	Other knowledge −intensive capital	Non-knowledge-intensive capital	Total	Knowledge-intensive labor. High	Knowledge-intensive labor. Medium	Non-knowledge-intensive labor	Total GVA
Electricity, gas, and water supply	18.17	3.58	14.59	45.07	34.95	13.32	21.63	1.81	100.00
Construction	10.18	1.24	8.94	5.67	77.87	22.49	55.38	6.29	100.00
Wholesale, retail trade; accommodation and food service	10.17	3.20	6.97	9.46	73.79	15.21	58.59	6.58	100.00
Transportation and communications	28.63	6.51	22.12	11.88	54.66	11.09	43.57	4.83	100.00
Financial, real state, and business services	12.05	4.08	7.97	40.09	46.38	21.27	25.12	1.47	100.00
Other services	7.32	1.63	5.69	9.29	80.16	33.70	46.46	3.22	100.00
Italy									
Total economy	11.23	2.68	8.55	25.80	47.62	12.98	34.63	15.35	100.00
Agriculture, forestry, and fishing	15.94	0.25	15.69	−0.62	42.24	5.87	36.37	42.45	100.00
Mining and quarrying	21.26	1.09	20.17	52.65	17.83	6.50	11.33	8.26	100.00
Manufacturing	22.33	2.61	19.72	5.38	48.02	10.44	37.57	24.28	100.00
Electricity, gas, and water supply	24.98	2.55	22.44	39.32	22.66	4.78	17.88	13.04	100.00
Construction	10.51	1.07	9.44	12.11	39.69	2.77	36.91	37.69	100.00
Wholesale, retail trade; accommodation and food service	8.26	1.62	6.64	11.11	54.84	6.60	48.24	25.79	100.00
Transportation and communications	21.45	7.07	14.38	26.11	36.59	5.44	31.14	15.85	100.00
Financial, real state, and business services	6.79	3.44	3.35	54.21	36.08	12.17	23.91	2.91	100.00
Other services	6.69	1.60	5.08	11.41	69.33	27.35	41.98	12.57	100.00

TABLE 14.6 Knowledge and non-knowledge compensation over GVA by industry. International comparison, 2015[a] (percentage of each industry GVA).—cont'd

	Knowledge-intensive capital				Knowledge-intensive labor				
	Total	ICT-knowledge-intensive capital	Other knowledge-intensive capital	Non-knowledge-intensive capital	Total	Knowledge-intensive labor. High	Knowledge-intensive labor. Medium	Non-knowledge-intensive labor	Total GVA
Spain									
Total economy	12.40	3.84	8.56	25.49	47.28	32.87	14.42	14.83	100.00
Agriculture, forestry, and fishing	26.73	0.22	26.51	37.32	14.83	6.74	8.09	21.12	100.00
Mining and quarrying	28.83	2.23	26.60	12.95	37.55	25.78	11.77	20.67	100.00
Manufacturing	20.54	3.50	17.03	21.06	40.61	26.57	14.04	17.79	100.00
Electricity, gas, and water supply	35.21	7.57	27.64	36.72	20.87	14.86	6.01	7.19	100.00
Construction	6.95	0.36	6.60	31.86	34.61	20.95	13.66	26.58	100.00
Wholesale, retail trade; accommodation and food service	10.49	2.13	8.36	13.04	48.04	24.03	24.01	28.42	100.00
Transportation and communications	28.07	10.66	17.41	19.48	37.70	21.70	15.99	14.75	100.00
Financial, real state, and business services	8.26	5.37	2.90	46.70	39.71	31.17	8.54	5.33	100.00
Other services	5.38	2.48	2.90	11.33	73.12	57.92	15.20	10.17	100.00
United Kingdom									
Total economy	11.51	2.89	8.62	22.10	58.32	35.61	22.71	8.08	100.00
Agriculture, forestry, and fishing	11.56	0.19	11.37	−14.73	79.84	40.31	39.53	23.33	100.00
Mining and quarrying	28.20	3.86	24.34	14.60	51.59	37.62	13.97	5.61	100.00
Manufacturing	17.15	2.51	14.64	4.23	67.80	37.92	29.88	10.82	100.00
Electricity, gas, and water supply	30.00	2.96	27.04	30.13	36.82	21.51	15.31	3.05	100.00
Construction	2.85	0.43	2.42	6.00	75.16	27.32	47.84	15.99	100.00
Wholesale, retail trade;	14.33	3.25	11.09	14.16	56.48	21.29	35.19	15.03	100.00

(Continued)

TABLE 14.6   Knowledge and non-knowledge compensation over GVA by industry. International comparison, 2015[a] (percentage of each industry GVA).—cont'd

	Knowledge-intensive capital				Knowledge-intensive labor				
	Total	ICT-knowledge−intensive capital	Other knowledge−intensive capital	Non-knowledge-intensive capital	Total	Knowledge-intensive labor. High	Knowledge-intensive labor. Medium	Non-knowledge-intensive labor	Total GVA
accommodation and food service Transportation and communications	20.27	5.21	15.06	6.99	56.99	28.72	28.27	15.75	100.00
Financial, real state, and business services	10.09	3.55	6.53	44.45	41.91	29.59	12.32	3.55	100.00
Other services	6.89	1.77	5.12	7.06	80.23	59.16	21.07	5.83	100.00

Note: In Germany, France, Italy, and United Kingdom capital compensation of non-knowledge assets is negative in the case of Agriculture, forestry, and fishing; and Mining and quarrying.

[a] 2013 for Brazil, 2014 for Canada, Colombia, and Italy.

Source: Bureau of Economic Analysis (BEA): Industry economic accounts, 2018. Available at: https://www.bea.gov/data/economic-accounts/industry. Bureau of Labor Statistics (BLS): Current employment statistics (CES), 2018. Available at: https://www.bls.gov/ces/. EU KLEMS: EU KLEMS growth and productivity accounts, 2018. Available at: http://www.euklems.net/. LA KLEMS: Productividad y crecimiento económico en América Latina, 2018. Available at: https://www.cepal.org/cgi-bin/getprod.asp?xml=/la-klems/noticias/paginas/9/40269/P40269.xml&xsl=/la-klems/tpl/p18f-st.xsl&base=/la-klems/tpl/top-bottom.xsl. Statistics Canada, World KLEMS and own elaboration.

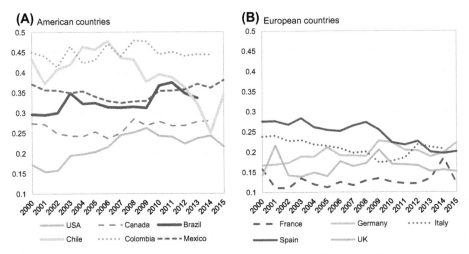

FIGURE 14.13   Dispersion of the knowledge-based GVA share among sectors. International comparison, 2000—15 (coefficient of variation). (A) American countries. (B) European countries. *Source: Bureau of Economic Analysis (BEA): Industry economic accounts, 2018. Available at: https://www.bea.gov/data/economic-accounts/industry. Bureau of Labor Statistics (BLS): Current employment statistics (CES), 2018. Available at: https://www.bls.gov/ces/. EU KLEMS: EU KLEMS growth and productivity accounts, 2018. Available at: http://www.euklems.net/. LA KLEMS: Productividad y crecimiento económico en América Latina, 2018. Available at: https://www.cepal.org/cgi-bin/getprod.asp?xml=/la-klems/noticias/paginas/9/40269/P40269.xml&xsl=/la-klems/tpl/p18f-st.xsl&base=/la-klems/tpl/top-bottom.xsl. Statistics Canada, World KLEMS and own elaboration.*

14.5.1 Shift-share analysis

Lastly, we will use the shift-share technique to analyze the determinants of the knowledge-based economy's share of GVA (represented in Fig. 14.1). Shift-share analysis is widely used to decompose the changes in an aggregate variable over time into three components: within-industry effect, sectoral static effect, and sectoral dynamic effect. It thus allows us to explain the changes in the knowledge intensity of GVA (Y^K_-/Y) over a specific period of time (0 to T) as follows:

(without distinguishing between static and dynamic), in Fig. 14.14. The main results can be summarized as follows. First, the within-industry effect is by far the most important determinant of the knowledge intensity variation in all countries. In all the countries except the United States and Canada, it is the within-industry effect that explains the intensification in the use of knowledge in production. The within-industry effect is especially large in Chile, Colombia, Mexico, France, and Spain. Second, the sectoral effect had a negative impact in all

$$\frac{Y^K_T}{Y_T} - \frac{Y^K_0}{Y_0} = \underbrace{\sum_{j=1}^{J} \theta_{j0}\left(\frac{Y^K_{jT}}{Y_{jT}} - \frac{Y^K_{j0}}{Y_{j0}}\right)}_{\text{Within–industry effect}} + \underbrace{\sum_{j=1}^{J}(\theta_{jT} - \theta_{j0})\frac{Y^K_{j0}}{Y_{j0}} + \sum_{j=1}^{J}(\theta_{jT} - \theta_{j0})\left(\frac{Y^K_{jT}}{Y_{jT}} - \frac{Y^K_{j0}}{Y_{j0}}\right)}_{\substack{\text{Static effect} \qquad\qquad \text{Dynamic effect} \\ \text{Sectoral effect}}} \tag{14.9}$$

where $\frac{Y^K_T}{Y_T} - \frac{Y^K_0}{Y_0}$ is the change in knowledge intensity between years 0 and T, j is the industry, and θ_{jT} is the share of GVA in industry j in year T.

The within-industry effect shows the growth of knowledge intensity that would have occurred even without any structural change, i.e., due to the aggregate knowledge intensity gains (positive sign) or losses (negative sign) arising from internal improvements in knowledge intensity within each industry. The sectoral effect captures the consequences of the reallocation of factors between sectors toward industries with a higher initial level of knowledge intensity (static effect) or with a higher rate of knowledge intensity growth (dynamic effect).

The results of this decomposition for the period 2000–15 appear in Table 14.7 and a summary of the within-industry and sectoral effects

the countries, with the sole exception of Spain. In most of the countries this negative impact is attributable to both the static and the dynamic effect. The dynamic component had a negative impact in all the countries, while the static component had a nil impact in Mexico and a positive impact only in Brazil and Spain. These results show that the change in the sectoral composition of GVA during these years did not contribute to the growth of knowledge-based GVA, except in the case of Spain.

The main conclusion to be drawn—from the perspective of designing public policies aimed at improving an economy's knowledge intensity—is that it is important to facilitate the penetration of knowledge-intensive assets (both capital and labor) in all sectors of the economy, since the structural change from less to more knowledge-intensive sectors does not seem to play a role.

TABLE 14.7 Shift-share analysis of the knowledge-based GVA weight. Average 2000−15[a] (percentage points).

	USA	Canada	Brazil	Chile	Colombia	Mexico	France	Germany	Italy	Spain	UK
Within-industry effect	−0.11	−0.04	0.26	0.46	0.41	0.44	0.44	0.16	0.30	0.50	0.32
Sectoral effect	−0.06	−0.12	−0.09	−0.13	−0.09	−0.03	−0.07	−0.05	−0.04	0.06	−0.07
Static effect	*−0.04*	*−0.10*	*0.02*	*−0.07*	*−0.08*	*0.00*	*−0.06*	*−0.03*	*−0.02*	*0.07*	*−0.05*
Dynamic effect	*−0.02*	*−0.03*	*−0.10*	*−0.06*	*−0.02*	*−0.03*	*−0.01*	*−0.02*	*−0.01*	*−0.02*	*−0.03*
Total	**−0.16**	**−0.16**	**0.17**	**0.33**	**0.31**	**0.41**	**0.37**	**0.11**	**0.27**	**0.56**	**0.25**

[a] *2000−13 for Brazil, 2000−14 for Canada, Colombia, and Italy.*
Source: Bureau of Economic Analysis (BEA): Industry economic accounts, 2018. Available at: https://www.bea.gov/data/economic-accounts/industry. Bureau of Labor Statistics (BLS): Current employment statistics (CES), 2018. Available at: https://www.bls.gov/ces/. EU KLEMS: EU KLEMS growth and productivity accounts, 2018. Available at: http://www.euklems.net/. LA KLEMS: Productividad y crecimiento económico en América Latina, 2018. Available at: https://www.cepal.org/cgi-bin/getprod.asp?xml=/la-klems/noticias/paginas/9/40269/P40269.xml&xsl=/la-klems/tpl/p18f-st.xsl&base=/la-klems/tpl/top-bottom.xsl. Statistics Canada, World KLEMS and own elaboration.

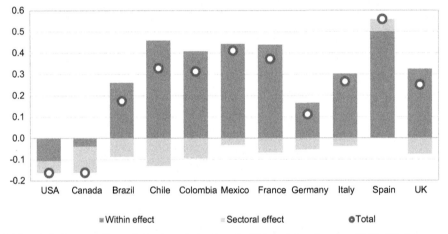

FIGURE 14.14 Shift-share analysis of the knowledge-based GVA weight. Average 2000−15* (percentage points). * 2000−13 for Brazil, 2000−14 for Canada, Colombia, and Italy. *Source: Bureau of Economic Analysis (BEA): Industry economic accounts, 2018. Available at: https://www.bea.gov/data/economic-accounts/industry. Bureau of Labor Statistics (BLS): Current employment statistics (CES), 2018. Available at: https://www.bls.gov/ces/. EU KLEMS: EU KLEMS growth and productivity accounts, 2018. Available at: http://www.euklems.net/. LA KLEMS: Productividad y crecimiento económico en América Latina, 2018. Available at: https://www.cepal.org/cgi-bin/getprod.asp?xml=/la-klems/noticias/paginas/9/40269/P40269.xml&xsl=/la-klems/tpl/p18f-st.xsl&base=/la-klems/tpl/top-bottom.xsl. Statistics Canada, World KLEMS and own elaboration.*

14.6 Conclusions

The proposed metric calculates the knowledge content of an economy based on more accurate and disaggregated measurements of human and physical capital services by branch of activity. To compute the size and composition of the knowledge economy, we have used a broad definition of knowledge-based inputs that includes ICT and machinery and equipment assets as capital inputs and the highest and medium levels of educational attainment as labor inputs. Once the knowledge-based inputs have been identified, we quantify the portion of income which remunerates the services these factors provide (capital and labor compensation, in KLEMS terminology) and, by extension, their contribution to GVA. This chapter analyzes the behavior followed by 11 countries: six American countries (the United States, Canada, and four Latin-American countries, namely, Brazil, Chile, Colombia, and Mexico) and five big European countries (France, Germany, Italy, Spain, and the United Kingdom). The period covered is 2000—15, which is the latest year available for all the countries. The information comes from the most updated releases of EU KLEMS, LA KLEMS, and the KLEMS databases for Canada and the United States.

The study confirms the important role of knowledge-intensive inputs in advanced economies, but also in less developed ones, as knowledge-based GVA accounts for more than 50% of total GVA in all countries analyzed (with the sole exception of Colombia). However, as expected, the more developed countries of North America and Europe (Germany, France, and the United Kingdom) have a higher penetration of the knowledge-based economy than the less developed ones. Among the Latin-American countries, Chile stands out, with higher levels of knowledge-based GVA than either Italy or Spain. All the countries except the United States and Canada have experienced an increase in the knowledge economy. In fact, the most dynamic countries in this respect have been the less developed ones, with Colombia and Chile taking the lead, followed by Brazil and Mexico, which points to a process of convergence during the period 2000—15. The convergence is the result of the countries that started out in last place having improved at a faster rate than the leader, Italy being the only exception to this general pattern.

At the same time, the four Latin-American countries also show a more dynamic behavior in the non-knowledge economy. The general picture is of less dynamic European countries, in contrast to very dynamic Latin-American countries. The United States and to a lesser extent Canada also show a more dynamic behavior than the European countries, especially in the non-knowledge economy.

In terms of knowledge-based GVA per capita, the United States leads, followed by Canada, the five European countries (in this order: Germany, France, the United Kingdom, Italy, Spain), and then the four Latin-American countries (with Chile in the lead and Colombia in last place). All 11 countries experienced an increase in knowledge-based GVA per capita between 2000 and 2015.

Of the six knowledge-intensive and non-knowledge-intensive components into which capital and labor are disaggregated, ICT-knowledge—intensive capital has the lowest share, below 5% in all countries. The component with the second lowest share is *Non-knowledge-intensive labor*. For the remaining four components of the decomposition the contributions vary between countries and years. Focusing on the last year (2015), the Latin-American countries stand out for their relatively higher share of *Non-knowledge-intensive capital* (linked to non-residential and residential structures) and their relatively lower share of medium-skilled labor. Medium-skilled labor has a significant share in Germany, Canada, and Italy, while in Spain, France, and the United Kingdom the share of high-skilled workers is larger. The United States has the highest contribution of ICT capital of all the countries and, together with Canada, one of the lowest contributions of low-skilled workers. The component with the largest contribution in the more advanced countries is high-skilled labor, followed by medium-skilled labor.

In terms of contribution to GVA growth (which is the result of combining GVA shares with the rates of growth of individual assets or types of labor), in most of the countries *Knowledge-intensive labor* contributed more than *Knowledge-intensive capital*. Within *Knowledge-intensive labor*, high-skilled workers generally contributed more than medium-skilled workers. The contribution of *Knowledge-intensive capital* was negative in France, the United Kingdom, and Italy; and the contribution of ICT capital was negative in Germany, Italy, and Brazil. In a set of countries the contribution of *Non-knowledge-intensive capital* was higher than that of its *Knowledge-intensive* counterpart. However, in all of the countries, without exception, the contribution of *Knowledge-intensive labor* was higher than that of its *Non-knowledge* counterpart.

The disaggregation by industry provides further insights into the composition of the knowledge economy. Generally speaking, the industries that contribute most to the knowledge-based economy in almost all the countries are *Other services* (basically, Public Administration, Health, and Education) and *Financial, real estate, and business services*. This is mainly due to the contribution of workers with higher levels of educational attainment. In contrast, *Agriculture, forestry, and fishing* and *Mining and quarrying* are, broadly speaking, non-knowledge activities, with responsibility split between labor and capital depending on the country analyzed. An interesting, though expected insight is that the more developed a country is, the higher the penetration of the knowledge-based economy in all sectors of its economy.

Overall, we can say that there are important differences among the countries analyzed in terms of their knowledge-based economy, but two facts are worth highlighting. First, as expected, the more developed countries have a higher share of knowledge-based GVA, but the less developed countries are the ones in which the knowledge economy is growing fastest. Thus, a certain process of convergence can be observed, though it is probably not fast enough to close the gap in the near future. In addition to the knowledge intensity differences between countries, the differences in knowledge intensity between sectors within the same country are important as well and there is no general pattern of convergence toward less dispersion between them.

Finally, the results of the shift-share analysis point to the within-industry effect as the main determinant of the shift toward a more knowledge-based economy. The main conclusion to be drawn—from the perspective of the design of public policy—is that it is important to facilitate the penetration of knowledge-intensive assets (both capital and labor) in all sectors of the economy, since the change in productive specialization from less to more knowledge-intensive sectors does not seem to play an important role.

References

Aravena C, Hofman AA, Escobar LE: Fuentes del crecimiento económico y la productividad en América Latina y el Caribe, 1990-2013, *Economia Chilena* 21(1):034–066, April 2018.

Bureau of Economic Analysis (BEA): *Industry economic accounts*. Available at: https://www.bea.gov/data/economic-accounts/industry.

Bureau of Labor Statistics (BLS): *Current employment statistics (CES)*. Available at: https://www.bls.gov/ces/.

Chen DH, Dahlman CJ: *The knowledge economy, the KAM methodology and World Bank operations*, Stock No. 37256, Washington DC, 2006, The International bank for Reconstruction and Development/The World Bank Institute.

Coremberg A, Pérez F, editors: *Fuentes del crecimiento y productividad en Europa y América Latina*, Bilbao, 2010, BBVA Foundation.

Corrado C, Haskel J, Jona-Lasinio C: Knowledge spillovers, ICT and productivity growth, *Oxford Bulletin Economics and Statistics* 79(4):592–618, 2017.

Corrado C, Haskel J, Jona-Lasinio C, et al.: Innovation and intangible investment in Europe, Japan, and the United States, *Oxford Review of Economic Policy* 29(2):261–286, 2013.

Corrado C, Hulten CR, Sichel DE: *Intangible capital and economic growth*, NBER Working Paper No. 11948, Cambridge (MA), 2006, National Bureau of Economic Research.

de Haan M, van Rooijen-Horsten M: *Knowledge indicators based on satellite accounts*, Final Report for NESIS-Work Package 5.1, The Hague, Statistics Netherlands.

EU KLEMS: *EU KLEMS growth and productivity accounts*. Available at: http://www.euklems.net/.

Eurostat: *Science, technology and innovation in Europe, 2013 Edition* Luxembourg, 2013, Publications Office of the European Union. Available at:. http://ec.europa.eu/eurostat/data/database.

Fukao K, Hamagata S, Miyagawa T, et al.: *Intangible investment in Japan: measurement and contribution to economic growth*, RIETI Discussion Paper Series 07-E-034, Tokyo, 2007, Research Institute of Economy, Trade and Industry.

Hatzichoronoglou T: *Revision of the high-technology sector and product classification*, STI Working Paper No. 59918, Paris, 1997, OECD.

Hulten CR: *Accounting for the knowledge economy*, Economics Program Working Paper Series 08-13, New York, 2008, The Conference Board.

Jorgenson DW: *Productivity, vol. 1: postwar U.S. economic growth*, Cambridge (MA), 1995, MIT Press.

Jorgenson DW, Gollop FM, Fraumeni BM: *Productivity and U.S. economic growth*, Cambridge (MA), 1987, Harvard Economic Studies.

Jorgenson DW, Ho MS, Stiroh KJ: *Productivity, vol. 3, information technology and the American growth resurgence*, Cambridge (MA), 2005, MIT Press.

LA KLEMS: *Productividad y crecimiento económico en América Latina*. Available at: https://www.cepal.org/cgi-bin/getprod.asp?xml=/la-klems/noticias/paginas/9/40269/P40269.xml&xsl=/la-klems/tpl/p18f-st.xsl&base=/la-klems/tpl/top-bottom.xsl.

López A, Niembro A, Ramos D: Latin America's competitive position in knowledge-intensive services trade, *CEPAL Review* 113(August):21–39, 2014.

López A, Ramos D: Pueden los servicios intensivos en conocimiento ser un nuevo motor de crecimiento en América Latina? *Revista Iberoamericana de Ciencia, Tecnología y Sociedad* 8(24):81–113, 2013.

Mas M, Hofman A, Benages E: Knowledge intensity in a set of Latin-American countries, *International Productivity Monitor* 36:204–233, 2019.

Maudos J, Benages E, Hernández L: *El valor económico de las actividades basadas en el conocimiento en España y sus regiones*, Madrid, 2017, Ramón Areces Foundation.

Marrano MG, Haskel J: *How much does the UK invest in intangible assets?*, Working Papers No. 578, London, 2006, Queen Mary, University of London.

Marrano MG, Haskel J, Wallis G: *What happened to the knowledge economy? ICT, intangible investment and Britain's productivity record revisited*, Working Paper No. 603, London, 2007, Queen Mary, University of London.

OECD: *Measuring capital OECD manual*, Paris, 2001, OECD.

OECD: *Measuring capital OECD manual*, Paris, 2009, OECD.

OECD: *OECD science, technology and industry scoreboard 2015*, Paris, 2015, Innovation for Growth and Society. OECD.

OECD: *Purchasing power parities (PPP) statistics*. Available at: https://stats.oecd.org/.

Oulton N: The mystery of TFP, *International Productivity Monitor* 31:68–87, 2016.

Pérez F, Benages E: *El PIB basado en el conocimiento: Importancia y contribución al crecimiento*, Valencia, 2012, ABACO. Available at: http://www.observatorioabaco.es/buscador?informe=115.

Pérez F, Benages E: The role of capital accumulation in the evolution of total factor productivity in Spain, *International Productivity Monitor* 33(Fall):24–50, 2017.

Schreyer P: User costs and bubbles in land markets, *Journal of Housing Economics* 18(3):267–272, 2009.

Solow R: A contribution to the theory of economic growth, *Quarterly Journal of Economics* 70(1):65–94, 1956.

Solow R: Technical change and the aggregate production function, *The Review of Economics and Statistics* 39(3):312–330, 1957.

Statistics Canada: *Multifactor productivity statistics*. Available at: https://www150.statcan.gc.ca/n1/en/subjects/economic_accounts/productivity_accounts/multifactor_productivity.

Timmer M, van Moergastel T, Stuivenwold E, et al.: *EU KLEMS growth and productivity accounts*, Version 1.0. Part I Methodology. Available at: http://euklems.net/data/EUKLEMS_Growth_and_Productivity_Accounts_Part_I_Methodology.pdf.

United Nations. World population prospects 2017. Available at: https://population.un.org/wpp/Download/Standard/Population/.

Van Ark B, Hulten CR: *Innovation, intangibles and economic growth: towards a comprehensive accounting of the knowledge economy*, EPWP#07-02 (December). New York, 2007, The Conference Board.

Van Rooijen-Horsten M, Tanriseven M, de Haan M: *R&D satellite accounts in The Netherlands*, A Progress Report, The Hague, 2008, Statistics Netherlands.

World Bank: *TradeCAN: database and software for a Competitiveness analysis of Nations: user guide*, 1999 Edition, The International Bank for Reconstruction and Development/The World Bank and Economic Commission for Latin America and the Caribbean (ECLAC).

World Bank: Measuring knowledge in the world's economies?. In *Knowledge assessment methodology and knowledge economy Index, knowledge for development program, Washington, DC*, The World Bank.

World Bank: Building knowledge economies. In *Advanced Strategies for development*, Washington, DC, 2008b, The World Bank.

World KLEMS: *World KLEMS data*. Available at: http://www.worldklems.net/data.htm.

Measuring consumer inflation in a digital economy

Marshall Reinsdorf[1], Paul Schreyer[2]

[1]International Monetary Fund, Washington, DC, United States; [2]OECD, Paris, France

15.1 Introduction and key findings

Whether estimates of GDP still provide a good measure of growth in a digitalized economy has become a topic of debate. Several academic and business economists[1] have suggested that the overlooked output generated by the digital economy, including from products perceived as welfare-enhancing, could be large enough to explain the productivity slowdown that began in the mid-2000s and that growth of material living standards has far outstripped growth as measured by GDP. Possible inadequacies of GDP concepts and methods for measuring the digital economy have even been a focus of articles, for instance, in *The Economist*,[2] *Les Echos*,[3] or *Computer Weekly*.[4]

On the other side of the debate, several analyses have found that many of the criticisms of GDP statistics are based on misunderstandings of the conceptual framework and purpose of GDP or on exaggerated perceptions of the likely size of the effects. Ahmad and Schreyer (2016) considered how nominal GDP measurement is affected by digitalization and concluded that existing GDP concepts remain sound. Syverson (2017) concluded that mismeasurement is unlikely to be explanation for the productivity slowdown. Ahmad et al. (2017) developed alternative price and welfare measures for several items and found relatively small impacts on GDP growth. Byrne et al. (2016) found that the mismeasurement of US productivity is small compared to the magnitude of the productivity slowdown and did not grow when productivity slowed. Similarly, based on a careful assessment of sources of bias in the measurement of output, prices, and productivity, Moulton (2018) found that the overstatement of the consumer price index (CPI) and of the deflator for personal

---

[1] Examples include Brynjolfsson and McAfee (2014), Bean (2016), and Feldstein (2017).

[2] https://www.economist.com/news/briefing/21697845-gross-domestic-product-gdp-increasingly-poor-measure-prosperity-it-not-even.

[3] Interview with Henri de Castries, Chief Executive AXA Assurance, *Les Echos* 31 August 2015.

[4] http://www.computerweekly.com/opinion/Why-were-measuring-the-digital-economy-in-the-wrong-way.

consumption expenditure in the United States has fallen, not risen, over the past 20 years.

Welfare changes from new and free digital products are conceptually relevant for understanding consumer inflation both as measured by the CPI and as measured by household consumption deflator. For the CPI, however, capturing many of these welfare changes will probably require a supplementary version of the index that can be revised (such as the chained CPI of the US Bureau of Labor Statistics). The official CPI has some important purposes that require a conservative approach to treating subjective increases in satisfaction from the appearance of novel goods as price reductions, and its compressed publication timetable with no revisions limits the extent of quality adjustment that is practical. Also, lags in bringing new goods into the CPI mean that early prices changes for new goods—often downward—tend to be missed. In contrast, the household consumption deflator is well-positioned to capture most of the welfare changes. Welfare from the appearance of novel kinds of new goods is conceptually appropriate to include in real consumption growth (though not always measurable in practice), and the revision process for the household consumption deflator affords opportunities for sophisticated quality adjustment and for additional consideration of early price changes of new goods.

In this chapter, we take a broad look at the possible sources of error in capturing digital products in the price and volume measures for household consumption in national accounts. While all the components of final demand could potentially play a role in mismeasurement of real GDP,[5] household consumption represents the most important part of GDP in OECD countries (somewhat more than 60% on average) and price measures of household consumption are a key gauge of inflation, with a multitude of applications. As summarized in Table 15.1, the claims that prices—and, by implication, growth—of household consumption are being mismeasured largely revolve around three potential sources of distortion:

(1) incomplete adjustment for quality change in products or distribution channels, i.e., the treatment of new, and often improved, varieties of existing digital products; the treatment of new digital products that replace existing nondigital products; and improved variety selection of digital and nondigital products;

(2) neglected welfare gains or cost savings from truly novel digital products when these are introduced into price indexes too slowly; and

(3) neglected welfare gains from free digital products when there is no imputation of shadow prices.

Although digitalization clearly poses some genuine measurement challenges, we argue in Section 15.2 that the welfare effects of truly novel products at their point of introduction (2) and free products (3) are best addressed as part of welfare measurement "beyond GDP" rather than within an official price index. The arguments for this are both conceptual and practical.

We calculate upper-bound impacts on the deflator for household consumption arising from the various effects that are part of (1)—quality change in existing digital products, digital replacement of nondigital products, and improved variety selection—by considering each effect in turn. We assume a bias in the price index for each of these categories that we view as the maximum plausible but not necessarily as the most plausible and apply an average weight calculated from detailed data sets on the weighting structure of household consumption in OECD countries. Using 2015 weights, the upper bound revision to the growth rate of the

---

[5] For instance, ICT investment deflators are identified as a source of downward bias by Byrne and Corrado (2017a,b,c).

TABLE 15.1 Sources of welfare effects.

1. Quality change in existing product lines	2. Appearance of truly novel products	3. Appearance and use of free products
(a) Quality change in existing digital products through evolving characteristics embodied in new varieties of digital products (e.g., computers)	e.g., smartphones	e.g., free communication services through apps
(b) Digital replacement of nondigital products (e.g., streaming services replacing CDs)		
(c) Improved variety selection among products, digital and other (e.g., clothing, books)		

Note: This categorization is for the present analytical purpose only and not necessarily a general classification of how industries are affected by digitalization.

household consumption deflator from completely adjusting for quality change in digital products is around -0.4 percentage points per year; the upper bound adjustment from cost savings from new digital products that directly replace a nondigital product is about -0.1 percentage points; and the impact of adjusting for the widespread, but small, welfare effect from improved variety selection is -0.05 percentage points. A correction in the order of over half a percentage point to annual real consumption growth would be significant. Nonetheless more than half of the gap between the postslowdown and preslowdown rates of productivity growth would remain even without considering the corrections for sources of mismeasurement in the preslowdown era.

15.2 Quality change in existing product lines, truly novel products, and free products

15.2.1 Quality change in existing product lines

Price indexes for aggregates like household final consumption are built from elementary price indexes that cover a single product, or narrow product stratum. The elementary indexes are compiled from microdata on individual prices of different product varieties and from different sellers.

Constructing a price index for a product would be rather straightforward if the characteristics of the varieties available for purchase never changed. For products with high technological content, however, new models embodying the latest technology often appear as replacements for older models or as new varieties. Accurate measurement of real growth when technology is changing therefore requires product-level price indexes that properly adjust for the quality change implied by changes in characteristics.

The basic approach used to construct elementary price indexes is to select a sample of representative varieties and sellers, and then compare prices of the same varieties and sellers over time. Because like is compared with like, such a matched-model approach produces a pure measure of price change with no risk of distortion from variation in quality. However, products' characteristics tend to evolve over time, with new models appearing in the market and existing ones disappearing. Replacement of items in the sample that disappear from the market ("forced replacements") is one of the challenges faced by price statisticians.

There are four possibilities for handling a forced replacement: direct comparison, quality-adjusted comparison, linking with price changes of the continuing items used to impute the change in the missing price, and linking with overlapping prices.[6] A direct comparison of the prices of the original and replacement models is appropriate when the replacement model has similar characteristics and can be assumed to represent the same quality level. In this case, the replacement model is treated as a continuation of the original model and the entire difference between the last observed price of the original model and the first observed price of the replacement model is identified as inflation. Inflation will be overstated if the replacement model is actually of significantly higher quality.

Second, the missing price may be imputed by adjusting the price of the replacement model for the quality change implied by the differences in characteristics from the original model. In effect, the quality adjustment makes it possible to treat the replacement item as a virtual continuation of the original model. The accuracy of the quality adjustment will determine whether the resulting price index suffers from an upward or downward bias.

Third, if the changes in characteristics are too extensive to estimate the value of the quality change given the resources available, the index must be linked. Often collection of the replacement model's price begins only after the original model has exited. In this case, the item is left out of the price comparison in the period of the exit, the initial price of the replacement model being set aside until it can be compared to a second price of the same model. Leaving the item out of the index amounts to assuming that the true, quality-adjusted price of the item at hand has moved at the same rhythm as the average price change of the other items in the product line. This is, in fact, an implicit way of making a quality adjustment based on the difference between

the (inflation-adjusted) final price of the exiting model and the initial price of the replacement model. Whether the method generates an upward or a downward bias in the price index depends on whether the implicit quality adjustment is less than or more than the true quality difference.

A less common case is when the price of the replacement model begins to be collected while the original model is still available. Overlapping prices make it possible to include the exiting model in the price comparison for the link month. The implicit assumption in a link with overlapping prices is that the price difference between the exiting and replacement models is entirely due to quality. The direction of the bias would again depend on whether the implicit quality adjustment understates or overstates the true quality change associated with the model replacement.

Whether reliance on these methods for handling changes in the sample over- or understates inflation is unclear a priori and cannot necessarily be judged on the observation of rising or falling quality of a product alone. However, many authors have examined the overall treatment of variety entry and exit, typically finding an overstatement of inflation due to underadjustment for quality improvements, or because the entering varieties that are linked into the index have high reservation prices. For example, Aghion et al. (2019) argue that using price changes of continuing products to approximate price changes of new varieties (method 3) leads to an overestimation of inflation.[7]

Forced replacements are not the only way new models and new products enter an elementary index. Planned item replacements sometimes occur as part of sample refreshments.

---

[6] For a full discussion of methods and consequences, see (Triplett, 2006, pp. 22—23), the International Consumer Price Index Manual (ILO et al., 2004), and Diewert et al. (2017a).

[7] However, these results must be interpreted with much caution because they rely on strong assumptions to identify the evolution of the market share of continuing products and to translate it into changes in a cost of living index.

Sample refreshments help to keep the sample representative and are also occasions for bringing in *new products and product varieties*. In a sample refreshment, a newly selected sample is "linked in," and the old sample is "linked out." The first period the new sample comes in is also the last period for which the old sample is used. Any quality difference between them that is not fully reflected in their relative prices will not be captured, as the linking procedure assumes that the market is always in a state of perfect equilibrium in which apparent price dispersion really stems from quality differences. In the case of a product undergoing significant quality improvement, the failure to adjust for the higher average quality of the items in the sample being linked in may cause the index to overstate the product's price change (Moulton and Moses, 1997).

An important question concerns the frequency of sample refreshment and how quickly new products are brought into the price index. Late introduction can lead to price declines early in the life cycle being missed, a problem that is particularly relevant for digital products. Goolsbee and Klenow (2018) constructed a digital price index as an alternative to the CPI for products sold online. They emulate the basic CPI matched-model methodology, where price changes are assessed as the weighted average of those models whose prices can be observed in consecutive comparison periods (method 3 above). The *Adobe* data set used by Goolsbee and Klenow (2018) allows for a much speedier and finer identification of entering and exiting products than standard CPI sampling procedures and they find a significantly lower rate of inflation in their digital price index (−1.6% per year for 2014−17) than in the corresponding categories of the CPI (−0.3%). Thus, the rapid

inclusion of new products and the timely exclusion of exiting products appear to be an important factor in matched-model price indexes.

Sample refreshments are also an occasion for bringing new outlets into the sample for an elementary index.[8] Reinsdorf (1993) investigated sample refreshments to update the outlet sample to reflect current shopping patterns for food and gasoline. The outlets in the newly selected samples had systematically lower prices, but the linking procedure prevented the index from reflecting consumers' savings from substitution to lower-priced outlets, a problem known as *outlet substitution bias*. Digitalization has again raised the question of outlet substitution bias as consumers have substituted online shopping for shopping in physical stores. The evidence on whether prices are lower online is mixed. On the one hand, retailers with both an online and offline presence tend to offer the same price both places (Cavallo and Rigobon, 2016). But on the other hand, Cavallo (2017) finds that Amazon's online prices are, on average, 5% lower than offline prices. If a product is 5% cheaper online, gains in the online market share at the rate of 2 percentage points per year would cause an overstatement of 0.1 percentage points in the growth rate of the product's price index.

Much less investigated, but not to be overlooked, is whether quality change of some digital products may systematically be *overstated*. Examples of quality declines that are not captured in price measures include programmed obsolescence of certain consumer products, after-sales services that are purely machine-based, or the requirement to purchase new models of mobile phones and computers in the absence of backward compatibility of new software with older hardware. There is also the case of digitally enabled services where the consumer must

---

[8] New outlets may also enter as forced replacements. In this case, the new outlet is linked into the index. The price observations from the new outlet are generally not treated as a continuation of the observations from the previous outlet, even if they both sell the same item.

supply a labor input as part of the transaction, for instance, self-checkout in stores or self-check-in on airports. Whether these constitute quality improvements or declines is a matter of debate and personal perception, but it is clear that these changes to self-service are not accounted for in official price indexes.

To summarize, quality adjustment of replacements for existing products within a sample, and of new products coming in during sample refreshments, may miss some quality change. The overlooked quality change and cost of living effects could be in either direction, but for digital products benefitting from new technology, insufficient capture of quality improvements is more likely. The consequences of possible biases can be significantly attenuated by bringing new products into the sample early in their life through frequent sample updates.

15.2.2 Truly novel products

In addition to the new products and varieties that replace existing products and varieties, truly novel products are occasionally invented. Such goods and services are recognizable by the entirely new characteristics and service flows that they offer, or by the entirely new way—and typically much more efficient way—by which service flows are generated; historical examples are the introduction of electricity, automobiles, or air conditioning ("tectonic shifts," in the terminology of Nordhaus, 1996).[9] These entirely new products (or associated services) are too different from any existing product to estimate the quality adjustment needed for a comparison to an existing product. They must therefore enter as an "added line" in the structure of product strata of the top-level index. This entails adjusting the weights to make room for the new elementary index and linking the new elementary index into the top-level index as part of a general updating of the item strata definitions and weights. The delay in bringing them into the index until the next update of the basket structure and weights poses a risk of bias because, depending on the pricing strategy and market conditions, novel products may initially exhibit distinctive price change behavior. The most common pattern is for prices of truly novel products to decline quickly at first, so the bias is upward. A key issue with entirely new products is, then, avoiding a delay in getting them into the price index.[10]

---

[9] Nordhaus (1996) distinguishes between transaction prices of the purchased products and the shadow prices of service flows derived from these purchased goods. He argues that a true cost-of-living index (COLI) should be an index of the cost of service flows, which implies regrouping products by their contribution to consumer services such as transportation or entertainment: "For revolutionary changes in technology, such as the introduction of major inventions, traditional techniques simply ignore the fact that the new good or service may be significantly more efficient [in producing flows of services]. Consider the case of automobiles. In principle, it would be possible to link automobiles with horses so as to construct a price of travel, but this has not been done in the price statistics for just the reasons that the true price of light was not constructed. Similar problems arise as televisions replace cinemas, air travel replaces ground travel, and modern pharmaceuticals replace snake oil" (p. 56).

[10] A chained index that tracks the entire path of the new good's price from its high starting point to its lower long-run equilibrium, with weights reflecting the rising quantities, could closely approximate the welfare gain. A pioneering study in this area dates back some 25 years: Berndt et al. (1993) found that prices of new pharmaceuticals fell relative to the prices of older pharmaceuticals, reflecting a pricing strategy by drug manufacturers that raised the prices of older brands when new generic drugs entered the market. The authors constructed an alternative price index that brought new pharmaceuticals in as soon as they became available. It showed substantively lower price change than the official US price index for pharmaceuticals. This led to a modified sampling procedure by the US Bureau of Labor Statistics (Triplett, 2006, p. 112).

There is another, more basic issue with new goods. Their standard treatment in price index compilation links them into the index basket in a way that prevents any immediate effect on the index. But from a conceptual point of view, consumer welfare in the period prior to introduction of the new good is the same as if a price existed that was just high enough to drive demand for that good to zero (Hicks, 1940). The difference between this unobserved "reservation price" and the observed price at the moment of entry is not captured in traditional price indexes. From a welfare perspective, the standard treatment misses part of the effect of new products on consumers' living standards.[11]

There is no agreed methodology for imputing reservation prices of new goods, and, in practice, no attempts have been made to include them in official price indexes.[12] There is thus a question of whether the unmeasured consumer welfare effects generated by the appearance of truly new digital products are significant. The answer is likely to be yes, but even rather large absolute welfare effects do not automatically entail large corresponding adjustments to aggregate deflators, and aggregate real growth. The reason is the small weight that typically attaches to recently introduced products.

15.2.3 Free products

Many empirical studies of the value of new and free products have found that important gains for consumers are insufficiently picked up by consumption price indexes. For instance,

Brynjolfsson and Oh (2012) investigate welfare gains from the Internet and conclude:

> Our key findings are as follows: the average incremental welfare gain from the Internet between the years 2002 and 2011 is about $38 billion per year [for the United States]. Of that amount, we estimate that about $25 billion accounts for the consumer surplus from the free digital services on the Internet. This corresponds to about 0.19% of annual GDP. In contrast, the welfare estimates are significantly lower when we estimate it in a traditional way, relying only on money-based expenditures. The best estimate of the annual incremental welfare gain is only about $2.7 billion when we do not consider the value of time. This is about 7% of the estimate derived from our preferred model.

In addition, Varian (2011) puts a $65 billion figure on the value to US consumers of time savings from Google's search engine, and Bughin (2011) estimates the consumer surplus from the Internet to be about $64 billion based on a survey where users stated their preferences. However, multiplying the $17,530 median willingness-to-accept to forego access to Internet search engines found by Brynjolfsson et al. (2018) by the number of adult Internet users in the United States would imply a surplus of almost $3.8 trillion, or 30% of personal consumption expenditures in the US national accounts.

Often, the digital goods examined in these studies are available free of charge to consumers. This increases consumer choice and consumer welfare. The question is whether, and if so, how and when, free goods should be reflected in consumption price indexes.

From a cost-of-living perspective, with all observed prices unchanged but new kinds of

---

[11] For reasons of symmetry, a reservation price should also be imputed for disappearing products. In the disappearing product case, the effect on the index of the imputation would be upward.

[12] Indeed, there is not even a consensus on the need to do so. Although proponents of the cost-of-living-index (COLI) approach take a sympathetic view of imputing a reservation price, as called for by theory, proponents of a more traditional cost-of-goods-index (COGI) approach do not favor imputation of reservation prices. For a discussion of the COGI approach, see National Research Council (2002). Hausman (1996) is a widely cited study of introducing a reservation price for new variants of cereals.

free digital services becoming available, the price index should decline to reflect the rise in living standards. This would occur by introducing free products into the price index and assigning shadow prices to them. Consider a situation where households' utility depends on a vector of products $q \equiv [q_1, q_2, ... q_N]$ with a positive price $p \equiv [p_1, p_2, ... p_N]$ and a set of "environmental variables" $z \equiv [z_1, z_2, ... z_M]$ for which there is no market price. This could be environmental variables in the sense of the term such as clean air or free digital products. Consumer utility is then given by $u = f(q,z)$[13] and the corresponding *variable or conditional cost function* (McFadden, 1978) is:

$$C(u, p, z) = \min_q (p \cdot q : f(q, z) \geq u). \quad (15.1)$$

$C(u,p,z)$ thus indicates the minimum expenditure consumers incur on market products q given p and z. It can be shown that C is linearly homogenous and nondecreasing in p and nonincreasing in z. A cost of living price index (Konüs, 1939) conditioned on environmental variables z is then given by:

$$P(u, p^1, p^0, z) = C(u, p^1, z)/C(u, p^0, z). \quad (15.2)$$

By holding z constant, Eq. (15.2) reflects the standard approach of defining the COLI as conditional on a fixed level of the environmental variables and considering only priced goods in constructing price indexes that estimate the COLI. Although it is generally necessary to hold the environmental variables constant—a point emphasized by the National Research Council (2002) panel—researchers have considered models in which the free products supplied by digital platforms are treated as an environmental

variable that could change. To compute a price index that estimates Eq. (15.2) from just market prices and quantities, the usual assumption is thus that the "free" goods z remain unchanged.[14] This is, however, a strong assumption in an environment of rapidly emerging free digital products. Another possibility is to follow Diewert (2000), who shows that under the assumption that the effects of the changes in z on the consumption basket are monotonic, the changes in z can be accommodated using a superlative price index number formula,[15] in the sense that the superlative index corresponds to some average level of z between the periods of comparison.

While the assumption of monotonic effects is a less stringent requirement than an unchanged z, it still makes the COLI *conditional on environmental variables*, including the free products, and therefore does not reflect cost-of-living decreases due to the introduction of free digital products. What would a price index that makes explicit allowance for such free products look like? Diewert and Fox (2016) demonstrate that the inclusion of free products into the consumers' cost minimization leads to a cost function of the form $C(u,p,w)$, where w represents shadow prices for each free product. Under cost minimization, it holds that $w \equiv -\nabla_z c(u,p,z)$, i.e., shadow prices correspond to the marginal change in total costs to consumers due to the use of one additional unit of a free product. As Diewert and Fox (2016, p.11) point out: "[these are] ... the appropriate prices to use when valuing the services of free goods in order to construct cost of living indexes or measures of money metric utility change." Given shadow prices and quantities of free products,

---

[13] The utility function $u(q,z)$ is continuous and quasi-concave, and increasing in q and z.

[14] The more formal assumption that allows z to be ignored is separability of the cost function $c(u,p,z) = f(u)h(p)g(z)$.

[15] Diewert (1976) defined a price index to be superlative if it is exact for a unit cost function capable of providing a second-order differential approximation to an arbitrary twice-differentiable linearly homogeneous function. The Fisher index formula used in the US national accounts is an example of a superlative form.

these would be introduced into the price index number formula just like any market product.

Unfortunately, there are two issues here. First, where would shadow prices to value the change in z come from? Another, more fundamental question is whether shadow prices should be introduced in a consumption price index in the first place. We consider these questions in turn.

If the free products are available in unlimited quantities, under the assumptions of cost minimization, consumption will expand to the point where $\nabla z\ c(u,p,z) = 0$, making the postentry shadow price equal to 0. However, the preentry reservation price is not zero, and the consumer surplus from the change in z from its preentry quantity of zero to the quantity consumed when it is freely available equals the area under the demand curve from the reservation price down to the postentry shadow price of zero. Quality improvements in existing free products also generate consumer surplus.

Concerning the measurement of the consumer surplus, one option is assessing the consumer's willingness to accept a payment to give up free products via surveys or indirect measurement tools.[16] One such indirect tool has been tried: Brynjolfsson et al. (2018) designed a sequence of discrete choice experiments to elicit US consumers' willingness-to-accept to forego access to various kinds of free Internet services. As mentioned above, the results imply large valuations for some of these free services.

Another option is to expand the model of consumer behavior to include the consumer's time budget as a second constraint alongside the normal monetary budget constraint. The opportunity cost of the time involved would then act to limit the consumption of free products. After all, the value of consumers' time constitutes the main impediment to increasing marginal use of free Internet and smartphone app products. The prices of the ICT equipment and services required to access the free products are, of course, relevant for the decision of whether or not to consume the package of services, but once those prices have been paid, the only constraint on marginal consumption of more services comes from the time budget (though quality improvements may increase real consumption with time held constant). Of course, given the need to pay for the services out of the time budget, the marginal willingness-to-pay from the monetary budget is zero, but the total consumer surplus from the appearance of the new free products and their subsequent quality improvements should have some relationship to the time budget expenditures.

A third consideration is that many "free" digital products are not, in fact free. Even ignoring the cost of the devices and telecommunication services needed to access these products, they generally involve an implicit payment through the consumer's acceptance of advertisements while using the free product (an app, for instance), or her acceptance to share personal data with the provider of free product. However, neither the valuation of time nor the valuation of implicit payments in exchange for viewing the free product is straightforward in practice, and these approaches also raise theoretical issues.[17] While extremely valuable as a research project,

---

[16] For a formal elaboration see for instance Diewert and Fox (2016).

[17] See Ahmad and Schreyer (2016) for a general discussion of the national accounting implications, and Nakamura and Soloveichik (2015) for a discussion of valuing free media. Also, Diewert et al. (2017b) discuss the conceptual and econometric issues in valuing consumer time for nonmarket activities and leisure. A simpler version with cross-country comparisons of full consumption (monetary consumption expenditure plus value of time) and the derivation of an associated consumer price index can be found in Schreyer and Diewert (2014).

the implementation of shadow prices in an official price index may raise questions of transparency, reproducibility, and, ultimately, credibility of the price index.

Concerning the more basic question of whether these free products should be part of the COLI in the first place, much depends on the purpose of measurement. If the purpose is to measure production, it would be difficult to justify including "free" digital products in the COLI while at the same time excluding other nonmarket products that also command a shadow price in terms of the value of time: child care, care of the elderly, or gardening, to name just a few examples. In contrast to the time spent using free digital products, which may fall under leisure, households' nonmarket work clearly involves production. But if the purpose is simply to measure welfare itself, the exclusion of important environmental variables such as "life expectancy" would be difficult to justify. The steady rise of life expectancy in many parts of the world has also raised consumer welfare for a given market consumption bundle (Deaton, 2013). Rising life expectancy has a massive welfare effect not captured in the consumption of market products. Full inclusion of nonmarket products and environmental variables would fundamentally change the character of the consumption deflator.

A COLI also might be used for CPI purposes. For some of these purposes, the answer to the question "Would the CPI be a better tool for policymaking if the welfare from free goods and services were captured?" seems to be "no." For example, monetary policy targets to maintain the purchasing power of money should consider the prices of things that money is used to buy rather than a rate of inflation that reflects imputations for free products produced by households or for environmental variables.[18] Also, pensions and other payments are often escalated by the CPI. Downward adjustments to the CPI for increases in welfare from truly novel inventions and improvements to the external environment would leave the recipients of the escalated payments no better off than if these gains had never happened, in effect excluding them from sharing in the benefits of progress.[19] There is also a conceptual consideration: it is impossible to include every aspect of the external environment in the COLI calculations, but including a selective set of free goods or other aspects of the external environment in an ad hoc way could leave the index with an unclear or confusing interpretation.

Nevertheless, measures of shadow values of free products, the associated full income including the time budget endowment, are needed for purposes of a full understanding of growth and productivity in the digital era regardless of their treatment in the consumption deflator and CPI. Their inclusion in an extended COLI would be an important step toward broader measures of consumer welfare.

In summary, quality change in existing products, the emergence of new products, and free goods are not new issues, but the digital

---

[18] Note also that even if shadow prices of free products are not a standard element of a consumption price index, the effects of free digital replacements (Section 15.2.1) should be captured under standard price index methodology: At the point of entry, the zero price of the replacement product is compared with the positive price of the old product. Weights will be positive and reflect the base period if a Laspeyres index is used, or an average of base period and comparison period if a Fisher index is used.

[19] The US National Academy of Sciences panel on COLIs and price indexes was unable to agree on whether the welfare from new goods like cell phones and Viagra would be conceptually desirable to include in the CPI even if it could be measured (National Research Council, 2002). Some of the panel members viewed adjusting the CPI for welfare effects of truly novel new goods as inconsistent with the main purposes of the CPI.

economy, with its fast pace of innovation, has brought them to the fore. Rapid change in available products and in product characteristics has increased the potential for price measurement shortcomings. Indeed, there is evidence of understatement of some price changes due to insufficient quality adjustment and long lags in bringing new products into the index. The failure of the official price and volume indexes to capture the welfare gains at the moment of entry of truly novel new products and the welfare effects of free products is well noted but practical—and, to some extent, conceptual—considerations support these omissions. Nevertheless, broader welfare effects are important to measure. This can be done as part of statistics "Beyond GDP," as will be discussed in Section 15.4.

15.3 What's the potential impact?

The next task is assessing the potential bias in consumption deflators that may arise in conjunction with digital products. The discussion in Section 15.2 has identified some reasons why current price index compilation practices may not reflect the welfare effects from quality change and from novel and free products:

a) Less-than-complete quality adjustment when new varieties of existing products and new products with similar functions to an existing product enter the sample, and lags in bringing in them into the index;

b) Lags in bringing truly novel new products into the price index, and no imputation of a reservation price; and

c) No imputation of shadow prices for free products.

Section 15.2 also argued that some of the omitted welfare effects are not appropriate to include in official indexes of consumption prices for reasons of transparency and credibility. In what follows, we shall therefore focus on issue

(a) because there is a consensus that quality change should be reflected in price index practice; indeed, this is recommended in international guidelines for price and volume measures. Therefore, no quantification will be provided for the absence of reservation prices for truly novel products and for shadow prices of free services, or more generally for effects of environmental variables. These are, however, good candidates for broader welfare measures.

It is sometimes forgotten that even significant biases in individual product strata only affect the aggregate picture in proportion to their weight. This oversight leads to what could be called "anecdotal fallacy," whereby the bias in the price change of one particular product is extrapolated to the index as a whole. To avoid this fallacy, we consider the question: "if prices of the affected products were corrected for the bias that could potentially be present, what would be the implications for the aggregate price index?"

Our approach to quantifying the potential inadequacies in quality adjustment techniques proceeds by examining "pessimistic" scenarios that assume that the official procedures largely overlook the quality changes in digital products. (Some of the relevant evidence has been summarized in Section 15.2.) The main tool for our analysis is a detailed set of 145 household consumption expenditure weights from the OECD Purchasing Power Parities database covering 34 OECD countries in recent years. Expenditure weights are not affected by the price measurement biases mentioned above, but they provide the link to translate measurement errors in price changes of individual products to aggregate price index. Our illustration of the plausible upper bound of the effects will be based on averages of the weights for each OECD member as of 2005 and 2015.

We proceed in two steps. First, we classify all expenditure items into three groups based on the degree to which the price measures are likely to be affected by difficulties in measuring digital products:

- *Affected products*: products that clearly fall under the label of "digital" and whose price measures are most prone to difficulties due to digitalization, such as information technology goods or communication services;
- *Unaffected products*: products whose prices are very unlikely to suffer from a measurement problem associated with the digital economy, such as food, tobacco or housing;
- *Possibly affected products*: products that are in-between, such as cars or other consumer durables where digital features may have gone unnoticed in price measurement.

The second step is to further break down the categories *Affected* and *Possibly Affected* by the type of effect identified earlier (Table 15.1). This breakdown is judgmental and ad-hoc and in no way constitutes an official categorization of digital economy products. But we consider the three categories as fit-for-use for the problem at hand of determining an upper bound of the plausible range for the mismeasurement of the deflator for household consumption. Three kinds of effects were distinguished under the category *Quality Adjustment* in Table 15.1:

- *Quality adjustments in deflators of existing digital products*: for digital products where *advances in technology* are causing rapid quality improvement, it is plausible that official price indexes underadjust for quality change. Affected products include telephone equipment, telephone services, and computers and software. A full list is shown in the top four rows of Table 15.A.1 in Annex A.
- Byrne and Corrado (2015, 2017a, 2017b) construct alternative price indexes for communication equipment, computer and peripheral equipment and computer software. They base their estimates on the existing literature on high-tech price change and on their own price indexes for detailed products of the relevant US industries which

they construct using a broad variety of statistical and industry sources. For communications equipment, the authors' price index declines at close to 10% per year between 2010 and 15, or 8 percentage points faster than the official price index (Byrne and Corrado, 2017b, Table.2). For computers and peripheral equipment, the authors incorporate indicators of price-performance trends in constructing their price index and find a downward difference from the official BEA index of 11 percentage points per year between 2010 and 15 (Byrne and Corrado, 2017b, Table 5). For software, Byrne and Corrado (2017b) construct an index using a refined version of the basic BEA approach (e.g., more granular structure for software products and more differentiated input cost measure). Overall, the alternative price index for ICT investment shows a rate of price change of −8% between 2004 and 2015, 5.9 percentage points below the official US price index.

- Greenstein and McDevitt (2010) quality adjust the broadband price index but find that this makes only a small difference to the official measures (2 percentage points per year). The quality characteristics in their hedonic approach are upload and download speed.
- Abdirahman et al. (2017) construct alternative communication services deflators for the UK with an economic perspective in one case and an engineering perspective in another case. At the core of both approaches are unit value measures based on the price per unit of data transported. The economic approach treats data transportation associated with different services (text, voice, …) as different products, the engineering approach treats them as a single product, assuming perfect substitutability of a unit of data transported between any type of usage. Given the exponential growth in the number of bytes transported, the resulting indexes decline rather steeply—about 8% annually in real

terms between 2010 and 2015 for the economic approach and around 35% per year in real terms for the engineering approach. Both figures are considerably larger in absolute terms than the 0.4% per year rate of decline of the official price index. The authors are very explicit about the fact that their engineering approach overstates the true fall in prices, which they suggest lies somewhere between the two estimates. The use of unit values as the basis for price indexes, especially when computed over heterogeneous categories of products, is, indeed, not recommended by international statistical standards.

- Byrne and Corrado (2019) develop a measure of household consumption of digital services that "[…] reflects the intensity with which households use their ICT equipment and software, along with the intensity with which consumers use purchased digital services, internet access, cellular and cable TV services as well as cloud services (via gaming or other entertainment services, and computing or storage)." Intensity of the consumer use of ICT capital services is captured in terms of Petabytes of Internet Protocol Traffic. Byrne and Corrado (2019) develop their argument as part of an extension of the production boundary where households deliver large volumes of own-account digital services (akin to owner occupied housing) that gives rise to a new digital access service price index, essentially a use-adjusted price index of subscription costs. This use-adjusted adjusted price index declines by 11% per year, as

compared to the official price index that is essentially unchanged.[20]

- Goolsbee and Klenow (2018) use online prices to estimate alternative indexes for several product categories in the US CPI. For information technology products, they derive a measure of annual inflation of −6.1% for the years 2014−17. This compares with a decline in the corresponding CPI category of −3.7%, suggesting an upward bias of 2.4 percentage points per year.
- The Boskin Commission (Boskin et al., 1996) estimated the missing quality adjustment for consumer durables in the US CPI in 1995 at around 0.6 percentage points per year. Bils (2009) found twice this estimate. Moulton (2018) updated some of the estimates and assessed the quality adjustment bias for the US personal consumption expenditure deflator at 0.34 percentage points per year.

In light of the evidence above, we assume a *5 percentage point per year overestimation of the price change* in the affected categories *of ICT equipment and communication services*. As communication services are also a product group where digital replacement occurs (see below) for them we add another *5 percentage points of possible upward bias*. Bearing in mind that most countries have procedures in place to capture at least some of the quality change, and that the large declines in experimental communication services prices reflect debatable adjustments in proportion to the volume of data transported, this figure is clearly an upper bound.

---

[20] Byrne and Corrado's (2019) approach raises a more general question, namely whether price indexes should reflect the actual intensity of use of a product by consumers (provided it can be measured). With rising prevalence of flat subscription fees for digital services, this is particularly relevant for the ICT area. While there is no doubt that changes in capacity or speed constitute quality criteria that should be reflected in price indexes, it is less clear whether the intensity of use of such capacity should make its way into the price index—this is not common practice for other products (car prices are not adjusted for average mileage). Nevertheless, adjustments for use intensity have been made for capital service flows, which is indeed the setting of Byrne and Corrado (2019).

In addition, we assume a *2 percentage point per year overestimation of the price change* in the possibly affected categories (next four rows of Table 15.A.1). Motor vehicles are the largest of possibly affected categories, and for them the existing procedures appear likely to capture most of the quality change. The composition of the other possibly affected categories gives a relatively low weight to digital items with quality changes.

15.3.1 Digital replacements

Some digital products provide a free or inexpensive replacement for a more expensive item that used to be the only option available. For example, in some places Uber services are cheaper than a taxi. Or digital cameras made photo processing services unnecessary, only to become largely unnecessary themselves as smartphones replaced separate digital cameras in many use cases. Official price indexes only partially capture the cost-of-living declines from lower-cost or free digital replacements. For the item categories that have been extensively replaced by digital alternatives (shown in the top five rows of Table 15.A.2), we assume that the cost of living index declines by *5% per year* relative to a conventional price index over the 10 years from 2005 to 2015. In some cases, digital replacements require some increases in spending elsewhere—one must first purchase a smartphone, or at least a computer and Internet access services to benefit from the replacement. Also, there is an upper limit to this kind of bias, because once everyone has switched to the digital replacement, there are no further gains to be made. For categories in the possibly affected group (in which items not replaced by a digital alternative predominate) we assume a *1 percentage point decline in the cost of living*.

15.3.2 Access and information enabling better selection of varieties

E-commerce has expanded consumers' access to varieties, and online sources of information have reduced search costs for finding the best match for one's individual needs and tastes. Brynjolfsson et al. (2003) provide some evidence on the welfare gains from increased access to variety for books, finding that "obscure" titles accessible only through online bookstores accounted for 2.35% of total book sales. With a plausible value of 4 for the elasticity of substitution, the Feenstra (1994) formula for the effect of new varieties on a cost of living index implies a decline of about 0.8 percentage points from newly accessible books (Byrne et al., 2016). If the expansion in the selection of books available online took 4 years, the average annual impact would be 0.2 percentage points. Second, better information that allows better selection of varieties affects almost any kind of differentiated product consumed by households. These welfare gains are part of Hulten and Nakamura's (2017) concept of "output-saving technological change" (which they capture in a complementary welfare measured that they call EGDP). Table 15.A.3 identifies the product categories that are relevant for the effects of online information or for both effects and finds that they had a budget share of almost 17% in 2005. In absence of much direct evidence, we will assume *0.3 percentage points per year* overestimation of the relevant prices as the upper bound for the variety effects. At least for recent years, this is probably too high as the gains from variety access and better information are concentrated in the early days of the Internet: once the variety set is already large, additional varieties have little marginal impact on welfare, and information is also subject to decreasing returns.

Table 15.2 shows the corrections to a household consumption price index whose purpose

TABLE 15.2 Corrections to growth rate of the consumption deflator if the goal is to estimate a broad cost-of-living index.

	Assumed measurement error in annual growth rate of prices (percentage points)	2005 weight (unweighted average across 33 OECD countries) (percent)	2015 weight (unweighted average across 34 OECD countries) (percent)	Correction to growth rate of the consumption deflator, 2005 weights (percentage points)	Correction to growth rate of the consumption deflator, 2015 weights (percentage points)
Significant potential for under adjustment for quality change (*"affected products"*) except communication services	5	0.79	0.99	−0.04	−0.05
Significant potential for under adjustment for quality change (*"affected products"*)—communication services	10	2.71	2.38	−0.27	−0.24
Some potential for under adjustment for quality change (*"potentially affected products"*)	2	7.38	6.16	−0.15	−0.12
Significant replacement by alternative product from the digital economy (*"affected products"*)	5	2.36	0.98	−0.12	−0.05
Some replacement by alternative product from the digital economy (*"potentially affected products"*)	1	5.79	6.06	−0.06	−0.06
Significant potential for improved variety selection (*"potentially affected products"*)	0.3	16.83	15.55	−0.05	−0.05
All potential effects on aggregate deflator		35.86	32.12	**−0.68**	**−0.57**

Source: *Authors' calculations using data from the OECD Purchasing Power Parities program database.*

is assumed to be to estimate a broad cost-of-living index that accounts for welfare gains from quality change, digital replacements, and expanded and improved selection of varieties. The first observation here is that the categories of *affected* and *potentially affected* products account for 31.5% of consumer expenditure in 2015 (unweighted average across 34 OECD countries). In other words, over *two-thirds* of household consumption expenditure is unlikely to be subject to a measurement bias linked to the digital economy. The second observation is for each kind of effect (quality adjustment, digital replacement, better choice of varieties) the expenditure share has declined between 2005 and 2015. This may reflect declining relative prices of the products (or transition to free products), possibly coupled with an elasticity of substitution below unity. Whatever the precise cause, the consequence is that the sensitivity of aggregate inflation to measurement errors in prices of digital products has declined.

In terms of the simulated effects of possible measurement errors, the upper bound correction to the index's growth rate for overlooked quality change is −0.41 percentage point in 2015, largely driven by the assumed 10% overestimation of the deflator for telecommunication services. The potentially unmeasured savings from digital replacements declines from about −0.18 percentage points based on 2005 weights to −0.11 percentage points based on the 2015 weights. Our upper bound correction for improved variety selection is −0.05 percentage point. Combining all the effects, we end up with an upper bound for the potential mismeasurement of digital products of −0.68 percentage point in 2005 and −0.57 percentage point in 2015. A correction in the order of half a percentage point to recent annual real consumption growth would not be insignificant. Nonetheless more than half of the gap between the postslowdown and preslowdown rates of productivity growth would remain. And some upward corrections for

sources of mismeasurement are also likely be needed in the preslowdown era.

15.4 Two unorthodox points and *beyond GDP*

15.4.1 Hulten Paradox

Hulten (1996)—in a discussion of the estimates of the price of light and potential measurement biases in long-term real income in Nordhaus (1996)—concluded that our ancestors would have suffered from an implausibly low standard of living had there been a long-term upward bias in price measures of the magnitude suggested by Nordhaus. Here, we transpose Hulten's thought experiment to a shorter and more recent period, but its basic spirit is unchanged.

The household consumption deflator in the US national accounts rose by 3.3% per year between 1959 and 2016. As shown in Table 15.3, in 1959, median household income was 5400 dollars at then-current prices. In today's prices, and given the 3.3% annual price increase, this 1959 income translates into 34,636 dollars/household. Compared with today's income of 59,039 dollars at current 2016 prices, there has thus been a 70% rise of real income over the past six decades.

Now assume that the annual growth rate of the household consumption deflator was biased upward by 1 percentage point, so that "true" inflation was only 2.3% per year. This yields a 1959 income of 19,588 dollars in 2016 prices, implying a tripling of material living standards over the six decades. And the 1959 median income, expressed in 2016 prices, would only be 11,077 dollars if a 2 percentage points upward bias is assumed, implying a *fourfold* rise in living standards in less than a lifetime (59,039/11,077 = 4.33). This seems implausibly high.

There is another telling comparison: By today's poverty threshold, the 1959 *median* income expressed in 2016 prices would lie just above the

TABLE 15.3 Median household income under alternative inflation assumptions (United States).

Year	Prices of:	HH Income—US dollars
2016	Current year	59,039
1959	Current year	5400
1959	2016, based on official PCE deflator	34,636
1959	2016, assuming bias of 1%/year	19,588
1959	2016, assuming bias of 2%/year	11,077
Year	**Household type**	**Poverty threshold**
2016	Household size 2	15,569
2016	Household size 3	19,705
Addendum:		
Period	**Assumed bias in deflator**	**Real income growth**
1959–2016	None	70.5%
1959–2016	1% per year	201.4%
1959–2016	2% per year	433.0%

Source: US Bureau of Economic Analysis and US Census Bureau.

poverty line (1% bias scenario), or markedly below it in the 2% bias scenario. To be sure, none of this is hard evidence, and the Hulten Paradox rests on a hypothetical scenario. Nevertheless, it puts some plausibility limits on any *persistent and significant* bias in overall inflation measurement.[21]

15.4.2 Perceived inflation

Central Banks, the European Commission, and other institutions have systematically monitored peoples' perceptions and expectations about consumer inflation. Expected inflation is obviously an important piece of information for central banks, given the role of expectations as a transmission channel of monetary policy. Yet, for the question at hand—whether there is a systematic upward bias in aggregate consumer inflation due to mismeasured prices of digital products—it is less the expectation of inflation than the gap between perceived inflation and measured inflation that is of interest. We take the European data, recently analyzed by Arioli et al. (2017) as representative of a finding that seems to hold broadly: despite differences between countries and over time, the level of perceived inflation is nearly always above the level of inflation as measured by CPIs (Fig. 15.1).

There are explanations for such a discrepancy: incorrect weighting of price changes by consumers (small, frequently purchased items tend to get disproportionate weight in perceptions), other psychological reasons (price rises are better remembered than price drops), and, often-quoted, the fact that consumers do not account

---

[21] A persistent bias may be less probable than a bias for shorter periods of time, as statisticians usually take measures to address known issues. For instance, hedonic quality adjustment methods for computers were introduced in the United States as early as 1986, and their use spread to other countries following the Boskin Commission.

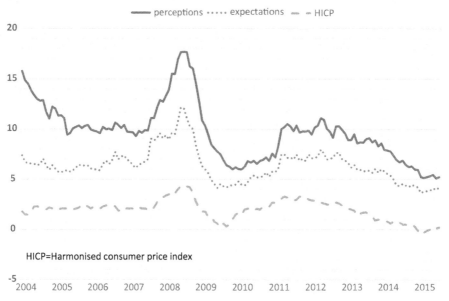

FIGURE 15.1 EU consumers' inflation perceptions and expectations. *Credit: Arioli, R, Bates CHD, Duca I, Friz R, Gayer C, Kenny G, Meyler A, Pavlova I: EU consumers' quantitative inflation perceptions and expectations: an evaluation, European Central Bank Occasional Papers Series, 186, Frankfort, 2017. https://www.ecb.europa.eu/pub/pdf/scpops/ecb.op186.en.pdf? bc91d1bc6ad64614b2d76abbd884b1ba, chart 4a.*

for quality change, whereas statisticians do. Thus, the 500-dollar cost of a new laptop today is registered as no price change over the 500-dollar laptop purchased 3 years ago, even if the new model offers vastly improved performance and weighs less than the old model. Another factor that may play out here is inequality. Households at different points of the income distribution may face different inflation rates and the survey results may summarize the experience of individual households differently from the aggregate CPI.

The implications of these observations for the question at hand are of a qualitative nature. First, we simply note that consumers tend to believe that their own cost of living has risen by *more* than is shown by aggregate official price indexes. Thus, if the official deflator is upward biased because it overlooks the welfare gains from digital products, correcting for such a bias will widen the gap between perceived and measured

inflation. Perceived, rather than official, inflation is what drives many elements of consumer behavior, so a wider gap may pose some issues both from a policy perspective and from a perspective of credibility of statistics.

Second, an observation of a more philosophical nature is that our theory of quality adjustment of consumer prices is firmly rooted in the picture of a utility-maximizing, well-informed representative consumer. The measurement of welfare gains that come with new products, free products, and digitally enabled products relies on the same consumer theory. However, as the discussion of perceived inflation shows, consumers do not appear to make rational and well-informed judgments on the rate of inflation. Are consumers increasingly well off even if this is contrary to their own judgment? Or are consumers indeed rational but equipped with a more elaborate intuitive perception of their net welfare gains than the economic models underlying price measurement? For instance, people might intuitively factor in certain disadvantages that come with digital products (24/7 connectedness, extended working hours, loss of privacy, cybersecurity incidents, etc.), or might attribute less of a quality improvement to their new computer than statisticians do because the higher-performing computer is simply necessary to accommodate more-demanding software that essentially performs the same tasks.

Any answer to this question is beyond the scope of this chapter, but a potentially wide gap between perceived and measured inflation is an issue that cannot be ignored as a matter of credibility and perceived quality of official statistics.

15.4.3 "Beyond GDP"

The welfare gains from digital products are, undoubtedly, large. But from a statistical perspective, the question is, how many of these welfare effects should be packed into our core macroeconomic measures—consumption, real income, and GDP? Or should these welfare effects instead be identified in data designed to gauge quality of life *Beyond GDP*? One consideration is whether the macroeconomic measures would remain fit for key macroeconomic policy-making purposes. While a consensus on this criterion will likely remain elusive, it can at least help with drawing the boundaries. For instance, a CPI that partly depends on shadow prices is unlikely to pass the criterion of being fit for interest rate targeting and may be hard to accept as a reference for escalating pensions and other payments. Reproducibility of results, objectivity, and transparency of methods are important criteria, along with purely practical considerations. For example, even if we set aside the conceptual problems, developing an estimate of a reservation price for a truly novel product is a major research project that would be impossible to conduct within the normal timeliness and resource constraints of statistical offices. At the same time, there are good reasons to go further in incorporating quality adjustments to the greatest extent possible, and in capturing new products early in their life cycle.

Another promising avenue is to attempt to systematically capture important dimensions of welfare and well-being in data sets that complement macroeconomic aggregates. On the one hand, some elements of this work are conceptually tied to the *System of National Accounts* and provide additional depth to existing data, such as introducing distributional information into measures of household consumption or real income (Jorgenson and Schreyer, 2017; Zwijnenburg et al., 2017). In the area of price statistics, an analogous complement would be an investigation of whether the implied price changes from new goods disproportionally affect certain income groups. This sort of analysis could also be relevant for free services from digital platforms, and platform-enabled services and rentals.

On the other hand, the "Beyond GDP" agenda clearly requires indicators on well-being and welfare that cover broader dimensions of life, economic and otherwise. The agenda has been set by Stiglitz et al. (2009) and work undertaken at national and international levels (for instance OECD, 2017). Current and more specific research in the context of the OECD's *Going Digital* Strategy (http://www.oecd.org/going-digital/) concerns the link between digitalization and well-being. It aims at assessing the effects of digitalization across major dimensions of the quality of life. These are highly relevant welfare effects, but none of them will be reflected in CPIs, nor should they be.

15.5 Conclusion

We divide the potential sources of distortion in the price index for household consumption into three categories: (1) neglected welfare gains from new and free goods, and from improved matching of variety characteristics with consumer tastes; (2) the cost savings from free or low-cost digital products that directly replace existing nondigital products; and (3) incomplete adjustment for changes in the quality of products embodying digital technology. We argue that welfare effects that require estimation of reservation prices or shadow values are relevant for a complementary welfare account but less suitable for the measurement in official GDP and consumer price statistics. We calibrate upper bounds for the impact of incorporating the remaining welfare effects in the household consumption deflator (though their inclusion in GDP may be debatable) using detailed data on the weighting structure of household consumption in OECD countries. We find that the products concerned account for about 35% of household expenditure in 2005, declining to 32% in 2015. Total plausible upper bound effects

on the growth rate of the consumption deflator amount to somewhat less than -0.6 percentage points in 2015, down from just under -0.7 in 2005. The implied upper bound adjustment to real household consumption growth would result in a more optimistic picture of growth and productivity change but would not overturn the conclusion that productivity has slowed substantially compared to the its performance in the early 2000s and late 1990s, particularly if the adjustments to the productivity growth also needed in the earlier years are also considered.

Annex 15.A. Weights in household consumption basket of product categories potentially affected by measurement errors in deflators

TABLE 15.A.1   Weights in household consumption of products with potentially overlooked quality improvements.

Product category	Potential source of measurement error	2005 weight (per mil)	2015 weight (per mil)
Telecommunication equipment	Overlooked quality change	2.1	4.1
Telecommunication services	Overlooked quality change and replacement by digital alternatives	27.1	23.8
Information processing equipment and software	Overlooked quality change	4.5	4.9
Photographic/cinematographic equipment	Overlooked quality change and replacement by the smartphone	1.3	0.9
Major and small HH appliances	Possibly/partially affected by overlooked quality change	11.2	9.5
Equipment for the reception and recording of sound and vision	Possibly/partially affected by overlooked quality change and replacement by online services	7.0	5.3
Motor vehicles and parts	Possibly/partially affected by overlooked quality change	50.8	42.6
Games, toys and hobbies	Possibly/partially affected by overlooked quality change	4.8	4.2
Total		**108.8**	**95.3**

Unweighted averages across OECD countries.
Source: *Authors' calculations based on the OECD Purchasing Power Parities Database.*

TABLE 15.A.2 Weights in household consumption of products subject to replacement by digital alternatives.[a]

Product category	Digital alternative providing replacement	2005 weight (per mil)	2015 weight (per mil)
Passenger transport, taxi or hired car with driver	Platform-enabled ridesharing	3.1	3.0
Prerecorded recording media	Digital media, downloads and streaming	2.2	1.2
Unrecorded recording media	Digital downloads and streaming	1.1	0.4
Newspapers and periodicals	Online media	6.8	4.5
Category containing film developing and printing	Digital cameras and storage media	10.4	0.7
Books[b]	e-books and used books bought online	4.7	3.3
Passenger transport by air[b]	Internet enables households to be their own travel agent	6.8	8.9
Package holidays[b]	Digital replacement for travel agents	8.1	9.3
Accommodation services[b]	Sharing economy replacement for hotels	14.1	15.6
Services for maintenance and repair of dwelling[b]	YouTube enables do-it-yourself repairs	4.6	4.1
Postal services[b]	Online billing paying (and quality improvement from online tracking of packages)	1.1	0.9
Jewellery, clocks and watches[b]	Smartphone replaces watches and clocks	4.3	3.9
FISIM[b]	Better rates of online banks and peer-to-peer lenders	14.2	14.6
Total		**81.5**	**70.4**

Unweighted averages across OECD countries.
[a] *The adjustment for quality change in communication services and photographic instruments and equipment for reception and recording of sound and vision is assumed to include effect of digital replacements, so they are omitted here.*
[b] *Replacement by digital alternative limited in scope.*
Source: *Authors' calculations based on the OECD Purchasing Power Parities Database.*

TABLE 15.A.3 Weights in household consumption of products where digitalization may have improved variety selection.

Product category	2005 weight (per mil)	2015 weight (per mil)
Cloth and clothing	51.6	44.5
Furniture, floor coverings, HH textiles, and repairs thereof	25.0	19.8
Games, toys and hobbies	4.8	4.2
Newspapers and periodicals	6.8	4.5
Books	4.7	3.3
Other durable and nondurable HH goods	18.3	16.9
Restaurants, cafes and dancing establishments	38.4	42.6
Accommodation services	14.1	15.6
Services for maintenance and repair of dwelling	4.6	4.1
Total	**168.3**	**155.5**

Unweighted averages across OECD countries.
Source: *Authors' calculations based on the OECD Purchasing Power Parities Database.*

Disclaimer

Views expressed are those of the authors and should not be attributed to the IMF, its Executive Board, or its Management, nor to the OECD or its member countries.

Acknowledgments

The authors are grateful to David Byrne and Carol Corrado for helpful comments.

References

Abdirahman M, Coyle D, Heys R, Stewart W: *A comparison of approaches to deflating telecoms services output*, ESCoE Discussion Papers, 2017-04, London, https://www.escoe. ac.uk/wp-content/uploads/2017/02/ESCoE-DP-2017-04.pdf.

Aghion P, Bergeaud A, Boppart T, Klenow P, Li H: Missing growth from creative destruction, *American Economic Review* 109(8):2795—2822, 2019. https://doi.org/10.1257/aer.20171745.

Ahmad N, Schreyer P: *Measuring GDP in a digitalised economy*, OECD Statistics Working Papers, 2016/07, Paris, 2016, OECD Publishing, https://doi.org/10.1787/5jlwqd81d09r-en.

Ahmad N, Ribarsky J, Reinsdorf M: *Can potential mismeasurement of the digital economy explain the post-crisis slowdown in GDP and productivity growth?*, OECD Statistics Working Papers, 2017/09, Paris, 2017, OECD Publishing, https://doi.org/10.1787/a8e751b7-en.

Arioli R, C Bates HD, Duca I, Friz R, Gayer C, Kenny G, Meyler A, Pavlova I: *EU consumers' quantitative inflation perceptions and expectations: an evaluation*, European Central Bank Occasional Papers Series , 186, Frankfort, https://www.ecb.europa.eu/pub/pdf/scpops/ecb.op186.en.pdf?bc91d1bc6ad64614b2d76abbd884b1ba.

Bean C: *Independent review of UK economic statistics*, London, https://www.gov.uk/government/publications/independent-review-of-uk-economic-statistics-final-report.

Berndt E, Griliches Z, Rosett J: Auditing the producer price index: micro evidence from prescription pharmaceutical preparations, *Journal of Business & Economic Statistics* 11(3):251—264, 1993. https://www.tandfonline.com/doi/abs/10.1080/07350015.1993.10509953.

Bils M: Do higher prices for new goods reflect quality growth or inflation? *Quarterly Journal of Economics* 124(2): 637—675, 2009.

Boskin M, Dulberger E, Gordon R, Griliches Z, Jorgenson D: Final report of the advisory commission to study the consumer price index Committee on Finance, US Senate. In William Jr VR, editor: *Chairman 104th Congress, 2nd Session, S Prt 104-72 Washington*, Government Printing Office. https://www.finance.senate.gov/download/final-report-of-the-advisory-commission-to-study-the-consumer-price-index-print-104-72.

Bughin J: The web's 100 billion surplus, *McKinsey Quarterly*, (January): 2011. https://www.mckinsey.com/industries/media-and-entertainment/our-insights/the-webs–and-8364100-billion-surplus.

Brynjolfsson E, Eggers F, Gannamaneni A: *Using massive online choice experiments to measure changes in well-being*, NBER Working Paper Series 24514, https://www.nber.org/papers/w24514.pdf.

Brynjolfsson E, McAfee A: *The second machine age: work, progress, and prosperity in a time of brilliant technologies*, New York, 2014, WW Norton & Company.

Brynjolfsson E, Oh JH: The attention economy: Measuring the value of free digital services on the internet. In *Proceedings of the 2012 international conference on information systems, Orlando*, 2012. https://aisel.aisnet.org/icis2012/proceedings/EconomicsValue/9/.

Brynjolfsson E, Hu Y, Smith M: Consumer surplus in the digital economy: estimating the value of increased product variety at online booksellers, *Management Science* 49(11): 1580—1596, 2003.

Byrne D, Corrado C: *Prices for communications equipment: rewriting the record*, FEDS Working Papers 2015-069, Washington, 2015, Board of Governors of the Federal Reserve System, https://www.federalreserve.gov/econresdata/feds/2015/files/2015069pap.pdf.

Byrne D, Corrado C: *ICT Prices and ICT Services: what do they tell us about productivity and technology?*, Finance and Economics Discussion Series 2017-015, Washington, 2017a, Board of Governors of the Federal Reserve System, https://doi.org/10.17016/FEDS.2017.015.

Byrne D, Corrado C: *ICT asset prices: marshaling evidence into new measures*, Finance and Economics Discussion Series 2017-016, Washington, 2017b, Board of Governors of the Federal Reserve System, https://doi.org/10.17016/FEDS.2017.016r1.

Byrne D, Corrado C: Accounting for innovation in consumer digital services: implications for economic growth and consumer welfare, Presented at the IMF Statistics Forum, 2019. https://www.imf.org/~/media/Files/Conferences/2017-stats-forum/correct-version-accounting-for-innovation-in-consumer-digital-services.ashx?la=en.

Byrne D, Fernald J, Reinsdorf M: *Does the United States have a productivity slowdown or a measurement problem?*, Brookings Papers on Economic Activity (Spring), pp 109—157. https://www.brookings.edu/wp-content/uploads/2016/03/byrnetextspring16bpea.pdf.

Cavallo A: Are online and offline prices similar: evidence from large multi-channel retailers, *The American Economic Review* 107(1):283—303, 2017. https://doi.org/10.1257/aer.20160542.

Cavallo A, Rigobon R: The billion prices project: using online prices for measurement and research, *The Journal of Economic Perspectives* 30(2):151–178, 2016. http://www.jstor.org/stable/43783711.

Deaton A: *The great escape: health, wealth and the origins of inequality*, Princeton, 2013, Princeton University Press.

Diewert WE: Exact and superlative index numbers, *Journal of Econometrics* 4(2):115–145, 1976. https://doi.org/10.1016/0304-4076(76)90009-9.

Diewert WE: *Notes on producing and annual superlative index using monthly data*, Economics Discussion Papers 00-08, Vancouver, 2000, University of British Columbia Department of Economics.

Diewert WE, Fox K: The digital economy, GDP and consumer welfare. In *Paper presented at the economic measurement group workshop, UNSW Sydney*, 2 December 2016.

Diewert WE, Fox K, Schreyer P: *The digital economy, new products and consumer welfare*, UBC Economics Discussion Papers 17-09, https://econ2017.sites.olt.ubc.ca/files/2018/02/pdf_paper_erwin-diewert-17-09DigitalEconomy-1.pdf.

Diewert WE, Fox K, Schreyer P: *The allocation and valuation of time*, UBC Economics Discussion Papers 17-04, https://econ.sites.olt.ubc.ca/files/2017/05/pdf_paper_erwin-diewert-17-04-AllocationandValuationetc.pdf.

Feenstra R: New product varieties and the measurement of international prices, *The American Economic Review* 84(1):157–177, 1994.

Feldstein M: Underestimating the real growth of GDP, personal income, and productivity, *The Journal of Economic Perspectives* 31(2):145–164, 2017.

Goolsbee A, Klenow P: *Internet rising, prices falling: measuring inflation in a world of E-commerce*, NBER Working Papers 24649, http://www.nber.org/papers/w24649.

Greenstein S, McDevitt R: *Evidence of a modest price decline in US broadband services*, NBER Working Papers 16166, https://www.nber.org/papers/w16166.

Hausman J: Valuation of new goods under perfect and imperfect competition. In Bresnahan T, Gordon R, editors: *The economics of new goods*, Chicago, 1996, University of Chicago Press, pp 209–237.

Hicks J: The valuation of the social income, *Economica* 7(26):105–124, 1940.

Hulten C: Comment. In Bresnahan T, Gordon R, editors: *The economics of new goods*, Chicago, 1996, University of Chicago Press, pp 66–70. http://www.nber.org/chapters/c6064.

Hulten C, Nakamura L: *Accounting for growth in the age of the internet: the importance of output-saving technical change*, NBER Working Paper No 23315 (revised in 2018), http://www.nber.org/papers/w23315.

ILO, IMF, OECD, United Nations, World Bank: *Consumer price index manual: theory and practice*, Geneva, 2004, International Labour Office.

Jorgenson D, Schreyer P: Measuring individual economic well-being and social welfare within the framework of the system of national accounts, *Review of Income and Wealth* 63(Supplement 2):460–477, 2017.

Konüs A: The problem of the true index of the cost of living, *Econometrica* 7(1):10–29, 1939.

McFadden D: Cost, revenue and profit functions. In , Amsterdam, 1978, North-Holland, pp 3–109. Fuss M, McFadden D, editors: *Production economics: a dual approach to theory and applications*, vol. 1. Amsterdam, 1978, North-Holland, pp 3–109.

Moulton B: *The measurement of output, prices and productivity: what has changed since the Boskin commission?*, Washington, 2018, Brookings Institution. https://www.brookings.edu/wp-content/uploads/2018/07/Moulton-report-v2.pdf.

Moulton B, Moses K: *Addressing the quality change issue in the consumer price index* (No. 1), 1997. Brookings Papers on Economic Activity, pp 305–366. https://www.brookings.edu/wp-content/uploads/1997/01/1997a_bpea_moulton_moses_gordon_bosworth.pdf.

Nakamura L, Soloveichik R: *Valuing 'free' media across countries in GDP*, Federal Reserve Bank of Philadelphia Working Papers 15-25, Philadelphia, 2015.

National Research Council: *At what price? Conceptualizing and measuring cost-of-living and price indexes*, Washington, 2002, National Academy Press.

Nordhaus W: Do real-output and real-wage measures capture reality? The history of lighting suggests not. In Bresnahan T, Gordon R, editors: *The economics of new goods*, Chicago, 1996, University of Chicago Press, pp 29–66. http://www.nber.org/chapters/c6064.

OECD: *How's life?: Measuring Well-being*, Paris, 2017, OECD Publishing Paris. https://doi.org/10.1787/how_life-2017-en.

Reinsdorf M: The effect of outlet price differentials on the U.S. consumer price index. In Foss M, Manser M, Young A, editors: *Price measurements and their uses*, Chicago, 1993, University of Chicago Press, pp 227–258. http://www.nber.org/chapters/c7805.

Schreyer P, Diewert WE: Household production, leisure and living standards. In Jorgenson D, Landefeld JS, Schreyer P, editors: *Measuring economic sustainability and progress*, Chicago, 2014, University of Chicago Press, pp 89–114. http://www.nber.org/chapters/c12826.

Stiglitz J, Sen A, Fitoussi J-P: *Report by the commission on the measurement of economic performance and social progress*,

Paris, https://ec.europa.eu/eurostat/documents/118025/118123/Fitoussi+Commission+report.

Syverson C: Challenges to mismeasurement explanations for the US productivity slowdown, *The Journal of Economic Perspectives* 31(2):165–186, 2017.

Triplett J: *Handbook on hedonic indexes and quality adjustments in price indexes, special application to information technology products*, Paris, 2006, OECD Publishing, https://doi.org/10.1787/9789264028159-en.

Varian H: *Economic value of Google, Presentation at Web 2.0 Expo san Francisco.* https://cdn.oreillystatic.com/en/assets/1/event/57/The%20Economic%20Impact%20of%20Google%20Presentation.pdf.

Zwijnenburg J, Bournot S, Giovannelli F: *Expert group on disparities in a national accounts framework: results from the 2015 exercise*, OECD Statistics Working Papers, 2016/10, Paris, 2017, OECD Publishing, https://doi.org/10.1787/2daa921e-en.

Further reading

Diewert WE: Aggregation problems in the measurement of capital. In Usher D, editor: *The measurement of capital*, Chicago, 1980, University of Chicago Press, pp 433–538.

Diewert WE: Exact and superlative welfare change indicators, *Economic Inquiry* 30(4):565–582, 1992. https://doi.org/10.1111/j.1465-7295.1992.tb01282.x.

16

Intangible capital, innovation, and productivity *à la* Jorgenson evidence from Europe and the United States

Carol Corrado[1], Jonathan Haskel[2], Massimiliano Iommi[3], Cecilia Jona-Lasinio[4]

[1]The Conference Board, New York, United States; Center for Business and Public Policy, McDonough School of Business, Georgetown University, Washington, DC, United States; [2]Imperial College Business School, London, United Kingdom; [3]Italian Statistical Institute, Rome, Italy; [4]LUISS University and Econometric Studies and Economic Forecasting Division, Italian Statistical Institute, Rome, Italy

The changing nature of the global economy has placed novel attention on intangible capital as a source of economic growth. This chapter demonstrates the increased relevance of intangible capital using the theoretical and empirical framework for analyzing factors affecting economic growth developed by Dale Jorgenson (and coauthors) over the years.

16.1 Intangible investment and capital

The links among intangible investment, productivity, and innovation have their roots in Jorgenson and Griliches (1967), and intangibles-related expansions of that work developed in closely related literatures: R&D became explicit in neoclassical and firm-level growth accounting in the 1970 and 1980s (Griliches, 1973, 1979, 1986); innovation was made explicit in endogenous growth models in the early 1990s (Romer, 1990; see also Aghion and Howitt, 2007); and the importance of intangibles other than R&D emerged with the IT-driven productivity "boom" years of the late 1990s (Brynjolfsson et al., 2002). The notion that there may be more to investments than captured in standard measures grew along with the gap between equity market and accounting valuations of firms (Lev, 2001; see also Lev and Gu, 2016).

Corrado et al. (2005, 2009, hereafter CHS) set out a framework that expanded the core concept of business investment in national accounts to treat long-lived spending on "intangibles"—computerized information (software and databases), R&D, design and other nonscience-based new product development costs, brand equity, firm-specific training, and business process reorganization—as fixed investment.

They used an economic view of investment to formalize the arguments for capitalizing this broad range of spending in company and national accounts.

An economic view of investment suggests that assets are created when today's resources are set aside and used to expand tomorrow's production capacity. The criterion applies equally to firms' expenditures on intangibles as it does to expenditures on tangibles because spending on, e.g., research, product, brand, and organizational development increases future production capacity through "organic growth," or innovation. This broad view of investment is common sense, yet it is firmly grounded in economic theory via the optimal growth literature (e.g., Weitzmann, 1976; Hulten, 1979).

CHS also set out methods to measure intangible investment for use in productivity analysis, methods based in part on Nakamura (2001). Although the fixed asset boundary in national accounts has been continuously expanded in recent decades to better account for the role of intangibles, official SNA-based estimates treat as investment only a limited range of intangible assets: R&D, mineral exploration, computer software and databases, and entertainment, literary and artistic originals.[1]

16.1.1 INTAN-Invest

A significant research effort has expanded the number of countries for which estimates of investment in intangible assets based on the CHS approach are available. Key work has focused on covering Europe and is comparative in nature; this applies to three projects funded by the European Commission under the Seventh Framework Programme and two efforts funded by the European Investment Bank.[2]

More recently, a collaboration of researchers—the authors of this chapter—produced harmonized national estimates that include the United States.[3] This has led to the publication of the INTAN-Invest data set, which initially covered 27 countries of the European Union, plus Norway and the United States, beginning with data for 1995 (Corrado et al., 2012, 2013). For further information, see http://www.intaninvest.net.

This chapter uses a newly revised release of the data set, INTAN-Invest©2018, covering the market sector of 20 European countries and the United States through 2016. Appendix A describes the sources and methods used to develop these estimates. Fig. 16.1 shows the tangible and intangible investment shares of GDP (adjusted to include intangibles) for the 20 INTAN-Invest economies averaged over years prior to the global financial crisis (1996–2007) and during and after this crisis (2008–16) using this new data set. Note of course that the latter period includes the European sovereign debt crisis years (2010–13), and that tangible investment excludes residential structures.

These data will be analyzed in the context of productivity in Section 16.3 of this chapter, and the following descriptive facts underscore the modeling approach used in the next section (Section 16.2): (1) intangible shares of GDP vary considerably across countries, ranging from 6 and 7% to 15 and 16% for the two lowest and two highest in the latter period; (2) the gap between countries above and below the median

---

[1] SNA refers to the *System of National* Accounts 2008, which are internationally agreed upon standards for national accounts (European Commission et al., 2009).

[2] The European Commission projects were COINVEST, INNODRIVE, and SPINTAN. The European Investment Bank results were reported in van Ark et al. (2009) and Corrado et al. (2016).

[3] "Harmonized" means that, to the extent possible, the same concepts, methods, and data sources are applied and used for each country.

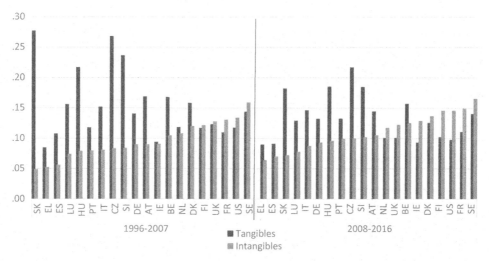

FIGURE 16.1 Intangible and tangible investment shares of GDP. Notes: GDP is adjusted to include intangibles. Country abbreviations are as follows: Austria (AT), Belgium (BE), Czech Republic (CZ), Germany (DE), Greece (EL), Denmark (DK), Hungary (HU), Spain (ES), Finland (FI), France (FR), Ireland (IE), Italy (IT), Luxembourg (LU), Netherlands (NL), Portugal (PT), Slovenia (SI), Slovakia (SK), Sweden (SE), United Kingdom (UK), United States (US). *Source: Authors' elaboration of data from INTAN-Invest @ 2018.*

intangible share did not narrow over the two periods, but (3) intangible investment shares for all countries rose or stayed the same, i.e., on average the rate of intangible investment appears to have grown (albeit slowly) despite the crises during the latter period. On the other hand, with the exception of Greece (EL), France (FR), Ireland (IE), Portugal (PT), and Sweden (SE) where tangible investment shares are flat or up a tad across the two periods, the rate of tangible investment in the other 15 countries is down.

16.1.2 Intangible capital

Our analysis of intangible investment relies on estimates of capital derived by applying the perpetual inventory model (PIM) to the INTAN-Invest @ 2018 investment estimates shown in Fig. 16.1. In the economic theory of capital due to Jorgenson (e.g., Jorgenson, 1963, 1989), geometric depreciation forms a component of the rental price of capital services. Capital services, or capital input, along with labor input and productivity, can then be combined to form the input

side of a production account in volume terms, as in Fraumeni and Jorgenson (1980, 1986); see also the earlier, simplified production accounts of Christensen and Jorgenson (1969, 1973).

Given the unexpected nature of returns to certain investments in intangibles, it is natural to question the plausibility of PIM-based estimates of net stocks of intangible capital based on geometric depreciation. In theoretical terms, intangibles are partially nonrival, and returns to investments in intangibles are not fully appropriable. Although this implies that the value of the investment to the firm or innovator is limited to the returns that can be captured, partial appropriability also provides a conceptual basis for using the rate of decline in appropriable returns as a measure of the asset's depreciation (Pakes and Schankerman, 1984).

Despite having a conceptual basis for measures of intangible capital, one often hears the question, "How can you treat [fill in the blank, say, employer-provided employee training] as an asset of the firm? The firm doesn't own [it.] Indeed [it] can walk out the door." This concern is akin to the "lemons" problem in asset valuation, i.e., the phenomenon where some, but not all, investments in an asset class tend to fail or need lots of repairs early in their lifetime. This problem exists for some tangible assets, too, and its resolution (due to Hulten and Wykoff, 1981a,b; see also OECD, 2009) is rather technical. But the bottom line is that, when the "lemons" problem is severe, the result is a relatively high geometric-like rate of economic depreciation for the asset class.[4]

Table 16.1 reports the geometric depreciation rates for the market sector intangibles used in this study, i.e., for each intangible asset type a, its net asset stock NS_t^a in period t is given by

$$NS_t^a = N_t^a + \left(1 - \delta_a^R\right)NS_{t-1}^a \qquad (16.1)$$

where N_t^a is real investment in intangible asset a and δ^a is its depreciation rate. As may be seen, the values in Table 16.1—more or less the assumptions developed by CHS—are relatively high. By contrast, geometric depreciation rates used to calculate tangible capital stocks in, e.g., EU KLEMS are rather lower—.033 (nonresidential structures), 0.01 (residential structures), 0.12 (machinery), and 0.15 (transport equipment).[5]

The initial CHS work postulated intangible depreciation rates using studies on R&D and informed guesstimates on, e.g., training via employee tenure. Later, direct estimates of intangible depreciation rates based on business survey data in the United Kingdom (Awano et al., 2010) supported the CHS rates.

TABLE 16.1 Geometric depreciation rates for market sector intangibles.

ASSET TYPE	DEPRECIATION RATE
Computerized information	
1. Software	0.315
2. Data and databases	0.315
Innovative property	
3. R&D	0.15
4. Entertainment, literary, and artistic originals	0.20
5. Mineral exploration	0.075
6. Design and other new product development	0.20
Economic competencies	
7. Brands	0.55
8. Organizational capital	
(a) Manager/strategic capital	0.40
(b) Purchased services	0.40
9. Employer-specific human capital	0.40

Note—Line 6 includes new financial products.
Source: Corrado C, Haskel J, Jona-Lasinio C, and Iommi M: Intangible capital and growth in advanced economies: measurement and comparative results. Working paper, The Conference Board and IZA, 2012.

16.2 The sources-of-growth model with intangibles

This section sets out a theoretical framework that can be used to analyze the relationship

---

[4] The probability that a given asset type will survive in productive use from one period to the next is summarized by a stochastic discard, or survival, function. The productivity of an asset as it ages, conditional on its survival from one period to the next, is described by a decay function. A decay function can be concave (i.e., possess an age-price profile bowed out from the origin) and have long-lasting effects conditional on survival from one period to the next. But Hulten and Wykoff showed that when a decay function implying long-lasting productivity conditional on survival is interacted with a discard function with a high early failure rate and age cohorts are aggregated, the result is a convex geometric-like profile with relatively rapid depreciation.

[5] The figure for nonresidential structures is the median rate across industries, which ranges from 0.023 to 0.069; see appendix table 1 (p. 55) in Timmer et al. (2007).

among intangibles, innovation, and productivity. Like the sources-of-growth (SOG) model of intangibles in CHS, its fundamentals stem from Jorgenson's works (e.g., Jorgenson, 1963, 1966; Jorgenson and Griliches, 1967; Christensen and Jorgenson, 1969; Jorgenson et al., 1987).

16.2.1 Upstream/downstream framework

The model has two sectors: an upstream, or knowledge-producing, sector and a downstream, or knowledge-using, sector. The upstream sector takes freely available concepts or ideas—basic knowledge—and produces "finished" ideas or commercial knowledge (e.g., blueprints), N_t. Another way of thinking about the two sectors is that one is the "innovation" sector and the other is the "production" sector.

Commercial knowledge, R_t, is an input to downstream production, modeled here as the sum of consumption and tangible investment and whose value is given by $P_t^Y Y_t = P_t^C C_t + P_t^I I_t$. The commercial knowledge is nonrival and appropriable, but only for a time, during which it is sold at a monopoly price to the downstream sector. The downstream sector is thus a price-taker for knowledge. This feature of the model—that product market power is temporary and located in the innovation sector—is similar to many models of innovation, e.g., Romer (1990); Aghion and Howitt (2007). Less obviously, it enables Jorgenson's user cost to be the price of knowledge services used by the downstream sector. The upstream/downstream framework is then set out as follows:

$$N_t = F^N(L_t^N, K_t^N, R_t^N; t);$$
$$P_t^N N_t = \mu_t(P_t^L L_t^N + P_t^K K_t^N) \tag{16.2}$$

$$Y_t = F^Y(L_t^Y, K_t^Y, R_t^Y; t);$$
$$P_t^Y Y_t = (P_t^L L_t^Y + P_t^K K_t^Y + P_t^R R_t^Y). \tag{16.3}$$

The first relationship in each equation is for production, which is governed by a production possibilities frontier following Jorgenson (1966). There are multiple outputs, multiple relative output prices, and product quality change. Production uses labor (L), tangible capital (K), and intangible capital (R) services as inputs.[6]

In the factor payment equations, the second relationship in Eqs. (16.2) and (16.3), the variables P^L and P^K are competitive factor prices paid for the services of L and K. The variable $\mu \geq 1$ in the upstream equation reflects the market power of the innovator, i.e., it is an "innovator markup" over the input cost of commercial knowledge production. The idea is that upstream firms produce, say, new designs over which they are assumed to have property rights and so can extract payments from downstream producers. But those new designs also add to the overall stock of knowledge upon which other inventors can draw without payment. Thus the nonrival design inputs are, overall, only partially appropriable, but at the same time may temporarily earn returns greater than their marginal cost.

In the downstream payments equation, P^R is the rental equivalence price for commercial knowledge produced by the upstream sector (e.g., a per period license fee for a patent or blueprint). Jorgenson's user cost expression gives the relationship between capital rental prices (which in practice are imputed prices) and asset replacement prices (usually transaction prices) for capital goods (Jorgenson, 1963). Applying this to the use of commercial knowledge stocks gives the following relationship between P^R and P^N

$$P_t^R = (r_t - \pi_t^R + \delta^R)P_t^N \tag{16.4}$$

---

[6] Input variables are services aggregates formed from the many types of each factor that are used in production. Intermediate inputs are ignored for simplicity. The detailed intangible asset types in R^Y were listed in Table 16.1, and in due course we will say more about the composition of other inputs.

where r_t is the net rate of return common to all capital in year t (taxes are ignored) and π_t^N is the expected capital gain (loss) on intangible capital, i.e., the expected rate of change of the asset price for commercial knowledge P^N. Note that even though P^N may reflect innovator market power, there is a limit to its exercise in downstream pricing via r, i.e., via arbitrage of returns to investments in innovation with returns to alternative long-term investments. This operates as an intertemporal constraint, implying the existence of "abnormal" firm-level profits for periods of time but zero profits (i.e., $\mu = 1$) in long-term equilibrium. From a practical point of view, this is perhaps best understood in an ex post sense. Combining upstream and downstream production, the common ex post r absorbs markups that may, of course, vary over time due to underlying variation in the pace and appropriability of innovation.[7]

There are no payments to basic knowledge in the upstream payments Eq. (16.2) because services from R^N are free, from universities say, and determined outside the model. This implies that, after log differentiation of the upstream Eq. (16.2), the term for the log change in N with regard to pure time, denoted a^N, will reflect knowledge spillovers from R^N. There are then two sources of knowledge spillovers in this model; i.e., upstream commercial knowledge production directly reflects "free" public knowledge as inputs, and downstream a^Y will reflect the diffusion of partially appropriable commercial knowledge R^Y—or directly appropriable R^N,

i.e., an "excess" return to R that accrues to society.[8]

Our model thus has key features of most models of innovation, namely, markups and knowledge spillovers. As noted by Romer (1990, p. S90), "There is little doubt that much of the value to society of any given innovation or discovery is not captured by the inventor, and any model that missed these spillovers would miss important elements of the growth process. Yet it is still the case that private, profit-maximizing agents make investments in the creation of new knowledge and that they earn a return on these investments by charging a price for the resulting goods that is greater than the marginal cost of producing the goods."

This model is closed by assuming competitive supply and rental prices of tangible capital; thus we have in parallel with Eq. (16.4),

$$P_t^K = \left(r_t - \pi_t^K + \delta^K\right)P_t^I \qquad (16.5)$$

where, as previously noted, compositional differences in the aggregate capital (and labor) services used in each sector are ignored.

16.2.2 Interpreting innovation

Without the capitalization of intangibles, GDP consists solely of downstream sector output Y, but when investments in innovation are capitalized, the growth of aggregate value added reflects current production in both sectors Q:

$$P^Q Q = P^Y Y + P^N N \equiv P^C C + P^I I + P^N N \quad (16.6)$$

---

[7] Note further that because the return over marginal cost accrues upstream and is part of the price of N in the upstream/downstream model, the innovator markup becomes an element of marginal production costs via P^R. Models of imperfect competition usually express markups as a producer markup γ, e.g., the price of goods P^Y is given by $P^Y = \gamma MC^Y$, where MC is the marginal production cost of Y. In our model there is no producer markup, but when MC is taken as the cost of conventional inputs K and L, then when $\gamma = \frac{1}{1 - P^R R^Y / Y}$, our model is observationally equivalent to models with producer markups.

[8] This is not to suggest that corporations do not conduct paid-for basic and applied R&D that creates productivity spillovers, but the simplified nature of the model, i.e., that it ignores intermediates and does not model the use of N to produce N; these spillovers are not separately accounted for even though they contribute both a^N and a^Y.

Now for some notation, let dz be the log change in Z, where "Z" is any variable in our model, and combine the conventional inputs L and K into X. Then let σ_Q^X and σ_Q^R be each input's payment share in total production; s_Q^N and s_Q^Y each sector's share of total final output; and s_Q^C, s_Q^I, and s_Q^N each final demand component's share of total final demand. Consider next two cases.

16.2.2.1 Case 1: "competitive" innovation

We first ignore the innovator markup, i.e., we set $\mu_t = 1$. Log differentiating Eqs. (16.2), (16.3), and using Eq. (16.6), we obtain the following SOG decomposition with intangible capital:

$$dq = s_Q^C dc + \underbrace{s_Q^I di + s_Q^N dn}_{\text{Expanded Investment}} \quad (16.7)$$

and

$$dq = \sigma_Q^X dx + \sigma_Q^R dr^Y + da \quad (16.8)$$

where

$$da = s_Q^Y da^Y + s_Q^N da^N. \quad (16.9)$$

In Eq. (16.8), dx reflects the combined change in (own-share-weighted) conventional inputs in total output.[9]

Likewise, da reflects the combined residual impact of exogenous influences on output growth (e.g., scientific progress) and knowledge spillovers in this model. What is different with the capitalization of intangibles, seen in all three equations above, is that growth in paid-for knowledge becomes a source of economic growth. Let us focus now on the implications of this difference for innovation.

In his evidence to the Gutierrez commission (Schramm et al., 2008), Jorgenson explained growth from innovation by stressing innovation

versus replication. To illustrate, let us ask: how might McDonalds sell more hamburgers? One way would be to issue more franchises: build more restaurants and employ more people. That would be growth via duplication; in this case more of K and L, and would likely lead to diminishing returns. The other path to growth would be to get more sales from existing K and L: reengineering the business supply process, managing inventories better, improving queuing methods so customers can be served more quickly. Jorgenson calls this growth via innovation. How might we measure this? Conceptually, innovation is growth after "netting out" growth from duplication, which via Eq. (16.8) suggests the following definition:

$$\text{Innovation} \equiv dq - \sigma_Q^X dx = \sigma_Q^R dr^Y + da \quad (16.10)$$

The innovation measure given by the RHS of Eq. (16.10) says innovation consists of two parts. The first part is the contribution of commercially valuable knowledge to growth, represented in Eq. (16.10) as services from intangible capital, $\sigma_Q^R r^Y$, i.e., services that firms pay for. The second is total factor productivity, da, the impact of knowledge that comes for free.

Adding paid-for knowledge to TFP as a description of innovation is a continuation of the Jorgenson research corpus that has shown how the "Solow" residual might be explained by better theory and better measurement. Regarding innovation and the addition of knowledge-based investments, Jorgenson and Griliches (1967, p. 275) were explicit: "*investment in scientific research and development could be separated from expenditures on current account and cumulated into stocks. The rate of return to research activity could then be computed.*" But the addition of intangible investment to their SOG model has a number of consequences, not all apparent at the time of their writing.

---

[9] That is let $P^X X = (P^L L^N + P^K K^N) + (P^L L^Y + P^K K^Y)$, then $dx = (P^L L^N / P^X X) dl^N + (P^K K^N / P^X X) dk^N + (P^L L^Y / P^X X) dl^Y + (P^K K^Y / P^X X) dk^Y$.

First, much knowledge spending continues to be treated as intermediate expenditure. Here, all such spending is treated as investment. Thus GDP is larger, a first-order impact of capitalizing intangibles.

Second, while TFP is common currency for economists and policy analysts, management scholars of innovation ignore it.[10] Perhaps they do so because they are of the view that innovation requires investment, which the intangibles-expanded framework captures and bridges, at least in part, the disparate treatment of productivity in the two literatures.

Third, many descriptions of innovation have attempted to distinguish between innovation and *diffusion*. One may use the above framework to capture this notion in various ways. One is to regard diffusion as the adoption of innovative ideas and technology via their embodiment in tangible capital, which is then included in inputs (dx). Another is to regard innovation as frontier developments requiring investments ($s_Q^N dn$), whereas diffusion is the free spread of those ideas (da^Y).

Fourth, science policy scholars long have distinguished between general knowledge and commercial knowledge, modeled here as the paid-for versus free distinction. To be clear, the notion is that, say, arithmetic is general knowledge (da^N), but specific mathematical processes for inventory management are paid-for knowledge services ($\sigma_Q^R dr^Y$).

Finally, the McDonalds example underscores that we might wish to consider a broad range of investments in knowledge beyond R&D, such as those in software, training, marketing, design, and organizational processes, i.e., following the CHS framework. Of course, this chapter's empirics do just that.

16.2.2.2 Case 2: costly innovation

The alternative $\mu > 1$ solution is given by

$$dq = s_Q^C dc + \underbrace{s_Q^I di + s_Q^N dn}_{\text{Expanded Investment}} \tag{16.11}$$

and

$$dq - \frac{\mu - 1}{\mu} s_Q^N dn = \sigma_Q^X dx + \sigma_Q^R dr^Y + da \tag{16.12}$$

where

$$da = s_Q^Y da^Y + \frac{s_Q^N da^N}{\mu}. \tag{16.13}$$

where we note the following: First, as shown on LHS of Eq. (16.12), the markup built into P^N (the excess charge for N) is a drag on output growth, i.e., more Q could be produced using the same factor inputs if the price of commercial knowledge was not so high. Second, as seen by the last term on the RHS of Eq. (16.13), the innovator markup reduces the impact of upstream TFP (da^N) on growth of the knowledge-producing sector (dn).

The costly innovation case helps underscore the importance of competitive commercial knowledge production to economies. In the limit (i.e., as μ grows very large), costly innovation is observationally equivalent to having a small or nonexistent domestic upstream sector, i.e., a situation in which (1) payments for the use of innovative commercial knowledge are subtractions from real output growth (imports) and (b) spending on basic science (e.g., university R&D) generates few productivity spillovers. Seen differently, this framework also illustrates the tensions inherent in a patent system. Polices that protect intellectual property

---

[10] A search for "total factor productivity" in any text in any Academy of Management publications since 1954, returned, out of a possible 35,796 hits, a mere 28. The same search on the Web of Science returned, out of over 5 million possible hits, 234 in Management journals and 232 in Business journals. This is not to imply that management scholars are somehow doing the wrong thing but to document that there is a large gap between the two literatures when it comes to productivity.

promote incentives to innovate via preserving high innovator markups, which then drag on growth.

16.2.3 Missing intangibles and TFP

A key point running through Jorgenson's work is that, in practice, da is measured residually and errors of measurement contaminate it in various ways. Here we focus on the possibility that intangibles are mismeasured in a first-order way: namely, that they are ignored, or that some of them are omitted (in which case the included portion can be thought of as in K). Note first that intangibles are sometimes purchased and sometimes generated internally within firms, and these cases have different accounting treatments, i.e., the ignored intangibles may (1) be treated as intermediates, not investment or (b) not counted at all, in which case they are unrecognized own-account production. To keep things simple (and consistent with the model in Section 16.2.1 that did not include intermediates), we consider the latter case.

So as to not confuse downstream production $P^Y Y$ with the case of missing intangibles, let aggregate economy activity when there are missing intangibles activity be denoted by $P^V V$, and its national income identity be given by

$$P^C C + P^I I \equiv P^L L + P^{K'} K \qquad (16.14)$$

where the rental price $P^{K'}$ is not the same as the P^K in the upstream/downstream model.[11]

Measured TFP growth is then

$$da_m = dv - dx' \qquad (16.15)$$

where dx' uses P^L and $P^{K'}$ as price weights. Subtracting (16.18) yields

$$da_m = da - (dq - dv) + \sigma_Q^R dr^Y + \sigma_Q^X dx - dx'. \qquad (16.16)$$

After rearranging terms gives, we have

$$
\begin{array}{rc}
da_m = & da \\
& \underbrace{} \\
& \text{Knowledge spillovers} \\
- & (dq - dv) \\
& \underbrace{} \\
& \text{Missing investment } N \\
+ & \sigma_Q^R(dr^Y - dx) \\
& \underbrace{} \\
& \text{Misstated returns to } R \\
- & (dx' - dx) \\
& \underbrace{} \\
& \text{Overweighted } K \text{ input}
\end{array}
\qquad (16.17)
$$

This equation says that when intangibles are ignored, TFP measured as the change in the sum of value added inputs subtracted from the change in value added output (da_m) will (1) understate actual TFP growth (da) to the extent the growth in intangible investment exceeds the growth in value added output, but on the other hand, (b) overstate actual TFP growth due to the fact that only some portion of the returns to fast-growing intangibles are captured in conventional input measures.

The final term (overweighted K effect) depends on the relative growth rates of the two conventional inputs; given that dk usually

---

[11] To explain, let $P^{K'}$ and P^K be ex post calculated gross rates of return. We have here $P^V V = P^L L + P^{K'} K$, and when we capitalize intangibles we (1) add $P^N N$ to both sides of the "old" national income identity (as a matter of accounting) and (b) restate the payments side as in the upstream/downstream model. Equating these gives

$$P^L L + P^{K'} K + P^N N = P^L L + P^K K + P^R R.$$

Dropping labor payments yields

$$P^{K'} K + P^N N = P^K K + P^R R$$

where note the difference between $P^{K'}$ and P^K vanishes as $P^R R$ approaches $P^N N$.

exceeds dl over time, the term likely reduces measured (relative to actual) TFP growth a tad.

16.2.4 The productivity slowdown

In the context of the current slowdown in measured productivity da_m, what does the intangibles-augmented SOG framework say about what might have caused it? Let us look first at Eqs. (16.11)–(16.13) of the upstream/downstream model and consider the following implications:

1. Productivity da might be slowed down because underlying scientific and technological knowledge growth dr^N has slowed. (Recall da^N is driven by unpaid R^N services.)
2. … or because commercial knowledge growth dr^Y has slowed for exogenous reasons (e.g., regulations) *and* productivity spillovers to R^Y are endogenous, i.e., if $da = \beta dr^Y$, where $\beta > 0$, then da slows when dr^Y slows.
3. … or because output growth has been limited by abnormally high innovator markups

Now, consider that productivity may be mismeasured due to uncounted intangibles, i.e., let us look now at Eq. (16.17). There are two important aspects to the impact of this mismeasurement:

4. There are unmeasured intangibles, and they are fast-growing, leading measured TFP growth (da_m) to understate actual TFP growth.
5. Or, unmeasured intangibles grow only slightly faster than conventional value added inputs, but they have a large share (σ^{R^Y}) and boost measured TFP growth.

Analysis of implication **1** is outside the scope of this chapter, except to the extent we are able to rule out all others. Implication **2** is compelling pursuit in light of recent evidence that there are productivity spillovers from non-R&D intangible investments (Corrado et al., 2017); evidence

for spillovers from R&D is well established (e.g., Griliches, 1992).

In recent work, Brynjolfsson et al. (2018) suggest the introduction and rise of artificial intelligence (AI) might be an example of bias to current measures of TFP. The sources of bias set out in Eq. (16.17) is in the spirit of their analysis, i.e., they suggest that implication **4** helps to explain the current productivity slowdown because AI investments are both fast-growing and missing, and that implication **5** points to why the slowdown might be expected to be temporary—the returns to AI have yet to come.

A belief that slow productivity growth is temporary due to lags in returns to innovation investments hinges on the expectation that returns eventually materialize. If they do not (or as one waits for them), we essentially have implication **3**, abnormally high innovator markups, i.e., Google makes massive investments in AI, paid for by very high prices charged to downstream producers for branding and selling on Google's search platform. At the same time, these same downstream producers pay high fees to IT consultants for AI-based data services with the expectation of future payoffs in organizational efficiency or return sales.

All told, when there are lags in returns to investments in innovation, upstream costs limit output and productivity growth in downstream sectors. This is one of the major implications of the model, and it seems especially useful in the context of recent productivity developments. For example, a recent analysis of US productivity (Byrne and Corrado, 2017) looked at relative productivity in the information and communication technologies (ICT) services—producing sector and a non-ICT general production sector; the study found industry-level evidence for "slow returns to spending on IT reorganization and/or data analytic services" as an explanation for the very weak relative TFP growth among non-ICT—producing industries in the Bureau of Labor Statistics (BLS) industry-level productivity measures during 2011–14.

16.3 Empirical analysis

In this section we first provide descriptive evidence on the dynamics of tangible and investment for 10 European countries and the United States for the years 1996–2016 and then examine (1) growth decompositions to analyze the relevance of intangible capital to understanding developments in productivity, and (2) intangibles-related hypotheses for explaining the productivity slowdown.

16.3.1 Coverage

We are unable to use the full INTAN-Invest @ 2018 data set in our productivity analysis—recall it covers 20 European countries—due to limited (historical) output and/or labor input source data for many countries. There are 10, primarily Western, European countries included in our empirical analysis. They are Austria (AT), Germany (DE), Denmark (DK), Spain (ES), Finland (FI), France (FR), Italy (IT), Netherlands (NL), Sweden (SE), and United Kingdom (UK).

Our coverage of these economies and the United States is for 11 NACE A21 industry sectors that represent most nonagricultural private business activity in the two geographies: mining, manufacturing, construction, wholesale and retail trade, transportation and storage, accommodation and food services, finance and insurance, professional services, administrative services, and other services.[12] See Table 16.2 for details.[13]

In the following discussion, "aggregate GVA" refers to the sum of gross value added (GVA) for included industries, i.e., NACE sectors B, C, F–K, M, N, and S per Table 16.2, including

TABLE 16.2 Industry sectors.

Sector	Description
A	Agriculture, forestry and fishing
B	Mining and quarrying
C	Manufacturing
D	Electricity, gas, steam and air conditioning supply
E	Water supply; sewerage, waste management and remediation activities
F	Construction
G	Wholesale and retail trade; repair of motor vehicles and motorcycles
H	Transportation and storage
I	Accommodation and food service activities
J	Information and communication
K	Financial and insurance activities
L	Real estate activities
M	Professional, scientific and technical activities
N	Administrative and support activities
O	Public administration and defense; compulsory social security
P	Education
Q	Human health and social work activities
R	Arts, entertainment and recreation
S	Other service activities
T	Activities of households
U	Activities of extraterritorial organizations and bodies

Note—INTAN-Invest covers all but the dark-shaded industry sectors. All shaded sectors (light and dark) are excluded from the SOG decompositions reported in this paper.
Source: NACE Rev. 2 A21 industry sectors as defined in Eurostat: NACE Rev. 2: Statistical classification of economic activites in the European community. Technical report, European Commission, 2008.

[12] NACE is the industry standard classification system used in the European Union.

[13] While INTAN-Invest covers the NACE A21 industry sectors except sectors L, O, P, Q, T, and U, our analysis also drops A, D, E, and R to better represent nonagricultural private business activity.

capitalized nonnational accounts (non-NA) intangibles investment. "Industry output" refers to adjusted industry GVA in real terms.

16.3.2 Europe and United States investment aggregates

We touched on the substantial cross-country variation in intangible and tangible investment intensity in the first section of this chapter. Here our focus is over time, both in the aggregate

and comparatively at the Europe versus United States level. The investment slowdown experienced by advanced economies has been highly debated since the onset of the global financial crisis in 2008, and analysis has often looked at the tangible–intangible divide between Europe and the United States (e.g., Corrado et al., 2016; European Investment Bank, 2018).

Fig. 16.2 shows data on the intangible and tangible investment shares of aggregate GVA in Europe and the United States in panel (a).

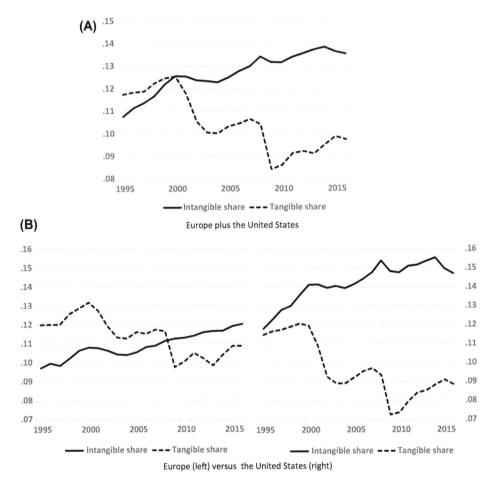

FIGURE 16.2   Intangible and Tangible Investment Shares. Note—See Section 16.3.1 for industry and country coverage. Shares are of aggregate GVA including all intangibles. *Source: Authors' elaboration of data from INTAN-Invest @ 2018, EU KLEMS, Eurostat, and national accounts for European countries and the United States.*

As may be seen, intangible investment overtook tangible investment after the global financial crisis, during which intangible investment fell comparatively less than tangible investment. Panel (b) of Fig. 16.2 distinguishes between investment shares for Europe versus the United States. The US intangibles share is higher and more variable than the aggregate share for our 10 European (EU) countries. The fallback in the US share in 2015 and 2016 is due to sharp contractions in mineral exploration in those years; excluding this component (not shown), the US share continues to rise. In the EU countries, the intangible investment share follows a steadily increasing trend over all years. The tangible share declines, on balance, in both geographies.

The trends in Fig. 16.2's picture of intangibles versus tangibles in Europe are largely unchanged when the Mediterranean countries of Italy and Spain are excluded, but as suggested by Fig. 16.1, investment in these countries is more tangible intensive. When these countries are excluded, the average rate of tangible investment in the covered industry sectors in the remaining countries is 2.1 percentage points lower than the rate of intangible investment (2008–16).

Before we use these data to develop productivity estimates, consider first the data set's possible biases following the discussion of missing intangibles in the previous section. We are not in a position to quantify investments in AI and then examine whether missing investments in AI "explain" part of the productivity slowdown using Eq. (16.17) because investments

in AI, such as spending for the creation and curation of databases, are not regularly broken out in the source data used to estimate market sector intangibles in INTAN-Invest.[14]

That said, we believe that INTAN-Invest is unlikely to be missing significant digital-related investments in intangibles by firms in market sector industries. Consider that (1) firm development of machine learning training algorithms is likely to be included in software development R&D; (2) software occupations used to estimate software produced on own-account in national accounts may overlap with workers who process and monetize databases; and (3) purchases of data analytic services are likely included in management and computer-related consulting services. We cannot affirm these conditions for all series in all countries, but we are able to appeal to two indicators of AI activities in the United States: private industry purchases of computer design consulting services and for-profit business investments in computer, software, and data-processing–related R&D. Byrne and Corrado (2017) argue at recent developments in these series are related to the demand for data analysis via cloud computing.

The US AI indicators are plotted in Fig. 16.3 relative to total US GDP. As may be seen, both indicators are dynamic and growing. While data on computer design consulting services for Europe are lacking, estimates of computer-related R&D based on industry-level estimates from EU KLEMS suggest the pace of these investments are generally stable relative to GDP in Europe.[15] This differential pattern is consistent

---

[14] Note, too, that the Brynjolfsson et al. (2018) study did not rely on investment data coherent with national accounts, which is our objective with INTAN-Invest. See Appendix A for further details on INTAN-Invest.

[15] The R&D component is included in INTAN-Invest intangibles of course. While a separate series for computer design consulting services is *not* now included in the INTAN-Invest harmonized industry sector estimates for Europe and the United States, the computer design consulting services shown in Fig. 16.3 is included in the aggregate nonharmonized series for intangible investment in the United States that begins in 1977. See www.intaninvest.net for further details.

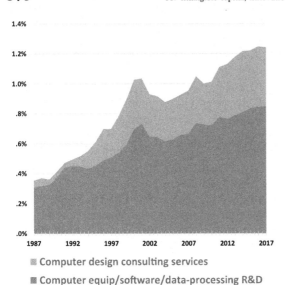

■ Computer design consulting services

■ Computer equip/software/data-processing R&D

FIGURE 16.3 Indicators of AI product development in the United States (percent of GDP). *Source: Authors' elaboration of data developed and described in Byrne DM and Corrado CA: ICT Services and their Prices: what do they tell us about Productivity and Technology? International Productivity Monitor, 2017. (33):150–181.*

with established patterns in EU–US productivity comparisons (e.g., those based on EU KLEMS; see O'Mahony and Timmer, 2009), namely, that ICT investment rates are relatively higher and more dynamic in the United States. Thus, there is evidence of an AI investment dynamic in the United States, though not so much in Europe and even in the United States, available indicators suggest these investment rates, which exclude government-funded research by universities, are still rather small.

16.3.3 Application of the SOG framework

In addition to theory, Jorgenson made substantive contributions to the practical application

of the SOG framework. Because output growth can be divided into contributions from input growth and total factor productivity growth *da*, major efforts addressed the measurement of *K* and *L* inputs to better understand the contribution of *da* to economic growth.

One way to better measure *K* and *L* inputs is to account for changes in their composition (a form of quality-change to the extent higher relative prices and better quality go together). This was originally done in Jorgenson and Griliches (1967) and expanded in SOG implementations with coauthors over the years (e.g., Jorgenson et al., 1987, 2005a). He highlighted ICT and its contribution to growth via rapid relative price declines in ICT capital in his presidential address to the American Economic Association (Jorgenson, 2001), an application of his production possibilities frontier.[16]

16.3.3.1 Methods for K and L inputs

Jorgenson's contributions to the measurement of *K* and *L* and the distinction between ICT and Non-ICT capital are the "state of the art" in productivity measurement today. This is demonstrated by methods used in (1) official TFP estimates for the United States that have been issued annually by the Bureau of Labor Statistics since 1981; (2) the EU KLEMS database project that has calculated—on a country-by-county basis—TFP estimates for Europe periodically since March 2007; and (3) the extensive worldwide network of researchers and practitioners involved in the WORLD KLEMS initiative founded by Jorgenson in 2010. In this section we apply these methods as closely as possible.

We follow EU KLEMS in our tangible capital estimation and look at aggregates for ICT equipment and Non-ICT equipment and structures in our analysis. We also follow EU KLEMS in using price deflators for ICT equipment that are harmonized to those for the United States; here

[16] See Jorgenson et al. (2005b) for further discussion.

we also harmonize price deflators for software based on estimates provided by the OECD.[17] Our tangible capital stocks are created using the geometric depreciation rates discussed in Section 16.1.2 (p. 1.2).

Regarding labor services, we look at labor input (L) decomposed into hours of all persons (H) and a composition index. The former is sourced from national accounts and composition indexes are from EU KLEMS for European countries and BLS for the United States.[18]

16.3.3.2 Methods for growth decompositions

Growth decompositions in this paper are calculated for industry value-added weighted labor productivity in Europe and the United States. Define labor productivity in industry i in country j as $(Q/H)_{i,j}$ and its log change as $d(q/h)_{i,j}$. Our decompositions are for the following bottom-up aggregates:

$$d(q/h) = \sum_i^I \sum_j^J \overline{\omega}_{i,j} d(q/h)_{i,j} \quad i = 1, I; j = 1, J$$

$$(16.18)$$

where aggregation for Europe is over 10 countries (indexed by j) and 11 industries (indexed by i); the aggregate for the United States is over industries only. The weights $\overline{\omega}_{i,j}$ are Divisia weights based on industry i in country j's purchasing-power-parity (PPP)—adjusted value added share in the relevant aggregate.[19] Inputs for Europe also are PPP-adjusted value-added weighted aggregates.

The labor productivity decompositions for Europe and the United States are then calculated as follows:

$$d(q/h) = \overline{v}_l d(l/h) + \overline{v}_k d(k/h) + \overline{v}_r d(r/h) + da_m$$

$$(16.19)$$

where da_m is measured TFP growth, here with intangibles. Our analysis and decompositions are for periods before and after the financial crisis.

Before we turn to our results, we first look at labor productivity calculated at an aggregate level $d(q^a/h^a)$, i.e., where Q and H are aggregated first and labor productivity is obtained as their ratio. Aggregate labor productivity is arguably a welfare measure (e.g., Hulten, 1978), and we first wish to know whether it is driven by underlying productivity gains, i.e., $d(q/h)_{i,j}$ weighted by value-added shares, or a reallocation of hours across sectors. Value-added share-weighted labor productivity misses the extra kick to aggregate labor productivity that comes when labor moves to high value-added per hour sectors, i.e., we have

$$d(q^a/h^a) \equiv \sum_i^I \overline{\omega}_{i,j} d(q/h)_{i,j} + \sum_i^I \overline{\omega} d(h_{i,j}/h).$$

$$(16.20)$$

where the final term represents the reallocation of hours as set out by Stiroh (2002) and the country dimension is ignored. In the graph below, we calculate this term for Europe and the United States, before and after financial crisis and it turns out to be small (Fig. 16.4).

16.3.4 Sources-of-growth results

Fig. 16.5 uses Eq. (16.18) (which is based on Eq. 16.8 from the previous section) and shows labor productivity growth and contributions to labor productivity growth from labor composition, tangible and intangible capital deepening, and total factor productivity. The decomposition are for Europe and the United States, and for both

---

[17] We thank Nadim Ahmad for supplying these deflators.

[18] Labor composition figures for Europe in 2016 are authors' estimates.

[19] The industry PPPs are from Eurostat.

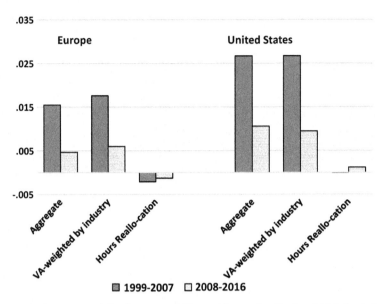

FIGURE 16.4 Labor Productivity and Reallocation of Hours. Notes—See Section 16.3.1 for industries and countries included. Figures are natural log differences. *Source: Authors' elaboration of data from INTAN-Invest@2018, EU KLEMS, and national accounts for European countries and the United States.*

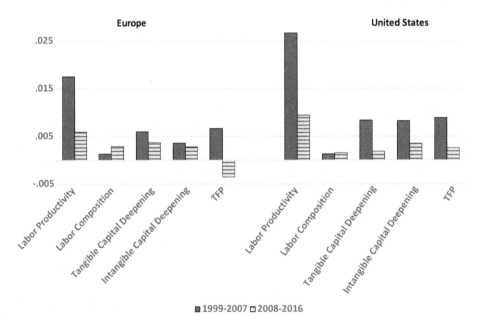

FIGURE 16.5 Decomposition of Growth in Labor Productivity. Notes—See Section 16.3.1 for industries and countries included. Figures are natural log differences. *Source: Authors' elaboration of data from INTAN-Invest@2018, EU KLEMS, and national accounts for European countries and the United States.*

before and during/after the global financial crisis.[20] The European sovereign debt crisis years (2010–12) are of course included in the second period.

In the precrisis years (1999–2007), labor productivity grew at faster pace in the United States (2.7% per year) compared with Europe (1.8% per year); both were largely driven by capital deepening that accounted for about 60% of the advances in labor productivity. Tangible capital provided a larger growth contribution compared to intangible capital but was a relatively more important driver in Europe. TFP growth was a relevant driver in both geographies during this period, accounting for 37% and 33% of labor productivity growth in the United States and Europe, respectively.

The overall picture is remarkably different in the during/after crisis period (2008–16), reflecting a combination of factors that negatively affected productivity dynamics in all advanced economies: increasing economic and political uncertainty, slow increase in demand, and low wage growth (Remes et al., 2018). Labor productivity slowed markedly, to 0.9 and 0.6% per year in the United States and Europe, respectively, driven by both a decline in capital intensity and weak/negative changes in TFP. On balance, TFP growth in Europe was negative over the period, reflecting an incomplete recovery from the large drops in 2008 and 2009.

Changes in real market sector output in 2008 and 2009 were somewhat larger in Europe than in the United States (−4.2% in Europe vs. −3.4% in the United States, at average annual rates), but downward adjustments to person hours were very sharp in the United States (−4.9%) whereas Europe curtailed hours more moderately (−2.3%). Thus, although capital deepening rose in both geographies in these

years, the drop in total factor productivity was especially large in Europe; it fell 1.6% in 2008 (compared with a 2.0% drop in the United States) and plunged nearly 6% in 2009 (compared with edging down 0.4% in the United States).

All told, TFP growth in Europe, after accounting for intangibles, slowed from 0.67% per year prior to the crisis (1999–2007) to −0.35% per year after the crisis (2008–16). In the United States, TFP growth slowed from 0.89% per year (before) to 0.26% on average (after). Thus we have total factor productivity slowdowns of 1.0 percentage point per year (Europe) and 0.63 percentage points per year (United States).

16.3.5 Productivity slowdown redux

What might account for these slowdowns? Let us first consider measured productivity excluding INTAN-Invest's non-NA intangible assets (lines 5–8 on Table 16.1). Although the weight on non-NA assets is fairly large, their investment path (in the aggregate) is not terribly dynamic after the early 2000s. If we had not capitalized non-NA intangible assets, the deceleration in TFP growth reported in Fig. 16.5 would have been 0.1 percentage point per year greater for both Europe and the United States. Thus ignoring non-NA intangibles creates a slighter larger downturn to explain.

Next, we consider that commercial knowledge spillovers are proportional to growth of intangible capital services, i.e., $da = \beta dr^Y$. Fig. 16.6 explores this relationship before (squares) and after (circles) the financial crisis. The figure points to a positive correlation between TFP and intangible capital services growth rates, consistent with a spillover relationship driven by partial appropriability and as

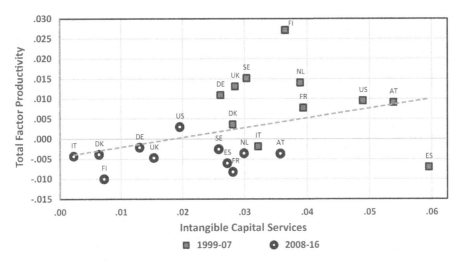

FIGURE 16.6 Spillovers to Intangible Capital Services. Notes—See text for industry sector coverage and methods for productivity calculations. Figures plotted are natural log differences. Dotted line is linear trend through all observations. *Sources: Authors' elaboration of data from INTAN-Invest@2018, EU KLEMS, Eurostat, and national accounts for European countries and the United States.*

reported (Corrado et al., 2017); the latter is a cross-country econometric analysis that found significant TFP spillovers to intangible capital after controlling for other factors of production and endogeneity of inputs. The study considered the precrisis years using data that since have been substantially revised. Fig. 16.6 suggests, however, that a relationship persists in recent years (no obvious slope difference between the pre- and postcrisis time periods) and that a significant slowdown in intangible capital services accompanied the postcrisis slowing in productivity (or vice versa).

Assuming the previously estimated spillover coefficient $\widehat{\beta}$ is applicable to recent experience and revised data, how much of the TFP decline can be accounted for by the slowing of intangible investment? The econometric analysis reported

in Corrado et al. (2017) generally finds that $\widehat{\beta} = .2$, consistent with results for R&D reported in Griliches (1992). When this $\widehat{\beta}$ is applied to the figures for the slowdown in intangible capital services, we find that knowledge spillovers can account for *nearly all* of the slowdown in productivity in the United States and one-third of the decline in TFP growth in Europe.[21]

16.4 Conclusions

This chapter develops a theoretical framework for the analysis of the relationship among intangibles, innovation, and productivity by setting out a Jorgenson-like model of economic growth. The model is first used to explore the

[21] Intangible capital services grew 3.4% per year in Europe prior to the crisis and decelerated to 1.9% thereafter. This is a slowdown of 1.5 percentage points, which when multiplied by 0.2 yields a productivity spillover of 0.3 percentage point. For the United States, intangible capital services grew 4.9% per year prior to the crisis and decelerated to 2.0% per year. This is a slowdown of 2.9 percentage points, which when multiplied by 0.2 yields a productivity spillover of −0.58 percentage point.

implications of the intangible-expanded growth framework for analyzing productivity and innovation, including how missing intangible investments might bias TFP estimates and how markups by innovators interact with growth and productivity.

The chapter also provides empirical evidence on the relevance of intangible capital to explaining productivity growth based on data for a sample of European countries and the United States from a new release of the INTAN-Invest data set. Our investigation of intangibles and the productivity slowdown found (1) the decline in capital deepening (tangible and intangible) directly accounts for a large part of the labor productivity slowdown after the financial crisis but that intangible capital growth recovered comparatively faster than tangible capital, especially in the United States; (2) the positive cross-country relationship between TFP and intangibles continues to suggest that knowledge spillovers arise from investments in both R&D and non-R&D intangible assets, i.e., as in Corrado et al. (2017); and (3) when the estimated spillover relationship is applied to recent data, the decline in intangible capital growth accounts for the decline in estimated TFP growth in the United States but explains very little of the larger TFP growth decline in Europe.

The work reported in this chapter suggests a number of avenues to explore in future work. The empirical implications of our model with innovator markups and intangibles deserve attention in light of recent work on markups (e.g., De Loecker and Eeckhout, 2017). And there is more to do on incorporating AI and the digital economy into intangibles measurement. The central point, however, is that these avenues potentially can be answered in a Jorgenson-style framework, even though it was developed in a time where such questions were in the realm of science fiction. That is eloquent testimony to the richness, power, and logical consistency of the neoclassical methods Dale Jorgenson developed and used in his work.

Appendix

The INTAN-Invest database

The main pillar of the INTAN-Invest estimation strategy is the adoption of the expenditure-based approach to measure the value of investment in intangible assets. Moreover, the project has the goal of generating measures of harmonized intangible investment satisfying (as much as possible) the following criteria: exhaustiveness, reproducibility, comparability across countries and over time, and consistency with official national accounts data. The latter goal is particularly important because our aim is to generate measures of intangible investment coherent with national accounts aggregates used to develop production accounts for the calculation of total factor productivity, i.e., output, investment in tangible assets, intermediate costs, compensation of employees, hours and employment.

The above characteristics are assured by the adoption of official data sources designed to be homogeneous across countries. But an implication of the adopted estimation strategy is that our estimation methods can be applied only for the years when national accounts data are available. For EU countries, the starting date of national accounts data from Eurostat database usually ranges from 1995 (for almost all countries) to 2000 (and even more recent years for detailed data on gross fixed capital formation [GFCF] by industry in a few countries). The relatively short time coverage for European countries is one of the main weaknesses of our database, because a longer time period would be preferred for the analysis of economic growth. Estimates for the United States are available from 1977 on although estimates beginning 1998 are more robustly estimated.

INTAN-Invest @ 2018 data cover total investment in industries from NACE sectors shown in

Table 16.2, namely, A to K, M, N, R and S up to 2015 and aggregate estimates for 2016.

The implementation of INTAN-Invest estimation strategy leads to the adoption of two different approaches for intangible assets not currently included in the SNA2008 asset boundary (design, brand, training, organizational capital, and new financial products) and for the assets already included (computer software and databases, research and development, mineral exploration, and entertainment, literary and artistic originals).

Methods and sources (EU countries)

National accounts intangible assets are based on official national accounts estimates of GFCF by industry. National accounts data on GFCF in intellectual property products (IPPs) by 21 industries and total GFCF (with no industry disaggregation) in computer software and databases (SFT) and in research and development (R&D) are available for all countries included in our analysis. Moreover, for almost all countries also data on SFT and R&D by 21 industries are available. For these countries, we estimate overall GFCF in mineral exploration and artistic and entertainment originals (MINART) by 21 industries as a residual. For countries where only total IPP by industry is available, we have adopted the following approach: First, we produce preliminary estimates of the industry distribution of GFCF in SFT, R&D, and MINART using the available indicators. Then we have rescaled preliminary estimates to make them consistent with total GFCF in IPP by industry and with aggregate GFCF in SFT, R&D, and MINART (using an iterative biproportional fitting procedure). The preliminary estimates have been derived from ESA95 national accounts data on GFCF by industry or from capital stocks estimates, depending on data availability.

The estimates of the purchased component of brand, design, and organizational capital in INTAN-Invest @2018 are obtained directly at the industry level using expenditure data by industry provided by the use tables, expressed according to the NACE Rev2 and related CPA2008 product classifications. Use tables consistent with latest guidelines for European national accounts (ESA2010) are available for all countries included in this chapter from 2010 until 2014, while use tables consistent with prior guidelines (ESA95) are available from 2008 until 2010.

The use tables compiled according to NACE Rev.2/CPA2008 classifications report intermediate costs of each industry for the following products: Advertising and Market Research Services (CPA M73), Architectural and engineering services, technical testing and analysis services (CPA M71), and Legal and accounting services, services of head offices and management consulting services (CPA M69 and M70). We take the data on total intermediate costs for these products as a proxy for total expenditure, respectively, in brand, design, and organizational capital.

The general approach is quite similar for all three assets. The first step is to make the initial data a better proxy of expenditure in the corresponding asset. We deem that in the case of Advertising and Market Research Services (CPA M73) and Architectural and engineering services, technical testing and analysis services (CPA M71) the products identified in the use table are good proxies of the corresponding assets and no further adjustments are needed. In contrast, this is not the case for Legal and accounting services, services of head offices and management consulting services (CPA M69 and M70). In this case, we computed the share of turnover of NACE M701 in turnover of NACE M69 plus M70 for each country and we apply the share to intermediate consumption in CPA M69 and M70. The above correction assumes that, in each country the share of CPA M701 (consulting services) in total intermediate consumption for CPA M69 and M70 is the same across all industries.

Finally, in each industry the capitalization factor is applied to total expenditure by market producers to obtain the value of total expenditure that we deem should be treated as GFCF instead than intermediate consumption. Capitalization factors are asset specific but not industry specific with the only exception of a special treatment for subcontracting. In fact, it is likely that part of Advertising and Market Research Services (CPA M73) bought by the Advertising and Market Research industry, that part of Design services (CPA M71) bought by the Architectural and engineering industry, and that part of Legal, accounting and consulting services (CPA M69 and M70) bought by the Legal, accounting and consulting industry are due to subcontracting activity. For this reason, we assume that the capitalization factors for CPA M73 in the Advertising and Market Research, for CPA M71 in the Architectural and engineering industry, and for CPA M69 and M70 in the Legal, accounting and consulting industry are 50% lower than in the other industries.

The approach outlined above is used to obtain estimates from 2010 until 2014 (the years in which use tables consistent with ESA2010 national accounts are available). The same approach has been applied to the use tables consistent with ESA95 available from 2008 to 2010 and the resulting estimates have been used as indicators to back-cast the level of the estimated intangible GFCF in 2010 until 2008. The back-casting procedure has been implemented at the industry level. For the years before 2008, we have produced intangible investment time series using the rate of change of the previous release of INTAN-Invest estimates of GFCF by industry as an indicator to back-cast the level of the estimated GFCF from 1995 to 2008. For each of the three assets, estimates for 2015 and 2016 have been derived updating 2014 using turnover of the corresponding industry available from Structural Business Statistics.

The estimates based on data available from the use tables guarantee the exhaustiveness of purchased GFCF in brand (based on product CPA M73) and organizational capital (based on product CPA M6970), but not that of design (based on product CPA M71). In fact, in the CPA classification, part of design activity is also classified in the CPA M741, "Specialized design activities." The use tables currently available from Eurostat do not allow identifying expenditure in CPA M741 because they only report data for the CPA M74−75 ("Other professional, scientific and technical services and veterinary services"). The Structural Business Statistics report data on turnover of NACE M741, however, and we have taken the turnover of NACE M741 as a proxy of total expenditure in CPA M741. We assume that only the market sector purchases "Specialized design activities" and obtain our GFCF estimate applying the same capitalization factor as CPA M71.

As for the own-account component, its estimate requires detailed employment data by type of occupation and by industry (e.g., from the Structure of Earning survey or the Labour Force survey) or a special survey. Eurostat available occupational data allow identifying only those occupations related to organizational capital. Therefore, at this stage, we measure only the own-account component of organizational capital, while for design and brand we only estimate the purchased component.

Methods and sources (United States)

The general methods outlined above are followed for the United States, but there are some departures and some significant differences in data availability.

For intangible assets included in the national accounts, separate data for artistic, literary, and entertainment originals, including five detailed components, are available, and thus all national accounts IPP components are available. Each IPP component is obtained from the U.S. Bureau of Economic Analysis (BEA) Fixed Asset Accounts (FAs), which covers 63 private industries and provides time series from 1901 on (where relevant). The US industry data follow the North American Industry Classification System (NAICS) and the 63 industries are grouped to the NACE sectors covered in INTAN-Invest (see above for NACE sectors covered).

Non-NA components of intangible investment are based on BEA's Annual Input-Output Accounts (IO), which are available at the 71 industry sector level; the 71 industries include the same 63 included in the FAs, plus 5 government sectors. Annual IO data are available from 1997 on and may be linked to earlier versions from 1977 on. Excluding training, discussed below, we are able to rely on only one commodity component in these accounts, miscellaneous professional and technical services (BEA code 5412OP, which covers NAICS 5412-4,6-9). The relevant individual components are first shared out using details from the benchmark IO table, which covers more than 600 industries. These results are then adjusted to a domestic spending indicator based on gross output less net exports; where relevant gross output and services trade components are not available, product line revenue data from Census Bureau surveys are used.

Official survey data on private industry spending on employer-provided training are scant for the United States. However, each year *Training Magazine* issues a "Training Industry Report" on US expenditures. The survey includes payroll of employees devoted to training and spending on external products and services for training; some major industry detail is provided. These data have been benchmarked to a comprehensive survey conducted by the BLS in 1996, which also provided major industry sector detail, and then controlled to the industry distribution of intermediate purchases of education services from BEA's Annual Input-Output Accounts. The own-account component is also benchmarked to the BLS survey, extended by information in the "Training Industry Report" on hours of training per employee and BEA wage data by industry.

References

Aghion P, Howitt P: Capital, innovation, and growth accounting, *Oxford Review of Economic Policy* 23(1): 79–93, 2007.

Awano G, Franklin M, Haskel J, Kastrinaki Z: Measuring investment in intangible assets in the UK: results from a new survey, *Economic & Labour Market Review* 4(7): 66–71, 2010.

Brynjolfsson E, Hitt LM, Yang S: Intangible assets: computers and organizational capital, *Brookings Papers on Economic Activity* 1:137–198, 2002.

Brynjolfsson E, Rock D, Syverson C: *The productivity J-Curve: how intangibles complement general purpose technologies*, NBER. Technical Report Working Paper 25148.

Byrne DM, Corrado CA: ICT services and their prices: what do they tell us about Productivity and Technology? *International Productivity Monitor* (33):150–181, 2017.

Christensen LR, Jorgenson DW: The measurement of US real capital input, 1929–1967, *Review of Income and Wealth* 15(4):293–320, 1969.

Christensen LR, Jorgenson DW: Measuring economic performance in the private sector. In Moss M, editor: *The measurement of economic and social performance*, NBER, pp 233–351.

Corrado C, Haskel J, Iommi M, Jona-Lasinio C: Growth, tangible and intangible investment in the EU and US before and since the great recession. In *Investment and investment finance in Europe 2016, annual report on investment and investment finance*, Luxembourg, 2016, European Investment Bank, pp 73–101. chapter 2.

Corrado C, Haskel J, Jona-Lasinio C: Knowledge spillovers, ICT, and productivity growth, *Oxford Bulletin of Economics & Statistics* 79(4):592–618, 2017.

Corrado C, Haskel J, Jona-Lasinio C, Iommi M: *Intangible capital and growth in advanced economies: measurement and comparative results*, Working paper, The Conference Board and IZA.

Corrado C, Haskel J, Jona-Lasinio C, Iommi M: Innovation and intangible investment in Europe, Japan, and the United States, *Oxford Review of Economic Policy* 29(2): 261–286, 2013.

Corrado C, Hulten C, Sichel D: Measuring capital and technology: an expanded framework. In Corrado C, Haltiwanger J, Sichel D, editors: *Measuring capital in the new economy, volume 66 of NBER Studies in Income and wealth*, Chicago, 2005, University of Chicago Press, pp 11–46.

Corrado C, Hulten C, Sichel D: Intangible capital and U.S. economic growth, *Review of Income and Wealth* 55(3): 661–685, 2009.

De Loecker J, Eeckhout J: *The rise of market power and the macroeconomic implications*, NBER. Technical Report 23687.

European Commission, International Monetary Fund, Organization for Economic Cooperation and Development, United Nations, World Bank: *System of national accounts 2008*, New York, N.Y., 2009, United Nations.

European Investment Bank: *EIB investment report 2018/2019: retooling Europe's economy*, Frankfurt, DE, 2018, Report, European Investment Bank.

Eurostat: *NACE Rev. 2: statistical classification of economic activites in the European community*, Technical report, European Commission.

Fraumeni BM, Jorgenson DW: The role capital in U.S. Economic growth, 1948–1976. In von Furstenberg G, editor: *Capital efficiency and growth*, 1980, pp 9–250. Ballinger.

Fraumeni BM, Jorgenson DW: The role of capital in U.S. Economic growth, 1949–1979. In Dogramaci A, editor: *Measurement issues and postwar productivity*, Martinus Nijhoff, pp 161–244.

Griliches Z: Issues in assessing the contribution of research and development to productivity growth, *The Bell Journal of Economics* 10(1):92–119, 1979.

Griliches Z: The search for R&D spillovers, *The Scandinavian Journal of Economics* 94(Supplement):S29–S47, 1992.

Grliches Z: Research expenditures and growth accounting. In Williams BR, editor: *Science and technology and economic growth*, MacMillan.

Grliches Z: Productivity, R&D, and basic research at the firm level, *The American Economic Review* 76(1):141–154, 1986.

Hulten CR: Growth accounting with intermediate inputs, *The Review of Economic Studies* 45(3):511–518, 1978.

Hulten C: On the 'importance' of productivity change, *The American Economic Review* 69(1):126–136, 1979.

Hulten CR, Wykoff FC: The estimation of economic depreciation using vintage asset prices, *Journal of Econometrics* 15: 367–396, 1981a.

Hulten CR, Wykoff FC: The measurement of economic depreciation. In Hulten CR, editor: *Depreciation, inflation & the taxation of income from capital*, The Urban Institute, pp 81–125.

Jorgenson DW: Capital theory and investment behavior, *The American Economic Review* 53(2):247–259, 1963.

Jorgenson DW: The embodiment hypothesis, *Journal of Political Economy* 74(1):1–17, 1966.

Jorgenson DW: Capital as a factor of production. In Jorgenson DW, Landau R, editors: *Technology and Capital Formation*, The MIT Press, pp 1–35.

Jorgenson DW: Information technology and the U.S. Economy, *The American Economic Review* 90(1):1–32, 2001.

Jorgenson DW, Gollop FM, Fraumeni BM: *Productivity and U.S. Economic growth*, Harvard University Press.

Jorgenson DW, Griliches Z: The explanation of productivity change, *The Review of Economic Studies* 34(3):249–283, 1967.

Jorgenson DW, Ho MS, Stiroh KJ: *Productivity, volume 3: information technology and the American growth resurgence*, Cambridge, Mass, 2005a, The MIT Press.

Jorgenson DW, Ho MS, Stiroh KJ: *Productivity volume 3: information technology and the American growth resurgence*, The MIT Press.

Lev B: *Intangibles: management, measurement and reporting*, The Brookings Institution Press.

Lev B, Gu F: *The end of financial accounting and the path forward for investors and managers. Wiley finance series*, John Wiley John Wiley & Sons, Inc.

Nakamura L: What is the US gross investment in intangibles?. In *(At least) one trillion dollars a year! Working paper No. 01-15*, Federal Reserve Bank of Philadelphia.

OECD: *Measuring capital: revised manual*, Paris, 2009, OECD.

O'Mahony M, Timmer MP: Output, input and productivity measures at the industry level: the EU KLEMS database, *Economic Journal* 119(538):F374–F403, 2009.

Pakes A, Schankerman M: The rate of obsolescence of patents, research gestation lags, and the private rate of return to research resources. In Griliches Z, editor: *R&D, patents, and productivity*, University of Chicago Press, pp 73–88.

Remes J, Manyika J, Bughin J, Woetzel J, Mischke J, Krishnan M: *Solving the productivity puzzle: the role of demand and the promise of digitization*, McKinsey global institute.

Romer PM: Endogenous technological change, *Journal of Political Economy* 95(5):S71–S102, 1990.

Schramm CJ, Arora A, Chandy RK, Cooper K, Jorgenson DW, Siegel DS, Bernd DL, Ballmer S, Blanchard J, Buckley G, Collins A, Eskew ML, Hodges L, Palmisano SJ, Menzer J: *Innovation measurement: tracking the state of innovation in the American economy*, Department of Commerce. Technical report.

Stiroh KJ: Information technology and the US productivity revival: what do the industry data say? *The American Economic Review* 92(5):1559–1576, 2002.

Timmer MP, Moergastel TV, Stuivenwold E, Ypma G, O'Mahony M, Kangasniemi M: *EU KLEMS growth and productivity accounts version 1.0: Part 1 methodology*Available at, www.euklems.net.

van Ark B, Hao J, Corrado C, Hulten C: Measuring intangible capital and its contribution to economic growth in Europe, *European Investment Bank Papers* 14(1):62–93, 2009.

Weitzmann ML: On the welfare significance of national product in a dynamic Economy, *Quarterly Journal of Economics* 90(364):156–162, 1976.

Getting smart about phones: new price indexes and the allocation of spending between devices and services plans in Personal Consumption Expenditures

Ana Aizcorbe[1], David M. Byrne[2], Daniel E. Sichel[3]

[1]Bureau of Economic Analysis, Washington, DC, United States; [2]Federal Reserve Board, Washington, DC, United States; [3]Wellesley College and NBER, Wellesley, MA, United States

17.1 Introduction

Since the introduction of the iPhone in 2007, smartphones have become one of the wonders of the modern age, providing a level of connectivity, data access, and functionality that was considered science fiction even 10 years earlier.[1] Moreover, smartphones have become far more capable during the past decade, with an iPhone X having about seven times as many transistors as the original iPhone (and about 51,000 times as many transistors as an early 1980s IBM personal computer).[2] As with many other information and communications technologies (ICTs), that rapid change in capabilities and characteristics poses challenges for estimating quality-adjusted price indexes.[3] Accurate estimates of quality-adjusted prices are crucial inputs

---

[1] Following Byrne and Corrado (2015), we define smartphones as "cellular phones with powerful operating systems that allow multitasking and installation of third-party applications." We also follow IDC's definition of mobile phones "as a device with a screen size of less than 7.0 inches as well as out-of-the-box cellular voice telephony with an in-built mic/speaker, capable of connecting to a cellular network for voice communication through a service provider plan." These definitions exclude tablets, non-telephony-enabled devices, and rugged devices.

[2] According to CNet (2018), the A12 chip powering an iPhone XS has about 6.9 billion transistors. An entry on Quora (2016) estimated that the processor on an original iPhone had about 1 billion transistors. Hennessy and Patterson (2012) report that an Intel 80286 powering early 1980s IBM PCs had 134,000 transistors.

[3] For discussions of these challenges and ICT examples, see Aizcorbe (2014), Byrne and Corrado (2017), and Triplett (2006).

Measuring Economic Growth and Productivity
https://doi.org/10.1016/B978-0-12-817596-5.00017-2

for measures of inflation, real GDP and productivity growth, capital stocks, as well as for gauging the pace of innovation in the technology sector.[4]

Moreover, until recently, many mobile phones[5] were purchased as part of a bundle; purchasers would receive a subsidy or discount on the phone reducing the upfront out-of-pocket cost in exchange for a commitment to a multimonth wireless service plan whose price would include payment for the remaining cost of the phone.[6] This bundling, when it occurs, is problematic for economic measurement both because a portion of spending on services actually includes payments for phones and because that misallocation could lead to the wrong deflators being applied to the portion of the wireless services spending that actually reflects this spending for phones.

In this chapter, we address both of those issues, developing new price indexes for mobile phones and proposing a methodology for disentangling the phone and service portions of spending on wireless services in recent years.

Regarding prices of mobile phones, we know of only a handful of studies that have attempted to construct constant-quality price indexes. For the United States, Byrne and Corrado (2015) developed matched-model indexes for mobile phones and other types of communications equipment. Their mobile phone index was based on a mix of price data—including prices of used

phones for the period studied in this chapter — and it declined at an average annual rate of 22% from 2010 to 2016.

Outside the United States, we are aware of only one published paper that provides price indexes for mobile phones: Watanabe et al. (2010) for Japan. Using their hedonic analysis for the prices for "feature" phones and smartphones, they found declines in prices of mobile phones of about 13% per year over the period from 2002 to 2007. For smartphones, preliminary findings for two studies have also been reported at conferences and international meetings. Chessa (2016) applied hedonic techniques to smartphone prices in the Netherlands for the 24-month period beginning in December 2013 and found average annual declines of 14%; similarly, the hedonic analysis by Karamti and Haouech (2018) for Tunisia for the six-quarter period beginning in 2016Q1 found annual average declines of around 15%.

Among US statistical agencies, the Bureau of Economic Analysis (BEA)—as part of the 2018 Comprehensive Revision of the National Income and Product Accounts—adopted the price index from Byrne and Corrado (2015) for mobile phones for equipment investment, Personal Consumption Expenditures (PCEs), and trade flows.[7] For the consumer price index (CPI), the Bureau of Labor Statistics (BLS) recently implemented two

---

[4] For discussions, see Byrne et al. (2016) and Byrne et al. (2017).

[5] We use "mobile phone" and "cell phone" interchangeably. In the period of our study, the terms are essentially synonymous. That is, nearly all mobile phones connect through a cellular network. Exceptions, like satellite phones, are out of scope for our analysis.

[6] Verizon's 2016 annual report provides a description of these bundled plans and their phaseout: "Historically, wireless service providers offered customers wireless plans whereby, in exchange for the customer entering into a fixed-term service agreement, the wireless service providers significantly, and in some cases fully, subsidized the customer's device purchase. Wireless providers recovered those subsidies through higher service fees as compared to those paid by customers on device installment plans. We and many other wireless providers have limited or discontinued this form of device subsidy." Available at: https://www.verizon.com/about/sites/default/files/annual_reports/2016/downloads/Verizon-AnnualReport2016_mda.pdf.

[7] This index is maintained and updated by the Federal Reserve Board and is available at https://www.federalreserve.gov/releases/g17/commequip_price_indexes.htm.

improvements to the traditional matched-model method that they had used for smartphones through the end of 2017. Beginning in January 2018, the BLS began adjusting prices for item substitutions in the index using coefficients from a hedonic regression; beginning in the April 2018 data, the BLS also increased the frequency with which smartphones in the "basket" are refreshed to twice a year. We cannot, however, compare the BLS price index for mobile phones (or smartphones) to other indexes because the index for mobile phones is not reported separately but rather is a component of a broader index for "telephone hardware, calculators, and other consumer information items."

Regarding the disentangling of bundled purchases of mobile phones and wireless service plans, we know of no past effort to separate out the phone and service components of spending on wireless service plans.

Our approach to these issues is as follows. On price indexes, we believe that it is important to see if hedonic techniques yield similar or different price trends than past studies. Accordingly, we develop new estimates for the United States of quality-adjusted prices for smartphones using data from IDC (International Data Corporation). These data track average selling prices and units for smartphones and have not previously been used to develop hedonic price indexes. Our preferred hedonic index—which allows coefficients to vary over time—declines

at an average annual rate of about 16% per year from the first quarter of 2010 to the first quarter of 2018. In addition, we combine our smartphone price index with a matched-model price index for feature phones to obtain an overall price index for mobile phones, which falls 17% per year from 2010 to 2018Q1.[8] These estimates provide useful points of comparison with other recent estimates of prices, including the index used by the Federal Reserve for the Industrial Production data (which closely tracks Byrne and Corrado (2015)). The price index for mobile phones developed here falls rapidly like the index in Byrne and Corrado (2015) but 4 percentage points slower in the overlap period. Yet, it has the appeal of higher frequency (quarterly vs. annual) and direct measurement of the price of new phones, whereas the Byrne and Corrado index relied on prices in the market for used phones. This index points to rapid technical change in smartphones since 2010, broadly in line with the double digit rates of advance for some other digital products as reported in Byrne et al. (2017) and Byrne and Corrado (2017).[9]

With regard to the allocation of spending between cellular equipment and services in PCE, we propose two adjustments to separate equipment and services. First, we use Service Annual Survey (SAS) data to identify upfront or out-of-pocket spending on phones that is included in the services category. Second, we use a comparison of phone prices from IDC and J.D. Power to

---

[8] To the extent that our preferred index differs from the deflators used in the national accounts, such differences likely would have limited implications for real GDP because smartphones largely are produced outside the United States. Federal Reserve Board estimates, based on Byrne and Corrado's (2015) reading of Census data and private sources, show US mobile phone production averaged around only $300 million a year from 2010 to 2016. At the same time, some recent research has highlighted that a considerable part of the value added of iPhones and some other products should be attributed to the United States rather than the country from which they are imported. If that adjustment were made, then our estimates could have more significant implications for real GDP and productivity. See Guvenen, Mataloni, Rassier, and Ruhl (2017).

[9] Price trends provide information about the pace of innovation via the "dual" relationship in which price changes reflect changes in input costs and total factor productivity. That being said, swings in margins and other factors may complicate the linkage between price trends and the pace of technological advance.

gross up equipment spending to the full cost of the phone, taking account of any subsidy offered by the service provider in exchange for a commitment to a long-term contract for cell service. In particular, the IDC data tracks the price of smartphones without any service commitment; that is, without netting out any discounts (or subsidies) to the upfront cost of the phone. In contrast, the J.D. Power data—which are based on consumer surveys—capture the upfront or out-of-pocket price paid net of any subsidies. Accordingly, the difference in prices across these datasets provides an estimate of the size of the subsidy. This comparison indicates that these subsidies were quite substantial prior to 2013, in the range of $200 to $300. Then, starting around the beginning of 2013, mobile phone providers began more frequently offering straight up purchase options without these discounts on purchasing a device. These subsidies or discounts largely, though not entirely, had disappeared by 2018.

With this information on discounts in hand, we can split out the portion of spending on wireless service plans that actually reflects spending for phones. We find that this share averaged 28% from 2010 to 2017, hitting a high of more than 36% in 2012 and falling to about 21% in 2017. And, we can then apply our deflator for phones to this portion of spending to get an adjusted estimate of an overall deflator for the spending on Cellular Telephone Services and, by implication, for real PCE for this category.

Our calculations indicate that, after making these corrections, the deflator for Cellular Telephone Services fell at an annual average rate of 7.7% from 2010 to 2017, about 4 percentage points faster than the currently published deflator for this category. Accordingly, real PCE for this category has grown 4 percentage points faster per year over this period than the currently published series.

We believe our results are valuable in their own right as a contribution to improved measurement of prices and PCE. In addition, our results contribute to the growing literature that documents the rapid technical change in and diffusion of products related to the digital revolution.

This chapter is organized as follows. Section 17.2 discusses the IDC data we use and highlights the rapid improvement of smartphone characteristics. We describe our methodology for estimating quality-adjusted price indexes in Section 17.3, and our new results for smartphone and overall mobile phone price indexes in Section 17.4. Section 17.5 describes how we use data from the SAS and a comparison of price data from IDC and J.D. Power to disentangle and allocate spending on phones and services when the two are bundled together. Section 17.6 concludes.

17.2 IDC data and smartphone characteristics

17.2.1 IDC data

We rely on data from IDC to develop smartphone price indexes. Specifically, we use data from the Worldwide Quarterly Mobile Phone Tracker dataset published by IDC. IDC estimates revenue, units, and prices by model for the US market using public and proprietary information from phone manufacturers, component suppliers, and distribution channel companies (e.g., retailers and wholesalers).[10] Unique models are distinguished in the data by four

---

[10] Data sources used by IDC are briefly described in "Worldwide Quarterly Mobile Phone Tracker," available at https://www.idc.com/getfile.dyn?containerId=IDC_P8397&attachmentId=47322790. The description of methodology in the text is based on "IDC's Worldwide Mobile Phone Tracker Taxonomy (2018)," which is only provided to subscribers, and on conversations with IDC analysts.

variables: the "model" in IDC nomenclature (e.g., "iPhone 4s"), the size of internal storage (e.g., 8 gigabytes), the mobile telecommunications generation (e.g., 3G), and the operating system (e.g., "Android Jelly Bean 4.1"). The database contains both consumer and commercial sales and does not provide model-level information by market, so we cannot produce a pure CPI; however, roughly 90% of the unit sales in the database are to the consumer market. There are 1294 phone models in the database.

The model prices reported are average selling prices (before point-of-sale taxes) offered by retailers or service providers *without a contract commitment*, including channel costs such as freight, insurance, shipping, and tariffs. As noted above and discussed below, it was common during a portion of the period covered in our analysis for service providers to bundle phones with service contracts, and the IDC dataset indicates over 80% of phones were sold through service providers in this period. A crucial feature of the dataset is that for phones sold through carriers, IDC analysts have been successful in collecting the price charged for each phone model *without a contract commitment*; that is, in all cases where phones were sold with a service contract commitment, the price recorded was the price for that model of phone, without contract, directly reported by the carrier. We also confirmed that IDC is collecting actual prices paid, rather than manufacturers' suggested retail prices (MSRPs), by examining cases where a prominent manufacturer publicizes MSRPs and

confirmed that prices do, in fact, appreciably deviate from the MSRP. In a small number of cases, we recoded price observations to eliminate implausible patterns.[11]

17.2.2 Smartphone characteristics

The IDC database also provides detailed information on phone model characteristics spanning 2010Q1 to 2018Q1. Table 17.1 reports values of key smartphone characteristics in the IDC data. The main inference we draw from these data is that the quality of smartphones improved significantly over the sample period. For example, processor speed increased at an average annual rate of 9% between 2010 and 2017, while the average number of cores in a phone's processor rose from 1 in 2010 to over 5 by 2017. Storage capacity also rose very rapidly, increasing at an average annual rate of 29% during 2010–17, and the amount of working memory (RAM) increased at an average annual rate of 33% during this period. Camera resolution also improved at a good clip during this period.

During our sample period, other important aspects of the market for mobile phones changed. The share of smartphones in the overall market for mobile phones rose from 38% in 2010 to 94% in 2017. And, market concentration in the market is substantial and climbs over this time period. The Herfindahl index calculated with manufacturers' revenue shares in the consumer smartphone market is 0.16 in 2010 and climbs to 0.44 by 2017.[12]

---

[11] In particular, we applied two rules. In cases of apparent missing values, defined as quarters where no units of a model were sold flanked by non–zero sales in both adjacent quarters, a price and a quantity were added using log-linear interpolation. In cases of a price spike, defined as a price increase of 10% or more in one quarter followed by a price decrease of 10% or more in the following quarter, or a price "pothole," defined symmetrically to spikes, we substituted the log-linear interpolated price for the reported price.

[12] There were 23 manufacturers in the market in 2017. If each manufacturer had an equal share of the market, the Herfindahl index would be 0.05.

TABLE 17.1   US Smartphone Characteristics, IDC Data. Average characteristics by year.

	2010	2011	2012	2013	2014	2015	2016	2017	Annual average growth rate (%)
Processor speed (GHz)	1.0	1.1	1.2	1.4	1.5	1.6	1.7	1.9	9
Cores	1.0	1.2	1.7	2.3	2.7	3.4	4.3	5.2	23
Storage (GB)	7.2	12.9	15.4	16.6	21.5	30.7	36.3	55.9	29
RAM (GB)	0.23	0.34	0.44	0.98	1.31	1.61	2.03	2.34	33
Camera resolution (megapixels)	4.2	5.2	6.5	7.8	8.7	9.7	10.1	10.4	13
Screen diagonal (inches)	3.3	3.5	3.8	4.2	4.5	4.7	4.9	5.1	6
Smartphone share of mobile phone units sold (%)	38	55	69	77	88	87	91	94	
Herfindahl index of market concentration	0.16	0.26	0.35	0.35	0.36	0.39	0.41	0.44	

Note: The Herfindahl index measure of market concentration is the sum of the squared revenue shares by manufacturer in the US consumer market for smartphones.
Source: IDC Mobile Phone Tracker database.

17.3   Methodology for quality-adjusted price indexes[13]

17.3.1   Matched-model indexes

We estimate both matched-model and hedonic price indexes to control for quality change though we emphasize hedonic indexes. The matched-model approach, the most common method employed by statistical agencies, relies in its most basic formulation on price changes over time for specific models of the good in question, holding quality constant by construction if models are specified in enough detail. This approach takes an average of price changes for specific models rather than calculating the change in the price average across models. Although the matched-model approach ideally strips out the effect of quality change on prices, this technique may fall short in cases

characterized by frequent model entry and exit for two reasons. First, in the period of entry, no price change relative to the previous period is available, and, of course, no price change is available in the period following the model's exit either. Second, if entering models have a lower price relative to quality than incumbent models and do not drive down the price of incumbent models—that is, the law of one (quality adjusted) price does not hold—before the older model exits the market, the quality improvement represented by the new model may not be reflected in the index. Both issues are a concern in the market for mobile phones.

For matched-model indexes, we consider first an index constructed as an unweighted geometric mean of price changes, known as the Jevons formula. We start with unweighted indexes because statistical agencies typically do not collect

---

[13] The description of hedonic methodology in this section draws heavily from Byrne et al. (2018), including a significant amount of text taken and adapted directly from that paper.

weights at the model level in each period.[14] In addition, researchers estimating hedonic indexes often do not have model-level weights.

Such a lack of weighting raises two issues. First, some models undoubtedly represent a greater share of the market than others—a particular concern in the mobile phone market where a handful of Apple models account for a disproportionate share of the market. Second, the relative importance of models changes over time. The importance of the issue of fixed weights in price indexes has been the subject of extensive research. Generally speaking, allowing weights to evolve over time is the preferred approach as that allows the index to reflect consumers' response to relative prices and substitution across models as discussed in Diewert (1998). Our second matched-model index addresses this issue; we calculate an index where the model-specific price changes are weighted by the average of their revenue share in the two periods used to calculate the price change (known as the Tornqvist formula).[15]

17.3.2 Hedonic price index methodology

Hedonic regression—estimating the statistical relationship between model prices and product characteristics and performance—provides information that can be used in a variety of ways to construct constant-quality indexes. One can impute model prices for the period prior to the model's appearance in the market and use the implied price change in a conventional matched-model formula (Pakes, 2003). Another approach is to adjust the price of a newly introduced model according to the implicit valuation of the difference in characteristics relative to an existing model.[16] In this chapter, we focus on a third approach, estimating "time-dummy" hedonic price indexes. In this setup, product characteristics act simply as control variables and the focus is on the quality-adjusted price trend implied by the coefficient on the dummy for each time period, with the quality change stripped out by the regression.[17] All of these approaches are valid uses of hedonic regression for the construction of constant-quality price indexes, and the choice of method is dictated largely by the circumstances.[18]

To fix ideas for our time-dummy hedonic price indexes, consider the following simple dummy-variable hedonic specification:

$$\ln(P_{i,t}) = \alpha + \sum_k \beta_k X_{k,i,t} + \sum_t \delta_t D_{i,t} + \varepsilon_{i,t}$$

$$(17.1)$$

where $P_{i,t}$ is the price of smartphone i in quarter t, $X_{k,i,t}$ is the value of characteristic or performance metric k for smartphone i in quarter t (measured in logs or levels, as appropriate), $D_{i,t}$ is a time dummy variable (fixed effect) that equals 1 if smartphone i is observed in quarter t and zero otherwise, and $\varepsilon_{i,t}$ is an error term.

An often-cited concern with Eq. (17.1) is that the coefficients on the characteristic or

---

[14] Survey participants may be asked to report a revenue-representative set of products when they first enter the survey sample, but then not be asked to report sales by model in subsequent periods.

[15] The Tornqvist index satisfies the criteria set out in Diewert (1976) for a "superlative" price index—one which provides a reasonable approximation to a true cost of living index.

[16] This "explicit quality adjustment" approach is used by BLS in their consumer price index for smartphones. (See "Measuring Price Change in the CPI: Telephone hardware, calculators, and other consumer information items," available at https://www.bls.gov/cpi/factsheets/telephone-hardware.htm.)

[17] The BLS used this approach for the first time for their producer price index for semiconductors beginning in 2018.

[18] Triplett (2006) notes these approaches are equivalent under fairly general conditions.

performance variables are constrained to remain constant over the full sample period as discussed in Berndt (1991) and Pakes (2003). We mitigate this concern by estimating each time dummy with a separate regression; that is, we estimate adjacent-period regressions as discussed in Triplett (2006).[19] Specifically, we estimate the following regression for each overlapping two-quarter period:

$$\ln\left(P_{i,t}\right) = \alpha + \sum_k \beta_k X_{k,i,t} + \delta D_2 + \varepsilon_{i,t} \quad (17.2)$$

where $P_{i,t}$ is a price observation for smartphone i in quarter t. The dummy variable D_2 equals 1 if the price observation is in the second quarter of the two-quarter overlapping period and 0 otherwise. In addition, we run weighted regressions, where observations are weighted according to the share of revenue the models represent in the market during the quarter when each price is observed. To construct a price index from this sequence of regressions, we spliced together the percent changes implied by the estimated coefficients on the D_2 variables.[20]

17.4 Smartphone price indexes

17.4.1 Matched-model

Price indexes constructed using different formulas and specifications with the IDC data are shown in Table 17.2. As shown in line 1, the simple average price of smartphones—with no

quality adjustment—edged down about 1% per year on average in the time period of our analysis, from the first quarter of 2010 to the first quarter of 2018. Roughly speaking, there are two noticeable periods—prices moved up through 2013, then fell, on balance, through 2017—a pattern visible in the quality-adjusted price indexes as well. The trend in the unweighted Jevons index, line 2, contrasts sharply with the path of average prices; the index falls 19% per year on average. Line 3 reports results for the revenue-weighted Tornqvist index. Clearly, weights matter a great deal for this market: the weighted index falls 10% per year on average, a full 9 percentage points more slowly than the Jevons index. Numerically, we attribute this difference to a prominent phone manufacturer which has a substantial market share by revenue but releases relatively few phone models and consequently plays a more important role in the Tornqvist index than it does in the Jevons index.[21] Phone models sold by this manufacturer have significantly slower price declines than those of other producers, on average. Accordingly, we weight price observations in the hedonic regressions we report below by model revenue for the relevant quarter.

17.4.2 Hedonic

For our hedonic indexes, we first consider the simple, time-invariant specification in Eq. (17.1), regressing (the natural log of) price on four continuous measures of engineering capability (storage capacity, screen size, camera resolution, and processor speed, all in natural log form) and

---

[19] An alternative approach, advocated by Pakes (2003), is to run a separate regression for each period and construct a price index using imputed prices for each period.

[20] We apply the adjustment suggested by van Dalen and Bode (2004) for adjacent-period regressions to correct for bias introduced when going from the natural log of prices to price levels, which is based on the standard error of the estimated coefficient on the second-period dummy. The adjustment reduces the annual average rate of decline for our preferred index by 0.1 percentage point over the period of our study.

[21] Our agreement with the data provider prevents us from disclosing the name of the manufacturer.

TABLE 17.2 Quality-Adjusted Price Indexes for Smartphones, IDC Data (average of quarterly percent changes, annual rate).

	2011	2012	2013	2014	2015	2016	2017	2011–13	2014–17	2010Q1–2018Q1
1. Average prices	3.0	1.6	0.4	−6.9	−0.4	−14.7	11.9	1.7	−2.6	−0.8
Matched-model indexes										
2. Unweighted (Jevons)	−14.2	−9.8	−21.9	−18.9	−26.7	−29.3	−21.1	−15.3	−24.0	−19.3
3. Weighted (Tornqvist)	−4.7	−9.1	−12.7	−11.9	−12.9	−12.5	−9.8	−8.9	−11.8	−10.0
Hedonic indexes										
4. Time invariant	−8.8	−16.6	−16.2	−18.5	−16.9	−28.6	−24.7	−13.9	−22.2	−19.6
5. Time-varying effects (adjacent quarter)	**−6.5**	**−11.1**	**−16.8**	**−16.9**	**−14.9**	**−24.8**	**−19.4**	**−11.4**	**−19.0**	**−15.5**
6. Manufacturer-specific	−13.4	−12.6	−13.3	−20.5	−16.4	−23.8	−16.5	−13.0	−19.3	−16.0
Memo										
Feature phones	−8.0	−16.8	−17.3	−48.6	−31.3	−7.8	−0.9	−14.0	−22.2	−18.5
Overall mobile phones	−9.6	−14.9	−15.2	−28.0	−18.8	−22.5	−15.3	−13.2	−21.1	−16.6
Byrne/Corrado index	−7.5	−19.9	−26.4	−28.8	−25.1	−25.0	NA	−17.9	−26.3	−22.1

Note: All hedonic indexes are revenue-weighted and control for manufacturer, processor speed, storage, screen size, camera resolution, operating system version, generation of wireless mobile technology, and input type. The manufacturer-specific regression index is a Fisher chain-weighted aggregate of indexes for six major manufacturers and a residual category. We apply to the results in lines 4 and 5 the adjustment suggested by van Dalen and Bode (2004) for adjacent-period regressions to correct for bias introduced when going from the natural log of prices to price levels, which is based on the standard error of the estimated coefficient on the second-period dummy. Average growth rates for Byrne/Corrado index extend through 2016. For the 2011–16 period, the average growth rate for the overall mobile phone price index developed in this paper is −18.2, roughly 4 percentage points slower than for the Byrne/Corrado index.

an array of dummy variables.[22] Specifically, we include dummies for phone manufacturer (there are 43 in our dataset), for operating system (there are 58 in our dataset, for example, "Android Froyo 2.2"), for telecommunications generation (2G, 3G, 3.5G, 4G), and for input type (QWERTY keyboard vs. touchscreen). We also include a dummy for models in their quarter of introduction.

Our rationale for including an introduction-quarter dummy is to account for price variation over the model life cycle that does not merit inclusion in measured quality-adjusted price trends. In particular, prices paid when models are first introduced may be affected by a number of factors that confound quality adjustment: When a model first appears, the novelty of the item may lead select early-adopter consumers to pay a

[22] We also experimented with including measures of smartphone performance from Passmark, following the emphasis in Byrne et al. (2018) on using performance measures in hedonic regressions. Our experimentation with a small set of models indicated that performance measures added relatively little once a full set of characteristics were included. Although we plan to pursue the approach further in future work, we did not do so in the current paper, and we do not report results from hedonic regressions using performance measures.

premium for the item that does not persist over time.[23] Alternately, the market may be in disequilibrium at first in the sense that the "law of one price" does not hold and the new item is sold at a lower quality-adjusted price than incumbent models (put another way, the price of the old model does not fall enough to equilibrate to the price-performance ratio of the new model).[24] Or, very early buyers may demand a discount in exchange for bearing the burden of testing the new features of the phone.[25] In addition, Apple typically introduces new models in September—the third month of the third quarter— implying that the average price observed in the IDC data for that quarter is not an average of 3 full months of price history as for other quarters, and that difference may distort estimates of the price change in the following quarter. Whatever the correct explanation, we find that adding a dummy variable for the first quarter a model appears in the market has a noteworthy impact on our results as discussed below.

To recap, the first hedonic regression we report includes quarterly time dummies, variables for engineering capability, dummy variables for manufacturer and operating system, and a dummy for the quarter a model is introduced in the market. As shown on line 4, the price index constructed by chaining the coefficients on the quarterly dummies falls 19.6% per year, on average, from 2010Q1 to 2018Q1. The regression results indicate this set of variables explains 83.9% of the variation in price.

We next consider the impact of allowing the effect of these characteristics on price to vary over time using the adjacent-quarter regressions in Eq. (17.2). For example, a particular mobile telecommunications generation (2G, 3G, 4G) will represent relatively high quality when first introduced and relatively low quality once the succeeding generation enters the market. Thus, one might expect a positive coefficient on 3G early in its life cycle and a negative coefficient once 4G phones are available. Likewise, when phones with the Android Ice Cream Sandwich operating system appeared, they commanded a premium over phones with Android Gingerbread, the predecessor operating system; once its successor—Android Jelly Bean—appeared, Ice Cream Sandwich phones sold at a discount. Dummies for these fine gradations of operating system have the added appeal of serving as proxies for an array of small features that are enabled by each operating system generation. This specification yields a price index—reported on line 5—that falls 15.5% on average, appreciably slower than the index derived from the regression with time-invariant coefficients. This set of adjacent-quarter regressions explains 92.3% of price variation on average across the time period, substantially more than in the time-invariant regression. For the reasons discussed below, this is our preferred specification. And, in this specification, the dummy for quarter of model introduction matters; when we exclude this dummy from this specification, the aggregate price index falls 2.6 percentage points slower per year on average.

We also experimented with separate adjacent-quarter regressions for each of the six phone manufacturers which accounted for 5% or more of the market by revenue in at least one quarter (Apple, Blackberry, HTC, LG Electronics, Motorola, and Samsung) and a seventh regression for the residual manufacturers. These separate manufacturer regressions also introduce yet another form of flexibility—characteristic effects are permitted to vary across manufacturers. The resulting price

---

[23] This phenomenon was first studied in Pashigian, P., B. Bowen, and E. Gould (1995) for the motor vehicle market. See Aizcorbe, Bridgman, and Nalewaik (2010) and Williams and Sager (2018) for more recent discussions.

[24] Cole et al. (1986) offer this explanation in the market for computers.

[25] We thank Erick Sager for suggesting this explanation.

TABLE 17.3 Summary statistics across regressions: Time-varying specification estimated with revenue-weighted observations.

	Mean	Minimum
Observations	417	145
r-squared	0.92	0.88
Adjusted r-squared	0.91	0.85
	Number of regressions significant out of 32	**Average coefficient**
Storage	31	0.12
Camera resolution	31	0.36
Screen size	25	1.04
Processor speed	23	1.00
Introduction-quarter dummy	19	−0.06
	Number of regressions out of 32 with at least one significant coefficient of category shown	**Average number of significant coefficients of category shown (Zeros excluded)**
Operating system version	28	5.4
Manufacturer	30	6.7
Input type	12	1.2
Mobile generation	5	1.2

Notes: Significance measured at the 10% level. Continuous variables (storage, camera resolution, screen size, and processor speed) are measured in natural log terms, so coefficients represent price elasticities.

All significant coefficients for storage, camera resolution, screen size, and processor speed are positive. 14 of 19 significant coefficients for the entry-quarter dummy are positive.

Input types include QWERTY keyboard, touchscreen, and the combination of both. Mobile generations are commonly referred to as "2G," "3G," and so on and represent significant advances in the efficiency of data transmission on the associated network.

indexes vary tremendously across vendors, ranging from a 12% to 29% annual average decline during 2010–18. Aggregating these price indexes using revenue weights yields a price index—shown on line 6—that falls 16.0% per year on average. Because this rate of decline is roughly the same as that for the regression which pools manufacturers—reported on line 5—and because the pooled price index is somewhat more precise, we prefer the pooled regression shown on line 5.[26]

Table 17.3 presents an overview of the regression results for our preferred specification—the adjacent-quarter specification run with

[26] The regression which pools all manufacturers is more precise in the sense that 22 of 32 quarterly time dummy coefficients are significantly different from zero at the 90% level in contrast to the manufacturer-specific regressions, for which the number of significant time dummies ranges from 4 to 11. Note that because our data cover the entire population of mobile phone models, P-values reflect population dispersion, rather than sampling variation.

revenue-weighted observations. As shown in the upper panel, individual adjacent-quarter regressions have 417 model observations on average, and no regression has fewer than 145 observations. The regressions explain 92% of price variation on average, as measured by the r-squared statistic, and no regression has an r-squared below 0.88.

The middle panel highlights that, among the continuous performance variables, internal storage and camera resolution are statistically significant as control variables at the 10% level in 31 out of the 32 adjacent-quarter regressions. Screen size and processor speed are significant in 25 and 23 out of the regressions, respectively. As noted previously, in this hedonic approach, model characteristics are treated as control variables and their estimated sign and magnitude are difficult to interpret.[27] That being said, we note that coefficients for all four of the performance variables are positive, both on average as shown in the table, and in all cases where the coefficient estimate is significant. The model-introduction quarter dummy variable discussed above is significant in 19 of 32 regressions, negative on average, and negative in 14 of 19 cases where the variable is significant.

The lower panel summarizes results for other discrete variables. In nearly all of the regressions, at least one operating system and manufacturer dummy was significant—28 and 30 cases, respectively. There are 54 distinct operating system versions in the data, but only a handful are relevant in any particular adjacent-quarter

regression.[28] Although on average, only 5.4 of these have significant coefficients in each regression, 39 of the 54 dummies are significant at least once. Similarly, 6.7 of the 41 manufacturer dummies are significant on average. The dummy variables for input type and for mobile generation play a role less frequently, with at least one of these dummies statistically significant in 12 and in 5 regressions, respectively. To provide additional background on our results, Table A17.1 in the Appendix shows complete regression results for two selected quarters for our preferred specification.

Bottom line: our preferred specification delivers a price index that falls at an average annual rate of 15.5% from 2010:Q1 to 2018:Q1.

We also created an index using the IDC data on feature phones (i.e., mobile phones that are not smartphones). The database does not provide model-level information for feature phones, but does allow us to construct a matched-model index using average prices for narrowly defined groups of phones.[29] Our feature phone price index falls at an average annual rate of 18.5% during 2010—18 as shown in a memo item in Table 17.2. We created a Fisher chain-aggregated index for all mobile phones using this feature phone index and our hedonic smartphone index—also shown in the table—which falls at an average annual rate of 16.6%. This rate of decline is similar to, but 4 percentage points slower than that of the Byrne and Corrado index—reported in the memo item in Table 17.2—that currently is being used by the

---

[27] Although the full vector of characteristics coefficients can be used to quality-adjust individual prices, we view the common practice of informally considering coefficients on individual characteristics as implicit prices as ill advised. Pakes (2003) notes that "the hedonic regression is a "reduced form," that is, its coefficients have no obvious interpretation in terms of economic primitives."

[28] The count of operating systems in our sample is 17 Android, 9 BlackBerry, 9 iOS, 8 Windows Mobile, and 11 miscellaneous others.

[29] The characteristics used to define narrow our narrow groups of phones are manufacturer, form factor (clamshell, bar, etc.), storage, generation, camera resolution, GPS capability, primary memory card, color display, and input type (QWERTY, touchscreen, etc.).

BEA for mobile phones. We prefer our new index to the Byrne and Corrado index because the new index relies on prices for new phones rather than used phones, draws on data with broader coverage, has revenue weights, and uses quarterly rather than annual observations.

17.5 Allocation of PCE spending between cellular devices and bundled service contracts

An improved price index is useful for proper deflation of nominal spending on mobile phones as recorded in PCE. However, in the NIPAs, nominal spending for mobile phone purchases is not reported in a single category. Although the PCE category "telephone and related communication equipment" includes purchases at retail outlets, the bulk of mobile phones purchased in the past decade were obtained directly from wireless carriers. Moreover, for reasons that we detail below, the value of those phones ends up misreported in PCE for Cellular Telephone Services.

In this section, we propose a method to identify the component of PCE for Cellular Telephone Services that represents spending on mobile phones. Extracting this component entails two corrections. First, we use data from the Census Bureau to identify the upfront cost of phones paid by purchasers. As described below, this reported upfront spending on phones does not represent the full cost if the phone was subsidized by the service provider. Accordingly, our second correction makes a further adjustment to account for these subsidies so that the full cost of the phone is captured as equipment spending at the time of purchase. This method corrects the misallocation of some phone purchases as services and thereby provides a way to apply the appropriate deflators to each category of spending.

17.5.1 Accounting for the upfront cost of phones

There are two potential data sources that could be used to estimate the upfront cost of phones (that currently is counted within the services category in PCE): both the Census Bureau's SAS and the quinquennial Economic Census provide some information on the detail underlying the top line estimate for total revenues of wireless service providers. In addition, because respondents to these surveys typically follow the accounting rules that they use in their annual reports, annual reports contain useful corroborating information. To sort through these accounting issues, we begin by considering how some hypothetical transactions are recorded in the annual reports, the SAS survey, and the quinquennial Census.

We illustrate the accounting underlying these transactions by considering four ways that one could have acquired an Apple iPhone 3G at introduction. Our first scenario considers a purchase of the phone at a subsidized price with a commitment to a 2-year service contract, and the second considers an outright purchase of the phone. Apple's initial announcement offered two prices: $199 if one was willing to commit to a 2-year contract with AT&T, and $499 if one did not commit to the contract. In these types of contracts, the $199 was commonly referred to as the subsidized price to reflect the fact that the service provider had held down the upfront cost of the phone. Because the accounting convention used by service providers in their annual reports was to record revenues as they were received, the cost of the phone (whether $199 or $499) was recorded in the SAS and in company annual reports as equipment revenue in the year the purchase was made.

What about the monthly payments for wireless service in these two scenarios? When consumers entered into (typically 2-year) contracts

TABLE 17.4   Accounting for Service Providers' Equipment Revenues: Four examples.

Scenario	Annual reports[a]		SAS survey[b]		Economic Census and PCE		Proposed PCE[c]	
	Equipment	Services	Equipment	Services	Equipment	Services	Equipment	Services
Phone purchase from wireless provider								
1. $199 subsidized phone; $62.50 monthly service charge over 2-year contract	$199	$62.50/mo	$199	$62.50/mo	0	$199; $62.50/mo	$499	$50/mo
2. $499 phone with full payment up front; $50 monthly service charge	$499	$50/mo	$499	$50/mo	0	$499; $50/mo	$499	$50/mo
3. $499 phone with payment in installments; $50 monthly service charge	$499	$50/mo	$499	$50/mo	0	$499; $50/mo	$499	$50/mo
Phone purchase at retail outlet								
4. $499 phone upfront; $50 monthly service charge	n.a.	$50/mo	$499	$50/mo	$499	$50/mo	$499	$50/mo

[a] *These are reported in the Income Statements, as equipment revenue and service revenue.*
[b] *Reported in SAS as "Reselling services for telecomm equipment, retail," Table 4 Sources of Revenue.*
[c] *Equipment category is Telephone and facsimile equipment; service category is recorded in Cellular Telephone Services.*

with the carriers, the providers would attempt to recoup the gap between the full and subsidized prices ($499 vs. $199), by elevating the monthly amount paid for wireless service over the course of the contract. In our example, suppose that this raised their monthly charge by $12.50 so that consumers who signed a contract made (inflated) monthly service payments of $62.50 for 2 years for services, whereas consumers who paid for the phone up front only paid $50 per month for services.[30]

The first two rows of Table 17.4 compare how spending for equipment and services would be recorded in each of these two scenarios. In service-provider annual reports, the revenue recorded for those who paid the full cost of phone up front (line 2 of the table) correctly includes the $499 for the phone as equipment and the monthly charges that only cover services as service revenue. For those who sign a contract (line 1), providers recorded part of the full cost of the phone—the upfront piece—as equipment revenue. But a convention prevalent through the end of 2017 was to report the additional cost of the phone paid in the elevated monthly service bill as service (not equipment) revenue. So, in this example, the $12.50 boost to monthly service bills that covers the cost of the phone is

[30] We assume the service provider recoups the unpaid portion of the noncontract price of the phone over the duration of the service contract. The service provider may ultimately recover less (or more) than the price for purchasing the phone outright (the IDC price) if, say, the price elasticity of demand differs systematically between customers who pay the full price up front and those who do not.

reported as revenue for services. That is, this practice would inappropriately allocate revenues received for the phone as services. Moreover, it also affected the timing for recording the phone purchase: only the upfront cost was reported on the day of the transaction, the other revenues collected over the service contract were spread over the span of the contract.

As shown in line 3, the accounting treatment when a consumer purchases the phone through an installment plan is the same as when consumers pay the full cost of the phone up front (line 2); the annual reports accurately exclude any payments for phones from service revenues. Similarly, line 4 shows the case where consumers purchase their phone at a retail outlet not affiliated with the carrier (like Best Buy) and sign up for wireless services separately. Again, the service revenues reported by providers correctly only include consumer payments for the services; the purchase of the phone is recorded separately in Best Buy's financial statements.

We confirmed that numbers reported in the annual reports lined up with those in the SAS survey. In the annual reports, firms report revenues received from equipment sales separately from service sales in a line item typically called "equipment revenue" in their income statements. Similarly, in the SAS survey, detail on the sources of revenues includes a line item called "Reselling services for telecomm equipment, retail" that gives the dollar value of equipment sales as reported by the carriers.[31] To see if these two series are capturing the same spending, we compare the ratio of equipment to total revenue in the annual reports to the ratio of SAS reselling revenues to total revenues. In 2012, for example, the ratios from the annual

reports for the top four carriers, Verizon, AT&T, Sprint, and T-mobile, were either 10% or 11%. In the SAS survey, the ratio of reselling revenues to total revenues was 11% that year.

So, again, for purchases that involve a contract, the SAS survey reports the $199 upfront cost of the phone as equipment and all other payments received on a monthly basis (including the part that covers the phone subsidy) as service revenue.

As in the SAS survey, the top line revenue estimate for wireless service providers in the Economic Census also includes revenues for equipment. However, unlike the SAS survey, the Economic Census does not provide a separate line item that one could use to split out the equipment revenue from the top line.

This feature of the Economic Census, that all equipment revenue received by wireless service providers is included as service revenue, has important implications for nominal PCE because in Census years, the level of nominal PCE for wireless services is set to match that in the Economic Census. Specifically, for Census years, BEA estimates current dollars for this category by applying a commodity-flow method to total receipts (business, consumer, and exports) reported by wireless carriers in the Economic Census. Those benchmarks are then extrapolated using data on receipts reported by wireless carriers in the SAS. Accordingly, the level of PCE for wireless services includes *all* the revenues received for mobile phones that they sold to subscribers (upfront and other).

Correcting for this problem, however, turns out to be straightforward because of the data described above from annual reports and the SAS survey that isolate the upfront revenue received by service providers for equipment.

---

[31] The coverage of this line in the SAS survey is broader than we would like in that it includes sales to all subscribers—not just consumers—and for all types of equipment—not just phones. We do not view the product coverage issue as a big problem because most of this spending is on phones and carriers only more recently began reselling tablets and other equipment.

TABLE 17.5   Allocation of PCE for wireless services between services and devices.

			2010	2011	2012	2013	2014	2015	2016	2017	2010–17
	Personal Consumption Expenditures										
(1)	Cellular Telephone Service	Bill $	98.0	105.1	107.0	110.6	119.4	120.7	124.5	127.6	114.1
	Service Annual Survey (SAS)										
(2)	Total revenues	Bill $	199.2	214.4	225.4	233.1	251.8	254.4	259.3	257.8	236.9
(3)	Reselling services for telecomm equipment, retail	Bill $	18.8	21.0	23.7	24.7	35.5	41.3	44.4	46.7	32.0
(4) = (3)/(2)	Share of total revenues	Percent	9.4	9.8	10.5	10.6	14.1	16.2	17.1	18.1	13.2
	IDC and J.D. POWER average prices										
(5)	Ratio of average prices: IDC/J.D. POWER	Ratio	2.79	3.27	3.48	2.93	2.16	1.59	1.21	1.16	2.3
(6) = (5) x (4)	**Adjusted share of reselling services to total revenues**	Percent	26.2	32.1	36.6	31.0	30.5	25.7	20.8	20.9	28.0
	Imputed detail for PCE for Cellular Telephone Services										
(7) = (1) x (6)	Phones	Bill $	25.7	33.7	39.1	34.3	36.4	31.0	25.9	26.7	31.6
(8) = (1) - (7)	Wireless services	Bill $	72.3	71.4	67.9	76.3	83.0	89.6	98.7	100.9	82.5

The relevant calculations are shown in Table 17.5. The top line shows current estimates of PCE for Cellular Telephone Service. Lines 2 and 3 are from the SAS survey: total revenues and revenues from reselling the phone equipment. The implied share of equipment to total revenue (line 4) averages just over 13% in the period during 2010–17; it increases steadily over the period, rising from a bit over 9% in 2010 to 18% in 2017.

17.5.2 Adjusting for subsidies (or "discounts") on smartphones

The more difficult problem is teasing out the part of monthly service payments that represent phone purchases. To solve this problem, we combine the IDC price data described above with additional price data from J.D. Power to estimate the discounts/subsidies implicit in the upfront equipment revenue reported by providers. We then use this ratio to form an adjustment factor to the share of equipment to total revenue that we formed from the SAS survey. This adjustment effectively augments the upfront revenues in the SAS data (the $199 in our example) to a noncontract purchase cost basis (the $499).

The IDC data we used above to estimate new price indexes provide average selling prices of smartphones without any discounts (or subsidies). In contrast, consumers surveyed by J.D.

Power report the upfront price they paid for their smartphones, net of discounts.[32] Thus, a comparison of prices in the IDC and J.D. Power datasets provides a reasonable gauge of the size of discounts. In our earlier example, the IDC dataset would record a price of $499 under all of the four transactions. In other words, units sold with a service contract are recorded by IDC with a price that does not include any cross-subsidy between device and service plan. Note that if the carrier dropped the no-contract price of the phone to $490 the following quarter, this price would be recorded in the IDC database, even if the "marquee" price on the Apple web-site continued to be $499.

In contrast, the J.D. Power survey reports the upfront price. In our example, prices for transactions that did not involve a contract would be the same as the IDC price, $499. However, in the transaction with a 2-year plan commitment in our example, respondents to the J.D. Power survey would (correctly) report they paid $199 and the survey would record the price as $199. That is, the J.D. Power price is the upfront price that nets out all discounts and subsidies. This difference in price concept allows us to identify the discounts or subsidies that were an important feature of smartphone pricing. Carriers began eliminating discounts in 2013 and, according to press reports, discounts largely—though not entirely—were gone by the end of 2016 and finally disappeared by 2018 as consumers paid

for the full price of smartphones up front or had an explicit charge on their wireless bill for installment payments.

To gauge the size of discounts or subsidies, Fig. 17.1 plots average smartphone prices from both the IDC and J.D. Power data (which also are reported in Table 17.6). By average prices, we mean the average of reported prices in the datasets prior to any quality adjustment. The difference in trends is stark. The IDC average prices are flat through about 2013 around $500 per phone. Prices then drift down through 2016 before popping back up in 2017 to $460 per phone. The average price in the J.D. Power data is about $160 per phone from 2010 to 2012. In 2013, these prices then begin rising rapidly (right around the time that plans with discounts were beginning to be removed) and by 2016 and 2017 were relatively close to the IDC average prices.[33] Although a portion of the difference in average prices between the datasets could reflect differences in coverage (e.g., a small share of the price observations in the IDC dataset are for sales to business customers), we believe that these differences largely reflect discounts or cross subsidies, and these discounts amounted to about $300 per phone between 2010 and 2012.[34] The removal of these discounts thereafter led to a steep up-trend in average prices as experienced by consumers beginning in 2013. And, to the extent that service providers recaptured those

---

[32] The reported price in the J.D. Power data is the respondents' answer to the question: "How much did your current wireless phone cost, including any rebates or cash-back deals received? Your best estimate is fine." Thus, this price reflects any discounts or subsidies received by the consumer.

[33] The line plotted in Figure 17.1 includes all reported positive or zero prices. Table 17.4 also reports average prices when observations with a reported price of zero are excluded.

[34] As further evidence of subsidies and their gradual disappearance, Verizon's annual reports indicate that their cost of purchasing wireless phones from manufacturers was *twice* the resale revenue of the equipment reported in 2013 and 2014, when most subscribers had the upfront cost of the phone subsidized. As consumers shifted away from traditional plans toward plans that required them to pay the full cost up front, this gap between the reported equipment cost and resale revenues narrowed significantly: that ratio dropped to 1.17 (from 2.0) by 2017, when the majority of subscribers were on plans that required that they pay the full cost of the phone up front.

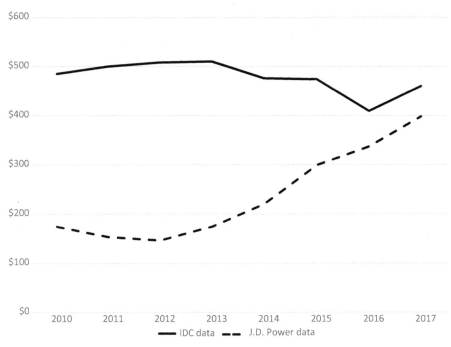

FIGURE 17.1   Average smartphone prices: IDC and J.D. Power data.

discounts in the prices set for wireless service plans, a substantial amount of spending recorded as for wireless service actually reflects payments for devices.[35]

To correct this understatement of equipment purchases, we use the ratio of IDC to J.D. POWER average prices (including "zero" price phones)—shown on line 5 of Table 17.4—as an adjustment factor to the equipment share of revenues reported in the SAS survey.[36] This ratio provides the key piece of information on the relationship between the recorded out-of-pocket cost of a phone and the actual full cost. Specifically, we multiply the ratio of average prices (shown in line 5) and the equipment share of revenues in line 4 to obtain an adjusted share (line 6). That adjusted share averaged about 28% from 2010 to 2017, rising until 2012, then falling appreciably

---

[35] That a large amount of equipment revenue from subsidized plans was actually reported as service revenue by firms was highlighted by service providers when the shift from subsidized plans (with a lot of equipment revenue recorded in services) toward no-subsidy plans (with no equipment revenue recorded in services) lowered the service revenues that providers showed in their financial statements. The declines were significant and required explanation. For example, Verizon's 2015 annual report included the following statement about the effect of increases in no-subsidy plans: "The increase in activations of devices purchased under the Verizon device payment program has resulted in a relative shift of revenue from service revenue to equipment revenue and caused a change in the timing of the recognition of revenue. This shift in revenue was the result of recognizing a higher amount of equipment revenue at the time of sale of devices under the device payment program."

[36] One caveat to our results is that the adjustment factor is based on prices for smartphones, whereas the spending is for all mobile phones.

TABLE 17.6   Average prices ($), US Smartphones.

	2007	2008	2009	2010	2011	2012	2013	2014	2015	2016	2017	Annual average growth rate (%)	
												2007–17	2010–17
IDC data	485	485	499	485	500	508	510	476	474	409	460	−0.5%	−0.8%
J.D. Power data	ND	ND	ND	174	153	146	174	220	299	337	398	ND	15.6%
Excluding zero-price phones	ND	ND	ND	174	173	175	203	252	359	393	457	ND	15.5%

through 2017, as average phone prices declined and an increasing share of phones were sold at retail outlets, for which only the wireless services would be recorded in the SAS.

We then use the adjusted share from line 6 to allocate spending for Cellular Telephone Service (line 1) into phones and wireless services. As seen in lines 7 and 8, our estimates suggest that a nontrivial share of what is reported as wireless services in PCE represents revenues from equipment sales by carriers.

17.5.3 Real PCE spending on phones and wireless services

Our derivation of the adjusted deflator and real PCE for spending currently categorized as Cellular Telephone Services is shown in Table 17.7. The new, adjusted index requires expenditure and price indexes for the two components: phones and services. Given the split derived above between phone and service revenues in the PCE Cellular Telephone Services category (lines 1 and 2), we can deflate the phone component using the new price index that we have developed and deflate the service spending using the CPI currently used in the NIPAs, "wireless telephone services."[37]

Our mobile phone price index falls substantially faster than the CPI currently used to deflate spending for mobile phone services; our phone index falls about 6.6% per year, compared with an average 3-$\frac{1}{2}$% decline in the CPI deflator during 2010–17. A new overall deflator calculated as a weighted average of the two indexes yields a new index for Cellular Telephone Services (line 4) that falls about 4 percentage points faster than the deflator currently used in the NIPAs (declines of 7.7% compared with 3.5%). This difference in deflators translates directly into a mirror image difference in real PCE growth for this category, implying about 4 percentage points of additional real PCE growth when adjusted deflators are used (lines 7 to 9).

For overall PCE, we note that nominal spending on Consumer Telephone Services makes up around 1% of overall PCE over this period. Using this share, our new, adjusted deflator for wireless services implies that the overall PCE deflator increased an average of about 4–5 basis point less per year from 2010

---

[37] We believe that falling constant-quality prices for the devices is not already captured by the matched-model methodology used for the CPI for wireless telephone services because the price of service plans collected for construction of the CPI do not vary depending on the device purchased by the customer. Note that explicitly collected installment payments for devices are not included in the CPI for wireless telephone services (see https://www.bls.gov/cpi/factsheets/telecommunications.htm).

TABLE 17.7   Price deflators and real PCE for Cellular Telephone Services.

	2010	2011	2012	2013	2014	2015	2016	2017	2010–17
Components									
Estimated expenditure shares									
1. Phone	0.26	0.32	0.37	0.31	0.30	0.26	0.21	0.21	0.28
2. Services	0.74	0.68	0.63	0.69	0.70	0.74	0.79	0.79	0.72
Proposed deflators (percent change)									
3. Mobile phones (this paper)		−9.6	−14.9	−15.2	−28.0	−18.8	−22.5	−15.3	−16.6[a]
4. Services (CPI wireless services)		−3.7	−0.8	−1.8	−2.2	−3.8	−1.0	−11.4	−3.5
Cellular Telephone Services (percent change)									
5. Prices: Tornqvist aggregate of components on lines 3 and 4 using shares on lines 1 and 2		−5.4	−5.6	−6.3	−10.1	−8.0	−6.0	−12.2	−7.7
6. Nominal spending		7.0	1.8	3.3	7.7	1.0	3.2	2.4	3.8
Real PCE spending									
7. Proposed		12.4	7.4	9.7	17.8	9.1	9.2	14.6	11.4
8. Current		10.7	2.6	5.1	9.8	4.8	4.2	13.8	7.3
9. Difference		1.7	4.8	4.5	8.0	4.2	5.0	0.8	4.2

[a] *Growth rate is from 2010Q1 to 2018Q1.*

to 2017, with a corresponding boost to overall real PCE growth. Our results also imply a small offset of about 1 basis point lower PCE growth from deflating the PCE spending on cell phones recorded in the "telephone and related communication equipment" by our new deflator, which falls more slowly than the price index currently used in the NIPAs.

Although we do not provide estimates for earlier years, our best guess is that our results do not imply *acceleration* in PCE growth. We have no reason to believe that the share of telecom service provider revenue accounted for by reselling equipment was different prior to the period of our analysis. And, Byrne and Corrado (2015) found that mobile phone prices have declined at similar rates in the past.

17.6 Conclusion

This chapter addresses two problems related to the measurement of smartphones. First, we develop new quality-adjusted price indexes for smartphones using data from IDC that have not previously been used for this purpose. Our preferred index—a hedonic index that allows coefficients on characteristics to change over time—falls at an annual average rate of 16% from 2010 to 2018. Combining this hedonic with a matched-model index for feature phones yields a price index for mobile phones overall that falls at an average rate of 17%. This rate of decline is close to, but about 4 percentage points slower than, that in Byrne and Corrado (2015) and to the index currently being used by the

BEA since the Comprehensive Revision of the GDP accounts in the summer of 2018.

Second, we develop a methodology for disentangling and correctly allocating spending on phones and wireless services when the two are bundled together, typically with a discount on the upfront out-of-pocket cost of the phone in exchange for a commitment to a multiyear service plan. This bundling causes measurement challenges because the accounting conventions used by wireless service providers led to some equipment purchases being counted as service revenues. We correct this misallocation using detail in the SAS. In addition, we use a comparison of price data from IDC and J.D. Power to adjust for the subsidies on phones that some purchasers received in exchange for committing to a long-term contract for wireless service. With these changes, the adjusted deflator for the PCE

category Cellular Telephone Services fell at an average annual rate of 7.7% during 2010–17, about a 4 percentage points faster decline than in currently published measures. Similarly, this adjustment implies faster growth in this category of real PCE by about 4 percentage points. Given the share of this category in overall PCE, our results imply 4 to 5 basis points faster growth in overall real PCE over this period.

Taken together, our results highlight the rapid decline in quality-adjusted prices for products related to the digital economy and, by implication, continued rapid technical advance in these products.

A17 Appendix

TABLE A17.1 Selected adjacent-quarter regressions.

Variable	2010Q1 to 2010Q2			2017Q4 to 2018Q1		
	Coefficient	Std. Error	T statistic	Coefficient	Std. Error	T statistic
Constant	6.886***	(1.417)	4.860	−14.21***	(5.298)	−2.681
Second quarter	−0.123***	(0.0432)	−2.842	−0.00347	(0.0116)	−0.300
Performance variables						
Storage	0.0464***	(0.0150)	3.094	0.145***	(0.00805)	17.97
Camera resolution	0.528***	(0.0695)	7.605	0.367***	(0.0507)	7.226
Processor speed	−0.209	(0.218)	−0.962	2.101***	(0.0755)	27.84
Screen size	−0.0978	(0.199)	−0.492	1.360***	(0.0713)	19.08
Manufacturer						
Manufacturer # 5				0.450	(5.279)	0.0852
Manufacturer # 6				0.136	(0.198)	0.685
Manufacturer # 7	−0.0791	(0.0688)	−1.150	−0.239	(0.694)	−0.344
Manufacturer # 8				−0.249	(0.166)	−1.501
Manufacturer # 9				−0.189	(1.717)	−0.110
Manufacturer # 11				−0.187	(0.214)	−0.873

(Continued)

TABLE A17.1   Selected adjacent-quarter regressions.—cont'd

Variable	2010Q1 to 2010Q2			2017Q4 to 2018Q1		
	Coefficient	Std. Error	T statistic	Coefficient	Std. Error	T statistic
Manufacturer # 12	−0.416*	(0.234)	−1.782			
Manufacturer # 14				0.238	(0.187)	1.274
Manufacturer # 15	−0.462	(0.475)	−0.972	0.927	(1.709)	0.542
Manufacturer # 16	−0.255**	(0.0984)	−2.586	0.209	(0.196)	1.067
Manufacturer # 17	−0.333*	(0.176)	−1.896	−0.598***	(0.227)	−2.633
Manufacturer # 18				0.867***	(0.159)	5.449
Manufacturer # 19	−0.277**	(0.123)	−2.247	0.202	(0.142)	1.423
Manufacturer # 23	−0.684***	(0.0861)	−7.941	0.294**	(0.143)	2.048
Manufacturer # 25	−0.352	(2.028)	−0.174			
Manufacturer # 28	0.00463	(0.335)	0.0138			
Manufacturer # 30				0.204	(0.270)	0.756
Manufacturer # 31				0.196	(0.385)	0.508
Manufacturer # 33	−0.347***	(0.0790)	−4.388	0.360**	(0.143)	2.522
Manufacturer # 36				−0.176	(0.202)	−0.873
Manufacturer # 37	−0.251	(0.271)	−0.929			
Manufacturer # 39				−0.144	(0.152)	−0.946
Manufacturer # 40	−0.324***	(0.0879)	−3.685			
Manufacturer # 43				−0.155	(0.146)	−1.063
Operating systems						
OS version # 2	0.297***	(0.108)	2.735			
OS version # 3	0.366***	(0.0559)	6.545			
OS version # 4	−0.0648	(0.0678)	−0.955			
OS version # 11				0.255	(5.283)	0.0482
OS version # 14				−0.182	(5.277)	−0.0345
OS version # 15				−0.293	(5.277)	−0.0555
OS version # 16				−0.162	(5.277)	−0.0307
OS version # 17				−0.225	(5.277)	−0.0427
OS version # 18				−0.00140	(5.331)	−0.000262
OS version # 21	0.198**	(0.0966)	2.050			
OS version # 22	0.238***	(0.0473)	5.040			

TABLE A17.1 Selected adjacent-quarter regressions.—cont'd

Variable	2010Q1 to 2010Q2			2017Q4 to 2018Q1		
	Coefficient	Std. Error	T statistic	Coefficient	Std. Error	T statistic
OS version # 23	0.121**	(0.0531)	2.273			
OS version # 24	0.0938**	(0.0363)	2.582			
OS version # 29	−0.178	(2.135)	−0.0832			
OS version # 30	0.162	(0.391)	0.415			
OS version # 31	0.353	(0.540)	0.654			
OS version # 32	−0.186	(2.034)	−0.0915			
OS version # 33	−0.270	(2.029)	−0.133			
OS version # 34	−0.361	(2.025)	−0.178			
OS version # 38				−0.788	(5.429)	−0.145
OS version # 39	0.214	(1.974)	0.108			
OS version # 40	0.0213	(0.0725)	0.293			
OS version # 41	−0.0381	(0.0705)	−0.540			
OS version # 46				−0.274***	(0.0464)	−5.902
OS version # 47				−0.124***	(0.0392)	−3.153
OS version # 48	0.123	(0.0902)	1.363			
OS version # 49	0.145*	(0.0738)	1.960			
OS version # 56	−0.363	(0.329)	−1.103			
Telecommunications generation						
2.5G	−0.333***	(0.110)	−3.037			
3G	−0.0740	(0.107)	−0.690			
4G	−0.0982	(0.150)	−0.653	0.137	(0.221)	0.619
Input method						
QWERTY	0.0805	(0.460)	0.175			
QWERTY and touchscreen	0.307	(0.468)	0.656			
Touchscreen	0.122	(0.467)	0.260	−0.791***	(0.141)	−5.624
Entry quarter	−0.0939**	(0.0440)	−2.135	0.0693***	(0.0149)	4.637

* *Represents coefficient estimate significance at the 10 percent level.*
** *Represents coefficient estimate significance at the 5 percent level.*
*** *Represents coefficient estimate significance at the 1 percent level.*
Note: 145 observations are used in the first regression and 689 observations are used in the second regression. Adjusted R-squared values for the first and second regressions are 0.886 and 0.956, respectively.

TABLE A17.2 Preferred quarterly and annual mobile phone price indexes based on IDC data.

	All mobile phones	Smartphones	Feature phones
2010 Q1	4.68	4.73	4.32
2010 Q2	4.64	4.65	4.28
2010 Q3	4.57	4.57	4.22
2010 Q4	4.56	4.56	4.21
2011 Q1	4.54	4.56	4.18
2011 Q2	4.54	4.53	4.20
2011 Q3	4.52	4.50	4.19
2011 Q4	4.46	4.39	4.15
2012 Q1	4.39	4.38	4.05
2012 Q2	4.38	4.38	4.03
2012 Q3	4.37	4.38	4.01
2012 Q4	4.33	4.35	3.95
2013 Q1	4.32	4.34	3.95
2013 Q2	4.27	4.28	3.92
2013 Q3	4.17	4.21	3.77
2013 Q4	4.10	4.13	3.71
2014 Q1	4.02	4.11	3.48
2014 Q2	3.96	4.05	3.39
2014 Q3	3.92	4.01	3.36
2014 Q4	3.84	3.96	3.18
2015 Q1	3.84	3.95	3.17
2015 Q2	3.78	3.91	3.04
2015 Q3	3.73	3.85	2.99
2015 Q4	3.64	3.76	2.96
2016 Q1	3.60	3.72	2.91
2016 Q2	3.54	3.66	2.92
2016 Q3	3.51	3.61	3.00
2016 Q4	3.44	3.54	3.01
2017 Q1	3.42	3.52	2.99

TABLE A17.2 Preferred quarterly and annual mobile phone price indexes based on IDC data.—cont'd

	All mobile phones	Smartphones	Feature phones
2017 Q2	3.38	3.48	2.96
2017 Q3	3.32	3.42	2.92
2017 Q4	3.36	3.45	2.93
2018 Q1	3.35	3.45	2.84
2010	4.61	4.61	4.61
2011	4.51	4.47	4.52
2012	4.36	4.35	4.36
2013	4.21	4.21	4.18
2014	3.93	4.01	3.70
2015	3.74	3.84	3.38
2016	3.52	3.61	3.31
2017	3.36	3.44	3.30

Acknowledgments

We thank Sarah Brown for excellent research assistance and Jeannine Aversa, Craig Brown, Kyle Brown, Carol Corrado, Nicole Nestoriak, and Erick Sager for helpful comments. The views expressed in this chapter are those of the authors alone and do not necessarily represent those of organizations with which they are affiliated.

References

Aizcorbe AM: *A practical guide to price index and hedonic techniques, practical econometrics*, 2014, United Kingdom, 2014, Oxford University Press.

Aizcorbe A, Bridgman B, Nalewaik J: Heterogeneous car buyers: a stylized fact, *Economics Letters* 109:50–53, 2010.

Berndt ER: The measurement of quality change: constructing an hedonic price index for computers using multiple regression methods. In *The practice of econometrics: classic and contemporary*, 1991, pp 127–131.

Bureau of Labor Statistics: *Measuring price change in the CPI: telephone hardware, calculators, and other consumer information items* (website). https://www.bls.gov/cpi/factsheets/telephone-hardware.htm.

Byrne DM, Corrado CA: Prices for communications equipment: rewriting the record. In *Finance and economics discussion series, Board of Governors of the Federal Reserve System*, 2015.

Byrne DM, Corrado CA: *ICT asset prices: marshaling evidence into new measures, Finance and economics discussion series*, 2017, Board of Governors of the Federal Reserve System.

Byrne DM, Fernald J, Reinsdorf M: *Does the United States have a productivity slowdown or a measurement problem? Brookings Papers on Economic Activity* vols. 109–182.

Byrne DM, Oliner SD, Sichel DE: Prices of high-tech products, mismeasurement, and the pace of innovation, *Business Economics* 52:103–113, 2017.

Byrne DM, Oliner SD, Sichel DE: How fast are semiconductor prices falling? *Review of Income and Wealth* 64:679–702, 2018.

Chessa, AG: Processing scanner data in the Dutch CPI: A new methodology and first experiences. *Proceedings of the meeting of the group of experts on consumer price indexes, Geneva, Switzerland, May 2–4.* (website) https://www.unece.org/fileadmin/DAM/stats/documents/ece/ces/ge.22/2016/Session_1._Netherlands_Processing_scanner_data_in_the_Dutch_CPI.pdf.

CNET: *iPhone XS A12 Bionic chip is industry-first 7nm CPU* (website) https://www.cnet.com/news/iphone-xs-a12-bionic-chip-is-industry-first-7nm-cpu/.

Cole R, Chen YC, Barquin-Stolleman JA, Dulberger E, Helvacian N, Hodge J: Quality-adjusted price indexes for computer processors and selected peripheral equipment, *Survey of Current Business* 66:41–50, 1986.

Diewert WE: Exact and superlative index numbers, *Journal of Econometrics* 4:115–145, 1976.

Diewert WE: Index number issues in the consumer price index, *The Journal of Economic Perspectives* 12:47–58, 1998.

Guvenen F, Mataloni Jr RJ, Rassier DG, Ruhl KJ: *Offshore profit shifting and domestic productivity measurement*, 2017,

National Bureau of Economic Research. Working Paper 23324.

Hennessy JL, Patterson DA: *Computer architecture: a quantitative approach*, 2012, Elsevier.

IDC Worldwide quarterly mobile phone tracker, 2018.

Karamti C, Haouech N: Introducing hedonic quality adjustment in the official price statistics: evidence from the Tunisian smartphones market. In *The conference: 61st ISI world statistics congress, . Marrakech, Morocco*, 2018.

Pakes A: A Reconsideration of hedonic price indexes with an application to PC's, *American Economic Review* 93: 1578–1596, 2003.

Pashigian B, Bowen B, Gould E: Fashion, styling, and the within-season decline in automobile prices, *The Journal of Law and Economics* 38:281–309, 1995.

QUORA. *How many transistors were on the first iPhones processor* (website) https://www.quora.com/How-many-transistors-were-on-the-first-iPhones-processor.

Triplett J: *Handbook on hedonic indexes and quality adjustments in price indexes: special application to information technology products*, Paris, 2006, OECD Publishing.

Van Dalen J, Bode B: Estimation biases in quality-adjusted hedonic price indices. In *Paper presented at the SSHRC international conference on index number theory and the measurement of prices and productivity, Vancouver*, June, 2004.

Watanabe N, Nakajima R, Ida T: Quality-adjusted prices of Japanese mobile phone handsets and carriers' strategies, *Review of Industrial Organization* 36:391–412, 2010.

Williams B, Sager E: A new vehicles transaction price index: offsetting the effects of price discrimination and product cycle bias with a year-over-year index. In *Proceedings of the meeting of the group of experts on consumer price indexes, Geneva Switzerland*, 2018.

Accounting for growth and productivity in global value chains

Marcel P. Timmer[1], Xianjia Ye[2]

[1]Faculty of Economics and Business, University of Groningen, Groningen, The Netherlands; [2]Utrecht School of Economics, Utrecht University, Utrecht, The Netherlands

18.1 Introduction

One of Dale Jorgenson's major contributions to the economics profession is the art of growth accounting. In a series of articles with numerous collaborators he outlined the theoretical and empirical foundation of measuring the contribution of factor input and productivity growth to output, culminating in an exhaustive analysis of US postwar growth (Jorgenson et al., 1987). This by now classic study set the gold-standard for the growth accounting technique which quickly became a powerful tool in the economists' tool box. With a lag, it also permeated into the confines of official statistics as the framework of the system of national accounts expanded with each revision, gradually incorporating the concepts of labor and capital services as well as multifactor productivity (MFP) (Jorgenson, 2018a). Progress was steady yet slow, not the least due to the high demands that productivity analysis puts on the data, in particular regarding proper investment and capital stock statistics. Nevertheless, Dale's tireless efforts over the decades bore fruit, influencing, energizing, and connecting researchers and statisticians all over the world, as shown, for example, by the progress being made in the EUKLEMS and World KLEMS projects (Jorgenson et al., 2016; Jorgenson, 2018b).

The growth accounting technique was originally developed for analyzing growth at the aggregate country or industry level. In this chapter we explore the usefulness of applying the growth accounting technique for analysis of a vertically integrated production process. There are both conceptual and empirical reasons for doing so. The main reason is the increasing occurrence of outsourcing and offshoring of production stages. This global fragmentation of production owes much to advances in information and communication technologies that bring down the costs of (cross-border) coordination of production across firms and countries (Baldwin, 2016). Other factors have also been important, notably market liberalization and economic restructuring in many countries, financial deregulation and the integration of global capital markets, and improved contract enforcement in many jurisdictions (Buckley and Strange, 2015). Offshoring has a long history going back to the

1960s, taking great flight in the past two decades, to a significant extent propelled by the accession of China to the WTO in 2001 (Johnson and Noguera, 2012; Los et al., 2015). This led to an increasing cross-country interdependence of production, exemplified by intermediate goods and services as well as technologies crossing borders. As a result nowadays a production process of a good typically consists of many activities which are carried out in different places around the world. For example, an iPad is designed in California, the United States, but assembled in Shenzhen, China on the basis of more than 100 components which are in turn manufactured in many places around the world. This is referred to as global value chain (GVC) production.

This new phenomenon invites new questions: what is driving output growth in a GVC? Is it mainly driven by increased use of labor and capital inputs, or has there been also improvements in productivity through technological change? When offshoring is simply a process of relocating a particular production stage from one country to another without any change in the production technology, productivity growth is expected to be nil yet production costs may decline. On the other hand, it might also be the case that offshoring is just one manifestation of a much larger wave of technical innovations that improve the efficiency in the use of factor inputs throughout the chain. Alternatively, one might hypothesize that the availability of cheap factor inputs might lead to the buildup of slacks or other inefficiencies in the process, if only during the transition phase during which stages are relocated. In this chapter we will show that the traditional growth accounting method can be used to shed light on these issues. To do so, it needs to be applied in the framework of a production function in which all stages of production are vertically integrated. We outline how this can be done in theory as well as in practice.

The remainder of this chapter is organized as follows. In Section 18.2 we outline our general approach to growth accounting for GVCs, and discuss the data sources used. In Section 18.3

we provide an example of a GVC growth account and present results for 273 GVCs of manufacturing products that have been finalized in advanced countries. In Section 18.4 we highlight the importance, and plausibility, of the assumption of perfect global factor input markets for the measurement of multi factor productivity in GVCs. Section 18.5 concludes.

18.2 General approach and data

18.2.1 Prior contributions

The analysis of productivity in vertical integrated production processes has a long history, going back at least to Domar (1961). To fix ideas, assume that a local industry produces a final good (Y_1) using domestic labor (L_1) and capital (K_1) as well as intermediate inputs (M_2) according to a constant returns to scale production function $Y_1 = A_1 F_1(L_1, K_1, M_2)$ with (Hicks neutral) technology A_1. Further suppose that the intermediates are produced abroad with labor in country 2 according to $M_2 = A_2 F_2(L_2, K_2)$. Combining the two stages, one can write the vertically integrated production function for the final good as $Y_1 = A_V F_V(L_1, K_1, L_2, K_2)$ with technology A_V a combination of technologies A_1 and A_2. We refer to this as a GVC production function that relates total capital inputs and labor inputs to the production of a final product. Measures of MFP growth in vertically integrated production were proposed by Rymes (1972), Pasinetti (1977), and Hulten (1978). A well-known result, inspired by Domar (1961), is that MFP growth in the chain is the weighted sum of MFP growth in the two industries that comprise the integrated production sector, where the weights are the ratios of industry gross output to the value of output of final product (Hulten, 1978). Other variations of vertically integrated measurement frameworks include Wolff (1994), Durand (1996), and Aulin-Ahmavaara (1999). All these measures were developed for a closed economy setting.

More recently, Gu and Yan (2017) and Timmer and Ye (2018) provide frameworks that extend the vertical integration approach to an open economy setting. In their analyses they cover all inputs in production, domestic as well as abroad, taking advantage of the new availability of data on factor use in a large set of countries through the World Input–Output Database (WIOD, Timmer et al., 2015). Gu and Yan (2017) compare standard MFP growth in a country with what they call "effective" MFP growth. The latter includes also MFP growth in other countries that is embodied in upstream foreign industries delivering inputs that are imported. Effective MFP growth will surpass standard aggregate MFP growth in an open economy if productivity growth is higher in the foreign industries producing the imported intermediates than the aggregate domestic economy. This is a useful measure to track when there is a tight relationship between the price development of final goods and the rate of effective MFP, such that technical improvements in any stage of production (home and abroad) are reflected in a lower price. In that case, one can link technical change in foreign upstream stages of production to the decline in prices of final goods in the domestic market. Surprisingly, Gu and Yan (2017) do not find that the relationship between final output prices and effective MFP is stronger than for final output prices and standard MFP. This may be due to a mismatch in the deflators of foreign output and the deflators for imported input at home. We will return to this price measurement issue later. Timmer and Ye (2018) provide a wider analysis of production patterns and productivity in GVCs. We will present their framework and extend it to a dual price setting to make the link with analyses of international price competitiveness. Perhaps most importantly, we will highlight and discuss some new conceptual issues that arise when applying traditional growth accounting in a GVC context.

18.2.2 Measuring productivity in GVCs

This section gives a mathematical exposition of a framework to measure productivity in a multi-country production setting, following and extending Timmer and Ye (2018). There are S sectors and N countries. Each country-sector produces one good such that there are SN products. We use the term country-sector to denote a sector in a country, such as the French chemicals sector or the German transport equipment sector. Output in each country-sector is produced using domestic production factors and intermediate inputs, which may be sourced domestically or from foreign suppliers. Let $\mathbf{y}$ be the vector of production of dimension (SN × 1), which is obtained by stacking gross output levels in each country-sector. Define $\mathbf{f}$ as the vector of dimension (SN × 1) that is constructed by stacking world demand for final output from each country-sector. World final demand is the summation of demand from any country. For a particular intermediate good, let i be the source country, j be the destination country, s be the source sector, and t be the destination sector. We define a global intermediate input coefficients matrix $\mathbf{A}$ of dimension (SN × SN). The elements $a_{ij}(s,t) = m_{ij}(s,t)/y_j(t)$ describe the output from sector s in country i used as intermediate input by sector t in country j, expressed as a ratio of output in the latter sector. Columns in the matrix $\mathbf{A}$ describe how the products of each country-sector are produced using a combination of various intermediate products, both domestic and foreign.[1]

For a given set of final output $\mathbf{f}$ one can write associated output as:

$$\mathbf{y} = (\mathbf{I} - \mathbf{A})^{-1}\mathbf{f} \qquad (18.1)$$

[1] Although we will apply annual data in our empirical analysis, time subscripts are left out in the following discussion for ease of exposition.

where $\mathbf{I}$ is an (SN × SN) identity matrix with ones on the diagonal and zeros elsewhere. The element in row m and column n of the $(\mathbf{I} - \mathbf{A})^{-1}$ matrix gives the total gross output of sector m needed for production of one unit of final output of product n. To see this, one can apply information in the A matrix in a recursive procedure as follows. Let $\mathbf{z}$ be an SN column vector with a one for the element representing say iPhones assembled in China, and all other elements are zero. Then $\mathbf{Az}$ is the vector of intermediate inputs, both Chinese and foreign, that are assembled, such as the hard-disk drive, battery, and processors. But these intermediates need to be produced as well and $\mathbf{AAz}$ indicates the intermediate inputs needed to produce $\mathbf{Az}$. This continues until the mining and drilling of basic materials such as metal ore, sand, and oil required to start the production process. Summing up across all stages, one derives the gross output levels for all SN country-industries generated in the production of iPods by $(\mathbf{I} - \mathbf{A})^{-1}\mathbf{z}$, since the summation over all rounds is a geometric series $\left(\sum_{k=0}^{\infty} \mathbf{A}^k \mathbf{z} \right)$ that converges to $(\mathbf{I} - \mathbf{A})^{-1}\mathbf{z}$. The matrix $(\mathbf{I} - \mathbf{A})^{-1}$ is famously known as the Leontief inverse.[2]

Using the Leontief inverse we can derive the total factor requirements of a unit of final output by netting out all intermediate input flows. Let us define $l_i(s)$ as the labor per unit of gross output in sector s in country i and create the row-vector l containing these "direct" labor coefficients. Then the total (direct plus indirect) labor requirements per unit of final output can be derived as

$$\Lambda = \hat{l}(\mathbf{I} - \mathbf{A})^{-1} \qquad (18.2)$$

in which a hat-symbol indicates a diagonal matrix with the elements of the vector on the

diagonal. Λ is the matrix of dimension (SN × SN) with an element (n,m) indicating the amount of labor in country-sector m needed in the production of one unit of final output by country-sector n, referred to as the total labor coefficient. (Note that we analyze the input needed *per unit of output* such that there is no need to post multiply with $\mathbf{f}$.)

Similarly for capital, let $k_i(s)$ be the capital per unit of gross output in sector s in country i and create the row-vector k containing the "direct" capital coefficients. Then the total (direct plus indirect) capital requirements per unit of final output can be derived as

$$\mathbf{K} = \hat{k}(\mathbf{I} - \mathbf{A})^{-1} \qquad (18.3)$$

with $\mathbf{K}$ the matrix of dimension (SN × SN) with an element (n,m) indicating the amount of capital in country-sector m needed in the production of one unit of final output by country-sector n, referred to as the total capital coefficient.

Using these total factor requirements matrices, we can define factor cost shares in a GVC of a final product. At this point we first need to define prices of output and factor inputs. Let $\mathbf{p}$ be a (row) vector of output prices for products from each country-sector, $\mathbf{w}$ the (row) vector of hourly wage rates, and $\mathbf{r}$ the (row) vector of capital rental prices. We allow output and factor input prices to differ across sectors and countries.[3] Value added in a country-sector is defined in the standard way as gross output value (at basic prices) minus the cost of intermediate inputs (at purchasers' prices), that is, it is given by $\mathbf{p}(\mathbf{I} - \mathbf{A})$. The rental price includes an "ex post" rate of return on capital in the parlance of the Jorgensonian framework such that capital compensation (the rental price times the quantity of capital) plus labor compensation (wage times

---

[2] This is under empirically mild conditions. See Miller and Blair (2009) for a good starting point on input–output analysis.

[3] For ease of exposition we assume here that there is only one price for the output of each country-sector, and this price is paid by all intermediate and final users. This assumption is loosened up in the empirical application later.

hours worked) equals gross value added. Then the following accounting identity holds:

$$\mathbf{p}(\mathbf{I} - \mathbf{A}) = \mathbf{w}\widehat{l} + \mathbf{r}\widehat{k} \qquad (18.4)$$

Postmultiplying both sides of Eq. (18.4) with the inverse of (I-A) and substituting from Eqs. (18.2) and (18.3) we arrive at an important result: the output price of a final product (from a given country-sector) can be rewritten as a linear combination of the prices of all factors that were directly *and indirectly* needed in its production, or

$$\mathbf{p} = \mathbf{w}\mathbf{\Lambda} + \mathbf{r}\mathbf{K} \qquad (18.5)$$

with $\mathbf{\Lambda}$ and $\mathbf{K}$ the matrices with total labor and capital coefficients as defined earlier. The identity in Eq. (18.5) forms the basis for deriving cost shares of labor and capital in the GVC of a particular product. Through appropriate selection of elements in the matrices $\mathbf{\Lambda}$ and $\mathbf{K}$, one may trace the country-sector origins of these factor costs. We will use this decomposition in the next section to investigate the shifting factor shares in GVCs of manufacturing products.

The cost shares and quantities derived above can be used to measure total factor productivity (TFP) growth in the production of a final good in a GVC. We use the concept of TFP here rather than MFP, as in the vertically integrated production function all factor inputs are accounted for (in any country-industry) in contrast to the standard industry (single stage) case which only covers factor inputs in that industry. The consolidated data provide the opportunity to use the standard approach in growth accounting in measuring productivity assuming a final output production function with arguments based on total (direct and indirect) labor and capital used. Let G be a translog production function for a final product j: $f_j = G_j(\lambda_j, \kappa_j, T)$ where λ_j is the column vector of total labor requirements for product j from $\mathbf{\Lambda}$, and similarly κ_j a column of $\mathbf{K}$. T denotes technology. Under the standard assumptions of constant returns to scale and perfect input markets such that input prices reflect marginal

revenue (an issue to which we will return later) we can define the (primal) TFP growth in the GVC of product j by the weighted rate of decline of its total labor and capital requirements (as these are given per unit of output):

$$\frac{\partial \mathrm{TFP}_j}{\partial t} \equiv -\alpha_j^L \frac{\partial \ln\lambda_j}{\partial t} - \alpha_j^K \frac{\partial \ln\kappa_j}{\partial t} \qquad (18.6)$$

where $\partial \ln\lambda_j / \partial t$ is a (column) vector containing the differentials of the logarithms of all elements in λ_j. The weights are given by α_j^L, a (row) vector of value shares with elements reflecting the costs of labor from all country-sectors used in the production of one unit of product j, and similarly for the capital value shares given in α_j^K. Summed over all contributing sectors and countries, the elements in α_j^L add up to the labor share in final output of j, and similarly for capital.

Adding log output growth to the left- and right-hand sides and rearranging delivers the familiar growth accounting decomposition, yet now in the context of a GVC:

$$\frac{\partial \ln y_j}{\partial t} \equiv \alpha_j^L \frac{\partial \ln\widetilde{\lambda}_j}{\partial t} + \alpha_j^K \frac{\partial \ln\widetilde{\kappa}_j}{\partial t} + \frac{\partial \mathrm{TFP}_j}{\partial t} \qquad (18.7)$$

with $\frac{\partial \ln\widetilde{\lambda}_j}{\partial t}$ the growth in total labor input, and similarly $\frac{\partial \ln\widetilde{\kappa}_j}{\partial t}$ the growth in total capital input. The equation shows that growth in (final) output in a country-industry can be decomposed into the contribution of growth in labor $\alpha_j^L \frac{\partial \ln\widetilde{\lambda}_j}{\partial t}$, the contribution of the growth in capital $\alpha_j^K \frac{\partial \ln\widetilde{\kappa}_j}{\partial t}$, and TFP growth $\frac{\partial \mathrm{TFP}_j}{\partial t}$ along the GVC. Note that TFP growth measured in this way represents the improvement in the overall efficiency with which factor inputs in the GVC are being used. To measure productivity growth rates over discrete time periods rather than instantaneously the average value shares over the sample period can be used as weights α_j^L and α_j^K according to the so-called Tornqvist-Divisia productivity index (see Jorgenson et al., 1987).

One might also be interested in the price competitiveness of the country-industry producing good j. To analyze this one can define the dual (price) representation of TFP growth in a GVC as follows:

$$\frac{\partial \text{TFP}_j}{\partial t} \equiv -\frac{\partial \text{p}_j}{\partial t} + \alpha_j^L \frac{\partial \ln \text{w}_j}{\partial t} + \alpha_j^K \frac{\partial \ln \text{r}_j}{\partial t} \quad (18.8)$$

such that

$$\frac{\partial \text{p}_j}{\partial t} \equiv \alpha_j^L \frac{\partial \ln \text{w}_j}{\partial t} + \alpha_j^K \frac{\partial \ln \text{r}_j}{\partial t} - \frac{\partial \text{TFP}_j}{\partial t} \quad (18.9)$$

Eq. (18.9) provides insights into the determinants of price competitiveness of the country-industry producing good j. It shows that the output price will decline when factor prices decline, which may be in the domestic economy, but also abroad. Also, output price will decline when there is positive TFP growth in the chain, again not necessarily in those stages that are carried out domestically. It indicates the impact of factor price and technology developments abroad for the price competitiveness of the domestic economy.

One important consequence is that international competitiveness of countries and firms are becoming increasingly connected. Arguably, much of the offshoring by advanced countries was driven by a search for lower labor costs in the newly opening economies and this would be reflected in a higher share of imported intermediates. The (price) competitiveness of an industry thus no longer depended only on domestic factor prices and MFP, but also on access to cheap foreign inputs. For example, a firm in an advanced country might improve its price competitiveness by offshoring to cheaper labor locations or by improving the efficiency with which existing inputs are being used.

18.2.3 Data

A key empirical obstacle in this line of research is the lack of statistical information on GVCs. Standard statistical firm-level surveys typically provide only the amount of inputs and outputs of the firm. These are recorded with little, or no, detail on the identity and location of the input providers and output buyers. Put otherwise, only one stage of production is identified with no information on the previous or next stage. Statistical institutes combine this information with other information, such as detailed trade and production data, in a coherent supply and use framework to generate national input—output (IO) tables. The IO tables can be used to construct "synthetic" value chains assuming the same technology is used in all stages of production, such that IO tables can be applied recursively as described above. Recently, national IO tables have been linked together with bilateral trade data to form world IO tables (WIOTs) that contain information on intersectoral as well as intercountry flows of goods and services, such as the OECD Tiva (see https://oe.cd/tiva) and the WIOD (see https://www.wiod.org). Los et al. (2015) show how one use the information from WIOTs to derive the value added contributions from all countries (and industries) in the GVC of a particular final output. Timmer et al. (2014) extend this with information on wages and employment from the WIOD to construct labor and capital shares in GVCs. We follow their lead using data from the WIOD 2013 release, which includes current as well as constant price WIOTs.

18.2.4 GVCs and the measurement of intermediate input prices

The GVC approach provides additional insights into the sources of competitiveness beyond the insights from the traditional growth accounting for a single country-industry. In the traditional approach developments abroad would be summarized into changes of a price measure of imported inputs without information on its drivers (productivity or factor price changes abroad). Moreover, it relies strongly on the assumption that prices of intermediate inputs are well measured. Only in that case the price of value added can be properly measured through separate deflation of gross output and all intermediate inputs, also known as double deflation. However, double deflation is becoming increasingly difficult as production fragmentation progresses. There is increasing doubt about the reliability of price indices for imported intermediates due to the practice of intrafirm transfer pricing and more generally inadequate statistical systems to monitor prices of imports (see Houseman et al., 2011). One area of concern is in the price measurement of intangible service flows such as the provision of marketing and technical knowledge including software and data-services. Intangibles are becoming increasingly important in production, but so far their measurement is elusive (see Corrado et al. (2012) for pioneering attempts and Houseman and Mandel (2015) for an overview).

A special case of mismeasurement that recently attracted attention is the measurement of input price change in the presence of offshoring. Reinsdorf and Yuskavage (2018) conclude that for the case of the United States, "changes in prices paid for intermediate inputs caused by offshoring are not tracked in any index. The U.S. Bureau of Economic Analysis (BEA) uses producer price indexes (PPIs) to deflate the domestically sourced items and MPIs to deflate foreign sourced items, but neither of these indexes would follow an item as it moved from domestic production to offshore production." In a conservative estimate, Reinsdorf and Yuskavage (2018) found that mismeasurement of import prices related to sourcing change appears to be responsible for about a tenth of the speedup in measured productivity growth during 1996−2005. They also found it to be highly unevenly distributed across sectors and particularly pertain to the manufacturing sector, as earlier suggested by Houseman et al. (2011). It seems reasonable to assume that these mismeasurements in productivity are proportional to the share of import in intermediate use, and thus to be larger for countries that are smaller and much more open than the United States.

Mismeasurement of intermediate input prices leads to a problem of attribution of productivity growth across industries (and countries). Triplett (1996) shows that in the case of measuring productivity in the US production of computers, the use of alternative quality-adjusted prices leads to radically different assessments of the location of productivity, which may be in the computer industry itself, or in the semiconductor industry that delivers the main inputs to the computer industry, or even further back in the chain, namely the manufacturing of semiconductor machinery. Similarly, mismeasurement of prices of imported intermediates might obscure the geographical location of productivity growth in GVCs. The robustness of analyses such as in Gu and Yan (2017) who allocate productivity growth in a GVC to various stages of production across countries depends crucially on the quality of the price statistics used. In this paper we will restrict ourselves to analyses of input and TFP growth for the chain as a whole which do not require the use of intermediate input deflators.

18.3 Growth accounts for global value chains

18.3.1 Illustrative example

We illustrate our GVC methodology by decomposing the growth of final output from the transport equipment industry (NACE rev. 1 industries 34 and 35) in South Korea, in short "Korean cars." Final output includes the value added in the last stage of production, which will take place in South Korea by definition, but also the value added by all other activities in the chain which take place anywhere in the world. To decompose value added in production, we make use of the decomposition method outlined in Section 18.2 and given in Eq. (18.5).

The geographical origin of the value added in production of Korean cars in 1995 and in 2008 reveals striking developments. Between 1995 and 2008, the share of domestic value added decreased from 76 to 70% of the value of a Korean car. Conversely foreign value increased from 24 to 30%. With the new availability of cheap and relatively skilled labor, firms from South Korea relocated parts of the production process to other countries. At the same time, the industry quickly globalized by sourcing more and more from abroad. With additional information on the quantity of factors used in each country we can provide a growth accounting decomposition of the growth rate of final output of Korean automotives using Eq. (18.7). Data on workers are measured by the number of hours, classified on the basis of educational attainment levels as defined in the International Standard Classification of Education (ISCED): low-skilled (ISCED categories 1 and 2), medium-skilled (ISCED 3 and 4), and high-skilled (ISCED 5 and 6). Capital stock volumes are measured on the basis of capital stocks of reproducible assets as covered in national account statistics measured at 1995 constant price. Note that we have information on inputs used in 35 industries in 41 economies such that contributions in a particular GVC can be made in potentially 1435 ($=35 \times 41$) country-industries.

The results are shown in Table 18.1: final output volumes of Korean automotives increased by 69 log points over the period from 1995 to 2007. This was mainly due to increases in the use of capital both domestically and abroad, together accounting for about a quarter of the increase in final output. The number of workers employed in production increased as well, yet with a clear difference between the structure and growth of labor demand domestically and abroad. Demand for low-skilled workers within South Korea declined rapidly,

while demand for low-skilled abroad increased. The highest growth is in demand for high-skilled workers both at home and abroad contributing 11 and 6% to final output growth, respectively. Productivity growth is derived as a residual as in Eq. (18.6). It is growing fast by more than 0.50 log points over this period, contributing 60% of final output growth over this period. Clearly, growth in the South Korean car GVC is mostly driven by a more efficient use of the factor inputs. These factor inputs are increasingly located abroad.

18.3.2 General patterns of productivity growth and input use in GVCs

What are the general patterns of input and productivity growth in GVCs? As for cars finalized in South Korea, we decompose growth in GVCs of manufactured goods that are finalized in 21 advanced countries, including 15 European countries, Australia, Canada, Japan, South Korea, Taiwan, and the United States. We have data for output from 13 manufacturing industries, which are groups of two digit industries according to ISIC rev.3. So all in all, we will study the production structure of 273 ($=13 \times 21$) GVCs. In Table 18.2 we provide the growth accounts for each of the 13 manufacturing product groups, weighted across the 21 finalizing countries with the shares in total final output across all advanced countries. The results are depicted in Fig. 18.1.

Global output growth has been high during 1995–2007 for final electronic goods (including computers and electrical machinery), transport equipment, and chemicals. It has declined for textiles (including wearing apparel), shoes, and wood products. Two observations stand out with respect to the contribution of labor to output growth. First, the quantity of low-skilled work used in GVCs has been declining in most GVCs. This is not so surprising for GVCs in which output is declining as well, but

TABLE 18.1   Growth accounting for vertical production of automotives from South Korea.

	Cost shares in GVC (%)		Quantities (1995 = 1)		Contribution to output growth	
	1995	2007	1995	2007	Log pts	%
Factors in South Korea						
Low-skilled labor	12.2	4.4	1.00	0.42	−7.2	−10.5
Medium-skilled labor	26.7	23.8	1.00	0.99	−0.3	−0.4
High-skilled labor	17.0	20.5	1.00	1.52	7.8	11.3
Capital	20.6	21.5	1.00	1.53	8.9	13.0
Factors outside South Korea						
Low-skilled labor	2.9	2.7	1.00	1.68	1.5	2.1
Medium-skilled labor	6.6	6.1	1.00	2.40	5.6	8.1
High-skilled labor	3.2	3.8	1.00	2.97	3.8	5.5
Capital	10.7	17.2	1.00	1.68	7.3	10.6
Total all factor inputs			1.00	1.31	27.3	39.7
Total factor productivity			1.00	1.51	41.5	60.3
Final output	100.0	100.0	1.00	1.99	68.8	100.0

Note and source: Own calculation based on Eq. (18.7) using data from WIOD, November 2013 release. The shares and volumes for factors abroad are based on summations across 39 countries and the rest-of-the-world region. Capital growth is proxied by growth in capital stocks. Input quantities are set to 1 in 1995. Numbers may not add due to rounding.

we find it to be also true for fast-growing products such as electronics and nonelectrical machinery. The quantity of unskilled work only increased in the rapidly expanding GVCs of transport equipment and chemicals. Second, the use of high-skilled work has increased in all industries, except the ones in which output declined. Even more strongly, it appears that there is a strict ordering: for each product group it is true that the growth rate of low-skilled work is lower than for medium-skilled work, which is again lower than for high-skilled work.

The bottom part of the graph shows the contribution of the growth in each input to final output growth. Growth in capital input appears to be an important source of growth in most GVCs, typically accounting for 40% of output growth or more. The notable exception is for electronics, as capital input growth was fast in

an absolute sense, but slow compared to output growth. Growth in high-skilled work contributed positively to all GVCs, except, again, in electronics. On the other hand, growth contributions from medium-skilled workers were small or even negative. Not surprisingly, growth contributions from low-skilled work are negative, given its absolute decline noted above. Note that for industries that are shrinking (negative growth of final output), contributions to growth from factor inputs are positive when the input shrinks as well. This explains the "positive" contributions of low-skilled worker growth to the growth in final output of textiles, for example.

Another main conclusion from the table is that TFP growth is positive in all GVCs. It ranges from 7.5% in basic metals to 72% in electronics. Clearly, technological change was such that inputs were used more efficiently in the global

TABLE 18.2   Final output growth decomposition for manufacturing product groups, 1995–2007.

Final output group	Food	Textile	Shoes	Wood	Paper	Chemical	Plastic	Non-metal	Metal	Machinery	Electronics	Transport equipment	Other manufacturing
ISIC	15t16	17t18	19	20	21t22	24	25	26	27t28	29	30t33	34t35	36t37
Cost shares (%) in 1995													
Low-skilled	15.6	22.8	27.9	18.0	12.9	11.9	14.8	16.3	16.3	14.7	12.3	13.2	18.1
Medium -skilled	29.3	31.4	27.2	35.2	31.2	26.1	31.7	30.7	33.0	35.3	32.8	35.5	34.7
High-skilled	14.4	14.1	12.3	13.4	17.8	16.6	15.3	14.0	14.2	16.7	18.9	17.6	15.9
Capital	40.7	31.6	32.6	33.4	38.1	45.5	38.2	39.0	36.5	33.2	36.0	33.7	31.4
Cost shares (%) in 2007													
Low-skilled	10.4	15.4	18.1	11.3	8.7	7.9	10.0	10.3	9.9	9.2	7.5	8.2	11.5
Medium -skilled	28.5	32.6	29.4	34.7	28.5	23.3	30.0	28.8	29.2	31.5	28.9	30.5	31.0
High-skilled	17.6	19.1	16.6	17.0	22.7	19.4	19.1	17.6	16.3	19.6	24.6	20.7	18.9
Capital	43.4	33.0	35.9	37.0	40.2	49.4	41.0	43.3	44.5	39.7	39.0	40.5	38.5
Quantity growth (log points)													
Low-skilled	−38.0	−79.8	−56.8	−61.0	−15.3	6.8	−18.6	−27.2	−27.2	−16.1	−35.0	5.2	−32.0
Medium -skilled	−5.8	−62.6	−37.9	−39.5	−7.0	18.8	−2.5	−4.1	−0.6	1.5	−8.3	21.2	−9.7
High-skilled	17.2	−31.2	−5.8	−11.2	22.4	43.1	23.3	26.7	28.3	28.6	17.0	45.5	17.4
Capital	11.0	−43.6	−24.7	−26.5	25.7	34.6	14.0	7.2	8.7	25.8	15.9	42.1	8.8
Final output	9.3	−44.2	−33.1	−18.4	20.9	38.1	20.9	14.7	6.5	26.3	66.5	43.2	5.2
TFP	9.3	22.3	11.2	16.6	13.7	15.2	21.0	15.2	7.5	20.8	72.3	21.6	13.0
Contribution to final output growth (%)													
Low-skilled	−64.9	41.1	53.8	53.1	−22.1	−6.0	−27.2	−41.8	−82.7	−19.2	−8.2	−8.1	−142.5
Medium -skilled	−35.1	62.3	46.2	88.4	−19.4	0.9	−21.5	−28.9	−63.5	−15.4	−14.2	2.8	−127.7
High-skilled	20.7	20.4	13.1	13.6	14.8	14.4	9.3	22.1	35.2	10.9	−0.9	13.6	20.1
Capital	78.4	26.7	20.7	35.0	61.4	50.6	38.7	45.4	94.8	44.7	14.6	41.7	101.1
TFP	100.8	−50.5	−33.9	−90.2	65.3	40.0	100.6	103.3	116.2	79.0	108.6	50.0	249.0

Note: See Table 18.1. Based on GVCs ending in 21 advanced countries, weighted by share in final output across all countries.
TFP, total factor productivity.

production of goods. TFP growth can account for all output growth in food, plastic, nonmetallic minerals, metal products, electronics, and other manufacturing. In some case it even accounts for more than 100% of output growth as the quantity of some inputs is shrinking. The contribution of TFP to growth in chemicals and transport equipment is relatively limited, although still accounting for 50 and 40% of output growth, respectively. It accounts for 65% of output growth in plastics, and for 79% in machinery.

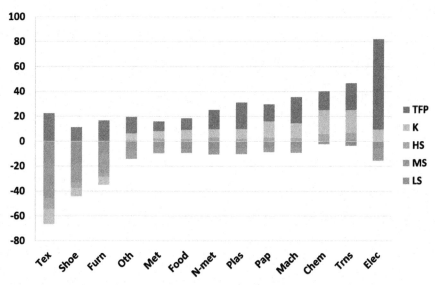

FIGURE 18.1 Accounting for final output growth of global value chains, 1995–2007. HS, high-skilled; K, capital; LS, low-skilled; MS, medium-skilled; TFP, total factor productivity. *Source: Table 18.2.*

18.4 Factor substitution bias in measuring GVC TFP

The application of growth accounting in GVCs raises new questions about the underlying fundamentals of the accounting framework. One key assumption in the growth accounting method is the assumption that each input is paid its marginal product. In that case, the growth of aggregate input can be measured as a weighted growth of the detailed inputs with cost shares as weights. Here we will focus on the case of labor input measurement and discuss to what extent this assumption is valid when applied in a GVC setting with labor input from various countries.

In the analysis so far, we have measured the growth of labor input of a given type as a weighted growth of labor of this type classified by country c. So

$$\Delta lnL_e = \sum_c \alpha_{c,e} \Delta lnL_{c,e} \qquad (18.10)$$

with $\alpha_{c,e} = w_{c,e}L_{c,e} \Big/ \sum w_{c,e}L_{c,e}$, the share of worker type e in country c in the overall wages

paid in the GVC to this type of worker. The implicit assumption is one of perfect competition in factor markets: for example, when Chinese workers (of a given educational attainment type) are paid $5 per hour (at exchange rate), while US workers (of the same type) are paid $10, then the contribution of growth in Chinese workers to output growth is assumed to be only half the contribution of a similar growth in US workers. This might be a reasonable assumption for high-skilled workers, but it is less obvious that this also holds for less skilled workers. We know that integration of labor markets across countries is still incomplete such that wage differentials are not necessarily arbitraged away. Interestingly, this measurement problem in labor input has a strong similarity to the problem of import substitution bias in the measurement of intermediate input prices discussed above. The price measurement problem arises as there is a substitution of a more expensive input for a similar cheaper variety. In analogy, shifts in the distribution of hours worked from lower- to higher-wage countries might not picked up correctly by the labor input index in Eq. (18.10) when the workers are comparable across countries, that is, have the same marginal productivity.[4] It seems clear that much of the off-shoring trends and GVC development is driven by a strong cost-saving motive of multinational firms. This hypothesis is congruent with a strong increase in the share of so-called "factorless income" in GVCs, that is, the part of value added that cannot be allocated to labor or capital (measured with an ex ante rate of return), as documented by Chen et al. (2018).

Can we put bounds on the size of the problem of labor substitution for TFP measurement in GVCs? To this end, we make an extreme assumption and assume that the marginal productivity of worker of a given type is equal across all countries. In that case, one can aggregate workers across countries, $L_e = \sum L_{c,e}$, such that growth in the aggregate labor input index is then given by

$$\widetilde{\Delta lnL}_e = \sum_c s_{c,e} \Delta lnL_{c,e} \qquad (18.11)$$

with weights $s_{c,e} = L_{c,e} / \sum L_{c,e}$. It can be easily shown that the difference between the aggregate labor indices in Eqs. (18.10) and (18.11) is given by difference in the weights α and s. The difference $\Delta lnL_e - \widetilde{\Delta lnL}_e$ is akin to what is called "labor quality" in the Jorgenson framework (see e.g., Jorgenson et al., 1987). But note that the interpretation here is the opposite: we assume that there is no quality difference across countries for a given type of worker, and hence the difference is an indicator of the mismeasurement of aggregate labor input in GVCs. When there is a shift in employment of identical jobs in the GVC from advanced to poor countries (with lower wages), then use of the standard index ΔlnL_e will lead to an *under*estimation of the labor

input, and an *over*estimation of TFP in the GVC as it is measured as a residual. Fig. 18.2 shows the magnitudes of the potential mismeasurement of TFP in GVCs when using the standard index.

Fig. 18.2 shows the Kernel density plots for TFP growth in 273 GVCs (the same set as above) for the period 1995–2007, measured according to four alternatives. TFPraw is the TFP growth in the GVC when using the standard methodology in which each input in each country-industry is treated as a different input, as in Eq. (18.10). TFP4 is the other extreme in which inputs are assumed to be identical across countries (and industries), as we discussed above. Put otherwise, growth in each factor input (low-, medium-, and high-skilled labor as well as capital) is calculated as the growth of the aggregate of the factor across all countries as in Eq. (18.11). These four inputs are subsequently weighted with their aggregate factor cost share. For

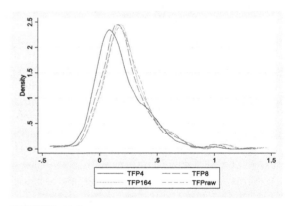

FIGURE 18.2   Alternative measures of total factor productivity (TFP) growth rates in global value chains (GVCs). Note: TFP growth rate in 273 GVCs according to four alternatives for the measurement of factor inputs: TFP4 (total input across all countries), TFP8 (domestic inputs and foreign inputs separately), TFP164 (inputs separately per country), and TFPraw (inputs per country-industry).

---

[4] This is most easily seen in the dual approach: assume no change in country-industry wages and a one-off shift of jobs to cheaper places. If the cost decline is fully reflected in output price, then there will be measured TFP growth, although there is no change in productivity as the same amount of labour inputs is being used as before.

comparison we also provide two intermediate alternatives: separate aggregation of domestic and foreign factor inputs, thus $2 \times 4 = 8$ inputs (TFP8), and separate aggregation of factor inputs within each of the 41 economies (across industries), thus $41 \times 4 = 164$ inputs (TFP164).[5]

We find that in general, the various TFP alternatives are highly correlated across GVCs. A GVC with a high TFP growth relative to other GVCs according to the standard method is likely to have also a high relative TFP growth when using the alternative measures. The correlation of TFPraw with TFP4 is 0.92 (0.89 for rank correlation), with TFP8 0.97 (0.96) and with TFP164 0.99 (0.99). The (unweighted) mean TFP growth in the set of 273 GVCs is 17.8 log points for TFP4, 21.3 for TFP8, 23.7 for TFP164, and 23.9 for TFPraw. So indeed TFPraw (the standard methodology) would overestimate TFP by 6.1 log points, in case our extreme case holds, namely that there is no difference in marginal productivity across countries for a given input type (TFP4). Thus we conclude that it is likely that TFP growth in GVCs will be overestimated when using the assumption of perfect competition in global factor markets. Our most extreme estimate suggest that the magnitude of this overestimation may be sizable, leading to an overestimation of TFP growth by almost a third.

18.5 Concluding remarks

In this paper we pioneered the application of the canonical KLEMS framework as developed by Dale Jorgenson and collaborators in the context of a GVC that spans countries across borders. We developed measures of factor inputs and of TFP growth in GVCs and showed how existing data from the WIOD can be used to make a decomposition of final output growth. We highlighted a particular issue that arises in the context of GVCs, which is the measurement of labor input when factor prices are not equalized across countries. We show that this might lead to sizable mismeasurement of TFP in GVCs, requiring further analysis into the validity of the perfect market assumption underlying growth accounting. All in all, the analysis presented here demonstrates that the canonical KLEMS framework is versatile and when appropriately modified, can also be applied outside the traditional confines of analyses of economic growth in individual countries and industries to wider analyses of GVCs. More than 50 years after its introduction the growth accounting framework of Jorgenson and Griliches (1967) is still a useful guide for the measurement of production output and inputs in the world economy.

References

Aulin-Ahmavaara P: Effective rates of sectoral productivity change, *Economic Systems Research* 11(4):349–363, 1999.

Baldwin R: *The great convergence*, Harvard University Press.

Buckley PJ, Strange R: The governance of the global factory: location and control of world economic activity, *Academy of Management Perspectives* 29(2):237–249, 2015.

Chen W, Los B, Timmer MP: *Factor incomes in global value chains: the role of intangibles*, NBER Working Paper No. 25242, 2018.

Corrado C, Haskel J, Iommi M, Jona-Lasinio C: *Intangible capital and growth in advanced economies: measurement and comparative results*, CEPR Discussion Papers 9061, 2012.

Domar ED: On the measurement of technological change, *The Economic Journal* 71(284):709–729, 1961.

Durand R: Canadian input–output-based multi-factor productivity accounts, *Economic Systems Research* 8(4):367–390, 1996.

Gu W, Yan B: Productivity growth and international competitiveness, *Review of Income and Wealth* 63: S113–S133, 2017.

[5] These alternatives are all using index numbers, invoking strong assumptions about the substitutability of factor inputs. Alternatively, TFP can be measured using an econometric approach (see Jorgenson (2000)). Timmer and Ye (2018) report on an application of the econometric approach to producer behavior in a GVC.

Houseman S, Kurz C, Lengermann P, Mandel B: Offshoring bias in US manufacturing, *The Journal of Economic Perspectives* 25(2):111–132, 2011.

Houseman SN, Mandel B, editors: *Measuring globalization: better trade statistics for better policy* (vol. 1). W.E. Upjohn Institute for Employment Research.

Hulten CR: Growth accounting with intermediate inputs, *The Review of Economic Studies* 45(3):511–518, 1978.

Johnson RC, Noguera R: Accounting for intermediates: production sharing and trade in value added, *Journal of International Economics* 86(2):224–236, 2012.

Jorgenson DW: *Econometrics, Econometric modelling of producer behavior*, vol. 1. MIT Press.

Jorgenson DW: Production and welfare: progress in economic measurement, *Journal of Economic Literature* 56(3): 867–919, 2018a.

Jorgenson DW: The world klems initiative: measuring productivity at the industry level. In Grifell-Tatjé E, Knox Lovell CA, Sickles RC, editors: *The Oxford handbook of productivity analysis*, Oxford University Press, pp 663–698.

Jorgenson DW, Fukao K, Timmer MP, editors: *The world economy: growth or stagnation?* Cambridge University Press.

Jorgenson DW, Gollop FM, Fraumeni BM: *Productivity and U.S. economic growth*, Harvard University Press.

Jorgenson DW, Griliches Z: The explanation of productivity change, *The Review of Economic Studies* 34(99):249–280, 1967.

Leontief WW: Quantitative input and output relations in the economic systems of the United States, *The Review of Economic Statistics* 18(3):105–125, 1936.

Los B, Timmer MP, de Vries GJ: How global are global value chains? A new approach to measure international fragmentation, *Journal of Regional Science* 55(1):66–92, 2015.

Miller RE, Blair PD: *Input-output analysis: foundations and extensions*, Cambridge University Press.

Pasinetti LL: *Lectures on the theory of production*, Columbia University Press.

Reinsdorf M, Yuskavage R: Offshoring, sourcing substitution bias, and the measurement of growth in US gross domestic product and productivity, *Review of Income and Wealth* 64(1):127–146, 2018.

Rymes TK: The measurement of capital and total factor productivity in the context of the Cambridge Theory of Capital, *Review of Income and Wealth* 18(1):79–108, 1972.

Timmer MP, Dietzenbacher E, Los B, Stehrer R, de Vries GJ: An illustrated user guide to the world input–output database: the case of global automotive production, *Review of International Economics* 23(3):575–605, 2015.

Timmer MP, Erumban AA, Los B, Stehrer R, de Vries GJ: Slicing up global value chains, *The Journal of Economic Perspectives* 28(2):99–118, 2014.

Timmer MP, Ye X: Productivity and substitution patterns in global value chains. In Grifell-Tatjé E, Knox Lovell CA, Sickles RC, editors: *The Oxford handbook of productivity analysis*, Oxford University Press, pp 699–724.

Triplett JE: High-tech industry productivity and hedonic price indices. In *OECD Proceedings: industry productivity, international comparison and measurement issues*, 1996, pp 119–142.

Wolff EN: Productivity measurement within an input-output framework, *Regional Science and Urban Economics* 24(1): 75–92, 1994.

Emissions accounting and carbon tax incidence in CGE models: bottom-up versus top-down

Richard J. Goettle[1], Mun S. Ho[2], Peter J. Wilcoxen[3]

[1]Northeastern University, Boston, MA, United States; [2]Harvard-China Project on Energy, Economy, Environment, SEAS, Harvard University, Cambridge, MA, United States; [3]Maxwell School of Citizenship and Public Affairs, Syracuse University, Syracuse, NY, United States

19.1 Introduction

Policies proposed to mitigate climate change range from discouraging fossil fuel use to promoting energy efficiency, to stimulating research into clean technologies. A wide range of methods are used to analyze the efficacy and impact of these policies, but we may broadly divide many of them into those using economy-wide models and those using more detailed sector-specific technology models. Our focus here is on the former. Specifically, we recognize the problems that abstractions from measurement in the physical world pose for economy-wide models that need to retain physicality in the conduct of policy assessment. We also recognize the distinct possibility of differences in model outcomes depending on whether policies are modeled to directly affect inputs bottom-up as they most likely would in technology models or outputs top-down as most likely occurs in economy-wide models.

Given the long-time scale of climate change policies, economy-wide models are often multisector, general equilibrium, market-clearing models. They are multisector because of the need to track the movement from energy-intensive industries to less-intensive ones and because of the intense interest of industry stakeholders in policies that affect their employment and profitability. They are general equilibrium because the time scale of the policies is decades and such models have simpler temporal aspects than macroeconomic models that focus on short-run disequilibrium effects.

The class of computable general equilibrium (CGE) models, or applied GE models, does not represent technologies in detail such as blast furnace versus electric arc furnace, but does represent all sectors of the economy, typically 10–100 industries. To use such an aggregation of the complex modern economy with thousands of distinctly identified 6-digit sectors, CGE models rely on input–output tables that represent dollar values of each (aggregated) industry output and input. A sector such as primary metals is represented in the National and IO Accounts as an aggregate index of the tons of different quality steel, iron, aluminum, and other metals. The output of fossil fuel industries such as coal mining and petroleum refining is represented by indexes of the various types of coal or liquid fuels.

The use of an aggregate variable, say $QI_{coal,t}$, to represent the output index of the coal mining industry at time t, is an abstraction that needs to be treated carefully in reconciling with the data on tons of coal and estimates of the CO_2 emitted. In the economic accounts the total dollar value of coal supply is equal to the sum of the value of coal purchases by all sectors, but the aggregate output index $QI_{coal,t}$ is not a simple sum of the quantities of coal purchased by each sector. Some models make the simplification that the supply quantity variable is the sum of the quantities purchased, and that all sectors pay the same average price for a bundle of representative coal, even though in reality the metallurgical coal purchased by the primary metals industry is very different from the thermal coal purchased by the electricity industry. Such simplifications lead to biases in the accounts for BTUs (British thermal units) of energy used and tons of CO_2 emitted. In our examples we show how a carbon price that leads to an 11% reduction in emissions under the average price accounting system becomes a 21% reduction using sector-specific prices.

In this chapter we highlight these biases, drawing on two important contributions of Dale Jorgenson. The first is his contribution to economic measurement and the use of proper indexing procedures. In his important work on the cost-of-capital and TFP measurement (Jorgenson and Griliches, 1967), he emphasized the need to distinguish between the stock and flow of capital services; different assets have different service lives and thus the different flows from a $1 billion stock of machines versus a $1 billion stock of structures must be aggregated carefully. Similarly, the calculation of effective labor input requires a careful aggregation of high-skill-high-wage labor and low-skill-low-wage labor (Jorgenson et al., 1987). We draw on these aggregation methods to illustrate the accounting pitfalls of the different ways of representing fuel quantity aggregates in the analysis of greenhouse gas policies. We compare the simple approach of assuming a common price (the top-down or supply-side approach) with the use of purchaser-specific prices (the bottom-up or demand-side approach).[1]

The second Jorgenson contribution we use is the construction of CGE models that are econometrically estimated to examine energy and environmental policies (Hudson and Jorgenson, 1976; Jorgenson and Wilcoxen, 1990). We illustrate the impact of the top-down versus bottom-up formulations in simulations of the effect of a carbon tax using our Intertemporal General Equilibrium Model (IGEM). In constructing IGEM we have followed the Jorgensonian strictures to carefully aggregate capital, labor, and intermediate inputs, and to estimate the parameters of the producer and consumer functions.

We should note that IGEM contains the results of other major contributions of Jorgenson. The model uses flexible cost functions that allow technical change to be non-neutral (i.e., biased toward or away from some input factor). These functions are first introduced in Jorgenson and Lau (1974a, 1974b) and extended in Jin and Jorgenson (2010). The cost-of-capital formulation

---

[1] Our use of the term "bottom-up" in this context is distinct from references to "bottom-up models" which refer to detailed energy models which are partial equilibrium models containing lots of technological detail. Our discussion here is entirely within the context of multisector general equilibrium models.

(Jorgenson, 1963), the consumer, function and social welfare functions originating in Jorgenson et al. (1982) and Jorgenson and Slesnick (1987) are also fully represented.

19.2 Accounting for energy inputs in CGE models

The accounting of carbon emissions and local pollutants involves an accounting of energy inputs into industry and households. Many analyses of carbon policies use multisector CGE models, for example, those used in the Energy Modeling Forum, EMF 32 (Fawcett et al., 2018). These models are often complex with tens of thousands of variables (or even hundreds of thousands), and model descriptions, unfortunately, often do not describe the energy accounting in detail. As we show here, knowing the exact equations and assumptions are crucial in fully understanding simulation results of industry responses to energy and environmental policies.

To illustrate the heterogeneity of energy inputs under the usual classification of coal, oil and gas, we give the industry-level prices paid per physical unit for various US industries in Table 19.1. The top part of the table reproduces the prices reported in the Manufacturing Energy Consumption Survey (MECS) by the Energy Information Administration (EIA) for 2010. The MECS provides detailed data on energy use in manufacturing industries every 4 years; for other sectors such as electricity and transportation, there are only less granular data that does not distinguish, for example, between commercial transportation and household transportation. These more aggregated data are given annually.

To supplement the EIA data for manufacturing, in the bottom part of Table 19.1, we give estimates for illustrative industries from our IGEM database, including electricity. The value data are estimated in Jorgenson et al. (2018a) and the physical quantity data are from the Monthly Energy Review. The value data are

the intermediate purchases from the 2010 Use table which give the value at the factory gate (or mine-mouth), whereas the expenditure data in the EIA reports are at purchaser's prices which include trade and transportation margins. The prices in the top and bottom sections of Table 19.1 are thus not directly comparable.

The price paid for a ton of coal, within the manufacturing group, ranges from $53 paid by food manufacturing to $135 paid by plastics and rubber. The price per 1000 ft^3 of natural gas ranges from $5.0 paid by chemicals to $8.9 paid by apparel. Using the factory-gate prices in the bottom part of Table 19.1, the price per ton of (thermal) coal to electric generators is $6.6, whereas the price of (metallurgical) coal to primary metals is $688, and the price to chemicals, rubber, and plastics is $68.

This heterogeneity in prices for energy is not unique; there is a similar large range of wage rates ($ per hour worked) and rental costs of capital across industries. Many models recognize the heterogeneity of labor input prices even if the model assumes a single labor market; they do this by using industry-specific coefficients to convert the market clearing average wage to the industry-specific wage. There is, however, a lot less discussion about the treatment of energy inputs in most documentations of the multisector models and we cannot make a parallel statement about energy coefficients. In the next section we give explicit examples of two approaches to energy consumption accounting.

19.2.1 Top-down and bottom-up accounting

We refer to the method which assumes that all sectors buy an identical bundle of energy input at a common price as "top-down" or "supply-side" accounting. That is, the method assumes that there is one coal market and one type of average coal. The other method that allows different sectors to pay a sector-specific price, even with the

TABLE 19.1 Prices of energy paid by US industries, 2010 ($ per unit).

		Total energy	Coal	Electricity	Diesel, dist. fuel oil	Natural gas
		$/mil. BTU	$/ton	$/kWH	$/gallon	$/1000 ft³
NAICS		Estimates from MECS 2010				
311	Food	9.12	53.43	0.070	2.58	6.02
312	Beverage and tobacco products	12.96	95.14	0.087	1.80	6.66
313	Textile mills	12.69	103.39	0.065	2.35	7.15
314	Textile product mills	13.33	89.47	0.075	2.00	6.96
315	Apparel	19.64	0.00	0.089	2.12	8.87
316	Leather and allied products	17.67	0.00	0.102	2.92	7.79
321	Wood products	8.92	128.64	0.076	2.23	6.77
322	Paper	6.93	80.14	0.056	2.23	5.71
323	Printing and related support	18.09	0.00	0.091	2.85	7.21
324	Petroleum and coal products	5.98	126.53	0.057	2.27	5.02
325	Chemicals	9.39	73.63	0.056	2.37	5.00
326	Plastics and rubber products	16.04	135.07	0.077	3.15	6.64
327	Nonmetallic mineral products	7.41	68.05	0.071	2.32	6.07
331	Primary metals	7.97	127.00	0.049	2.08	5.53
332	Fabricated metal products	14.86	113.73	0.084	2.97	6.92
333	Machinery	16.10	0.00	0.085	2.74	7.26
334	Computer and electronic products	18.27	0.00	0.079	2.75	6.75
335	Electrical equipment and components	13.24	0.00	0.078	2.55	6.97
336	Transportation equipment	14.30	112.09	0.075	2.99	6.82
337	Furniture and related products	17.86	58.52	0.094	2.78	8.86
339	Miscellaneous	20.56	80.35	0.097	2.53	8.56
	All manufacturing	9.12	91.71	0.065	2.40	5.51

Values from IGEM-NAICS; physical units from EIA

	IGEM sector	Coal at mine-mouth			Natural gas at factory gate		
		mil. $	mil. tons	$/ton	mil. $	Bil. ft³	$/1000 ft³
6	Electric utilities	6432	975.1	6.6	6203	7387	0.84
12	Primary metals	11,702	17	688	4102	548	7.5
23	Petroleum and coal products	129	6	21	21,179	956	22.2
24	Chemicals, rubber, plastic	614	9	68	14,642	2162	6.8

Notes: "MECS 2010" price data are taken from Table 7.1 of the Manufacturing Energy Consumption Survey (2010). Our table only gives the total coal; the MECS gives separate prices for Anthracite, Bituminous, and Lignite. In the second section with the IGEM classification, the tons data come from Table 7.6 of the MECS (2010), and Table 6.2 of the MER (2016). The value data are estimated by us from BEA time series use tables.

assumption of a single market, is labeled "bottom-up" or "demand-side" accounting.[2]

To simplify the discussion, we use an input–output framework here where there is no distinction between industries and commodities. In some models, including our IGEM, these are distinguished; there is a Use table that gives the commodity inputs for each industry, and a Make (or Supply) table that gives the industry sources of supply for each commodity. In Jorgenson et al. (2013) we thus have distinct industry prices (PI_j) and commodity prices (PC_i). In the discussion below, we only use the i index for sector i, where PI_i is the producer price of output i, and QI_i is the output quantity index. AA_{ij} denotes the quantity of input i used by sector j. It is most meaningful to think of i as "coal mining," "petroleum refining," or "gas utilities" in this section.

Under the top-down method, the value of supply of good i is equal to the demand for i summed over the industry purchasers (intermediate) and final demanders (households, investment, government, and exports).[3] Total supply (QS_i) of a good comes from the domestic industry (QS_i) and imports (QM_i). We thus have these value equations:

$$PS_{it}QS_{it} = PI_{it}^{tt}QI_{it} + PM_{it}QM_{it} \quad (19.1)$$

$$PS_{it}QS_{it} = \sum_j^n PS_{it}\overline{AA}_{ijt} + PS_{it}\overline{C}_{it} + PS_{it}\overline{I}_{it}$$
$$+ PS_{it}\overline{G}_{it} + PS_{it}\overline{X}_{it} \quad (19.2)$$

where PM_{it} is the price of the imported variety, PI_{it}^{tt} is the sales tax-inclusive price of the domestic variety (to be distinguished from the seller price PI_i), and PS_i is the price of aggregate supply. C_{it},

I_{it}, G_{it}, X_{it}, respectively, denote the final demand for consumption, investment, government, and exports. The $j = 1, 2, ...n$ index runs over all the n industries identified in the model. The bars over the variables indicate that these are measured in economy-wide average units, not the units given in Table 19.1.

The supply price is expressed as an Armington function of the domestic and imported prices in almost all models reviewed (Armington, 1969). This supply quantity QS_i thus also has aggregation aspects that should be carefully spelt out since imported varieties are often very different from the average domestic variety, but we do not discuss them here. We note that multiregion models have an added complexity of having regional varieties that need to be considered (e.g., Saudi crude vs. Venezuelan crude), in addition to the different domestic varieties discussed here.

Since the top-down method assumes a common price PS, Eq. (19.2) simplifies to a quantity balance equation for homogenous quantities:

$$QS_{it} = \sum_j^n \overline{AA}_{ijt} + \overline{C}_{it} + \overline{I}_{it} + \overline{G}_{it} + \overline{X}_{it} \quad (19.3)$$

Energy content (in BTUs) is given by the (net) energy coefficient θ_i^{BTU}, while the CO_2 emissions are given by the (net) CO_2 coefficient $\theta_i^{CO_2}$:

$$E_{it}^{BTU} = \overline{\theta}_{it}^{BTU}QS_{it}; \quad E_{ijt}^{BTU} = \theta_{it}^{BTU}AA_{ijt}; \text{ etc} \quad (19.4)$$

$$E_{it}^{CO_2} = \overline{\theta}_{it}^{CO_2}QS_{it}; \quad E_{ijt}^{CO_2} = \theta_{ijt}^{CO_2}AA_{ijt}; \text{ etc} \quad (19.5)$$

---

[2] The lexicon for this topic is far from settled. Top-down or supply-side accounting also could be considered as upstream or output-driven. Bottom-up or demand-side accounting could be labeled downstream or input-driven.

[3] Investment includes changes in inventories. In the latest version of the official US input–output tables, there is a Government industry which accounts for the nondurable purchases of fuels by the government, and a Government final demand column that accounts for purchases from the Government industry and purchases of investment goods.

Let us elaborate on these coefficients. It is clear what is meant by the energy content per ton of coal (or oil) combusted, it is the average over all the different types of coal (or oil) that the EIA identifies. CO_2 emission coefficients should similarly be the average of the coefficients of different types of coal, liquid fuel, or gas. However, not all purchased fuel is combusted, some coal is converted to coke, gas converted to chemical products, and crude converted to lubricants. The θ_i^{**} coefficients are thus net values, equal to actual emission coefficients (e_{it}^{**}) multiplied by combustion ratios, e.g.:

$$\theta_{ijt}^{CO2} = e_{ijt}^{CO2} \rho_{ijt}^{comb} \qquad (19.6)$$

In the bottom-up (or demand-side) accounting, each buyer j pays a distinct price PB_{ijt} for input i. The supply equal demand value equation is changed from Eq. (19.2) to:

$$PS_{it}QS_{it} = \sum_j PB_{ijt}AA_{ijt} + PB_{i,Ct}C_{it} + PB_{i,Gt}G_{it}$$
$$+ PB_{i,Xt}X_{it}$$
$$(19.7)$$

Most models assume that there is only one market for each good i, and one corresponding market clearing price. In our case that is the supply price, PS_{it} (the import market is a separate market with a separate price, PM_{it}). The individual buyer-specific price is expressed as a fixed coefficient multiplied by the endogenous market clearing price:

$$PB_{ijt} = \xi_{ij0}PS_{it} \quad j = 1, \dots n, C, I, G, X \qquad (19.8)$$

These ξ_{ij0} coefficients may be derived from base year data such as those given in Table 19.1. They are analogous to the wage rate coefficients derived from value compensation and number of workers (or hours) in each industry. In the historical data these coefficients change over time

since there are changes in relative prices (e.g., anthracite relative to bituminous) and changes in the relative quantities bought by industry j. We do not discuss the projection of future changes and assume a fixed ξ_{ij0} for all periods in our simulations, but model builders should keep this in mind.

With the expression for buyer-specific prices in Eq. (19.8), we may rewrite the supply equal demand Eq. (19.7) as the quantity equation:

$$QS_{it} = \sum_j \xi_{ij0}AA_{ijt} + \xi_{iC0}C_{it} + \dots \qquad (19.9)$$

Unlike Eq. (19.3), the quantity variables in this equation are measured in sector-specific units, that is, the tons of coal correspond to the data in Table 19.1. To illustrate this, consider an example with the industry 1 buying 90 tons at a price of $1 per ton and industry 2 buying 10 tons at $10. The total supply value is $190, the total tons are 100, and the average price is thus $1.9 per ton. Eq. (19.2) for the top-down method and Eq. (19.9) for the bottom-up method for this market are, respectively:

$$1.9 * 100 = 1 * 90 + 10 * 10$$
$$= 1.9 * \frac{90}{1.9} + 1.9 * \frac{10}{0.19}$$
$$= 1.9 * 47.4 + 1.9 * 52.6 \qquad (19.10a)$$

$$100 = \frac{1}{1.9}90 + \frac{10}{1.9}10 = 0.52 * 90 + 5.2 * 10;$$
$$\xi_{i1} = 0.52, \quad \xi_{i2} = 5.2$$
$$(19.10b)$$

That is, $AA_{coal,1} = 90$ in natural physical units, and $\overline{AA}_{coal,1} = 47.4$ in average coal units.

In the top-down system, the emission coefficient for coal is given by the total tons of CO_2 from coal use in j divided by the quantity $AA_{coal,j}$. Say, for i = coal in the example above, the CO_2 from national coal combustion is 180 tons. We then have:

$$\bar{\theta}_{coal,t}^{CO2} = \frac{180}{100} = 1.8 \qquad (19.11)$$

Under the top-down system (Eq. 19.5) we would attribute the total 180 tons of CO_2 emissions to industries 1 and 2 as:

$$E_{coal,1}^{CO2} = \bar{\theta}_{it}^{CO2}\overline{AA}_{coal,1} = 1.8 * \frac{90}{1.9} = 85.3;$$

$$E_{coal,2}^{CO2} = 1.8 * \frac{10}{0.19} = 94.7$$

$$(19.12a)$$

Under the bottom-up system, the 180 total tons are allocated as:

$$E_{coal,1}^{CO2} = \theta_{coal,1}^{CO2}AA_{coal,1} = 1.8 * 90 = 162;$$

$$E_{coal,2}^{CO2} = 1.8 * 10 = 18$$

$$(19.12b)$$

That is, in the top-down system we would attribute more coal consumption and more emissions to industry 2 even though it uses 1/9th of the physical tons used by industry 1.

Physical units and actual \$ prices are not often used in CGE models since models are based on economic accounts which are given in values. The time series in the US economic accounts are given as quantity and price indexes, say with prices (base year 2005) = 1, and quantities in billions of \$2005. The discussion above applies equally to such constant dollar QS_{it}'s which are aggregates of the constant dollar series of different types of coal, just as we have interpreted QS_{it} as tons of average coal. We should recognize that the constant dollar aggregate could be trending distinctly from the total tons of all types of coal, just as the average emission coefficient could be trending over time even if the true emission coefficient e_{it}^{CO2} is constant. The key point that top-down accounting gives very different industry attributions from bottom-up accounting applies to constant dollar measures in the same way that it applies to physical unit measures.

For the remainder of the chapter we are going to interpret QS and AA as constant dollar units and if we wish to convert them to physical tons (barrels or ft^3) we simply apply the base year conversion coefficients (η_{coal}^{tons} tons of coal per dollar):

$$Q_{coal,j}^{tons} = \eta_{coal}^{tons}AA_{coal,j} \qquad (19.13)$$

Using the numerical example above, in constant dollar terms we have $QS_{coal} = 190$, $AA_{coal,1} = 90$, and $AA_{coal,2} = 100$, and the tons for industries 1 and 2 using Eq. (19.13) are:

$$90 = 1 * 90; \; 10 = 0.1 * 100 \qquad (19.14)$$

In the top-down system the emission coefficient is 180/190 tons per dollar. The total CO_2 emissions are thus allocated as:

$$E_{coal,1}^{CO2} = \bar{\theta}_{it}^{CO2}\overline{AA}_{coal,1} = \frac{180}{190}90 = 85.3;$$

$$E_{coal,2}^{CO2} = \frac{180}{190}100 = 94.7$$

$$(19.15a)$$

Under the bottom-up system, the 180 total tons are allocated with industry-specific θ_{ij}^{CO2} coefficients (tons of emissions per dollar):

$$E_{coal,1}^{CO2} = \theta_{coal,1}^{CO2}AA_{coal,1} = 1.8 * 90 = 162;$$

$$E_{coal,2}^{CO2} = 0.18 * 100 = 18$$

$$(19.15b)$$

Eqs. (19.15a) and (19.15b) match exactly with the physical tons accounting in Eqs. (19.12a) and (19.12b).

19.2.2 Emission coefficients in IGEM

In Section 19.3 we illustrate the differences between the two energy and emission accounting approaches by simulating a carbon tax with IGEM, a model with 36 industries based on the NAICS classification. In the implementation of IGEM described in Jorgenson et al. (2018a,b) we calibrate the θ_i^{CO2} emission coefficients by using the CO_2 inventories in the

Energy Information Administration's (EIA's) *Annual Energy Outlook 2016* (AEO 2016) and IGEM's constant dollar output and intermediate input values. Table 19.2 gives an updated set of emission coefficients for 2015, aggregated over the 36 industries in IGEM to match the familiar EIA tables.[4] These are θ_i^{CO2}'s interpreted as tons of CO_2 per 1000\$ in \$2005 (or million tons of CO_2 per billion \$2005). (This is the inverse of the \$ per ton of CO_2 in Table 19.1.) Measured from the supply side, the economy-wide average CO_2 content is 57.7 tons of CO_2 per 1000\$ of total coal output, i.e., domestic production plus imports. Measured from the payments and tons for each purchasing sector, the emission coefficient is only 9.4 tons/1000\$ for industrial users paying high prices, and 146 tons/1000\$ for electric utilities paying for cheap steam coal. While the range of coefficients for petroleum and gas is not as wide as that for coal, it is still substantial; for example, 3.46 tons of CO_2/1000\$ for commercial gas use to 28.6 for electric utilities gas.

The disparities between bottom-up and top-down coefficients matter because they change the impact of carbon pricing on the relative prices of fossil fuel inputs, and because of variations in the price elasticities of energy use among the consuming sectors. For coal, electric utilities bear a higher carbon tax burden in the bottom-up system than they do in the top-down system with the opposite for commerce and industry. For petroleum, taxing carbon bottom-up results in higher petroleum prices to households, commercial transportation, and electric utilities than occurs under top-down taxation, whereas the reverse holds for commerce and industry. For natural gas, industry, transportation, and

TABLE 19.2 IGEM's 2015 Carbon emission coefficients (metric tons of CO_2 per 1000 \$2005 of output or input).

	Coal	Petroleum	Gas
Top-down coefficients for supply (domestic output plus imports)			
Coal mining	57.69		
Petroleum products		4.79	
Gas mining			4.13
Gas distribution			6.69
Bottom-up coefficients for purchases (commodity inputs)			
Household (residential)		11.3	5.86
Commercial and government	50.14	0.32	3.46
Industrial (agriculture, mining, manufacturing)	9.4	3.24	8.23
Transportation		11.3	15.54
Electric utilities	146.19	14.75	28.55

electric utilities face higher gas prices under bottom-up as opposed to top-down carbon pricing, while residential and commercial users experience the higher prices with top-down taxation.

As an example, at unit prices, the own-price elasticities for coal, petroleum, and gas inputs in the cost function for electric utilities are -1.05, -1.90, and -0.85, respectively. For primary metals, these same elasticities are -0.65, -1.04, and -0.58, respectively.[5] Thus, fossil fuels are across-the-board less elastic in primary metals than in electric utilities. For a given carbon price, top-down pricing would greatly reduce coal and petroleum price

---

[4] In IGEM, unlike the EIA accounts, residential petroleum use includes gasoline and other products related to household transportation. Petroleum use in IGEM's transportation sector (industry-commodity no. 27) refers to commercial transportation only.

[5] These elasticities are calculated from cost function coefficient estimates reported in Jorgenson et al. (2018b, Appendix B) which is an update of *Double Dividend* (Jorgenson et al., 2013).

increases to electric utilities, relative to bottom-up, with an opposite effect for primary metals. Given that the CO_2 emissions coefficient (per dollar) of coal input is much larger for electric utilities than they are for primary metals, taxing carbon bottom-up would achieve greater emissions reductions in these two sectors than taxing carbon under the top-down system where they have a common emissions coefficient. For natural gas, both sectors would benefit from top-down taxation with electric utilities receiving the relatively greater reduction in price increases. With top-town carbon taxes, the emissions reductions by electric utilities would be much smaller than under bottom-up taxation because they would be driven by much smaller price increases.

Emissions reductions by primary metals would be larger, driven by larger price increases in the top-down system, but since its fuel inputs are less price elastic than those of electric utilities, its larger reductions here would not be enough to compensate for the smaller reductions by electric utilities and total CO_2 reductions would be smaller under the top-down system than total reductions in the bottom-up system. These differences are shown next in the simulation results.

19.3 The contrast between bottom-up and top-down accounting of a carbon tax

To show the impacts of using different energy and emission accounting approaches we simulate a carbon tax with IGEM. We show how a tax on the price of coal has a very different effect if placed on the average ton of coal supplied (the top-down, supply-side method) or on the actual tons purchased (the bottom-up, demand-side

method). We follow the methods used earlier in Jorgenson et al. (2018a) so that readers have a complete description and focus on the accounting comparisons here.

19.3.1 Model features summary

IGEM (version 17) is described in detail in Jorgenson et al. (2013) and we summarize the main features here. That version is based on the SIC and we have now constructed a NAICS version of IGEM (version 20) with updated annual input—output tables, 1960—2010. This updated version is described in Jorgenson et al. (2018b). It is a perfect foresight model with one capital stock that is mobile across sectors. 36 sectors are recognized including 6 energy, 15 manufacturing, and 12 service industries; this reflects the proportions of the modern US economy more closely than typical models that have only one or two service industries. Each industry may make several commodities. Production is represented by a nested set of translog cost functions, with a KLEM function at the top tier.[6] The energy bundle consists of the six energy commodities identified—coal, oil mining, gas mining, electric utilities, gas distribution, petroleum refining and coal products. There is Hicks-neutral technical change which continues at historical rates which means that the high TFP growth sectors continue to experience a reduction in their relative prices in the projection period. There is also biased technical change which means that input prices affect the rate of TFP growth. The estimates in Jorgenson et al. (2013, Fig. 4.12) show that most industries have energy-using technical change which means that higher energy prices slow down TFP growth.

[6] KLEM—capital (K), labor (L), energy (E), and materials (M)—data sets and modeling originated in the 1970s. Berndt and Wood (1975) estimated and analyzed a transcendental logarithmic (translog) KLEM production model of US manufacturing. Hudson and Jorgenson (1974) pioneered the use of translog KLEM models of producer and consumer behavior in their computable general equilibrium (CGE) of US structure and growth, the forerunner of IGEM.

The household sector is represented at the top tier by an aggregate Euler equation that determines aggregate full consumption and savings in each period. Full consumption refers to the aggregate of commodity consumption and leisure. In the next tier, full consumption demand is derived from household utility functions that are consistently aggregated over different household types where different types are allowed to have different full consumption baskets. The utility function at this stage has nondurables, services, capital services, and leisure as arguments and it gives us price and income effects of policy changes on these four bundles. A nested set of indirect utility functions allocate these top tier bundles to 36 consumption items; these functions are estimated over aggregate time series. The consumption items based on National Account classifications are then bridged to the 36 commodities of IGEM.

At the stage where we aggregate over different demographic groups using data from the Consumer Expenditure Survey there are 244 types of households cross-classified by region, number of children, number of adults, sex and race of household head.[7] Welfare for each household type (a dynasty), V_d, is the present value of the stream of utility derived from full consumption. This welfare measure is monetized by a dynastic expenditure function, $\Omega_d(\{p_t\}, V_d)$, that depends on the whole path of prices and interest rates. The equivalent variation due to a policy change for each household type is calculated from this intertemporal expenditure function. A social welfare function is defined as an aggregate over these dynastic welfare values; this function gives a measure of efficiency and a measure of inequality.

Import demand is given by a translog price function that treats imported and domestic varieties as imperfect substitutes. IGEM is a 1-country model and world relative prices (price of good i relative to j) are assumed to change at the same rate as changes in US total factor productivity for each industry. The current account balance is set exogenously and the current account equation is satisfied by adjusting the terms-of-trade through an endogenous exchange rate.

The government imposes taxes on capital and labor income, sales, imports, property, and wealth. Tax rates are calibrated to the revenue projections of the Congressional Budget Office (CBO, 2013). Government deficits are exogenous and set to CBO (2013) and government purchases (final demand) are endogenous in the base case path. In policy cases, the real purchases are held equal to the base case as explained below.

IGEM is an infinite horizon model; in the implementation we find a date T such that the transition path from the first period to T ends up within a convergence bound of a separately calculated steady state equilibrium. In practice, this means that by 2130 the costate variable, full consumption, is within a tolerance criterion of the separately calculated steady state value. We construct a smooth transition that is consistent with projections of population, public deficit, and other exogenous variables by following official projections of population out to 2060 and then holding it constant thereafter. Government deficits follow CBO mid-term projections out for 10 years and then are set to taper to zero by 2060. A similar treatment is given to current account deficits. The productivity terms in the production functions follow the estimated trends and then are required to taper to zero growth by 2060. This procedure gives the state variables enough time (2060−2130) to converge to their steady state values.

For the EMF 32 comparisons (Fawcett et al., 2018) all models involved were asked to calibrate

---

[7] The model of consumer behavior in the current NAICS version of IGEM (version 20) employs the data from the 2006 Consumer Expenditure Survey (CEX).

the GDP growth and fossil fuel consumption to the projections in EIA's *Annual Energy Outlook 2016* (AEO 2016). For comparison with those runs, we follow the same calibration procedures as described in Jorgenson et al. (2018a).

19.3.2 The carbon policies analyzed

We analyze a set of carbon tax policies, each with the same path of taxes on CO_2 emissions but different revenue recycling options. These policies are summarized in Table 19.3. The carbon tax starts at $25 per ton of CO_2 in 2020 and rises at 5% per year until 2050. All prices are measured in 2010 dollars. After 2050 all tax rates are at a steady-state level, constant relative to the GDP deflator (i.e., the tax buys the equivalent bundle of goods for all remaining years). Under bottom-up accounting, the tax burden falls on the inputs of fossil fuels for combustion for everyone—residential, commercial, industrial, transportation, electric utility, and government sectors. Exports are exempt from the carbon tax. Under top-down accounting, the carbon tax incidence is on fossil fuel supplies—domestic output plus imports—so that all uses including feedstocks and exports share in its burden.

We simulate the carbon policy scenarios under conditions of debt and deficit neutrality for both government and the rest of the world. We also assume that there are no border taxes or other restrictions on all commodity trade flows, energy-intensive or otherwise. Carbon tax receipts are recycled back to the private sector through tax swaps that preserve the real purchases of the government in the base case path.[8] We employ three common recycling mechanisms to illustrate the range of effects—lump sum redistribution, capital tax rate reductions, and labor tax rate reductions.

IGEM distinguishes between taxes on capital income, on property and on wealth (estate taxes). The corporate income tax system and the personal income tax system are combined into one average tax rate for capital income in this version. The capital tax cut option cuts only the tax on capital income. The model includes separate variables for the average tax on labor income and marginal tax on labor income. The price of leisure depends on the marginal tax rate while revenue and disposable income depends on the average rate. In the labor tax cut option, we cut both average and marginal rates in a consistent fashion.

TABLE 19.3 Carbon tax scenarios ($(2010) per metric ton CO_2).

| | Tax in 2020 | Growth rate | Transition to steady state | |
			Year	Tax
$25 @ 5%	$25.00	5.00%	2050	$108.05
Revenue recycling scenarios				
Lump sum	Lump sum rebate to households, equal rebate per capita			
Capital	Cut tax on capital income (property and wealth taxes unchanged)			
Labor	Cut tax on labor income (change both average and marginal rates)			

[8] This constraint limits the amount of carbon tax revenue that can be recycled and does have general equilibrium consequences in terms of governments' claims on the economy. The revenue "haircut" is discussed in detail in Jorgenson et al. (2018a).

A lump sum distribution may be implemented in many ways; some proposals call for an equal per-capita payment, others include a special treatment for the poorest households. The simplest policy to simulate is a transfer that adds to aggregate disposable income which is a straightforward matter in a model with only one aggregate household. In a model with different households, such a transfer would be equivalent to giving each household a sum proportional to their current incomes. We choose a more complicated implementation which gives the same sum per-capita; households of different sizes receive different distributions, but rich and poor households of a given type get the same sum.

The carbon tax is a unit tax (as opposed to an ad valorem tax) and we represent it as a $tx^u_{CO2,t}$ tax per ton of CO_2. The subscript CO_2 for tx denotes that the externality tax is for carbon dioxide, the model allows for other externality taxes such as SO_2 taxes. Recall that emissions are given by Eq. (19.15) where the emissions coefficient θ^{CO2}_{it} is multiplied by QS_{it} or AA, the constant dollar variables. The price PS_{it} is normalized to 1 in the base year 2005, and so the carbon tax is $tx^u_{CO2,t}\theta^{CO2}_{it}$ per unit of QS_{it} (per billion \$2005) in the top-down system. The revenue from this tax is $tx^u_{CO2,t}\theta^{CO2}_{it}QS_{it}$ dollars.

In the *top-down accounting system* the carbon thus tax raises the price of output of industry i, in addition to existing sales taxes (tt_{it}), to:

$$PI^{tt}_{it} = (1 + tt_{it})PI_{it} + tx^u_{CO2,t}\theta^{CO2}_{it}$$
$$i = \text{coal, oil mining, gas mining} \tag{19.16}$$

The tax is also placed on the imports of i, which has an emission coefficient of $\theta^{M,CO2}_{it}$:

$$PM_{it} = (1 + tr_{it})PM^*_{it} + tx^u_{CO2,t}\theta^{M,CO2}_{it}$$
$$i = \text{coal, oil mining, gas mining} \tag{19.17}$$

Eqs. (19.16) and (19.17) give us the buyer's prices corresponding to those in Eq. (19.1) giving the total supply price, PS. Every industry which

buys fuel i faces the same percentage change in price when the carbon tax is imposed: $tx^u_{CO2,t}\theta^{CO2}_{it}/PS_{it}$.

In the *bottom-up accounting system* the price paid by buyer j for fuel input i is given by an industry-specific emissions coefficient:

$$PB_{ijt} = PS_{it} + tx^u_{CO2,t}\theta^{CO2}_{ijt} \quad j = 1,...,n,C,I,G,X \tag{19.18}$$

where PS_{it} is the supply price of i that includes only the existing sales tax and tariffs. In this case the percentage change in input price is $tx^u_{CO2,t}\theta^{CO2}_{ijt}/PS_{it}$ which differs by industry of use.

19.3.3 Emissions and fossil fuel impacts

We begin our discussion of the different simulated impacts of the two accounting systems by describing the carbon tax rates and CO_2 emission targets. There are two distinct issues: one is the choice of the emission equation, Eq. (19.15a) or Eq. (19.15b), and the other is the implementation of the tax, Eq. (19.16) or Eq. (19.18). Table 19.4 shows the cumulative 2015–50 CO_2 emissions from fossil fuel combustion in gigatonnes (GtCO2) for the three recycling cases under (1) bottom-up and top-down accounting (the two columns), and (2) bottom-up and top-down tax incidence (the two rows).

Over the period from 2015 through 2050 the cumulative emissions in the base case is 194 Gt. Consider first the figures in bold. In the lump sum redistribution case, there is a 21% reduction under the bottom-up tax equation (and bottom-up emission accounting) but only as 12% reduction under the top-down tax system. The capital tax cut and labor tax cut cases have similar differences between the bottom-up and top-down tax systems, −21% versus −11%. Clearly, measuring and taxing emissions according to their actual attribution as opposed to an economy-wide average achieves greater abatement.

TABLE 19.4 Cumulative CO_2 emissions from fossil fuel combustion, 2015−50 gigatonnes (billion metric tons) CO_2, $GtCO_2$.

Scenario title	Bottom-up emissions accounting $GtCO_2$		Top-down emissions accounting $GtCO_2$	
Base case	194.4	% From base	194.4	% From base
Lump sum redistribution				
Bottom-up tax incidence	**152.8**	−21.4%	170.3	−12.4%
Top-down tax incidence	171.4	−11.8%	**170.9**	−12.1%
Capital tax recycling				
Bottom-up tax incidence	**153.7**	−20.9%	171.8	−11.6%
Top-down tax incidence	172.6	−11.2%	**172.6**	−11.2%
Labor tax recycling				
Bottom-up tax incidence	**154.0**	−20.8%	171.7	−11.7%
Top-down tax incidence	173.2	−10.9%	**172.4**	−11.3%

Note: Bottom-up tax incidence uses Eq. (19.18); top-down tax uses Eq. (19.16).

Of equal interest are the off-diagonal elements in Table 19.4—the situations in which carbon is priced bottom-up while emissions are measured top-down and vice versa. In each case, we see emissions levels and their percentage reductions approximately equal to those arising from top-down measurement and top-down taxation. Only the bottom-up—bottom-up pairing yields greater abatement. This indicates that it is less about the aggregates of fossil fuel demands and supplies but more about their compositions in explaining the differences between bottom-up and top-down.

The evidence in Table 19.5 confirms this composition effect. Here, we show the changes in fossil fuel quantities demanded by the major sectors corresponding to the EIA groups (residential including household transportation, commercial, industrial, commercial transportation, electric utilities), and the change in the total quantity supplied by domestic producers and imports.[9] We report these changes for a single year, 2050, the year in which the carbon tax reaches its peak. In the bottom-up system, we see that the high tax on coal for electric utilities (tax per dollar of coal input) reduce its consumption by about 56%, whereas the lighter tax rate on industrial coal reduces their coal use by only 17% −19% in all three recycling options (recall the different emissions per dollar of coal in Table 19.2). The carbon tax virtually eliminates the small amount of commercial coal use. When emissions coefficients are economy-wide averages and the carbon tax is imposed top-down, the reductions in coal by electric utilities and commerce are far less than in the bottom-up columns,

[9] The fossil fuel demands exclude inventory changes and exports, while the supplies refer to commodity supplies which are distinct from industry output; the Make (Supply) matrix is not diagonal, especially for the oil and gas industries.

TABLE 19.5 Contrasting fossil fuel quantities in a bottom-up versus a top-down system (percent change from base case, 2050).

	Coal		Petroleum		Natural gas	
	Bottom-up	Top-down	Bottom-up	Top-down	Bottom-up	Top-down
Lump sum recycling						
Fuel demands by major groups						
Residential			−23.0%	−9.9%	−8.5%	−11.5%
Commercial	−98.7%	−65.1%	−1.8%	−7.6%	−9.1%	−10.8%
Industrial	−19.2%	−34.5%	−11.6%	−11.4%	−12.9%	−19.4%
Transportation			−22.3%	−11.1%	−55.1%	−9.0%
Electric utilities	−55.8%	−30.4%	91.0%	9.0%	−43.1%	−12.9%
Total	−31.4%	−33.2%	−11.5%	−9.6%	−15.8%	−15.7%
Industry supplies	−31.3%	−33.8%	−11.3%	−9.5%	−16.0%	−16.3%
Capital tax recycling						
Fuel demands by major groups						
Residential			−22.9%	−9.6%	−8.2%	−11.2%
Commercial	−98.7%	−66.2%	−1.7%	−7.4%	−9.0%	−10.7%
Industrial	−16.8%	−32.3%	−10.0%	−9.4%	−12.1%	−18.5%
Transportation			−21.5%	−9.9%	−54.8%	−8.0%
Electric utilities	−55.6%	−29.7%	92.9%	9.8%	−42.9%	−12.5%
Total	−29.7%	−31.5%	−10.8%	−8.6%	−15.3%	−15.0%
Industry supplies	−29.6%	−32.1%	−10.5%	−8.5%	−15.5%	−15.7%
Labor tax recycling						
Fuel demands by major groups						
Residential			−21.2%	−6.8%	−6.9%	−9.6%
Commercial	−98.7%	−65.6%	−0.4%	−6.1%	−8.4%	−10.0%
Industrial	−17.2%	−33.0%	−9.6%	−8.9%	−11.4%	−17.9%
Transportation			−20.9%	−8.7%	−54.8%	−7.0%
Electric utilities	−55.6%	−29.3%	96.7%	11.5%	−42.9%	−11.7%
Total	−29.9%	−31.8%	−9.7%	−7.2%	−14.6%	−14.2%
Industry supplies	−29.9%	−32.5%	−9.5%	−7.1%	−14.9%	−15.0%

in the ranges of 30% and 66%, respectively, while industrial reductions are far greater, in the 30% range.

In the case of petroleum under bottom-up accounting, we see that the high carbon tax rate (tax per dollar of petroleum products) for commercial transportation and households reduces their consumption by more than 20%, whereas the lower tax rate for industrial users only reduces their use by 10%–12%. Interestingly, the small amount of petroleum use by electric utilities almost doubles. In the top-down scheme, the percentage reductions in petroleum use are much more uniform across the residential, commercial, industrial, and transportation sectors, and they are more in line with the reductions in total demands, Also, the substitution of petroleum for coal and gas by electric utilities is greatly diminished.

For natural gas under bottom-up accounting, electric utilities and transportation get the cheapest gas and thus the higher tax burden reduces gas use by 55% and 43%, respectively, whereas households, commerce, and industry buying more expensive gas reduce their use by only 7% −13% among the three recycling options. When measuring and taxing top-down, the demand reductions again are more uniform with reductions in the 10%–19% range for households, commerce, and industry and in the 7%–13% range for electric utilities and transportation.

Next, we compare these changes in demands by the various sectors with the changes in total supplies in the rows marked "industry supplies." With aggregate coal reductions in the 30%–34% range for the three recycling options, aggregate petroleum reductions of 7%–12%, and aggregate gas reductions of 14%–16%, it is clear that variations in changes of sector demands greatly exceed changes in their totals; there are substantial composition effects that distinguish bottom-up from top-down.

19.3.4 Economic impacts

Table 19.6 summarizes the macroeconomic consequences of taxing carbon under the two accounting and tax schemes and the three recycling options.[10] Within a given recycling policy, there are common qualitative outcomes bottom-up and top-down. Capital tax reductions lower the user cost of capital. These favor saving, investment, and leisure over consumption and labor supply. The result is a double dividend in overall production and spending, i.e., real GDP changes, averaging +0.2% bottom-up and +0.5% top-down.[11] Labor tax reductions have a cost-price diminution effect—by lowering the pretax wages paid by industries, production costs, and, hence, output prices, fall. With a fixed after-tax nominal wage, this yields an increase in real wages which favors consumption and labor supply over saving, investment, and leisure. On average, the real GDP effects are minimal, averaging minus 0.1% bottom-up and plus 0.1% top-down. With lump sum redistributions, there are no relative price effects from recycling; there are only income effects. Here, the trade-off is between consumption, saving, and leisure as households substitute the latter for less labor income at the expense of saving and, to a lesser extent, consumption. The losses in real GDP under lump sum average 1.2% in both accounting schemes.

The major differences between bottom-up and top-down relate to consumption and trade. The size of the adjustments in exports and imports is

---

[10] The mechanisms and details of the adjustments to carbon pricing are discussed thoroughly in Jorgenson et al. (2018a) and are not repeated here. Our emphasis here is on the model outcomes that differ between the bottom-up and top-down emissions modeling and tax incidence.

[11] Jorgenson et al. (2018a) discuss the few cases where a double dividend arises; at higher carbon prices there is no GDP gain.

TABLE 19.6 Contrasting macroeconomic impacts of a CO_2 price in a bottom-up versus a top-down system.

	Bottom-up emissions accounting			Top-down emissions accounting		
	Lump sum	Capital tax	Labor tax	Lump sum	Capital tax	Labor tax
Cumulative CO_2, 2015–50;						
Percent change from base case	−21.4	−20.9	−20.8	−12.1	−11.2	−11.3
Average percent change from base, 2015–50						
GDP	−1.2	0.2	−0.1	−1.2	0.5	0.1
Consumption	−1.0	−0.5	0.3	−0.5	0.1	1.0
Investment	−2.1	1.3	−0.8	−2.0	2.2	−0.5
Government	0.0	0.0	0.0	0.0	0.0	0.0
Exports	−2.4	−0.2	−1.4	−3.6	−1.0	−2.5
Imports	−2.3	−0.7	−1.2	−1.2	0.9	0.2
Capital stock	−1.2	0.9	−0.7	−1.1	1.4	−0.6
Labor demand and supply	−0.8	−0.1	0.7	−0.9	−0.1	0.9
Leisure demand	0.3	0.1	−0.3	0.4	0.0	−0.4
Full consumption	−0.1	0.0	−0.1	0.1	0.2	0.0
Exchange rate (terms-of-trade)	1.0	0.8	−1.1	−0.5	−0.6	−2.8

similar in the cases of bottom-up compared to the bigger adjustments for exports in top-down. This result is consumption bearing a bigger burden of the GDP change in the bottom-up case, whereas, top-down, the bigger reductions in exports absorb more of the GDP change and consumption has smaller changes. The impacts on the terms-of-trade, i.e., the exchange rate, are key to explaining these patterns (a negative change is an appreciation). Preserving rest-of-world debt neutrality under bottom-up conditions requires the dollar to depreciate by an average of 1.0% with lump sum recycling and 0.8% with capital tax reductions, but an appreciation of 1.1% under the labor tax option. In the top-down scheme, the dollar appreciates under all recycling options by an average of 0.5% under lump sum redistribution, 0.6% with capital tax reductions, and 2.8% under labor tax recycling. To understand the forces at work here, we turn to prices.

The consequences of carbon taxation and revenue recycling are price driven. Under top-down accounting, the domestic and imported supplies from gas mining, coal mining, gas utilities, and refined petroleum are directly taxed at their economy-wide average rates (again, recall Table 19.2). No buyer can avoid the resulting price shock; inventory valuations and feedstock and export purchasers all are affected. Under bottom-up accounting, only selected users of gas mining, coal mining, gas utilities, and refined petroleum supplies are directly taxed, at their respective rates of emissions. Table 19.7 shows the direct and indirect effects of carbon taxation on the prices to buyers under the bottom-up and top-down pairings averaged over the period 2015–50. Table 19.8 shows these same effects on the prices to foreign buyers but only for 2050, the year of peak carbon taxation.

TABLE 19.7 Contrasting price effects to buyers of a CO_2 price in a bottom-up versus a top-down system (average percent change from base case, 2015−50).

		Bottom-up emissions accounting			Top-down emissions accounting		
		Lump sum	Capital tax	Labor tax	Lump sum	Capital tax	Labor tax
1	Agriculture	1.1	0.4	−0.8	0.8	0.0	−1.4
2	Oil mining	−1.9	−1.9	−3.4	−2.1	−2.1	−3.8
3	Gas mining	2.9	2.8	1.5	2.3	2.3	0.8
4	Coal mining	32.3	31.1	30.2	41.0	40.0	38.7
5	Nonenergy mining	1.4	0.9	−0.5	1.5	0.9	−0.7
6	Electric utilities	11.6	10.9	9.8	5.0	4.1	3.0
7	Gas utilities	11.2	10.6	9.5	12.6	11.9	10.7
8	Water and wastewater	0.6	−0.1	−1.3	0.5	−0.4	−1.7
9	Construction	0.7	0.4	−1.4	0.6	0.2	−1.8
10	Wood and paper	1.4	0.9	−0.6	1.0	0.4	−1.2
11	Nonmetal mineral products	1.9	1.4	−0.2	1.6	1.1	−0.8
12	Primary metals	1.9	1.6	−0.1	3.7	3.2	1.3
13	Fabricated metal products	1.0	0.5	−1.1	1.0	0.5	−1.4
14	Machinery	1.0	0.5	−1.0	0.6	0.0	−1.7
15	Information technology equipment	0.8	0.5	−1.3	0.0	−0.4	−2.4
16	Electrical equipment	0.8	0.4	−1.2	0.2	−0.2	−2.1
17	Motor vehicles and parts	1.0	0.7	−1.1	0.4	0.1	−1.9
18	Other transportation equipment	0.8	0.3	−1.3	0.5	−0.1	−1.9
19	Miscellaneous manufacturing	0.8	0.4	−1.3	0.2	−0.2	−2.1
20	Food, beverage, tobacco	1.1	0.5	−0.9	0.7	0.0	−1.5
21	Textiles, apparel, leather	1.0	0.7	−1.1	−0.2	−0.4	−2.5
22	Printing and related	0.7	0.2	−1.4	0.5	−0.1	−1.9
23	Petroleum and coal products	8.9	8.6	7.2	7.0	6.7	5.1
24	Chemicals, rubber, plastics	1.1	0.6	−0.8	0.9	0.2	−1.4
25	Wholesale trade	0.5	0.0	−1.5	0.5	−0.2	−1.8
26	Retail trade	0.5	0.0	−1.5	0.4	−0.2	−2.0
27	Transportation, warehousing	2.5	2.0	0.4	1.0	0.4	−1.3
28	Publishing, broadcast, telecom.	0.5	−0.2	−1.4	0.4	−0.5	−1.8
29	Software, IT services	0.5	0.1	−1.5	0.4	−0.2	−2.0

(Continued)

TABLE 19.7   Contrasting price effects to buyers of a CO_2 price in a bottom-up versus a top-down system (average percent change from base case, 2015−50).—cont'd

		Bottom-up emissions accounting			Top-down emissions accounting		
		Lump sum	Capital tax	Labor tax	Lump sum	Capital tax	Labor tax
30	Finance and insurance	0.5	−0.2	−1.4	0.4	−0.5	−1.8
31	Real estate and leasing	0.7	−0.4	−1.0	0.6	−0.7	−1.4
32	Business services	0.4	−0.1	−1.7	0.4	−0.2	−2.0
33	Educational services	0.5	0.0	−1.5	0.6	0.0	−1.7
34	Health care, social assistance	0.5	0.0	−1.6	0.4	−0.2	−2.0
35	Accommodations and other services	0.6	0.1	−1.4	0.5	−0.1	−1.9
36	Other government	0.5	0.0	−1.5	0.6	0.0	−1.8

If the exchange rate is key to understanding the trade and consumption differences between bottom-up and top-down, then export prices (Table 19.8) are the keys to understanding the weakening or strengthening of the dollar. In IGEM, the oil and gas mining industries are modeled under the resource limitations of fixed capital stocks yielding upward sloping supply curves. When demand and output falls, domestic unit production costs fall. Under the bottom-up treatment, domestic oil and gas production decline more than in the top-down case. More importantly, fossil fuel export prices are sheltered from the carbon tax in the bottom-up system. Thus, export prices for oil and gas mining and finished gas and petroleum products all decline as domestic (seller) prices fall. Export prices for coal increase slightly due to general equilibrium effects while electricity export prices rise dramatically as a result of the heavier carbon tax burden this sector incurs for its fossil fuel use. Under bottom-up accounting nonenergy export prices increase slightly more compared to top-down accounting in all sectors and recycling options, except for primary metals

and nonenergy mining under lump sum recycling. To maintain the base case trade balance, these changes in export prices require the dollar to weaken under lump sum and capital tax recycling, and strengthen under labor taxes recycling.[12]

Under the top-down pairing, the export prices for coal, oil, and gas increase significantly because they are taxed upstream, but the export prices for most manufactures rise by less than in the bottom-up case. (An exception is that the export price for primary metals rises significantly because it bears the burden of a heavier tax on coal.) The small benefits of slightly smaller increases in nonenergy export prices under top-down do not compensate the large price increase for energy exports, which are among IGEM's most expensive export commodities. In the bottom-up case the dollar has to weaken to compensate for the higher prices of nonenergy exports under lump sum and capital tax recycling and strengthen slightly when reducing labor taxes. In the top-down pairing, the dollar must strengthen in all three recycling mechanisms. This appreciation (improvement in the

---

[12] Recall that labor tax reductions lower unit prices making US goods and services more competitive internationally. Maintaining the current account therefore necessitates a stronger dollar.

TABLE 19.8 Contrasting price effects to foreign buyers of a CO_2 price in a bottom-up versus a top-down system (percent change from base case 2050).

		Bottom-up emissions accounting			Top-down emissions accounting		
		Lump sum	Capital tax	Labor tax	Lump sum	Capital tax	Labor tax
1	Agriculture	2.3	1.0	−1.3	1.9	0.2	−2.5
2	Oil mining	−6.1	−6.3	−8.1	−5.4	−5.6	−7.7
3	Gas mining	−14.1	−14.4	−16.2	4.7	4.4	2.1
4	Coal mining	3.7	2.3	0.1	54.2	52.4	49.7
5	Nonenergy mining	2.9	1.8	−0.8	3.0	1.7	−1.5
6	Electric utilities	19.7	18.3	16.0	8.0	6.4	3.8
7	Gas utilities	−1.7	−2.8	−4.8	23.9	22.5	20.0
8	Water and wastewater	1.3	0.0	−2.4	1.0	−0.5	−3.5
9	Construction	1.4	0.7	−2.5	1.2	0.4	−3.6
10	Wood and paper	2.9	1.8	−0.8	2.3	0.9	−2.2
11	Nonmetal mineral products	3.7	2.8	−0.1	3.3	2.3	−1.3
12	Primary metals	3.9	3.1	0.2	7.9	6.9	3.3
13	Fabricated metal products	1.6	0.6	−2.2	2.2	1.0	−2.5
14	Machinery	2.1	1.0	−1.6	1.9	0.5	−2.7
15	Information technology equipment	1.2	0.1	−2.5	0.9	−0.4	−3.7
16	Electrical equipment	1.4	0.4	−2.3	1.3	0.1	−3.3
17	Motor vehicles and parts	2.0	1.0	−1.8	1.7	0.6	−2.9
18	Other transportation equipment	1.5	0.5	−2.3	1.2	0.0	−3.5
19	Miscellaneous manufacturing	1.6	0.6	−2.1	1.2	0.0	−3.4
20	Food, beverage, tobacco	2.2	1.0	−1.5	1.6	0.2	−2.9
21	Textiles, apparel, leather	2.0	1.1	−1.8	1.2	0.1	−3.4
22	Printing and related	1.2	0.3	−2.6	0.9	−0.2	−3.8
23	Petroleum and coal products	−1.2	−2.0	−4.0	12.2	11.2	8.7
24	Chemicals, rubber, plastics	2.3	1.0	−1.3	2.3	0.8	−2.1
25	Wholesale trade	1.1	0.1	−2.7	0.9	−0.3	−3.7
26	Retail trade	1.1	0.1	−2.7	0.8	−0.5	−3.9
27	Transportation, warehousing	4.6	3.7	0.8	1.9	0.9	−2.7
28	Publishing, broadcast, telecom.	1.1	−0.2	−2.5	0.9	−0.7	−3.6
29	Software, IT services	1.0	0.2	−2.8	0.8	−0.2	−3.9

(Continued)

TABLE 19.8 Contrasting price effects to foreign buyers of a CO_2 price in a bottom-up versus a top-down system (percent change from base case 2050).—cont'd

		Bottom-up emissions accounting			Top-down emissions accounting		
		Lump sum	Capital tax	Labor tax	Lump sum	Capital tax	Labor tax
30	Finance and insurance	1.1	−0.2	−2.6	0.9	−0.7	−3.6
31	Real estate and leasing	1.5	−0.4	−2.0	1.2	−1.1	−3.1
32	Business services	0.8	−0.1	−3.0	0.8	−0.3	−4.0
33	Educational services	1.1	0.2	−2.7	1.2	0.2	−3.6
34	Health care, social assistance	1.0	0.2	−2.8	0.8	−0.3	−3.9
35	Accommodations and other services	1.3	0.4	−2.5	1.0	−0.1	−3.7
36	Other government	1.1	0.2	−2.7	1.1	0.0	−3.5

terms-of-trade) leads to the bigger reductions in export quantities and the expected smaller reductions or actual increases in import quantities in the top-down case.

Table 19.9 shows the effects of carbon taxation on domestic industry output. These are most influenced by the changes in buyers' prices (Table 19.7). In the lump sum case using bottom-up accounting, we see that the more expensive energy reduces coal output by 23.7% (averaged over 2015–50), petroleum products by 7.0%, gas mining by 9.7%, and gas utilities by 8.7%. The higher fuel prices underlying these effects lead to higher electricity prices and electric utilities output falls by 7.7%. The output of energy-intensive industries falls by much more than the other industries; nonmetallic mineral products (−3.9%), primary metals (−3.8%) and transportation (−4.6%) versus printing (−0.7%), food manufacturing (−1.1%), IT hardware (−1.3%) and software (−1.4%), finance (−1.0%), and health care (−0.6%). While all sectors except education experience output reductions, there is a slight bias that favors consumption-related industries.

The industry restructuring for the capital and labor tax recycling options shows patterns of responses that clearly reflect their respective incentives. Capital tax reductions promote construction, machinery, IT hardware and software, electrical equipment, motor vehicles, and real estate over such industries as food, textiles, health care, and accommodations. Labor tax recycling has the opposite effects.

For each recycling option, we observe the following when comparing bottom-up to top-down. Refined petroleum output declines more bottom-up than it does top-down as households and transportation bear a larger tax burden relative to commerce and industry. Oil mining as its supplier and transportation as its primary consumer show consistent behaviors. On the other hand, chemicals output falls more top-down as it is a large consumer of petroleum and gas products and is taxed more heavily when the tax is based on the economy-wide average emissions rate.

Gas mining output declines more bottom-up while gas utilities declines more top-down. This aligns with the findings in Table 19.6. The gas mining industry supplies heavy industry, electric utilities, and transportation while gas utilities supply residential, commercial, and light industry users. Under bottom-up, the heavier tax burden falls on gas mining consumers while, under top-down, it falls on gas utility consumers.

Reductions in electric utilities output are larger bottom-up than top-down, whereas the

TABLE 19.9 Contrasting domestic industry output effects of a CO_2 price in a bottom-up versus a top-down system (Average percent change from base case, 2015–50).

		Bottom-up emissions accounting			Top-down emissions accounting		
		Lump sum	Capital tax	Labor tax	Lump sum	Capital tax	Labor tax
1	Agriculture	−1.5	−0.8	0.0	−1.5	−0.6	0.2
2	Oil mining	−4.5	−4.2	−3.8	−3.6	−3.2	−2.8
3	Gas mining	−9.7	−9.4	−9.2	−8.3	−7.9	−7.8
4	Coal mining	−23.7	−22.1	−23.3	−24.1	−22.6	−23.8
5	Nonenergy mining	−2.8	0.5	−1.6	−2.1	1.8	−0.8
6	Electric utilities	−7.7	−7.2	−6.6	−4.8	−4.2	−3.6
7	Gas utilities	−8.7	−8.0	−7.9	−9.9	−9.1	−9.0
8	Water and wastewater	−2.6	−2.4	−1.4	−1.6	−1.3	−0.2
9	Construction	−1.8	0.6	−0.6	−1.8	1.2	−0.4
10	Wood and paper	−2.6	−0.9	−1.4	−2.4	−0.4	−1.1
11	Nonmetal mineral products	−3.9	−1.9	−2.8	−3.8	−1.3	−2.6
12	Primary metals	−3.8	−1.3	−2.8	−8.0	−5.1	−7.0
13	Fabricated metal products	−2.2	0.1	−1.1	−3.0	−0.3	−1.8
14	Machinery	−2.4	0.7	−1.2	−2.6	1.2	−1.3
15	Information technology equipment	−1.3	0.9	−0.3	−1.6	1.1	−0.5
16	Electrical equipment	−1.5	1.1	−0.4	−1.7	1.5	−0.5
17	Motor vehicles and parts	−2.4	0.5	−1.1	−2.4	1.1	−1.0
18	Other transportation equipment	−1.1	0.5	−0.4	−1.5	0.5	−0.6
19	Miscellaneous manufacturing	−1.7	1.0	−0.3	−2.0	1.3	−0.5
20	Food, beverage, tobacco	−1.1	−0.8	0.7	−0.8	−0.5	1.2
21	Textiles, apparel, leather	−1.7	−0.9	0.1	−1.3	−0.3	0.8
22	Printing and related	−0.7	0.3	0.5	−0.7	0.6	0.7
23	Petroleum and coal products	−7.0	−6.5	−6.1	−5.7	−5.1	−4.6
24	Chemicals, rubber, plastics	−2.0	−0.4	−0.7	−2.7	−0.7	−1.3
25	Wholesale trade	−1.1	0.5	0.5	−1.4	0.5	0.3
26	Retail trade	−1.3	0.4	0.5	−1.1	0.9	0.9
27	Transportation, warehousing	−4.6	−3.4	−3.3	−2.7	−1.3	−1.3
28	Publishing, broadcast, telecom.	−0.9	0.4	0.2	−0.8	0.8	0.5
29	Software, IT services	−1.4	0.9	−0.3	−1.5	1.3	−0.3

(Continued)

TABLE 19.9 Contrasting domestic industry output effects of a CO_2 price in a bottom-up versus a top-down system (Average percent change from base case, 2015−50).—cont'd

		Bottom-up emissions accounting			Top-down emissions accounting		
		Lump sum	Capital tax	Labor tax	Lump sum	Capital tax	Labor tax
30	Finance and insurance	−1.0	−0.2	0.2	−0.8	0.1	0.5
31	Real estate and leasing	−1.3	0.8	−0.7	−1.2	1.3	−0.6
32	Business services	−1.4	−0.2	−0.2	−1.4	0.1	0.1
33	Educational services	0.4	0.4	0.8	0.2	0.2	0.6
34	Health care, social assistance	−0.6	−0.6	0.8	−0.2	−0.3	1.4
35	Accommodations and other services	−1.1	−1.1	0.3	−0.6	−0.7	1.0
36	Other government	−0.1	0.0	0.0	−0.1	0.0	0.0

reverse holds for primary metals. When accounting and taxing bottom-up, the electric sector faces steep price increases for its fossil fuel use which, in turn, lead to larger price increase than occur top-down. These then result in larger electricity demand reductions. For primary metals, the relatively cheaper electricity and gas top-down versus bottom-up are not enough to compensate the much heavier tax burden the industry experiences for their coal use. This also helps explain the slightly larger reductions in domestic coal production top-down as compared to bottom-up.

Finally, except for primary metals, the bottom-up pairing leaves nonenergy output losses (gains) slightly larger (smaller) than their counterparts under the top-down pairing, again for a given recycling option. For example, food, retail trade and health care decline more (lump sum and capital tax) and rise less (labor tax) when comparing bottom-up to top-down.

The differences in the effects of top-down versus bottom-up accounting are large as we noted above but are not very different across the three recycling options. In Table 19.9 we see that the reduction in the output of electric utilities under the bottom-up system are 7.7%, 7.2%, and 6.6% under lump sum, capital tax, and labor tax cut, respectively. Under the top-down system the reductions are much lower but correspondingly similar: 4.8%, 4.2%, and 3.6%. The similarity of effects within an accounting scheme is not surprising since the same mechanisms are at work using the same relative prices of coal, petroleum, and gas appropriate to each scheme. The differences across accounting schemes depend on whether the relative prices to different buyers are the same (top-down) or different (bottom-up).

These same reasons apply to other industries. For example, under bottom-up accounting, primary metals output falls by averages of 3.8%, 1.3%, and 2.8% and transportation by averages of 4.6%, 3.4%, and 3.3%. The differences in the top-down system reflect the differences in effective carbon tax rates to each. For primary metals where its coal use is taxed more heavily top-down, the percentage losses average 8.0%, 5.1%, and 7.0%, i.e., the losses are greater. For transportation where its petroleum use is taxed more heavily bottom-up, the average percentage losses top-down are 2.7%, 1.3%, and 1.3%, i.e., the losses are smaller.

19.3.5 Welfare effects

The inclusion of demographic detail in IGEM's model of aggregate consumer behavior broadens, enriches, and informs our discussions of policy. We first focus on household welfare and the policy impacts by demographic attribute. Here, we compute equivalent variations (changes measured at base case prices) in lifetime full wealth and expenditure—goods, services, and leisure—for 244 household types defined by family size (numbers of children from 0 to 3+ and numbers of adults from 1 to 3+), region of residence (Northeast, Midwest, South, or West), race of head (nonwhite or white), sex of head (female or male), and household location (rural or urban). Table 19.10 shows the population-weighted average results by demographic group for the two accounting and tax schemes and the three revenue recycling options.[13]

We note that within an accounting scheme, capital tax recycling is most favorable for households and lump sum redistributions are least favorable to households with the effects of labor tax reductions lying in between. The effects are small. The largest average welfare cost is 0.70% of household full wealth occurring under bottom-up accounting with lump sum recycling. The largest average welfare gain is 1.49% of full wealth occurring under the top-down-lump sum pairing.

Under lump sum recycling, some households experience welfare gains, but generally there are costs no matter the accounting scheme. Bottom-up, the welfare gains are smaller and the welfare costs are larger than under top-down accounting and taxation. Under capital tax recycling, there are welfare costs bottom-up but welfare gains top-down, i.e., there is a double dividend in the top-down option. Under labor tax recycling, there are welfare costs bottom-up and some households are adversely affected under top-down as well, although not as much. Generally,

however, labor tax recycling is welfare beneficial top-down.

Under lump sum recycling, there are consistencies in the rankings of outcomes by demographic group across the two accounting methods. In both schemes, rural households fare better than urban ones, households headed by females or nonwhites fare better than their counterparts, and those in the South fare best followed by those in the Midwest, the Northeast and, lastly, the West. When there are no children, larger households fare better than smaller ones. For households with one or two children, single adult households fare best followed by those with three or more adults and, lastly, two adult households. The lone reversal across the two accounting schemes occurs for households with three or more children. Under bottom-up, single adult households fare better than those with three or more adults who, in turn, fare slightly better than those with two adults. However, under top-town, for households with three or more children, the strictly fewer adults, the better.

With capital tax recycling, there again are consistencies in the demographic rankings. For region and location, the patterns are the reverse of those under lump sum. Here, in both the bottom-up and top-down worlds, urban households fare better than rural ones and the regional ranking from best to worst is West, Northeast, Midwest, and, lastly, South. The reversals under capital tax recycling come when considering family size, race, and gender. Moreover, these appear dependent on whether there are welfare costs or welfare benefits. Under bottom-up, there are welfare costs. Larger households fare better than smaller ones, households headed by males fare better than those headed by females, and those headed by nonwhites fare better than those headed by whites. Under top-down, there are

---

[13] While the emissions, energy, and economic details focus on the policy period, 2015–50, individual, household, and social welfare are determined for an infinite horizon, with a small weight for distant years given our rate of time preference.

TABLE 19.10 Contrasting household welfare effects of a CO_2 price in a bottom-up versus a top-down system (change from base case lifetime full expenditure).

	Bottom-up emissions accounting			Top-down emissions accounting		
	Lump sum	Capital tax	Labor tax	Lump sum	Capital tax	Labor tax
Children, adults per household						
3+, 3+	0.030%	−0.036%	−0.204%	0.204%	0.131%	−0.065%
2, 3+	−0.133%	−0.033%	−0.192%	0.012%	0.138%	−0.050%
1, 3+	−0.309%	−0.019%	−0.198%	−0.213%	0.138%	−0.072%
0, 3+	−0.461%	0.004%	−0.203%	−0.421%	0.139%	−0.104%
3+, 2	0.020%	−0.044%	−0.168%	0.226%	0.158%	0.012%
2, 2	−0.191%	−0.035%	−0.158%	−0.028%	0.166%	0.021%
1, 2	−0.379%	−0.027%	−0.161%	−0.261%	0.165%	0.006%
0, 2	−0.580%	−0.007%	−0.165%	−0.522%	0.166%	−0.021%
3+, 1	1.029%	−0.071%	−0.119%	1.493%	0.192%	0.135%
2, 1	0.336%	−0.061%	−0.106%	0.667%	0.203%	0.149%
1, 1	−0.202%	−0.046%	−0.111%	0.011%	0.206%	0.128%
0, 1	−0.701%	−0.026%	−0.112%	−0.600%	0.212%	0.108%
Region of household						
Northeast	−0.500%	−0.001%	−0.155%	−0.410%	0.191%	0.008%
Midwest	−0.446%	−0.032%	−0.148%	−0.328%	0.171%	0.034%
South	−0.417%	−0.043%	−0.149%	−0.292%	0.161%	0.036%
West	−0.508%	0.007%	−0.152%	−0.423%	0.197%	0.008%
Race and gender of household head						
Nonwhite female	−0.145%	−0.025%	−0.151%	0.027%	0.177%	0.028%
White female	−0.462%	−0.030%	−0.123%	−0.328%	0.195%	0.084%
Nonwhite male	−0.386%	−0.008%	−0.181%	−0.295%	0.162%	−0.042%
White male	−0.509%	−0.020%	−0.156%	−0.416%	0.173%	0.013%
Location of household						
Urban	−0.474%	−0.016%	−0.150%	−0.371%	0.181%	0.022%
Rural	−0.284%	−0.089%	−0.156%	−0.113%	0.127%	0.048%

welfare benefits and these patterns are the exact opposites. Now, it is the smaller, female-headed and white-headed households that do better.

When labor taxes are reduced, the demographic consistencies relate to family size, race, and gender. Under both accounting schemes and for a given number of children, smaller households are better off than larger ones. In addition, households headed by females and whites fare better than their male and nonwhite counterparts. The demographic inconsistencies befalling labor tax recycling occur for the rankings by region and location. Under bottom-up, urban households lose proportionally less than rural ones; however, under top-down, they gain proportionally less than do rural households. As for regions, bottom-up, labor tax recycling favors the Midwest over the South, West, and, lastly, the Northeast. In the top-down scheme, it is the South that fares better than the Midwest with the West and Northeast now

tied for last. These reversals, like those for capital tax recycling, appear to be linked to the distinction between the welfare costs of bottom-up and the welfare benefits of top-down.

In Jorgenson et al. (2018a), we use family size to determine the size distribution in lifetime full expenditure per capita and compute equivalent variations by quintiles of persons irrespective of their demographic characteristics. Table 19.11 shows the equivalent variations expressed as percentages of lifetime full expenditure *per person*. There are both winners and losers at the levels of individual welfare. However, like the household results, the changes are small for this level of carbon price—respectively, the

TABLE 19.11 Contrasting individual and social welfare effects of a CO_2 price in a bottom-up versus a top-down system (Change from base case lifetime full expenditure).

	Bottom-up emissions accounting			Top-down emissions accounting		
	Lump sum	Capital tax	Labor tax	Lump sum	Capital tax	Labor tax
Quintile 1	0.111%	−0.052%	−0.160%	0.345%	0.158%	0.031%
Quintile 2	−0.245%	−0.033%	−0.164%	−0.099%	0.162%	0.006%
Quintile 3	−0.416%	−0.024%	−0.172%	−0.319%	0.154%	−0.020%
Quintile 4	−0.590%	−0.015%	−0.153%	−0.516%	0.176%	0.013%
Quintile 5	−0.651%	0.009%	−0.161%	−0.608%	0.184%	−0.017%
Social welfare changes in $(2010) billions						
Egalitarian						
Due to equity	$1445	−$17	$811	$1314	−$444	$528
Due to efficiency	−$6780	−$257	−$2206	−$5292	$2578	$270
Total	−$5335	−$274	−$1395	−$3978	$2134	$798
Utilitarian						
Due to equity	$496	−$1	$331	$479	−$117	$272
Due to efficiency	−$6780	−$257	−$2206	−$5292	$2578	$270
Total	−$6284	−$258	−$1875	−$4813	$2461	$542
Indices of progressivity						
Absolute	Progressive	Regressive	Progressive	Progressive	Regressive	Progressive
Relative	Regressive	Regressive	Progressive	Progressive	Progressive	Progressive

maximum gain and loss are 0.35 and 0.65% of individual lifetime expenditure.

In the case of lump sum recycling, the poorest individuals are protected from the adverse effects of carbon taxation by the equal lump sum redistribution. The wealthier individuals in quintiles 2 through 5 experience welfare losses. The gain for quintile 1 in the top-down system is larger than in the bottom-up—0.35% versus 0.11%—while the welfare losses for all other quintiles are smaller given that CO_2 reductions are much smaller in the top-down system. It is worth noting that the welfare gap favoring top-down over bottom-up systematically diminishes as full wealth increases. For quintile 1, the benefit is 0.23 percentage points while, for quintile 5, it is only 0.04 percentage points. Under the lump sum option and in both accounting and tax schemes, each quintile fares better than the next higher quintile and thus appears progressive.

In the bottom-up system, the carbon tax with capital tax recycling has almost trivial welfare consequences. The burden on quintile 1 is just over 0.05% of their lifetime expenditure, whereas the gain for quintile 5 is just under 0.01% of theirs. Because the welfare costs to individuals fall and give way to gains as wealth increases, capital tax recycling is regressive. In the top-down system, the capital tax option yields a double dividend in welfare for all individuals. The benefits range from 0.15 percentage points for quintile 3 to 0.18 points for quintile 5. Because quintile 3's gain is smaller than those for quintiles 1 and 2, the regressivity of capital tax recycling is more ambiguous in top-down accounting than it is in bottom-up accounting.

Labor tax recycling has the least systematic welfare effects of the three redistribution options. Under bottom-up, the welfare losses relative to full wealth range from 0.15% (quintile 4) to 0.17% (quintile 3). Considering the subgroups of quintiles 1, 2, and 3 and quintiles 4 and 5

separately, labor tax recycling appears progressive as within-group losses rise with rising wealth. However, with smaller losses for quintiles 4 and 5 compared to the others, there is some evidence for regressivity in the bottom-up—labor-tax pairing. In the top-down system, the welfare consequences of carbon taxation combined with reductions in labor taxes are trivial, like bottom-up and capital. Quintiles 1, 2, and 4 gain slightly, while quintiles 3 and 5 experience small losses. Given the relative changes over the five quintiles, there is no clear progressivity pattern.

This brings us to our next important point—social welfare. The quintiles are accumulations of averages for individuals and result from adding up full wealth and equivalent variations in it. These aggregations cannot be construed as either group or societal welfare because of the nonidentical and nonhomothetic preferences specific to IGEM's household utility model. Furthermore, we need to determine unambiguously whether a particular accounting method and revenue recycling pairing is progressive or regressive. We remedy both issues through use of our social welfare function.

Jorgenson and Slesnick (1987) and Jorgenson et al. (1992) pioneered in the creation of a monetary measure of social welfare using an exact aggregation of lifetime full expenditures over the 244 household types.[14] Within this framework, social welfare increases as household welfare increases, transfers from richer to poorer households are social welfare improving, and the range of society's preferences for equality from the purely egalitarian to the purely utilitarian is definable.

The framework also allows the decomposition of social welfare into components of efficiency and equity. Welfare efficiency is the maximum level achievable from reallocations of lifetime full expenditure that equalize household utility.

---

[14] The Jorgenson, Slesnick, Wilcoxen contributions are covered extensively in Jorgenson (1997).

Welfare equity is the difference between actual social welfare and welfare efficiency. A policy is progressive in the *absolute* sense if the equity gap shrinks and is otherwise regressive. A policy is progressive in the *relative* sense if the ratio of actual-to-efficient welfare increases and is otherwise regressive.

The results for the social welfare from carbon taxation also are given in Table 19.11. Like individual welfare, the social welfare changes are extremely small in relation to their base. National full wealth (the present value of consumption and leisure) stands at $1,100,515 billion. The largest changes in social welfare are the losses associated with lump sum recycling and these represent only 0.48 and 0.36% of this amount for bottom-up and top-down, respectively.

Considering only the social welfare metric, capital tax recycling is the most advantageous, lump sum redistribution is the least favorable alternative, and labor-tax reductions yield results that are in-between. Under bottom-up accounting, there are no double dividends. For the capital tax option, equity losses reinforce the loss in efficiency leading to overall losses in social welfare exceeding $250 billion. For the lump sum and labor tax alternatives, respectively, equity gains partially compensate efficiency losses yielding social welfare losses in the ranges of $5.3-$6.3 trillion and $1.4-$1.9 trillion, depending on society's aversion to inequality.

Under top-down accounting, there is the familiar social welfare penalty associated with lump sum redistribution. Equity gains partially offset the efficiency loss, netting losses in total welfare in the range of $4.0-$4.8 trillion. However, the other recycling options give rise to double dividends. The larger of these occurs when capital taxes are reduced. Here, losses in equity are not large enough to swamp the gain in efficiency; the result is social welfare benefits in the range of $2.1-$2.5 trillion, depending on egalitarian versus utilitarian preferences. When labor taxes are reduced, there are equity gains that complement the gain in efficiency with overall improvements in the range of $0.5-$0.8 trillion.

The conclusions for progressivity versus regressivity are mixed. In the *absolute* sense, there is agreement across the two accounting schemes. The lump sum and labor tax options are absolutely progressive while recycling through capital tax reductions is absolutely regressive. In the *relative* sense, this pattern is broken. Labor tax recycling is still progressive under both accounting methods. Capital tax recycling is still regressive but only under bottom-up accounting; it is relatively progressive when emissions are taxed top-down. The opposite occurs for lump sum redistribution. It is still progressive top-down but becomes relatively regressive bottom-up. These differences demonstrate the care in definition that needs to be taken when considering the effects of tax policy.

19.4 Conclusion

Fossil fuel production and use involve a heterogeneous mix of products, prices, technologies, and externalities. These pose few problems for models or submodels that express the details in physical units, e.g., tons, gallons, cubic feet, BTUs. However, the need to reduce complexities generally leads to homogenization. For CGE models, there is an additional challenge—the contents of the social accounting matrices from which they derive are transactions in nominal value, with quantities and prices as indices over time. This creates even more distance between the model and physical worlds.

No matter the units of account, modelers must consciously choose where to attach their emissions coefficients. The choice is use, or input-demand-driven (our bottom-up), make or output-supply driven (our top-down), or some blend of the two. In a single model, IGEM, we demonstrate that the extremes yield significant differences in model outcomes. We can only imagine how, in a multimodel exercise, the lack of clarity in emissions accounting and carbon tax incidence clouds any conclusive consensus. The issues we raise here are not usually discussed in the CGE literature nor described in model documentation; however, we believe that these are just as important as equations and elasticities. Our hope from this effort is for greater detail in describing all the attributes and mechanisms that go into modeling environmental policy.

References

Armington P: A theory of demand for products distinguished by place of production, *International Monetary Fund Staff Papers* 16:159–178, 1969.

Berndt ER, Wood DO: Technology, prices, and the derived demand for energy, *The Review of Economics and Statistics* 57(3):259–268, 1975 (August).

Bureau of Economic Analysis (BEA): *Industry economic accounts*. https://www.bea.gov/industry/input-output-accounts-data.

Bureau of Labor Statistics (BLS): *Consumer expenditure surveys: aggregate expenditure shares tables*. https://www.bls.gov/cex/csxashar.htm.

Congressional Budget Office (CBO), The budget and economic outlook: fiscal years 2013 to 2023, February 5, 2013. https://www.cbo.gov/publication/43907.

Fawcett AA, McFarland JR, Morris AC, Weyant JP: Introduction to the EMF 32 study on U.S. Carbon tax scenarios, *Climate Change Economics* 9(1), 2018, 1840001: 1-7.

Hudson EA, Jorgenson DW: U.S Energy policy and economic growth, 1975-2000, *Bell Journal of Economics and Management Science* 5(2):461–514, 1974 (Autumn).

Hudson EA, Jorgenson DW: U.S Tax policy and energy conservation. In Jorgenson DW, editor: Econometric Studies of U.S. Energy policy *Amsterdam*, North Holland, pp 7–94.

Jin H, Jorgenson DW: Econometric modeling of technical change, *Journal of Econometrics* 157:205–219, 2010.

Jorgenson DW: Capital theory and investment behavior, *The American Economic Review* 53(2):247–259, 1963 (May).

Jorgenson DW: *Welfare, Measuring social welfare*, vol. 2. Cambridge MA, 1997, The MIT Press.

Jorgenson DW, Gallop FM, Fraumeni BM: *Productivity and U.S. economic growth*, Cambridge MA, 1987, Harvard University Press.

Jorgenson DW, Goettle RJ, Ho MS, Wilcoxen PJ: *Double Dividend: Environmental taxes and fiscal reform in the United States*, Cambridge, MA, 2013, The MIT Press.

Jorgenson DW, Goettle RJ, Ho MS, Wilcoxen PJ: The welfare consequences of taxing carbon, *Climate Change Economics* 9(1), 2018a. pp1840013: 1-39.

Jorgenson DW, Goettle RJ, Ho MS , Wilcoxen PJ: *IGEM: a model of US Growth and the Environment. Version 20. Appendix A* and revised chapters of *Jorgenson et al. (2013) double Dividend* https://github.com/openigem/naics36/tree/master/docs and http://www.igem.insightworks.com/docs/2018b.

Jorgenson DW, Lau LJ: Duality and differentiability in production, *Journal of Economic Theory* 9(1):23–42, 1974a (September).

Jorgenson DW, Lau LJ: The duality of technology and economic behavior, *The Review of Economic Studies* 41(2): 181–200, 1974b. no.126 (April).

Jorgenson DW, Lau LJ, Stoker TM: The transcendental logarithmic model of aggregate consumer behavior. In , Greenwich CT, 1982, JAI Press, pp 97–238. Basmann RL, Rhodes G, editors: *Advances in Econometrics*, vol. 1. Greenwich CT, 1982, JAI Press, pp 97–238.

Jorgenson DW, Griliches Z: The explanation of productivity change, *The Review of Economic Studies* 34(99):249–280, 1967 (July).

Jorgenson DW, Slesnick DT: Aggregate consumer behavior and household equivalence scales, *Journal of Business & Economic Statistics* 5(2):219–232, 1987.

Jorgenson DW, Slesnick DT, Wilcoxen PJ: *Carbon taxes and economic welfare*, Brookings Papers: Microeconomics, 1992, pp 393–454.

Jorgenson DW, Wilcoxen PJ: Environmental regulation and U.S. Economic growth, *The RAND Journal of Economics* 21(2):314–340, 1990.

U.S. Energy Information Administration (EIA): *Manufacturing energy consumption Survey 2010*. https://www.eia.gov/consumption/manufacturing/data/2010/.

U.S. Energy Information Administration (EIA): Monthly energy review. https://www.eia.gov/environment/data.php. https://www.eia.gov/totalenergy/data/monthly/.

U.S. Energy Information Administration (EIA): *Annual energy outlook*. https://www.eia.gov/outlooks/archive/aeo16/2016.

U.S. Environmental Protection Agency (EPA): *Inventory of U.S. greenhouse gas emissions and sinks: 1990–2014*. https://www.epa.gov/ghgemissions/us-greenhouse-gas-inventory-report-1990-2014.

CHAPTER

20

Analyzing carbon price policies using a general equilibrium model with household energy demand functions

Jing Cao[1],*, Mun S. Ho[2],*, Wenhao Hu[3],*

[1]School of Economics and Management, Tsinghua University, Beijing, China; [2]Harvard-China Project on Energy, Economy, Environment, SEAS, Harvard University, Cambridge, MA, United States; [3]School of Economics, Tianjin University, Tianjin, China

20.1 Introduction

China is the largest consumer of fossil fuels in the world and generated 10.4 billion tons of CO_2 in 2016 compared to the 5.0 billion tons from the United States, the next biggest emitter.[1] There is obviously great interest in China greenhouse gas control policy in the international community. The Chinese government has set CO_2 emission goals as part of its Nationally Determined Contribution (NDC) coming out of the Paris Agreement in 2015 as part of the United Nations Framework Convention on Climate Change. The aim is to cut CO_2 emissions per unit of gross domestic product (GDP) by 60–65% by 2030, compared to 2005 levels. While these are not binding targets, the government also announced the 13th Five-year Plan with firmer goals to reduce energy per unit GDP by 15% between 2015 and 2020 and to reduce CO_2 per unit GDP by 18%.

Given this intention to reduce energy use and carbon emissions, there have been a vigorous discussion of carbon policy proposals and analyses of their likely impacts in China. Policies analyzed include energy-efficiency targets, emission trading systems (ETSs), and carbon taxes

---

* Cao is Professor at the School of Economics and Management, Tsinghua University. Ho is a Visiting Scholar at the Harvard-China Project on Energy, Economy and Environment and also at Resources for the Future. Hu is a Post-Doctoral Fellow at the Ma Yinchu School of Economics, Tianjin University. Ho is supported by the Harvard Global Institute under an award to the Harvard-China Project titled "China 2030/2050: Energy and Environmental Challenges for the Future."

[1] CO_2 emissions estimates from the European Commission, Janssens-Maenhout et al. (2017). These include non-combustion sources.

(e.g. Aunan et al., 2007; Zhang, 2015; Pang and Duan, 2016; Cao and Ma, 2018). The important communiqué issued by the then new leaders of the Communist Party in November 2013 emphasized the desire to make the market a "decisive function in resource allocation" and also emphasized "protection of ecology and the environment." The discussion of using carbon prices to reduce energy use and pollution flows from taking these stated aims seriously.

Some of the analyses of carbon prices have used multisector general equilibrium models, since these models can capture interindustry effects: how higher energy prices feed into the energy-intensive sectors such as electricity, metals, and cement, which then make investment goods more expensive relative to consumption goods and thus change the structure of the entire economy. Energy is used by every sector of the economy, and enterprise owners and workers are concerned about how carbon prices would affect jobs and profits. An economy-wide analysis of detailed industries is thus very useful to the many stakeholders. Alternative methods of analysis use sector-specific technology models (sometimes referred to as bottom—up models) which provide valuable insights into how exactly a carbon price affects the production processes and technologies in a given industry.[2] These methods, however, do not trace through the interindustry linkages in the rest of the economy.

The studies that use such multisector computable general equilibrium (CGE) models for China policies include Aunan et al. (2007), Liang et al. (2007), Cao et al. (2013), and Wu and Tang (2015) among many others. These models have provided useful insights into the economy-wide impacts of greenhouse gas policies. There is, however, a more limited discussion of distributional impacts. Furthermore, many of these models represent the consumption side of the economy using simple, easily implementable consumption

functions such as linear expenditure systems (LESs) or constant elasticity of substitution (CES) functions. These functions have only the own-price elasticity, and the CES is homothetic in contrast to more flexible forms with cross-price elasticities and nonunit income elasticities.

There is now a large literature on household energy demand that shows that some energy types are income inelastic while others are income elastic including a literature specific to China. Cao et al. (2016) find that coal is income inelastic, whereas gasoline is a luxury good. They also find that demands are heterogenous across household types—different shares of the budget are allocated to food for example, depending on the number of children, age, and source of employment. Zhou and Teng (2013) estimate a relatively low income elasticity for electricity (0.1—0.3). It has been rare, however, to include such elasticity estimates into large-scale simulation models. Caron et al. (2017) find a complex relation between household energy consumption and income using a function that resembles the flexible Exact Affine Stone Index. That paper and Cao et al. (2018a) are some of the few studies that include such information into a China CGE model.

General equilibrium models which incorporate more flexible forms should be able to represent the consumption baseline more accurately as well as estimating responses to policy shocks better. Models that allow for household heterogeneity have a richer description of distributional impacts of policies. This paper analyzes a carbon tax using a flexible model of household demand that allows for heterogeneity across households. Unlike Cao et al. (2018a) which does not explicitly identify energy items in their consumption function, here we use a demand model which is a function of electricity, household fuels, and transportation.

Dale Jorgenson has made important contributions to these issues of energy demand modeling,

---

[2] An example is Zhang et al. (2014).

household heterogeneity and social welfare functions, and the use of CGE models to analyze environmental policies. Jorgenson et al. (1982) introduced the translog consumption function as a flexible form that allows for heterogeneity across household types while Jorgenson et al. (1988) used a two-stage function to model energy demand. Jorgenson discussed social welfare functions in his Presidential Address to the Econometric Society (Jorgenson, 1990). Hudson and Jorgenson (1974) is a pioneering study of energy policies using a CGE model, while Jorgenson and Wilcoxen (1990) introduces the use of a translog consumption function that allows for household heterogeneity into CGE modeling. Jorgenson's contributions to productivity measurement and specification of production functions underlie the analysis and models of many chapters in this volume. These econometric production functions are also reflected in the development of the growth models in Hudson and Jorgenson (1974) and Jorgenson and Wilcoxen (1990).

In this paper, we use a two-stage flexible consumption model of household energy demand in a dynamic multisector model of China to allow for a better representation of price and income effects of carbon price policies. We draw on the major contributions of Jorgenson noted above—the use of an econometrically estimated two-stage demand model, the use of a demand function that recognizes the differences among household types, and the application of a general equilibrium model to simulate an environmental policy. The projection of total factor productivity (TFP) growth is informed by the China industry productivity accounts presented in Cao et al. (2009). Unlike most CGE models which use simple working-age population measures for projecting labor supply, we use an index of effective labor input that takes into account the differences in marginal products of different demographic groups; this is an approach emphasized long ago in Jorgenson and Griliches (1967).

In Section 20.2, we describe our econometric model of household energy demand. In Section 20.3, we describe how this demand model is

included in our dynamic growth model of China and describe the representation of carbon taxes and emissions. Section 20.4 reports the effects of a carbon tax simulated using the growth model and effects on energy demand in general and household demand in particular.

20.2 A two-stage model of household energy demand

Our econometric model of household energy demand is taken from Hu et al. (2018), and we briefly summarize the model and estimation here. We follow the two-stage budgeting model of consumer behavior described in Jorgenson et al. (1988). Households are assumed to maximize utility in two stages, conditional on leisure choice, location choice and the stock of durables including housing. The demand functions from both stages are integrable. In the first stage, total expenditures in period t are allocated to electricity, other home energy (OHE), transportation, and consumer goods and services. In the second stage, the transportation bundle is allocated to vehicle fuel and transportation services (fares and vehicle maintenance).

The conditions required for a well-defined two-stage system are strict; one of the stages must be homothetic, i.e. must have unit income elasticities. In our model, here we require the second stage to be homothetic, whereas in Cao et al. (2016), we have a homothetic linear expenditure system (LES) in the first stage and an Almost Ideal Demand System (AIDS) function in the second.

20.2.1 Demand model theory

20.2.1.1 First stage

For the first stage, we assume a translog indirect utility function for household k:

$$\ln V_k = \ln\left(\frac{p}{M_k}\right)' \cdot \alpha_p + \frac{1}{2}\ln\left(\frac{p}{M_k}\right)' \cdot B \cdot \ln\left(\frac{p}{M_k}\right)$$
$$+ \ln\left(\frac{p}{M_k}\right)' \cdot B_A \cdot A_k$$

$$(20.1)$$

where:

$p = (p_1, p_2, \ldots, p_N)-$ vector of prices of consumption bundles,

$x_k = (x_{1k}, x_{2k}, \ldots, x_{Nk})-$ vector of quantities consumed by household k,

$M_k = \sum_{n=1}^{N} p_n \cdot x_{nk}-$ total expenditures of household k,

$w_{nk} = p_n \cdot x_{nk}/M_k-$ expenditure share of the n-th commodity,

$w = (w, w, \ldots, w_{Nk})-$ vector of expenditure shares,

A_k- vector of (0,1) attribute indicators.

In this form, the preference differences among households are introduced through the attribute vector A_k. These include household size, presence of children, region, area of home, cooling degree days, and heating degree days. The matrices α, B, and B_A are constant parameters that are the same for all households. The five consumption bundles are index by:

n = {1,2,3,4,5} = {electricity, OHE, transportation, cons. goods, services}

The conditions required for exact aggregation (i.e. the restrictions needed so that an aggregate demand function is obtained by explicit aggregation over households) are that the expenditure shares be linear in functions of A_k and M_k. These conditions are:

$$\iota'B\iota = 0; \quad \iota'B_A = 0 \quad (20.2)$$

where i is a vector of 1's. In addition, homogeneity of the demand function allows us to choose a normalization, $\iota'\alpha = -1$.

The vector of expenditure shares derived by Roy's identity is:

$$w_k = \frac{1}{D(p)}[\alpha + B \ln p - B_M \ln M_k + B_A A_k] \quad (20.3)$$

where the denominator takes the following form under the aggregation conditions:

$$D(p) = -1 + B'_M \cdot \ln p \quad (20.4)$$

$$B_M = B\iota$$

Integrability of the demand system also requires that the matrix of price substitution effects be symmetric and nonpositive definite:

$$B' = B \quad (20.5)$$

The demand function (20.3) is nonlinear in log prices, and the expenditure (income) elasticity is a function of B_M. The uncompensated price elasticities are:

$$\eta_{ij} = -\delta_{ij} + \frac{\beta_{ij}/\omega_i - \beta_{M_i}}{-1 + \sum_k \beta_{Mk} \cdot \ln(p_k/M)} \quad (20.6)$$

where δ_{ij} is the Kronecker indicator (see Hu et al., 2018). Expenditure elasticities are given by:

$$\eta_{iM} = 1 - \frac{\sum_j \beta_{ij}/\omega_i}{-1 + \sum_k \beta_{Mk} \cdot \ln(p_k/M)} \quad (20.7)$$

20.2.1.2 The second stage

In the second stage, we assume that total transportation expenditures be allocated to vehicle fuels (gasoline and diesel) and transportation services (fares, vehicle rentals, own-vehicle maintenance) via a homothetic translog utility function:

$$\ln T_k = \ln q'\gamma + \ln M_k^T + \frac{1}{2}\ln q'\Delta \ln q$$
$$+ \ln q'\Delta_A A_k \quad (20.8)$$

where:

$q = (q_1, q_2)-$vector of prices q_m, m = {1,2} = {fuel, transportation services},

$y_k = (y_{1k}, y_{2k})-$vector of quantities consumed by household k,

$M_k^T = \sum_m q_{mk} y_{mk}-$total expenditures on transportation bundle of household k,

$v_{mk} = q_{mk} y_{mk}/M_k^T-$expenditure share of input m = {1,2},

The vector of expenditure shares of household k derived by Roy's identity is:

$$-v_k = \gamma + \Delta \ln q + \Delta_A A_k \quad (20.9)$$

The conditions for exact aggregation, that expenditure shares are linear in functions of attributes and total expenditures, are satisfied by Eq. (20.9). This is unlike the first stage (20.3) which is nonhomothetic. We can express the transportation bundle price index (the third consumption bundle in the top tier) in terms of the second-stage utility function:

$$\ln p_{3k} = \ln M_k^T - \ln T_k$$

$$= -\left[\ln q' \gamma + \frac{1}{2}\ln q' \Delta \ln q + \ln q' \Delta_A A_k\right]$$

$$(20.10)$$

Thus, under the homothetic assumption, expenditures on the transportation bundle are the product of the price and quantity indexes:

$$M_k^T = p_{3k} * T_k = \sum_m q_{mk} y_{mk} \qquad (20.11)$$

20.2.1.3 Econometric method

The above system may be implemented if most households purchase both motor fuels and transportation services as the case in the United States. However, for our sample period 1992–2009, a large fraction of households in China do not own gasoline-using vehicles. We thus break the second stage into two steps: first, whether to own a car, and second, how much fuel (gasoline or diesel) to consume. To correct for selection bias, we first estimate a probit function for choosing vehicle fuels in period t, $P(y_{1kt} > 0 | q_{1kt}, q_{2kt}, M_{kt}, A_{kt}) = \Phi(y_{1kt} \cdot v)$, where Φ is the cumulative distribution function (CDF) of the standard normal distribution, and the selection function depends on prices, total transportation expenditures, and demographic characteristics. From this, one could obtain the inverse Mills ratio, $\widehat{\lambda}_{1kt} = \lambda(y_{1kt} \cdot v) = \frac{\phi_{ikt}(\cdot)}{\Phi_{ikt}(\cdot)}$, where ϕ is the normal density function.

To correct for sample selectivity, one would usually add this inverse Mills ratio on the right-hand side of Eq. (20.9). However, as noted by Cao et al. (2016), this will result in a bias when there are many zero values, and we use the following equation to correct for sample selectivity:

$$-v_{1kt} = \widehat{\Phi}_{1kt} \cdot (\gamma + \Delta \ln q + \Delta_A A_k) + \xi \widehat{\phi}_{1kt}$$
$$+ v_{1kt}$$

$$(20.12)$$

For the first stage, we use repeated cross-sections, pooling all years (1992–2009) with household observations, where prices vary across region and time.[3] That is, while we do not have prices unique to each household type k, we have prices for different regions in each province, with the price vector denoted p_{rt}. We assume that the disturbances in the demand system (20.3) are additive so that the system of estimating equations is:

$$w_{kt} = \frac{1}{D(p_{rt})}[\alpha + B \ln p_{rt} - B_M \ln M_k + B_A A_k]$$
$$+ \widetilde{\varepsilon}_{kt}$$

$$(20.13)$$

We drop one equation since the shares add to one and express four prices relative to the fifth. Similarly, in the second stage, we estimate only the equation for vehicle fuels; the share for transportation services is given residually. The share demand systems are estimated subject to the constraints (20.4) and (20.5) and concavity.

The demographic characteristics used to control for heterogeneity in household behavior include:

1. Age of household head: Under 35, 35–55, above 55
2. Gender of household head: Female, male

---

[3] Jorgenson and Slesnick (2008) estimate both rank 2 and rank 3 demand systems but have only four consumption bundles. We have five consumption items and only estimate a rank 2 system.

3. Employment of household head: Private sector, public sector
4. Education of household head: Less than secondary school, secondary school, and college (or above)
5. Has child: A 0−1 indicator showing if there is someone under age 16 in the household
6. Has aged: A 0−1 indicator showing if there is someone aged 60 or older
7. Number of members in the household: 1−2, 3, 3+
8. Location: West, East, and Middle

20.2.2 Data and estimation results

The detailed data on energy use by households are only available from the Urban Household Income and Expenditure Survey (UHIES) conducted by the National Bureau of Statistics (NBS). We are unable to find a corresponding level of detail for rural households; such information is only available for the most recent years. The UHIES is conducted every year where one-third of the sample households are replaced each year. These data are not available to the public, and we obtained a subsample of the UHIES, covering nine provinces from 1992 through 2009.[4] The nine provinces were selected to represent all regions and income levels of China. Our sample size is between 5000 and 6000 households per year before 2001, and 15,000−17,000 after that.

The five consumption bundles are made of the following items given in the UHIES:

1. Electricity (EL)—electricity
2. Other home energy (OHE)—coal, gas, heat, and other energy in homes except electricity
3. Transportation (TR)—vehicle fuels (gasoline and diesel), transportation services (bus, taxi, trains, etc.), and vehicle maintenance

4. Goods (GD)—food (including in-kind and dining out), clothing, household equipment, medical goods, educational goods, transportation equipment, communications equipment, recreational goods, and other goods
5. Services and housing (SH)—expenditure on medical care, educational services, communication services, recreation services, other services, and rental equivalents of housing and water utilities.

Note that vehicle purchases are included in the consumer goods bundle and not in transportation. Hu et al. (2018) describe how we impute rentals equivalents, given that more than 90% of urban households own their homes. The UHIES do not have information on the value of durables owned by households, and we make an average imputation using the data on purchases of durables for each income and demographic group.

In 2009, the sample average share of expenditures for electricity, OHE, transportation, goods, and services are 2.3%, 2.2%, 2.8%, 56.5%, and 36.2%, respectively. Averaged over the whole period, only 3.8% of urban households have a car, however, by 2009, it was 11%. About 90% of households have a washing machine and refrigerator, while 28% have two or more TV sets. 29% have only one air conditioner, while 16% have two or more.

Fig. 20.1 shows the average shares of the five bundles in the first stage over the sample period 1992−2009 when per-capita GDP rose at 9.5% per year. There is a big fall in the share for consumer goods which include food, and an offsetting rise in the services (including housing). Given the big price gap in housing between small and large cities, there is a distinct pattern of shares between regions, with bigger shares

---

[4] This subsample comes from the China Data Center (CDC), Tsinghua University, and covers these provinces: Beijing, Liaoning, Zhejiang, Anhui, Hubei, Guangdong, Sichuan, Shaanxi, and Gansu.

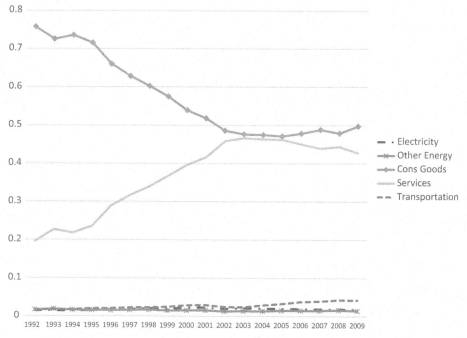

FIGURE 20.1 Expenditure shares of households in large cities, 1992–2009.

for housing in the big cities. The share for transportation rises as gasoline expenditures rise with incomes in both types of cities while the share of OHE is essentially flat. The share for electricity rose between 1992 and 2000 and then flattened out.

20.2.2.1 Prices

The UHIES records the RMB expenditures on hundreds of items, but quantities are only given for certain types of food, clothing, durable goods, and energy. We supplemented the unit values derived from these UHIES data with data from National Development and Reform Commission (NDRC) surveys of prices in many cities, from the provincial Development Research Center's (DRC's) and from companies. This gives us the cross-section of prices across cities for 2009. We find that there is a distinct difference in price levels between small and large cities and thus construct separate indices for

them. With this division between large versus small cities, our nine provinces result in 17 distinct regions (Beijing is not divided), and we aggregate the detailed commodities to our five price bundles, p_{irt}, $i = 1, 2, ..., 5$. We then extrapolate these five prices for each of the 17 regions back to 1992 using regional CPIs.

The prices in large cities are higher relative to those in small cities for all bundles except for transportation where the small-city average is a few percentage points higher. Services (including housing) price rose rapidly during 1992–2001 but then decelerated. The price of the consumer goods bundle, which includes food, rose rapidly in the 1990s due to food inflation, but then fell with the falling prices of electronic equipment. The price of OHE rose the most of these five bundles, while electricity prices were flat after the late 1990s.

We exploit the big differences in price levels between large and small cities within each province and between provinces to help identify price elasticities. Hu et al. (2018) show how the share versus price graphs differ by province where some exhibit a positive slope indicating price-inelastic demand, while others have a negative slope showing very elastic responses. If one were to ignore the provincial patterns then one would be estimating a flat curve or a unit price elasticity.

20.2.2.2 Estimation results

Hu et al. (2018), Appendix, give the detailed estimates of the parameters in Eqs. (20.12) and (20.13). We derive the price and income elasticities from these estimates using Eqs. (20.6) and (20.7). The elasticities are calculated for the reference household in 2005: household size 3, with child, no aged member, East, and head of household is male, aged 35–55, secondary school educated, and employed in the private sector.

These elasticities for the top tier are given in Table 20.1. The expenditure (income) elasticities are estimated with very small standard errors; consumer goods is slightly income inelastic (0.95) since it is a mix of inelastic food and more elastic electronic goods; services, including housing, is income elastic (1.1). Electricity and OHE have low-income elasticities, while transportation, which consists of motor fuels, daily passenger fares, and holiday travel, is elastic.

All the price elasticities are well estimated with small standard errors. The own-price (uncompensated) elasticity is negative for all goods; −0.49 for electricity and −0.35 for OHE, while transportation is the most price elastic with −0.71.

For the second stage, the share of motor fuels is a function of the prices of fuel and transportation services. The price coefficient is significantly negative (−0.23) and the demographic terms are almost all significant at the 5% level. The own-price (uncompensated) elasticity for fuels is −0.26. Since we have to impose homotheticity in the second stage, the income elasticity is inherited from the stage one value for total transportation, 1.22.

20.3 Carbon policy assessment methodology

The government's current carbon policy is an ETS which is now in a pilot phase in five major cities and two provinces. A national ETS is being set

TABLE 20.1 Price and income elasticities (standard error in parenthesis).

Good	Uncompensated price elasticity	Compensated price elasticity	Expenditure elasticity
Electricity	−0.491	−0.474	0.690
	(0.021)	(0.023)	(0.002)
Other home energy	−0.348	−0.337	0.492
	(0.015)	(0.004)	(0.001)
Transportation	−0.707	−0.671	1.225
	(0.020)	(0.008)	(0.002)
Consumer goods	−0.447	0.067	0.952
	(0.019)	(0.054)	(0.001)
Service and housing	−0.550	−0.119	1.100
	(0.016)	(0.011)	(0.002)

Reference household: 35–55, Male, Private sector, Secondary School, Has child, No aged, Size 3, East, in 2005.

up for the electricity sector with the aim of actual trading beginning in 2020. The ETS proposed is complicated and instead we consider a simple national tax on carbon emissions. A China national tax has been discussed and analyzed by many authors as noted in the Introduction, but these used simpler consumer demand functions. In this section, we describe the main points of our method to simulate the impact of a carbon tax.

20.3.1 Consumption demand

In Cao et al. (2013), we used a CGE model with a simple Cobb–Douglas consumption function. Such a function has unit income elasticities and if used as is, would give projections of consumption shares that are not in accord with the history shown in Fig. 20.1. To avoid that, we changed the share parameters based on consumption patterns observed in rich countries. Here we simulate the impact of a carbon tax using an updated version of our China economic growth model which includes the two-stage demand function described in Section 20.2 above in place of the Cobb–Douglas version.

The first step is to derive an aggregate consumer demand function from the household demand in Eq. (20.3) following Jorgenson et al. (1988). The national share demand vector, w_t, is given by summing over all households:

described in Cao et al. (2018b), Section 4, which projects consumption patterns using a similar translog consumption function but for food, consumption goods, services, and housing. Recall that households are distinguished by demographic characteristics including age, education, and size of household; there are a total of 1296 types of households counting all combinations. The $\sum M_k A_k / \sum M_k$ distribution term in Eq. (20.14) gives the share of national expenditures going to each of those 1296 types. We replace that term with one derived from a population projection model that gives the age and education distribution of the population:

$$
w_t = \frac{\sum\limits_k M_k w_k}{\sum\limits_k M_k} = \frac{1}{D(p_t)} \left[\alpha + B \ln p_t - B_M \right.
$$

$$
\left. \left(\xi_t^d + \ln M_t \right) + B_{pA} \xi_t^L \right]
$$

(20.15)

where $M_t = \sum\limits_{K=1}^{1296} n_{Kt} M_{Kt}$, and n_{Kt} is the number of households of type K.

The construction of the ξ_t^d and ξ_t^L distribution terms is given in detail in Cao et al. (2018b), Section 4. We assume that the relative expenditures of household type k1 and k2 are fixed at base year ratios (i.e. M_{Kt}/M_t is constant). The projection of n_{Kt} is linked to population projections

$$
w_t = \frac{\sum\limits_k M_k w_k}{\sum\limits_k M_k} = \frac{1}{D(p_t)} \left[\alpha + B \ln p_t - B_M \frac{\sum M_{kt} \ln M_{kt}}{M_t} + B_{pA} \frac{\sum M_{kt} A_{kt}}{M_t} \right]
$$

(20.14)

$$
M_t = \sum M_{kt}
$$

To implement this function for a projection model, we need to replace the distribution of M_k's observed in the sample period with external projections. We do this using the procedure

where we assume no further changes in the distribution of location and household size. Fig. 20.2 gives the projected share of national expenditures by the different age and education of head of household types. Under our assumption of fixed relative expenditures, the expenditure

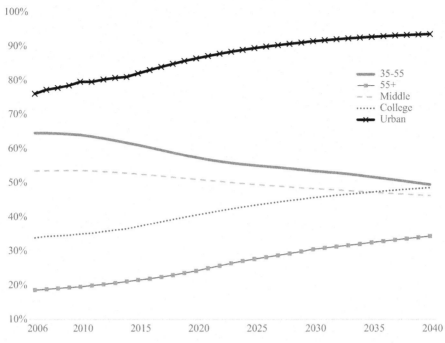

FIGURE 20.2   Projection of expenditure shares by household type.

share of households with head over age 55 is projected to rise from 18.9% in 2006 to 34.4% in 2040, while that of households with a college-educated head rises from 34.0% to 48.6%.

The second step to implement an aggregate demand function in a CGE model from our econometric estimates is to recognize that we have only an urban sample but need to use it for the national economy. We have to use the estimated price elasticities but calibrate the α's to match the national shares of consumption in the two tiers. In recent years, the urban component dominates the national total and the adjustment is small; the electricity share among urban households in 2014 is 1.89% compared to the national share of 1.79%, OHE is 1.68% versus 1.40%, transportation is 3.63% versus 3.74%.

20.3.1.1 Cross-section versus time-series estimates of elasticities and projections

There is a complication about long-term baseline projections that confront model builders that we should note here. Estimates of elasticities using a large cross-section of households in a particular year, or repeated cross-sections like ours, are generated by comparing the behavior of poor and rich households. These income elasticities may differ from those derived by observing an average household over time. If one assumes that the average household changes its consumption patterns as it gets richer over time like the change between poor and rich in the base year, then one might overstate the changes.[5]

---

[5] Yu et al. (2003) discuss one aspect of the difficulties of projecting demand—the use of simple functional forms and the difficulty of calibrating elasticities in CGE models.

The projections we make here illustrate some of these difficulties. We first simulated our model out to 2040 using the parameters estimated with our repeated cross-sections. This results in the electricity share falling from 1.8% in the base year 2014 to 0.1% by 2030 and the OHE falling to zero. This is clearly untenable, and we recalibrated the income coefficient so that the shares approach the United States. 2015 shares by 2040 as explained in the next subsection. That is, we gradually change the B_{Mi}'s each year toward zero, so that the shares by 2040 are equal to the targets, observing the $\iota'B_M = 0$ constraint every period.

20.3.1.2 Consumption subtiers and commodity classification

The household demand model given in Section 20.2 covers the five bundles in the top tier and the allocation of transportation to motor fuels and transportation services in the second tier. We next allocate these bundles to 27 detailed consumption items ranging from food to health care. This is done using exogenous shares, that is using a Cobb—Douglas function. A major task confronting modelers, related to the identification of appropriate income elasticities just noted, is the projection of these shares for a rapidly growing economy. While the income effects are well known for particular items, there is not a systematic estimate of income elasticities for all products and countries. We take a simple approach and assume that the China shares will converge gradually to the shares observed in the recent US Personal Consumption Expenditures data.[6] We set the China shares in 2040 to equal the US shares observed for 2015. In the base case projection shown in Table 20.2, GDP per capita in 2040 is 3.2 times that in 2014 or $27,000 in 2005 purchasing power parity (PPP)-adjusted dollars.

An issue not often discussed in descriptions of CGE modelers is the link between commodity classifications used in household surveys and classifications used in input—output (IO) accounts. Consumption expenditures recorded in the surveys are at purchasers' prices that include trade and transportation margins whereas IO accounts are at factory gate values. That is, the yuan paid for coal by households is shared by the coal mining, trade, transportation, and other service industries. We thus have to allocate our 27 detailed consumption items to the 33 IO commodities identified in the model. The official China IO tables do not provide such a link but the US IO benchmark tables include a Personal Consumption Expenditures Bridge Table[7], and we use the 2002 US table as a starting point to estimate a bridge for our China 2014 consumption and IO data. This gives us a link to relate the consumption prices in Eq. (20.15) to the prices in the IO model.

20.3.1.3 Welfare

The utility function (20.1) gives the welfare of household k as a function of the demographic indicators. Jorgenson and Slesnick (1984) introduces household equivalent indexes to allow a comparison of expenditures required for two different types of households (say size 2 vs. size 3) to reach the same level of utility. The equivalent index (m_0) is a function of prices, the parameters of Eq. (20.1) and the demographic in-

---

[6] The US Personal Consumption Expenditures are given in the National Accounts published by the US Bureau of Economic Analysis (Table 2.5.5) which are available at https://apps.bea.gov/iTable/index_nipa.cfm.

[7] The 2002 US benchmark input—output accounts, including the bridge tables, are given in the *Survey of Current Business*, October 2007 which is available at https://apps.bea.gov/scb/.

TABLE 20.2   Base case projection.

Variable	2017	2020	2030	2017-30 growth rate
Population (million)	1387	1403	1416	0.16%
Effective labor supply (bil. 2014 yuan)	27,624	27,433	25,527	−0.61%
GDP (billion 2014 yuan)	77,419	93,066	151,414	5.30%
Consumption/GDP	0.42	0.46	0.53	
Energy use (million tons sce*)	4504	4776	5564	1.64%
Coal use (million tons)	4171	4212	4745	1.00%
Oil use (million tons)	554	608	707	1.90%
Gas use (million cubic meters)	236,742	295,560	474,327	5.49%
Electricity use (TWh)	6060	6520	7580	1.74%
CO_2 emissions (fossil fuel, million tons)	9391	9740	11,293	1.43%
CO_2 emissions (total, million tons)	11,044	11,435	12,983	1.25%
Carbon intensity (kg CO_2/yuan)	0.143	0.123	0.086	−3.84%
Primary PM emissions (mil tons)	17.6	17.9	16.7	−0.42%
SO_2 emissions (mil tons)	19.8	19.6	18.7	−0.44%
NOx emissions (mil tons)	20.2	19.5	17.4	−1.11%
GDP per capita (2014 yuan)	55,812	66,341	106,966	
GDP per capita; PPP US$2005	9872	11,734	18,920	

GDP, gross domestic product; *PM*, particulate matter; *PPP*, purchasing power parity.
Note: sce denotes "standard coal equivalent."

dicators, and using it, the utility of household of type k may be rewritten as:

$$\ln V_k = \ln p'\alpha + \frac{1}{2}\ln p'B \ln p$$
$$- D(p)\ln[M_k / m_0(p, A_k)]$$

(20.16)

The money metric of this utility level is given by the expenditure function, $M(p,V)$, which is derived as:

$$\ln M_k = \frac{1}{D(p)}\left[\ln p'\alpha + \frac{1}{2}\ln p'B \ln p - \ln V_k\right]$$
$$+ \ln m_0(p, A_k)$$

(20.17)

We have about 17,000 observations in 2009, and we compute (20.17) for each of them, separately for the base case and policy cases. The households are cross-classified by age, education, gender of head, household size and location, etc. and instead of reporting the result for each of these cells, we give the welfare effects for the component categories of the major groups: location, household size, and income quintiles. The money metric for the group welfare effect is a formula like (20.17) but with V_k replaced by group average welfare and m_0 replaced by the sum of all household equivalents in that group.

TABLE 20.3 The effects of carbon taxes to achieve official CO_2-intensity goals.

Variable	Base case 2020	2020 (% change)		Base case 2030	2030 (% change)	
		62.5% case	65% case		62.5% case	65% case
GDP (billion yuan 2014)	93,100	−0.006	−0.104	151,400	−0.13	−0.48
Consumption (bil yuan 2014)	41,100	−0.006	−0.012	76,000	−0.13	−0.29
Investment (bil yuan 2014)	39,600	−0.011	−0.022	57,100	−0.17	−0.37
Government consumption (bil yuan 2014)	10,300	0.000	0.000	13,200	0.00	0.00
Energy use (million tons of sce)	4780	−0.86	−1.63	5560	−6.8	−12.2
Coal use (million tons)	4210	−1.26	−2.40	4740	−10.0	−17.9
Oil use (million tons)	608	−0.19	−0.37	707	−1.9	−3.8
Gas use (billion cubic meters)	295,600	−0.53	−1.02	474,300	−6.0	−11.4
Electricity (billion kWh)	6520	−0.32	−0.61	7580	−2.7	−5.1
CO_2 emissions (inc cement; mil tons)	11,400	−0.95	−1.80	13,000	−7.7	−13.9
Primary PM emissions (mil tons)	17.86	−0.46	−0.87	16.7	−3.6	−6.7
SO_2 emissions (mil tons)	19.63	−0.84	−1.60	18.7	−6.4	−11.7
NOx emissions (mil tons)	19.51	−0.63	−1.21	17.4	−4.6	−8.4
Emission permit price (Y/ton CO_2)		9.5	18.4		158	323
Permit value and carbon taxes as %total revenue		0.30%	0.57%		1.9%	3.7%

20.3.2 Economic-energy model

We now turn to the rest of the economic-energy growth model of China that we use. Our model identifies 33 sectors including six energy-related sectors (see Table 20.4 for the list of sectors). Output growth is driven by capital accumulation, population growth, and TFP growth. An earlier version of the model is described in Nielsen and Ho (2013); Appendix A, and we summarize the key features of the current version here with more information in the Appendix.

The model is a dynamic recursive one where an exogenous savings rate determines investment. Enterprises pay value-added tax (VAT) and taxes on capital income and retain part of the profits for investment, resulting in a "dividend payout" rate that is smaller than 1. A change in tax rates due to a carbon policy would thus affect the after-tax income and investment. The GDP growth rate in the base case is thus affected by the savings rate, the dividend rate, the TFP growth rate, and the growth of effective labor. The parameters for these growth factors are discussed in the Appendix and given in Table 20.A1.

The main variables of the base case path are given in Table 20.2. GDP is projected to grow at 6.5% during 2014−20, then decelerating to 5.0% in 2020-30[8]. Energy consumption is

---

[8] This is consistent with the deceleration observed during 2010−16 and with the government target of 6.5% growth for the 13th Five-Year Plan. These growth projections are also similar to those in World Bank-DRC-PRC (2013) and IEA (2014).

TABLE 20.4 Industry effects of carbon taxes in 2030 (% change from base case).

Scenario	62.5% case		65% case	
	Change in price	Change in quantity	Change in price	Change in quantity
Agriculture	0.31	0.03	0.60	0.06
Coal mining	18.94	−8.10	38.60	−14.98
Crude petroleum mining	3.81	−0.28	7.80	−0.75
Natural gas mining	7.15	−0.85	14.57	−1.98
Nonenergy mining	0.64	−1.55	1.27	−3.01
Food products, tobacco	0.12	0.23	0.26	0.42
Textile goods	0.50	0.43	1.00	0.80
Apparel, leather	0.19	1.18	0.39	2.28
Sawmills and furniture	0.32	0.45	0.64	0.83
Paper products, printing	0.47	−0.16	0.95	−0.35
Petroleum refining, coking	2.90	−2.30	5.89	−4.52
Chemical	0.98	−1.61	1.96	−3.14
Nonmetal mineral products	1.44	−1.54	2.85	−3.00
Metals smelting	1.56	−2.63	3.07	−5.02
Metal products	0.95	−1.76	1.88	−3.36
Machinery and equipment	0.70	−1.04	1.38	−2.01
Transport equipment	0.47	−0.04	0.93	−0.11
Electrical machinery	0.70	−1.24	1.38	−2.39
Electronic and telecom. equip	0.55	−0.54	1.09	−0.97
Water services	0.47	−0.54	0.93	−1.07
Other manufacturing	0.67	−1.57	1.31	−3.00
Electricity, steam, hot water	4.11	−2.66	8.15	−5.10
Gas production and supply	4.92	−2.77	9.86	−5.39
Construction	0.38	−0.08	0.77	−0.21
Transportation	0.45	−0.48	0.91	−0.97
Communications	0.12	0.11	0.25	0.19
Trade	−0.30	0.63	−0.54	1.19
Accommodation and food	0.01	0.18	0.04	0.33
Finance and insurance	−0.13	0.21	−0.23	0.39
Real estate	0.05	0.12	0.11	0.20

TABLE 20.4 Industry effects of carbon taxes in 2030 (% change from base case).—cont'd

Scenario	62.5% case		65% case	
	Change in price	Change in quantity	Change in price	Change in quantity
Business services	0.17	0.03	0.35	0.04
Other services	0.09	0.04	0.18	0.07
Public administration	0.10	0.02	0.21	0.05

calibrated to the projections in IEA (2016) and total energy use grows at 1.6% during 2017-30 with a substantial switch from coal to oil, gas, and renewables. With this fall in coal use, total CO_2 emissions only grow at 1.4% per year during 2017—30.

The projection of the consumption shares is plotted in Fig. 20.3. Recall that these are the results of adjusting the income elasticities in the first-stage function (20.15) every year to avoid untenably small values and to target the 2040 shares at recent US values. The share for consumer goods continues to fall from 45% in 2014 to 37% in 2030 while services rise to 56%. The share of electricity falls from 1.8% to 1.5%, while other home energy fall from 1.4% to 1.1%. Motor fuels, given by the second-stage demand function, rise from 1.3% to 1.6% in 2040, while transportation fares fall from 1.9% to 1.2%.

We assume competitive markets and production in each industry are represented by a constant returns-to-scale function that implies zero profits. That is, we assume that there is no price regulation on output, or equivalently, assume that regulated prices are changed to reflect costs. Our model distinguishes between industry and commodity; an industry has a production function that uses various commodity inputs, and

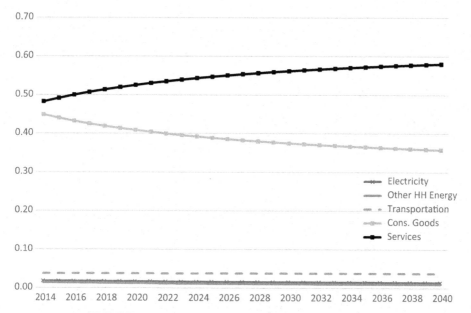

FIGURE 20.3 Projection of consumption shares in base case.

each industry may "make" or "supply" more than one commodity (e.g. the primary metals industry may also make "coking products"). The relationships are given by endogenous Use and Make Matrices.

20.3.3 Implementing CO_2 policies in economic model

Our procedure is to first simulate a base case path where there are no carbon taxes and only the existing taxes on output, value-added, profits, labor income, profits, and imports. We then introduce a CO_2 tax by taxing all fossil fuels in proportion to the CO_2 emission intensity and taxing the process emissions from cement production. Other greenhouse gases are ignored here.

The price paid by industry j for fuel input i in year t is denoted by PB_{ijt} (B for buying) and is equal to the total supply price (PS) plus the carbon tax, t_{it}^{CO2}:

$$PB_{ijt} = PS_{it} + t_{it}^{CO2} \ \rho_{ij}^{cmb}$$

$$i = \{\text{coal mining, oil mining, gas mining}\}$$
$$(20.18)$$

$$t_{it}^{CO2} = tx_{CO2,t}^{u} XP_{i}^{CO2} \qquad (20.19)$$

The supply price, PS_{it}, is the aggregate of the domestically produced commodity and the imported variety. This includes the domestic sales tax and tariffs. The tax per unit of fuel i is given by the carbon tax rate $tx_{CO2,t}^{u}$ (¥ per ton of CO_2) multiplied by XP_{i}^{CO2}, the emission coefficient (tons of CO_2 per unit of i). The unit of measurement of industry or commodity output is billion 2014 yuan. The carbon tax is multiplied by a combustion ratio, ρ_{ij}^{cmb}, which is less than one

for cases such as the use of oil as feedstocks in the chemicals industry. It is one in most cases.

Households also pay the carbon tax on their fossil fuel purchases (denoted by a C superscript to represent consumption):

$$P_{it}^{C,IO} = \left(1 + t_{it}^{c}\right) PS_{it} + t_{i,hh,t}^{CO2} \qquad (20.20)$$

China has a large nonmetallic mineral (NMM) products sector which includes cement. The production process for cement generates a lot of CO_2 beyond those generated from fuel burning. We thus set the purchaser price for NMM as the sum of the seller price (PI_j) plus the regular sales taxes (t_j^t) and the process CO_2 tax:

$$PI_j^t = \left(1 + t_j^t\right) PI_j + t_j^{xpu}$$
$$j = \text{Nonmetallic Mineral Products} \qquad (20.21)$$

$$t_j^{xpu} = tx_{CO2}^{u} \ XP_j^{proCO2}$$

The process tax is given by the carbon tax rate multiplied by the process emission coefficient XP_j^{proCO2} (tons of process CO_2 per unit of output j).

Total national CO_2 emissions is thus the sum of primary emissions and process emissions:

$$EM_t^{CO2} = \sum_j \sum_{i \in fossil} \rho_{ij}^{cmb} XP_{it}^{CO2} A_{ijt}$$
$$+ XP_{NMM}^{proCO2} QI_{NMM,t} \qquad (20.22)$$

where A_{ijt} is the quantity of input i in industry j, and QI_{jt} is the quantity of industry output.

The carbon tax will raise new revenues for the government. The issue of how different methods of revenue recycling affect overall welfare costs of environmental policies and have different distribution effects is discussed in a large literature.[9] Here we maintain fiscal neutrality by cutting all existing taxes, for example, the VAT tax rate (t_t^V)

---

[9] Fawcett et al. (2018) introduces the studies of many models in a special issue of Climate Change Economics devoted to this topic. Study by Jorgenson et al. (2011) is a contribution to a special issue devoted to distributional impacts of carbon policies.

and capital income tax rate (t_t^K) are cut from base case rates by a tax scaling factor $\lambda_t^{taxscale}$:

$$t_t^V = \lambda_t^{taxscale} t_{t;Base}^V; \quad t_t^K = \lambda_t^{taxscale} t_{t;Base}^K \quad (20.23)$$

This tax cut factor is determined endogenously to maintain "real revenue neutrality" by requiring aggregate government purchases to equal the base case levels in real terms in each period[10]. Keeping the level of public goods unchanged allow us to focus on the changes in private consumption and investment due to the carbon price, simplifying the welfare comparisons.

20.4 The impact of a carbon tax

The discussions of a carbon tax for China have not arrived at a consensus of the level of tax that the government could likely consider. The announced plans for the national ETS so far have also not included a specific target for the cap. What we have are the government CO_2-intensity goals in the 13th five-year plan for 2016−20 and the intensity goal in the NDC submitted in 2016 to the United Nations Framework Convention on Climate Change. That goal is to cut the CO_2-GDP intensity by 60−65% by 2030 compared to 2005 levels. The 10.5 billion tons of CO_2 emitted in 2014 is a 27% reduction in intensity from 2005 (Janssens-Maenhout et al., 2017). In the base case shown in Table 20.2 the intensity falls from 0.143 kg CO_2/¥ in 2017 to 0.086 in 2030, a 59.4% reduction from 2005 levels.

We thus chose two carbon price paths to illustrate the effects simulated by our model; the first meets the midpoint of the NDC target—a 62.5% reduction in CO_2-GDP intensity by 2030 starting from the actual fuel consumption in our 2014 base year, and the second price path meets the 65% target. We chose a linear increase in the carbon tax level start from 2020 and iterated on a path of carbon tax rates (¥ per ton of CO_2) until we reach that targeted 62.5% or 65% reduction in the 2030 CO_2-GDP ratio (note that both emissions and GDP are endogenous). For the 62.5% reduction, the path turns out to start from 10 ¥/ton in 2020 and rise to 160¥ in 2030 (US$24), while the 65% reduction requires a price of 320¥ in 2030.

The impact of this carbon tax path on the main economic and energy variables is given in Table 20.3; we report the percent change in the key variables between the base case and policy cases for 2020 and 2030. The key advantage of a market instrument like a carbon price, as opposed to, say, a regulation on production standards, is the impact on prices to encourage conservation of all carbon-intensive products. We report the impact on industry prices and output in 2030 in Table 20.4 and plot the change in prices for 2020 and 2030 in Fig. 20.4 for the 62.5% case.

We first focus on the 62.5% intensity reduction case. The carbon tax results in much higher prices for coal, +2.2% in the first year and +19% by 2030, encouraging all industries and households to reduce coal use. This leads to a reduction in the domestic output (and total use) of coal, −1.2% in 2020 and −8.1% in 2030. Oil mining prices rise by 3.8% by 2030 and gas mining prices by 7.1%. The higher cost of fuels raises the price of electricity by 0.5% in the first year and by 4.1% in 2030 (note that this is the price of delivered electricity, the generator price rises by much more).

The higher cost of fossil fuels and electricity causes the energy-intensive industries to raise their prices and output to fall by more than the changes in the less-energy-intensive sectors. Electricity output falls by 2.7% by 2030, NMM products, metals smelting, and chemicals fall by 1.5%, 2.6%, and 1.6%, respectively, while the less carbon-intensive manufacturing

---

[10] This targeting of real purchases is explained in equation (A62) in the Model Appendix (Cao and Ho, 2017).

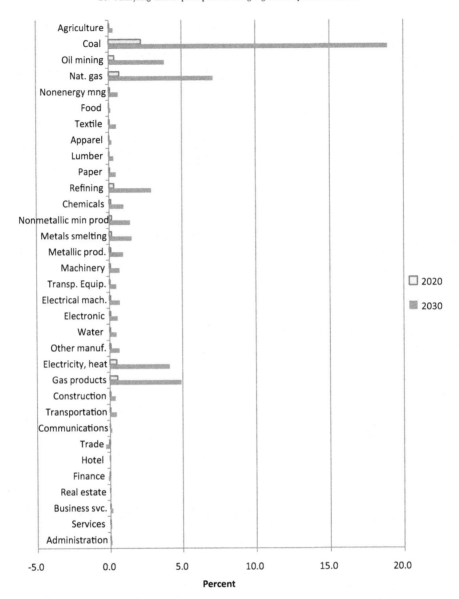

FIGURE 20.4 Impact of carbon taxes on industry output prices; 62.5% reduction case.

sectors—food, electronic equipment, transportation equipment—fall by less than 0.6%. Oil faces a moderate carbon tax and refined products price rise by 2.9% by 2030; this leads to an increase in transportation services price of 0.45% and a reduction in output of 0.48%.

The changes in industry output are caused by the changes in prices and by the changes in the composition of final demand. Recall that the new carbon tax revenues are recycled back by cutting existing taxes, taxes that are dominated by the VAT, and capital income tax. These recycled taxes come to about 2.1% of total government revenues. The biggest beneficiary of the tax cut is enterprises which distribute part of their profits as "dividends," and use the retained earnings for investment. The distribution of value added in China is tilted more toward capital income compared to the rich market economies, the share of GDP at factor cost going to capital (including land) income being over 50% in 2014 compared to 44% for the United States.[11] That is, labor income has a smaller weight in China's GDP compared to the richer countries. Households do get a cut in their labor income tax and an increase in dividends, but their increase in nominal income is smaller than the increase in enterprise retained earnings. The tax recycling thus results in a small shift in nominal expenditures away from consumption to investment in the main categories of final demand (GDP is the sum of consumption, investment, government, and exports less imports).

Investment goods are dominated by construction, machinery, electrical equipment, and transportation equipment, which in turn means a demand for metals and cement (NMM products). The output effects are thus complicated; on one hand the energy-intensive goods like metals and NMM products face higher costs, but on the other hand they enjoy a small shift in demand from consumption to investment. The net effect of aggregate consumption and investment is given in Table 20.3. In the first year, real GDP and consumption fall by a tiny 0.01%, while real investment falls by a bit more. This lower investment, however, cumulates into a smaller capital stock over time. Thus by 2030, there is the same number of workers as in the base case, but the capital stock is 0.1% smaller. This reduction in factor supplies and the distortion of the carbon tax leads to GDP being

0.13% smaller in 2030 and aggregate investment being 0.17% lower. The impact on GDP over time is plotted in Fig. 20.5 and shows the rising gap with the base case GDP.

The composition of household consumption is significantly altered by the direct price effects of the carbon tax and the indirect effects of the cuts in other taxes. The income effect is small, and the main effect is through prices. First recall that in the discussion of consumption classifications in Section 20.3.1, we noted how the first-stage demands for electricity, OHE, transportation, consumer goods, and services bundles are allocated to the detailed consumption items valued at purchaser's prices that include trade and other margins. These are then bridged to the commodity classification in the IO accounts valued at factory gate prices. The changes in energy consumption for both classifications are given in Table 20.5 for 2030 to illustrate the importance of keeping these distinct concepts clear. The change in the main energy purchases at the IO commodity classification is plotted in Fig. 20.6 for 2020-30 (percent change from the base case).

The reduction in real consumption of OHE is 1.5% in 2030 and that is composed of a reduction in coal and heating by 1.0% and gas by 1.7% in the consumption classification. The reduction in total transportation demand is 0.58% and that is composed of motor fuels (−0.43%), vehicle maintenance (−0.46%), and transportation services (−0.58%). These reductions are translated to changes in the IO classifications for petroleum refining and cooking products of −1.9%, coal −14%, and gas −2.7%. In the IO accounts, transportation services demand falls by 0.39% and electricity and hot water by 2.8%.

The rising path of carbon prices generates a steady reduction in the use of household

---

[11] The National Accounts in both countries do not make estimates to the contribution of capital by the self-employed, noncorporate entities. We make a simple estimate for land rent in China, and the US value-added estimates, including noncorporate capital, are taken from Jorgenson et al. (2019).

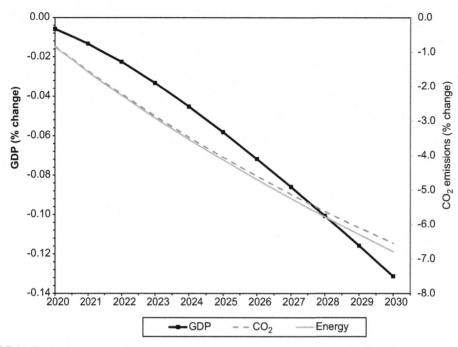

FIGURE 20.5   Carbon tax impact on gross domestic product (GDP), energy, and emissions; 62.5% reduction case.

energy. From Fig. 20.5 (using the IO classifications), we see that household electricity consumption is reduced by only 0.34% in the first year, but with the lower GDP (and household incomes) and much higher electricity prices in 2030, it is then reduced by 2.9%. The change in coal consumption rises from −1.9% to −14% in 2030.

Emissions of CO_2 are linked to the physical units of coal, oil, and gas in tons or cubic meters. This is best linked to the factory gate measures of the output of coal, oil, and gas. Given our discussion of the two distinct concepts of consumption measures, we emphasize that it is important to measure emissions in a way that is closest to the physical units; the changes in the constant dollar quantities of motor fuels as classified in the consumption expenditure accounts may understate the changes in physical units due to the inclusion of margins which vary over time.

The changes in industry output and fuel use lead to significant changes in emissions of local pollutants and CO_2. As shown in Table 20.3, coal use falls by 10% in 2030 and that is the major contributor to a reduction in primary particulate matter (PM) of 3.6% and a reduction in sulfur dioxide of 6.4%. The reduction in PM is smaller than the change in coal use because there is a large emission of PM from industrial processes, and the reduction of, say, NMM products is only 1.5%. There is thus a substantial cobenefit in the effort to reduce CO_2 emissions—a major reduction in local air pollution. The reduction in oil use is 1.9% and that contributes to a total CO_2 reduction of 7.7% in 2030. In terms of energy (measured as tons of standard coal equivalent in the China accounts), the reduction is only 6.8% in 2030 due to the shift from coal to oil and gas. The change in energy use and CO_2 emissions over time is also plotted in Fig. 20.5 (scale

TABLE 20.5 Effect of carbon tax on household energy consumption in 2030; 62.5% case (% change from base case).

Consumption commodity bundles (including trade and other margins)	
Electricity	−2.0
Other home energy	−1.5
Coal and heating	−1.0
Gas	−1.7
Transportation	−0.58
Motor fuels	−0.43
Vehicle maintenance	−0.46
Transportation services	−0.58
Input−output commodity at factory gate prices	
Coal	−14.1
Petroleum refining and coking	−1.9
Electricity and hot water	−2.8
Gas utilities	−2.7
Transportation services	−0.39

on the right-hand axis). We see that the gap between the policy path and the base case is rising over time but at a diminishing rate, unlike the GDP gap that is accelerating due to the investment effect.

20.4.1 Distributional effects

The equivalent variation of the policy effect is given by first evaluating the expenditure function (20.17) for the base case and the policy case, both using the base case prices, and then taking the difference between them. We report the effects for different income quintiles, regions, and household sizes in Table 20.6. The difference in effects among the different demographic groups is small. This is due to two

reasons, first, the energy shares are very small, and second, there are two opposing effects of the higher energy prices. Electricity and OHE are income inelastic, but transportation is income elastic; the higher energy prices hurt the poorer groups more for their use of electricity and OHE, whereas they hurt the richer groups more for their transportation demand. The result is that there is not a smooth progressive or regressive effect among the five income quintiles; in the 62.5% case, the fourth quintile suffers the least and the second quintile, the most. The East region has the highest shares of electricity, OHE, and transportation in consumption and suffers the largest loss in welfare. The size 4 + households have the highest electricity and home energy shares while the size 1-2 households have the highest transportation shares, and these two groups have bigger welfare losses than the size 3 households.

20.4.2 The 65% intensity reduction case

We also considered an alternative path of higher carbon taxes that would be required to hit the upper end of the CO_2-GDP intensity goal of the government, a 65% reduction in 2030 compared to 2005 levels. The main results are also given in Tables 20.3 and 20.4. To achieve this target, we simulated a path that rises from 18¥ per ton of CO_2 in 2020 to 320¥ (about $47), slightly more than double the taxes in the 62.5% case.

The effects on industry prices and output also about doubled. The reduction in coal output in 2030 is 15% instead of the 8.1% in the less ambitious case. GDP in 2030 is lower by 0.48% compared to 0.13%. The industry effects are not linear depending on the elasticities of substitution. The reduction of coal use is a bit less than doubled while the reduction in oil use is doubled (−3.8% vs. −1.9%). This means that

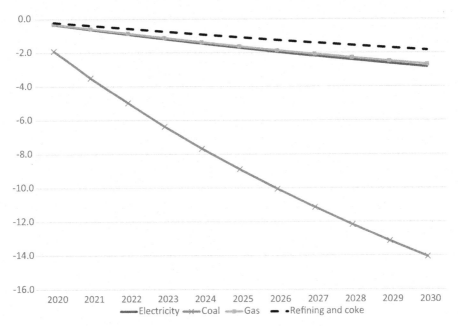

FIGURE 20.6   Effect of carbon tax on household energy use; 62.5% case (% reduction from base case).

the reduction in local pollutants is less than doubled. The more than proportionate reduction in GDP indicates the steepness of the marginal cost curve for emission reduction. The ranking of distributional impacts is the same as that in the 62.5% case.

20.5 Conclusion

The Special Report issued by the Intergovernmental Panel on Climate Change in October 2018 noted the immense challenges of limiting global warming to 1.5C above preindustrial levels.[12] The government of China has announced ambitious targets as part of the Paris Agreement—reducing the carbon intensity of GDP by 60%–65% by 2030 compared to 2005 levels. Given the expected continued growth of GDP at more than 5% per year, achieving this target would still very likely mean rising CO_2 emissions from China up to 2030. The government is set to introduce a national emissions trading system (ETS), but implementation difficulties have delayed the program and limited its scope as discussed in Cao et al. (2018b). Many analysts have argued for considering a carbon tax that would cover the entire economy and avoid putting the burden on only a limited set of industries as under the ETS.

We examine how a carbon tax could meet the 60%–65% intensity reduction goal using an economic-energy model of China. We incorporated an econometric model of household demand that explicitly accounts for electricity, household energy, and transportation. That consumption function is based on the pioneering work of Jorgenson and Slesnick and is estimated over repeated cross-sections of household

---

[12] The Summary for Policymakers is available at https://www.ipcc.ch/news_and_events/pr_181008_P48_spm. shtml, which also provides a link to the full IPCC report.

TABLE 20.6 Impact of carbon taxes on different household groups; equivalent variation in 2030 (% change in money measure of welfare from base case).

Nation	62.5% case	65% case
Income groups		
First quintile	−0.30922	−0.65117
Second quintile	−0.30931	−0.65124
Third quintile	−0.30923	−0.65120
Fourth quintile	−0.30920	−0.65116
Fifth quintile	−0.30928	−0.65124
Region		
East	−0.30926	−0.65122
Central	−0.30922	−0.65125
West	−0.30918	−0.65121
Household size (households with children)		
1–2	−0.30924	−0.65120
3	−0.30921	−0.65119
4+	−0.30924	−0.65112

consumption data (1992−2009), giving good estimates of price and income elasticities. The consumption model distinguishes households by demographic characteristics allowing us to discuss the distributional impacts of policies.

Our simulations indicate that a tax that rises to 160 yuan (about US$25) per ton of CO_2 by 2030 would be sufficient to meet midpoint of that goal. Such a tax would reduce coal use by 10% in 2030 and reduce GDP by a modest 0.1% when the carbon tax revenues are recycled by reducing existing taxes. Household electricity use falls by 3% and transportation demand falls by 0.4%. The reduction in fossil fuel use will also reduce significantly the emissions of local pollutants that cause the very poor air quality in China—sulfur dioxide, nitrogen oxides, and PM.

Our use of a general equilibrium model that is based in part on econometrically estimated functions is in the tradition strongly emphasized by Jorgenson. The value of having a flexible consumption function in such simulation models is clear—it allows a richer set of substitution possibilities and the use of empirically grounded income elasticities. We also highlighted Jorgenson's significant contribution to welfare measurement that is tied to using a tractable model that accounts for heterogeneity among households. Jorgenson's lifetime contribution to productivity measurement and modeling is substantial and we hope is obvious in our application here.

Appendix. Economic-energy growth model of China

An economic growth model of China is used to estimate the impact of policy on industrial output, energy use, and household consumption. It is a myopic model where savings and investment are determined using a simple savings rule (often called a dynamic recursive model). The model has 33 industries, including coal mining, electricity, transportation, and 16 manufacturing sectors. Labor and new capital is mobile across sectors in any given period. The electricity sector includes generation from all sources as well as transmission and distribution; it is assumed to have constant returns to scale and the price of electricity clears the market. The government collects taxes on valued added, output, capital income, labor income, and imports. Enterprises use part of their after-tax income for investment and the remainder is given to households as dividends. This is a revised version of the model given in Nielsen and Ho (2013); the model details, including equations, are given in a technical appendix, Cao and Ho (2017).

In this version of the model, the production functions are nested CES functions shown in Fig. 20.A1. We assume a common rate of total factor productivity growth across all industries, but the share parameters are projected forward starting from the 2014 base year using

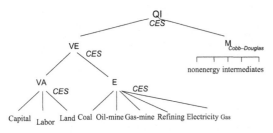

FIGURE 20.A1　Production structure.

information from the US IO table for 2007. This means that we are projecting energy conservation (sometimes called autonomous energy efficiency improvement), and also projecting a shift in the composition of energy away from coal and toward electricity. The base case energy consumption is calibrated to the projections given by the International Energy Agency (IEA, 2016).

Household demand is given by an "exact aggregation" over household types that are distinguished by size, age of head. and region. This function is estimated over household survey data that allow us to estimate the different shares allocated to various consumption baskets by the different household types. This function also gives us income elasticities that are different from 1; we estimated that as incomes rise, a smaller share is devoted to electricity and consumer goods and a bigger share to transportation and services. Our model allows us to discuss the distribution impact of a policy change, e.g., how poor households, or those in the West, are affected differently compared to other households. We express household welfare as a function of the level of consumption of each item in

the basket, and each household type has its own function. The welfare impact of a policy change is measured as the "equivalent variation" of the policy compared to the no-policy case; this is a money measure of this welfare function. (These welfare calculations are described in Jorgenson et al. (2013 Chapter 3).) This welfare measure only covers private consumption; environmental quality and government-supplied public goods are not included, and policy scenarios are designed to keep public expenditures constant. The household demand function contributes an endogenous source of structural change in the economy in the base case. The household supplies labor, and effective labor supply is given by population growth, adjusted for aging and improvement in the level of education.

The total supply of each commodity is a CES aggregate of a domestically produced variety and an imported one, that is, they are regarded as imperfect substitutes. The export of each commodity is given by a constant-elasticity transformation function of domestic and world prices. The current account balance is equal to the trade balance plus exogenous terms for transfers and net interest/dividend flows. The exogenous current account balance in each period is met by an endogenous terms-of-trade (real exchange rate) variable.

The exogenous drivers of growth are the working-age population, labor quality (which determines the effective labor force), investment (driven by an exogenous savings rate and the rate of retained earnings), capital quality, and total factor productivity growth. The projections of these drivers are given in Table 20.A1. We expect

TABLE 20.A1　Parameters of growth model for the base case.

	Savings rate	Dividend rate	Population	Workers	Labor input (quality adjusted)	Productivity index
Base year 2014	38.9%	41.7%	1368	773	100.0	100.0
2020	30.8%	52.8%	1403	765	99.9	109.4
2040	20.1%	63.9%	1395	712	93.0	121.6

the current effort to restructure the economy from investment to consumption to continue, and project that savings rate will fall steadily from 38.9% in the base year to 20.1% in 2040. While the working age population is expected to fall from 890 million in 2014 to 844 in 2030, rising labor quality meant that effective labor input continues to rise modestly until 2019 before falling gradually. The last column of Table 20.A1 gives the industry-level TFP index; we project that this grows at 1.5% during 2014−20. Over the period 2014−20 GDP growth is projected at 6.5% per year, and at 5.0% for 2020−30. There is substantial energy conservation projected; the growth of energy consumption is only 1.5% per year during 2020−30; CO_2 emissions growth is even lower at 1.2% with the falling share of coal in total energy.

References

Janssens-Maenhout G, Crippa M, Guizzardi D, Muntean M, Schaaf E, Olivier JGJ, Peters JAHW, Schure KM: *Fossil CO_2 and GHG emissions of all world countries, EUR 28766 EN, 2017*, Luxembourg, 2017, Publications Office of the European Union.

Aunan K, Berntsen T, O'Connor D, Persson TH, Vennemo H, Zhai F: Benefits and costs to China of a climate policy, *Environment and Development Economics* 12:471−497, 2007.

Cao J, Ho MS: *Economic-environmental model of China (version 18)*, Harvard China Project Working Paper, 2017.

Cao J, Ho MS, Jorgenson D: The economics of environmental policy in China. In Nielsen C, Ho M, editors: *Clearer skies over China: reconciling air quality, climate and economic goals*, 2013, Cambridge, MA, 2013, MIT Press.

Cao J, Ho MS, Liang H: Household energy demand in Urban China: accounting for regional prices and rapid income change, *Energy Journal* 37:87−110, 2016.

Cao J, Ma R: *Who bears the costs of environmental mandates? Evidence from the top 10,000 enterprise energy saving program in China*, Harvard China Project Working Paper, 2018.

Cao J, Ho MS, Jorgenson D, Ren R, Sun L, Yue X: Industrial and aggregate measures of productivity growth in China, 1982-2000, *Review of Income and Wealth* 55(s1):485−513, July, 2009.

Cao J, Ho MS, Hu W, Jorgenson D: *Household consumption in China*, 2018a, Harvard China Project Working Paper.

Cao J, Ho MS, Hu W, Jorgenson D, Zhang Q: *Welfare and Inequality measures for China based on consumption*, Harvard China Project Working Paper, 2018b.

Caron J, Karplus V, Schwarz G: *Modeling the income dependence of household energy consumption and its implications for climate policy in China*, MIT Joint Program on the Science and Policy of Global Change, Report 314, July, 2017.

Fawcett A, McFarland J, Morris A, Weyant J: Introduction to the EMF 32 study on U.S. Carbon tax scenarios, *Climate Change Economics* 9(1):1−7, 2018.

Hu W, Ho MS, Cao J: *Energy consumption of urban households in China*, 2018, Harvard China Project Working Paper.

Hudson E, Jorgenson D: U.S. Energy policy and economic growth, 1975-2000, *Bell Journal of Economics and Management Science* 5(2):461−514, 1974.

International Energy Agency (IEA): *World energy outlook 2014*, 2014, Paris, 2014, IEA.

International Energy Agency (IEA): *World energy outlook 2016*, 2016, Paris, 2016, IEA.

Jorgenson D: Aggregate consumer behavior and the measurement of social welfare, *Econometrica* 58(5):1007−1040, 1990.

Jorgenson D, Griliches Z: The explanation of productivity change, *The Review of Economic Studies* 34(99):249−280, 1967.

Jorgenson D, Goettle R, Ho MS, Wilcoxen P: The distributional impact of climate policy, *the B.E* (Symposium), Article 17 *Journal of Economic Analysis and Policy* 10(2), 2011.

Jorgenson D, Goettle R, Ho MS, Wilcoxen P, Dividend D: *Environmental taxes and fiscal reform in the United States*, 2013, Cambridge, 2013, MIT Press.

Jorgenson D, Ho MS, Jon Samuels J: Education attainment and the revival of U.S. economic growth. In Hulten C, Ramey V, editors: *Education, skills and technical change: implications for future U.S. GDP growth*, 2019, Chicago, 2019, University of Chicago Press, pp 23−60.

Jorgenson D, Lau LJ, Stoker TM: The transcendental logarithmic model of aggregate consumer behavior. In , Greenwich, CT, 1982, JAI Press, pp 97−238. Basmann R, Rhodes G, editors: *Advances in econometrics*, vol. 1. Greenwich, CT, 1982, JAI Press, pp 97−238.

Jorgenson D, Slesnick D: Aggregate consumer behavior and the measurement of inequality, *Review of Economic Studies* 51(3):369−392, 1984.

Jorgenson D, Slesnick D: Consumption and labor supply, *Journal of Econometrics* 147(2):326−335, 2008.

Jorgenson D, Slesnick D, Stoker TM: Two-stage budgeting and exact aggregation, *Journal of Business & Economic Statistics* 6(3):313−325, 1988.

Jorgenson D, Wilcoxen P: Environmental regulation and U.S. Economic growth, *The RAND Journal of Economics* 21(2):314−340, 1990.

Liang Q, Fan Y, Wei Y: Carbon taxation policy in China: how to protect energy and trade-intensive sectors? *Journal of Policy Modeling* 29:311–333, 2007.

Nielsen C, Ho MS, editors: *Clearer skies over China: reconciling air quality, climate and economic goals*, 2013, Cambridge, MA, 2013, MIT Press.

Pang T, Duan M: Cap setting and allowance allocation in China's emissions trading pilot programmes: special issues and innovative solutions, *Climate Policy* 16(7): 815–835, 2016.

World Bank, Washington DC, Development Research Center (DRC) and People's Republic of China, China 2030, 2013.

Wu L, Tang W: *Efficiency or equity? Simulating the carbon emission permits trading schemes in China based on an interregional CGE model*, Australian National University Centre for Climate economics and policy, working paper 1505, 2015.

Yu W, Hertel T, Preckel P, Eales J: Projecting world food demand using alternative demand systems, *Economic Modelling* 21(1):99–129, 2003.

Zhang S, Bauer N, Luderer G, Kriegler E: Role of technologies in in energy-related CO2 mitigation in China within a climate-protection world: a scenario analysis using REMIND, *Applied Energy* 115(C):445–455, 2014.

Zhang Z: *Carbon emissions trading in China: the evolution from pilots to a nationwide scheme*, Australian National University, Centre for Climate Economic and Policy (CCEP) Working Paper 1503, April, 2015.

Zhou S, Teng F: Estimation of urban residential electricity demand in China using household survey data, *Energy Policy* 61:394–402, 2013.

GDP and social welfare: an assessment using regional data[1]

Daniel T. Slesnick

Department of Economics, University of Texas at Austin, Austin, TX, United States

21.1 Introduction

There is an old saying in the economics profession that microeconomics is what we understand but macroeconomics is what we care about. Dale Jorgenson understood this maxim from the beginning of his career as a graduate student. All of his work has brought microeconomics and econometrics to bear on questions of deep import in terms of their larger macroeconomic impacts and consequences. You can see this in his work related to economic growth, productivity, investment behavior, tax policy, index number theory, applied general equilibrium analysis, and producer and consumer behavior. Dale has never wasted his time on trivial problems, and he has changed the way generations of economists think about these issues in profound and permanent ways.

There is perhaps no field in economics where the aggregation problem is more vexing than the measurement of economic welfare. For years, economic well-being has been based on the traditional theoretical paradigm of individual utility maximization. Well-being is generated by consumption decisions, and individual welfare is represented to be a function of income or consumption. In this framework, the assessment of the impacts of policies on welfare is typically made using either Marshall's (1920) concept of consumer's surplus, or Hicks' (1942) equivalent or compensating variation.

Over the last several decades, the domain of welfare measurement expanded to accommodate alternative conceptual frameworks. Some researchers have suggested that material well-being is overly restrictive as the sole determinant of welfare and have proposed subjective measures of well-being or happiness as alternatives.[2] Largely inspired by Sen's (1985, 1987, 1992) work, others have moved beyond the ubiquitous utility-based framework to incorporate elements

[1] I would like to thank Mun Ho and Barbara Fraumeni for helpful comments and suggestions on an earlier draft of this paper.

[2] Van Praag (1971, 1994) provides early examples of subjective welfare measurement. More recent research is summarized by Fleurbaey (2009), Kahneman and Krueger (2006), and Stevenson and Wolfers (2008).

that clearly influence individual and social welfare such as the levels social justice and personal freedom.

These efforts have focused on measurement issues related to individuals. As the old saying suggests, policies are rarely evaluated on the basis of their impact on specific individuals. Instead, policy-makers care about the welfare effects on groups of individuals and usually groups representing entire countries. This aggregation problem is often resolved by an assumption that economy-wide outcomes are consistent with the behavior of a rational representative agent. Unfortunately, there is a large body of empirical evidence that shows that aggregate outcomes are inconsistent with this assumption.[3]

One does not need to be a student of the history of economic thought to notice that the problem of social welfare measurement has drawn the attention of the greatest minds of generations of economists including Adam Smith, Bentham, Marshall, Kaldor, Robbins, Scitovsky, Kuznets, Hicks, Arrow, Samuelson, Tobin, Sen and Dale Jorgenson. While widely considered, economists have failed to reach a consensus on the appropriate foundation for measuring social welfare. Inspired by Arrow's (1951) famous impossibility theorem, social choice theorists have devoted their intellectual energy to demonstrations of the robustness of Arrow's central conclusion of the inconsistency of a social welfare function with core principles of social choice.

In parallel, gross domestic product (GDP) has served as a workhorse in empirical work that measures aggregate output and economic growth. GDP has the practical advantage of being calculated by virtually every country, which facilitates comparisons within countries over time and across countries at a point in time. Analyses of aggregate and industry-specific growth help us understand the process of production, but the focus on output growth is often motivated by concern for social welfare. Although not always stated explicitly, higher levels of production are simply assumed to translate to higher levels of well-being, and GDP is taken to be a measure of aggregate economic welfare.

The influential report by Stiglitz et al. (2009) is by no means the first to suggest that GDP is not a reasonable measure of social welfare.[4] From the very inception of national income accounting, it was recognized that GDP falls short as an indicator of aggregate well-being. Dynan and Sheiner (2018) quote Kuznets as stating in a 1934 report to Congress that "… the welfare of a nation …. can scarcely be inferred from a measure of national income."[5] The inadequacy of GDP as a measure of social welfare spawned the era of the "New Welfare Economics" in the 1940s and 1950s. Prominent economists of the time attempted to supplement national income statistics and index numbers with a theoretical framework that was grounded on welfare theoretic principles based on the Pareto principle. In the end, this approach ranks social states based on potential levels of welfare and is less useful for the evaluation of observed outcomes.[6]

---

[3] Kirman (1992) provides a summary of conceptual and empirical arguments that show that the assumption of a representative agent is untenable. An important alternative to the representative consumer assumption is described in the seminal paper by Jorgenson et al. (1982) who developed an approach to welfare measurement based on exact aggregation. See Slesnick (1998) for a survey of other empirical approaches to welfare measurement.

[4] See Jorgenson (2018) for a summary of the shortcomings associated with the use of GDP as a measure of social welfare.

[5] See Dynan and Sheiner (2018), p. 5.

[6] Chipman and Moore (1971, 1973) also noted that consistent rankings of social states using compensation principles can only occur under restrictive conditions on individual preferences.

Although many would agree that the conceptual basis for GDP as a social welfare measure is weak, it is possible that it performs well as a proxy. Jones and Klenow (2016) presented a compelling alternative framework for social welfare measurement that depends on consumption, leisure, and life expectancy and incorporates distributional concern in ranking outcomes. This is an impressive empirical study, and a key finding is that cross-country comparisons of social welfare are highly correlated with per capita GDP. In this paper, I revisit this issue and assess the performance of GDP as a proxy for social welfare.

I perform this evaluation by comparing GDP to a measure of social welfare developed within the traditional framework in which individual welfare functions depend on consumption and serve as arguments of an explicit Bergson–Samuelson social welfare function. By design, the social welfare function satisfies principles of social choice and depends on the distribution of individual welfare in ranking social states. Regional data published by the Bureau of Economic Analysis (BEA) are used to compare levels and trends of GDP with alternative measures of social welfare calculated for the four major Census regions of the United States. The use of regional information has the practical advantage of (partially) mitigating significant conceptual and measurement problems that often plague cross-country comparisons even within the standardized framework of national income accounting.

The organization of the paper is as follows. Section 21.2 presents regional estimates of levels and growth rates of per capita GDP for the United States. In Section 21.3, I propose alternative consumption-based measures of individual welfare that are comparable to per capita GDP and as easy to compute. These welfare functions depend on expenditure levels that are estimated

using household survey data. They also depend on household-specific price indexes that account for regional variation of price levels for a variety of goods and services. The individual welfare functions serve as arguments of social welfare functions that are designed to be consistent with core principles of social choice. The social welfare functions are defined in Section 21.4 and compared to per capita GDP using information for the entire US economy. I assess the empirical performance of per capita GDP as a proxy for regional welfare using over 5 decades of data in Section 21.5.

21.2 Regional Gross Domestic Product as a welfare measure

As a component of the national income and product accounts, the BEA produces GDP as a measure of domestic production. By design, it can be represented either by final expenditures or by the incomes earned through the production process.[7] Using the final expenditure account, GDP is the sum of personal consumption expenditures (PCE), gross private domestic investment, net exports, and government expenditures and gross investment.

It is difficult to see how any reasonable process of aggregation of individual welfare functions would yield GDP as a measure of social welfare. Dynan and Sheiner (2018) note that GDP includes items that are not typically associated with personal well-being such as investment by businesses, governments, and households as well as production related to the replacement of depreciated physical capital. Nordhaus and Tobin (1972) highlight the broader concern that there are factors other than output or material well-being that influence individual and social welfare. For example, higher levels of production may be associated

---

[7] For an excellent description of the US national income and product accounts, see Jorgenson and Landefeld (2006).

with negative externalities such as pollution that lower welfare. Nonmarket factors related to household production also influence well-being in ways that are not captured by GDP.[8] Others have noted that aggregate levels of production do not account for potentially important distributional effects that would be included in equity-regarding social welfare functions.[9]

Nevertheless, GDP has persisted as a de facto measure of social welfare driven by its ease of access through the national accounts. An unanswered empirical question is the extent to which social welfare levels, trends, and growth rates are misrepresented by an index of aggregate production such as real per capita GDP. This is of practical concern to applied welfare economists but also has implications for empirical questions related to growth and development. For example, neoclassical theories of economic growth have the refutable implication that, with diminishing returns to capital, per capita growth is inversely related to initial levels of per capita income. If GDP accurately represents economic well-being, the implication is that the process of economic growth leads to convergence in the standards of living of rich and poor countries.[10]

The absence of long time series of comparable estimates of economic variables across countries makes empirical assessments of relative levels of social welfare difficult. This has precipitated a resurgence of interest in regional economics as analysts assess the extent of convergence across states or regions of the United States. For the purpose of assessing the performance of GDP as a proxy for economic well-being, I follow the empirical strategy used by Barro and Sala-i-Martin (1992) and examine state-level estimates

of GDP produced by the BEA over the period between 1963 and 2017. Using Gross State Products and the populations of all US states, regional estimates of per capita GDP are obtained by aggregating over the following partition of states:

Northeast: Connecticut, Maine, Massachusetts, New Hampshire, New Jersey, New York, Pennsylvania, Rhode Island, Vermont.
Midwest: Illinois, Indiana, Iowa, Kansas, Michigan, Minnesota, Missouri, Nebraska, North Dakota, Ohio, South Dakota, Wisconsin.
South: Alabama, Arkansas, Delaware, District of Columbia, Florida, Georgia, Kentucky, Louisiana, Maryland, Mississippi, North Carolina, Oklahoma, South Carolina, Tennessee, Texas, Virginia, West Virginia.
West: Alaska, Arizona, California, Colorado, Hawaii, Idaho, Montana, Nevada, New Mexico, Oregon, Utah, Washington, Wyoming.

A GDP-based welfare measure is defined to be the log of real per capita GDP for each region:

$$GDP_{rt} = ln\left(\frac{Y_{rt}}{P_t N_{rt}}\right) \qquad (21.1)$$
$$(r = 1, 2, \ldots 4; \ t = 1963, \ldots, 2017)$$

where

GDP_{rt} is the log of real per capita GDP of region r at time t.
Y_{rt} is the aggregate GDP of region r at time t.
P_t is the US GDP price deflator.
N_{rt} is the number of persons in region r at time t.

---

[8] Attanasio et al. (2015) provide an example of this type of welfare measurement in their examination of the evolution of income, consumption, and leisure inequality over time.

[9] The Stiglitz et al. (2009) report has stimulated a renewed interest in incorporating distributional effects in assessing social outcomes. Jorgenson and Slesnick (2014) and Piketty et al. (2018) have proposed frameworks for social welfare measurement in the national accounts that incorporate principles of equity.

[10] See, for example, Barro and Sala-i-Martin (1991,1992).

Note that a national price index is used to deflate regional GDP out of practical necessity. Although the BEA has produced estimates of regional price parities recently, only economy-wide price indexes are available over the entire sample period between 1963 and 2017.

In 2017 nominal levels of GDP of both the Northeast and Midwest regions were $3.9 trillion, while GDP in the West and the South were $4.9 trillion and $6.6 trillion. This would place all four regions among the largest economies in the world. In assessing regional welfare levels, it is important to note at the outset that there were significant changes in the regional distribution of the US population between 1963 and 2017. These changes were undoubtedly endogenous, and affected and were affected by regional differences of welfare levels. Fig. 21.1 shows the South grew over time from 31% of the population in 1963 to 38% in 2017. The West also showed higher than average population growth and accounted for almost 24% of the total population by 2017. This growth was at the expense of largely equivalent proportionate reductions in the fractions of the populations in the Northeast and Midwest.

The log of real per capita GDP defined in (21.1) is shown for each region in Fig. 21.2. In the early 1960s, there were small differences between the Northeast and the West, while levels in the Midwest were between 5 and 10% lower depending on the year. Per capita GDP in the South was well below the other regions; in some years as much as 30% lower than levels attained in the Northeast. Over the 1960s and the 1970s, growth in the South was higher than in the other regions which resulted in significant regional convergence through the mid-1980s. Over this period, the highest levels of per capita GDP were in the West followed by the Northeast, while levels in the South eventually matched those in the Midwest. Beginning around 1985, growth in the Northeast exceeded that of the other regions, and by the early 1990s, the Northeast had the highest levels of

per capita GDP followed by the West, Midwest, and the South. In 2017, per capita GDP in the South remained almost 30% below the level in the Northeast and differences between all regions were large.

To more precisely quantify regional patterns of growth, Table 21.1 shows average growth rates for each region and the aggregate economy over subperiods. Over the entire 54 years, the national growth rate averaged 2.0% per year although there was substantial intertemporal variation. The lowest growth occurred over the decade that covered the Great Recession and the highest average growth rate was between 1963 and 1970. Consistent with Fig. 21.2, average growth rates between 1963 and 1980 were substantially higher in the South but lower than average over the latter half of the sample period. The Northeast had an average growth rate that exceeded the national average over the 5 decades, but the temporal pattern was the reverse of the South, below-average growth early in the sample period and higher than average growth after 1980. The Midwest and West experienced below-average growth rates over the entire sample period which contributed to the divergence of levels of per capita GDP seen in 2017.

PCE represent economy-wide levels of (mostly) household expenditures and comprise approximately two-thirds of total GDP. Conceptually, per capita PCE is an appealing alternative to GDP as a measure of social welfare, because it reflects aggregate consumption levels. How do the results change if we substitute PCE for GDP in Eq. (21.1)? Define the log of real per capita PCE for each region as:

$$PCE_{rt} = ln\left(\frac{M_{rt}}{P_t^* N_{rt}}\right) \tag{21.2}$$
$$(r = 1, 2, \ldots 4; \ t = 1997, \ldots, 2016)$$

where

PCE_{rt} is the log of real per capita PCE of region r at time t.

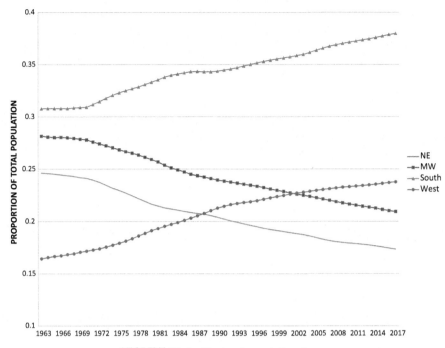

FIGURE 21.1   Regional population shares

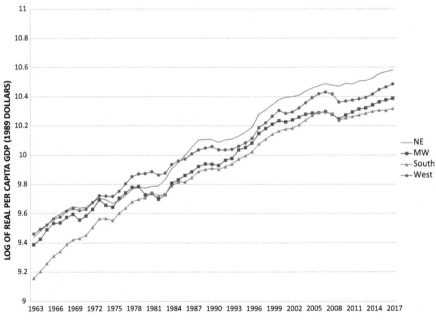

FIGURE 21.2   Regional real per capita Gross Domestic Product (GDP).

TABLE 21.1   Average annual growth of real per capita GDP: 1963−2017.

	National	Northeast	Midwest	South	West
1963−70	2.89%	2.84%	2.42%	3.90%	2.28%
1970−80	2.09%	1.37%	1.72%	2.77%	2.53%
1980−90	2.30%	3.31%	2.09%	2.02%	1.84%
1990−2000	2.66%	2.75%	2.98%	2.55%	2.49%
2000−10	0.75%	1.10%	0.38%	0.90%	0.63%
2010−17	1.31%	1.30%	1.63%	0.92%	1.66%
1963−2017	1.99%	2.12%	1.85%	2.15%	1.90%

GDP, gross domestic product.

M_{rt} is the PCE in region r at time t.
P^{*}_{t} is the US PCE price deflator.
N_{rt} is the number of persons in region r at time t.

The BEA provides state-level PCE data over the period from 1997 through 2016, and Fig. 21.3 shows the regional levels of the log of real per capita PCE over this period. The ordinal rankings of per capita PCE across regions are similar to those based on GDP. The Northeast had the highest levels over the 2 decades and the South had the lowest. By 2016, the proportionate gap between the two regions reached approximately 25% which generally matches what was found in Fig. 21.2 with GDP. The most obvious difference between the PCE- and GDP-based indexes is the fact that per capita GDP showed a much larger gap between the West and the Midwest compared with per capita PCE.

Table 21.2 compares the growth rates of real per capita PCE with those based on real per capita GDP over the shorter sample period. The consumption-based index increased at higher rates both nationally and across regions compared with GDP. Between 1997 and 2016, per capita PCE had average annual growth rates that were approximately 0.5% higher than corresponding rates based on GDP.[11] The regional patterns of growth were similar, with the highest growth rates in the Northeast and lower growth rates in the Midwest and South.

Do either of these indexes support conclusions of convergence of regional welfare levels? I show the standard deviation of the population-weighted log variance of the regional indexes for both the GDP- and PCE-based measures in Fig. 21.4. Between-region dispersion of real per capita GDP fell between the early 1960s and the early 1980s. This reflects the sharp increase in per capita GDP in the South shown in Fig. 21.2. After the 1980s, there was a U-turn and dispersion in regional per capita GDP increased as growth in the Northeast outpaced the other regions. Fig. 21.4 also shows between-region inequality of real per capita PCE was generally below that of per capita GDP. Between-region dispersion of the PCE-based index increased after 1997 and generally matched the trend of the inequality index based on GDP. Neither index supports the hypothesis of convergence of regional welfare levels over time.

To summarize these results, data from the national accounts allow assessments of regional welfare levels based on real per capita GDP. Early in the sample period, real per capita GDP in the South was well below the Northeast, West, and Midwest regions. Between the 1960s and the 1980s, growth in the South was higher than the other regions which served to narrow the gap in per capita GDP. This level of growth was not sustained, and between-region dispersion began to increase beginning in the early

---

[11] The lower growth rate of GDP relative to PCE was largely the result of a lower than average increase of government consumption expenditures and gross investment.

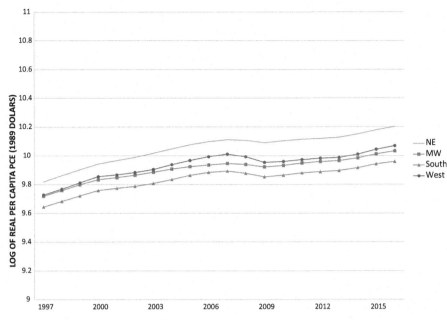

FIGURE 21.3   Regional real per capita personal consumption expenditures (PCE).

TABLE 21.2   Average annual growth of real per capita PCE: 1997–2016.

	National	Northeast	Midwest	South	West
1997–2000	3.95%	4.12%	3.80%	3.81%	4.23%
2000–10	1.13%	1.62%	0.98%	1.06%	1.05%
2010–16	1.65%	1.65%	1.69%	1.56%	1.82%
1997–2016	1.74%	2.02%	1.65%	1.65%	1.79%

Average annual growth of real per capita GDP: 1997–2016

	National	Northeast	Midwest	South	West
1997–2000	3.24%	3.31%	2.92%	2.94%	3.99%
2000–10	0.75%	1.10%	0.38%	0.90%	0.63%
2010–16	1.30%	1.33%	1.72%	0.85%	1.60%
1997–2016	1.31%	1.52%	1.21%	1.21%	1.47%

GDP, gross domestic product; *PCE*, personal consumption expenditures.

1990s. Over the latter half of the sample period, the highest levels of per capita GDP were attained in the Northeast followed by the West,

Midwest, and the South. Replacing the GDP-based measure with real per capita PCE yields qualitatively similar results although the latter shows higher average growth rates over the shorter period between 1997 and 2016. Neither the GDP- nor the PCE-based indexes support a conclusion of regional convergence over time.

21.3 Individual welfare, consumption, and prices

While GDP has served as a frequently used measure of social welfare, measures of individual welfare in the United States are often represented to be functions of income. Official measures of poverty depend on household income, and inequality is predominantly assessed using either individual earnings, individual income, family income, or household income. The reliance on income to measure individual welfare has largely been the result of practical

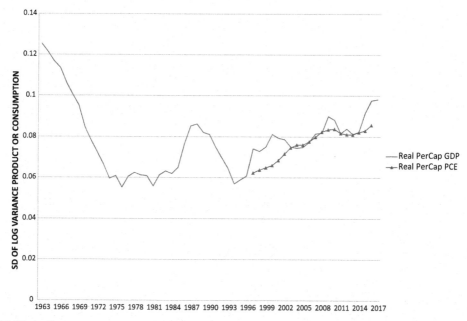

FIGURE 21.4 Between-region inequality. GDP, gross domestic product; PCE, personal consumption expenditures.

considerations of data availability; historically only income data were available at annual frequencies.[12]

There are theoretical reasons to expect consumption-based measures to provide more accurate representations of individual welfare in both static and intertemporal contexts. In modeling consumer behavior, the traditional framework assumes individual utility is derived from the consumption of goods and services. In an intertemporal context, Friedman's (1957) permanent income hypothesis suggests that consumption decisions are made on the basis of permanent income, implying that total consumption would serve as a more accurate proxy for lifetime income.[13]

To define an individual welfare function based on consumption, specifications are used that are as easy to compute as real per capita GDP or PCE. The welfare function is similar to (21.1), so that differences between the measure of social welfare and per capita GDP cannot be ascribed to the choice of functional form. I begin with additional notation:

p_{ik}—the price of the ith good faced by individual k (i = 1,2, ..., I; k = 1,2, ..., N).

x_{ik}—the quantity consumed of the ith good by individual k (i = 1,2, ..., I; k = 1,2, ..., N).

$M_k = \sum_{i=1}^{I} p_{ik} x_{ik}$—total expenditure of individual k (k = 1,2, ...,N).

---

[12] In the United States, annual income-based measures of poverty and inequality are often based on the Current Population Surveys produced by the Bureau of the Census.

[13] For additional discussion, see Attanasio and Pistaferri (2016) and Slesnick (2001).

Analogous to (21.2), the individual welfare function is taken to be the log of total expenditure deflated by an individual-specific Paasche price index:

$$W_k(P_k, M_k) = ln\left(\frac{M_k}{P_k}\right) \quad (k = 1, 2, ...N)$$

(21.3)

and

$$P_k = \frac{M_k}{M_k^0} = \frac{\sum\limits_{i=1}^{I} p_{ik} x_{ik}}{\sum\limits_{i=1}^{I} p_i^0 x_{ik}}$$

(21.4)

where p_i^0 is the reference price of the ith commodity and M_k^0 is the level of total expenditure evaluated at reference prices. By contrast with real per capita GDP defined in (21.1), individual welfare is evaluated under the more realistic assumption that prices vary across the population, and the impacts of price changes depend on individuals' expenditure patterns. For example, the welfare function (21.3) accounts for the fact that housing prices may be higher for individuals living in the Northeast compared to the South and increases in the prices of necessities have a larger negative impact on the poor relative to the rich. This treatment of prices will turn out to be particularly influential in the empirical results.

Although the welfare function is defined for individuals (as opposed to households), the simplicity of the specification omits features that could be important. First, all individuals with the same level of total expenditure are assumed to have the same level of welfare if they face the same prices. This may be counterfactual if the needs of individuals differ based on their demographic characteristics (such as adults vs. children). Living arrangements and the associated economies of scale in consumption may also influence well-being beyond what is measured in Eq. (21.3). Finally, while use of a Paasche price index greatly simplifies calculations, it is "inexact" as a true cost-of-living index in the sense originally defined by Diewert (1976).[14]

21.3.1 Measuring consumption

Calculation of the consumption-based measure of individual welfare requires estimates of expenditures and prices. The only comprehensive sources of microlevel expenditure data that can be compared with GDP over an extended time period are the Consumer Expenditure Surveys (CEX) published by the Bureau of Labor Statistics (BLS). These surveys are representative national samples that were created for the purpose of estimating the weights needed to compute the CPI. They were administered approximately every 10 years until 1980 when the data were collected annually. Our sample includes the surveys covering 1960−61, 1972, 1973, and 1980 through 2016.

Expenditures in the 1961 survey were estimated using a single interview and the results were reported on an annual basis. In the 1972 and 1973 surveys, the consumer unit was interviewed over five quarters for most items but, as in 1961, only the annual expenditures were reported. Beginning in 1980, the CEX changed to a rolling panel format in which each consumer unit was in the sample for five quarters. The first interview in the first quarter collected

[14] The advantage of using a Paasche index is its computational simplicity and minimal data requirements. It can be computed for each individual using only current period prices and expenditures along with reference prices. An alternative approach was proposed by Jorgenson and Slesnick (1983) who estimated household-level true cost-of-living indexes using an econometric model that allowed recovery of the household expenditure function.

demographic information and a partial inventory of consumer durables. In the remaining four interviews, detailed expenditure information was collected and reported on a quarterly basis.

To avoid issues of attrition and the weighting of nonrepresentative samples, I use observations from the second quarter of each survey year from 1980 through 2016. Each quarterly data set is designed to be a representative sample of the US population. For the welfare calculations, quarterly expenditures are multiplied by four to obtain total expenditure on an annual basis. The sample size for the 1961 survey was approximately 13,000 households, in 1972 and 1973, the sample sizes were around 9500, and the post-1980 samples ranged from between 4000 and 7500 households.

The CEX reports the out-of-pocket expenditures of the consumer unit. I divide total expenditure into six commodity groups: energy, food, consumer goods, durables, housing (rental or owner occupied), and consumer services. I use a definition of total expenditure that differs from that used by the BLS in several ways. Gifts and cash contributions are deleted because altruistic spending requires a conceptual framework that is different from the current framework for measuring individual and social welfare. Pensions, retirement contributions, and Social Security payments are also removed because they represent components of saving

rather than consumption. Outlays on owner-occupied housing are replaced with consumer units estimated rental equivalents. The purchases of durables are replaced with estimates of the services received from the households' stocks.[15]

A consumer unit in the CEX is a group of individuals who are related by blood or marriage, financially independent single individuals, or a group of individuals who make joint financial decisions. The expenditures of all individuals within a consumer unit are aggregated which makes it difficult to directly identify the spending of each individual in multiperson units. For the measurement of welfare, we take the unit of observation to be an individual and assume total spending is allocated equally among all members of the consumer unit. This is clearly an oversimplification of the intrahousehold allocation process but, in the current context, has the advantage of maintaining consistency with the assumption implicit in the use of real per capita GDP as a measure of social welfare.[16]

Before developing an explicit social welfare function, it is useful to assess whether the substitution of CEX-based expenditure data for GDP changes conclusions concerning regional welfare levels and patterns of growth. For this purpose, I recalculate real aggregate expenditure per capita using the PCE deflator as in (21.2) but substitute estimates of

---

[15] The methods used to compute the rental equivalent of owner-occupied housing and the service flows from consumer durables are described by Slesnick (2001).

[16] An alternative approach is to evaluate and compare household welfare and assume every individual in the household attains the same welfare level. In this framework, comparisons of welfare across households are typically made by deflating income or total expenditure by household equivalence scales. Early examples of this approach include Jorgenson and Slesnick (1984a, 1984b, 1987). Slesnick (2001) assesses the sensitivity of household welfare measures to alternative representations of household equivalence scales including the per capita adjustment. Recent approaches tackle the issue of intrahousehold allocation decisions directly and measure the welfare levels of individuals living in the household. See Browning et al. (2013), Lewbel and Pendakur (2008) and Lise and Seitz (2011).

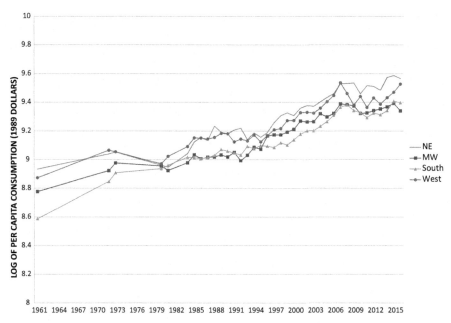

FIGURE 21.5   Consumer Expenditure Surveys (CEX)-based- per capita consumption.

regional expenditures and population from the CEX:

$$CEX_{rt} = ln\left(\frac{\sum M_{krt}}{P^*_t N_{rt}}\right)$$

$$(r = 1, 2, ...4;\ t = 1961, ..., 2016)$$

$$(21.5)$$

where

CEX_{rt} is the log of real per capita CEX-based total expenditure of region r at time t.
$\sum M_{krt}$ is the CEX-based sum of total expenditure over all individuals in region r at time t.
P^*_t is the US PCE price deflator.
N_{rt} is the number of persons in region r at time t as tabulated in the CEX.

Fig. 21.5 shows regional levels of per capita consumption for each year for which the CEX was administered. Comparison of Fig. 21.5 with Fig. 21.2 shows that many of the qualitative conclusions concerning regional levels and growth rates of per capita expenditure and per capita GDP are similar. In 1961, per capita expenditure in the South was approximately 35% below the Northeast. From 1961 through the early 1980s, growth in the South exceeded the other regions, and differences in levels of real per capita expenditure narrowed to such an extent that between-region dispersion was virtually eliminated. Beginning in the mid-1980s, growth in the Northeast and West exceeded the other regions, and, by 2016, levels of real per capita expenditure in these two regions exceeded levels attained in the Midwest and the South. After the mid-1980s, the highest levels of per capita expenditure were found in the Northeast followed by the West, Midwest, and South in most years. These patterns match those tabulated using real per capita GDP quite closely.

TABLE 21.3 Average annual growth of real per capita expenditure (CEX): 1961−2016.

	National	Northeast	Midwest	South	West
1961−73	1.73%	1.00%	1.66%	2.66%	1.51%
1973−80	−0.52%	−1.32%	−0.29%	0.41%	−1.20%
1980−90	1.52%	2.19%	0.63%	1.23%	2.10%
1990−2000	1.14%	1.27%	1.93%	0.79%	0.92%
2000−10	1.58%	1.51%	1.10%	1.89%	1.67%
2010−16	1.20%	1.80%	0.30%	1.16%	1.46%
1961−2016	1.21%	1.15%	1.02%	1.47%	1.19%

CEX, consumer expenditure surveys.

While qualitative conclusions concerning relative welfare levels across regions are preserved, Table 21.3 shows that between 1961 and 2016 the average growth rates based on real per capita expenditures in the CEX were slightly over one-half of those tabulated using GDP (which, in turn, were less than PCE growth rates). Comparison of Fig. 21.5 with Fig. 21.3 shows that the levels of estimated expenditures in the CEX were also substantially below those based on the PCE. This suggests that the CEX underestimates expenditures relative to the PCE and the gap has been widening over time. This feature of the household survey data will have an important impact on comparisons of growth rates between real per capita GDP and the CEX-based measures of the standards of living across the four regions.[17]

21.3.2 Household-specific prices

The calculation of individual welfare also requires the prices paid for goods and services. The CEX records expenditures on hundreds of items but provides no information on prices. While the BLS publishes time series of price indexes for different cities and regions, they do not provide information on differences in price levels across geographic areas. Kokoski et al. (1994) use the 1988 and 1989 CPI database to estimate the prices of goods and services in 44 urban areas. I use their estimates of prices for rental housing, owner-occupied housing, food at home, food away from home, alcohol and tobacco, household fuels (electricity and piped natural gas), gasoline and motor oil, household furnishings, apparel, new vehicles, professional medical services, and entertainment. In 1988 and 1989, these items constituted approximately 75% of all expenditures.

I aggregate these prices to obtain indexes for seven commodity groups:

Energy: Electricity and piped natural gas, gasoline and motor oil
Food: Food at home, food away from home, tobacco and alcohol
Consumer goods: Apparel
Consumer durables: Household furnishings and operation, and new vehicles
Rental housing
Owner-occupied housing
Consumer services: Professional medical services and entertainment

---

[17] Differences in population coverage and the definition of expenditure can explain some of the divergence between the two series. Households surveyed in the CEX record out-of-pocket expenditures while PCE estimates are based on the receipts of businesses which could include third-party payments. The rapid growth of expenditures on health care without commensurate increases in out-of-pocket spending would account for some of the gap between CEX and PCE aggregates. Also, PCE includes several items that are not captured in the CEX such as the expenditures by private nonprofit institutions and a category described as the "services furnished without payment by financial intermediaries." See Slesnick (1992) for additional discussion.

Given 1988—89 price levels for these groups, prices before and after this period are extrapolated using price indexes published by the BLS. Most of these indexes cover the period from December 1977 to the present at either monthly or bimonthly frequencies depending on the year and the commodity group. A detailed description of the extrapolation procedure can be found in Slesnick (2002).

Although Kokoski et al. provide estimates of prices for 44 urban areas across the United States, the publicly available CEX data do not report households' cities of residence in an effort to preserve the confidentiality of survey participants. This necessitates aggregation across urban areas to obtain prices for the four major Census regions. Because the BLS does not collect nonurban price information, rural households are assumed to face the prices of class D—sized urban areas. These areas correspond to nonmetropolitan urban areas which are cities with less than 50,000 persons. The monthly prices are linked to consumer units in the CEX by region of residence, housing tenure, and the date at which they were interviewed.

Fig. 21.6 presents price indexes aggregated over the seven commodities for each of the four urban Census regions and rural areas. Of particular relevance for the analysis of individual and social welfare are the relative price levels. Per capita GDP defined in (21.1) is deflated by a national price index (the GDP deflator) that does not account for geographic price differences. The series shown in Fig. 21.6 show that adjusting for price levels could have an important impact on assessments of regional welfare levels and trends. The Northeast and the West have higher than average levels of per capita GDP but also face the highest prices. The reverse is true for individuals who live in the South and the Midwest. Rural households face the lowest prices and are concentrated in the Midwest and the South. Given the positive correlation between regional levels of GDP and regional price levels, accounting for price variation is likely to have an impact on conclusions about relative levels of regional welfare. In addition, average inflation rates are higher in the Northeast and the West relative to the national average. This will have the added effect of reducing estimated regional growth rates relative to what is obtained using a national price index.[18]

To summarize, CEX-based estimates of real per capita expenditure for the four Census regions yield results that are surprisingly similar to those based on real per capita GDP. In 1961, per capita expenditures in the Northeast and the West were of the same magnitude while the level in the South was substantially lower. Higher than average growth in the South resulted in regional convergence through the 1980s, but high growth in the Northeast after the 1990s resulted in increased regional dispersion through 2016. In most years after the mid-1980s, the highest levels of per capita

---

[18] While inclusion of regional price variation is clearly an improvement over a single national price index such as the PCE or GDP price deflators, potentially important sources of measurement error remain. Accurate estimates of price level differences require that one control for product heterogeneity. This is particularly true of owner occupied and rental housing which are influential elements of the overall variation of regional prices. Kokoski et al. control for this heterogeneity using hedonic regression methods using observable characteristics of the housing unit, but one suspects that unobservable characteristics are likely to be statistically important as well. Although empirically less important, similar issues arise with other expenditure items. Also, the prices of only approximately 75% of all items are covered which implies that price variation within the broad commodity groups is ignored for a nontrivial fraction of each household's spending.

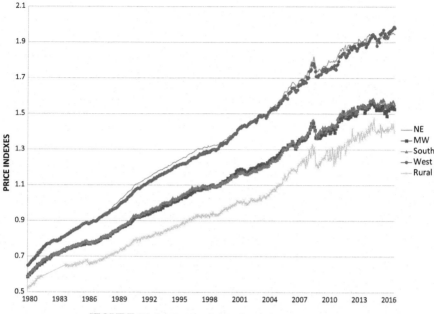

FIGURE 21.6   Regional price levels (NE, 1989 = 1.0).

expenditure were in the Northeast followed by the West, Midwest, and South. These key features match what was found using the GDP-based index despite definitional and coverage differences between the CEX and the national accounts. I have also estimated price levels for seven commodity groups and, in the aggregate, find higher prices in the Northeast and the West and lower prices in the South and Midwest. This price variation alone will influence conclusions about the relative levels of individual and social welfare and the associated growth rates.

21.4 The measurement of social welfare

Individual welfare functions are aggregated to obtain measures of well-being using Bergson–Samuelson social welfare functions. These functions are consistent with social orderings that

are assumed to satisfy the Arrovian axioms of unlimited domain, independence of irrelevant alternatives, and the weak Pareto principle. Unlimited domain requires the social ordering to be defined over all possible individual welfare functions. Independence of irrelevant alternatives implies the ordering of any two states be independent of a third, and the Pareto principle requires a social state to be socially preferred if every individual prefers it.[19]

Arrow's assumption of ordinally noncomparable welfare functions can be replaced by assumptions that allow for both the measurability and comparability of individual welfare. As demonstrated by Sen (1977) and Roberts (1980), relaxing Arrow's assumption of ordinal noncomparability expands the set of possible social welfare functions significantly. Roberts shows, for example, that the assumption that welfare functions are cardinal and unit

---

[19] See Roberts (1980) for additional discussion of the axiomatic basis for the social welfare functions described below.

comparable (i.e., welfare differences between states are comparable across individuals) yields a utilitarian social welfare function defined as the weighted sum of individual welfare functions:

$$W(\mathbf{u}) = \frac{\sum_k W_k}{N} = \overline{W} \qquad (21.6)$$

where $\mathbf{u} = (W_1, W_2, ..., W_N)$ denotes the vector of welfare functions of every individual in the population.

An assumption that individual welfare functions are cardinal and fully comparable yields a social welfare function that is the sum of average welfare and a linearly homogeneous function of welfare deviations from the mean. Cardinal full comparability allows both welfare levels and differences to be comparable between individuals. An example of a social welfare function that is consistent with this assumption is an egalitarian specification that is the utilitarian social welfare function with an additive penalty for dispersion in the distribution of individual welfare:

$$W(\mathbf{u}) = \overline{W} - \left(\frac{1}{2}\right) \sum \left(\frac{1}{N}\right) |W_k - \overline{W}| \quad (21.7)$$

The social welfare functions (21.6) and (21.7) have several advantages over per capita GDP as measures of aggregate well-being. Both specifications represent aggregations of individual welfare functions that are consistent with principles of social choice. This provides an explicit, axiomatic foundation for what has often been an ad hoc normative exercise. Second, arguments of the social welfare function are consumption-based welfare functions that depend on expenditures and prices. The estimates of prices account for geographic differences in price levels. This yields a microeconomic foundation for the individual welfare functions that are aggregated to measure

social welfare. Lastly, both social welfare functions are sensitive to the distribution of well-being across individuals. All else being equal, social welfare will be lower for more unequal distributions of individual welfare.

Both social welfare functions can be decomposed into measures of efficiency and inequality[20]:

$$W(\mathbf{u}) = W^{EFF} - W^{INEQ} \qquad (21.8)$$

The efficiency index, W^{EFF}, is the maximum level of social welfare that is attainable with a fixed level of aggregate (constant dollar) expenditure. If the social welfare functions are equity-regarding, efficiency is attained at the perfectly egalitarian distribution of individual welfare at which expenditure per person is equalized. At this distribution, both the utilitarian and the egalitarian social welfare functions reduce to:

$$W^{EFF} = ln\left(\frac{\sum M_k^0}{N}\right) \qquad (21.9)$$

where M_k^0 is the level of total expenditure of individual k evaluated at reference prices. Note the functional similarity between the measure of efficiency and real per capita GDP defined in (21.1).

A measure of absolute inequality is the difference between the potential level of social welfare attained at the perfectly egalitarian distribution of welfare and the actual level of social welfare[21]:

$$W^{INEQ} = W^{EFF} - W(\mathbf{u}) \qquad (21.10)$$

The index W^{INEQ} represents the loss of social welfare due to an unequal distribution of individual welfare. It is greater than zero and, all else being equal, increases as the distribution of individual welfare becomes more unequally distributed.

---

[20] This decomposition was originally proposed by Jorgenson and Slesnick (1984a, 1984b).

[21] Absolute measures of inequality are discussed by Kolm (1976a, 1976b) and Blackorby and Donaldson (1980).

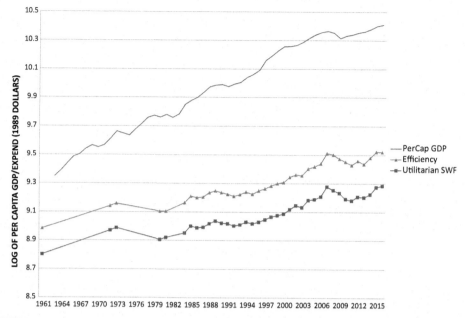

FIGURE 21.7   Measures of aggregate welfare. GDP, gross domestic product; SWF, social welfare function.

Before I compare regional welfare levels, I evaluate social welfare and its components for the aggregate economy. Fig. 21.7 shows national levels of real per capita GDP, the level of efficiency defined in (21.9), and the level of social welfare as defined by the utilitarian specification in (21.6) using the individual welfare functions defined in (21.3). The GDP-based index and the consumption-based measure of efficiency are distribution-free measures of aggregate welfare. The former shows an average annual growth rate of 2.0% per year between 1963 and 2017. The average growth rate of the measure of efficiency is 1.0% per year which reflects the sharply lower growth of CEX-based expenditures described in the previous section.

The gap between the measure of efficiency and the social welfare function reflects the bias that would occur if distributional effects are excluded from the measure of social welfare. For the utilitarian specification, the bias (on a logarithmic scale) is large ranging from 0.18 to 0.26 depending on the year. Of course, the magnitude of the bias would be even larger with the egalitarian specification because of the added penalty for inequality. Although distributional effects have an important effect on measured levels of social welfare, Fig. 21.7 also shows that the trend of the utilitarian social welfare function is similar to the measure of efficiency. In the aggregate, changes in efficiency dominate changes in inequality in determining the long-run trend of social welfare in the United States.

To address the issue of inequality more directly, I present estimates of the inequality index (21.10) in Fig. 21.8. This isolates the vertical difference between the measure of efficiency and the measure of social welfare. Although efficiency is clearly most influential in reflecting the trend of social welfare, inequality has changed over time in the US. Dispersion of individual welfare decreased between 1961 and 1973 but

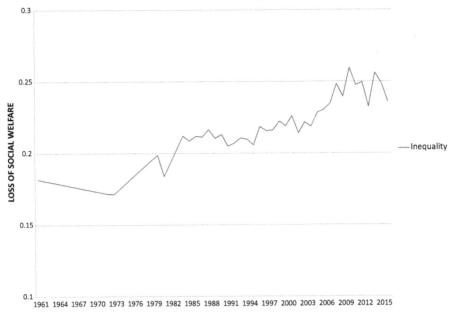

FIGURE 21.8   Measure of aggregate inequality.

subsequently increased through the mid-1980s.[22] Over the 2 decades between 1985 and 2005, the consumption-based index of absolute inequality did not exhibit much change. After 2005, inequality increased through the end of the sample period although the change was modest by comparison with the changes in efficiency.

21.5 Regional welfare in the United States

The specification of an explicit social welfare function provides a benchmark against which real per capita GDP can be compared. To assess the performance of GDP as a proxy for social welfare, I examine the extent to which it provides consistent conclusions concerning the ordering of regional welfare levels. I also assess how qualitative features of regional trends differ depending on the index utilized. The comparison between economy-wide real per capita GDP and the CEX-based measure of social welfare shown in Fig. 21.7 suggests that significant differences between the two measures across regions are likely.

The utilitarian and egalitarian social welfare functions are calculated for each region using individual welfare functions that depend on total expenditure and person-specific Paasche price indexes. Fig. 21.9 shows social welfare levels for each of the four Census regions between 1961 and 2016 using the utilitarian specification. In 1961 welfare levels in the Northeast, Midwest, and West were of similar magnitudes but

---

[22] The increase in inequality between 1973 and the early 1980s may reflect the change in the CEX from annual to quarterly reports of expenditures. It seems likely that households smooth consumption decisions over the course of a year which would yield less observed dispersion of expenditures in the annual data compared with the quarterly observations.

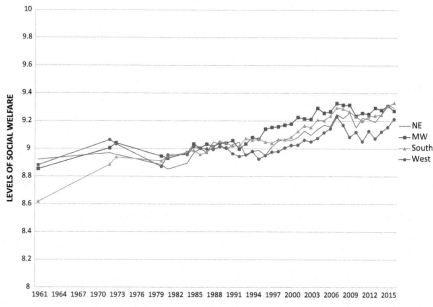

FIGURE 21.9 Utilitarian social welfare.

welfare in the South was substantially lower. The gap between the Northeast and the Midwest was 0.07 (on a logarithmic scale) compared with a difference of 0.30 between the Northeast and the South. Between 1961 and the mid-1980s the consumption-based social welfare function showed regional convergence to such an extent that between-region dispersion was essentially eliminated. This reflects the higher than average growth rate of social welfare in the South. Beginning in the 1990s, welfare in the Midwest and the South increased faster than the other two regions and, by 2016, the Northeast, Midwest, and South had comparable welfare levels while social welfare in the West was below the other regions.

Fig. 21.10 shows regional welfare levels calculated using the egalitarian specification defined in (21.7). Despite the added penalty for inequality associated with this social welfare function, the ordinal ranking of relative welfare levels across regions is the same as that based on the utilitarian specification. Welfare levels in the Northeast, Midwest, and West were approximately equal in 1961 and welfare in the South was much lower;

the difference between the Northeast and the South was 0.38. As with the utilitarian welfare function, there was convergence in regional welfare levels through the early 1990s, but, by 2016, welfare levels in the Northeast, South, and Midwest were little different and higher than welfare attained in the West. The heavier penalty for inequality has the effect of widening the gaps between regions early and late in the sample period but preserves the qualitative features of the relative welfare levels.

Conclusions drawn from the social welfare functions differ markedly from those based on real per capita GDP both in terms of the ordering of regional welfare levels as well as the trends. Recall from Fig. 21.2 that early in the sample period, the levels of per capita GDP in the Northeast, Midwest, and West were of similar magnitudes and much higher than welfare in the South. Moreover, between 1961 and 1981, growth of real per capita GDP in the South exceeded that of the other regions. This matches what is found in Figs. 21.9 and 21.10. However, through the 1980s and early 1990s, there was more dispersion

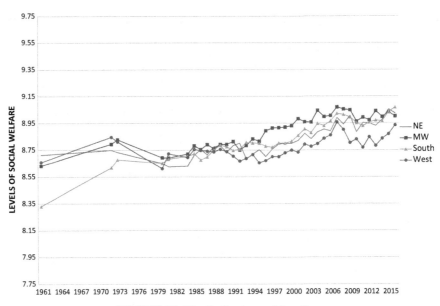

FIGURE 21.10   Egalitarian social welfare.

found with the GDP-based index compared with the social welfare functions. After the 1990s, the Northeast exhibited the highest level of growth and consistently had the highest levels of per capita GDP followed by the West, Midwest, and the South. The differences between regions in 2017 were large. This contrasts with Figs. 21.9 and 21.10 that show that the Midwest had the highest welfare level and the West had the lowest over the same period. In 2016, social welfare differences between the Northeast, Midwest, and South were small and welfare in the West was approximately 10–15% lower.

What accounts for the differences between the social welfare functions and real per capita GDP? The possibilities include:

1. The substitution of expenditures for GDP in measuring individual and social welfare.
2. The use of cross-sectional expenditure data from the CEX rather than comparable PCE data from the national accounts.
3. The inclusion of cross-sectional price variation in measuring individual and social welfare.

4. The incorporation of distributional effects in the measurement of social welfare that is absent from per capita GDP.

We consider the empirical impact of each factor in turn.

21.5.1 PCE consumption versus GDP-based measures

The direct impact of using expenditures rather than GDP to measure social welfare is assessed by comparing per capita GDP with per capita PCE as in Section 21.2. Over the 2 decades between 1997 and 2016, the latter index shows orderings of regional welfare that match those obtained using GDP. Welfare was highest in the Northeast followed by the West, Midwest, and the South. Average growth rates based on the PCE-based index were higher than those obtained using GDP, but both indexes show between-region dispersion increased over the sample period. Substitution of PCE expenditures for GDP alone cannot explain the different conclusions that emerge from the consumption-based social welfare functions and real per capita GDP.

21.5.2 Consumption measurement in the Consumer Expenditure Surveys (CEX)

The isolated effect of substitution of nominal CEX-based expenditures for GDP can be assessed by comparing real per capita GDP with real per capita expenditures defined in (21.5). The latter index deflates CEX expenditures by a national (PCE) price deflator. As noted in Section 21.3, substitution of CEX estimates of aggregate expenditure for GDP has the effect of lowering the average growth rate over the 5 decades by almost one-half both nationally and for each region. Nationally, real per capita GDP increased at an average annual rate of 2.0% per year between 1963 and 2017 compared with 1.2% per year for the comparable index tabulated using the CEX. Despite the lower average growth rates, Fig. 21.5 shows that the CEX-based index largely preserves the ordering of welfare levels across regions obtained using per capita GDP. In most years after 1990, the Northeast had the highest levels of welfare followed by the West, Midwest, and the South.

Lower levels of estimated expenditures in the CEX relative to the PCE have been well-documented.[23] Slesnick (1992, 2001) showed that not only are the CEX levels lower but the correspondence between the two estimates have deteriorated over time. This, in turn, results in substantially lower growth of per capita expenditures in the CEX relative to the PCE. This divergence is only partially explained by definitional and coverage differences between the CEX

and the PCE. More recent work by Meyer et al. (2015) demonstrates that this is also related to increasing measurement error found in a broad array of household surveys.[24]

21.5.3 Regional price effects

The impact of regional price variation can be assessed by comparing real per capita expenditure calculated using the PCE price deflator (defined in (21.5)) with the measure of efficiency (21.9) calculated with the person-specific Paasche price indexes. The only difference between these two measures is the treatment of prices. Comparison of Fig. 21.5 with Fig. 21.11 shows that incorporation of regional price differences largely explains the reordering of welfare levels. The efficiency index shows greater convergence over subperiods and different rankings of regional welfare particularly over the latter half of the sample period. The assumption that prices are the same across regions leads to the conclusion that after 1990 the highest welfare levels were in the Northeast followed by the West, the Midwest, and the South. Over the same period, incorporation of regional price variation shows the highest welfare levels were in the Midwest followed by the South, Northeast, and West.

Does the measure of efficiency change conclusions related to welfare convergence over time across the four regions? As I did with real per capita GDP, I tabulate the between-region standard deviation of log per capita consumption using (21.9). Fig. 21.12 compares the between-region dispersion of the GDP-based index (21.1) and the consumption-based measure of efficiency. The latter shows consistently significantly less between-region variation in welfare

---

[23] Houthakker and Taylor (1970) examined the 1960–61 survey and Gieseman (1978) compared the 1972–73 surveys to the PCE. Slesnick (1992) extended the comparisons to include surveys in the 1980s. See Passero et al. (2015) for more recent assessments.

[24] See, also, Bee et al. (2015) and Attanasio and Pistaferri (2016).

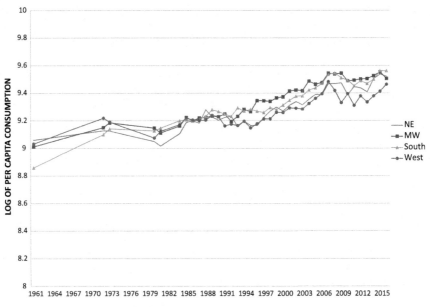

FIGURE 21.11   Measure of efficiency.

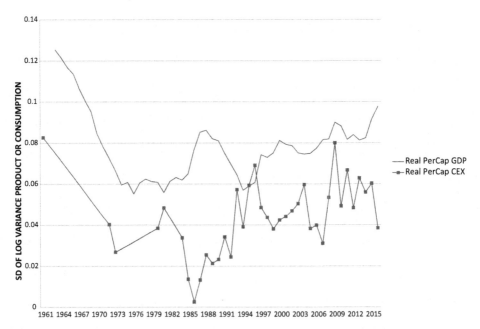

FIGURE 21.12   Between-region inequality. GDP, gross domestic product; CEX, Consumer Expenditure Surveys.

levels in virtually every year compared with the GDP-based index. Regional inequality based on the efficiency index fell sharply between 1961 and 1990. After (1990), between-region dispersion increased but remained lower than the index based on real per capita GDP. Over the entire sample period, neither index leads to an unequivocal conclusion of regional welfare convergence over the 55-year sample period.

21.5.4 Distributional effects

The report by Stiglitz et al. (2009) and subsequent work by Fleurbaey (2009), Jorgenson and Slesnick (2014), and Piketty et al. (2018) point to the fact that GDP-based measures are at best incomplete indicators of social welfare because they do not account for inequality in the distribution of welfare in ranking social states. I can evaluate the impact of welfare dispersion on the measured levels of social welfare directly by comparing the regional levels of inequality as defined in (21.10). The within-region inequalities for each of the four regions are tabulated using

the utilitarian social welfare function and presented in Fig. 21.13.

The impact of inequality on the regional welfare measures varied over the years. At the beginning of the sample period, inequality in the South was substantially higher than in the other three regions. Between 1961 and the early 1980s, dispersion in the South decreased sharply while inequality in the Northeast, Midwest, and West increased. The sharp decrease in welfare dispersion in the South and resultant increase in social welfare over this period had the effect of sharply reducing the between-region welfare dispersion that is seen in Fig. 21.9.

From 1985 to 2005, within-region inequality in the South, Midwest, and Northeast did not change appreciably which implies that distributional effects had little impact on the respective trends of social welfare. By contrast, inequality in the West increased more than the other regions which amplified the deterioration of its position relative to the other regions. The lower levels of inequality in the Midwest from the early 1980s through 2005 partially explain the higher

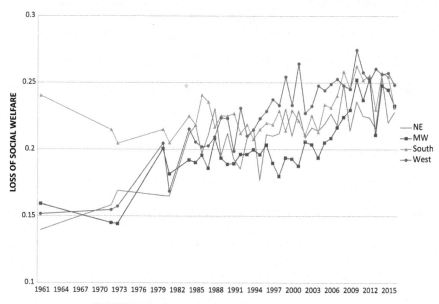

FIGURE 21.13 Within-region inequality—utilitarian.

FIGURE 21.14   Within-region inequality—egalitarian.

levels of social welfare found in this region and the reverse is true for the West. After 2005 inequality levels in the Midwest and South increased while corresponding levels in the Northeast and West showed little net change. Fig. 21.14 repeats the inequality calculations for the egalitarian social welfare function. The measured levels of dispersion are higher as expected but the qualitative conclusions are the same.

To summarize, both the utilitarian and egalitarian social welfare functions show levels and trends of regional welfare that are distinctly different from those based on real per capita GDP. The two indexes order the relative welfare levels across regions differently and show substantially different growth rates. For most years after 1990, real per capita GDP indicates that the highest welfare levels are in the Northeast followed by the West, Midwest, and South. The social welfare functions show much less dispersion of regional welfare levels and indicate that the highest welfare levels are in the Midwest

followed by the South, Northeast, and West. These differences are the result of accounting for regional price variation in the social welfare functions. Distributional effects also affect both levels and trends of regional welfare levels in important ways. Real per capita GDP shows higher levels of growth compared with the social welfare functions, but this reflects differences between estimates of aggregate expenditure in the CEX compared with PCE in the national accounts.

21.6 Summary and conclusions

From the inception of national income accounting, it has been understood that there are conceptual problems associated with the application of GDP as a measure of social welfare. GDP is intended to measure aggregate production and may not accurately reflect social well-being. GDP-based indexes are not functions of individual welfare measures, and there are no well-defined principles of social choice to support their use. The absence of an explicit normative framework leads to the use of measures such as real per capita GDP that ignore distributional effects in assessing social outcomes.

Although these shortcomings have been known for decades, GDP continues to be used either explicitly or implicitly to measure social welfare. It seems natural to simply assume that growth of production translates to an increase of aggregate well-being, and even if GDP does not exactly fit the bill as a measure of social welfare, it may serve as a reasonable proxy. In this paper, I have assessed the empirical performance of real per capita GDP as a representation of aggregate welfare using long time series of regional data for the United States. Each region represents a large (open) economy and the use of regional data produced by the BEA avoids many difficult data problems that plague international comparisons of standards of living. The evolution of regional welfare levels is of independent interest in evaluating changes in efficiency and equity and the extent to which welfare levels converge as regional economies grow.

To address the empirical performance of GDP as a proxy for social welfare, I have specified explicit social welfare functions to serve as benchmarks against which an index such as real per capita GDP can be compared. The arguments of these functions are individual welfare functions that depend on consumption levels. Axioms of social choice serve to limit the set of social welfare functions to specifications that are sensitive to changes in the underlying distribution of individual welfare. The social welfare functions are defined to be equity-regarding so that, all else being equal, more dispersed distributions of individual welfare serve to lower measured levels of social welfare.

The ubiquity of applications that use real GDP as a measure of aggregate welfare largely reflects the ease with which the index can be implemented. Calculation of a measure of social welfare that incorporates the distribution of well-being across the population is inherently more difficult. Individual-level information that records the consumption of goods and services and the associated prices is required. In the United States, the CEX provides household-level information on expenditures but no information on the prices paid. The measurement of social welfare therefore requires splicing data on expenditures with price information from other sources.

Several important conclusions emerge from regional comparisons of real per capita GDP with the consumption-based social welfare measures. As with cross-country studies, assessments of within-country regional standards of living must confront daunting challenges related to data access and quality. Aggregate estimates of total expenditure from the CEX are significantly lower than estimates based on PCE in the national accounts, and the gap between the two data sources has been growing. This implies CEX-based estimates of welfare show significantly lower levels of growth in the standards of living relative to comparable estimates based on the national income accounts. Price-level differences across geographic areas are large which implies that the use of a single national price index to measure individual and social welfare introduces significant errors.

Even with these challenges, several overarching conclusions can be made in assessing the performance of real per capita GDP as a measure of social welfare in regions of the United States. First, GDP clearly does not provide an accurate representation of relative welfare levels compared with the consumption-based social welfare functions. Real per capita GDP was consistently highest in the Northeast and lowest in the South. Substitution of PCE for GDP does not change this result. The CEX-based social welfare function generally matches this ordering of relative welfare levels early in the sample but shows the Northeast, South, and Midwest regions as having standards of living that were of similar magnitude and higher than well-being in the West after the 1990s.

The divergence of the ordinal ranking of welfare levels is related to differences in price levels that are not included in a measure of per capita GDP deflated by the national GDP price deflator. Price levels were significantly higher in the Northeast and the West relative to the Midwest and South, and incorporation of this variation serves to reorder regional welfare levels and increase the observed level of convergence. In most years, between-region dispersion of consumption-based welfare levels was much lower than corresponding measures based on GDP.

The use of a social welfare function also allows an assessment of the empirical importance of distributional effects in assessing welfare levels. Within-region inequality differed across regions and exhibited different trends over the 5 decades. Early in the sample, inequality in the South was much larger than in the other regions but also decreased sharply between 1961 and the mid-1980s. Inequality in the West was among the lowest in 1961 but increased more than the other regions after the 1970s. This variation had differential impacts on the levels and trends of the CEX-based measures of social welfare that were absent from the estimates of real per capita GDP.

What are the broad lessons learned about GDP as a measure of social welfare? The Stiglitz et al. (2009) report suggests a number of possible extensions to traditional models of welfare measurement. Other than the inclusion of distributional effects, these extensions have not been included in the regional comparisons presented in this paper. Within the usual framework of Marshallian individual welfare functions and Bergson—Samuelson social welfare functions, real per capita GDP performs poorly as a proxy for aggregate well-being. One would expect expansion of the scope for welfare measurement beyond the traditional paradigm, such as the inclusion of nonmarket factors or accounting for negative externalities, would exacerbate measurement error further.

The regional comparisons also highlight the importance of accurate estimates of the prices faced by individuals. This issue is discussed by Jorgenson (2018) in the context of international comparisons of GDP as part of the World Bank's International Comparison Program. Conversion of GDP across countries using exchange rates is flawed and should be replaced with Purchasing Power Parities. The importance of price differences across Census regions suggests that an accurate accounting of international variation of price levels is likely to be highly influential in the measurement of relative levels of social welfare across countries and their respective trends.

Finally, it is clear that the incorporation of distributional effects is likely to have an important impact on the measurement of the social standard of living. Even within regions of the United States, inequality influences levels and trends of regional welfare in empirically significant ways. The widely reported rise of income and wealth inequality within and between countries suggests this is likely to have an important effect on cross-country comparisons of social welfare. Failure to account for distributional effects in measuring the social standard of living would be a significant source of measurement error.

References

Arrow KJ: *Social choice and individual values*, New York, 1951, John Wiley and Sons.

Attanasio OP, Pistaferri L: Consumption inequality, *The Journal of Economic Perspectives* 30(2):3—28, 2016.

Attanasio OP, Hurst E, Pistaferri L: The evolution of income, consumption, and leisure inequality in the US 1980-2010. In Chicago, 2015, University of Chicago Press, pp 100—140. Carroll CD, Crossley TF, Sabelhaus J, editors: Improving the measurement of consumer expenditures, *studies in income and wealth*, vol. 74. Chicago, 2015, University of Chicago Press, pp 100—140.

Barro RJ, Sala-i-Martin X: Convergence across states and regions, *Brookings Papers on Economic Activity* (1): 107—182, 1991.

Barro RJ, Sala-i-Martin X: Convergence, *Journal of Political Economy* 100(2):223–251, 1992.

Bee A, Meyer BD, Sullivan JX: The validity of consumption data: are the consumer expenditure interview and diary surveys informative? In Chicago, 2015, University of Chicago Press, pp 204–240. Carroll CD, Crossley TF, Sabelhaus J, editors: Improving the measurement of consumer expenditures, *studies in income and wealth*, vol. 74. Chicago, 2015, University of Chicago Press, pp 204–240.

Blackorby C, Donaldson D: A theoretical treatment of indices of absolute inequality, *International Economic Review* 21(1):107–136, 1980.

Browning M, Chiaporri P-A, Lewbel A: Estimating consumption economies of scale, adult equivalence scales, and household bargaining power, *The Review of Economic Studies* 80:1267–1303, 2013.

Chipman JS, Moore J: The compensation principle in welfare economics. In Zarley A, Moore J, editors: *Papers in quantitative economics*, Lawrence, 1971, University Press of Kansas, pp 1–77.

Chipman JS, Moore J: Aggregate demand, real national income, and the compensation principle, *International Economic Review* 14(1):153–181, 1973.

Diewert WE: Exact and superlative index numbers, *Journal of Econometrics* 4(2):115–145, 1976.

Dynan K, Sheiner L: *GDP as a measure of economic well-being*, Hutchins Center on Fiscal and Monetary Policy Working Paper No. 43, August, 2018.

Fleurbaey M: Beyond GDP: the quest for a measure of social welfare, *Journal of Economic Literature* 47(4):1029–1075, 2009.

Friedman M: *A theory of the consumption function*, Princeton, N.J., 1957, Princeton University Press.

Gieseman R: *A comparison of the 1972-73 consumer expenditure survey results with personal consumption expenditures in the national income and product accounts*, Bureau of Labor Statistics Working Paper, January, 1978.

Hicks JR: Consumer's surplus and index numbers, *The Review of Economic Studies* 9(2):126–137, 1942.

Houthakker HS, Taylor LD: *Consumer demand in the United States: analyses and projections*, ed 2, Cambridge, 1970, Harvard University Press.

Jones CI, Klenow PJ: Beyond GDP? Welfare across countries and time, *The American Economic Review* 106(3):2426–2457, 2016.

Jorgenson DW: Production and welfare: progress in economic measurement, *Journal of Economic Literature* 56(3):867–919, 2018.

Jorgenson DW, Landefeld JS: Blueprint for expanded and integrated U.S. accounts: review, assessment and next steps. In Chicago, 2006, University of Chicago Press, pp 13–112. Jorgenson DW, Landefeld JS, Nordhaus W, editors: *A new architecture for the U.S. National Accounts, studies in income*

and wealth, vol. 66. Chicago, 2006, University of Chicago Press, pp 13–112.

Jorgenson DW, Slesnick DT: Individual and social cost of living indexes. In Diewert WE, Montmarquette C, editors: *Price level measurement*, Ottawa, 1983, Statistics Canada, pp 241–323.

Jorgenson DW, Slesnick DT: Aggregate consumer behavior and the measurement of inequality, *The Review of Economic Studies* 51(166):369–392, 1984a.

Jorgenson DW, Slesnick DT: Inequality in the distribution of individual welfare. In Greenwich, 1984, JAI Press, pp 67–130. Basmann RL, Rhodes GF, editors: *Advances in Econometrics*, vol. 3. Greenwich, 1984b, JAI Press, pp 67–130.

Jorgenson DW, Slesnick DT: Aggregate consumer behavior and household equivalence scales, *Journal of Business & Economic Statistics* 5(2):219–232, 1987.

Jorgenson DW, Slesnick DT: Measuring social welfare in the US national accounts. In Chicago, 2014, University of Chicago Press, pp 43–88. Jorgenson DW, Landefeld JS, Schreyer P, editors: Measuring economic sustainability and progress, *studies in income and wealth*, vol. 72. Chicago, 2014, University of Chicago Press, pp 43–88.

Jorgenson DW, Lau LJ, Stoker TM: The transcendental logarithmic model of aggregate consumer behavior. In Greenwich, CT, 1982, JAI Press, pp 97–238. Basmann RL, Rhodes JF, editors: *Advances in Econometrics*, vol. 1. Greenwich, CT, 1982, JAI Press, pp 97–238.

Kahneman D, Krueger A: Developments in the measurement of subjective well-being, *The Journal of Economic Perspectives* 20(1):3–24, 2006.

Kirman AP: Whom or what does the representative individual represent, *The Journal of Economic Perspectives* 6:117–136, 1992.

Kokoski MF, Cardiff P, Moulton B: *Interarea price indices for consumer goods and services: an hedonic approach using CPI data*, Bureau of Labor Statistics Working Paper No. 256, 1994.

Kolm SC: Unequal inequalities I, *Journal of Economic Theory* 12(3):416–442, 1976a.

Kolm SC: Unequal inequalities II, *Journal of Economic Theory* 13(1):82–111, 1976b.

Lewbel A, Pendakur K: Estimation of collective household models with Engel curves, *Journal of Econometrics* 147:350–358, 2008.

Lise J, Seitz S: Consumption inequality and intra-household allocations, *The Review of Economic Studies* 78:328–355, 2011.

Marshall A: *Principles of economics*, London, 1920, Macmillan.

Meyer BD, Mok W, Sullivan J: Household surveys in crisis, *The Journal of Economic Perspectives* 29(4):199–226, 2015.

Nordhaus WD, Tobin J: Is growth obsolete? In New York, 1972, National Bureau of Economic Research, pp

Measuring growth: fiftieth anniversary colloquium, vol. 5. New York, 1972, National Bureau of Economic Research.

Passero W, Garner TI, McCully C: Understanding the relationship: CE survey and PCE. In Chicago, 2015, University of Chicago Press, pp 181–203. Carroll CD, Crossley TF, Sabelhaus J, editors: Improving the measurement of consumer expenditures, *studies in income and wealth*, vol. 74. Chicago, 2015, University of Chicago Press, pp 181–203.

Piketty T, Saez E, Zucman G: Distributional national accounts: methods and estimates for the United States, *Quarterly Journal of Economics* 133(2):553–609, 2018.

van Praag B: The welfare function of income in Belgium: an empirical investigation, *European Economic Review* 2: 337–369, 1971.

van Praag B: Ordinal and cardinal utility: an integration of the two dimensions of the welfare concept. In Blundell R, Preston I, Walker I, editors: *The measurement of household welfare*, Cambridge, 1994, Cambridge University Press, pp 86–110.

Roberts KW: Possibility theorems with interpersonally comparable welfare levels, *The Review of Economic Studies* 47(147):409–420, 1980.

Stevenson B, Wolfers J: Economic growth and well-being: reassessing the Easterlin paradox, *Brookings Papers on Economic Activity* 39:1–102, 2008.

Sen A: On weights and measures: informational constraints in social welfare analysis, *Econometrica* 45(7):219–231, 1977.

Sen A: *Commodities and capabilities*, Amsterdam, 1985, North Holland.

Sen A: *The standard of living*, Cambridge, 1987, Cambridge University Press.

Sen A: *Inequality reexamined*, Cambridge, MA, 1992, Harvard University Press.

Slesnick DT: Aggregate consumption and saving in the postwar United States, *The Review of Economics and Statistics* 74(4):585–597, 1992.

Slesnick DT: Empirical approaches to the measurement of welfare, *Journal of Economic Literature* 36(4):2108–2165, 1998.

Slesnick DT: *Consumption and social welfare: living standards and their distribution in the United States*, New York, 2001, Cambridge University Press.

Slesnick DT: Prices and the regional variation in welfare, *Journal of Urban Economics* 51(3):446–468, 2002.

Stiglitz JE, Sen A, Fitoussi J-P: *Report by the commission on the measurement of economic performance and social progress*, INSEE.

Accumulation of human and market capital in the United States, 1975–2012: an analysis by gender

Barbara M. Fraumeni[1,2,3,5], *Michael S. Christian*[4]

[1]Central University of Finance and Economics, Haidian, Beijing, China; [2]Hunan University, Changsha, Hunan, China; [3]National Bureau of Economic Research, Cambridge, MA, United States; [4]Education Analytics, Madison, WI, United States; [5]IZA Institute of Labor Economics, Bonn, Germany

Since the mid-1970s in the United States, there have been significant increases in female labor force participation including early-on during child-bearing ages, substantial change in total and by gender human capital arising from higher levels of both male and female educational attainment, a narrowing wage gender gap, and reallocation of time by both males and females. Including an analysis of human capital by gender points to many of the underlying causes of trends in economic growth; including human capital in national accounts is also critical to understanding any trends in economic growth. For example, when contributions to gross private domestic product with and without human capital are examined, the 1995–2000 subperiod looks less remarkable because investment in human capital is less important than in the previous subperiod, while in the 2007 to 2009 subperiod the impact of increases in investment in tertiary education by

both males and females, among other factors, leads to healthier economic growth than would be expected during recession-affected years. This paper, although presenting national accounts, emphasizes human capital factors by gender as these impact longer-term trends across subperiods.

Part I of this chapter outlines human capital and national accounts methodology. Part II describes the underlying factors by gender. Part III presents national-level accounts with and without human capital. Part IV looks at components of human capital by gender over time. Part V concludes.

22.1 Part I: methodology

22.1.1 Human capital

The human capital model employed in this chapter is based on the model of Jorgenson and

Fraumeni (1989, 1992). The Jorgenson–Fraumeni approach is often referred to as a lifetime-income approach, in which the human capital associated with a person is equal to his or her current and future lifetime earnings in present discounted value. The stock of human capital is equal to the sum of lifetime earnings across all persons in a population. Events that add to the stock of human capital (births, education, and immigration) are considered human capital investment, while events that subtract from the stock of human capital (deaths, aging, emigration) are considered human capital depreciation. Jorgenson and Fraumeni's (1989, 1992) measures of human capital include not only a market component based on lifetime earnings in market work, but also a nonmarket component based on time spent in nonmarket work, defined as time outside of market work, schooling, and personal maintenance, valued at an hourly opportunity cost equal to market wage adjusted for the marginal tax rate.

The specific human capital measures employed in this paper, which measure human capital in the United States from 1975 to 2012, are the same measures as in Christian (2017). In the nominal human capital measures, per capita human capital in year y for a person of sex s, age a, and years of education e is equal to

$$i_{y,s,a,e} = yi_{y,s,a,e} + (1+\rho)^{-1}(1+g)sr_{y,s,a+1}$$
$$[senr_{y,s,a,e}\, i_{y,s,a+1,e+1}$$
$$+ (1 - senr_{y,s,a,e})i_{y,s,a+1,e}]$$

$$(22.1)$$

where

s = sex (male or female);
a = age (0–79);
e = years of education (0–18);
$i_{y,s,a,e}$ = per capita lifetime income in year y of persons of sex s, age a, and years of education e;
$yi_{y,s,a,e}$ = per capita yearly income in year y of persons of sex s, age a, and years of education e;

$sr_{y,s,a}$ = survival rate in year y of persons of sex s from age a-1 to age a;
ρ = discount rate;
g = real income growth rate;
$senr_{y,s,a,e}$ = school enrollment rate in year y of persons of sex s, age a, and years of education e.

This approach measures lifetime income in a way that takes into account the probabilities of survival and of school attendance, both in the present and in the future. The primary source of data for measuring yearly income $yi_{y,s,a,e}$ is the March demographic supplement of the Current Population Survey (CPS); that for measuring the school enrollment rate $senr_{y,s,a,e}$ is the October school enrollment supplement of the CPS; and that for measuring the survival rate $sr_{y,s,a}$ is the life tables of the Centers for Disease Control. It is assumed that school enrollment only takes place between ages 5 and 34 (at other ages, $senr_{y,s,a,e} = 0$), and that income is only earned at ages 14 and older (at earlier ages, $yi_{y,s,a,e} = 0$). As in Jorgenson and Fraumeni (1989), the real income growth rate g is assumed to be 2%, while the discount rate ρ is assumed to be 4%.

An exception to Eq. (22.1) is persons aged 80 and older. For these persons, per capita human capital is equal to

$$i_{y,s,80+,e} = \left[1 - (1+\rho)^{-1}(1+g)sr_{y,s,81+}\right]^{-1}$$
$$yi_{y,s,80+,e}$$

$$(22.2)$$

This is the sum of an infinite series and is equal to expected lifetime income given a yearly income $yi_{y,s,80+,e}$ that increases at an annual rate of g, a constant rate of survival $sr_{y,s,81+}$, and a discount rate ρ.

To compute per capita human capital at a given age a, sex s, and level of education e, one begins by first computing per capita human capital for persons aged 80 and older using Eq. (22.2), and then working backward to ages

79, 78, etc., all the way to age a by applying Eq. (22.1). To compute the stock of human capital, one computes the sum of per capita human capital times population across all combinations of age, sex, and education:

$$hc_y = \sum_s \sum_a \sum_e \left(pcount_{y,s,a,e} \times i_{y,s,a,e}\right) \qquad (22.3)$$

where

$pcount_{y,s,a,e}$ = population in year y of persons of sex s, age a, and years of education e.

The change in the stock of human capital from 1 year to next can be broken out into net investment and revaluation as follows:

$$hc_{y+1} - hc_y = inv_{net(y)} + reval_y \qquad (22.4)$$

where

$$inv_{net(y)} = \sum_s \sum_a \sum_e \left[\left(pcount_{y+1,s,a,e}\right. \right.$$
$$\left.\left. - pcount_{y,s,a,e}\right) \times i_{y,s,a,e}\right] \qquad (22.5)$$

and

$$reval_y = \sum_s \sum_a \sum_e \left[pcount_{y+1,s,a,e}\right.$$
$$\left. \times \left(i_{y+1,s,a,e} - i_{y,s,a,e}\right)\right] \qquad (22.6)$$

Net investment in human capital is the effect on human capital of changes, from 1 year to the next, in the size and distribution of the population by age, sex, and education, weighted using lifetime earnings from the earlier of the 2 years. Revaluation is the change in the nominal value of lifetime earnings—the "price" of human capital—from 1 year to the next, weighted using the size and distribution of the population in the later of the 2 years.

In the measures used in this paper, net investment is not only measured as a whole, but also broken down into five components: investment from births; investment from education, net of aging while in school; depreciation from aging of persons not enrolled in school; depreciation from deaths; and residual net investment. These are equal to:

$$inv_{births(y)} = \sum_s \left[pcount_{y,s,0,0} \times i_{y,s,0,0}\right] \qquad (22.7)$$

$$dep_{deaths(y)} = -\sum_s \sum_a \sum_e \left[pcount_{y,s,a,e}\left(1 - sr_{y,s,a+1}\right)\right.$$
$$\left. \times i_{y,s,a,e}\right] \qquad (22.8)$$

$$inv_{ed(y)} = \sum_s \sum_a \sum_e \left[pcount_{y,s,a,e}sr_{y,s,a+1}senr_{y,s,a,e} \times \left(i_{y,s,a+1,e+1} - i_{y,s,a,e}\right)\right]$$
$$= \sum_s \sum_a \sum_e \left[\left(pcount_{y,s,a-1,e-1}sr_{y,s,a}senr_{y,s,a-1,e-1} - pcount_{y,s,a,e}sr_{y,s,a+1}senr_{y,s,a,e}\right) \times i_{y,s,a,e}\right]$$
$$(22.9)$$

$$dep_{aging(y)} = -\sum_s \sum_a \sum_e \left[pcount_{y,s,a,e}sr_{y,s,a+1}\left(1 - senr_{y,s,a,e}\right) \times \left(i_{y,s,a+1,e} - i_{y,s,a,e}\right)\right]$$
$$= -\sum_s \sum_a \sum_e \left[\left(pcount_{y,s,a-1,e}sr_{y,s,a}\left(1 - senr_{y,s,a-1,e}\right)\right.\right. \qquad (22.10)$$
$$\left.\left. - pcount_{y,s,a,e}sr_{y,s,a+1}\left(1 - senr_{y,s,a,e}\right)\right) \times i_{y,s,a,e}\right]$$

$$inv_{resid(y)} = inv_{net(y)} - inv_{births(y)} - inv_{ed(y)}$$
$$+ dep_{deaths(y)} + dep_{aging(y)}$$

$$(22.11)$$

Of the above components of net investment, two are substantive departures from the original Jorgenson–Fraumeni approach and deserve further discussion.

The first of these, investment in education, net of aging, is the combined effect of having both increased 1 year in age and 1 year in education while in school. This is different from the approach of the original Jorgenson–Fraumeni papers, which measured the effect on human capital from education alone. The effects of education and aging are combined here to avoid making the assumption that the future schooling outcomes of persons not currently enrolled in school (who, among children of school age, are falling "off track" of typical educational progress) are the same as what the future schooling outcomes of persons currently enrolled in school would be in a counterfactual in which they were not currently enrolled in school. This assumption can lead to very high measures of gross educational investment, which are not robust to alternative assumptions (see Christian, 2010, for more discussion). It is useful to note that, because investment in education is measured net of aging, measures of depreciation from aging only include persons not enrolled in school.

The second of these, residual net investment, is the combined effect of net migration into and out of the United States and of measurement error. Net migration is included in residual net investment because, unlike births, deaths, education, and population, it is not measured in such a way as to be easily incorporated into the human capital account. Measurement error exists because the measures of births, deaths, education, and population used in the paper are not perfectly integrated, which means that there will be some differences in measured population

from 1 year to the next that are not explained by births, deaths, aging, education, or migration.

When we measure gross investment, we include residual net investment, as well as investment from births and education:

$$inv_{gross(y)} = inv_{births(y)} + inv_{ed(y)} + inv_{resid(y)}$$

$$(22.12)$$

As in the original Jorgenson–Fraumeni accounts, both market and nonmarket components of human capital are measured. To measure these separate components, we begin by measuring market yearly income and nonmarket yearly income separately. Market yearly income is measured using average wage, salary, and self-employment income by year, age, sex, and education, using data from the March CPS. To measure nonmarket yearly income, we first compute per capita hours in nonmarket production, equal to per capita hours spent outside of market work, school (set to 1300 hours per year times the school enrollment rate), or personal maintenance (set to 10 h per day) by age, sex, and education. This is multiplied by the hourly opportunity cost of not participating in market work, which is equal to the wage times 1 minus the marginal tax rate. We compute wages and hours in market work by age, sex, and education using the March CPS; school enrollment rates by age, sex, and education from the October CPS; and marginal tax rates using the Internet version of TAXSIM (Feenberg and Coutts, 1993). Combining market and nonmarket yearly income produces total yearly income:

$$yi_{y,s,a,e}(\text{total}) = yi_{y,s,a,e}(\text{market})$$
$$+ yi_{y,s,a,e}(\text{nonmarket}) \qquad (22.13)$$

We compute market, nonmarket, and total lifetime income by alternatively using market, nonmarket, or total yearly income as the measure of yearly income $yi_{y,s,a,e}$ in Eqs. (22.1) and (22.2). Similarly, we compute market, nonmarket, and total human capital stock and investment by alternatively using market, nonmarket, or total lifetime income as the measure of lifetime income $i_{y,s,a,e}$ in Eqs. (22.3) through (22.12).

We compute real measures of the human capital stock by producing a chained Fisher volume index in which volume is population by age, sex, and education and weight is lifetime income by age, sex, and education. This is computed separately for market human capital, nonmarket human capital, and total human capital, using market lifetime income, nonmarket lifetime income, and total lifetime income as a weight. The real human capital stock in a given year y is equal to the nominal human capital stock in the base year times the ratio of the value of the Fisher volume index in year y to the value of the Fisher volume index in the base year:

$$hc_y(\text{real}) = hc_{base} \times (F_y / F_{base}) \qquad (22.14)$$

where F_y and F_{base} are values of the Fisher volume index in year y and in the base year. Real investment from births and education and depreciation from deaths and aging are similarly computed using a Fisher volume index that uses lifetime income as a weight and the terms multiplied by lifetime income on the right-hand sides of Eqs. (22.7) through (22.10) as the disaggregated volume.

Real net investment is computed by subtracting the real stock of human capital from a 1-year lead of the real stock:

$$inv_{net(y)}(\text{real}) = hc_{y+1}(\text{real}) - hc_y(\text{real}) \qquad (22.15)$$

Real residual net investment is computed as the residual left over from real net investment after subtracting real investment from births and education and adding real depreciation from deaths and aging of individuals not enrolled in school.

22.1.2 National accounts

The national accounts methodology for all five national accounts is described in detail in Fraumeni et al. (2017).[1] In this paper, a 2009 production account is shown in Table 22.1.[2]

As in the "new architecture" accounts (Jorgenson and Landefeld, 2006, 2009), the core production account of the U.S. Bureau of Economic Analysis (BEA) national and income and product accounts (NIPA) is modified in a number of ways, but the estimates presented in this table, aside from the human capital components, are all but one from the U.S. BEA NIPA (U.S. Bureau of Economic Analysis, various dates). In the product account to allow for integration with productivity accounts, property-type taxes are included, but some other types of taxes, such as primarily sales taxes, are not included. Imputations for market capital services (see line 16 of the product account) add into gross private domestic product (GPDP) several capital services that are not in U.S. BEA NIPA Gross Domestic Product (GDP). These include those for consumer durables and real estate held by institutions and producer durable equipment held by institutions. The other imputation included in

---

[1] The five accounts are (1) production, (2) full (expanded) private national labor and gross national property income, (3) full (expanded) gross private national receipts and expenditures, (4) full (expanded) gross private national capital accumulation, and (5) full (expanded) private national wealth. Tables in the main body of Fraumeni et al. (2017) outline the accounts; Appendix B of that paper presents the underlying data for 1948–84 and 1998–2009 for that previous version of the accounts.

[2] 2009 is the base year for the national income and product accounts of the U.S. Bureau of Economic Analysis (BEA). Table 1 comes from p. S396 of Fraumeni et al.(2017), except for the human capital components: lines 18–21 of the entries under "product" and line 5 of the factor entries under "factor outlay." These human capital components were computed by Christian for this paper.

TABLE 22.1 Production in 2012 (billions of dollars).

		Product		
1		Gross national product (table 1.7.5, line 4)	16,497.4	
2	−	Rest-of-world gross national product (table 1.7.5, line 2 minus line 3)	252.9	
3	−	Compensation of government employees (table 6.2D, line 86)	1,742.8	
4	−	Government consumption of fixed capital (table 5.1, line 17)	493.6	
5	=	Gross private domestic product (NIPA definition)		14,008.1
6	−	Federal taxes on production and imports (table 3.5, line 2)	118.0	
7	−	Federal current transfer receipts from business (table 3.2, line 17)	28.7	
8	+	Capital stock tax (table 3.5, line 12)	0.0	
9	−	State and local taxes on production and imports (table 3.5, line 13)	1,004.9	
10	−	State and local current transfer receipts from business (table 3.3, line 18)	41.9	
11	+	Business property taxes (table 3.5, line 27)	440.0	
12	+	Business motor vehicle licenses (table 3.5, line 28)	9.8	
13	+	Business other taxes (table 3.5, sum of lines 29–31)	80.3	
14	+	Subsidies less current surplus of federal government enterprises (table 3.2, line 32 minus line 19)	70.2	
15	+	Subsidies less current surplus of state and local government enterprises (table 3.3, line 25 minus line 20)	14.8	
16	+	Imputations for nonhuman capital services	789.0	
17	=	Gross private domestic product (Christensen-Jorgenson*)		14,218.7
18	+	Time in household production and leisure	14,886.0	
19	+	Investment in human capital, births	9,916.3	
20	+	Investment in human capital, education, net of aging	8,032.8	
21	+	Investment in human capital, residual	2,258.9	
22	=	Expanded gross private domestic product		49,312.8
		Factor outlay		
1		Compensation of employees, all private industries (table 6.2D, line 3)	6,877.2	
2	+	Entrepreneurial labor income (imputation)	1,114.6	
3	+	Full property outlay (line 17 from the product account, minus lines 1 and 2 from the factor outlay account)	6,226.9	6,226.9
4	=	Gross private domestic factor outlay (Christensen-Jorgenson*)		14,218.7
5	+	Imputations for human capital services from product account above (lines 18–21)	35,094.0	
6	=	Expanded gross private domestic factor outlay		49,312.8

Notes: Totals may differ slightly from the sums due to rounding. Table numbers refer to the National Income and Product Accounts (U.S. Bureau of Economic Analysis, various dates).
* Christensen and Jorgenson developed what is called the U.S. Worksheets, which modified NIPA GDP and factor outlay as outlined above. The worksheets have never been published, but the earliest published production account using them appears on p. 23 of Christensen LR, Jorgenson DW: U.S. real product and real factor input, 1929-1967, Review of Income and Wealth 16(1):19–50, 1970.

line 16 of the product account is the difference between the value of household real estate capital services imputed in the "new architecture" accounts and that included in U.S. BEA NIPA GDP. These modifications are relatively minor in scale. It is the human capital components (lines 18 through 21) that substantially change the magnitude of GPDP.

In the production account, human capital components appear both in product and factor outlay. Expanded consumption includes market consumption as well as time in household production and leisure.[3] Time in household production and leisure, which is valued at the market wage, excludes time in school and time in sleep and maintenance. Expanded (gross) investment includes market investment as well as investment in births, education, and the residual. Human capital components are part of labor factor outlay. In Table 22.1, expanded labor factor outlay is equal to the sum of all components except for line 3: property outlay. Human capital labor factor outlay combines time in household production and leisure and human capital investment. As there are no human capital property factor outlay components, property outlay includes only market property outlay.

Net investment does not appear in the production account, but its components are of interest. Net investment is equal to investment (gross) which appears in the production account,

minus depreciation due to aging of individuals not enrolled in school and deaths.

In nominal values, this period's human capital stock is equal to the stock in the previous period plus this period's net investment and the previous period's revaluation. Because some underlying estimates in the complete Christian (2017) data base, such as residual net investment, are negative, all real net investment estimates are constructed using additive aggregation.[4] In 2009 dollars, this period's human capital stock is equal to the stock in the previous period plus this period's net investment.

22.2 Part II: underlying trends by gender

As noted in the introduction, the period from the mid-1970s to 2012 is a period of significant changes impacting on human capital.

Between 1970 and 2010, there were relatively minor changes in the male civilian labor force rates by age, but significant changes in the female civilian labor force rates by age.[5] As Fig. 22.1 shows, between 1970 and 1980, the shape of the civilian female labor force participation rate by age profile changed significantly, from one in which the impact of child-bearing could clearly be seen to one in which this was no longer true. The apex of civilian female labor force participation rate by age profile rose by

---

[3] The adjective "expanded" refers to constructs that include both human and market components. In previous published versions of this research (Jorgenson and Fraumeni, 1989; Fraumeni et al., 2017) the adjective "full" was used instead of the adjective "expanded." In addition, the adjective "nonhuman" was frequently used when referring to market (nonhuman) components.

[4] However, contributions by gender to human components by market, nonmarket, and household production and leisure are constructed with a Törnqvist index as the totals for these categories are all positive numbers (for example, see Fig. 22.8).

[5] The sources for figures 1 and 2 are: For years prior to 2010: U.S. Census Bureau, *Statistical Abstract of the United States: 2000*, Table no. 644. Civilian Labor Force and Participation Rates with Projections (1970) to 2008, p. 403; for 2010: Toossi, Mitra "Employment outlook: 2010–20, Labor force Projections to 2020: a More Slowly Growing Workforce" Table 3. Civilian labor force participation rates, by age, gender, race, and ethnicity, 1990, 2000, 2010, and projected 2020, U.S. Bureau of Labor Statistics, *Monthly Labor Review*, January 2012, pp. 50–51.

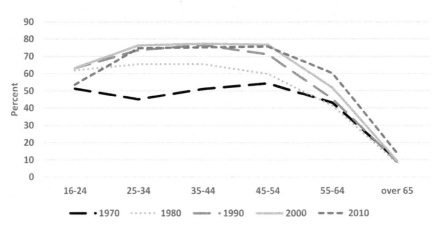

FIGURE 22.1 Civilian female labor force participation rates, 1970, 1980, 1990, 2000, and 2010.

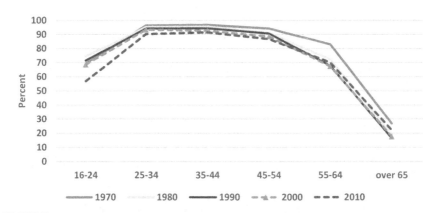

FIGURE 22.2 Civilian male labor force participation rates, 1970, 1980, 1990, 2000, and 2010.

over 10 percentage points between 1970 and 1980 and again between 1980 and 1990, to end up at around 75%, before the whole profile showed minor changes between 1990, 2000, and 2010. As Fig. 22.2 shows, the apex of the male civilian male labor force profile did drop from around 95% in 1970, 1980, and 1990 to around 92% in 2000 and 2010.

Over the period 1975 to 2010, average educational attainment for both males and females aged 15 and over increased substantially.[6] The

difference between genders is at most 0.4 years of school; the average for both began in 1975 at about 11.5 years and ended at something just over 13 years in 2010. However, a comparison of average number of years of school by gender for those aged 25–34 versus 55–64 is striking. Until 1995 as Fig. 22.3 shows, the difference between years of school for the younger versus the older individuals is at least 1.5 years. Beginning in 1995 the difference decreases substantially for both genders, most notably starting in

---

[6] The source of the educational attainment (years in school) data is Barro and Lee (2016).

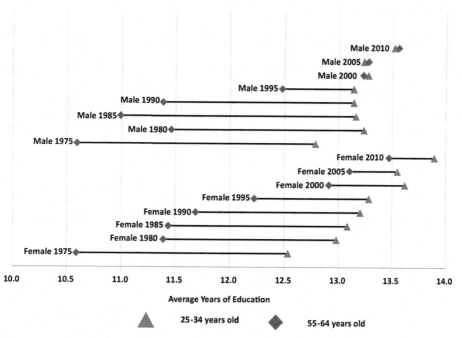

FIGURE 22.3　Educational attainment comparisons by gender, ages 25–34 versus ages 55–64, 1975, 1980, 1985, 1990, 1995, 2000, 2005, 2010.

2000 there is no appreciable difference between younger and older males. In fact, in 2005 and 2010, years of school of younger males is slightly less than for older males. In contrast, the number of years of school of younger females continues to be greater than for older females. By 2010, the years of school of younger females is greater than either that of younger or older males. It is expected that the female pipeline will lead to a higher 15 and over average for females than males as younger females age. This development is clearly in part a function of a larger percentage

of 18- to 24-year-old females than males enrolled in postsecondary degree-granting institutions beginning in 1991 (Fig. 22.4).[7]

Between 1975 and 2012 the labor income gender gap narrowed.[8] The average income of a full-time year-round female worker as a percent of males rose from 56.2% in 1975 to 72.5% in 2012. The increase in the percent is not monotonic, notably it declined in 1999, 2000, and 2008. The percent peaked at 72.9% in 2007, subsequently hovering at around 72% from 2010 to 2012.

[7] The source of the data underlying Fig. 22.4 is table 302.60 of the National Center for Education Statistics (NCES), *Digest of Education* Statistics 2016, https://nces.ed.gov/programs/digest/d15/tables/dt15_302.60.asp, accessed March 15, 2018.

[8] Table P-37 of U.S. Census Bureau, *Current Population Survey, Annual Social and Economic Supplements,* Accessed online March 13, 2018. Note that individuals 15 years old and over beginning with March 1980, and individuals 14 years old and over as of March of the following year for previous years are included in the source table estimates.

FIGURE 22.4   Percentage of 18- to 24-year-olds enrolled in postsecondary degree-granting institutions by gender, 1975–2012.

At the same time that females' average wages as a percent of males' rose, the allocation of time between market work and time in household production and leisure changed.[9] As a share of time excluding sleep and maintenance, in 1975 males on average spent a larger share of their time in school than females; the probability that a male was enrolled in school is greater than that for a female. By 2012, this share of time is almost equal for males and females because the probability that a female is enrolled in school caught up to that of males. Of greater interest are the changes in shares of time in market work and household production and leisure excluding time in school over this time period. It is not surprising that as a larger percentage of females moved into the labor force, they substituted market work time for household production and leisure time, to the tune of about

0.05 percentage point in the shares (see Table 22.2). Males substituted household production and leisure time for market work time, but they reallocated their time on average to a much lesser degree as the change amounted to only 0.006 percentage point in the shares.

22.3 Part III: national level accounts

Including human capital in any analysis is key to understanding economic growth. Figs. 22.5 and 22.6 show the growth accounting components with and without human capital.[10] On the output side, the contributions to economic growth are those from consumption and investment. On the input side, the contributions to economic growth are those from capital, labor, and change in multifactor productivity growth.

[9] Time use and all human capital data, which were computed for this paper based on Current Population Survey data, come from Christian.

[10] All real estimates in this paper combining human and market components are constructed with a Törnqvist index.

TABLE 22.2 Shares of time in market work and household production of leisure all ages, including children, 1975 and 2012.

	Male hours share		Female hours share	
	Market work	Household production and leisure	Market work	Household production and leisure
1975	0.225	0.775	0.112	0.888
2012	0.219	0.781	0.164	0.836

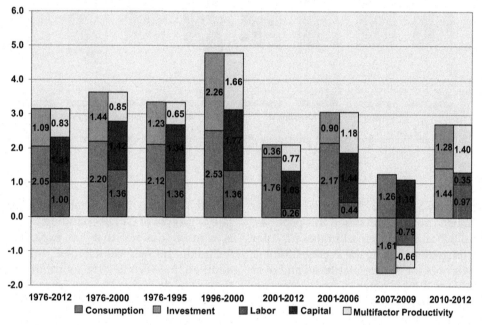

FIGURE 22.5 Contributions to gross private domestic product and economic growth without human capital, 1976–2012.

Fig. 22.6 includes the expanded GPDP components, while Fig. 22.5 does not. As Table 22.1 shows, the expanded GPDP human capital components, which include investment in education, net of aging, time in household production and leisure, and the residual, are very large relative to GPDP. Growth in human capital components depends upon population growth by category, and increasing levels of education and wage growth as reflected in lifetime income weights. These all grow slowly compared to GDP. According to the World Bank, US population

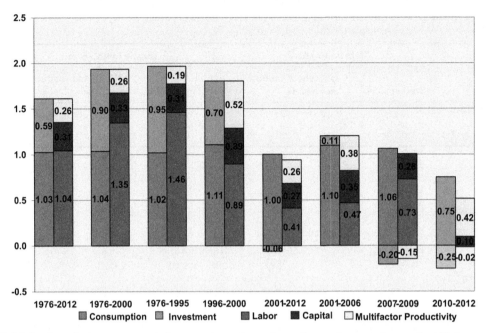

FIGURE 22.6 Contributions to expanded gross private domestic product and economic growth with human capital, 1976–2012.

growth from 1975 to 2012 averaged 1.04% per year.[11] Human capital estimates in this paper assume a real labor income growth rate of 2% per year. The progress in raising the average number of years in school for the population 15 and over (Barro and Lee, 2016) is notable, the increase per year averages at most 0.4% per year from 1975 to 2010. The average rate of growth in real GDP is 2.9% per year from 1975 to 2012.[12] Individuals are more highly educated on average, but population growth is slow. Accordingly for the whole

period 1975 to 2012, it is not surprising that the rate of growth of GPDP excluding human capital is almost double that of expanded GPDP including human capital (see Table 22.3); in addition, the 1976 to 2012 contribution of multifactor productivity change excluding human capital is about three times that in the accounts including human capital.[13]

In all subperiods starting with 1996 or later there are notable differences in the contributions with and without human capital as well as

---

[11] World Bank, World Bank Indicators, last updated March 1, 2018, accessed online April 14, 2018.

[12] U.S. BEA NIPA, table 1.1.1, accessed April 14, 2018.

[13] As the quantities of human capital investment and time in household production and leisure on the output side appear as nonmarket labor input on the input side, human capital components do not contribute to multifactor productivity.

TABLE 22.3 Real rate of growth of gross private domestic product (GPDP) with and without human capital, 1975–2012.

Years	GPDP	GPDP	Ratio of growth rates of GPDP without human capital to with human capital
	Without human capital	With human capital	
1975–2012	3.14	1.61	1.95
1975–2000	3.64	1.93	1.88
1975–1995	3.35	1.97	1.70
1995–2000	4.79	1.81	2.65
2000–12	2.12	0.94	2.26
2000–06	3.06	1.20	2.55
2006–09	-0.36	0.86	-0.42
2009–12	2.71	0.50	5.45

changes in the relative growth rate of GPDP across subperiods.[14,15] Between 1995 and 2000 and 2000 and 2006, the quantity of human capital investment either rose slightly or fell. As Fig. 22.3 shows, 1995 is the year in which the average years of school of 25–34 year olds compared to 55–64 year olds for both genders narrowed. In subsequent years, as previously noted, there is almost no difference in years of school for the younger and older males. The subperiod 1996–2000 is a remarkable time for the impact of computers on economic growth, but

[14] In the "Contributions to Expanded Gross Private Domestic Product and Economic Growth" charts, the following growth rates are included in the calculation of contributions by subperiods.

1976–2012	1975–76 ... 2011–12
1976–2000	1975–76 ... 1999–2000
1976–95	1975–76 ... 1994–95
1996–2000	1995–96 ... 1999–2000
2001–12	2000–01 ... 2011–12
2001–06	2000–01 ... 2005–06
2007–09	2006–07 ... 2008–09
2010–12	2009–10 ... 2011–12

[15] Contributions are calculated as a weighted rate of growth of quantities in logs, where the weights are the average share of this period's and last period's nominal values. The multifactor productivity change contribution is the exception as it is the rate of growth of the quantity of output minus the contributions of all inputs.

not for human capital investment.[16] When human capital is included, there is little difference between this and previous subperiods. In 2001–06, the contribution of investment including human capital is only one-tenth of consumption including time in household production and leisure.

During the 2007 through 2009 Great Recession years, tertiary enrollment and time use by both men and women differs compared to other subperiods.[17] Changes in tertiary enrollment percentages and time use shares by either gender are small or nonexistent in the prior and the later subperiod. From 2006 to 2009, the percentages of individuals aged 18 to 24 enrolled in a postsecondary degree-granting institution increased substantially and the share of time devoted to work dropped by almost the identical amount that the share of time in household production and leisure increased as the share of time devoted to school stayed almost constant. From 2006 to 2009, the percent of 18- to 24-year-old males enrolled in a postsecondary degree-granting institution increased by 4.3 percentage points from 34.1% to 38.4%; for females the comparable figures are 3.6 percentage points from 40.6% to 44.2%.[18] Over the same period, considering time devoted to household production and leisure and market work, the male share of time devoted to household production and leisure (market work) rose (decreased) by 2.4 percentage points; for females the comparable figure is 0.8 percentage points.

From 2007 to 2009, as shown in the output side of the contributions charts, the contributions of both consumption and investment are larger

in absolute value terms when human capital is excluded; however, output growth is positive only when human capital is included. The increase in tertiary enrollment is a positive investment in education, net of aging, contribution to economic growth as is the increase in consumption from a larger share of time devoted to household production and leisure. In addition, from 2006 to 2009, in spite of the recession beginning in late 2007, the quantity of market consumption increases, while the quantity of market investment as expected decreases substantially.

During the same period, the fact that human labor input is so large relative to market labor input, ranging from about 80 to 83% of total nominal labor input, changes the growth picture substantially. Human labor input is set equal to human capital investment, including the residual, plus time in household production and leisure. First, the positive contribution of human labor input outweighs the negative contribution of market labor input. Second, although in both charts capital input is all market capital input, because the share of market capital input is much smaller in the chart including human capital given the large magnitude of human labor input, the contribution of capital to output is substantially less than in the chart without human capital. The contribution of multifactor productivity change is negative both with and without human capital, but it is substantially less negative when the positive influence of human labor input is factored into the analysis. The contribution of multifactor productivity change is negative both with and without

---

[16] Human capital investment in education occurs when individuals are in school.

[17] The official dates for the "Great Recession" from the National Bureau of Economic Research Business Cycle Dating Committee are December 2007 (peak) to June 2009 (trough). Annual growth rates in real GDP declined substantially from 2004 through 2007, accordingly it is not surprising that time use and enrollments are impacted beginning in 2007. U.S. BEA NIPA real GDP annual growth rates are: 3.8% in 2004, 3.3% in 2005, 2.7% in 2006, and 1.8% in 2007.

[18] Table 302.60, NCES, *Digest of Education* Statistics 2016. https://nces.ed.gov/programs/digest/d15/tables/dt15_302.60.asp.

human capital, with the contribution of multifactor productivity change without human capital being more than four times more negative than that with human capital.

In the next subperiod: 2010–12, market investment recovers; the quantity of market investment increases by about 25% between 2009 and 2012, but the quantity of human investment declines by over 4% in the same time period. On net, expanded labor input decreases, and capital input (which is all market) increases, and the contribution of multifactor productivity growth to growth in expanded GPDP is almost a full percentage point less than the contribution of multifactor productivity growth to growth in GPDP, excluding human capital.

22.4 Part IV: human capital components by gender

Delving into the components of human capital investment and stock and allocation of time by gender reveals additional trends over time. Gross investment is the sum of births, education, net of aging, and residual components (Eq. 22.12). Net investment subtracts depreciation due to aging of individuals not enrolled and

deaths. Both investment and stock can be separated into market and nonmarket components. The nonmarket component includes human capital investment and time in household production and leisure. As residual net investment and some elements of detailed investment by gender, age, and education can be negative, contributions cannot be calculated for human capital gross or net investment except by market human and nonmarket human components.

In most cases between 1975 and 2012, male nominal investment shares and stock shares of totals for the country generally trend downward and female nominal shares generally trend upward. In all cases, the pace of the share changes slowed sometime in the 1990s and the percent change between 1975 and 2012 is larger for females than for males. It is not surprising that the biggest percent change in any share at 15.8% is for female investment in births (see Table 22.4); however, the female percent changes for investment in education, net of aging, depreciation due to deaths, and human capital stock are all between 13.4% and 14.0%. No female share of total for the country is at or above 50%, but all but one are close to 45% or above by 2012. All female shares begin in the range of about 35%–40%. The largest decrease in the

TABLE 22.4 Human capital components nominal shares, 1975 and 2012.

Year	Gross investment		Investment in births		Investment in education, net of aging	
	Male	Female	Male	Female	Male	Female
1975	0.592	0.408	0.614	0.386	0.611	0.389
2012	0.556	0.444	0.553	0.447	0.556	0.444

Year	Depreciation				Stock	
	Aging from individuals not enrolled in school		Deaths			
	Male	Female	Male	Female	Male	Female
1975	0.590	0.410	0.651	0.349	0.591	0.409
2012	0.545	0.455	0.604	0.396	0.537	0.463

TABLE 22.5   Human capital investment and time in household (HH) production and leisure, nominal Shares, 1975 and 2012.

	Male			Female		
Year	Market human capital	Nonmarket human capital	Time in HH production and leisure	Market human capital	Nonmarket human capital	Time in HH production and leisure
1975	0.316	0.333	0.351	0.165	0.416	0.419
2012	0.266	0.331	0.403	0.191	0.360	0.449

	Male		Female	
	Market human capital	Nonmarket human capital	Market human capital	Nonmarket human capital
1975	0.487	0.513	0.284	0.716
2012	0.446	0.554	0.347	0.653

male percent share is for investment in births, foretelling future changes in human capital stocks.

Table 22.2 demonstrated that women are spending less of their time in household production and leisure, but the nominal share of household production and leisure, relative to market and nonmarket human capital investment nominal shares, has increased (see Table 22.5). This occurs as a result of wages paid to women rising by more than enough to compensate for the reduction in time. In Table 22.5, three-way and two-way nominal shares are both presented. Although the share of male nonmarket human capital is essentially unchanging between 1975 and 2012, it is in part because there is a reallocation of time between market work and time in household production and leisure as Table 22.2

shows.[19] In both two-way and three-way comparisons, the female market and nonmarket human capital investment nominal shares remain substantially below those for men compared to the time in household production and leisure nominal share. In addition, in both comparisons, the female nominal share of time in household production and leisure remains substantially above those for men.

Examining real net investment components: investment in births and education, net of aging, residual, and aging from individuals not enrolled in school and death depreciation, underscores gender and subperiod differences. In absolute value terms, the size of the real net investment components are significantly different between the first major subperiod: 1975 to 2000, and the second: 2001 to 2012. Fig. 22.7

---

[19] The nominal value of time in household production and leisure only depends on time spent today and the current market wage. Since market and nonmarket human capital are lifetime income constructs, there are a number of factors which affect their nominal value, such as expected future education, number of working years, and survival rate. The real income growth rate is 2% for all future years.

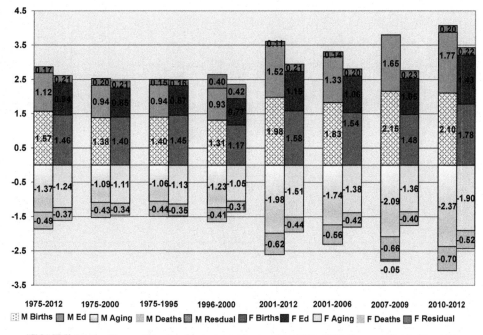

FIGURE 22.7　Shares of real net investment by gender, 1975–2012 (percent divided by 100).

shows that the positive and negative components for both genders become significantly larger.[20,21] The increasing levels of education, particularly tertiary education, influence both investment in education, net of aging, and investment in births, the latter as the expectation of higher future enrollments increases newborns' expected lifetime income. In 2000, although the average years of school of males aged 25–34 is almost the same as the average years of school of males aged 55–64, the average years of school for those younger is substantially greater than it is in 1995 (Fig. 22.3). Female average years of school for those aged 25–34 continued to increase over the second major subperiod. As

individuals age, their lifetime income decreases as they have fewer years before they die. Baby boomers births, those born between mid-1946 and mid-1964, which created a demographic bulge, by 2001 are between 37 and 55 years of age, and by 2012 are between 48 and 66 years of age.[22] Accordingly, it is not surprising that the male share of real net investment for both aging for individuals not enrolled in school and death depreciation becomes more negative in each of the subperiods 2001–06, 2007–09, and 2010–12. Although the female share of net investment for aging for individuals not enrolled in school and death depreciation does not become more negative in each of the three

---

[20] The sum of the real net investment percent shares is 100, but in Fig. 22.7 the percent shares are divided by 100 to fit them within the bars. Accordingly, the percent shares in Fig. 22.7 sum to 1.0.

[21] Contributions cannot be computed by these components of real net investment as residual investment is negative in a number of years. For the same reason, net investment is computed with additive aggregation.

[22] Colby and Ortman (2014).

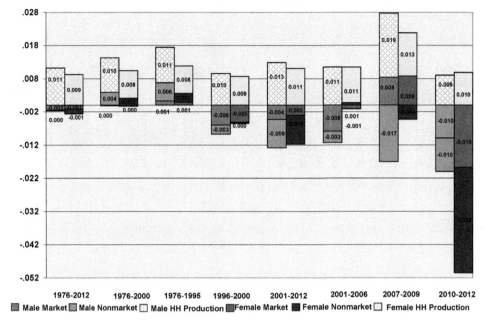

FIGURE 22.8 Expanded GDP contributions by gender 1975–2012.

subperiods, these shares are significantly more negative than those for the first major subperiod. In general, depreciation from aging for individuals not enrolled in school is greater for more highly educated individuals than for less highly educated individuals. Women live longer than males on average and are becoming more highly educated, but even in 2010 older males are more highly educated on average than older females (Fig. 22.3).

Another way to examine gender differences is to consider contributions of the expanded GDP components: market human capital net investment, nonmarket human capital net investment, and time in household production and leisure net investment to human components by gender as shown in Fig. 22.8.[23,24] In all but the earliest

lowest level subperiod: 1976–95, for both genders, there are at least some negative contributions, but the time in household production and leisure contribution is always positive. As the time that men spend in household production and leisure is going up, it is expected that the contribution of this component will be positive. The fairly consistent downward trend in female time in household production and leisure per capita ends in 2000, yet female total time in household production and leisure increases in all years as population growth more than offsets the decrease in time per capita. In the 2007–09 subperiod the contribution of male time in household production and leisure is substantially larger than it is for other years. In the same subperiod, the female contribution is larger

[23] These contributions can be presented as nonmarket labor outlay is estimated with a Törnqvist index from the aggregate quantities of market and nonmarket human capital investment and time in household production by gender, which are always positive.

[24] The investment in human capital, residual is included in the respective net investment totals.

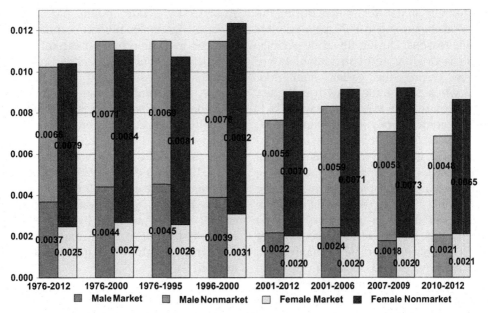

FIGURE 22.9   Human capital stock contributions by gender, 1975–2012.

than in any other subperiod. In both cases, the cause is a reallocation time away from market work time to time in household production and leisure during the U.S. Great Recession as already described. Beginning in 1996–2000, for both genders, the contribution of market and nonmarket net investment in human capital is negative or very small, except in 2007–09. Investment in education, net of aging, which occurs only when individuals are in school, is one of two positive additions to net investment in human capital. As previously described, 2007–09 is a subperiod in which the percentage of individuals 18–24 who enrolled in tertiary education increased substantially. However, between 2009 and 2010, this enrollment leveled off, before decreasing between 2011 and 2012. From 1975 to 1990, births increased in every

year but two.[25] Subsequently births declined from 1990 through 1997, then increased in most years, but then declined again from 2007 through 2012.[26] The impact of the decrease in births starting in 2007 is most felt in nonmarket net investment in human capital. It is not surprising that births decreased during the recession because of the uncertainty the recession created. In 2010–12, the rate of growth of the quantity of net investment is a negative 1.1% for males and a negative 4.1% for females. In this subperiod, the share of real net investment for both depreciation from aging for individuals not enrolled in school and death is significantly larger than for any other subperiod, reflecting the aging of the baby boomers.

The final figure shows the contribution to human capital stock by gender (see Fig. 22.9).

---

[25] U.S. Census Bureau, *Statistical Abstract of the United States: 2012*, Section 2: Births, Marriages, and Divorces, Table no. 78. Live Births, Deaths, Marriages, and Divorces: 1960 to 2008, p. 65.

[26] Hamilton and Kirmeyer (2017).

Growth in human capital stock slows during the later subperiods beginning in 2000, primarily for demographic reasons. During this time population growth is slowing and baby boomers are aging. Even during the earlier subperiod: 1975–2000, when population growth is higher, population growth still averages only 1.1%.[27] Accordingly, contributions to human capital stock are all fairly small. Investment in education, net of aging, is still an important source of growth in the stock, but the pace of increases in educational attainment, particularly among those 25–34, has slowed. Female labor force participation and the ratio of females to male wages stagnate by the end of this second major period. It is notable that female human capital stock contributions exceed those of males in each of the subperiods beginning in 1996. There are clear differences between the first major subperiod: 1975–2000 and the second: 2001 to 2012. Between 1975 to 2000 and 2001 to 2012, the male market contributions dropped by 0.15 percentage points and the male nonmarket contribution dropped by 0.11 percentage points. Between the same two periods, the female market contribution dropped only 0.04 percentage points and the female nonmarket contribution by just 0.09 percentage points. In addition, the share of male market contributions in total male contributions fell by over 16 percentage points; the female market share of contributions to human capital stock also dropped, but only by just over 2 percentage points. As Fig. 22.6 previously demonstrated, there are clear differences between the earlier major subperiod and the second.

22.5 Part V: conclusion

This paper has documented that there have been significant changes in human capital in the United States over the period 1975–2012.

Analysis by gender points out that although changes in male human capital occur, the changes in female human capital arising from significant underlying trends in labor force participation, educational attainment, relative wages, and time use are even greater. In addition, the first major subperiod: 1975–99, typically looks quite different than the second major subperiod: 2000–12. The future is more likely to look like the second major time period: 2000–12, than the first: 1975–99, as the underlying trends have not continued to more recent years. Without an analysis including human capital and an analysis by gender, important elements of past, present, and potential future economic growth in the United States would be missed.

References

Barro R, Lee JW: *Barro-Lee educational attainment data set* 2016. www.barrolee.com.

Christensen LR, Jorgenson DW: U.S. real product and real factor input, 1929-1967, *Review of Income and Wealth* 16(1):19–50, 1970.

Christian MS: Human capital accounting in the United States, 1994-2006, *Survey of Current Business* 90(6):31–36, 2010.

Christian MS: Net investment and stocks of human capital in the United States, 1975-2013, *International Productivity Monitor* 33:128–149, Fall 2017.

Colby SL, Ortman JM: *The baby boom cohort in the United States: 2012 to 2060, population estimates and projections, current population reports*, May 2014. P25-1141.

Feenberg D, Coutts E: An introduction to the TAXSIM model, *Journal of Policy Analysis and Management* 12(1):189–194, 1993.

Fraumeni BM, Christian MS, Samuels JD: Accumulation of human and nonhuman capital, revisited, *Review of Income and Wealth* 63(Suppl 2):S381–S410, 2017.

Hamilton BE, Kirmeyer SE: Trends and variations in reproduction and intrinsic rates: United States, 1990–2014, *National Vital Statistics Reports* 66(2), February 22, 2017.

Jorgenson DW, Fraumeni BM: The accumulation of human and nonhuman capital, 1948-1984. In Lipsey R, Tice H, editors: *The measurement of saving, investment and wealth*,

[27] World Bank, World Bank Indicators, last updated March 1, 2018, accessed online April 14, 2018.

Chicago, 1989, University of Chicago Press, NBER, pp 227–282.

Jorgenson DW, Fraumeni BM: The output of the education sector. In Griliches Z, editor: *Output measurement in the service sectors*, Chicago, 1992, University of Chicago Press, NBER, pp 303–341.

Jorgenson DW, Landefeld JS: Blueprint for expanded and integrated U.S. accounts: review, assessment, and next steps. In Jorgenson DW, Landefeld JS, Nordhaus WD, editors: *A new architecture for the U.S. national accounts*, Chicago, 2006, University of Chicago Press, NBER, pp 13–112.

Jorgenson DW, Landefeld JS: Implementation of a new architecture for the U.S. National accounts, *American Economic Review, Papers and Proceedings* 99(2):64–68, May 2009.

National Bureau of Economic Research: *US business cycle expansions and contractions. (website)* 2018. www.nber.org/cycles.html.

National Center for Education Statistics: *Digest of education statistics* 2016 (website), nces.ed.gov/programs/digest/d15/tables/dt15_302.60.asp.

Toossi M: Employment outlook: 2010–2020, labor force projections to 2020: a more slowly growing workforce, *Monthly Labor Review*, 2012:50–51, 2012.

U.S. Bureau of Economic Analysis: *National income and product accounts, Washington, D.C., U.S Department of Commerce* 2018. www.bea.gov.

U.S. Census Bureau: Current population survey, annual social and economic supplements *(website)* 2018. www.census.gov/data/tables/time-series/demo/income-poverty/historical-income-people.html.

U.S. Census Bureau: *Statistical abstract of the United States*, Washington, DC, 2000, U.S. Census Bureau (website), www.census.gov/library/publications/2000/compendia/statab/120ed.html.

U.S. Census Bureau: *Statistical abstract of the United States*, Washington, DC, 2012, U.S. Census Bureau (website), www.census.gov/library/publications/2011/compendia/statab/131ed.html.

World Bank: *World Bank indicators* 2018. worldbank.org/indicator/SP.POP.TOTL?locations=US&view=chart.

Index